walkermaths

AF583574

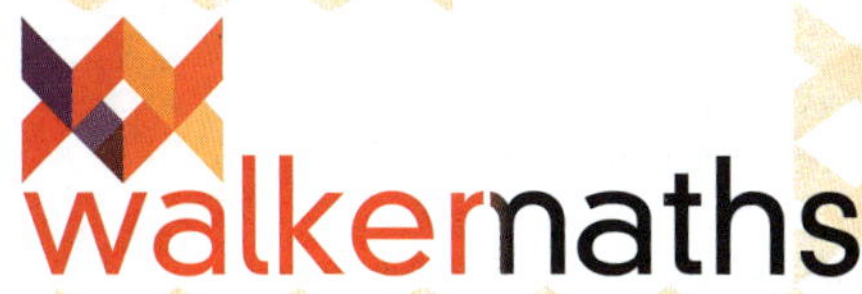

PHASE 4: FOUNDATION

Victoria and Charlotte Walker

Walker Maths — Phase 4: Foundation
1st Edition
Victoria and Charlotte Walker

Cover designer: Cheryl Smith, Macarn Design
Text designer: Cheryl Smith, Macarn Design
Production controller: Siew Han Ong

Any URLs contained in this publication were checked for currency during the production process. Note, however, that the publisher cannot vouch for the ongoing currency of URLs.

Acknowledgements
We wish to acknowledge the trusted kindred spirits throughout the country for your help in preparing this title.

We also thank CensusAtSchool New Zealand for the use the Data detective poster image on page 262 (www.censusatschool.org.nz).

For product information and technology assistance,
in Australia call **1300 790 853;**
in New Zealand call **0800 449 725**

For permission to use material from this text or product, please email **aust.permissions@cengage.com**

National Library of New Zealand Cataloguing-in-Publication Data
A catalogue record for this book is available from the National Library of New Zealand.

978 0 17 049797 8

Cengage Learning Australia
Level 5, 80 Dorcas Street
Southbank, VIC 3006, Australia

Printed in China by 1010 Printing International Limited.
2 3 4 5 6 7 27 26

CONTENTS

NUMBER ... **6**

The language of mathematics ... **6**

Words to operations ... 6

Integers ... **7**

Adding and subtracting ... 7

Multiplying and dividing ... 9

Types of numbers ... **12**

Multiples ... 12

Factors ... 13

Prime numbers ... 14

Square numbers ... 18

Mixing it up ... 19

Powers ... **20**

Roots ... **22**

Mixing it up ... 23

Order of operations ... **24**

Words to calculations ... 25

Fractions ... **26**

Numerators and denominators ... 26

Equivalent fractions ... 27

Converting between improper and mixed fractions ... 29

Adding and subtracting fractions ... 31

Multiplying fractions ... 34

Dividing fractions ... 35

Ordering fractions ... 38

Comparing fractions ... 39

Fraction of a quantity ... 41

Increasing and decreasing by a fraction ... 42

Given a fraction, find the whole amount ... 44

Decimals ... **46**

Place value ... 46

Decimals on number lines ... 49

Challenge ... 50

Comparing decimals ... 51

Recurring decimals ... 53

Using decimals to compare fractions ... 54

Percentages ... **55**

Converting between decimals and percentages ... 56

Converting between fractions and percentages ... 57

Converting between fractions, decimals and percentages ... 58

Challenges ... 59

Calculating percentages ... 60

Finding percentages of amounts ... 61

Increasing by a percentage ... 63

Decreasing by a percentage ... 64

Given a percentage, find the whole amount ... 65

Rounding ... **67**

Rounding to whole numbers ... 67

Rounding decimals ... 69

Significant figures ... 70

Rounding to significant figures ... 71

Appropriate rounding ... 73

Estimations/approximations ... 74

Scientific notation ... **75**

What is scientific notation? ... 75

Powers of 10 ... 75

Converting numbers from scientific notation to ordinary form ... 76

Converting numbers from ordinary form to scientific notation ... 77

Scientific notation on your calculator ... 79

Rates ... **80**

Ratios ... **82**

Simplifying ratios ... 82

Using ratios where the total is given ... 83

ISBN: 9780170497978

Financial mathematics 85
Calculations with money 85
GST 86
Interest 87
Profit and loss 88

ALGEBRA 89
The language of algebra 89
Phrases to expressions 89
More about variables 91
Simplifying expressions 92
Multiplying 92
Dividing 93
Like terms 94
Adding and subtracting 95
Mixing it up 96
Powers 97
Multiplying powers 97
Dividing powers 98
Powers of powers 100
Mixing it up 101
Brackets 102
Expanding 102
Factorising 104
Straight lines 106
Coordinates 106
Linear patterns with discrete data 107
The gradient of a line 112
Drawing straight lines – continuous data 117
1 Plotting points using the equation 117
2 Drawing straight lines using the gradient and intercept 120
3 Drawing horizontal and vertical lines 124
Writing equations from graphs 126
Solving linear equations 130
One-step equations 130
Forming and solving linear equations 133
Two-step equations 135
Equations with variables on both sides 138
Find the errors 141
Equations with brackets 142
Mixing it up 144
Inequations 145
Inequations with integers 145
Inequations on a number line 146
Solving inequations 147
Substitution and formulae 149
Substitution with one variable 149
Formulae with one variable 150
Substitution with several variables 153
Formulae with two or more variables 154
Rearrangement of formulae 156
Understanding instructions in algebra 158
Non-linear relationships 160
Linear or not? 160
Quadratic patterns 162
Drawing parabolas 164
1 In the form $y = x^2 \pm b$ 164
2 In the form $y = -x^2 \pm b$ 167
Putting it together 169

MEASUREMENT 170
The language of measurement 170
Measuring devices 171
Units 172
Abbreviations (shortened versions) for units 172
Length 173
Mass 175
Capacity (volume) 177
Appropriate units 179
Estimating quantities 180
Time 181
Converting units 181
Stopwatches 183
Speed 184
Scales 186
Reading scales 186
Showing values on scales 188
Perimeter 190
Shapes with linear sides 190
Circles 192
Compound shapes 194
Area 196
Units of area 196
Quadrilaterals 197
Square and rectangle 197
Parallelogram and rhombus 198
Trapezium 200
Kite 202

 ISBN: 9780170497978

Triangles.......203
Circles.......205
Compound shapes.......207

Volume.......210

Units of volume.......210
Cuboids.......211
Compound cuboids.......213

Scaling.......215

Scale factor.......215
Scale factors for perimeter, area and volume.......216

The Theorem of Pythagoras.......218

Finding the length of the hypotenuse.......219
Finding the lengths of short sides.......222
Mixing it up.......224

GEOMETRY.......225

The language of geometry.......225

Angles.......226

Angle revision.......226
Triangles.......228
- Naming triangles.......228
- Angles in a triangle.......229

Quadrilaterals.......231
- Angles in a quadrilateral.......231
- Angles in special quadrilaterals.......232

Parallel lines.......234

2D and 3D shapes.......237

2D and 3D language.......237
Nets.......238
Isometrics.......240
- Copying isometric shapes.......240
- Drawing isometric shapes from numbers in each column.......242
- Different views of isometric diagrams.......244

Transformation geometry.......245

Translation.......246
Reflection.......249
Rotation.......252

Position and orientation.......256

Directions.......256
Scales.......258

STATISTICS.......262

Statistical enquiry cycle.......262

Problem, plan and data.......263

Thinking about the data.......263
Investigative questions.......264
Types of questions and identifying variables and groups of interest.......265
Expected findings.......267
Collection of data.......269

Data display.......271

Reading axes.......272
Data interpretation.......274
Scatter plots.......277

Data analysis.......284

Measures of centre (averages).......284
Measures of spread.......287
Unusual features.......289

Decision trees.......291

Conclusions.......293

PROBABILITY.......296

The probability scale.......296
Events, outcomes and sample space.......297

Ways of calculating probabilities.......300

Calculating theoretical probability.......301
Calculating probabilities from observations.......304

Experimental probability investigation.......306

Simulations.......308

ANSWERS.......310

NUMBER

The language of mathematics

Words to operations

Write down the most appropriate operation (+, −, x or ÷) for each of the following terms.

	Term	Operation
1	Find twelve **divided by** four.	÷
2	Calculate five **and** one.	
3	What is sixteen **take away** ten?	
4	Find six **multiplied by** four.	
5	If thirty is **decreased by** fourteen, what is the result?	
6	What is thirteen **plus** three?	
7	What is the **total of** nineteen and five?	
8	What is twenty **increased by** seven?	
9	What is eighteen **shared between** six?	
10	Find a half **of** twenty-four.	
11	Calculate the **difference between** nine and two.	
12	What is the **product of** five and twelve?	
13	What is eleven **subtracted from** forty?	
14	Find the **sum of** two and eight.	
15	What is twenty-two **added to** seven?	
16	Find a number that is **smaller than** nine.	
17	What is seven **times** ten?	
18	Find the result when eleven is **reduced by** four.	
19	Calculate six **less than** twenty.	
20	What is three **more than** five?	

ISBN: 9780170497978

Integers

Adding and subtracting

- **-** means move **left**.
- **+** means move **right**.
- Remember that **- - = +**

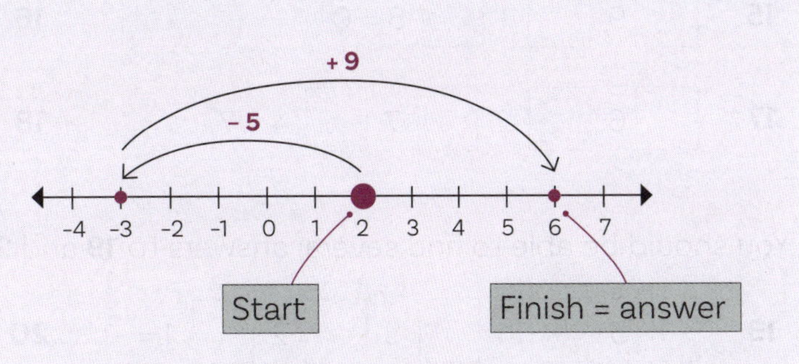

Example: 2 - 5 - -9 = 2 - 5 + 9

= 6

- - ⇒ +

Add arrows and dots to these number lines in order to complete the calculations.

1 -2 + 9 =

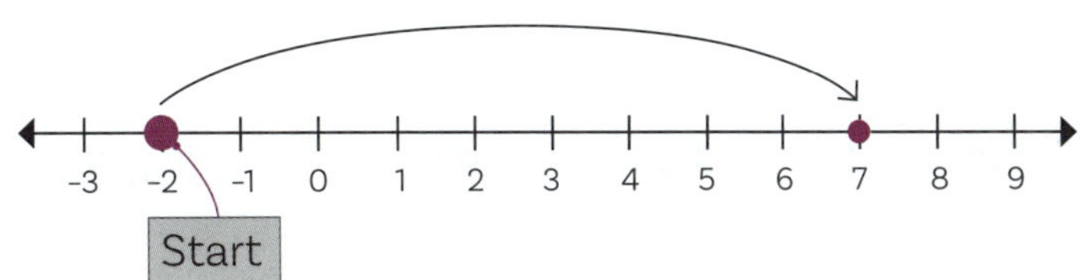

2 -1 - 4 =

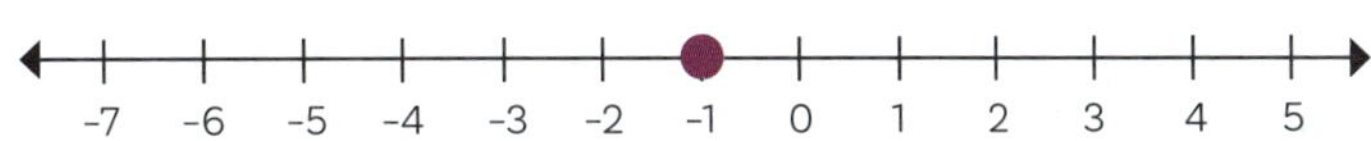

3 2 - 5 - -8 =

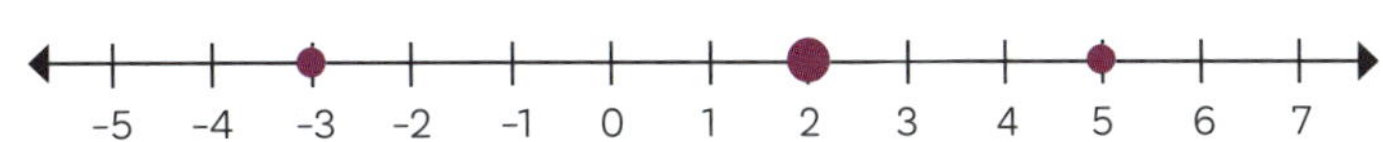

4 -4 + 10 - 7 =

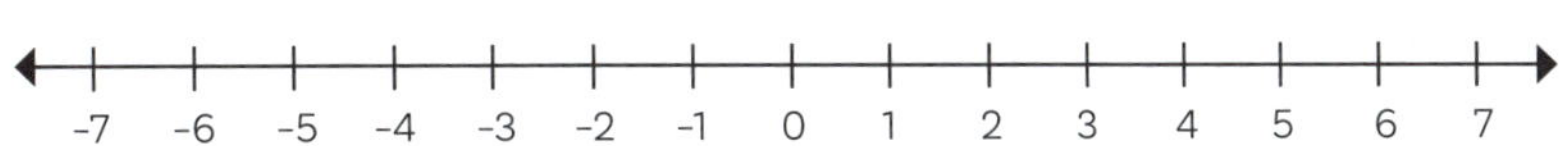

Complete the calculations.

5 -8 + 12 = ______________________

6 5 - 11 = ______________________

7 -3 + 6 - 10 = ______________________

8 -4 + 1 - 9 = ______________________

9 2 - -12 - 3 = ______________________

10 9 + -2 - -7 = ______________________

ISBN: 9780170497978

Write + or – signs in the boxes in order to create true statements.

11 □ 10 □ 2 □ 5 = 7

12 □ 2 □ 5 □ 4 = -1

13 □ 7 □ 2 □ 1 = -10

14 □ 3 □ 9 □ 2 = 8

15 □ 9 □ 1 □ 8 = 0

16 □ 2 □ 8 □ 12 = -6

17 □ 6 □ 2 □ 7 □ 4 = 7

18 □ 13 □ 7 □ 9 □ 1 = -12

You should be able to find several answers to **19** and **20**. Check your answers with your neighbour.

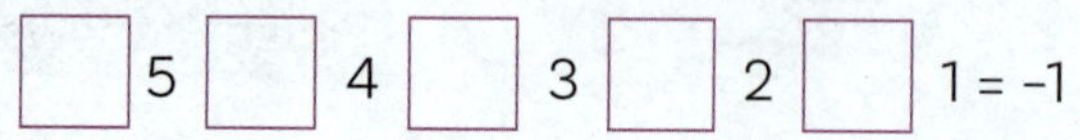

19 □ 5 □ 4 □ 3 □ 2 □ 1 = -1

□ 5 □ 4 □ 3 □ 2 □ 1 = -1

□ 5 □ 4 □ 3 □ 2 □ 1 = -1

20 □ 2 □ 4 □ 6 □ 8 □ 10 = -2

□ 2 □ 4 □ 6 □ 8 □ 10 = -2

□ 2 □ 4 □ 6 □ 8 □ 10 = -2

Write the calculation and answer shown by each diagram (start at the big dot).

21

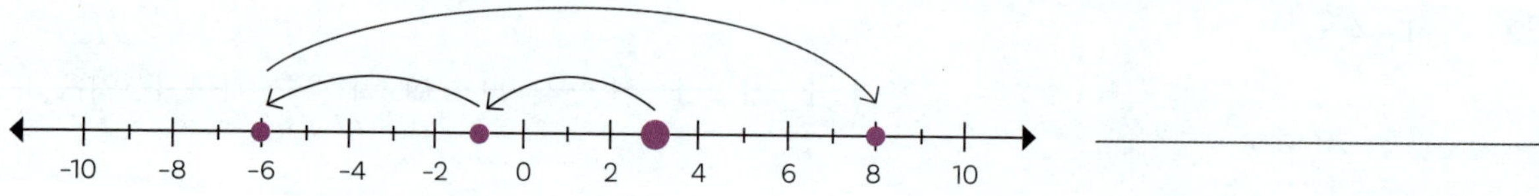

____

22

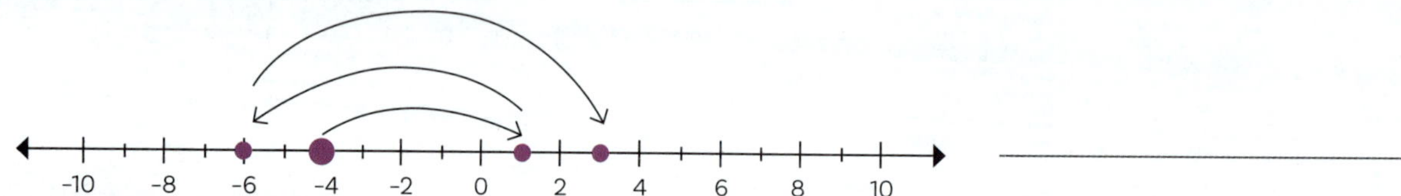

____

23

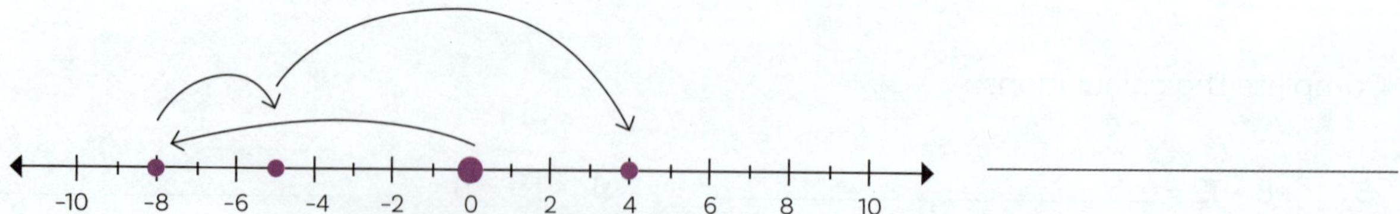

____

24

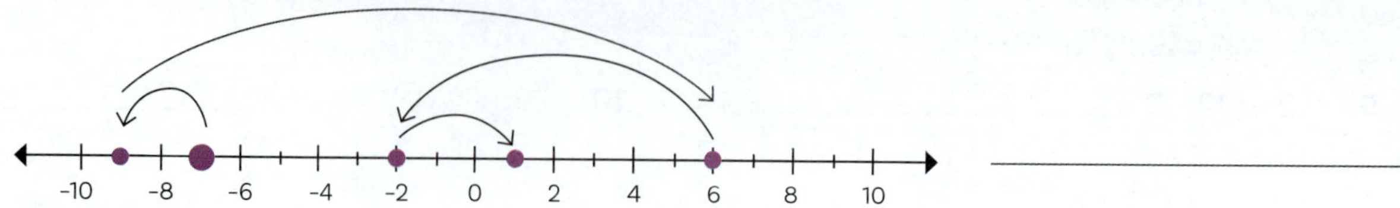

____

 ISBN: 9780170497978

Multiplying and dividing

- There are a number of ways of thinking about multiplying and dividing integers.

Multiplying integers

- Multiplying integers can be thought of as repeated addition or subtraction.

Examples:

1 Repeated addition: $8 \times 3 = 8 + 8 + 8$
$= 24$

2 Repeated subtraction: $-8 \times 3 = -8 + -8 + -8$
$= -8 - 8 - 8$
$= -24$

Fill in the gaps for the repeated additions/subtractions and then solve them.

1 5 x 4 = + [ ] + [ ] + [ ] + [ ]

= ________

2 7 x 5 = + [ ] + [ ] + [ ] + [ ] + [ ]

= ________

3 -7 x 4 = - [ ] - [ ] - [ ] - [ ]

= ________

4 -6 x 3 = - [ ] - [ ] - [ ]

= ________

Dividing integers

- Integers can be divided using the **inverse** (opposite) of division, which is multiplication.

Examples:

1 $-18 \div 9 = ?$ Consider the inverse operation: 9 **x** ? = −18
9 x **−2** = −18
This means that −18 ÷ 9 = −2
A shorter way of writing this: −18 ÷ 9 = **−2** because 9 x **−2** = −18

2 −18 ÷ −2 = 9 because −2 **x** 9 = −18

3 $\frac{18}{-3}$ = −6 because −3 **x** −6 = 18

Remember: 18 **÷** −3 means the same as $\frac{18}{-3}$

Write each division as two different multiplications.

5 8 ÷ 4 = 2

[4] x [2] = [8]

[ ] x [ ] = [ ]

6 15 ÷ −5 = −3

[ ] x [ ] = [ ]

[ ] x [ ] = [ ]

7 $\frac{-24}{8} = -3$

[ ] x [ ] = [ ]

[ ] x [ ] = [ ]

8 $\frac{-30}{-6} = 5$

[ ] x [ ] = [ ]

[ ] x [ ] = [ ]

ISBN: 9780170497978

Fill in the gaps for these calculations.

9 $-10 \div 5 = \square$ because $5 \times \square = -10$

10 $-27 \div -3 = \square$ because $-3 \times \square = \square$

11 $30 \div -5 = \square$ because ______________________

12 $\frac{-24}{8} = \square$ because ______________________

Families of facts

- When considering multiplication and division, facts using three numbers can be grouped into 'families'.

Examples:

1	4, 5 and 20	$4 \times 5 = 20$	$5 \times 4 = 20$	$20 \div 5 = 4$	$20 \div 4 = 5$
2	2, -6 and -12	$2 \times -6 = -12$	$-6 \times 2 = -12$	$-12 \div 2 = -6$	$-12 \div -6 = 2$
3	-2, -7 and 14	$-2 \times -7 = 14$	$-7 \times -2 = 14$	$14 \div -2 = -7$	$14 \div -7 = -2$
4	-3, 9 and -27	$-3 \times 9 = -27$	$9 \times -3 = -27$	$-27 \div -3 = 9$	$-27 \div 9 = -3$
5	6, $\frac{1}{3}$ and 2	$6 \times \frac{1}{3} = 2$	$\frac{1}{3} \times 6 = 2$	$2 \div \frac{1}{3} = 6$	$2 \div 6 = \frac{1}{3}$

This answer might seem surprising, but it's like saying 'How many thirds are there in two whole pizzas?'

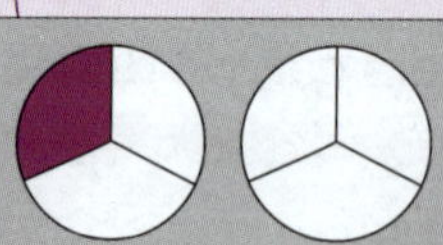

Fill in the gaps in order to complete these families.

13	4, 9 and 36	$4 \times 9 = 36$	$9 \times 4 = 36$	$36 \div 9 = 4$	$36 \div 4 = 9$
14	7, -6 and -42				
15	-2, -8 and 16				
16	8, $\frac{1}{4}$ and 2				
17	10, $\frac{1}{5}$ and 50				

 ISBN: 9780170497978

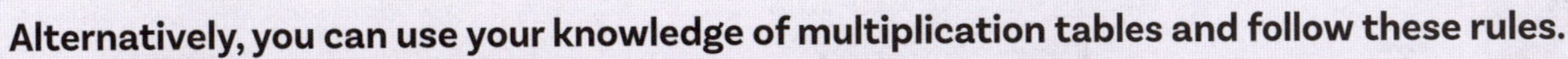

Alternatively, you can use your knowledge of multiplication tables and follow these rules.

Sign of integers	Answer sign	Examples
+ x ÷ +	positive	4 x 9 = 36
− x ÷ −	positive	-32 ÷ -4 = 8
+ x ÷ −	negative	4 x -6 = -24
− x ÷ +	negative	-12 ÷ 3 = -4

Same signs ⇒ +

Different signs ⇒ −

If there is more than one multiply or divide sign, work from left to right.

-3 x -2 x -5 = (-3 x -2) x -5
= (6) x -5
= -30

Highlight the correct answer for each of the following.

18	-8 x -2	16	-16
		-4	4
20	4 x -6	24	-2
		-10	-24

19	-15 ÷ 3	45	5
		-5	-45
21	-21 ÷ -3	18	7
		24	-7

Calculate the following.

22 -7 x 4 = ______________

23 -22 ÷ 11 = ______________

24 -2 x -9 = ______________

25 -18 ÷ -6 = ______________

26 12 x -3 x -1 = ______________

27 36 ÷ -4 x 2 = ______________

28 -10 ÷ 5 x -1 = ______________

29 -4 x -3 ÷ -2 = ______________

Fill in the gaps in order to complete correct calculations.

30 7 x ☐ = -35

31 -11 x ☐ = -66

32 ☐ ÷ 6 = -4

33 -72 ÷ ☐ x -1 = 9

34 8 x ☐ x -2 = -48

35 -4 ÷ -2 x ☐ = -26

ISBN: 9780170497978

Types of numbers

Multiples

- Multiples of a number are the results of **multiplying** the number by another number.

Examples: The multiples of **4** are **4, 8, 12, 16, 20, ...**
The multiples of **7** are **7, 14, 21, 28, ...**

These are the answers from the times tables.

1 Complete the table.

Number	First five multiples
3	3, 6, 9, 12, 15
5	
7	
6	
9	

2 Complete the table by stating if these are true or false.

Statement	True or False
21 is a multiple of 3	
16 is a multiple of 2	
20 is a multiple of 6	
9 is a multiple of 1	
18 is a multiple of 4	

Lowest common multiple (LCM)

- The lowest common multiple of two numbers is the **smallest multiple** of **both** numbers.

Example: The multiples of **3** are 3, 6, 9, 12, **15**, 18, 21, 24, 27, **30**, ...
The multiples of **5** are 5, 10, **15**, 20, 25, **30**, ...

The multiples they have in **common** (i.e. that are on both lists) are **15**, **30**, ...

The **lowest common multiple** of **3** and **5** is **15**.

Write enough multiples of these numbers in order to identify common multiples, and then write down the lowest common multiple.

3 Multiples of 5: ______________________
Multiples of 7: ______________________
The lowest common multiple of 5 and 7 is __________

4 Multiples of 6: ______________________
Multiples of 10: ______________________
The lowest common multiple of 6 and 10 is __________

5 Multiples of 8: ______________________
Multiples of 12: ______________________
The lowest common multiple of 8 and 12 is __________

6 Hannah can run round a track in 7 minutes, Hemi can bike round it in 4 minutes. If they start at the same time, how long will it take for them to complete a lap together?

____

ISBN: 9780170497978

Factors

- Factors of a number are all the whole numbers that **divide** into it exactly.

Examples: The factors of **12** are 1, 2, 3, 4, 6, 12.
The factors of **30** are 2, 3, 5, 6, 10, 15, 30.

1 Complete the table.

Number	Factors
8	1, 2, 4, 8
15	
10	
14	
38	

2 Complete the table by stating if these are true or false.

Statement	True or False
2 is a factor of 27	
1 is a factor of 13	
3 is a factor of 24	
5 is a factor of 35	
4 is a factor of 22	

Highest common factor (HCF)

- The highest common factor of two numbers is the **largest** common factor of **both** numbers.

Example: The factors of **20** are **1**, **2**, 4, 5, 10, 20.
The factors of **18** are **1**, **2**, 3, 6, 9, 18.

The factors they have in **common** are **1** and **2**.

The **highest common factor** of **20** and **18** is **2**.

Write all the factors of these numbers, highlight the common ones and then identify the highest.

3 Factors of 15: ______________________
Factors of 21: ______________________
The highest common factor of 15 and 21 is __________

4 Factors of 14: ______________________
Factors of 16: ______________________
The highest common factor of 14 and 16 is __________

5 Factors of 30: ______________________
Factors of 24: ______________________
The highest common factor of 30 and 24 is __________

6 A physical education teacher wants to split her class of 18 right-handers and 6 left-handers into even groups with the same number of right- and left-handers in each. There should be no one left out. What are some options she has?

She could have ____ groups with ____ right-handers and ____ left-hander(s) in each group.

She could have ____ groups with ____ right-handers and ____ left-hander(s) in each group

Prime numbers

- A prime number has **exactly two factors**: 1 and itself.

Examples: 2 **is** a prime number because it has exactly **two** factors: **1** and **2**.
7 **is** a prime number because it has exactly **two** factors: **1** and **7**.
6 **is not** a prime number because it has **four** factors: **1**, **2**, **3** and **6**.

Note: 1 **is not** a prime number because it has only **one** factor: **1**.

Highlight the prime numbers between 1 and 50. (Hint: You should find 15.)

1

1	2	3	4	5	6	7	8	9	10
11	12	13	14	15	16	17	18	19	20
21	22	23	24	25	26	27	28	29	30
31	32	33	34	35	36	37	38	39	40
41	42	43	44	45	46	47	48	49	50

2 Are all prime numbers odd? Give a reason for your answer.

____

3 What is the next prime number after 50?

____

4 Place these numbers in the correct area: 11, 28, 2, 9, 13, 19, 31, 1, 27, 38, 55.

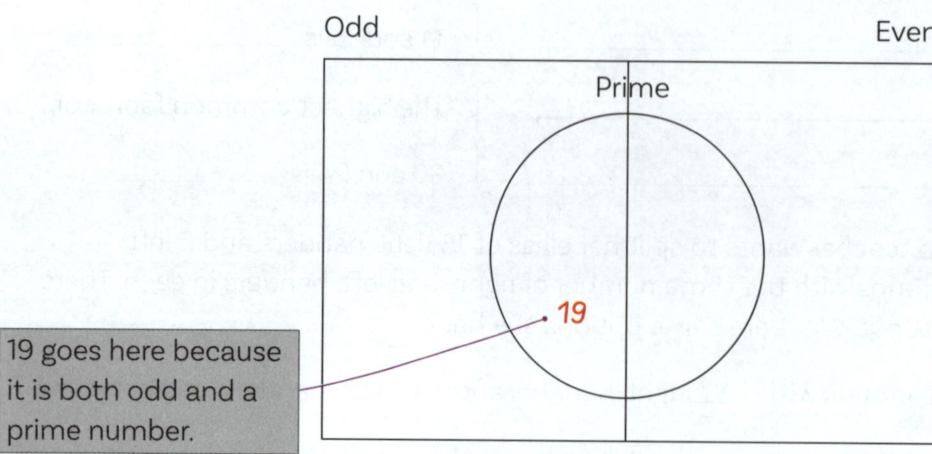

ISBN: 9780170497978

Prime factors

- All non-prime numbers can be written as products of prime factors.
- Prime numbers and factors are very important in cryptography (writing and using codes), especially for use in for cyber security.

Examples:

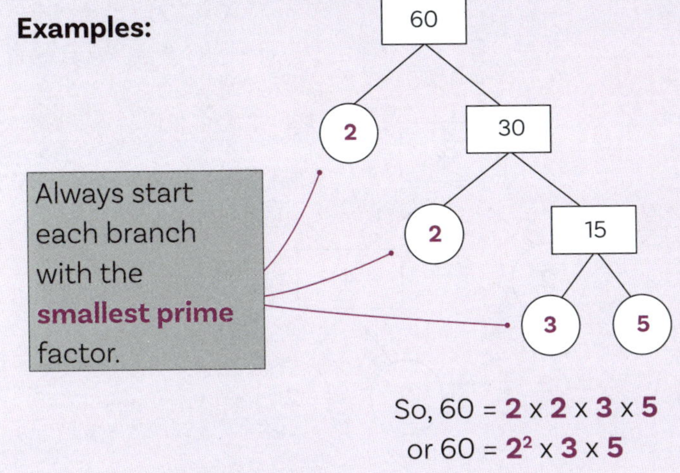

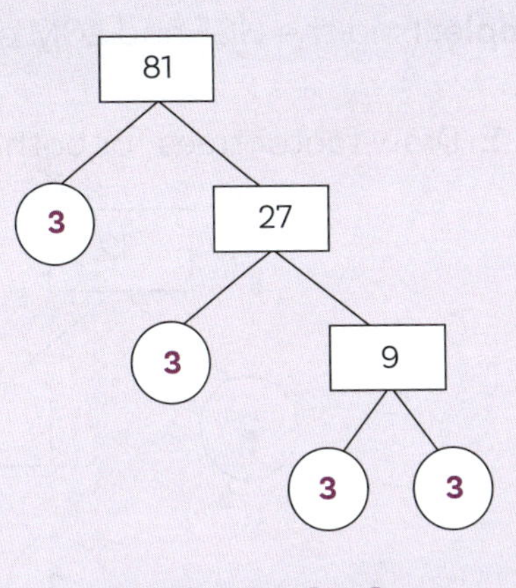

So, 60 = **2** x **2** x **3** x **5**
or 60 = $\mathbf{2^2}$ x **3** x **5**

81 = **3** x **3** x **3** x **3**
or 81 = $\mathbf{3^4}$

Complete these prime factor trees.

5

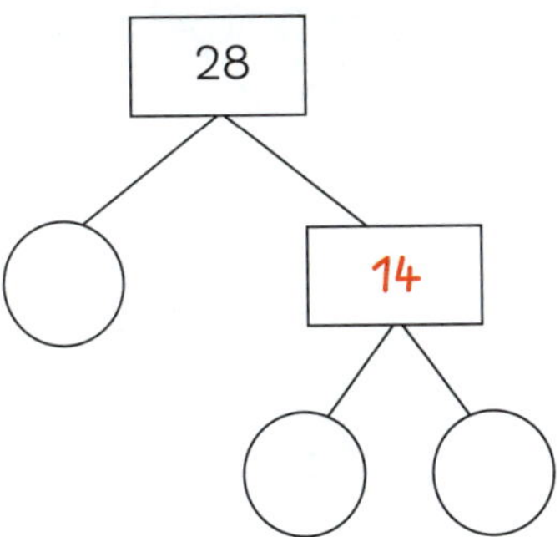

28 = ______________________

6

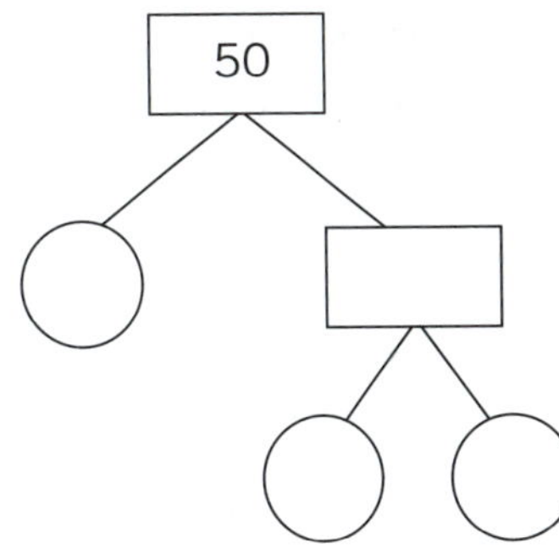

50 = ______________________

7

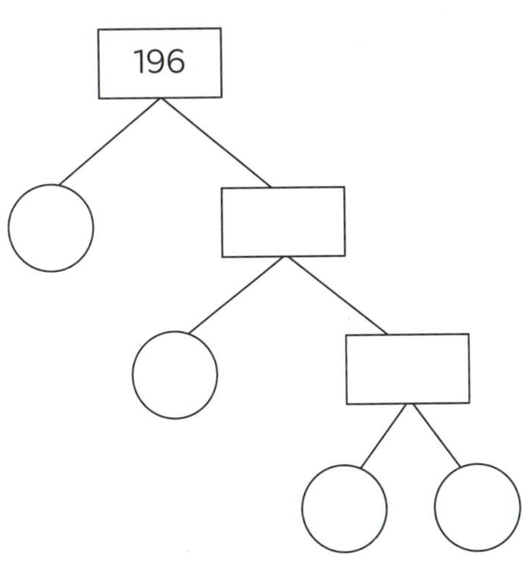

196 = ______________________

8

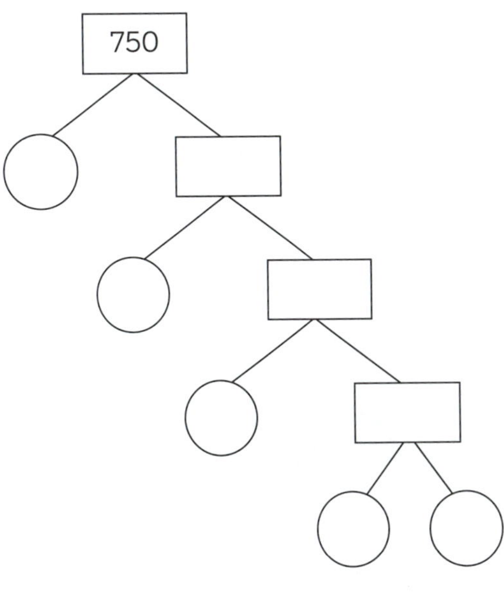

750 = ______________________

ISBN: 9780170497978

Using factor trees to find HCF and LCM

- Factor trees can be used to find the highest common factor and the lowest common multiple.

Example: Find the HCF and LCM of 12 and 8.

Step 1: Draw factor trees for both numbers.

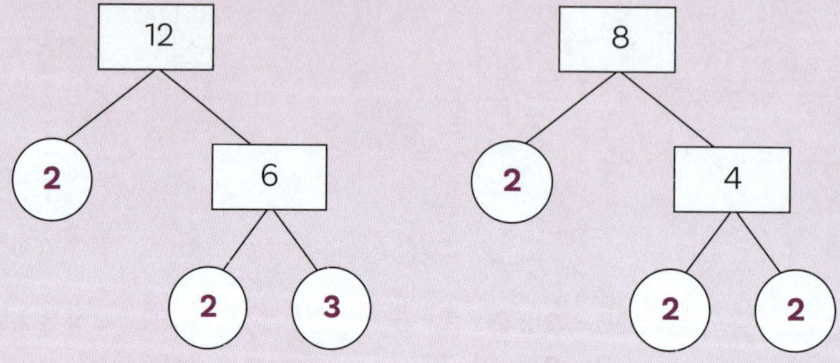

Step 2: Write each out as products of primes and highlight the numbers they have in common.

Step 4: Multiply the prime factors they have in common to calculate the HCF.

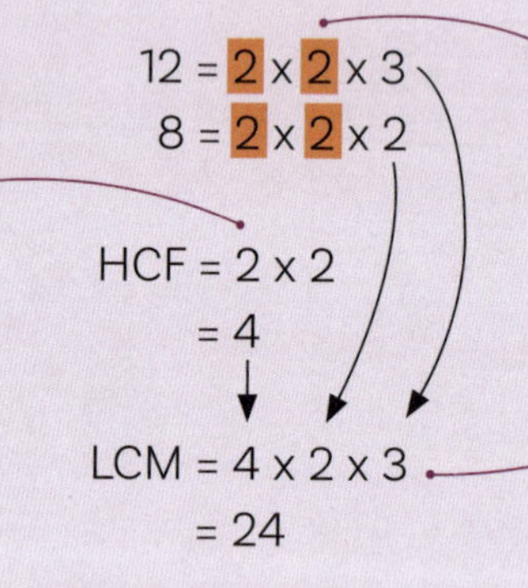

Step 3: Highlight the prime factors they have in common.

Step 5: Multiply the HCF and the leftover prime factors to calculate the LCM.

Find the HCF and LCM of these numbers using factor trees.

9

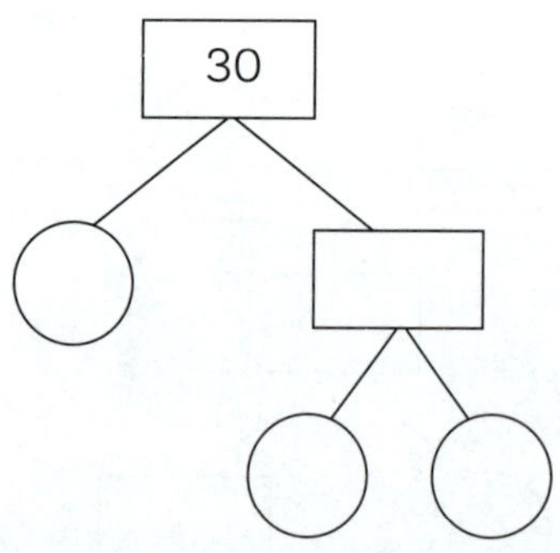

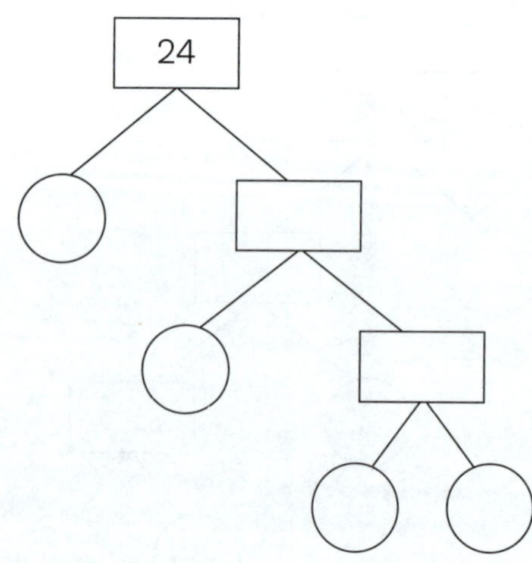

30 = ______________________

24 = ______________________

HCF = ______________________

LCM = ______________________

= ______________________

ISBN: 9780170497978

10

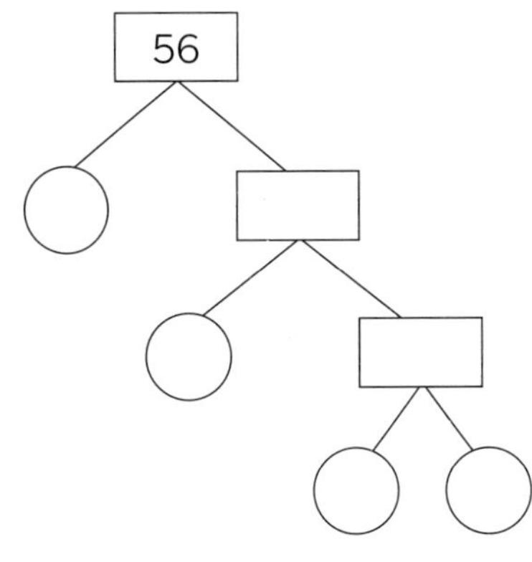

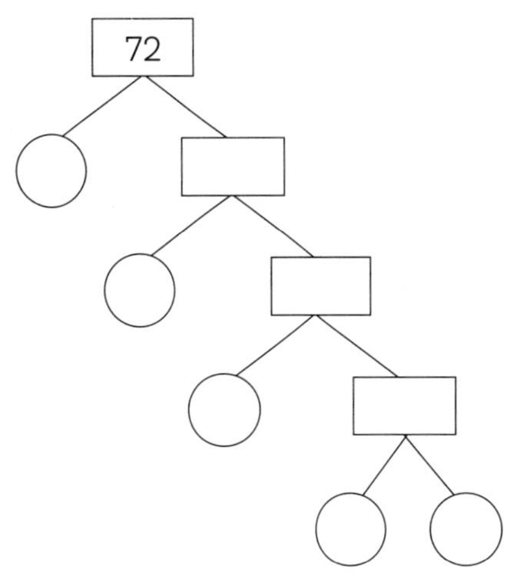

56 = ______________________

72 = ______________________

HCF = ______________________

LCM = ______________________

11

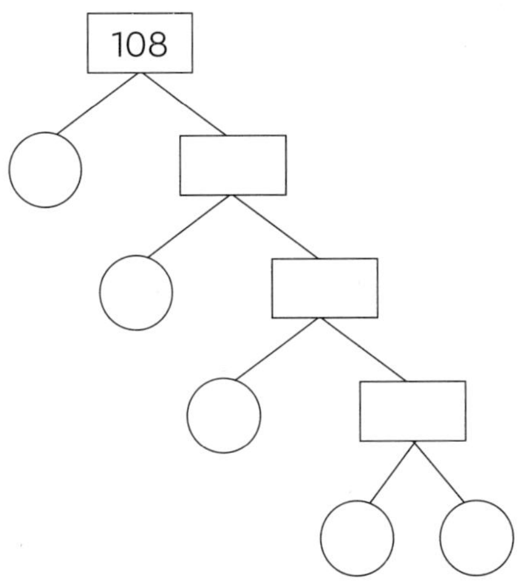

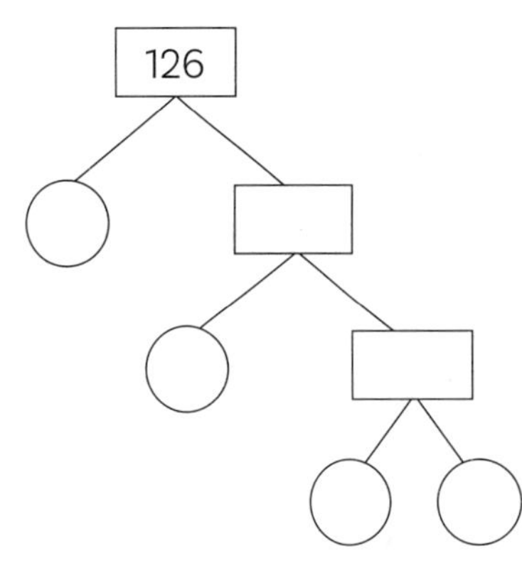

108 = ______________________

126 = ______________________

HCF = ______________________

LCM = ______________________

12

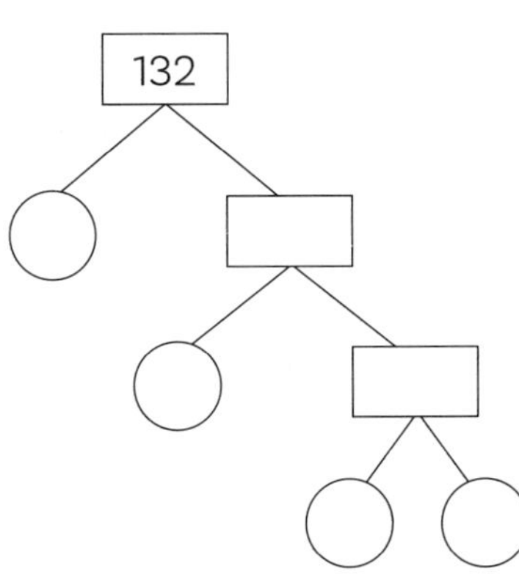

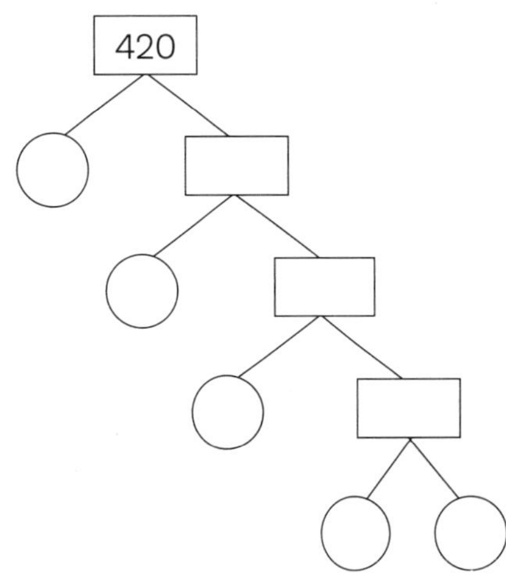

132 = ______________________

420 = ______________________

HCF = ______________________

LCM = ______________________

ISBN: 9780170497978

Square numbers

- A square number is a product of two equal integers (e.g. $4 = -2 \times -2, 9 = 3 \times 3$).
- Square numbers are written as n^2 (said 'n **squared**').
- Square numbers can be drawn as a square pattern of dots.

Examples: 9 **is** a square number because it is a product of 3 and 3, and it equals 3^2.
6 **is not** a square number because it cannot be written as a product of two equal numbers. Nor can six dots be drawn in a square.

Answer the following.

1 Complete the pattern and fill in the missing numbers.

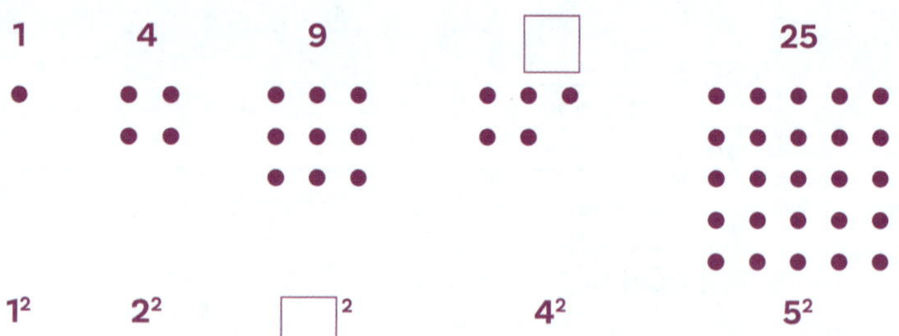

2 List the first 10 square numbers. ____________

3 The digits of 25 add to 7 (2 + 5 = 7). Write down at least three square numbers whose digits add to 9. (Some are more than 100.)

____

4 Write down two square numbers that add to 25. ____________

5 Write down two square numbers that add to 100. ____________

6 Find three square numbers that add to 49. ____________

7 **a** Study the diagram on the right, and fill in the gaps below.

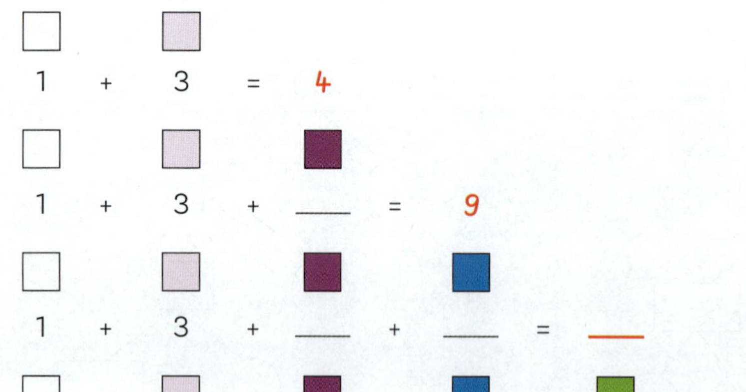

b What do you notice about the red numbers? ____________

c Write the next row of numbers. ____________

 ISBN: 9780170497978

Mixing it up

1 **a** The lowest temperature ever recorded in the Antarctic is −89.2°C and the highest is 19.8°C. How much warmer is the highest temperature than the lowest temperature?

____

b The average daytime temperature at McMurdo Station in winter is −26°C, and in summer it is −3°C. How much colder is it in winter than in summer?

____

2 **a** Mike is making up bags of mixed fruit to sell at the school fair. He has 78 apples, 104 pears and 143 feijoas. If each bag must contain the same number of each fruit, what is the maximum number of bags he can make?

____

____

b How many of each type of fruit will be in each bag?

____

3 **a** Huia is making up bags of stationery to be given away in backpacks for students starting school. Pens come in packs of 20, pencils in packs of 12 and highlighters in packs of 5. If each pack is to contain one of each, and she doesn't want any leftovers, what is the smallest number of bags she can make?

____

____

b How many packs of each item will she need to buy?

____

4 **a** One is a prime number. True or false? ____________

b Justify your answer.

____

c Write down the smallest prime number that is bigger than 40. ____________

d Write down the biggest prime number that is less than 110. ____________

5 **a** Some square tiles are sold in boxes of 140. Tai wants to cover the largest square possible with just one box of tiles. How many tiles will there be along each edge of the square?

____

b How many tiles will he have left over?

____

ISBN: 9780170497978

Powers

- Powers are used to indicate how many times a number (the base) is multiplied by itself.

The **3** is called the **base**.

The **5** is known as the **power** or the **exponent** or the **index**.

Example: $3^5 = 3 \times 3 \times 3 \times 3 \times 3$
$= 243$

When a power is **2**, we say the number is **squared**, e.g. 6^2 means six **squared** ($6 \times 6 = 36$).
When a power is **3**, we say the number is **cubed**, e.g. 4^3 means four **cubed** ($4 \times 4 \times 4 = 64$).

Important: **anything^1 = itself** e.g. $15^1 = 15$
anything^0 = 1 e.g. $15^0 = 1$

The power indicates how many times you need to multiply.

The brackets are important:
$-5^4 = -5 \times 5 \times 5 \times 5$
$= -625$

Examples: $7^2 = 7 \times 7$
$= 49$

$(-5)^4 = -5 \times -5 \times -5 \times -5$
$= 625$

Finding powers on your calculator

- Powers of numbers can get really big, so knowing how to find them on your calculator is **very** useful.

For squares, use a button that looks like this: x^2 e.g. show that $12^2 = 144$.

For cubes and all other powers, use a button that looks like this: $x^{■}$ e.g. show that $4^9 = 262\,144$.

Write the following as powers.

1 $3 \times 3 \times 3 \times 3$ = ______________

2 $12 \times 12 \times 12$ = ______________

3 -7×-7 = ______________

4 $-2 \times -2 \times -2 \times -2 \times -2$ = ______________

5 16 = ______________

6 1000 = ______________

7 27 = ______________

8 -27 = ______________ or ______________

9 32 = ______________

10 -32 = ______________ or ______________

11 -4 = ______________

12 -10 000 = ______________

 ISBN: 9780170497978

Without using your calculator, find the values of the following.

13 $8^2 =$ ______ **14** $2^6 =$ ______

15 $(-9)^2 =$ ______ **16** $-4^3 =$ ______

17 $-10^2 =$ ______ **18** $16^0 =$ ______

19 $10^5 =$ ______ **20** $19^1 =$ ______

21 $2^5 =$ ______ **22** $2^2 \times 2^3 =$ ______

23 Are your last two answers the same? ______

What number should go in the box in $2^2 \times 2^3 = 2^{\square}$? ______

Fill in the boxes in order to create correct statements.

24 $3^{\square} = 81$ **25** $7^{\square} = 343$

26 $-2^{\square} = -64$ **27** $(-4)^{\square} = 16$

28 $\square^2 = 121$ **29** $\square^3 = 1$

30 $\square^3 = -8$ **31** $\square^5 = -1$

Use your calculator to find the values of the following.

32 $2^9 =$ ______ **33** $12^4 =$ ______

34 $21^3 =$ ______ **35** $-13^2 =$ ______

36 $(-15)^5 =$ ______ **37** $2.9^3 =$ ______

38 $(-0.2)^3 =$ ______ **39** $0.08^4 =$ ______

40 Match these calculations with their answers.

Calculation		Answer
$10^3 \times 10^2$ •		• -10 000
$10^8 \div 10^2$ •		• 10 000
$-10^3 \times 10^1$ •		• 100 000
$(-10)^4 \times 10^0$ •		• 0.001
$10^0 \div 10^3$ •		• 1 000 000

ISBN: 9780170497978

Roots

- Finding a root is the opposite of finding a power.
- The **square root** is written as $\sqrt{\ }$. You do not need to write $\sqrt[2]{\ }$.

  e.g. $\sqrt{25} = \sqrt{5 \times 5}$
  $= 5$

  Notice $5^2 = 25$ and $\sqrt{25} = 5$.
- The **cube root** is written as $\sqrt[3]{\ }$.

  e.g. $\sqrt[3]{64} = \sqrt[3]{4 \times 4 \times 4}$
  $= 4$

  Notice $4^3 = 64$ and $\sqrt[3]{64} = 4$.
- The **fourth root** is written as $\sqrt[4]{\ }$, the **fifth root** is written as $\sqrt[5]{\ }$, etc.

  e.g. $\sqrt[5]{243} = \sqrt[5]{3 \times 3 \times 3 \times 3 \times 3}$
  $= 3$

  Notice $3^5 = 243$ and $\sqrt[5]{243} = 3$.

You can do this on your calculator with either $\sqrt{\blacksquare}$ ($\sqrt[3]{\blacksquare}$) or $x^{\blacksquare}$ ($\sqrt[\blacksquare]{\square}$).

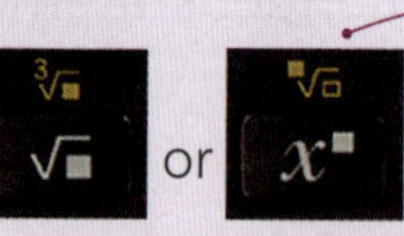

To access the yellow function, use the shift key. SHIFT

Complete the values from these missing families.

1 $\sqrt[3]{\square} = 2 \Rightarrow 2^{\square} = 8$

2 $\sqrt[\square]{81} = 9 \Rightarrow 9^{\square} = \square$

3 $\square^5 = 1 \Rightarrow \sqrt[\square]{1} = \square$

4 $\square^{\square} = 16 \Rightarrow \sqrt[\square]{16} = \square$

Without using your calculator, find the following roots.

5 $\sqrt{64} =$ ______________________

6 $\sqrt[3]{125} =$ ______________________

7 $\sqrt[3]{-27} =$ ______________________

8 $\sqrt[5]{100\,000} =$ ______________________

9 $\sqrt[5]{243} =$ ______________________

10 $\sqrt[4]{1} =$ ______________________

Use your calculator to find the values of the following.

11 $\sqrt{72.25} =$ ______________________

12 $\sqrt{47\,524} =$ ______________________

13 $\sqrt[3]{0.729} =$ ______________________

14 $\sqrt[3]{-3375} =$ ______________________

15 $\sqrt[5]{7776} =$ ______________________

16 $\sqrt[4]{0.1296} =$ ______________________

 ISBN: 9780170497978

Mixing it up

Remember: **>** means 'is greater than'.
< means 'is less than'.
= means 'is equal to'.

Examples: **1** $100 > 99$ **2** $99 < 100$

99 is **less than** 100.

Add one of these three symbols (<, > or =) in order to complete correct statements.

1 1^0 ◯ 1

2 $(-10)^2$ ◯ -10^2

3 $(-2)^3$ ◯ -2^3

4 0.9^3 ◯ 0.9^2

5 10^{-1} ◯ -1

6 $10^3 \times 10^0$ ◯ 10^3

7 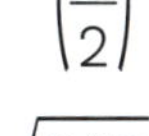 $\left(\frac{1}{2}\right)^2$ ◯ $\frac{1}{2}$

8 10^0 ◯ 10

9 $\sqrt{200}$ ◯ 14

10 $\sqrt{64}$ ◯ $\sqrt[3]{64}$

11 $\sqrt{25} + \sqrt{4}$ ◯ $\sqrt{29}$

12 $\sqrt{25} - 1$ ◯ $\sqrt{24} - 1$

13 $\sqrt{9 + 16}$ ◯ $\sqrt{9} + 16$

14 $\sqrt{10\,000}$ ◯ $\sqrt[3]{1\,000\,000}$

Estimating the size of a root

You can estimate the size of a square root by considering the sizes of the square numbers on either side.

Example: Estimate $\sqrt{20}$

$4^2 = 16$

← 20 lies between 16 and 25.

$5^2 = 25$ $\therefore \sqrt{20}$ must lie between 4 and 5.

15 Complete the table **without** using a calculator, and selecting the correct value from this list.

5.477	4.243	2.449	9.487	~~3.464~~	7.746

Square root	Square numbers on either side	Lower and upper limits for square root	Value
$\sqrt{12}$	9 and 16	3 and 4	3.464
$\sqrt{6}$			
$\sqrt{90}$			
$\sqrt{60}$			
$\sqrt{18}$			
$\sqrt{30}$			

Order of operations

- **BEDMAS** or **GEMA** are acronyms that help us to remember the order of operations.
- If you have several division signs or several multiplication signs, work from left to right.
- A horizontal division symbol in a fraction means you must bracket the numerator and bracket the denominator, e.g. $\frac{6+2}{4} = \frac{(6+2)}{4}$.
- A square root sign acts like a bracket, e.g. $\sqrt{16+9} = \sqrt{(16+9)} = 5$.

Fill in the tables below with words from the list. Some will appear twice. Use whichever table suits to help you remember the order to use in calculations.

Brackets	Exponents	Division	Multiplication	Addition	Subtraction	Groupings

B		( ) { } [ ]
E		2^3 or $\sqrt{}$
D		÷
M		x
A		+
S		−

G		( ) { } [ ]
E		2^3 or $\sqrt{}$
M	____________ and ____________	x ÷
A	____________ and ____________	+ −

Highlight the correct answer for each of the following. Do **not** use your calculator.

1	$5 + 3^2$	8	14
		64	11
3	$12 - 6 \div 2 + 7$	16	10
		22	17

2	$\frac{10+\sqrt{36}}{2}$	16	13
		8	11
4	$8 + 3(4 - 1)$	33	43
		19	17

Using BEDMAS or GEMA, calculate the following. Do **not** use your calculator.

5 $-2 + 7 \times 3 =$ ____________

6 $(-4 + 8) \times 3 =$ ____________

7 $5 + 3^2 =$ ____________

8 $\sqrt{25 - 16} =$ ____________

9 $11 \times -2 \div \sqrt{4} =$ ____________

10 $10 \div -2 \times 3 =$ ____________

11 $28 \div -4 \div 2 =$ ____________

12 $2^3 + (-3 + 4) =$ ____________

13 $\frac{72}{3+5} =$ ____________

14 $3 - (6 - 2)^2 - 5 =$ ____________

15 $7 - -1(4 + 6) =$ ____________

16 $-12 \div 3(-4 + 2) =$ ____________

17 $(-1)^2 \times 3 - 8 =$ ____________

18 $10 + -5 - 2 \times 3^2 =$ ____________

ISBN: 9780170497978

Words to calculations

Match the calculations with the stories below, and calculate the answer to each. You will not need to use all of these calculations.

$-16 + 2 \times (12 - 3)$	$16 \times 2 + 12 \times 3$	$(16 \times 2) - 12 \times 3$	$16 \div 2 - (12 + 3)$
$16 + 2 + 12 \div 3$	$-16 + 2 \times 12 - 3$	$16 + 2 + (12 \div 3)$	$\frac{16}{2} + 12 \times 3$
$16 + 2 - 12 + 3$	$16 \times (2 - 12) \times 3$	$16 \times 2 - 12 \div 3$	$(16 + 2 + 12) \div 3$
$\left(\frac{16}{2} + 12\right) \times 3$	$16 \times (2 + 12) \times 3$	$\frac{16}{2} - 12 \div 3$	$(16 \times 2 - 12) \times 3$

	Story	Calculation	Solution
1	Tia did two hours of housework, at a pay rate of $16 an hour. In the afternoon she went to the community fair and bought 12 secondhand books for $3 each. If she started the day with nothing, how much did she have to borrow from her mum?		$________
2	Brothers Ben and Oscar shared equally the $16 they were paid for stacking wood. Then, with their sister, they shared the cost of buying a $12 bunch of flowers for their mum. How much more or less money did each brother have at the end of the day?		$________
3	Mason earned $16 during the morning. He repaid half to his brother, then paid $12 to visit the local wildlife sanctuary and $3 for an ice cream. How much more or less money did he have at the end of the day?		$________
4	Ava paid $16 for a stall at the fair. She sold 12 baby plants for $2 each, and bought some lollies for $3. How much more or less money did she have at the end of the day?		$________
5	In the morning, Miru did two hours' gardening for her aunt at $16 per hour. Later in the day she shared the $12 cost of hiring a paddleboard with two friends. How much more or less money did she have at the end of the day?		$________
6	Teina and his sister cleaned the cars in the morning and shared equally the $16 they earned. Then Teina did three hours' housework for his grandfather, at $12 per hour. How much money did he earn in total?		$________
7	For their father's birthday, Jack and his two sisters bought a mug for $16, a $2 sheet of wrapping paper and some chocolate which cost $12. They shared the cost equally. How much did each have to pay?		$________

ISBN: 9780170497978

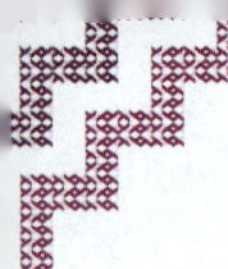

Fractions

Numerators and denominators

$\frac{3}{7}$

The **top** number is called the **numerator**.

The **bottom** number is called the **denominator**.
Hint: d stands for **downstairs**.

1 Shade the fraction represented in each diagram and cross out the word to make a true statement.

a

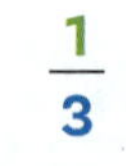

$\frac{1}{3}$

$\frac{2}{3}$

When the **numerator** increases, the size of the shaded section increases/decreases.

b

$\frac{1}{4}$

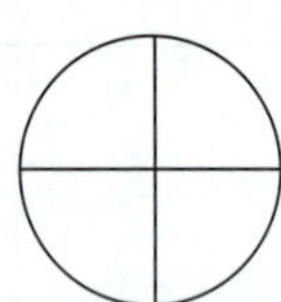

$\frac{1}{5}$

When the **denominator** increases, the size of the shaded section increases/decreases.

2 Place these fractions in the correct ascending order (smallest to biggest).

$\frac{11}{25}$	$\frac{1}{25}$	$\frac{7}{25}$	$\frac{12}{25}$	$\frac{16}{25}$	$\frac{2}{25}$	$\frac{25}{25}$

				$\frac{12}{25}$		

3 Place these fractions in the correct ascending order (smallest to biggest).

$\frac{1}{2}$	$\frac{1}{10}$	$\frac{1}{5}$	$\frac{1}{4}$	$\frac{1}{1}$	$\frac{1}{3}$	$\frac{1}{8}$

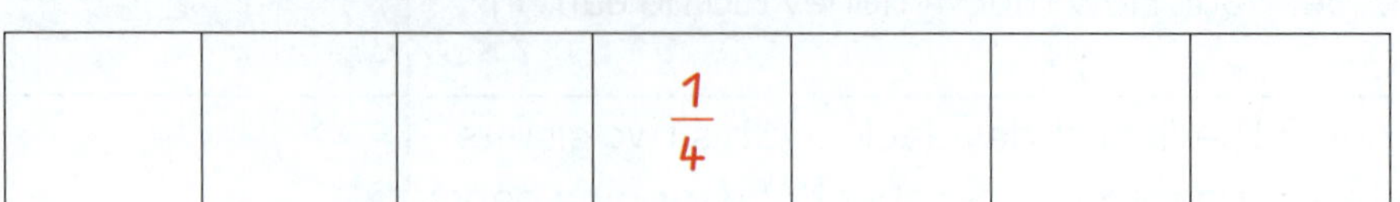

			$\frac{1}{4}$			

 ISBN: 9780170497978

Equivalent fractions

- Equivalent fractions are fractions that are written with different **denominators**, but which have the same value. For example:

$$\frac{1}{3} = \frac{2}{6}$$

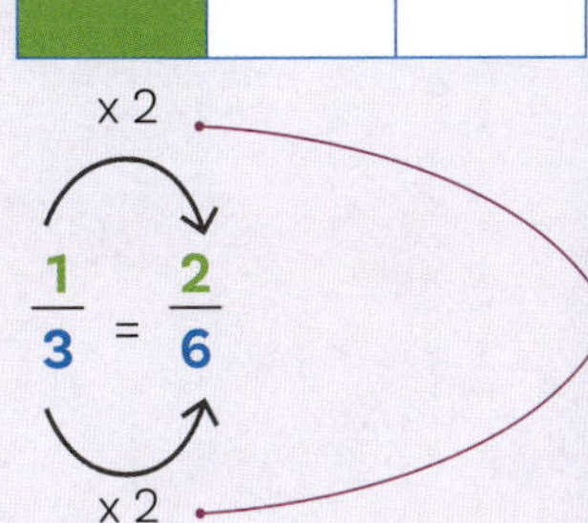

Equivalent fractions are obtained by multiplying or dividing the **numerator** and **denominator** by the **same** number.

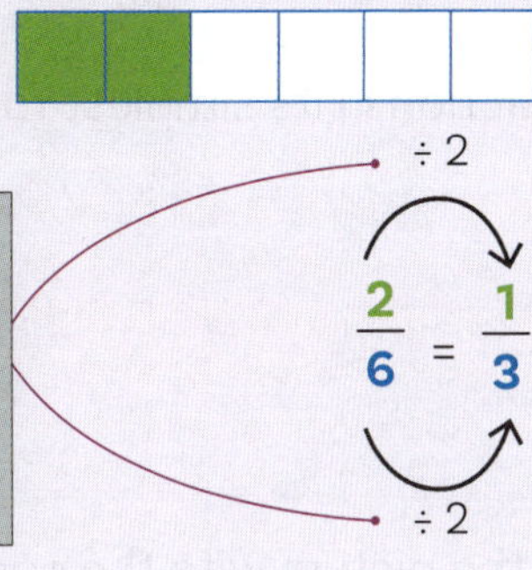

Shade the diagrams and fill the gaps to create equivalent fractions.

1

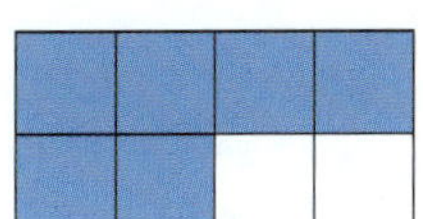

$\frac{6}{8} = \frac{\square}{4}$

2

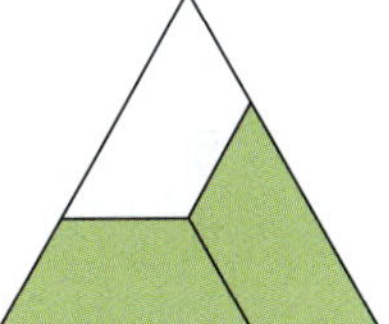

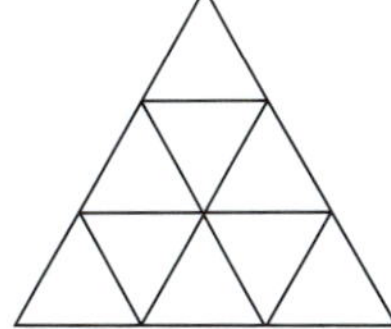

$\frac{2}{3} = \frac{\square}{9}$

3

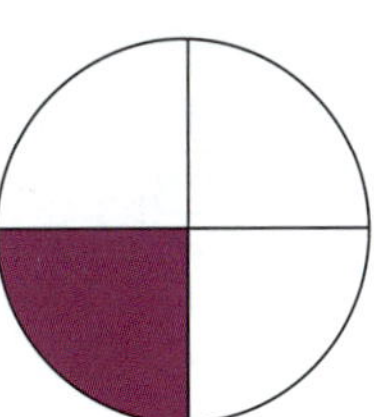

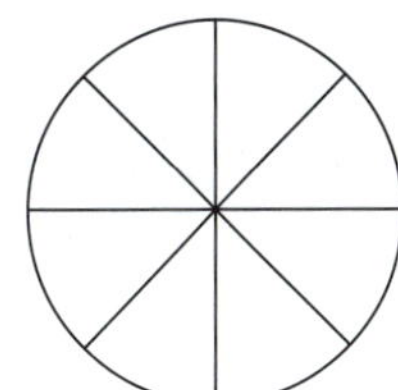

$\frac{1}{\square} = \frac{\square}{8}$

4

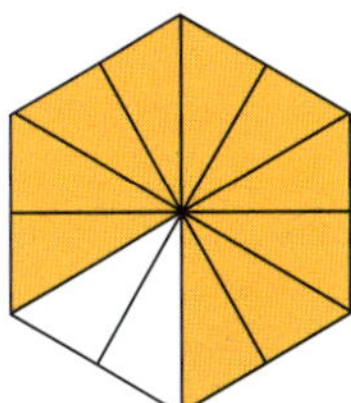

$\frac{\square}{12} = \frac{\square}{\square}$

5

$\frac{\square}{\square} = \frac{1}{\square}$

ISBN: 9780170497978

Fill in the gaps to create equivalent fractions.

6 $\frac{10}{16} = \frac{\square}{8}$

7 $\frac{6}{9} = \frac{2}{\square}$

8 $\frac{\square}{20} = \frac{3}{5}$

6 $\frac{5}{\square} = \frac{25}{120}$

Write each fraction in its simplest form.

10 $\frac{8}{24} =$

11 $\frac{10}{14} =$

12 $\frac{15}{25} =$

13 $\frac{16}{52} =$

14 Match the picture with the equivalent fraction.

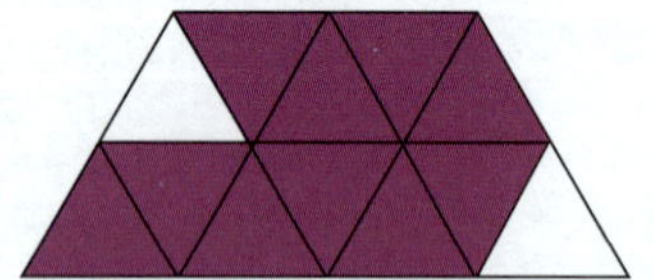 • • $\frac{18}{30}$

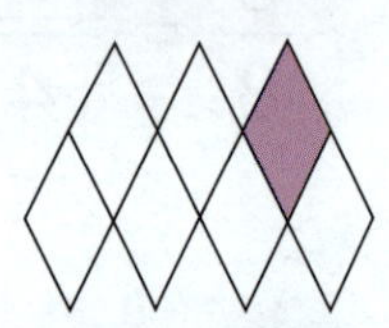 • • $\frac{4}{5}$

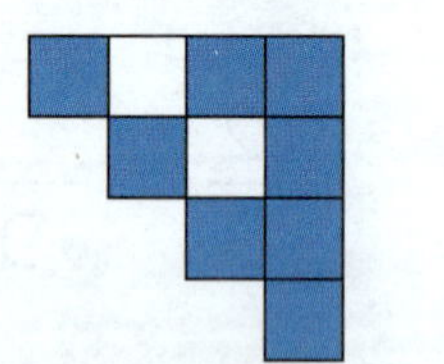 • • $\frac{5}{6}$

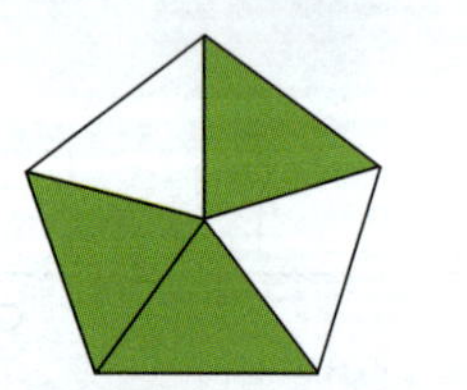 • • $\frac{5}{35}$

Find the missing values to make the fractions equivalent.

15 $\frac{1}{3} = \frac{\square}{6} = \frac{3}{\square} = \frac{\square}{12} = \frac{\square}{15} = \frac{6}{\square} = \frac{10}{\square}$

16 $\frac{1}{3} = \frac{\square}{18} = \frac{2}{\square} = \frac{\square}{108} = \frac{8}{\square} = \frac{24}{\square}$

17 $\frac{12}{15} = \frac{36}{\square} = \frac{\square}{25} = \frac{16}{\square} = \frac{24}{\square} = \frac{\square}{35} = \frac{\square}{5}$

 ISBN: 9780170497978

Converting between improper and mixed fractions

- An **improper** fraction (sometimes called a top-heavy fraction) is one with a numerator that is bigger than the denominator.

Example: $\frac{3}{2}$

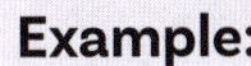
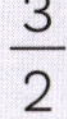
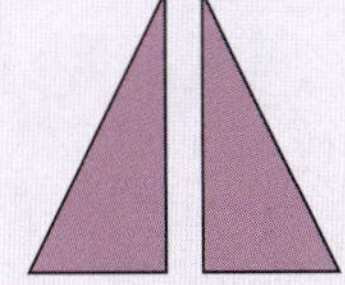
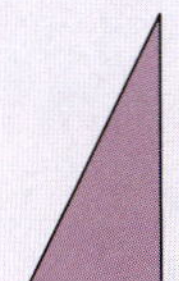

- A **mixed** fraction is a combination of a whole number and a fraction.

Example: $1\frac{1}{2}$

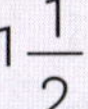
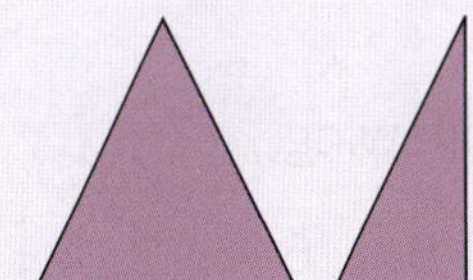

Complete the table. The first one has been done for you.

	Improper fraction	Mixed fraction
1	$\frac{5}{4}$ Five quarters	$1\frac{1}{4}$ One and one quarter
2	___ ______________	___ ______________
3	___ ______________	___ ______________
4	___ Thirteen fifths	___ ______________

ISBN: 9780170497978

Converting improper fractions to mixed fractions

Example: Convert $\frac{21}{5}$ to a mixed fraction.

$$\frac{21}{5} = \left(\frac{5}{5} + \frac{5}{5} + \frac{5}{5} + \frac{5}{5}\right) + \frac{1}{5}$$

$$= 4\frac{1}{5}$$

Remember, $\frac{5}{5} = 1$.

There are **4** lots of 5 in 21, with **1** fifth left over.

Complete the following.

5 $\frac{23}{6} = \frac{6}{6} + \frac{6}{6} + \frac{6}{6} + \frac{\square}{6} = 3\frac{\square}{6}$

6 $\frac{14}{3} = \frac{3}{3} + \frac{3}{3} + \frac{3}{3} + \frac{3}{3} + \frac{\square}{3} = \square\frac{\square}{3}$

7 $\frac{21}{2} = 10\frac{\square}{2}$

8 $\frac{31}{7} = \square\frac{3}{7}$

9 $\frac{16}{3} =$

10 $\frac{24}{5} =$

11 $\frac{51}{7} =$

12 $\frac{31}{8} =$

13 $\frac{27}{6} =$

14 $\frac{24}{9} =$

Converting mixed fractions to improper fractions

Example: Convert $3\frac{1}{4}$ to an improper fraction.

$$3\frac{1}{4} = \left(\frac{4}{4} + \frac{4}{4} + \frac{4}{4} + \frac{1}{4}\right)$$

$$= \frac{13}{4}$$

There are **3** lots of **four** fourths (**12** fourths), with **1** fourth left over.

A shortcut is to multiply the whole number by the denominator and add the numerator.

3 x 4 + 1 = 13

Complete the following.

15 $4\frac{1}{5} = \frac{5}{5} + \frac{5}{5} + \frac{5}{5} + \frac{5}{5} + \frac{1}{5} = \frac{\square}{5}$

16 $2\frac{4}{9} = \frac{9}{9} + \frac{9}{9} + \frac{4}{9} = \frac{\square}{9}$

17 $1\frac{1}{6} = \frac{\square}{6}$

18 $3\frac{2}{7} = \frac{\square}{7}$

19 $8\frac{1}{2} =$

20 $3\frac{3}{5} =$

21 $10\frac{3}{4} =$

22 $11\frac{1}{6} =$

23 $5\frac{6}{7} =$

24 $4\frac{7}{12} =$

ISBN: 9780170497978

Adding and subtracting fractions

With the same denominators

- To add or subtract fractions with the **same denominator**, you **add or subtract the numerator**. The denominator does not change.

Example: $\frac{1}{3} + \frac{1}{3} = \frac{2}{3}$

1 + **1** is **2**.

The **denominator** remains a **3**.

Add or subtract these fractions.

1 $\frac{3}{5} + \frac{1}{5} =$

2 $\frac{5}{6} - \frac{4}{6} =$

3 $\frac{2}{8} + \frac{3}{8} =$

4 $\frac{5}{7} - \frac{2}{7} =$

5 $\frac{7}{10} + \frac{2}{10} =$

6 $\frac{3}{4} - \frac{2}{4} =$

Use each fraction from the list once only in order to complete the calculations below.

$\frac{4}{7}$	$\frac{2}{7}$	$\frac{1}{7}$	$\frac{6}{7}$	$\frac{4}{6}$	$\frac{7}{7}$	$\frac{5}{7}$	$\frac{3}{6}$	$\frac{5}{6}$

7 $\frac{1}{6}$ + ☐ = $\frac{4}{6}$

8 ☐ − $\frac{2}{7}$ = 

9 ☐ − $\frac{4}{7}$ = 

10 $\frac{5}{7}$ + ☐ = 

11 ☐ − $\frac{1}{6}$ = ☐

ISBN: 9780170497978

With different denominators

- To add or subtract fractions with a **different denominator**, you must first change the **denominator(s)** so that they are the **same**.

Examples:

1 $\frac{1}{4} + \frac{1}{2} = \frac{1}{4} + \left(\frac{1}{2} \times \frac{2}{2}\right)$

$= \frac{1}{4} + \frac{2}{4}$

$= \frac{3}{4}$

This **denominator** needs to become 4.

Because the **denominators are the same**, we can **add the numerators**.

 + 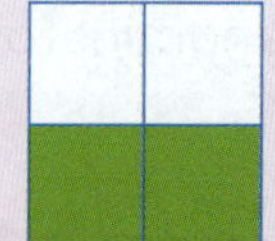 = 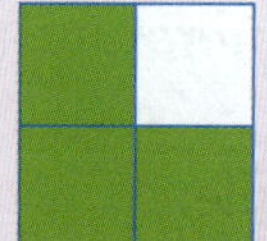

2 $\frac{1}{2} - \frac{1}{3} = \left(\frac{1}{2} \times \frac{3}{3}\right) - \left(\frac{1}{3} \times \frac{2}{2}\right)$

$= \frac{3}{6} - \frac{2}{6}$

$= \frac{1}{6}$

We need to change both **denominators**. The easiest way to do this is to multiply by each other.

6 is called a **common denominator** because it is the same for both fractions.

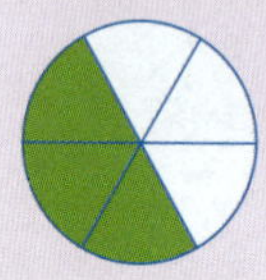 −  = 

Join the dots to match each calculation with its correct picture. Then complete the calculation.

12 $\frac{1}{6} + \frac{2}{3} =$ ________

= ________

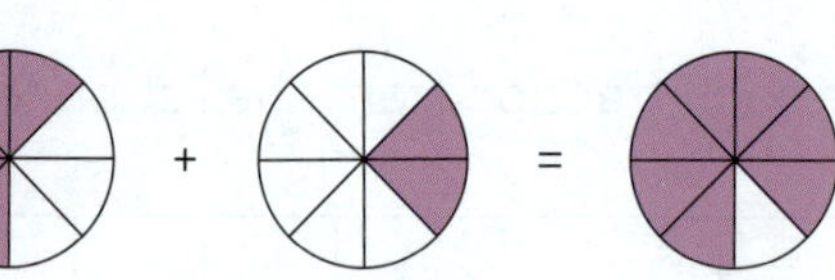

13 $\frac{3}{4} - \frac{1}{2} =$ ________

= ________

 = 

14 $\frac{5}{8} + \frac{1}{4} =$ ________

= ________

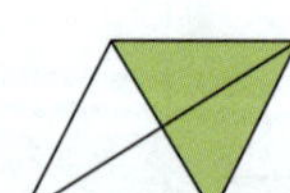 = 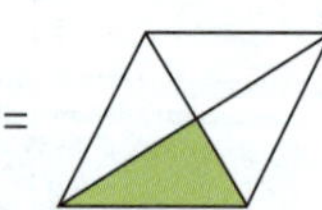

15 $\frac{7}{9} - \frac{1}{3} =$ ________

= ________

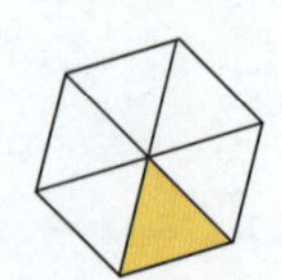 + 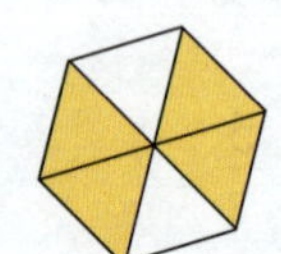 = 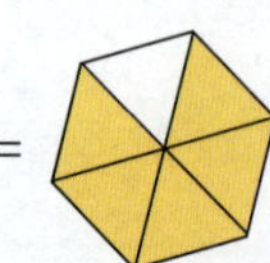

16 $\frac{9}{10} - \frac{3}{5} =$ ________

= ________

 − 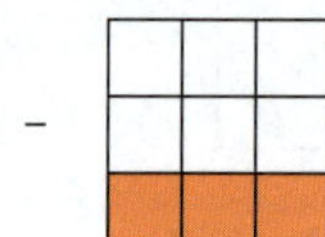 = 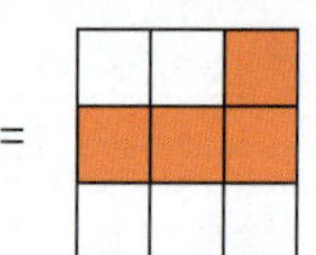

ISBN: 9780170497978

Add or subtract these fractions. Where possible, write your answers as simplified mixed fractions.

17 $\frac{3}{6} + \frac{1}{3} =$ ______________________

= ______________________

18 $\frac{1}{4} + \frac{3}{8} =$ ______________________

= ______________________

19 $\frac{5}{14} - \frac{2}{7} =$ ______________________

= ______________________

20 $\frac{7}{9} - \frac{2}{3} =$ ______________________

= ______________________

21 $\frac{5}{9} - \frac{1}{7} =$ ______________________

= ______________________

22 $\frac{7}{8} - \frac{1}{3} =$ ______________________

= ______________________

23 $\frac{4}{7} + \frac{1}{5} =$ ______________________

= ______________________

24 $\frac{10}{11} - \frac{4}{5} =$ ______________________

= ______________________

25 $\frac{2}{3} + \frac{1}{2} =$ ______________________

= ______________________

= ______________________

26 $\frac{11}{10} + \frac{3}{4} =$ ______________________

= ______________________

= ______________________

27 $\frac{9}{12} + \frac{7}{8} =$ ______________________

= ______________________

= ______________________

28 $\frac{5}{8} + \frac{3}{5} =$ ______________________

= ______________________

= ______________________

Using your calculator

It is very important that you learn to do calculations with fractions manually.
However, sometimes it is useful to use your calculator.
Once you can add using your calculator, you will be able to use other operations as well.

Examples: Use your calculator to find the answers.

1 $\frac{5}{12} + \frac{2}{5}$ 5  12   2  5 = $\frac{49}{60}$

2 $\frac{7}{8} - \frac{2}{3}$ 7 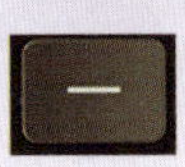 8   2 3 = $\frac{5}{24}$

Repeat some of questions **17–28** and check that you get the same answers.

Multiplying fractions

- To multiply fractions, **multiply the numerators** and then **multiply the denominators**.
- Mixed fractions must be converted to improper fractions first.
- If possible, simplify the answer and write it as a mixed fraction.

Examples:

1 $\frac{1}{3} \times \frac{3}{4} = \frac{1 \times 3}{3 \times 4}$

$= \frac{3}{12}$ ← Simplify.

$= \frac{1}{4}$

2 $2\frac{1}{2} \times 1\frac{3}{8} = \frac{5}{2} \times \frac{11}{8}$ ← First convert mixed fractions to improper fractions.

$= \frac{5 \times 11}{2 \times 8}$

$= \frac{55}{16}$

$= 3\frac{7}{16}$ ← Then back again.

Multiply these fractions and simplify when possible.

1 $\frac{1}{3} \times \frac{1}{5} = \frac{1 \times 1}{3 \times 5}$

$=$ ______

2 $\frac{1}{4} \times \frac{2}{3} =$ ______

$=$ ______

3 $\frac{5}{7} \times \frac{6}{7} =$ ______

$=$ ______

4 $\frac{4}{5} \times \frac{1}{6} =$ ______

$=$ ______

5 $\frac{1}{5} \times \frac{3}{8} =$ ______

$=$ ______

6 $\frac{5}{6} \times 3 =$ ______

$=$ ______

7 $1\frac{1}{3} \times \frac{1}{2} =$ ______

$=$ ______

8 $2\frac{3}{4} \times 2\frac{1}{5} =$ ______

$=$ ______

Fill in the gaps in order to complete correct calculations.

9 $\frac{3}{4} \times \frac{\square}{5} = \frac{12}{20}$

10 $\frac{6}{\square} \times \frac{3}{4} = \frac{\square}{20} = \frac{9}{\square}$

11 $\frac{\square}{5} \times 4 = \frac{8}{\square}$

12 $\frac{\square}{6} \times \frac{3}{\square} = \frac{\square}{42} = \frac{5}{14}$

13 $\frac{\square}{2} \times \frac{5}{\square} = \frac{15}{\square} = \frac{\square}{2} = 2\frac{1}{2}$

14 $\frac{\square}{10} \times \frac{8}{\square} = \frac{\square}{60} = \frac{6}{\square} = 1\frac{1}{5}$

 ISBN: 9780170497978

Dividing fractions

Dividing by whole numbers

10 ÷ 5 means 'How many fives are there in 10?' We know the answer is 2 because if we have 10 dots, these can be split into two groups of five.

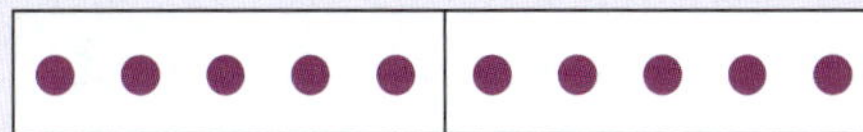

Reciprocals

The **reciprocal** of the fraction $\frac{a}{b}$ is $\frac{b}{a}$.

- You may like to think of this as '**turning the fraction upside down**'.
- To find the reciprocal of a mixed fraction, you must convert it to an improper fraction first.

Examples: **1** The reciprocal of $\frac{6}{7}$ is $\frac{7}{6}$.

2 $5\frac{2}{3} = \frac{17}{3}$, so the reciprocal of $5\frac{2}{3}$ is $\frac{3}{17}$.

3 $8 = \frac{8}{1}$, so the reciprocal of 8 is $\frac{1}{8}$.

Write reciprocals of the following numbers.

1 $\frac{6}{15}$ Reciprocal = ____________

2 $\frac{11}{3}$ Reciprocal = ____________

3 $4\frac{1}{3}$ Reciprocal = ____________

4 $5\frac{3}{4}$ Reciprocal = ____________

5 21 Reciprocal = ____________

6 $120\frac{3}{5}$ Reciprocal = ____________

Dividing by fractions

$2 \div \frac{1}{4}$ means 'How many quarters are there in 2?'

Consider pizzas: how many quarters are there in two pizzas?

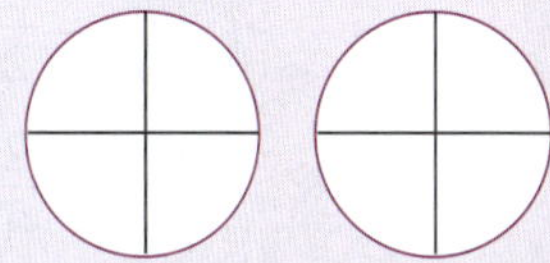

We can see there are eight (= 2 **x 4**) quarters.

So $2 \div \frac{1}{4} = 2$ **x 4** = 8: we need to **multiply** two by **four**.

We call 4 (or $\frac{4}{1}$) the **reciprocal** of $\frac{1}{4}$.

Complete the following.

7 Use the diagram to help you fill in the gaps.

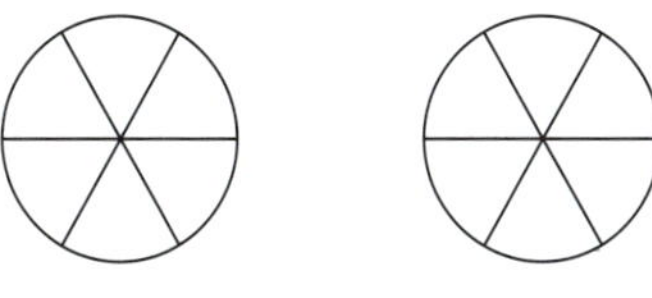

$2 \div \frac{1}{\square} = 2 \times \square = \square$

$2 \div \frac{1}{\square}$ means 'How many ____________ are there in ____________?

8 Use the diagram to help you fill in the gaps.

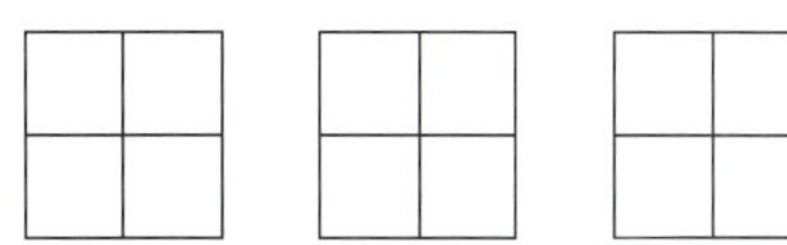

$3 \div \frac{1}{\square} = 3 \times \square = \square$

$3 \div \frac{1}{\square}$ means 'How many ____________ are there in ____________?

ISBN: 9780170497978

Rules for dividing fractions

- Mixed fractions must be converted to improper fractions first.
- Trick to dividing fractions:
  1 Leave the first fraction unchanged.
  2 Write the reciprocal of the second fraction.
  3 Multiply the two together.

If possible, simplify the answer and write it as a mixed fraction.

Examples:

1

$$10 \div \frac{\mathbf{1}}{\mathbf{5}} = \frac{10}{1} \times \frac{\mathbf{5}}{\mathbf{1}}$$ Multiply by the reciprocal of the second fraction.

$$= \frac{10 \times \mathbf{5}}{1 \times \mathbf{1}}$$

$$= 50$$ Simplify.

This means there are 50 fifths in 10.

2

$$\frac{3}{4} \div \frac{\mathbf{2}}{\mathbf{5}} = \frac{3}{4} \times \frac{\mathbf{5}}{\mathbf{2}}$$ Multiply by the reciprocal of the second fraction.

$$= \frac{3 \times \mathbf{5}}{4 \times \mathbf{2}}$$

$$= \frac{15}{8}$$

$$= 1\frac{7}{8}$$ Change to a mixed fraction.

3

$$3\frac{1}{4} \div 7\frac{1}{2} = \frac{13}{4} \div \frac{\mathbf{15}}{\mathbf{2}}$$ Turn both mixed fractions into improper fractions.

$$= \frac{13}{4} \times \frac{\mathbf{2}}{\mathbf{15}}$$ Multiply by the reciprocal of the second fraction.

$$= \frac{26}{60}$$ Divide the numerator and the denominator by the HCF, in this case 2.

$$= \frac{13}{30}$$

Divide these fractions and simplify when possible. Where appropriate, write your answers as mixed fractions.

9 $2 \div \frac{1}{3} = \frac{2}{1} \times \frac{\square}{\square}$

$= \_\_\_\_\_\_$

$2 \div \frac{1}{3} =$ ______ means 'There are ______ *thirds* in ______.'

10 $5 \div \frac{1}{10} =$ ______

$= \_\_\_\_\_\_$

$5 \div \frac{1}{10} =$ ______ means 'There are ______ ______ in ______.'

 ISBN: 9780170497978

11 $\frac{3}{4} \div \frac{1}{8} = \frac{3}{4} \times \frac{8}{1}$

$= \_\_\_\_\_\_$

$= \_\_\_\_\_\_$

$\frac{3}{4} \div \frac{1}{8} =$ ______ means 'There are ______ ______ in ______ ______.'

12 $\frac{1}{3} \div \frac{2}{3} =$ ______

$= \_\_\_\_\_\_$

$= \_\_\_\_\_\_$

$\frac{1}{3} \div \frac{2}{3} =$ ______ means 'There is ______ of two thirds in ______ ______.'

Divide these fractions and simplify when possible. Where appropriate, write your answers as mixed fractions.

13 $\frac{2}{3} \div \frac{5}{6} =$ ______

$= \_\_\_\_\_\_$

14 $\frac{1}{7} \div \frac{3}{8} =$ ______

$= \_\_\_\_\_\_$

15 $\frac{5}{8} \div \frac{2}{9} =$ ______

$= \_\_\_\_\_\_$

$= \_\_\_\_\_\_$

16 $\frac{2}{5} \div \frac{2}{7} =$ ______

$= \_\_\_\_\_\_$

$= \_\_\_\_\_\_$

17 $\frac{8}{9} \div 5 =$ ______

$= \_\_\_\_\_\_$

$= \_\_\_\_\_\_$

18 $\frac{3}{4} \div 1\frac{1}{3} =$ ______

$= \_\_\_\_\_\_$

$= \_\_\_\_\_\_$

19 $1\frac{1}{2} \div 2\frac{2}{5} =$ ______

$= \_\_\_\_\_\_$

$= \_\_\_\_\_\_$

20 $1\frac{4}{5} \div 9 =$ ______

$= \_\_\_\_\_\_$

$= \_\_\_\_\_\_$

Fill in the gaps in order to complete correct calculations.

21 $\frac{3}{5} \div \frac{1}{4} = \frac{\square}{5} \times \frac{4}{\square} = \frac{\square}{5}$

22 $\frac{7}{9} \div \frac{4}{\square} = \frac{7}{9} \times \frac{\square}{4} = \frac{49}{36}$

23 $\frac{2}{7} \div \frac{1}{2} = \frac{\square}{7}$

24 $\frac{5}{6} \div \frac{2}{3} = \frac{15}{\square} = \frac{5}{\square}$

25 $\frac{\square}{8} \div 2 = \frac{3}{\square}$

26 $\frac{7}{9} \div \frac{1}{\square} = 4\frac{2}{3}$

ISBN: 9780170497978

Ordering fractions

Ordering fractions is easiest if they all have the same **denominator**.

Example: Which is bigger? $\frac{2}{3}$ or $\frac{3}{4}$?

The **LCM** of **3** and **4** is 12, so use **12** as a **denominator**:

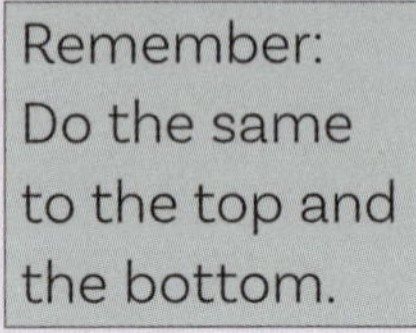

$\frac{2}{3} = \frac{8}{12}$ (x 4) and $\frac{3}{4} = \frac{9}{12}$ (x 3)

So, $\frac{3}{4}$ is bigger than $\frac{2}{3}$ or $\frac{3}{4} > \frac{2}{3}$

In the second row, rewrite the fractions in the first row so they have the same denominator.
In the third row, write the fractions in ascending order (smallest to biggest).

1

$\frac{3}{5}$	$\frac{7}{20}$	$\frac{1}{4}$	$\frac{1}{2}$	$\frac{9}{10}$	$\frac{3}{10}$	$\frac{4}{5}$	$\frac{13}{20}$
$\frac{12}{20}$							

Smallest → Biggest

				$\frac{3}{5}$			

2

$\frac{4}{50}$	$\frac{5}{25}$	$\frac{7}{10}$	$\frac{2}{5}$	$\frac{12}{25}$	$\frac{1}{2}$	$\frac{4}{5}$	$\frac{3}{10}$
				$\frac{24}{50}$			

Smallest → Biggest

In the second row, rewrite the fractions in the first row so they have the same denominator.
Then place the fractions on the number line.

3

$\frac{1}{4}$	$\frac{2}{3}$	$\frac{7}{12}$	$\frac{1}{2}$	$\frac{5}{6}$	$\frac{3}{4}$	$\frac{1}{6}$	$\frac{5}{12}$
$\frac{3}{12}$							

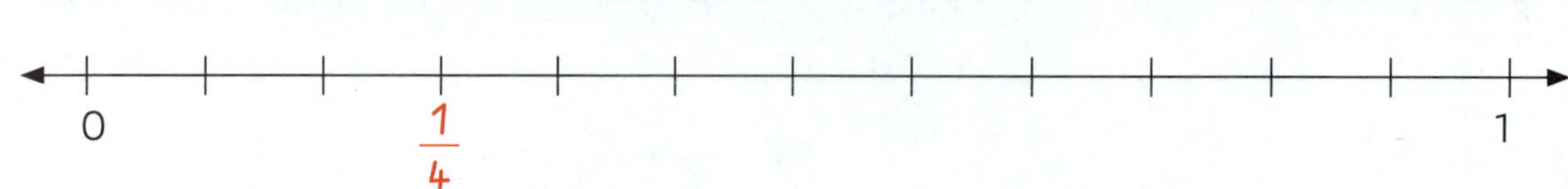

 ISBN: 9780170497978

Comparing fractions

Symbols you need to know:

> means '**is greater than**'
< means '**is less than**'
≥ means '**is greater than or equal to**'
≤ means '**is less than or equal to**'

Insert any of the above four symbols, in order to create true statements.

1 8 ☐ 3

2 2 ☐ 6

3 -3 ☐ -6

4 10^0 ☐ 4

5 10^3 ☐ 999

6 80 ☐ 3^4

To compare fractions

1 If the **denominators** are the **same**, compare the numerators.

Example: $\frac{5}{7}$ is greater than $\frac{2}{7}$ because 5 is larger than 2.

2 If the **denominators** are **different**:

Examples:

1 Which fraction is greater, $\frac{3}{5}$ or $\frac{2}{3}$?

Sometimes you can compare pictures: 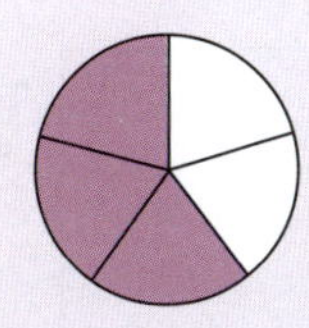 < 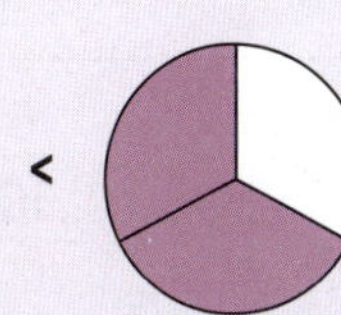 so $\frac{2}{3}$ is greater.

Otherwise you need to convert one or both fractions so they have a common denominator.

Because the denominators are 5 and 3, the **common denominator** needs to be **15**.

So $\frac{3}{5} \times \frac{3}{3} = \frac{9}{15}$ and $\frac{2}{3} \times \frac{5}{5} = \frac{10}{15}$

$\frac{9}{15} < \frac{10}{15} \therefore \frac{3}{5} < \frac{2}{3}$, so $\frac{2}{3}$ is greater.

2 Which fraction is greater, $\frac{6}{10}$ or $\frac{2}{3}$?

Denominators are **10** and **3**, so the common **denominator** is **30**.

So $\frac{6}{10} \times \frac{3}{3} = \frac{18}{30}$ and $\frac{2}{3} \times \frac{10}{10} = \frac{20}{30}$

$\frac{18}{30} < \frac{20}{30} \therefore \frac{6}{10} < \frac{2}{3}$, so $\frac{2}{3}$ is greater.

ISBN: 9780170497978

Shade the diagrams and write a > or < symbol between each fraction. The first one has been done for you. Hint: Start from 12 o'clock and shade in the same direction.

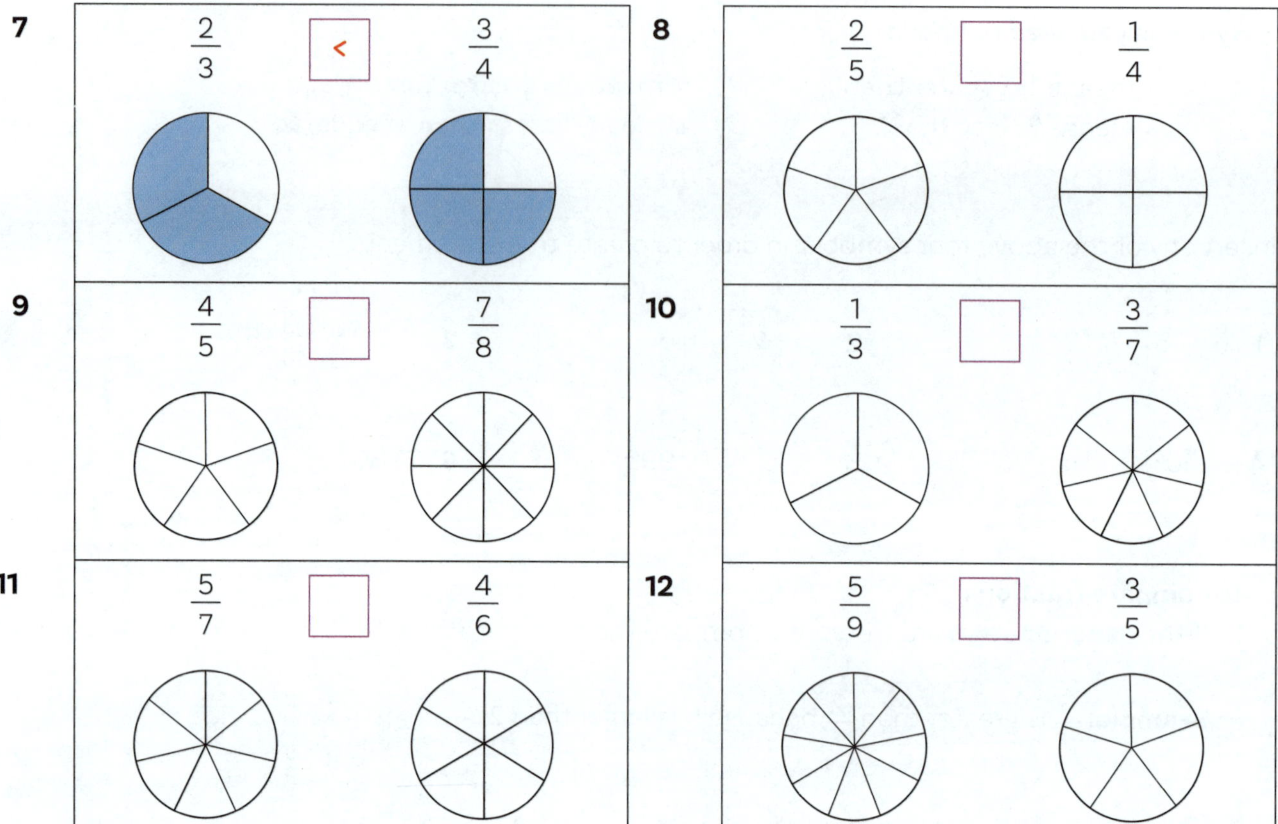

Rewrite each of the following pairs of fractions so that they have a common denominator, and then insert a < or > sign between them.

13 $\frac{2}{3}$ > $\frac{6}{10}$

$= \frac{20}{30}$ $= \frac{18}{30}$

14 $\frac{3}{4}$ ☐ $\frac{2}{5}$

$= \frac{☐}{☐}$ $= \frac{☐}{☐}$

15 $\frac{5}{8}$ ☐ $\frac{2}{3}$

$= \frac{☐}{☐}$ $= \frac{☐}{☐}$

16 $\frac{2}{7}$ ☐ $\frac{1}{3}$

$= \frac{☐}{☐}$ $= \frac{☐}{☐}$

17 $\frac{5}{6}$ ☐ $\frac{7}{8}$

$= \frac{☐}{☐}$ $= \frac{☐}{☐}$

18 $\frac{4}{5}$ ☐ $\frac{5}{7}$

$= \frac{☐}{☐}$ $= \frac{☐}{☐}$

19 $\frac{7}{10}$ ☐ $\frac{5}{7}$

$= \frac{☐}{☐}$ $= \frac{☐}{☐}$

20 $\frac{8}{11}$ ☐ $\frac{25}{35}$

$= \frac{☐}{☐}$ $= \frac{☐}{☐}$

 ISBN: 9780170497978

Fraction of a quantity

Remember that '**of**' means you must '**multiply**'.

Example: $\frac{1}{4}$ **of** $32 = \frac{1}{4}$ **x** 32

$= \frac{1}{4} \times \frac{32}{1}$

$= \frac{32}{4}$

$= 8$

Replace the word '**of**' with a **x** sign.

Remember that '32' means 32 wholes, or $\frac{32}{1}$.

Answer the following questions.

1 $\frac{1}{3}$ of 42 = ______
= ______
= ______

2 $\frac{3}{4}$ of 28 = ______
= ______
= ______

3 $\frac{3}{5}$ of 55 = ______
= ______
= ______

4 $\frac{1}{7}$ of 63 = ______
= ______
= ______

5 $\frac{5}{6}$ of 48 = ______
= ______
= ______

6 $\frac{3}{2}$ of 36 = ______
= ______
= ______

7 $1\frac{1}{3}$ of 27 = ______
= ______
= ______

8 Three aunts each paid a third of the cost of their niece's birthday present. Its total cost was $117. How much did each aunt pay?

______

______

9 Ten students share two cakes equally between them. What fraction of a cake does each student get?

______

______

10 Each flatmate paid a fifth of the cost of a new fridge. If the fridge cost $1591, how much did each flatmate pay?

______

______

ISBN: 9780170497978

Increasing and decreasing by a fraction

- Find the required fraction and add it to or subtract it from the original.

Increasing by a fraction

Example: Increase 135 by a fifth.

Method 1: Find a fifth of 135 and add it on. $135 \times \frac{1}{5} = 27$

$135 + 27 = 162$

Method 2: Find $1 + \frac{1}{5}$ or $1\frac{1}{5}$ or $\frac{6}{5}$ of 135. $135 \times \frac{6}{5} = 162$

Another way to think about it:

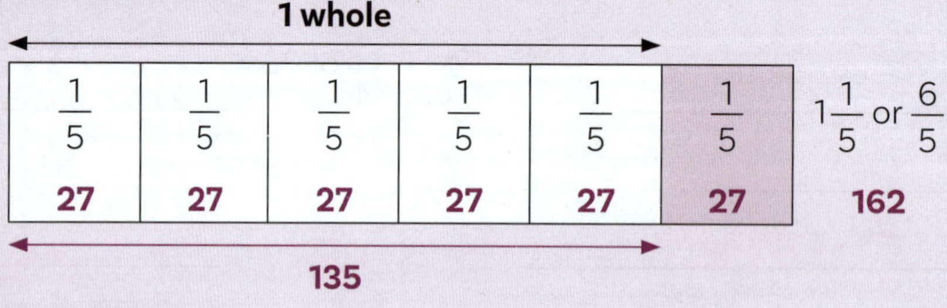

Answer the following questions.

1 Increase 24 by a sixth.

2 Increase 40 by an eighth.

3 Increase 540 by a tenth.

4 Increase 81 by a third.

5 Increase 292 by a quarter.

6 Increase 100 by two fifths.

7 Increase 60 by five sixths.

8 Increase 60 by three quarters.

9 Martin gets a holiday job. His father says that he will add a tenth of whatever Martin earns as a bonus. If Martin earned $352.00 at his job, how much did he earn altogether?

10 A company manufactures bars of soap that are 108 g each. The bars are shipped in boxes of 10. They find that their packaging adds an eighth to the mass of the soap. What will be the mass of a box of soap, including the packaging?

 ISBN: 9780170497978

Decreasing by a fraction

Example: Decrease 472 by a quarter.

Method 1: Find a quarter of 472 and subtract it. $472 \times \frac{1}{4} = 118$

$472 - 118 = 354$

Method 2: Find $1 - \frac{1}{4}$ or $\frac{3}{4}$ of 472. $472 \times \frac{3}{4} = 354$

Another way to think about it:

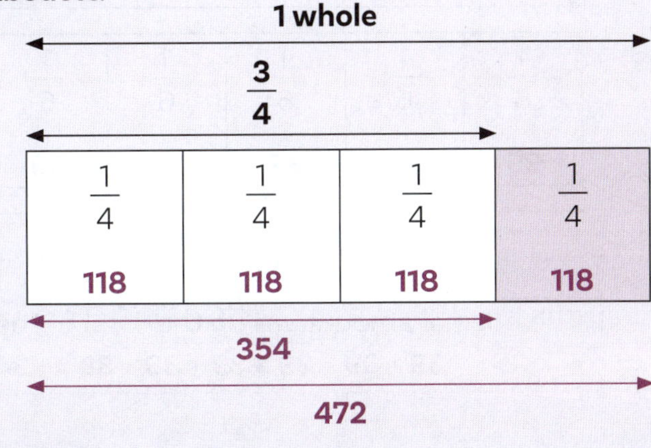

Answer the following questions.

11 Decrease 24 by a sixth.

12 Decrease 500 by a tenth.

13 Decrease 186 by a sixth.

14 Decrease 192 by a third.

15 Decrease 650 by two fifths.

16 Decrease 240 by three tenths.

17 Decrease 1000 by five eighths.

18 Decrease 567 by three sevenths.

19 A section of land is 522 m^2. The council rules say that the maximum area for a house is a third of the area of a section. If the house is the maximum allowable size, what area will be left for paths and garden?

20 Angus is making apricot jam. He has 4.5 kg of apricots. If $\frac{3}{50}$ of the mass of an apricot is the stone, what mass of apricots will he have once he has removed the stones?

ISBN: 9780170497978

Given a fraction, find the whole amount

- Find the required fraction and add it to or subtract it from the original.

Examples:

Method 1: This method will work only if the **numerator is 1**.

One sixth of an amount is 39. What is the original amount?

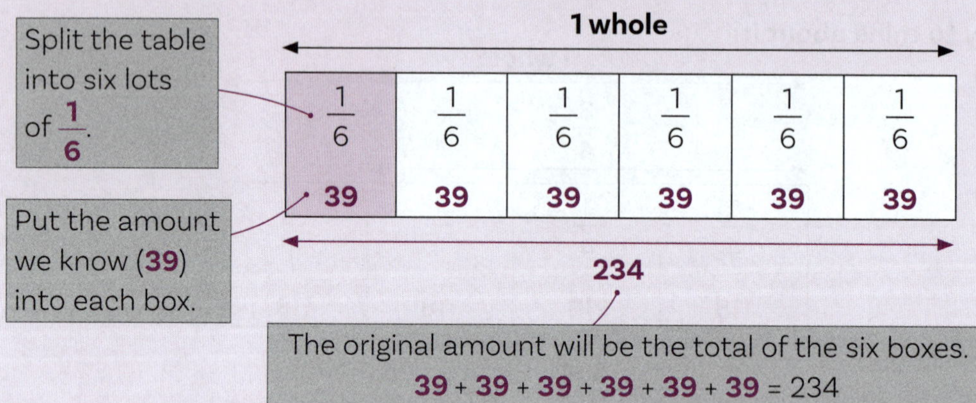

Method 2: This method will work for **any fraction**.

Three fifths of an amount is 189. What is the original amount?

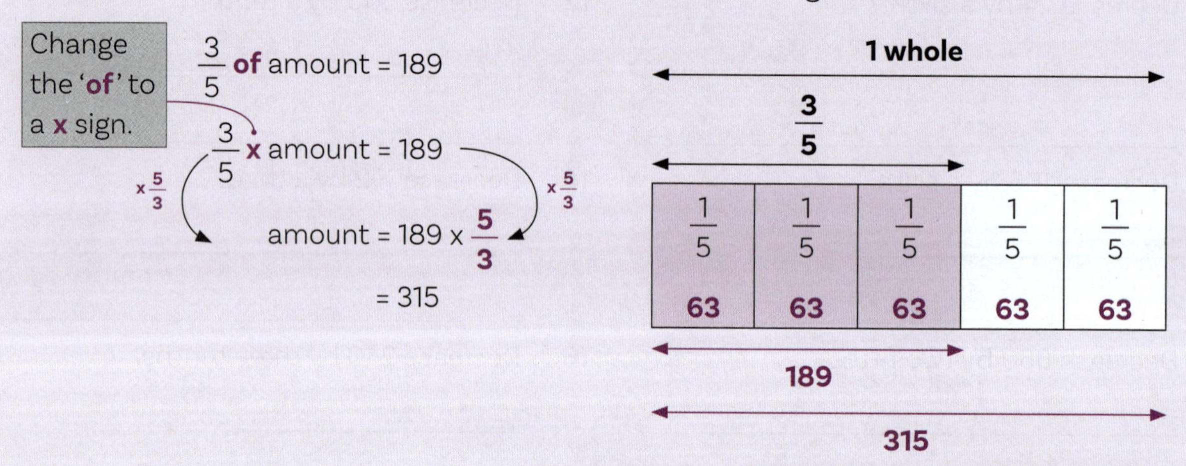

Complete the table and answer the following questions.

1 One fifth of what amount is 16?

1 whole

$\frac{1}{5}$	$\frac{1}{5}$	$\frac{1}{5}$	$\frac{1}{5}$	$\frac{1}{5}$

Amount is ____________

2 One eighth of what amount is 24?

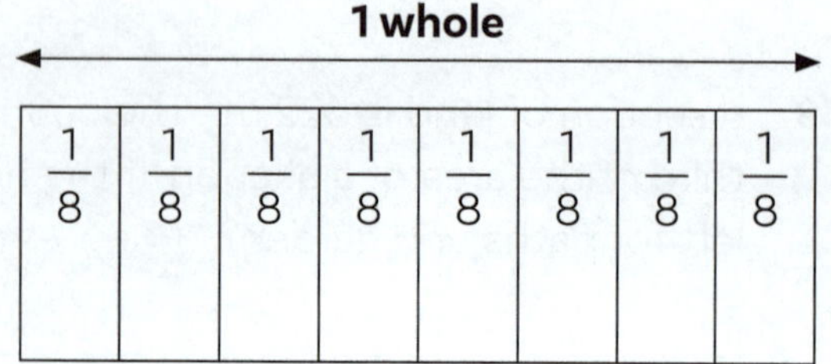

Amount is ____________

 ISBN: 9780170497978

3 A third of what amount is 91?

1 whole

Amount is ______________

4 A sixth of what amount is 204?

1 whole

Amount is ______________

5 A quarter of what amount is 28?

6 A fifth of what amount is 654?

7 Three tenths of what amount is 45?

8 Three fifths of what amount is 36?

9 Two thirds of what amount is 212?

10 Three quarters of what amount is 51?

11 Seven twelfths of what amount is 441?

12 Three twentieths of what amount is 27?

13 Three fifths of those who attended a concert were locals. If 738 locals attended it, how many people were there altogether?

14 The company that makes Loopy Lollies maintains there are equal numbers of each of six different colours in a bag. Anna found there were 18 blue lollies. How many Loopy Lollies should there be in the bag?

15 Two out of every 19 people on the school grounds are the 72 staff members. How many people are on the school grounds altogether?

ISBN: 9780170497978

Decimals

Place value

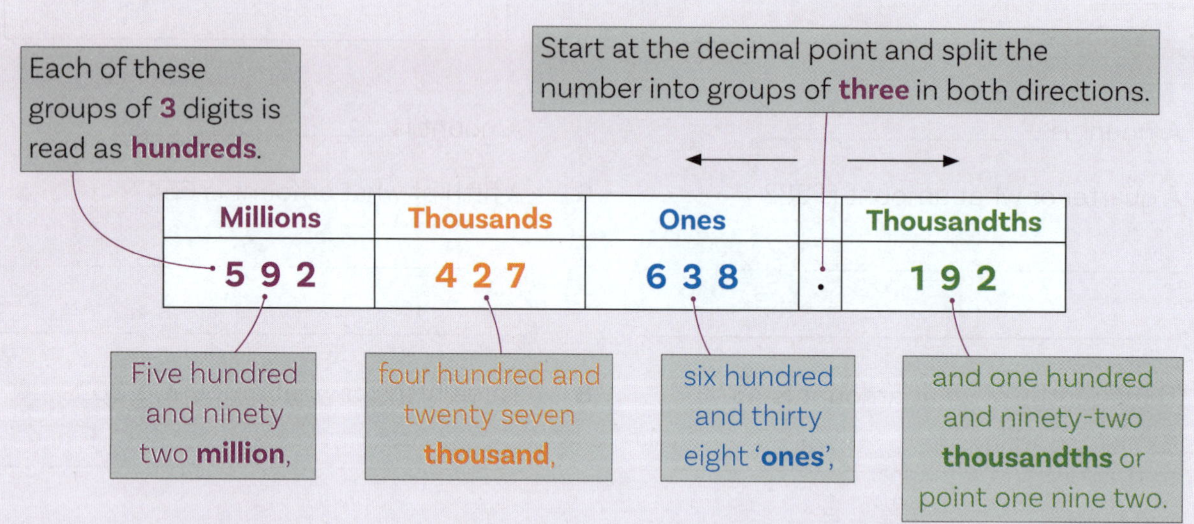

Writing decimals as words

Remember, if there is no decimal point, it is understood that it is after the last digit.

Examples:

1 Write 25 083 472 in words.

Millions	Thousands	Ones		Thousandths
25	083	472	.	

Twenty-five million, **eighty-three thousand**, **four hundred and seventy-two**.

2 Write 400 003 010.81 in words.

Millions	Thousands	Ones		Thousandths
400	003	010	.	81(0)

Be careful: if there are fewer than three digits in this column, and you want to express the number in thousandths, you need to add zeros to make it up to three digits.

Four million, **three thousand** **and ten** **point eight one** or **and eight hundred and ten thousandths**.

ISBN: 9780170497978

Write down the value of the purple numerals as numbers and in words.

		Number	Words
1	7 **2**54	200	
2	26**5** 971		Five thousand
3	**7**9		
4	4 3**6**5 194		
5	**8**01 035		
6	32**9** 247 840		
7	51 2**4**1		
8	**3**06 128 324		
9	20 **1**99		
10	9**8**2 105 075		

Write down the value of the purple numerals as decimals, fractions and in words.

		Decimal	Fraction	Words
11	0.**7**12			Seven tenths
12	0.56**4**		$\frac{4}{1\,000}$	
13	14.1**2**7	0.020		
14	98.**5**01			
15	19.8**3**2			
16	600.02**0**			
17	1.00**9**			
18	0.0**7**5			

ISBN: 9780170497978

Write the numbers using words.

19 826

____

20 12 441

____

21 3 507

____

22 82.6

____

23 715 624.5

____

24 203 473 614

____

25 0.63

____

26 300 060.2

____

27 980 010.47

____

Write the numbers using numerals.

28 Nine thousand and fifteen ______________

29 Forty-three and five tenths 43.5

30 Two million, seven hundred and thirty-one ______________

31 Six hundred thousand and four ______________

32 Three and twenty-two thousandths ______________

33 One million, eight hundred and thirty thousand and four ______________

34 Five and nine thousandths ______________

35 Eight tenths and six hundredths ______________

36 Forty-three million, one hundred and ninety-one and two hundredths ______________

 ISBN: 9780170497978

Decimals on number lines

To work out the size of each gap between ticks on a number line:

Step 1: Calculate the **distance** between two **labelled** points. **Distance** = 0.70 − 0.45 = **0.25**

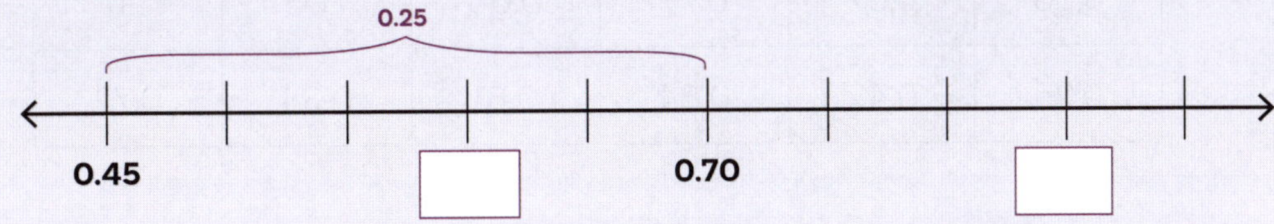

Step 2: Count the **number of gaps** between 0.45 and 0.70. **Number of gaps = 5**

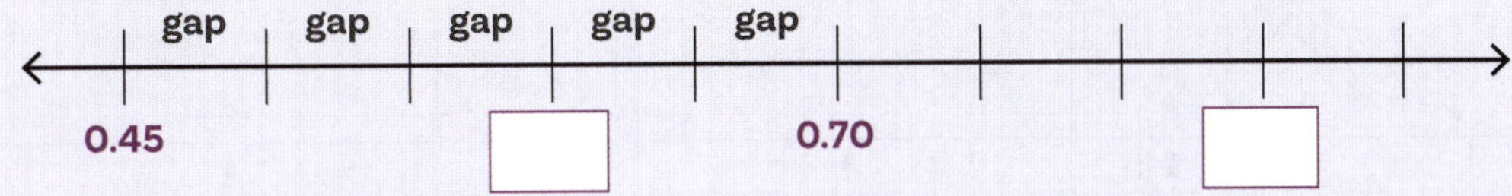

Step 3: Divide the distance by the number of gaps to give the size of each gap. $\frac{0.25}{5} = 0.05$

Step 4: Add 0.05 after each tick along the number line.

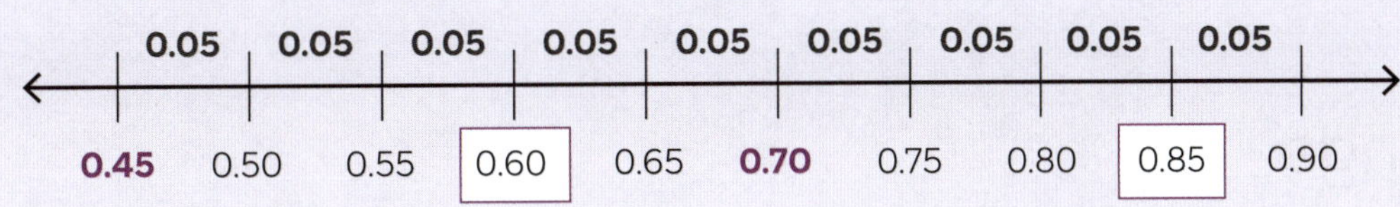

Write the missing decimals on the number lines.

1 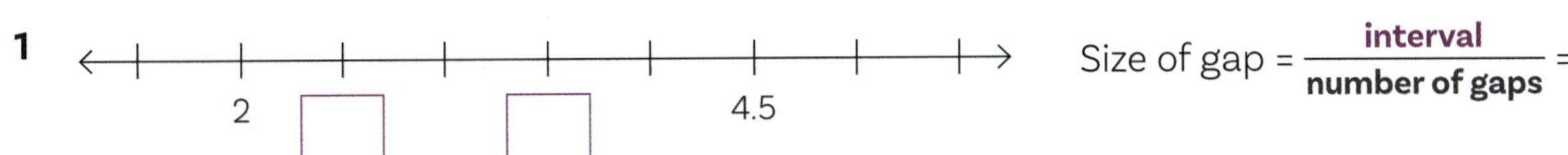

Size of gap = $\frac{\textbf{interval}}{\textbf{number of gaps}}$ =

2 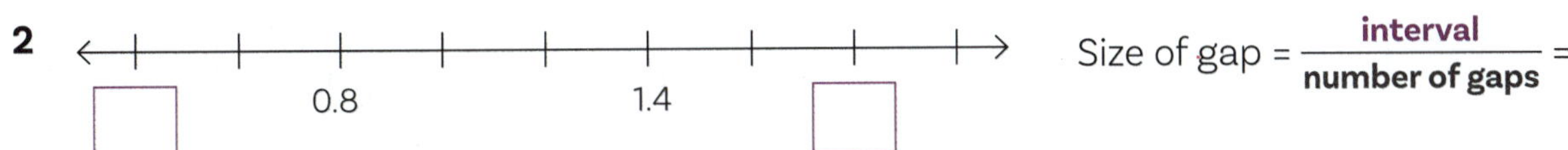

Size of gap = $\frac{\textbf{interval}}{\textbf{number of gaps}}$ =

3 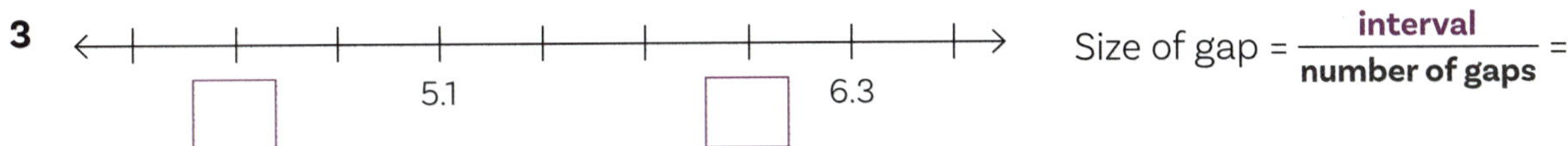

Size of gap = $\frac{\textbf{interval}}{\textbf{number of gaps}}$ =

4 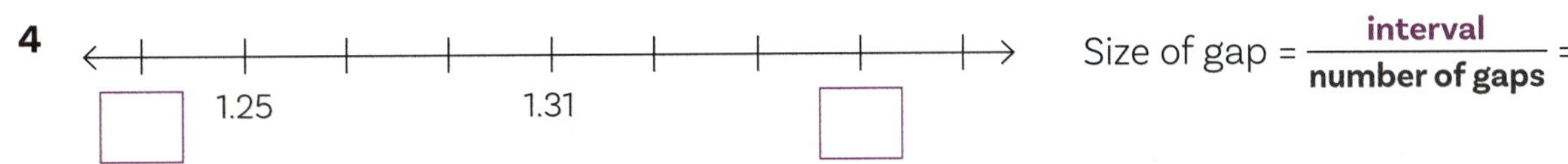

Size of gap = $\frac{\textbf{interval}}{\textbf{number of gaps}}$ =

5 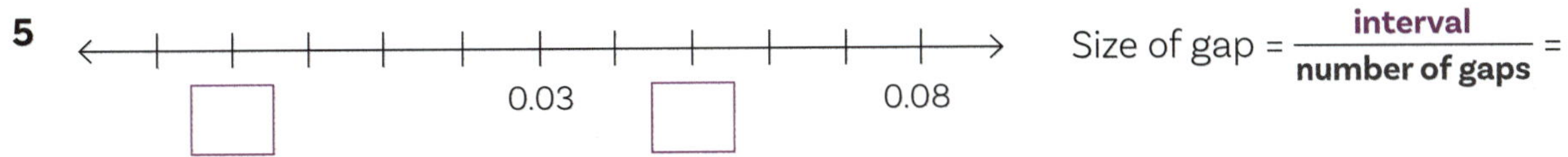

Size of gap = $\frac{\textbf{interval}}{\textbf{number of gaps}}$ =

ISBN: 9780170497978

6 Write decimal values for each point along the number line. Choose the most appropriate values from the list below. You will not need all the points on the list.

0.97	0.11	0.47	0.19	0.67	0.28
0.03	0.57	0.79	0.06	1.05	1.11
0.25	0.42	0.84	0.81	0.34	0.72

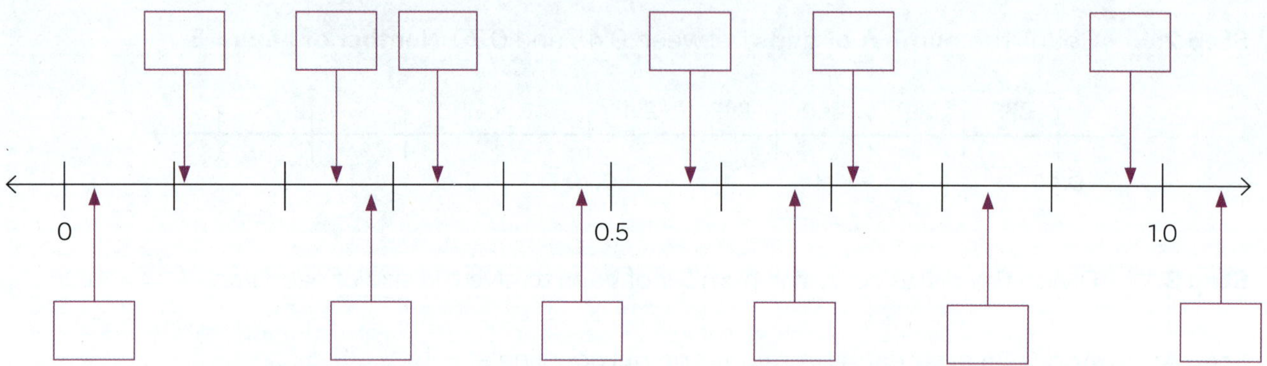

Challenge

Write decimal values for each point along the number line. Choose the most appropriate values from the list below. You will not need all the points on the list.

- 0.48	- 0.17	- 0.28	- 0.66	- 0.05	0.14
- 0.73	- 0.81	0.04	0.22	- 0.12	- 0.55
0.12	- 0.41	0.09	- 0.34	0.18	0.02

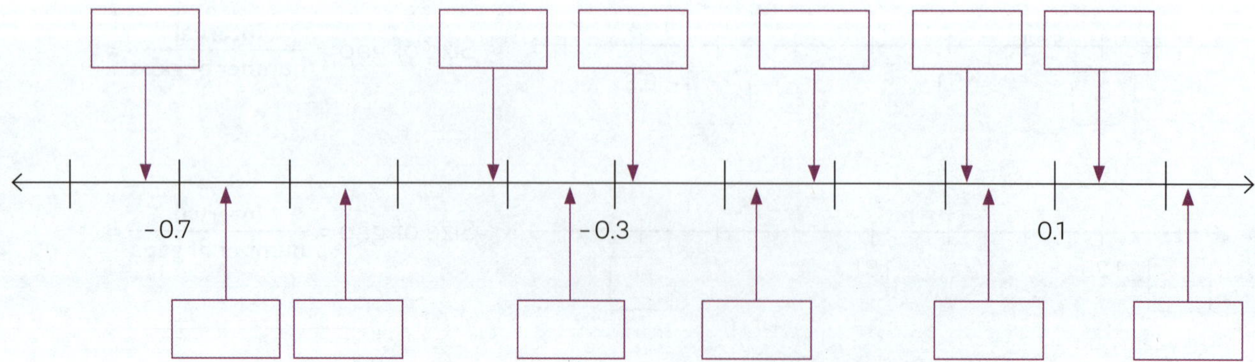

ISBN: 9780170497978

Comparing decimals

- To determine which decimal is largest, you need to consider the place values of each digit, starting from the left.

Examples: Place a < or a > sign between each pair of decimals.

1 

53.67 ☐ 53.82

Remember, < and > symbols **point to the smaller** number.

Step 1: Arrange the numbers with the **decimal points lined up** vertically:

53.67
53.82

The decimal points **must** be in line.

Step 2: Start at the left, and look for the **first pair of digits that is different**:

53 | .67
53 | .82

The first **two** digits are the same.

Step 3: Decide which is larger or smaller: **6** < **8**, so 53.**6**7 < 53.**8**2.

2 27.030 ☐ 27.009

Step 1: Arrange the numbers with the decimal points lined up vertically:

27.030
27.009

Step 2: Start at the left, and look for the **first pair of digits that is different**:

27.0 | 30
27.0 | 09

The first **three** digits are the same.

Step 3: Decide which is larger or smaller: **3** > **0**, so 27.0**3**0 > 27.0**0**9.

Highlight the bigger number.

1	24.42	24.24
2	1 789	1 798
3	5.42	5.4
4	3.167	3.12
5	10.01	10.10

Place a > or < or = to make each statement true.

6	0.9	☐	0.90
7	864.03	☐	863.40
8	9.603	☐	9.630
9	4.011	☐	4.110
10	0.759	☐	0.75

ISBN: 9780170497978

Write down the following decimals.

11 0.11 increased by three tenths 0.41

12 5.114 increased by four thousandths ______

13 61.003 increased by five hundredths ______

14 100.020 increased by seven tenths ______

15 4.172 increased by twelve thousandths ______

16 9.033 increased by fifteen hundredths ______

17 0.591 increased by three hundred and twenty-one thousandths ______

18 85.109 increased by eighteen thousandths ______

19 Complete the calculations shown in the diagram. If you do this correctly, your final answer should be 1.

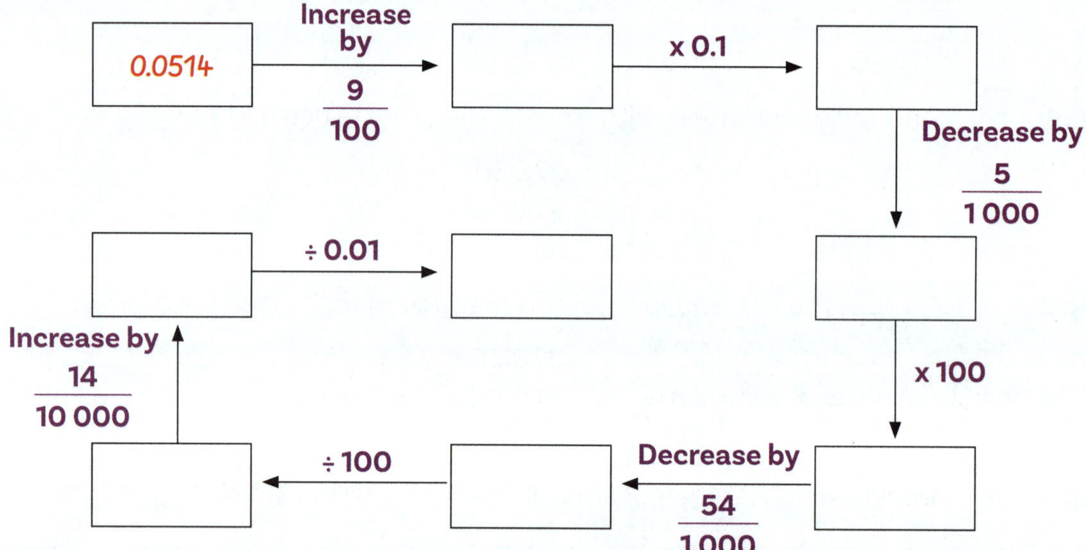

Place these decimals in ascending order.

20 7.077 7.707 7.007 7.770 ______ ______ ______ ______

21 0.101 0.111 0.110 0.011 ______ ______ ______ ______

22 4.340 4.304 4.043 4.403 ______ ______ ______ ______

23 0.998 0.898 0.889 0.989 ______ ______ ______ ______

24 0.055 0.050 0.505 0.550 ______ ______ ______ ______

  ISBN: 9780170497978

Recurring decimals

- Recurring decimals are decimals that have a **pattern of repeating digits** which never stops.
- To identify these, a dot is placed over the first and last digits that repeat.

Examples:

1 0.666666... can be written as $0.\dot{6}$.

2 8.1242424... can be written as $8.1\dot{2}\dot{4}$.

Notice that only the digits with dots are repeated.

3 0.103103103... can be written as $0.\dot{1}0\dot{3}$.

This means that the 103 must be repeated.

Why are these important?

Compare: 0.3 of \$1 000 = \$300

$0.\dot{3}$ of \$1 000 = \$333.33

That's a difference of over \$33!

More examples:

Fraction	Decimal	Notation
$\frac{4}{9}$	0.44444...	$0.\dot{4}$
$\frac{8}{11}$	0.727272...	$0.\dot{7}\dot{2}$
$\frac{4}{15}$	0.266666...	$0.2\dot{6}$

Fraction	Decimal	Notation
$\frac{9}{22}$	0.4090909...	$0.4\dot{0}\dot{9}$
$\frac{16}{27}$	0.592592592...	$0.\dot{5}9\dot{2}$
$\frac{4}{7}$	0.571428571428...	$0.\dot{5}7142\dot{8}$

Write these decimals in full. Use ... at the end to show that they carry on.

1 $0.\dot{7}$ = ______________

2 $0.\dot{2}\dot{3}$ = ______________

3 $0.\dot{7}1\dot{8}$ = ______________

4 $0.\dot{6}43\dot{2}$ = ______________

Write these using recurring decimal notation.

5 0.19191919... = ______________

6 0.143143143... = ______________

7 0.0967967967... = ______________

8 0.00888888... = ______________

Write these fractions using recurring decimal notation.

9 $\frac{1}{3}$ = ______________

10 $\frac{2}{11}$ = ______________

11 $\frac{19}{27}$ = ______________

12 $1\frac{7}{15}$ = ______________

13 $\frac{10}{22}$ = ______________

14 $7\frac{4}{11}$ = ______________

ISBN: 9780170497978

Using decimals to compare fractions

You can compare fractions by:

1 converting the fractions to decimals using your calculator,

2 then use < or > symbols between the fractions.

Example: Place a **<** or a **>** sign between the pair of fractions: $\frac{1}{3}$ ☐ $\frac{667}{2\,000}$

$\frac{1}{3} = 0.\dot{3} = 0.333|\mathbf{33}...$

$\frac{667}{2\,000} = 0.333|\mathbf{5}$

To get the decimal on your calculator, divide 1 by 3:

1 [÷] 3 [=] $1.\dot{3}$

$\mathbf{3} < \mathbf{5}$, so $\frac{1}{3} < \frac{667}{2\,000}$

Calculate the decimal value of each fraction and show which is bigger using a < or > sign.

1 $\frac{1}{3} =$ $0.\dot{3} = 0.33|33...$
 $\frac{17}{50} =$ $0.34|$
 $\frac{1}{3}$ [<] $\frac{17}{50}$

2 $\frac{1}{4} =$ _____
 $\frac{3}{11} =$ _____
 $\frac{1}{4}$ ☐ $\frac{3}{11}$

3 $\frac{4}{7} =$ _____
 $\frac{5}{9} =$ _____
 $\frac{4}{7}$ ☐ $\frac{5}{9}$

4 $\frac{7}{15} =$ _____
 $\frac{5}{11} =$ _____
 $\frac{7}{15}$ ☐ $\frac{5}{11}$

5 $\frac{5}{6} =$ _____
 $\frac{9}{11} =$ _____
 $\frac{5}{6}$ ☐ $\frac{9}{11}$

6 $\frac{1}{7} =$ _____
 $\frac{3}{16} =$ _____
 $\frac{1}{7}$ ☐ $\frac{3}{16}$

7 $\frac{2}{15} =$ _____
 $\frac{1}{8} =$ _____
 $\frac{2}{15}$ ☐ $\frac{1}{8}$

8 $\frac{8}{11} =$ _____
 $\frac{7}{9} =$ _____
 $\frac{8}{11}$ ☐ $\frac{7}{9}$

9 $\frac{1}{9} =$ _____
 $\frac{2}{17} =$ _____
 $\frac{1}{9}$ ☐ $\frac{2}{17}$

10 $\frac{21}{9} =$ _____
 $\frac{16}{7} =$ _____
 $\frac{21}{9}$ ☐ $\frac{16}{7}$

11 $1\frac{4}{9} =$ _____
 $1\frac{3}{7} =$ _____
 $1\frac{4}{9}$ ☐ $1\frac{3}{7}$

12 $\frac{7}{11} =$ _____
 $\frac{17}{27} =$ _____
 $\frac{7}{11}$ ☐ $\frac{17}{27}$

ISBN: 9780170497978

Percentages

- Percentages are a way of expressing a number **out of 100**.

Example:

42 out of 100 squares are **purple**.

42% is the same as $\frac{42}{100}$.

58 out of 100 squares are white.

58% is the same as $\frac{58}{100}$.

100 squares altogether.

42 **purple** squares.

100 - 42 = 58 white squares.

State the percentages shown in these diagrams.

1

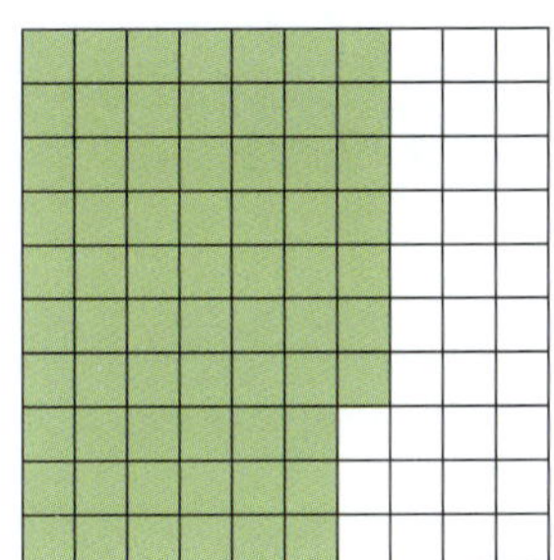

Percentage **green** ____________

Percentage white ____________

2

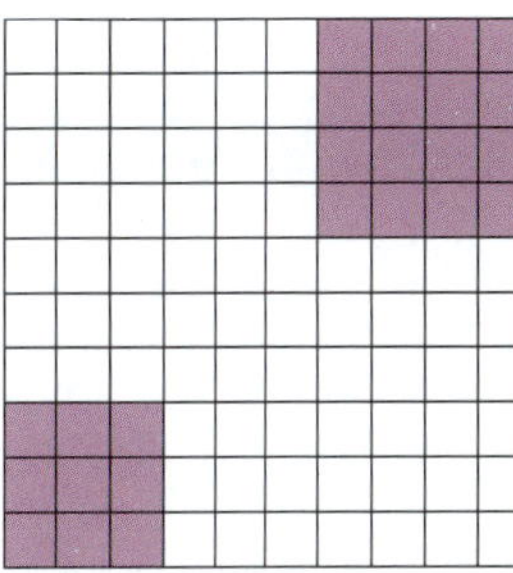

Percentage **purple** ____________

Percentage white ____________

3

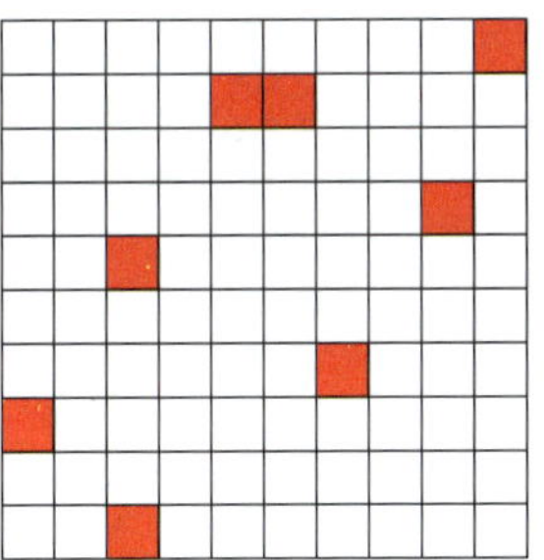

Percentage **red** ____________

Percentage white ____________

4

Percentage **blue** ____________

Percentage **yellow** ____________

Percentage white ____________

Answer the following.

5 13% of students at the school are left-handed. What percentage are not left-handed?

____

6 In a garden, 46% of the plants are flowers and 23% are shrubs. What percentage of the plants are neither flowers nor shrubs?

____

ISBN: 9780170497978

Converting between decimals and percentages

Because percentages are out of 100,

- to change a decimal to a percentage, you **multiply by 100**
- to change a percentage to a decimal, you **divide by 100**.

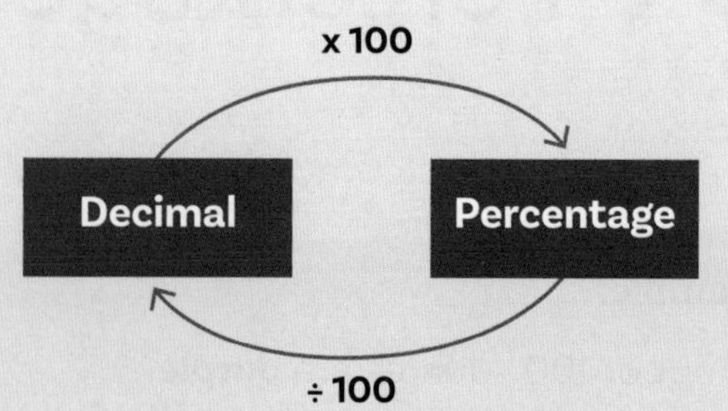

Examples: **1** 1.15 = 115%

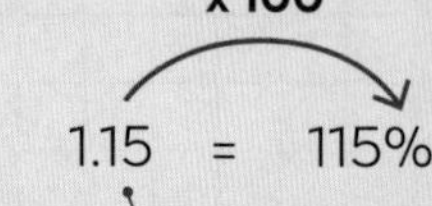

Notice that **multiplying** by 100 is the same as moving the decimal point two places to the **right**.

2 23.9% = 0.239

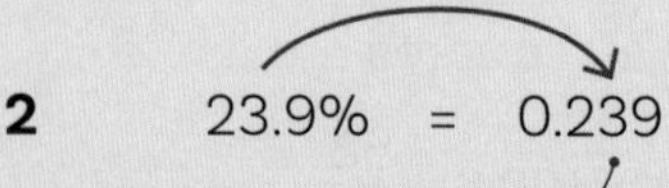

Notice that **dividing** by 100 is the same as moving the decimal point two places to the **left**.

Convert the following decimals to percentages.

1 0.85 = ____________________ **2** 0.13 = ____________________

3 0.04 = ____________________ **4** 0.845 = ____________________

5 0.9 = ____________________ **6** 0.027 = ____________________

7 7 = ____________________ **8** 1.3 = ____________________

Convert the following percentages to decimals.

9 36% = ____________________ **10** 8% = ____________________

11 98% = ____________________ **12** 120% = ____________________

13 40% = ____________________ **14** 0.3% = ____________________

15 102% = ____________________ **16** 99.99% = ____________________

17 200% = ____________________ **18** 0.01% = ____________________

ISBN: 9780170497978

Converting between fractions and percentages

Fractions to percentages: If possible, use equivalent fractions to make the denominator 100.

Examples: 1 $\frac{13}{20} = \frac{65}{100} = 65\%$ (× 5 numerator and denominator)

2 $\frac{74}{200} = \frac{37}{100} = 37\%$ (÷ 2 numerator and denominator)

Remember, you must multiply or divide both numerator and denominator by the **same number**.

- If this is too hard, use your calculator to multiply the fraction by 100, or use the % button on your calculator.

13 [÷] 20 [SHIFT] [%] [=] 65

Percentages to fractions: Use equivalent fractions to simplify the fraction.

Examples: 1 $36\% = \frac{36}{100} = \frac{9}{25}$

2 $37.5\% = \frac{37.5}{100} = \frac{75}{200} = \frac{3}{8}$

Avoid having combinations of fractions and decimals.

Complete the table below.

	Fraction	Fraction out of 100	Percentage
1	$\frac{7}{10}$	$\frac{\_\_}{100}$	%
2	$\frac{3}{4}$	$\frac{\_\_}{100}$	%
3	$\frac{2}{5}$	$\frac{\_\_}{100}$	%
4	$\frac{60}{400}$	$\frac{\_\_}{100}$	%
5	___	$\frac{\_\_}{100}$	16%
6	___	$\frac{\_\_}{100}$	85%
7	___	$\frac{\_\_}{100}$	6%
8	___	$\frac{\_\_}{100}$	120%

ISBN: 9780170497978

9 Use the terms in the box and match them to the most appropriate image.

37.5%	$83.\dot{3}\%$	$91.\dot{6}\%$	62.5%
75%	$33.\dot{3}\%$	24%	$66.\dot{6}\%$

Converting between fractions, decimals and percentages

Fill in the gaps.

	Fraction	Fraction out of 100	Decimal	Percentage
1		$\frac{25}{100}$		
2				7%
3	$\frac{3}{5}$			
4			$0.\dot{6}$	
5				95%
6	$\frac{7}{8}$			
7		$\frac{18}{100}$		
8			1.10	

ISBN: 9780170497978

Challenges

Place the numbers in ascending order. Hint: Change them all to decimals first.

1

42%	$\frac{2}{5}$	0.45	~~39%~~	$\frac{5}{8}$	50%	$\frac{7}{20}$	0.36
			0.39				

Smallest | Largest

		39%					

2

82%	0.89	$\frac{16}{20}$	84.5%	$\frac{8}{9}$	0.81	$\frac{7}{8}$	85%

Smallest | Largest

Place these numbers on the number line. Hint: Change them all to decimals first.

3

$\frac{4}{21}$	0.102	12%	$\frac{27}{200}$	0.21	$\frac{19}{110}$	0.151	11.2%

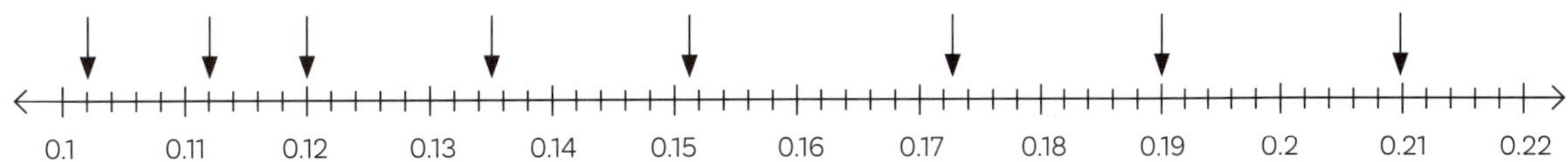

0.1 0.11 0.12 0.13 0.14 0.15 0.16 0.17 0.18 0.19 0.2 0.21 0.22

4

1.01	$\frac{27}{25}$	107%	$1\frac{1}{25}$	102.8%	1.10	$\frac{21}{20}$	1.065

1 1.05 1.1

Calculating percentages

- Remember, 'percent' means out of 100, so turning a fraction into a percentage means **multiplying by 100**.

Example: There are 224 students in Year 10, of which 126 play in the kī-o-rahi competition. What percentage of Year 10 students participate in the kī-o-rahi competition?

$$\% = \frac{126}{224} \times 100 = 56.25\%$$

Write **126** out of **224** as a fraction.

x by 100.

Otherwise use the % button on your calculator.

126 [÷] 224 [SHIFT] [%] [=] 56.25%

Write the following amounts as percentages.

1 56 out of 70 = ______________
= ______________

2 84 out of 140 = ______________
= ______________

3 21 out of 84 = ______________
= ______________

4 755 out of 1000 = ______________
= ______________

5 26.25 out of 3500 = ______________
= ______________

6 1500 out of 12 000 = ______________
= ______________

7 42 out of 63 = ______________
= ______________

8 5.25 out of 6 = ______________
= ______________

9 A 5 kg watermelon contains 4.7 kg of water. What percentage of the watermelon is water?

____

10 The average dairy cow has a mass of 600 kg. If the cow produces 25 kg of milk per day, what percentage of the cow's body mass is the milk produced in a single day?

____

11 A 2.2 kg kiwi lays an egg which has a mass of 0.44 kg. Before it was laid, what percentage of the kiwi's mass was egg?

____

ISBN: 9780170497978

Finding percentages of amounts

- There are many ways of doing this.

Example: Find 20% of 450. — You should be able to do this without a calculator.

Either: convert the percentage to a decimal: 20% **of** 450 = 0.2 **x** 450
= 90

Remember, '**of**' means **x**.

Or: convert the percentage to a fraction: 20% **of** 450 = $\frac{20}{100}$ **x** 450
= 90

Or: for some numbers, find 10% and then multiply or divide:
10% **of** 450 = 45
20% = 45 x 2 = 90

Or: if the percentage is a factor of 100, you could work it out by using a diagram like this:

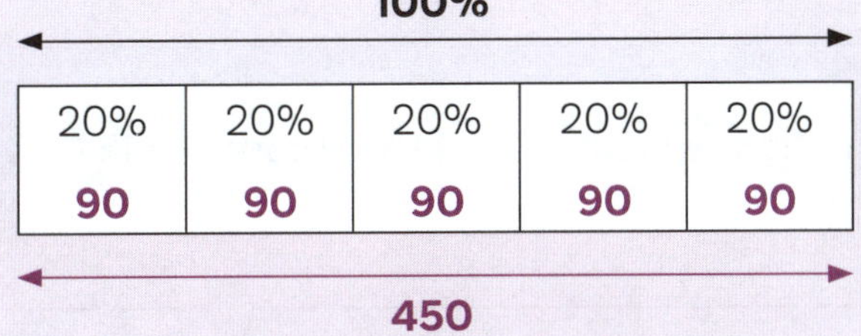

- Sometimes the numbers are not easy, so use your **calculator**.
- Not all calculators are the same, so you will need to experiment until you find how yours works. One example is shown below.

450 [×] 20 [SHIFT] [% (] [=] 90

Calculate these without using a calculator.

1 10% of 94 = ____________
= ____________

2 20% of 45 = ____________
= ____________

3 5% of 600 = ____________
= ____________

4 1% of 440 = ____________
= ____________

5 70% of 300 = ____________
= ____________

6 10% of 0.8 = ____________
= ____________

7 40% of 1200 = ____________
= ____________

8 25% of 5000 = ____________
= ____________

ISBN: 9780170497978

Use your calculator to work out these answers.

9 15% of 860 = ______

10 16% of 1300 = ______

11 66% of 44 = ______

12 22% of 6050 = ______

13 96% of 145 = ______

14 11% of 550 = ______

15 4.5% of 5600 = ______

16 3.8% of 250 000 = ______

Answer the following, and show appropriate calculations.

17 15% of the volume of a bottle is filled with juice. If the bottle has a total volume of 600 mL, how many millilitres of juice does it contain?

______

18 60% of the books in a library are fiction. If the library has 15 000 books, how many fiction books are there?

______

19 A factory produces 1500 toys in a day. If 18% of the toys are defective, how many defective toys are produced each day?

______

20 About 60% of your body mass is water. If you are 70 kg, how much of your mass is not water?

______

21 **a** Liam wanted to buy a jacket. The price on the tag was $85, but the store was offering a 20% discount on all items. How much will Liam save by buying the jacket during the sale?

______

b Calculate the sale price of the jacket.

______

22 **a** A gym is offering a 35% discount on membership fees for new members. The regular membership fee is $50 per month. By how much will the price be reduced?

______

b Calculate the price of a monthly membership to the gym.

______

ISBN: 9780170497978

Increasing by a percentage

- There are several ways of doing this.

Example: Increase 62 by 45%. — This means that we need 100% **plus** 45%.

Increased amount = 62 + 45% of 62
= 62 + 0.45 x 62
= 62 + 27.9
= 89.9

or

100% + 45% = 145%

Increased amount = 62 x 145%
= 62 x 1.45
= 89.9

Otherwise use the % button on your calculator.

62  145 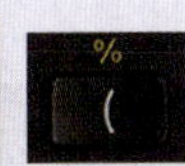

89.9

Calculate the following.

1 Increase 120 by 25% ____________

2 Increase 35 by 60% ____________

3 Increase $230 by 40% ____________

4 Increase 460 g by 15% ____________

5 Increase 52 km by 30% ____________

6 Increase 55 kg by 14% ____________

7 Increase 35.90 by 23% ____________

8 Increase 96 by 4% ____________

9 A town has a population of 12 000 people. If the population increases by 8%, how many people will live in the town?

____

10 A petrol station sells fuel for $2.60 per litre. If the price increases by 5%, what will the new price per litre be?

____________ per litre

11 A builder buys materials for $4500. He must pay the government 15% GST on this amount. How much will the materials have cost him altogether?

$____________

12 Toby bought a car using hire purchase. The price of the car was $5600. He has to pay for the car within a year, plus interest at 18%. How much will the car cost him altogether?

$____________

ISBN: 9780170497978

Decreasing by a percentage

- Once again, there are several ways of doing this.

Example: Decrease 90 by 25%. — This means that we need to find 90 minus 25% of 90.

Decreased amount = 90 - 25% of 90
= 90 - 0.25 x 90
= 90 - 22.5
= 67.5

or

100% - 25% = 75%

Decreased amount = 90 x 75%
= 90 x 0.75
= 67.5

Otherwise use the % button on your calculator.

90  75   67.5

Calculate the following.

1 Decrease 65 by 20%

____

2 Decrease 120 by 45%

____

3 Decrease 160 g by 10%

____

4 Decrease $620 by 15%

____

5 Decrease 65 km by 16%

____

6 Decrease 98 kg by 70%

____

7 Decrease $235 by 65%

____

8 Decrease 123 cm by 4%

____

9 The value of a $32 000 car decreases by 7%. What is its decreased value?

$______________________

10 A sports store advertises '30% off all equipment'. Calculate the sale price for the following items. Round your answers to the nearest 10 cents.

a A basketball which is normally $49.50. $______________________

b A pair of running shoes normally priced at $89.99. $______________________

11 It is estimated that the value of a new laptop drops 15% each year. Estimate the value of Emma's $1500 laptop a year after she bought it.

$______________________

 ISBN: 9780170497978

Given a percentage, find the whole amount

- You might be given an amount that is a percentage of a whole and asked to find the original or whole amount.

Examples:

Method 1: This method will work only if the **percentage is a factor of 100**.

20% of an amount is 24. What is the original amount?

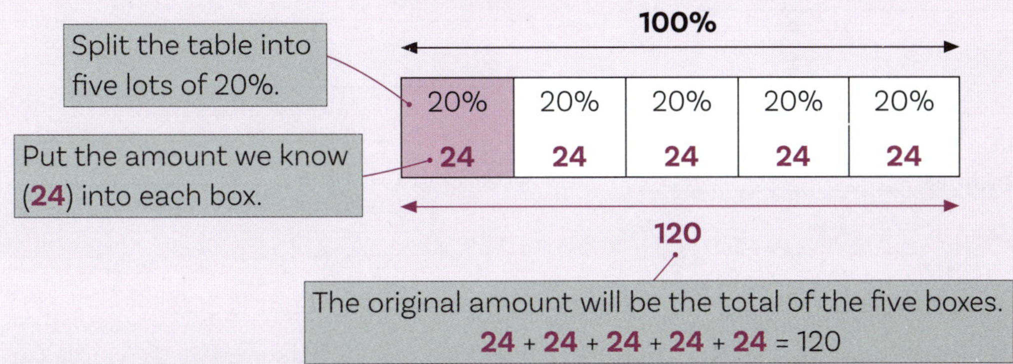

Method 2: This method will work for **any percentage**.

75% of an amount is 489. What is the original amount?

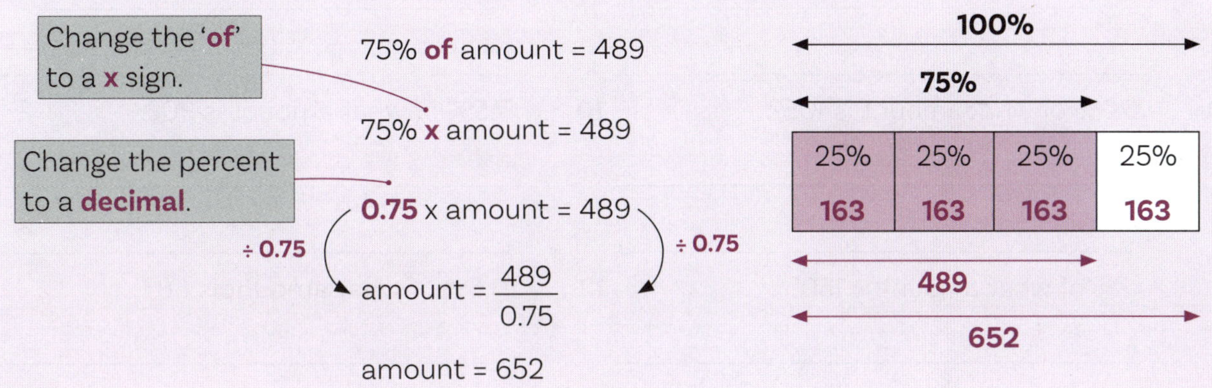

Method 3: This method will work for **any percentage**.

45% of an amount is 351. What is the original amount?

$$\text{Original amount} = \frac{351}{\mathbf{0.45}} = 780$$

x 0.45

Original amount 780 → **Percentage of amount** 351

÷ 0.45

Complete the boxes to find the original amounts.

1 20% of what amount is 18?

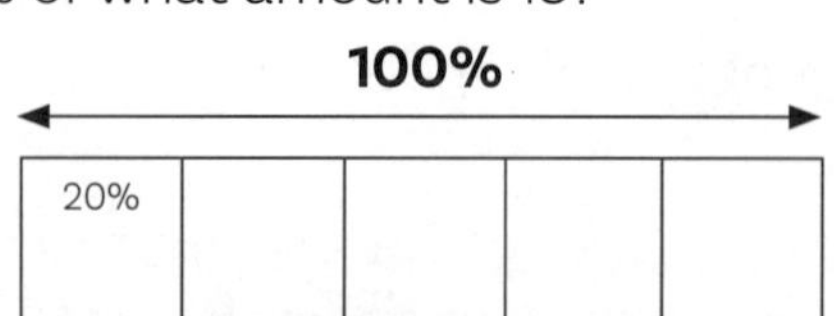

Original amount is ____________

2 10% of what amount is 13?

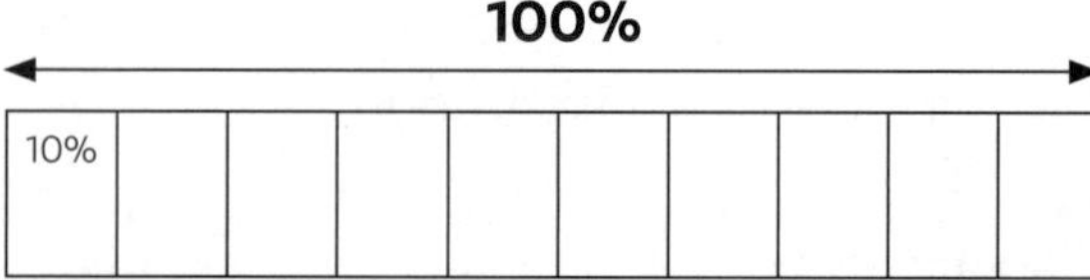

Original amount is ____________

3 25% of what amount is 32?

100%

Original amount is ____________

4 30% of what amount is 36?

Original amount is ____________

Find the following.

5 40% of what amount is 80?

6 80% of what amount is 30?

7 70% of what amount is 112?

8 35% of what amount is 28?

9 20% of what amount is 105?

10 7.5% of what amount is 30?

11 2% of what amount is 150?

12 0.5% of what amount is 68?

13 Kirsty scored 21 points in her test which was 70%. How many points in total were in the test?

14 Lee saved $18 on a top that was on sale for 20% off. What was the original price of the top?

15 In a school, 330 students are left-handed; this is 12% of the roll. How many students are enrolled in the school?

16 At a doggy daycare, 7 dogs are labradors. They make up 35% of the total. How many dogs are at the daycare?

 ISBN: 9780170497978

Rounding

- Often we need to round numbers to sensible and/or meaningful values.
- Never round until **after** you have completed your calculations.

Rounding to whole numbers

Locate the digit you have to round to. Is the digit to its **right** 5 or more?

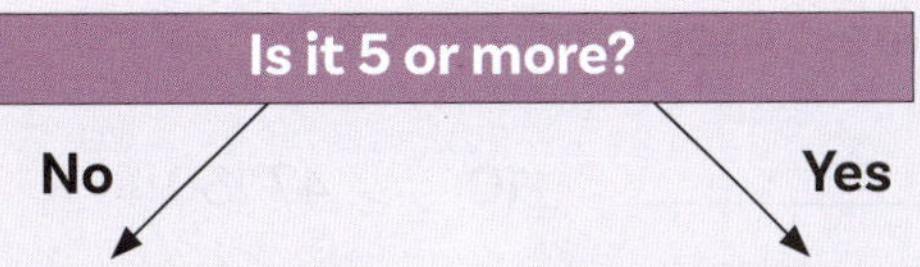

Replace it and everything after it with 0s. | Increase the previous digit by one and replace everything after it with 0s.

Examples: **1** Round 2349 to the nearest hundred.

The hundreds digit is **3**. The digit to its right is **4**.

So 2349 to the nearest hundred = 2300.

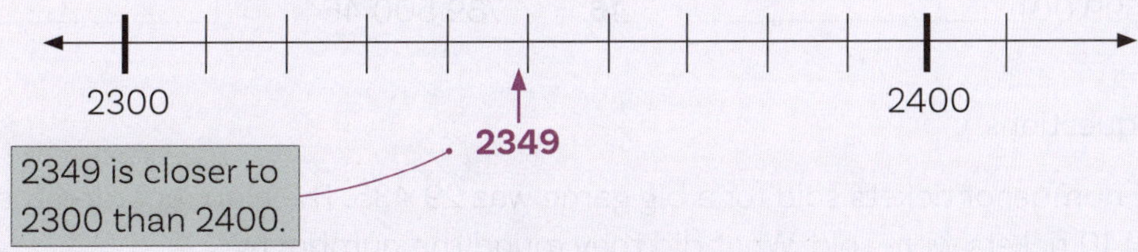

2 Round 127 500 to the nearest thousand.

The thousands digit is **7**. The digit to its right is **5**.

So 127 500 to the nearest thousand = 128 000.

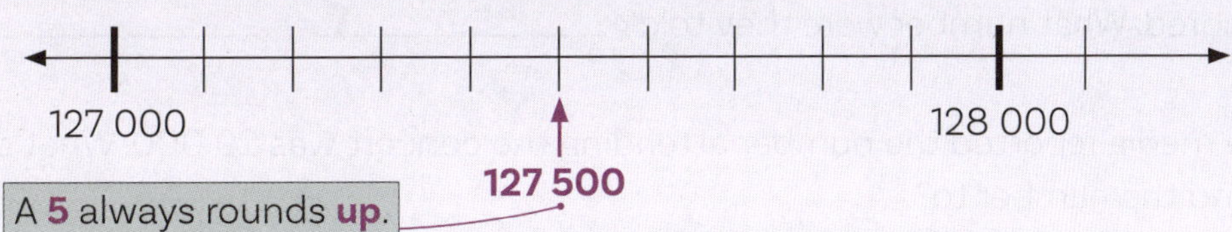

More examples:

	Rounded to the nearest:	Last required digit	Answer
125	ten	125	130
3 162 348.1	thousand	3 162 348.1	3 162 000
51 287 421	ten thousand	51 287 412	51 290 000
19 502 394	million	19 502 394	20 000 000

ISBN: 9780170497978

Round these numbers to the nearest ten.

1 18 ______________ **2** 2132 ______________

3 20 185 ______________ **4** 13.92 ______________

Round these numbers to the nearest hundred.

5 265.3 ______________ **6** 76 482 ______________

7 23 514 349 ______________ **8** 4 141 961 ______________

Round these numbers to the nearest thousand.

9 198 765 ______________ **10** 47 150 ______________

11 563.05 ______________ **12** 99 500 ______________

Round these numbers to the nearest million.

13 843 199 ______________ **14** 591 844 095 ______________

15 2 316 599 001 ______________ **16** 789 500 464 ______________

Answer these questions.

17 **a** The number of tickets sold for a big game was 29 435. The club recorded that 29 440 tickets were sold. What did they round the number to?

The nearest ______________________

b The portable toilet supplier needed to know the number attending to the nearest hundred. What number were they told? ______________________

c The media reported the number attending the concert was 29 000. What did they round the number to?

The nearest ______________________

d Based on previous experience, the caterers estimated that 36% of those attending would buy a pie. How many pies should they expect to sell?

____

e Pies come in boxes of 20. They would rather have too few pies than have pies left over. How many boxes of pies should they bring?

____

ISBN: 9780170497978

Rounding decimals

- The number of decimal places is the number of digits after the decimal point.

Examples:

Number	7	7.**0**	7.04	7.042	7.042**0**
Number of decimal places	0	1	2	3	4

Notice that a **0** at the **end** counts as a decimal place.

- When asked to round to 1 dp (one decimal place), there should be **exactly** one digit after the decimal point.
- The process is the same as for rounding to whole numbers.

Examples:

	Rounded to the nearest:	**Digit to the right of the last required digit**	**Answer**
5.354	1 dp	5.3**5**4	5.4
265.1829	2 dp	265.18**2**9	265.18
91.6275	3 dp	91.627**5**	91.628
0.24995	4 dp	0.2499**5**	0.2500

You **must** add the 0s so there are exactly **4** dp.

Complete the table.

	0 dp	**1 dp**	**2 dp**
4.2564			
23.8888			
7.6019			
0.28364			
9.0951			
0.0647			

ISBN: 9780170497978

Significant figures

Rules for deciding if a digit is significant

1 All non-zero digits are significant.

2 At the **start** of a number: zeros are **never significant**.

Example: 0.0**53** has **2** significant figures

In the **middle** of a number: zeros are **always significant**.

Example: **23009** has **5** significant figures

At the **end** of a number: zeros **are significant** if they are after a decimal point.

Example: **256.0** has **4** significant figures

Zeros **are not significant** if there is no decimal point.

Example: **895**00 has **3** significant figures

Highlight the last significant figure in each number.

1 288

2 280

3 2880

4 2.08

5 280.0

6 2.800

Write down the number of significant figures in the following.

7 0.2008 ____________

8 0.00280 ____________

9 280 000 ____________

10 280 000.0 ____________

11 20 008 ____________

12 0.0280 ____________

13 0.0028 ____________

14 0.280 ____________

15 20 ____________

16 20.080 ____________

17 0.2080 ____________

18 0.0280 ____________

19 280 ____________

20 2080.0 ____________

ISBN: 9780170497978

Rounding to significant figures

- When asked to round to 2 sf (two significant figures), this means there should be **exactly** two significant figures in the answer.

Locate the first digit to the **right** of the last required significant figure.

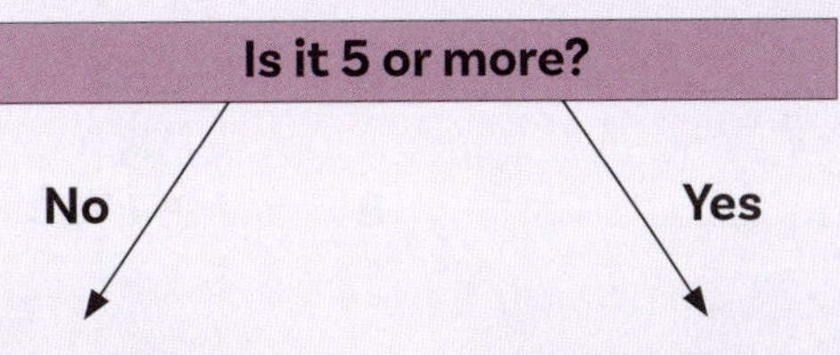

Leave the previous digit alone. | Increase the previous digit by one.

Examples:

1 Round 2.04**39** to 3 sf.

The **3** is **not** 5 or more
⇒ leave the 4 alone
∴ 2.0439 = 2.04 (3 sf)

2 Round 2.04**59** to 3 sf.

The **5 is** 5 or more
⇒ increase the 4 to 5
∴ 2.0459 = 2.05 (3 sf)

2.0439 is closer to 2.04 than 2.05.

2.0459 is closer to 2.05 than 2.04.

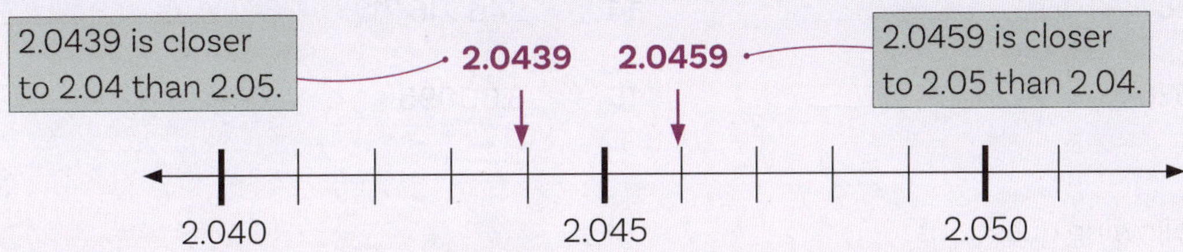

Some more examples:

Unrounded number	Number of significant figures	Rounded number
51**2** 759	2	510 000
2.4**7**90	2	2.5
94.02**6**4	4	94.03
39.**5**	2	40
189.**6**04	3	190
2 472 **7**14	4	2 473 000
5.79**8**	3	5.8**0**
0.029**6**3	2	0.03**0**
0.05099**9**	4	0.051**00**

Sometimes you get an answer that looks as though it is rounded to fewer significant figures than you were asked for.

You **must** have the required number of significant figures, so don't omit the **0**s at the end.

Round these numbers to 1 sf.

1 541 ______ **2** 1312 ______

3 13.567 ______ **4** 0.086 ______

Round these numbers to 2 sf.

5 2860 ______ **6** 19 264 ______

7 0.2055 ______ **8** 7 251 734 ______

Round these numbers to 3 sf.

9 284 136 ______ **10** 193 590 ______

11 2.0196 ______ **12** 0.01885 ______

Round these numbers to 4 sf.

13 9.00287 ______ **14** 946 216 712 ______

15 0.020764 ______ **16** 8.00095 ______

Answer the following questions.

17 7 is the same as 7.0. True or false? ______

Explain your answer.

______

______

______

18 The fun fair has come to town and the number of people who took part in each activity were recorded to two significant figures. Calculate the lowest and highest numbers of people that could have used the rides.

	Reported	Lowest number	Highest number
Ferris wheel	6600		
Rollercoaster	13 000		
Carousel	8100		
Bumper cars	16 000		

  ISBN: 9780170497978

Appropriate rounding

- Rounding is commonly used in everyday life.
- The degree of rounding used should depend on the context.
- Measurements are **always** rounded, e.g. if the length of a car is said to be 5.8 m, this could mean any length greater than 5.75 and less than $5.84\dot{9}$.
- You **must round** if you are dealing with numbers that must be integers, such as numbers of people, animals or objects, e.g. 55% of 826 students = 454.3 students, so round this to 454 students.
- As a general rule, if **safety** of people is involved, **little or no rounding** should be used.
- In everyday life, we round all the time, e.g.
  - if you are 13 years, 7 months, 18 days, 22 hours and 14 seconds old, and you are asked your age, you might answer 'Thirteen' or 'Thirteen and a half'
  - if you are estimating the volume of paint needed to redecorate a room, you will probably need to round up to 1, 2 or 4 litres, depending on the size of cans.

1 Complete the table to indicate whether or not rounding is appropriate in these situations and why.

	Little or no rounding	Rounding okay	Reason
Dose of a medicine	✓		
Buying wood for making a deck			
Savings goal for a new bike			
Time allowed for sitting an NCEA examination			
Time needed to drive to a holiday destination			
Strength of steel needed for a bridge			

2 Complete the table to indicate whether or not the value has been appropriately rounded in these situations, and if not, round the number appropriately.

	Appropriately rounded or not? (✓ or ×)	If not, a more appropriate figure or expression
I have saved five thousand three hundred and nineteen dollars and 42 cents.		
I am 156.3 cm tall.		
A car tyre pressure should be 28 psi.		
Canterbury godwits migrate 10 875 km.		
In New Zealand, 90% of the 96 species of seabird are threatened with extinction. So 86.4 species are threatened.		

ISBN: 9780170497978

Estimations/approximations

- Sometimes an exact answer isn't necessary, so you can just estimate the answer.
- In order to estimate, round every number to a **maximum of 2 significant figures**.
- Sometimes rounding to a nearest multiple works well.
- Don't forget to use BEDMAS or GEMA.

This symbol means 'is approximately equal to'.

Examples:

1 A list of prices:

Apples	$5.99 ≈ $6.00
Carrots	$4.54 ≈ $5.00
Potatoes	$3.15 ≈ $3.00

Round each value to 1 significant figure (the nearest dollar).

The approximate total is $14.00. — 6 + 5 + 3 = 14

2 Kaea is making jam. When it is cooked, the measure on her saucepan tells her she has made about 4.7 L (4700 mL). Her jars each hold 325 mL. Approximately how many jars will she need?

Rounding to 1 sf:

$$\text{Number of jars} = \frac{5000}{300} \approx 17$$

Rounding total volume to 4800 and jars to nearest multiple of 300:

$$\text{Number of jars} = \frac{4800}{300} \approx 16$$

Estimate the answers to the following. Do not use a calculator.

1 5.39 + 13.06 ≈ ______________________

2 1.37 + 6.51 + 4.27 ≈ ______________________

3 21.53 − 6.38 ≈ ______________________

4 4.49 x 2.05 − 3.1 ≈ ______________________

5 19.1 + 6.1 x 3 ≈ ______________________

6 49 ÷ 7.2 + 12.18 ≈ ______________________

7 24 100 ÷ 40.045 ≈ ______________________

____

8 42.4 x 9.8 + 59.01 ≈ ______________________

____

9 $\frac{17\,976}{612} \approx$ ______________________

____

10 1.7(24.59 − 9.021) ≈ ______________________

____

11 Jamie has $125.45 in her bank account. She went out for dinner, which cost her $19.60, bought a book for $12.80, and took a scooter home that cost her $7.20. Estimate the amount left in her bank account.

____

12 Three friends made a total of $120 at a bake sale. They spent $25 on ingredients. If they split the remaining amount equally, roughly how much does each friend get?

____

ISBN: 9780170497978

Scientific notation

What is scientific notation?

- Scientific notation is a way of writing either very large or very small numbers without writing all the place holders (0s).
- It is used a lot in science, social science, technology, etc., so it is really important that you understand it.
- Scientific notation is also known as standard form.
- Your calculator will sometimes give you answers in scientific notation.

Powers of 10

Remember:

$10^0 = 1$
$10^1 = 10$
$10^2 = 100$
$10^3 = 1000$
$10^5 = 100\ 000$
$10^8 = 100\ 000\ 000$, etc.

Hint: The exponent matches the number of 0s.

Another way to think about it:

Millions	Thousands			Ones		
1	7	4	2	3	6	5
x 10^6	x 10^5	x 10^4	x 10^3	x 10^2	x 10^1	x 10^0

Calculations with powers of 10

Examples: **1** 5.49×10^4 = 5 . 4 9 0 0 .
= 54 900

This means the decimal point shifts **4** places to the **right**.

This is the same as 5.49 x 10 000 = 54 900

2 0.00356×10^6 = 0 . 0 0 3 5 6 **0** .
= 3560

You must not forget to include the place-holding **0** before the decimal point.

3 $96.04 \div 10^5$ = 0 . 0 0 0 9 6 . 0 4
= 0.0009604

This means the decimal point shifts **5** places to the **left**.

This is the same as 96.04 ÷ 100 000 = 0.0009604

Perform the following calculations **without** using your calculator.

1 0.00456×10^3 = ______________ **2** 513×10^4 = ______________

3 0.926×10^2 = ______________ **4** $7.63 \div 10^3$ = ______________

5 $12\ 493 \div 10^4$ = ______________ **6** $0.06 \div 10^2$ = ______________

7 $4 \times 10^3 + 3 \times 10^4$ = ______________ **8** $6 \times 10^5 \div 6$ = ______________

Converting numbers from scientific notation to ordinary form

- In scientific notation, numbers are written in three parts:

A number between 1 and 10 | **x** | **a power of 10**

- Converting to ordinary form involves moving the decimal point to the right as you did for multiplying by powers of 10 on page 75.

Examples: **1** $5.3 \times 10^5 = 530\ 000$ **2** $1.3 \times 10^0 = 1.3$

Scientific notation — Ordinary form — Remember: $10^0 = 1$

Highlight the correct answer for each of the following.

1	1.3×10^2	13	130
		0.13	1300
3	6.0×10^4	60	6000
		0.0006	60 000

2	0.085×10^3	85	850
		8.5	0.85
4	2.47×10^0	2.74	24.7
		2.47	0

Convert these numbers to ordinary form.

5 2.8×10^4 = ______________ **6** 12.675×10^2 = ______________

7 1.33×10^5 = ______________ **8** 3.71×10^0 = ______________

9 8.6823×10^4 = ______________ **10** 4.00201×10^4 = ______________

11 5.5×10^6 = ______________ **12** 7.6207×10^3 = ______________

13 8.0×10^4 = ______________ **14** 1.11×10^6 = ______________

ISBN: 9780170497978

Converting numbers from ordinary form to scientific notation

Example: Convert 53 000 to scientific notation.

Step 1:
Shift the decimal point to the **left** until there is exactly **one** non-zero digit on its left.
(This will give you a number between 1 and 10.)

5. 3 0 0 0 . ⇒ **5**.3

The decimal point is moved four places to the left.

Step 2:
Multiply by 10 to the power of however many places the decimal point was moved (**4**).

5.3×10^4

Examples:

Number	Number between 1 and 10	x	Power of 10	Number in scientific notation
8400	8.4	x	3	8.4×10^3
1 346 000	1.346	x	6	1.346×10^6
60	6.0	x	1	6.0×10^1
2	2	x	0	2×10^0

Highlight the correct answer for each of the following.

1	8100	8.1×10^2	81.0×10^4
		8.1×10^3	0.81×10^1
3	55 000	$55\ 000 \times 10^4$	55.0×10^3
		5.5×10^4	5.5×10^5

2	12.35	1.235×10^2	1.235×10^1
		12.35×10^1	12.35×10^0
4	169.30	1.6930×10^4	1693.0×10^4
		16.93×10^2	1.6930×10^2

Write each of the following in scientific notation.

5 46 000 = ____________________

6 89 = ____________________

7 164.2 = ____________________

8 7 = ____________________

9 899 000 = ____________________

10 3.5 = ____________________

11 15 410 000 = ____________________

12 90.45 = ____________________

ISBN: 9780170497978

Highlight the bigger number.

13	3.6×10^4	3600	**14**	0.9×10^2	9000
15	24 999	2.5×10^3	**16**	1070	1.7×10^3
17	520 000	5.2×10^6	**18**	0.01×10^0	0.001
19	8.91×10^3	8.19×10^4	**20**	4.5×10^2	four and a half hundreds
21	1.25×10^8	one and a half million	**22**	eight thousandths	0.8

Place the numbers in ascending order. Hint: Change them all to ordinary form first.

23

2.45×10^5	5.42×10^1	4.25×10^3	5.24×10^2	2.54×10^4	4.52×10^0
		4250			

Smallest					Biggest
			4.25×10^3		

24 Complete the puzzle below by using values in the list. Hint: You will not need all the values in the list.

13.5	1.35×10^2	135	135 000	1.35×10^5
1.35×10^1	0.135	0.0135	1.35×10^4	1.35×10^6

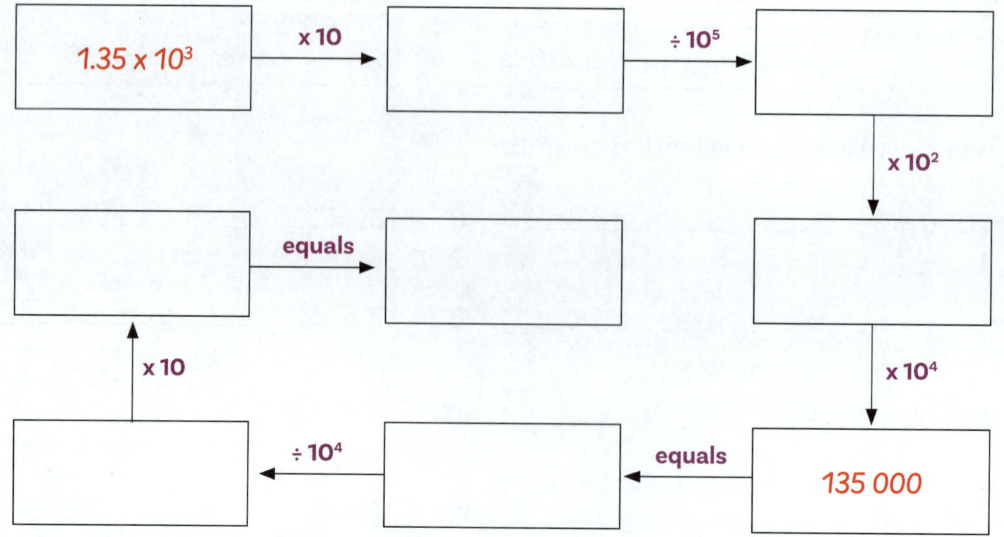

ISBN: 9780170497978

Scientific notation on your calculator

- You probably have a key that looks like this: 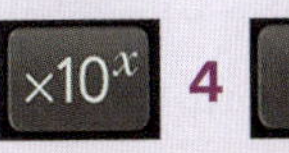 or this: 
- Both mean '10 to the power of something'.

Examples:

1 2.36×10^4 Enter 2.36 [$\times10^x$] **4** [=] Answer: 23 600

2 $81.71 \div 10^3$ Enter 81.71 [÷] [$\times10^x$] **3** [=] Answer: 0.08171

Perform the following calculations **using** your calculator. If necessary, round your answer to 4 sf.

1 $0.0386 \times 10^5 =$ ____________________

2 $2.9 \times 7.1 \times 10^4 =$ ____________________

3 $0.93 \times 0.14 \times 10^3 =$ ____________________

4 $18.34^2 \div 10^3 =$ ____________________

5 $3.4 \times 10^2 \div 2.6 =$ ____________________

6 $1.9(5.23 \times 10^4) =$ ____________________

7 $2.6 \times 10^2 \times 1.83 \times 10^4 =$ ____________________

8 $8.7 \times 10^3 \div 9^2 =$ ____________________

9 $\sqrt{4.3} \times 10^4 =$ ____________________

10 $\dfrac{1.47 \times 10^6}{\sqrt{3\,519}} =$ ____________________

11 Complete the calculations shown in the diagram. If you do this correctly, your final answer should be 1. Write all your answers in scientific notation.

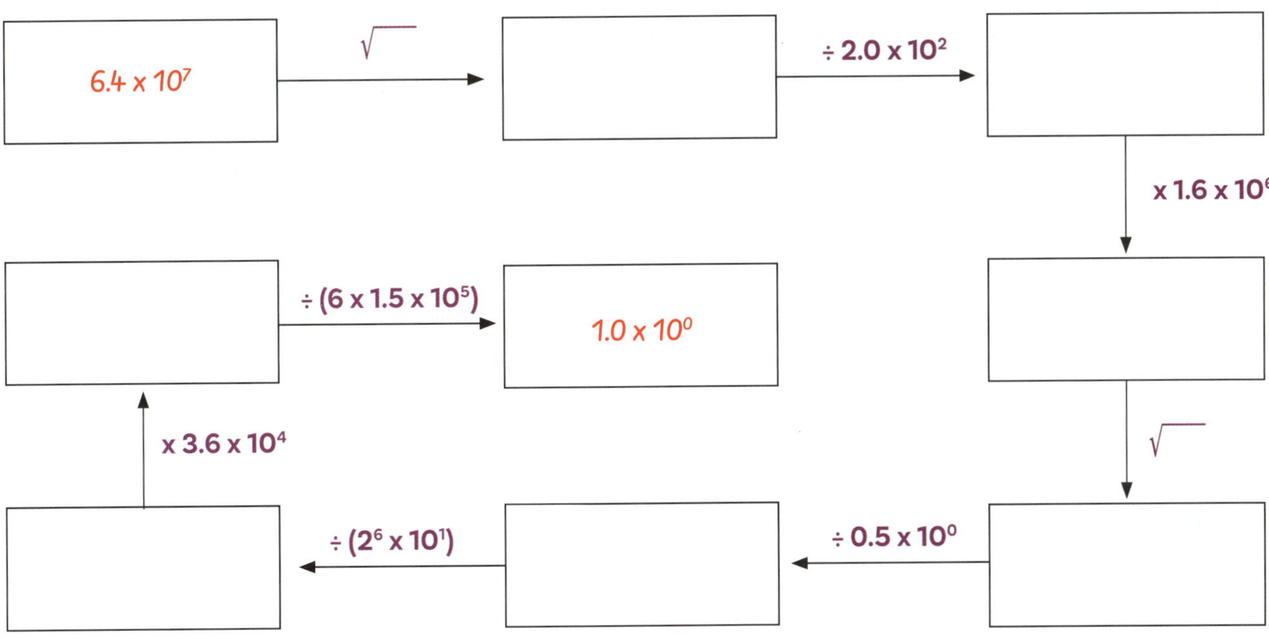

ISBN: 9780170497978

Rates

- A rate is a relationship between two quantities.
- Rates are usually written using the word '**per**'.
- Examples: the amount paid per hour for babysitting; the speed of a car in kilometres per hour.

Examples:

1 If 4 kg of apples cost $17.96, calculate the cost of 3 kg of apples.

Method 1:

Step 1: Write the information you are given in a brief statement.

4 kg cost **$17.96**

Because you are trying to find a price, put the **price** on the **right**.

Step 2: Underneath write a parallel statement about what you want to know.

4 kg cost **$17.96**

copy ↓

3 kg cost **$17.96** x $\frac{3}{4}$ = $13.47

Multiply by either $\frac{3}{4}$ or $\frac{4}{3}$. Use $\frac{3}{4}$ here because 3 kg will cost **less**.

Method 2:

Step 1: Work out how much 1 kg costs.

1 kg of apples costs $17.96 ÷ 4 = $4.49

Step 2: Multiply the cost of 1 kg by the number of kilograms you need.

3 kg of apples cost $4.49 x 3 = $13.47

2 If Marcel bikes home from town, he can travel at 15 kph and it takes him 11 minutes. How long would it take him to walk home from town at 4 kph?

Method 1:

Step 1: Write the information you are given in a brief statement.

At **15** kph he takes **11 min**

Because you are trying to find a time, put the **time** on the **right**.

Step 2: Underneath write a parallel statement.

At **15** kph he takes **11 min**

copy ↓

At **4** kph he takes **11** x $\frac{15}{4}$ = 41.25 min or 41 min 15 s

Multiply by either $\frac{4}{15}$ or $\frac{15}{4}$. Use $\frac{15}{4}$ here because it will take him **longer** to walk.

Method 2:

Step 1: Work out how long he takes at 1 kph.

At 1 kph he will take 11 x 15 = 165 min

Step 2: Work out how long he takes at 4 kph.

At 4 kph he will take $\frac{165}{4}$ = 41.25 min or 41 min 15 s

ISBN: 9780170497978

Answer the following questions.

1 It costs $27 for 2 kg of sunflower seeds. How much would it cost for 3 kg of sunflower seeds?

2 If 3 kg of brown onions cost $5.97, calculate the cost of 5 kg of brown onions.

3 If Tama jogs to the park at 6 kph, it takes him 30 minutes. How long would it take him if he rides his scooter at 18 kph?

4 A 5 kg bag of Sunny Rice costs $12.50, while a 2 kg bag of Budget Rice costs $5.60. Which rice is cheaper per kilogram? Justify your answer.

5 A supermarket sells three different-sized bags of dog biscuits:

- a 500 g bag costs $3.49
- a 1.5 kg bag costs $8.99
- a 3 kg bag costs $16.50.

Calculate the price per kilogram for each bag. Which one is the best value?

6 A weekly bus pass costs $15.50. Alternatively, buying a single ticket costs $2.70 each for a one-way trip. If you take the bus five days a week, with two trips per day, which option is cheaper? Explain your reasoning.

7 It took five workers nine hours to build a fence. How long would the job have taken if only three workers were available?

8 The scale on a map shows that 4 cm = 1 kilometre. The distance between two towns on the map is 18 cm. How many kilometres is it from one town to the other?

ISBN: 9780170497978

Ratios

Simplifying ratios

- Ratios show how an amount is split into several shares, usually of different sizes.
- Before you convert quantities into ratios, both quantities should be in the **same units**.
- Ratios are usually given in whole numbers, not decimals or fractions.
- A **colon** (**:**) is used to separate the parts, e.g. 2**:**3 means 'two **to** three'.
- Like fractions, ratios should be written in their simplest form.

Remember: Highest common factor (HCF) is the biggest number that will divide into several numbers. For example, the HCF of 20 and 25 is 5.

Examples:

1 Write the ratio 21:49 in its simplest form.

2 Write the ratio 5.5 m:150 cm in its simplest form.

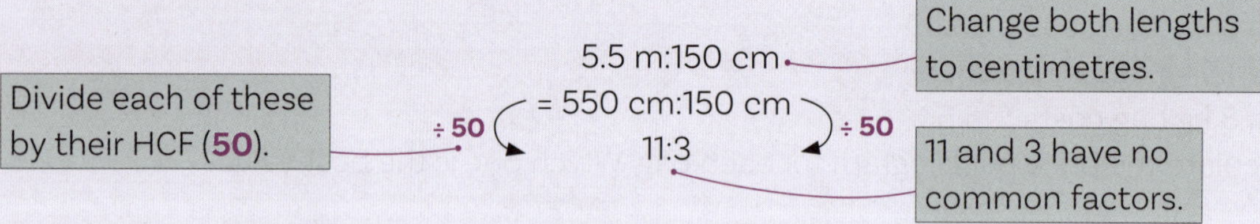

Write these ratios in their simplest forms.

1 15:10 = ______

2 24:60 = ______

3 200:650 = ______

4 18:27 = ______

5 10 000:750 = ______

6 $7:14^2$ = ______

7 250 g:10 kg = ______
= ______

8 3.6 kg to 300 g = ______
= ______

9 \$2:50c = ______
= ______

10 100 mm:18 cm = ______
= ______

11 150 m:2 km = ______
= ______

12 30 s:2 hours = ______
= ______

ISBN: 9780170497978

Using ratios where the total is given

- When there is a quantity that needs to be split using a ratio, follow the steps below.

Example: \$56 needs to be shared between Chloe and Davina in the ratio 3:4.

Step 1: Calculate the **total number of parts** by adding the **numbers in each share**: 3 + 4 = 7

Step 2: Calculate the **value of each part** by dividing the total amount by the **number of parts**: \$56 ÷ 7 = \$8

Step 3: Calculate the **value of each share** by multiplying the **number in each share** by the value of each part: 3 x \$8 : 4 x \$8

Ratio of money is \$24 : \$32

So Chloe gets \$24 and Davina gets \$32. (Check: \$24 + \$32 = \$56.)

Another way to think about it:

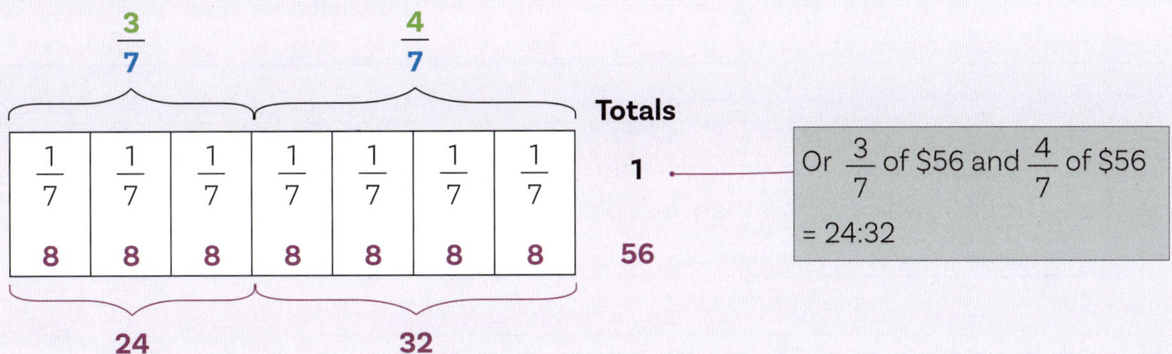

Note: While the ratio doesn't have units or decimals, your answer could have these.

Share the quantities in the given ratios.

1 \$90 in the ratio 2:3

2 \$60 in the ratio 5:7

3 850 g in the ratio 4:1

4 450 mL in the ratio 1:5

5 600 m in the ratio 9:3

6 \$15.75 in the ratio 2:5

ISBN: 9780170497978

7 The ratio of sugar to flour for making biscuits is 1:3. If you want to bake a batch using 24 cups of ingredients in total, calculate the number of cups of sugar and flour needed.

8 At Paradise High School, the ratio of students who participate in the production to those who don't is 7:5. If there are 720 students in total at the school, how many students participate in the production?

9 Grandma hired the kids next door to water her plants and feed her cat for 10 days while she was on holiday. She promised to pay them $55 in total. Ava took care of everything for six days and Mia handled the remaining four days. How much should each person be paid?

10 The ratio of people who own electric cars compared to those who don't is 1:24. If 960 000 people in the city own cars, how many people would you expect to own electric cars?

11 The ratio of cats to dogs at an animal shelter is 4:7. If the shelter houses 220 animals in total, how many of them are cats?

12 The global annual number of deaths due to crocodile attacks is approximately 1000, while deaths caused by assassin bugs are around 10 000. Write the ratio of crocodile deaths to assassin bug deaths in its simplest form.

13 On Earth, the ratio of the total mass of bacteria to the total mass of humans is 70:0.06. If your mass is 60 kg, what is the mass of your 'share' of bacteria?

ISBN: 9780170497978

Financial mathematics

Calculations with money

- Remember, money calculations are the same as those for decimals.
- Sometimes you will need to **round** your answers to 2 dp.
- Remember, never round until **after** you have completed your calculations.

Money rounding in New Zealand

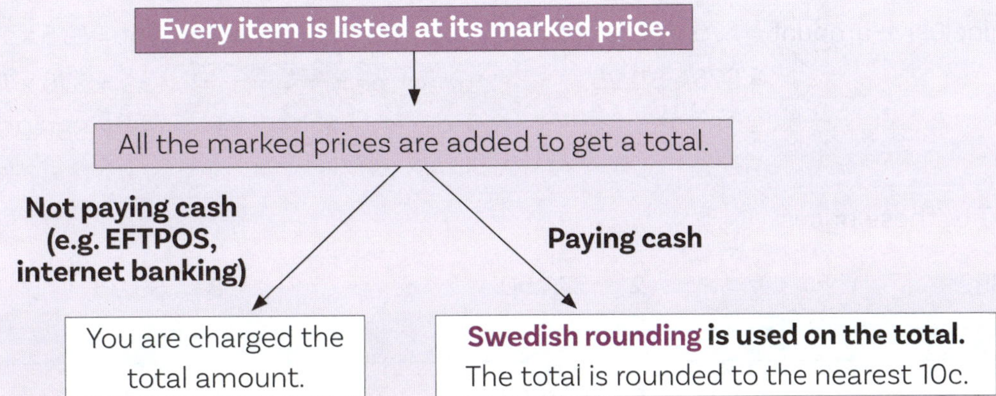

You can save money by choosing what you pay with.

Examples:

Total price (digital price)	Swedish rounding (paying by cash)
$11.98	$12.00
$9.47	$9.50
$518.51	$518.50
$180.02	$180.00

Cheaper to pay digitally (e.g. EFTPOS)

Cheaper to pay cash

Complete the table.

Total price (digital price)	Swedish rounding (paying by cash)	Cheaper with cash or digital payment?
$97.18	$97.20	Digital
$26.31		
$5.49		
$2359.96		
$990.81		
$37.54		

ISBN: 9780170497978

GST

- **GST** stands for **G**oods and **S**ervices **T**ax.
- It is added to everything you buy and it goes to the government to fund the running of the country.
- The standard current GST rate on all products in New Zealand is **15%**.
- Don't forget to add units and round when necessary.

Adding GST

Example: If the GST-exclusive price is $75, calculate the GST-inclusive price.

GST-inclusive amount = $75 + (15% of $75)
= $75 + $11.25
= $86.25

OR

GST-inclusive amount = $75 x **115%**
= $75 x **1.15**
= $86.25

Convert the percentage to a decimal and add 1.

Add GST to these prices.

1 $92

2 $24.50

3 $9.95

4 $103.32

5 $3152.99

6 $91.75

7 $0.36

8 $55.90

9 $720.00

10 The pre-GST price of a mountain bike is $520.87.

a How much is the GST on the mountain bike?

b Calculate its GST-inclusive price.

11 The pre-GST price of a milkshake is $5.22.

a How much is the GST on the milkshake?

b Calculate its GST-inclusive price.

12 The pre-GST price of a new car is $5500.

a How much is the GST on the car?

b Calculate its GST-inclusive price.

ISBN: 9780170497978

Interest

- When you deposit money in the bank, the bank pays you **'interest'** for the use of that money.
- When you borrow money, you have to pay **'interest'** because you are using the bank's money.
- Interest may be simple interest or compound interest.

Simple interest

- The same amount of interest is paid to you at regular intervals, usually per annum (yearly).
- This interest is paid separately into another account: it is not added to your deposit.

The original amount is sometimes called the 'principal'.

Examples:

1 Sofia borrowed $6000 from her uncle to start a small business. Her uncle agreed to charge her 4% interest each year.

a How much interest does she pay per annum?

'Per annum' means annually or each year.

Interest = 4% of $6000
= $240

b If she pays all the money back after three years, how much interest will she have paid to her uncle in total?

Interest = 3 x $240
= $720

2 Ngaio deposits $8500 into a savings account. The bank will pay 3% interest annually.

a How much interest does she earn after a year?

3% of $8500 = 0.03 x 8500
= $255

b If she leaves it in there for six years, how much interest will she have earned?

6 x $255 = $1530

Complete the table. All interest rates are annual.

Value of loan	Rate of interest	Interest per year	Number of years	Total to be paid back
$2000	4%	$80	3	$2000 + ($80 x 3) = $2240
$500	3%		5	
$14 000	6.5%		4	
$158 000	8.2%		6	

ISBN: 9780170497978

Profit and loss

- **Profit** is how much extra money is **earned** on a transaction.
- **Loss** is how much money is **lost** on a transaction.
- These can be written as an amount of money or a percentage.

Examples:

1 Toby bought a new bike for $1800 and sold it after a year for $1150.

a How much money did he lose?

He lost $1800 - $1150 = $650.

b Calculate his percentage loss.

$$\text{Percentage loss} = \frac{1800 - 1150}{1800} \times 100$$
$$= \frac{650}{1800} \times 100$$
$$= 36.1\% \text{ (1 dp)}$$

2 Clara invested $1000 at an annual simple interest rate of 4% for two years.

a How much interest did she earn?

Interest = Profit
= 2 x 4% x 1000
= $80

b What percentage profit did she make on her investment?

$$\text{Percentage profit} = \frac{80}{1000} \times 100$$
$$= 8\%$$

1 Complete the table for buying and then selling items. Round the percentages to 1 dp.

Buying price	Selling price	Profit	Loss	%
$90	$108	$18	–	20%
$16	$12			
$225	$270			
$1280	$768			
$150	$145.50			
$50	$115			

2 **a** Calculate the simple interest earned each year when $4500 is invested at 5%.

____

b If it is invested for three years, calculate the overall percentage profit.

____

3 **a** Hamish borrows $3000 from his brother to buy a computer. Hamish pays him 6% interest each year. How much interest does he pay each year?

____

b If he pays all the money back after four years, how much will the computer have cost him in total?

____

c Five years after he bought the computer, he sold it for $2300. What was his loss in dollars?

____

d Calculate his percentage loss.

____

____

ISBN: 9780170497978

ALGEBRA

The language of algebra

Phrases to expressions

- In algebra we use **operations** along with **variables** and numbers to write **expressions**.
- A **variable** is represented by a **letter of the alphabet**, which may be the initial of what it represents, e.g. *m* for mass.

Some tricks:

- We do not write in the times sign between a number and a variable, e.g. 7*m* means 7 **x** *m*.
- We do not write an exponent for powers of one, e.g. m^1 is written as *m*.

Phrase	Expression
Double or twice *m*	$m + m$ or $2 \times m$ or $2m$
Treble or triple *m*	$m + m + m$ or $3 \times m$ or $3m$
Four *m*	$m + m + m + m$ or $4 \times m$ or $4m$
m squared	$m \times m = m^2$
m cubed	$m \times m \times m = m^3$
m to the power of five or *m* to the fifth	$m \times m \times m \times m \times m = m^5$
Square root of *m*	$\sqrt[2]{m}$ or $\sqrt{m}$
Cube root of *m*	$\sqrt[3]{m}$
Fourth root of *m*	$\sqrt[4]{m}$
Half of *m*	$m \div 2$ or $\frac{1}{2}m$ or $\frac{m}{2}$
Quarter of *m*	$m \div 4$ or $\frac{1}{4}m$ or $\frac{m}{4}$
Sum of *m* and *n*	$m + n$
Product of *m* and *n*	$m \times n$ or mn

Note that $2 \times m = m \times 2$, but we write the **number first**: 2*m*.

Note that the '2' is not needed.

Examples:

Phrase	Operation	Variable	Expression
15 more than *c*	+	*c*	$c + 15$ or $15 + c$
Eleven (times) *g*	x	*g*	$11g$
t reduced by 3	−	*t*	$t - 3$
An eighth of *y*	÷	*y*	$y \div 8$ or $\frac{y}{8}$ or $\frac{1}{8}y$

Remember that order doesn't matter when we add, so we can write $c + 15$ or $15 + c$.

ISBN: 9780170497978

Match each phrase below with the correct expression from the box.

$7 - b$	$\sqrt{b}$	$\frac{b}{7}$	b^7	$\frac{7}{b}$
$\sqrt[3]{b}$	$7b$	b^3	$b - 7$	$7 + b$

	Phrase	Expression
1	The product of 7 and *b*	
2	*b* cubed	
3	7 divided by *b*	
4	7 reduced by *b*	
5	The square root of *b*	
6	7 less than *b*	
7	A seventh of *b*	
8	The sum of 7 and *b*	
9	The cube root of *b*	
10	*b* to the seventh	

Write an expression for these phrases. Use the variable *y*.

11 Half a variable ________

12 A variable squared ________

13 Four less than a variable ________

14 The cube root of a variable ________

15 Double a variable ________

16 Eight divided by a variable ________

Write a phrase for these expressions.

17 $\sqrt{p}$

____

18 $\frac{p}{5}$

____

19 p^4

____

20 $3p$

____

 ISBN: 9780170497978

More about variables

- We use letters of the alphabet to represent variables.
- A variable is a quantity that can change.

Example: Two brothers help their father with maintenance jobs at the marae. He pays them different amounts, depending on the job. The brothers share the work and the money equally. They are paid:

- \$24 for mowing the lawns. Each brother gets $\$\frac{24}{2} = \$12$.
- \$14 for sweeping the paths. Each brother gets $\$\frac{14}{2} = \$7$.
- \$20 for weeding around the harakeke. Each brother gets $\$\frac{20}{2} = \$10$.

We call the total amount they were **paid** for each job **p**, so each brother was paid $\$\frac{p}{2}$ for each job.

p is called the **variable** and it represents the amount that the father **pays** for each job. *p* **changes** depending on how much is paid for each job.

$\frac{p}{2}$ is called an **expression**.

Identify the variable and the expression.

1 Kahu delivers papers to letterboxes. He is paid 8c per paper. He found that the total he was paid (\$) each day was given by the expression **Total = 0.08*p***.

a The variable is ______ and it stands for ________________________________.

b Use the expression to calculate how much he would be paid if he delivers 240 papers to letterboxes.

____

2 Angus collects cacti plants. He already has 13 in his collection. He is going to a cactus sale and has saved enough to buy some more. When he comes home, his total number of cactus plants will be given by the expression **Total = c + 13**.

a The variable is ______ and it stands for ________________________________.

b Use the expression to calculate how many cactus plants he will have if he buys eight more.

____

3 Huia is calculating the number of fence posts needed for the distance along one side of a paddock. She has done some research and found that they need to be 3 m apart, and she will need one extra post at the end. The total number of posts she will need is given by the expression **Total** = $\frac{d}{3} + 1$.

a The variable is ______ and it stands for ________________________________.

b Use the expression to calculate how many posts she will need for a paddock 360 m long.

____

ISBN: 9780170497978

Simplifying expressions

Multiplying

The order within simplified expressions should be:

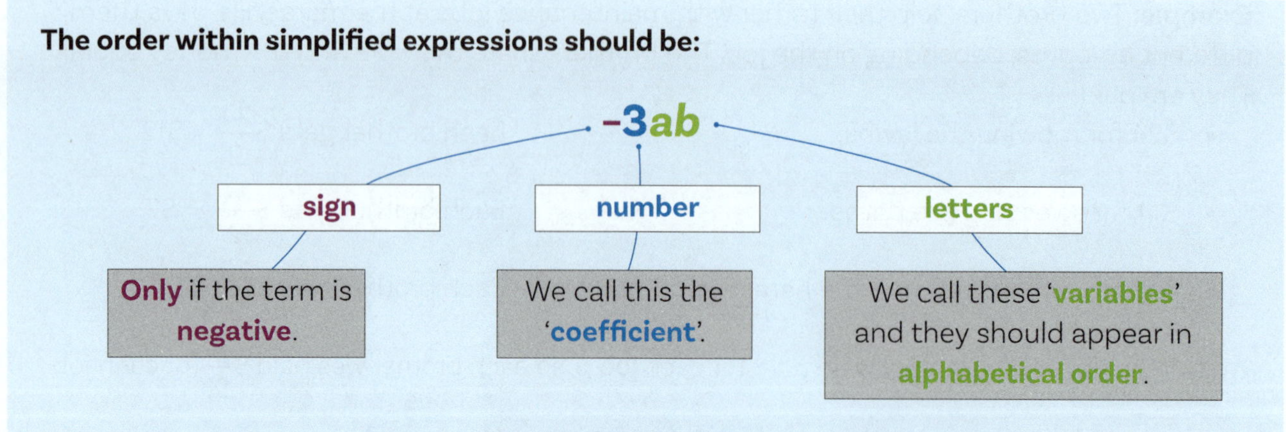

Examples:

Unsimplified expressions	Simplified expressions
a x 5	5a
a x a x a	a^3
7 x a x b	7ab
5a x 2a	$10a^2$
3a x -6b	-18ab
b x c x 3 x a	3abc

Index form or **power form**. (a^3 and $10a^2$)

Highlight the best simplified answer for each of the following.

1	p x p x p	^3p	3p
		p3	p^3
3	2d x 3	d6	5d
		6d	$16d^2$
5	3m x 4m	12m	$7m^2$
		$12m^2$	7m

2	5 x w	w5	5 + w
		5w	w^5
4	4c x 2d	cd^8	6cd
		cd8	8cd
6	3a x 5b x 1c	15abc	9cba
		9abc	15cba

Simplify the following expressions.

7 7 x n = ____________________

8 5a x 4b = ____________________

9 y x y = ____________________

10 h x 9 x j = ____________________

11 p x f x b = ____________________

12 -5 x y = ____________________

ISBN: 9780170497978

Dividing

- 'x divided by y' can be written as either $x \div y$ or $\frac{x}{y}$.
- Fully factorise the numerator and the denominator.
- Because $\frac{x}{x} = 1$, you can 'cancel'.

Example: $\frac{20p}{5} = \frac{4 \times \cancel{5} \times p}{\cancel{5}}$ or $\frac{20p}{5} \overset{\div 5}{=} \frac{4p}{1} = 4p$

$= 4p$

More examples:

Unsimplified expressions	Simplified expressions
$b \div 7$	$\frac{b}{7}$ or $\frac{1}{7}b$
$10 \div c$	$\frac{10}{c}$
$\frac{3d}{12}$	$\frac{d}{4}$ or $\frac{1}{4}d$
$\frac{14g}{7h}$	$\frac{2g}{1h}$ or $\frac{2g}{h}$

Circle/highlight the expression which is the best match for each of the following.

1 $m \div 3$

$\frac{3}{m}$	m^3
$\frac{m}{3}$	$3m$

2 $7 \div c$

$\frac{7}{c}$	$\frac{c}{7}$
$7c$	$c7$

3 $\frac{4}{12}a$

$\frac{2}{6}a$	$\frac{2}{6a}$
$3a$	$\frac{a}{3}$

4 $\frac{30}{6y}$

$5y$	$\frac{5}{y}$
$\frac{10}{2y}$	$\frac{y}{5}$

Simplify the following expressions.

5 $5p \div 10 =$ ____________________

6 $27d \div 9e =$ ____________________

7 $18 \div 6z =$ ____________________

8 $20bc \div 4e =$ ____________________

9 $\frac{50h}{10} =$ ____________________

10 $\frac{7}{28c} =$ ____________________

ISBN: 9780170497978

Like terms

- Terms can only be added or subtracted if they are '**like**' terms.
- 'Like' terms must have exactly the **same variables**, and each variable must be raised to exactly the **same power**.
- The coefficient does not matter.
- Order does not matter.
- The sign does not matter.

These are all like terms because they have x^1 and y^1.

Examples: The following **are** like terms: xy, $2xy$, yx, $-xy$.

The following are **not** like terms:

x^3y^5 and x^3y^2 — The y is to the power of **2**, not **5**.

x^2y^3 and y^3x^2z — Includes a '**z**'.

State whether each of the following pairs are like terms or unlike terms.

1	a and b	________	**2**	a and $5a$	________
3	$4ab$ and ab	________	**4**	$2b$ and $4b^2$	________
5	$3a$ and a^2	________	**6**	a and $-5a$	________
7	$7ab$ and $3ba$	________	**8**	4 and 6	________
9	a and $20a$	________	**10**	ab and $-ab$	________
11	a^5b^7 and b^5a^7	________	**12**	a^2b^5 and a^3b^5	________

13 Join the dots on the left to match the like terms on the right.

st •	• $5sr^2t^2$
rt •	• $11ts^2$
r^2st^2 •	• $10t^2sr$
trs •	• $8ts$
rst^2 •	• $6ts^2r^2$
$2rs^2$ •	• $-rt$
r^2s^2t •	• $7s^2r$
s^2t •	• $-r^2$
$6r^2$ •	• $9tsr$

 ISBN: 9780170497978

Adding and subtracting

- When adding or subtracting, you can **combine only like terms**.
- Only the terms with exactly the same variables and powers can be combined.

Hint: It is helpful to circle, underline or highlight terms that are 'like' each other with the same colour.

Examples: Simplify the following.

1 $9d + 3e - 2d = 7d + 3e$

9d and −2d are like terms, so they can be combined → 7d.

2 $11x^2 - 3y + 9z + x^2 + y = 12x^2 - 2y + 9z$

$11x^2$ and $+x^2$ are like terms, so they can be combined → $12x^2$.
$-3y$ and $+y$ are like terms, so they can be combined → $-2y$.

Fill the boxes with letters and/or numbers in order to complete a correct simplification.

1 $3p + p + p =$ ☐

2 $8a - 2a + a =$ ☐

3 $5f - 9f + 3f =$ ☐

4 $9x + 7 - 2x - 2 = 7x +$ ☐

5 $5a + 7b - a - 4b = 4a +$ ☐

6 $9c + 3d - c - 2d =$ ☐ $+ d$

7 $5e^2 - 3f + e^2 - f =$ ☐ − ☐

8 $12y^2 - 9y - 7y^2 + 2y =$ ☐ − ☐

9 $2x^2 + x - 2 - x - 5 =$ ☐ − ☐

10 $3p - p^2 + 1 - 9p + 3p^2 =$ ☐ − ☐ $+ 1$

Simplify these by adding or subtracting like terms.

11 $5a + b + a =$ ______

12 $11 - c + 3 =$ ______

13 $8d + 5e + d - e =$ ______

14 $8f + g + 2f - 5 =$ ______

15 $6j + 4k - 7j + 4 =$ ______

16 $8m + n - 2m - 2n - 9 =$ ______

17 $3p - q - p + 4q =$ ______

18 $2a + 7ab - 2b - ab =$ ______

19 $4c - 3d - 2c - c - d =$ ______

20 $g + g^2 - g - 2gh =$ ______

21 $4y^2 + 5 - 2y - xy^2 =$ ______

22 $2c^2 + 1 - d^2 - c^2 - 5 =$ ______

ISBN: 9780170497978

Mixing it up

Circle/highlight the correct/best simplified answer for each of the following.

	Expression	Option	Option
1	$\frac{12}{6a}$	$\frac{1}{2}a$	$\frac{2}{a}$
		$\frac{1}{2a}$	$2a$
2	$5a + 2b - 4a - b$	$a - b$	$a + b$
		$a - 2$	$a + 2$
3	$4a^2 + a - 3a - a^2$	$3a - 2a^2$	$3a^2 - 2a$
		$4 - 2a$	$3a^2 - 2a^2$
4	$5a \times 2b$	$7ab$	$7ba$
		$10ba$	$10ab$

5 Highlight the boxes which contain an expression that is equivalent to the central expression.

Central expression: **$12d$**

$7d - d + 6d$	$\frac{24d}{2}$	$2d \times 6d$	$\frac{48}{4}d$
$16d - 4$			$13d^2 - d$
$3 \times 4d$			$d \times 12$
$\frac{24}{2d}$	$12 + d$	$36d \div 3$	$d + 10d - p + p$

Simplify the following.

6 $\frac{15gh}{3g} =$ ____________

7 $2p + 5q - q - p =$ ____________

8 $\frac{24a}{8a^2} =$ ____________

9 $4f + 2g - 9f - g =$ ____________

10 $c \times 9c \times 3 =$ ____________

11 $\frac{3k}{18k} =$ ____________

12 $20z \div 5z =$ ____________

13 $1 \times m \times m \times 3 =$ ____________

14 $8ab - a + 5a^2 - 6ab - b =$ ____________

15 $-w + 2w^2 + 2w - 5w^2 =$ ____________

16 $4p^3 - p^2 - p + 2p^2 + p =$ ____________

 ISBN: 9780170497978

Powers

The words **power**, **exponent** and **index** all mean the same thing.

$5a^4$ — coefficient: 5; base: a; power, exponent, index: 4

You need to know that:
- a^4 means **a x a x a x a**
- a^1 is the same as **a**
- $a^0 = 1$ — This is important but often forgotten. It only works as long as $a \neq 0$.

Multiplying powers

When multiplying, we **add** the indices: $a^m \times a^n = a^{m+n}$

Examples:

1. $a^3 \times a^2 = a \times a \times a \times a \times a$ (If you are not sure, expand each term.)
   $= a^5$ ($3 + 2 = 5$)

2. $2ab \times 7ab^2 = 2 \times a \times b \times 7 \times a \times b \times b$
   $= 14a^2b^3$

3. $3a^4 \times 5a^9 = 15a^{13}$ (It helps to deal with the **coefficients** first.)

Highlight the best answer for each of the following.

1	e x e x e x e	4e	e4
		e^4	e^3e
2	$g^5 \times g^2$	g^{10}	g^7
		$10g$	$7g$
3	$h^3 \times 5h$	$5h^3$	h^8
		$8h^4$	$5h^4$
4	$3p^3 \times 2p^2$	$5p^5$	$6p^5$
		$6p^6$	$5p^6$

Simplify the following.

5 $z \times z =$ ______________________

6 $n \times n^7 =$ ______________________

7 $a^5 \times a^3 =$ ______________________

8 $b^2 \times b^4 \times b =$ ______________________

9 $c^5 \times 3c =$ ______________________

10 $3g^2 \times 7g^3 =$ ______________________

11 $6cd^5 \times 3d^2 =$ ______________________

12 $4r^2s^4 \times 3rs^5 =$ ______________________

ISBN: 9780170497978

Dividing powers

When dividing, we **subtract** the indices: $a^m \div a^n = a^{m-n}$

Examples:

1 $a^6 \div a^4 = \frac{a^6}{a^4}$

$a^6 \div a^4 = \frac{a \times a \times \not{a} \times \not{a} \times \not{a} \times \not{a}}{\not{a} \times \not{a} \times \not{a} \times \not{a}}$

$= a^2$

You can expand each term and then 'cancel' terms that are common to the numerator and denominator.

A quicker way is to subtract the index in the denominator from that in the numerator: **6** – **4** = **2**.

2 $\frac{20a^5}{4a^2} = \frac{5 \times \not{4} \times a \times a \times a \times \not{a} \times \not{a}}{\not{4} \times \not{a} \times \not{a}}$

$= 5a^3$

Deal with the **coefficients** first.

3 $\frac{10a^3}{4a^5} = \frac{5 \times \not{2} \times \not{a} \times \not{a} \times \not{a}}{2 \times \not{2} \times a \times a \times \not{a} \times \not{a} \times \not{a}}$

$= \frac{5}{2a^2}$

Your answer might have a variable in the denominator.

Circle/highlight the correct/best simplified answer for each of the following.

	Question		
1	$y^4 \div y$	y^3	$\frac{1}{y^3}$
		$3y$	y^5
2	$\frac{z^5}{z^3}$	$\frac{1}{z^2}$	$2z$
		z^8	z^2
3	$\frac{a^3}{a^9}$	$\frac{1}{a^6}$	a^3
		$\frac{1}{a^3}$	a^6
4	$\frac{6g^4}{18g}$	$3g^3$	$\frac{3g^3}{9}$
		$2g^3 \div 6$	$g^3 \div 3$
5	$\frac{6a^8}{a^2}$	$6a^4$	$6a^6$
		$\frac{6}{a^6}$	$\frac{6}{a^4}$
6	$4m^2 \div 8mn$	$\frac{m}{2n}$	$\frac{2m}{n}$
		$\frac{m^3}{2n}$	$\frac{2m^3}{n}$
7	$\frac{c^8 d^5}{c^2 d^{10}}$	$\frac{c^4}{d^2}$	$\frac{c^4}{d^5}$
		$\frac{c^6}{d^5}$	$\frac{c^6}{d^2}$
8	$\frac{6a^2 b^6}{2a^8 b^2}$	$\frac{3b^4}{a^6}$	$\frac{3b^4}{a^4}$
		$\frac{3b^3}{a^4}$	$\frac{3b^3}{a^6}$

ISBN: 9780170497978

9 Highlight the boxes which contain an expression that is equivalent to the central expression.

$2a^2$	$2a^6 \div 4a^4$	$14a^3b^5 \div 7ab^5$	$\frac{1}{2}a^2$
$\frac{6a^8}{12a^6}$	**$\frac{a^2}{2}$**		$2a^2 \div 4a^4$
$2a^4bc^2 \div 4a^2bc^2$			$\frac{2a^2}{4}$
$4a^4 \div 2a^2$	$\frac{12a^5b}{24a^3b}$	$6a^7b^2 \div 12a^5b^2$	$\frac{24a^{10}b}{12a^8b}$

Simplify these.

10 $z^6 \div z^9 =$ ____________

11 $\frac{p^6}{6p^2} =$ ____________

12 $\frac{12e^3}{4e} =$ ____________

13 $\frac{8y}{2y^2} =$ ____________

14 $\frac{mn^2}{mn} =$ ____________

15 $\frac{ab}{b^3} =$ ____________

16 $\frac{s^3t^4}{st^3} =$ ____________

17 $\frac{x^5y}{x^4y^3} =$ ____________

18 $\frac{cd^6}{4c^2d^2} =$ ____________

19 $\frac{12p^7q^2}{6p^3q} =$ ____________

Find the missing terms needed to make these expressions equivalent.

20 $y = \frac{\square}{1} = \frac{\square}{6} = \frac{3y}{\square} = \frac{\square}{y^3} = \frac{5y^2}{\square}$

21 $\frac{3}{z} = \frac{3z}{\square} = \frac{\square}{2z} = \frac{3z^2}{\square} = \frac{15z^4}{\square}$

22 $\frac{s}{r^2} = \frac{2s}{\square} = \frac{\square}{r^3} = \frac{3s^2}{\square} = \frac{5r^2s}{\square}$

ISBN: 9780170497978

Powers of powers

When finding a power of a power, we **multiply** the indices: $(a^m)^n = a^{m \times n}$

Examples:

1 $(a^4)^2 = (a^4) \times (a^4)$
$= (a \times a \times a \times a) \times (a \times a \times a \times a)$
$= a^8$

Once again, if you are not sure, expand each term.

$4 \times 2 = 8$

2 $(5a^2)^3 = (5a^2) \times (5a^2) \times (5a^2)$
$= (5 \times a \times a) \times (5 \times a \times a) \times (5 \times a \times a)$
$= 125a^6$

Deal with the **coefficient** first: $5^3 = 125$.

3 $3(2a^5)^4 = 3 \times (2a^5) \times (2a^5) \times (2a^5) \times (2a^5)$
$= 3 \times 16a^{20}$
$= 48a^{20}$

Expand the **brackets** first: $(2a^5)^4 = 16a^{20}$. Then multiply by 3.

Circle/highlight the correct/best simplified answer for each of the following.

1	$(x^6)^2$	x^3	x^8
		x^{12}	x^4
3	$(5d^4)^3$	$125d^{12}$	$125d^8$
		$15d^{12}$	$15d^8$
5	$(2g^4h^5)^3$	$6g^7h^8$	$6g^{12}h^{15}$
		$8g^{12}h^{15}$	$8g^7h^8$

2	$(4c^3)^2$	$8c^5$	$8c^6$
		$16c^5$	$16c^6$
4	$(7y^6z)^2$	$14y^8z^3$	$14y^{12}z^2$
		$49y^8z^3$	$49y^{12}z^2$
6	$2(3a^5b^6)^3$	$54a^{15}b^{18}$	$18a^{15}b^{18}$
		$36a^{15}b^{18}$	$12a^{15}b^{18}$

Simplify the following.

7 $(p^7)^2$ = ____________________

8 $(s^6)^3$ = ____________________

9 $(6b^5)^2$ = ____________________

10 $(4x^5)^3$ = ____________________

11 $(gh^4)^2$ = ____________________

12 $(3b^4c^5)^2$ = ____________________

13 $2(5m^6n^{10})^2$ = ____________________

14 $10(5d^4e)^3$ = ____________________

ISBN: 9780170497978

Mixing it up

1 Select the correct simplified expression below for each of the following expressions.

$8a^6b^2$	$5a^4$	$3a^3b^4$	$5a^3$	$3a^5$	$3a^4b^3$	$3a^3b$	$8a^6b^3$

$\dfrac{5a^6}{a^2}$ = ________ $(2a^2b)^3$ = ________ $\dfrac{6a^6b^3}{2a^2}$ = ________ $3a \times a^4$ = ________

$\dfrac{3(2a^2b)^2}{4ab}$ = ________ $8(a^3b)^2$ = ________ $a^2b^3 \times 3ab$ = ________ $\dfrac{15a^4b}{3ab}$ = ________

Simplify the following.

2 $2c^{10} \div c^5$ = ________

3 $3m^6 \times m^5$ = ________

4 $(p^4)^3$ = ________

5 $\dfrac{e^8}{e^2}$ = ________

6 $\dfrac{d^2}{d^6}$ = ________

7 $(3y^5)^2$ = ________

8 $3n \times 5n^4$ = ________

9 $4(2p^3)^5$ = ________

10 $5z \div 10z^4$ = ________

11 $\dfrac{20y}{4y^5}$ = ________

Find the error in each of the following, explain what has been done incorrectly and write the correct answer.

		Explanation	Correct answer
12	$6f^3 \times 2f^4 = 12f^{12}$		
13	$18e^{12} \div 6e^3 = 3e^4$		
14	$(2c^2)^3 = 8c^8$		
15	$2(3d^5)^2 = 36d^{10}$		

Brackets

Expanding

- In algebra, '**expand**' means **multiply** out all the **brackets**.
- After expanding, you are expected to **collect the like terms** in order to simplify the expression.

Example:

5(a + 3) means '5 lots of (a + 3)'.

In other words:

$$\begin{array}{r} a + 3 \\ + \quad a + 3 \\ + \quad a + 3 \\ + \quad a + 3 \\ + \quad a + 3 \\ \hline = 5a + 15 \end{array}$$

A quicker way to get this answer is to multiply each term in the bracket by 5.

$$5(a + 3) = 5 \times a + 5 \times 3$$
$$= 5a + 15$$

If there is **no sign** between a term and a bracket, it is understood that you should **multiply**.

More examples: Expand the following.

1 $3(a - 6) = 3a - 18$ — $3 \times a - 3 \times 6$

2 $-2(b + 3) = -2b - 6$ — $-2 \times b + -2 \times 3$

3 $-4(3c - 2) = -12c + 8$ — $-4 \times 3c - -4 \times 2$

4 $d(d - 5) = d^2 - 5d$ — $d \times d - d \times 5$

Remember that the negative of (or times) a negative is a **positive**.

Fill the boxes with letters and/or numbers in order to complete a correct expansion.

1 $5(p + 3) = \square\, p + 15$

2 $7(y + 2) = 7y + \square$

3 $3(w - 6) = 3\square - 18$

4 $2(v - 4) = 2v - \square$

5 $4(5 + m) = \square + 4m$

6 $9(3d + 4) = \square\, d + 36$

7 $8(2h + 3) = \square\, h + 24$

8 $5(4 - 3x) = 20 - \square\, x$

9 $-3(n + 7) = -3n - \square$

10 $-6(3z + 5) = -18\square - 30$

11 $-(5s - 11) = \square\, s + 11$

12 $-10(4x - 7) = -40x + \square$

ISBN: 9780170497978

Circle/highlight the correct expanded answer for each of the following.

13	$4(x + y)$	$x + 4y$ $4x + 4y$ $4x + y$ $4xy$
15	$3(y - 4)$	$3y + 12$ $y - 12$ $3y - 12$ $3y - 4$
17	$-6(x + 4)$	$-6x + 24$ $6x + 24$ $-6x - 24$ $6x - 24$
19	$x(4x - 9)$	$4x^2 - 9x$ $4x - 9x$ $4x^2 - 9$ $4x - 9x$

14	$5(x + 2)$	$5x + 10$ $x + 10$ $5x - 10$ $2x + 10$
16	$7(2x + 5)$	$14x - 35$ $7x + 35$ $2x + 35$ $14x + 35$
18	$-2(y - 8)$	$-2y - 16$ $2y + 16$ $-2y + 10$ $-2y + 16$
20	$-x(2y - z)$	$-2xy - z$ $-2xy + z$ $-2xy + xz$ $-2xy - xz$

Expand the following.

21 $5(2z - 4) =$ ______________________

22 $p(p - 4) =$ ______________________

23 $-6(3 - g) =$ ______________________

24 $-b(c + 4) =$ ______________________

25 $5(2r + s) =$ ______________________

26 $7(x - 2 + z) =$ ______________________

27 $-2u(u - 3) =$ ______________________

28 $2f(6g - 3) =$ ______________________

29 $-4(a - 2b) =$ ______________________

30 $-2(3 - 7p) =$ ______________________

31 $-x(1 - 2x) =$ ______________________

32 $m^2(2m - 5) =$ ______________________

33 $-(7y - 4) =$ ______________________

34 $-10a(1 - 3a^2) =$ ______________________

ISBN: 9780170497978

Factorising

- Factors are terms that are **multiplied** together (rather than added or subtracted), e.g. 3 and 5 are factors of 15 because 3 **x** 5 = 15.
- In algebra, factorising is the **'undoing' of expanding**.
- Expressions with brackets are usually in **factorised form**.

Examples:

Remember, if there is **no sign** between a term and a bracket, it is understood that you should **multiply**.

Expand →

Factorised form	Unfactorised (expanded) form
$3(x + 6)$	$3x + 18$
$4(p + q)$	$4p + 4q$
$-4(3 - 2y)$	$-12 + 8y$
$y(y - 9)$	$y^2 - 9y$

← Factorise

Finding the biggest factor

- When factorising, you must factorise **completely**. There must be **no common factor** for the terms inside the brackets.
- You need to ask yourself: '**What is the biggest term (highest common factor or HCF) that will divide into every term?**'
- Do not use fractions or decimals when factorising.

Examples:

Terms	Common factors	Highest common factor (HCF)
8 and 16	1, 2, 4, 8	8
$6p$ and $12p$	$1, 2, 3, 6, p, 2p, 3p, 6p$	$6p$
15 and 20	1, 2, 3, 5	5
$12ab$ and $9ab$	$1, 3, a, 3a, b, 3b, ab, 3ab$	$3ab$

List the common factors of these terms, then highlight the highest.

1 3, 9 ______________________ **2** 4, 12 ______________________

3 10, 18 ______________________ **4** 24, 30 ______________________

5 5, 11 ______________________ **6** 3, 21 ______________________

7 8, 24 ______________________ **8** y, 25 ______________________

List the common factors of these terms.

9 $g, 10g$ ______________________ **10** st, su ______________________

11 $10e, 20e$ ______________________ **12** $3cd, 12c$ ______________________

 ISBN: 9780170497978

Hints: 1 If you are asked to **factorise**, check your answer by **expanding**.

2 If you are asked to **expand**, check your answer by **factorising**.

Fill the boxes with letters and/or numbers in order to complete a correct factorisation.

13 $12x - 3 = 3(\square x - 1)$

14 $20x + 15 = 5(4x + \square)$

15 $18x + 12 = 6(\square x + 2)$

16 $4x - 20 = 4(x - \square)$

17 $x^2 + 9x = x(\square + 9)$

18 $14x + 21 = 7(\square x + 3)$

Fill the boxes with letters and/or numbers in order to complete a correct factorisation.

19 $4x + 24 = \square(x + 6)$

20 $12 + 2x = \square(6 + x)$

21 $8x - 24 = \square(x - 3)$

22 $36 + 12x = \square(3 + x)$

23 $15x - 10 = \square(3x - 2)$

24 $100x - 30 = \square(10x - 3)$

Write the contents of each bracket in order to complete a correct factorisation.

25 $20x + 15 = 5($ ______ $)$

26 $7x - 21 = 7($ ______ $)$

27 $27 - 18x = 9($ ______ $)$

28 $6x - 30 = 6($ ______ $)$

29 $25x + 5 = 5($ ______ $)$

30 $35x - 14 = 7($ ______ $)$

31 $2x^2 + 5x = x($ ______ $)$

32 $18x - 6x^2 = 6x($ ______ $)$

Factorise the following.

33 $8x + 8y =$ ______

34 $14x - 7y =$ ______

35 $12x - 6 =$ ______

36 $x^2 - 4x =$ ______

37 $xy + 2y =$ ______

38 $20x^2 - 5 =$ ______

39 $24 - 8x =$ ______

40 $2x^2 + 4x =$ ______

41 $-7x^2 + 14x =$ ______

42 $18x - 6x^2 =$ ______

43 $4xy - 20x^2 =$ ______

44 $-15xy - 5xyz =$ ______

ISBN: 9780170497978

Straight lines

Coordinates

- A positive **x** coordinate tells you how far to move to the **right**.
- A positive **y** coordinate tells you how far to move **up**.
- Coordinates are written in brackets in **alphabetical order**: **(x, y)**.
- We use the word 'ax**i**s' for one axis, and the word 'ax**e**s' for more than one.

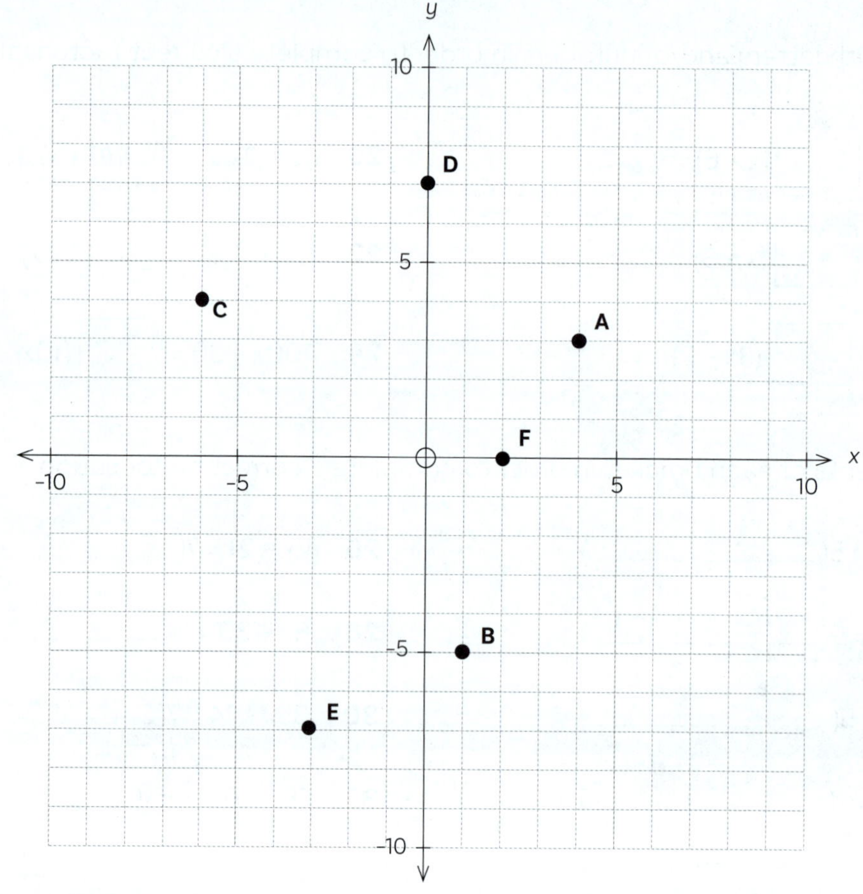

1 Write down the coordinates of the lettered points below.

A (______, ______) **B** (______, ______)

C (______, ______) **D** (______, ______)

E (______, ______) **F** (______, ______)

2 Plot these points on the graph above.

G (-3, 7) **H** (7, -3)

I (-4, 0) **J** (8, 6)

K (0, -9) **L** (-8, -4)

 ISBN: 9780170497978

Linear patterns with discrete data

- Discrete data is data that can be counted, e.g. number of people, heights measured to the nearest centimetre.
- You need to be able to continue a pattern, plot these on a graph, find a rule and use it.

Example: Emily made these designs with matchsticks:

Design 1

Design 2

Design 3

a She created a table.

To find out the number of matchsticks needed for design 0, start at design 1 and do the opposite of the pattern (**−2**).

Design number (n)	Number of matchsticks (M)
0	1
1	3
2	5
3	7
4	**9**
5	**11**

−2, +2, +2, +2, +2

Look for the pattern: in this case **+2**.

b Then she plotted the points on a graph.

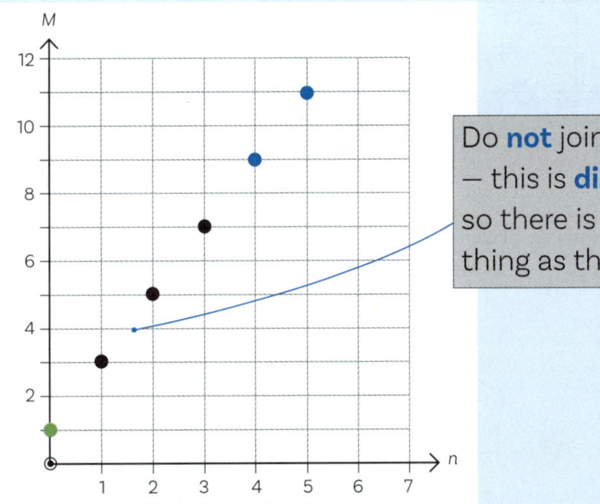

Do **not** join the points – this is **discrete** data so there is no such thing as the $1\frac{1}{2}$th point.

c She worked out the equation for the number of matchsticks (**M**) in any design (**n**).

She used the format $M = \underline{+2}\,n + \underline{+1}$

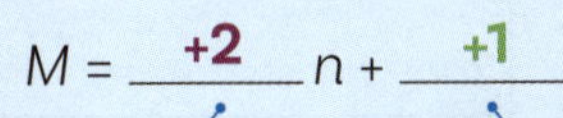

So the equation is $\mathbf{M = 2n + 1}$

She inserted the **+2** from the pattern in the table.

She inserted the number of matchsticks that would be in design number 0 (**1**).

d Explain how the equation relates to the designs.

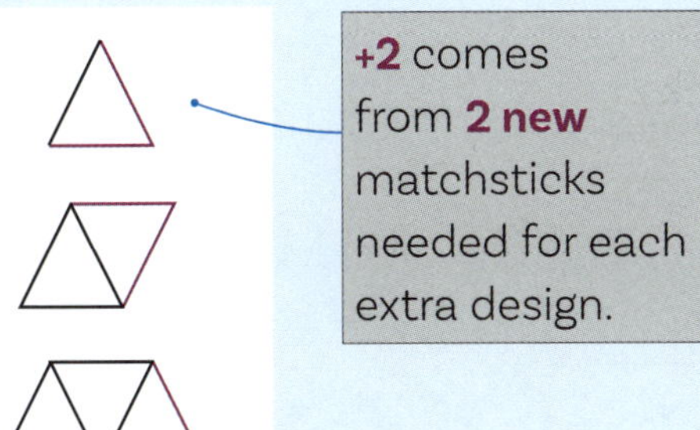

+2 comes from **2 new** matchsticks needed for each extra design.

$M = 2n + 1$

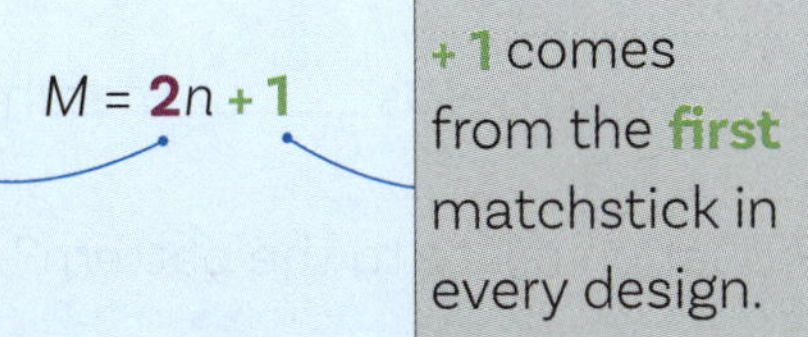

+ 1 comes from the **first** matchstick in every design.

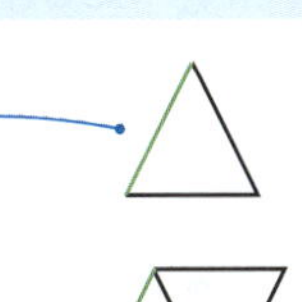

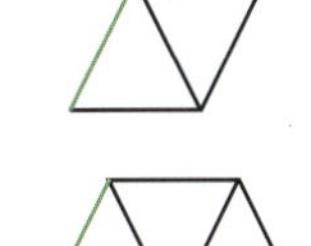

Answer the following questions.

1 Bryn makes the following designs with matchsticks.

a Complete the table, and use it to find the equation for the number of matchsticks in each design.

Design number (n)	Number of matchsticks (M)
0	
1	4
2	7
3	10
4	
5	
6	

Equation: M = ☐ n + ☐

b Plot the points on the graph.

c How many matchsticks are needed for the 30th design?

30th design ⇒ $n = 30 \therefore M =$ ______ x 30 + ______ = ______

So the 30th design needs ______ matchsticks.

d How does the equation relate to the pattern?

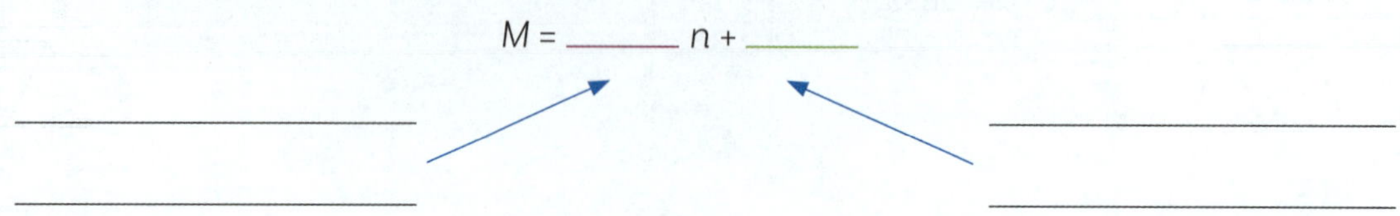

 ISBN: 9780170497978

2 Zoe is creating designs using buttons.

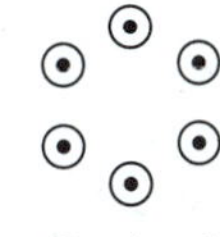

Design 1

Design 2

Design 3

a Complete the table, and use it to find the equation for the number of buttons needed for each design.

Design number (n)	Number of buttons (B)
0	
1	6
2	10
3	
4	
5	
6	

Equation: B = ______ n + ______

b Plot the points on the graph.

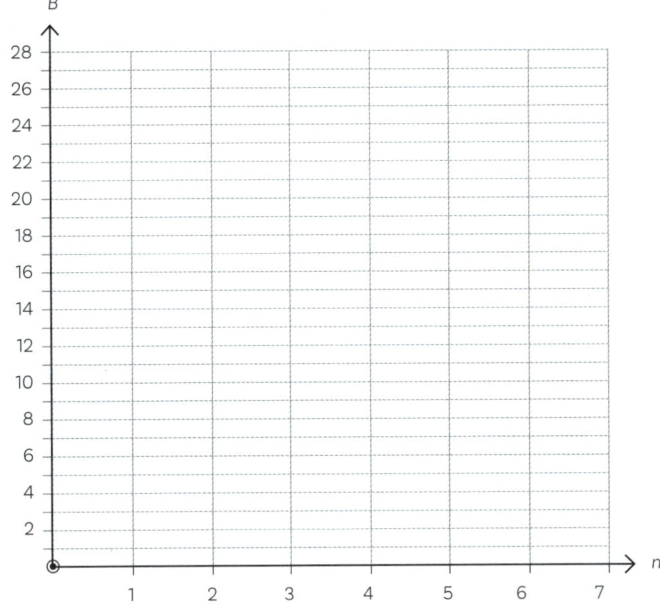

c How many buttons are needed for the 20th design?

20th design ⟹ n = 20 ∴ B = ______ x 20 + ______ = ______

So the 20th design needs ______ buttons.

d How does the equation relate to the pattern?

B = ______ n + ______

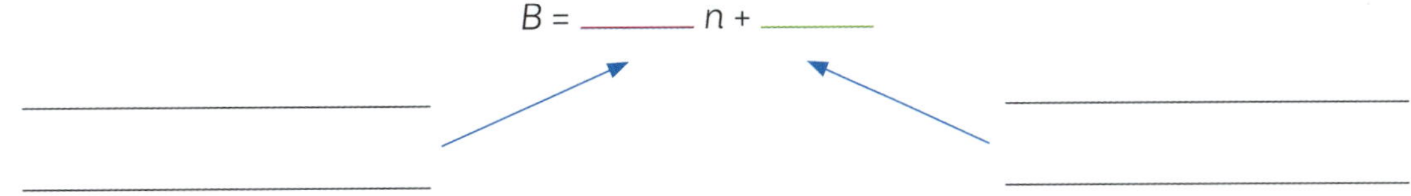

3 Tia makes the following designs as part of a tukutuku panel.

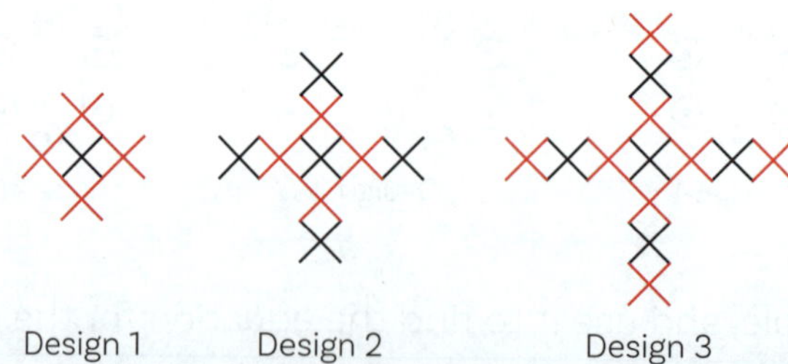

a Complete the table, and use it to find the equation for the number of crosses needed for each design.

Design number (n)	Number of crosses (C)
0	
1	
2	
3	
4	
5	
6	

Equation: C = ______ n + ______

b Plot the points on the graph.

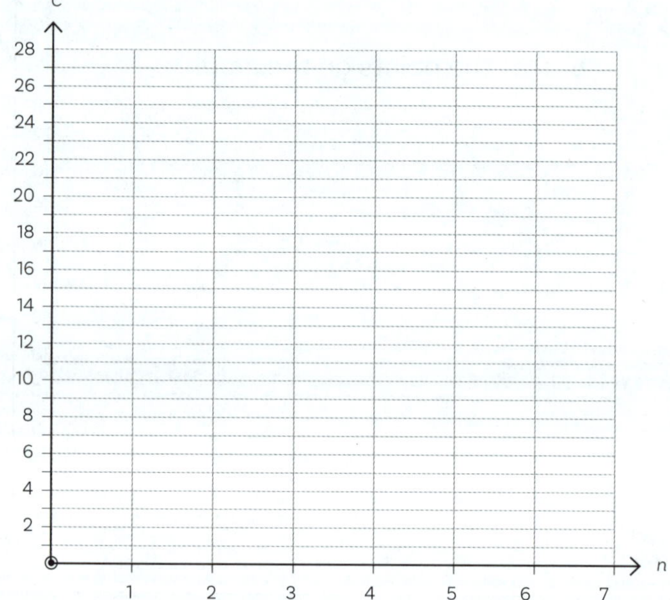

c How many crosses are needed for the 15th design?

15th design ⇒ $n = 15 \therefore C =$ ______ x 15 + ______ = ______

So the 15th design needs ______ crosses.

d How does the equation relate to the pattern?

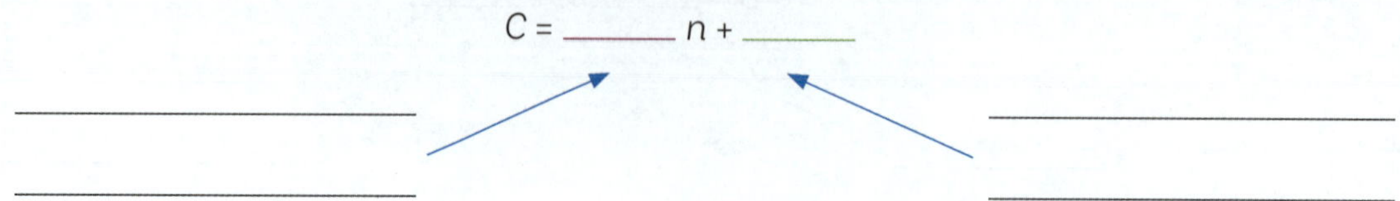

  ISBN: 9780170497978

4 Annie is going to the community fair. It costs \$5 to get in, and each activity costs another \$2.

a Complete the table, and use it to find the equation for the total cost of going to the fair.

Number of activities (A)	Cost (C)
0	
1	
2	
3	
4	
5	
6	

Equation: $C =$ ______ $A +$ ______

b Plot the points on the graph.

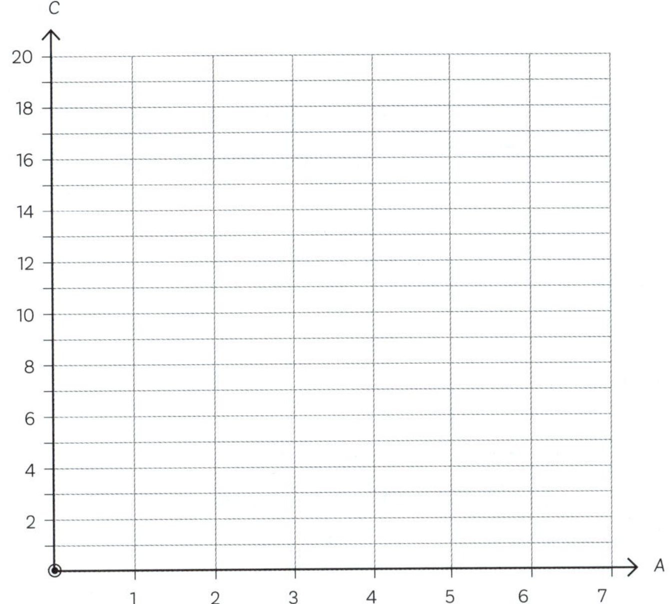

c How much would it cost if she participated in nine activities?

Nine activities $\Rightarrow A = 9 \therefore C =$ ______________ = ______

So the total cost if she did nine activities would be __________.

d How does the equation relate to the number of activities?

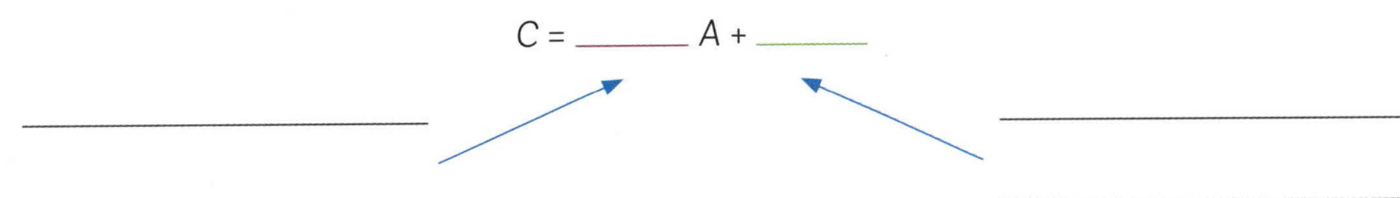

The gradient of a line

- The gradient is the **steepness**, or **slope**, of a line.
- The gradient is usually denoted by the letter **m**.

These lines all have **positive** gradients.

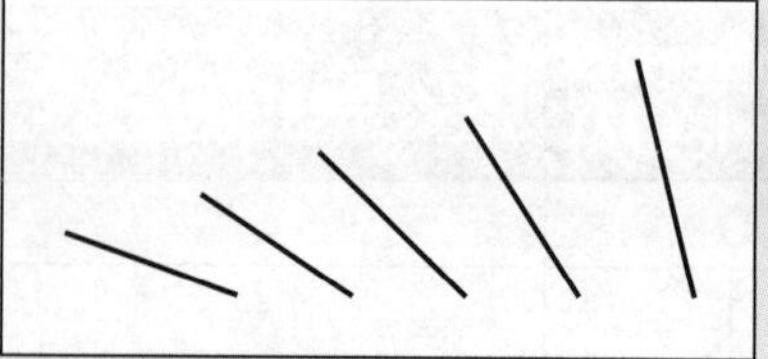

These lines all have **negative** gradients.

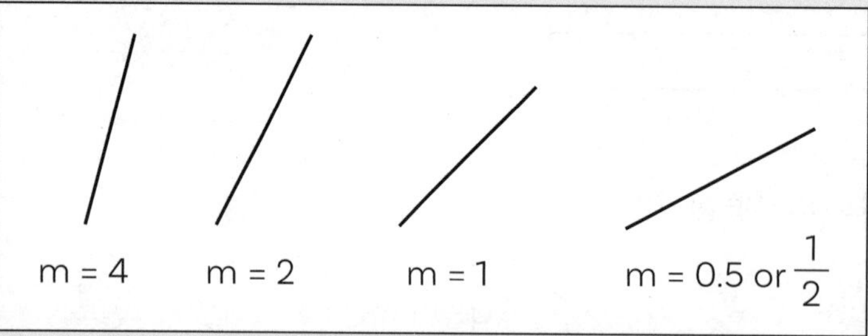

The steeper the line, the bigger the gradient.

The gradient is calculated using the formula **m** = $\frac{\textbf{change in } y}{\textbf{change in } x}$ or $\frac{\textbf{rise}}{\textbf{run}}$.

Example 1:

Step 1: Pick two points where the line goes **through the intersections of the grid**.

Step 2: Draw a right-angled triangle connecting these points and count the number of squares across (**run**) and up (**rise**).

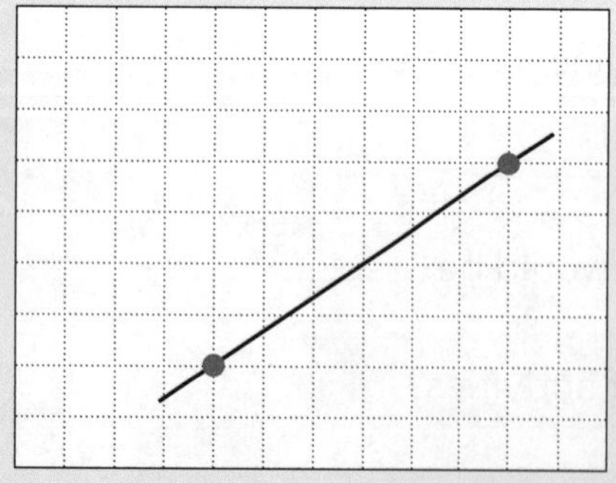

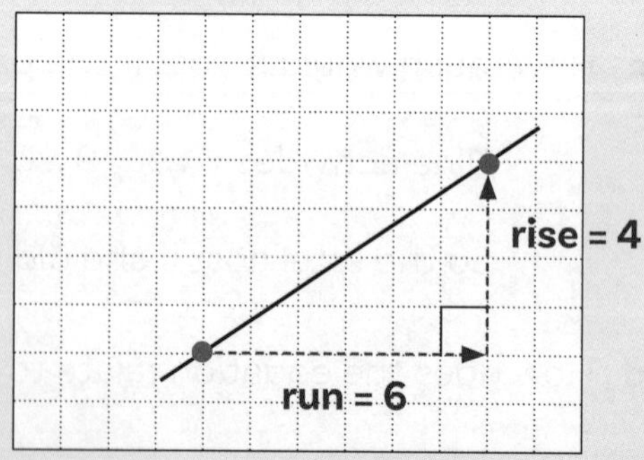

Step 3: $\mathbf{m} = \frac{\textbf{rise}}{\textbf{run}} = \frac{4}{6}$ or $\frac{2}{3}$ or $0.\dot{6}$

Do **not** round a gradient.

 ISBN: 9780170497978

Example 2:

Step 1: Pick two points where the line goes **through the intersections of the grid**.

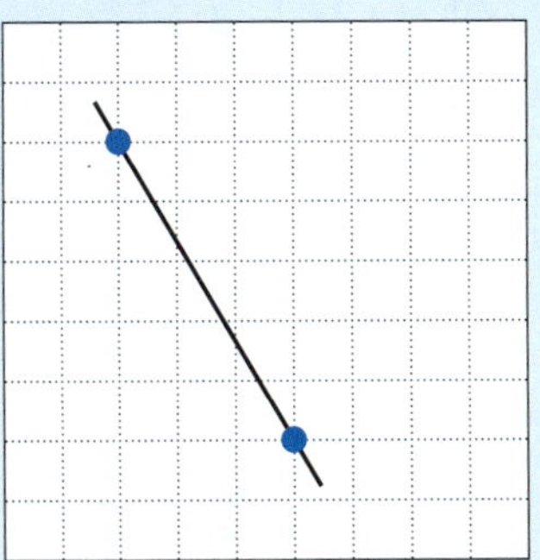

Step 2: Draw a right-angled triangle connecting these points and count the number of squares across (**run**) and up or down (**rise**).

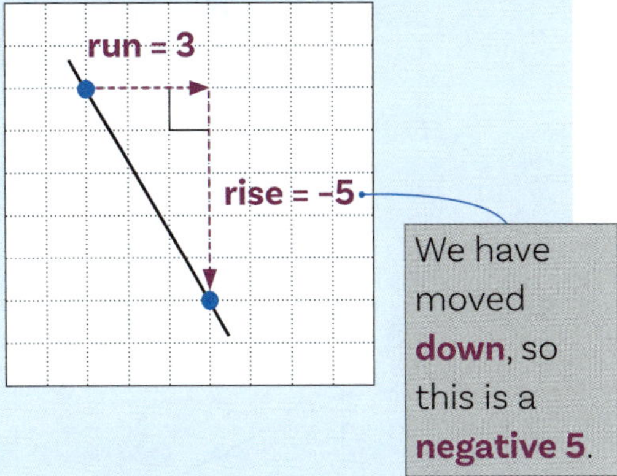

Step 3: $m = \frac{\text{rise}}{\text{run}} = \frac{-5}{3}$ or $-\frac{5}{3}$

Notice:

1 You get the same answer whichever way the arrows go.

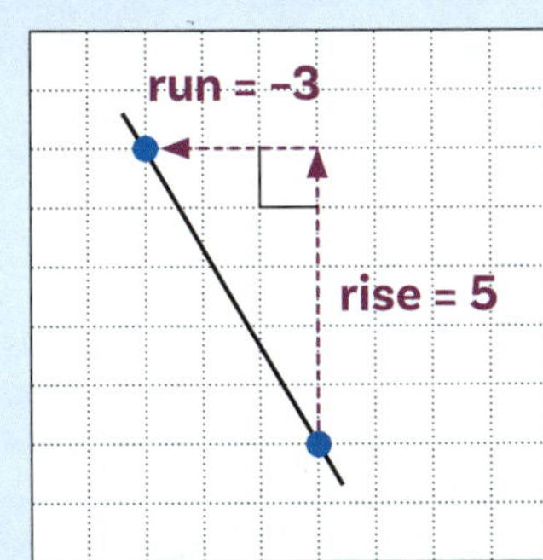

$m = \frac{\text{rise}}{\text{run}} = \frac{5}{-3}$ or $-\frac{5}{3}$

2 You get the same answer whichever side of the line you draw your triangle.

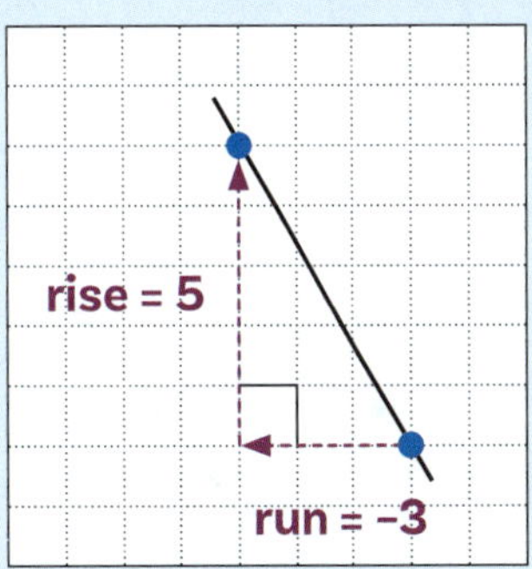

$m = \frac{\text{rise}}{\text{run}} = \frac{5}{-3}$ or $-\frac{5}{3}$

Example 3:

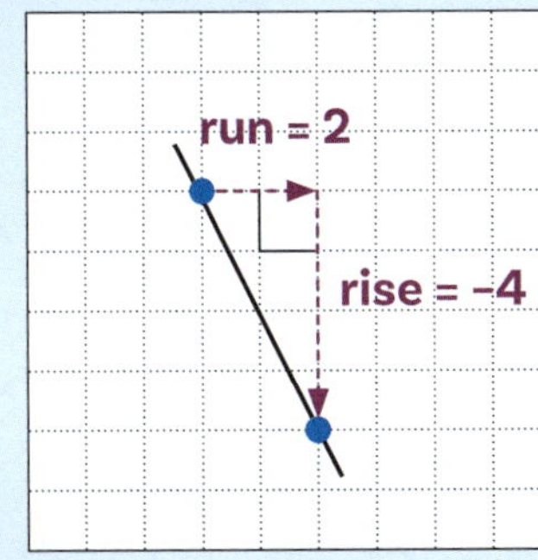

$m = \frac{\text{rise}}{\text{run}} = \frac{-4}{2} = -\frac{2}{1}$ or -2

Any of these answers is acceptable. Some gradients simplify to single digits.

Example 4:

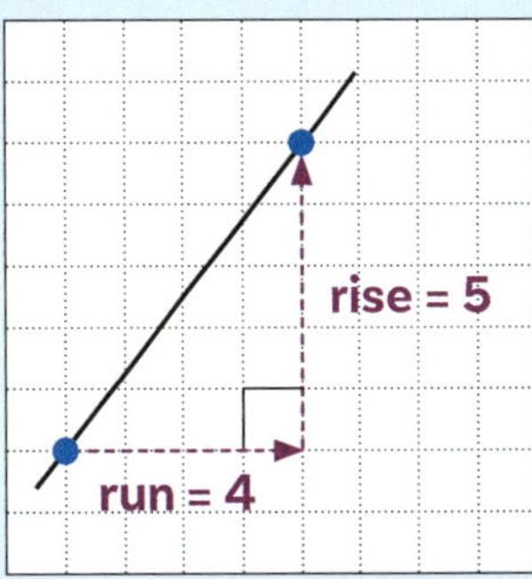

$m = \frac{\text{rise}}{\text{run}} = \frac{5}{4} = 1\frac{1}{4}$ or 1.25

Improper fractions are the most convenient form for writing gradients.

ISBN: 9780170497978

Find the gradients of these lines. Write your answers as improper fractions or whole numbers.

1

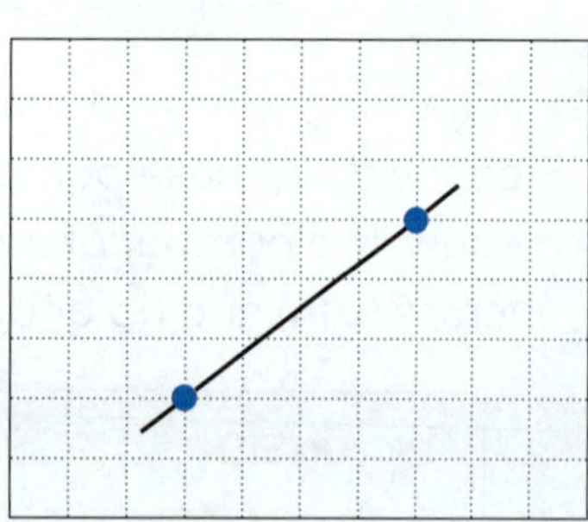

m = ________

2

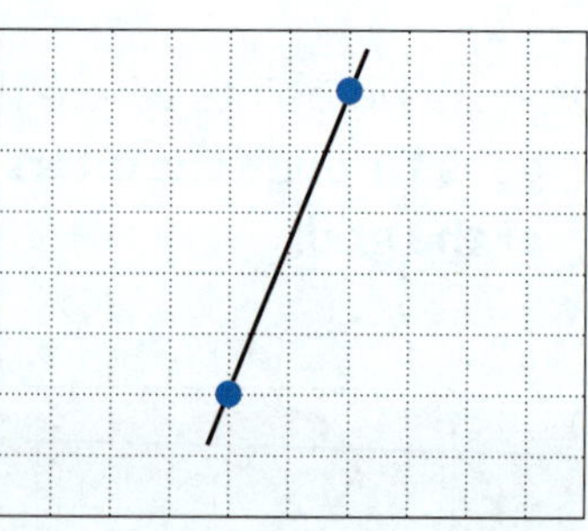

m = ________

3

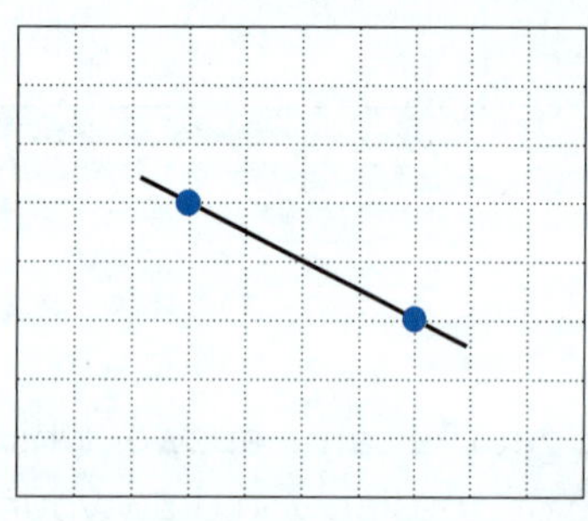

m = ________

4

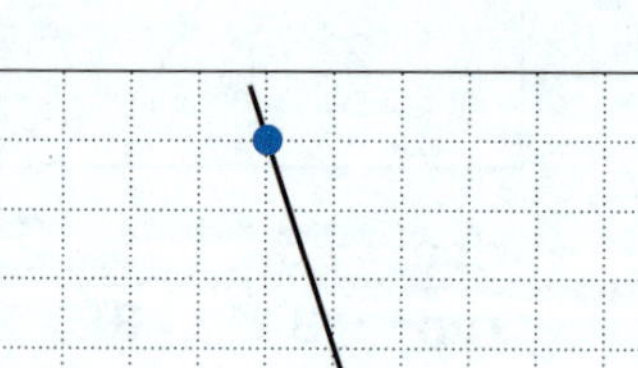

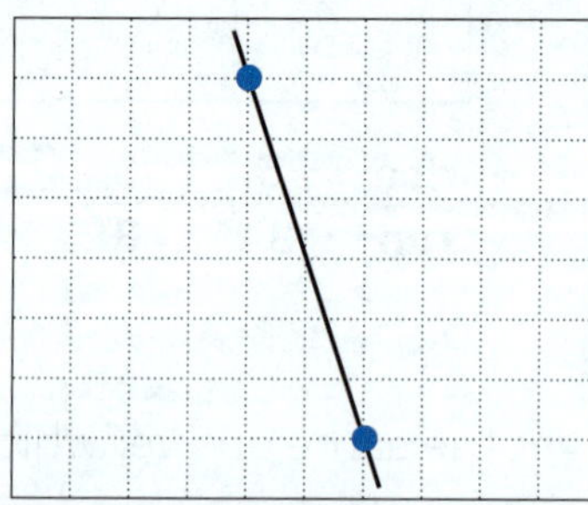

m = ________

5

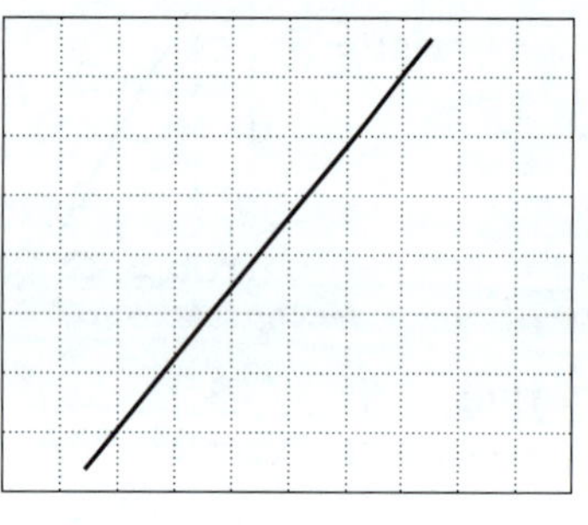

m = ________

6

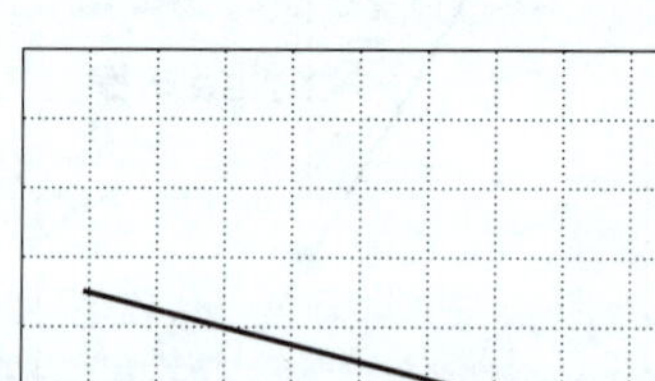

m = ________

7

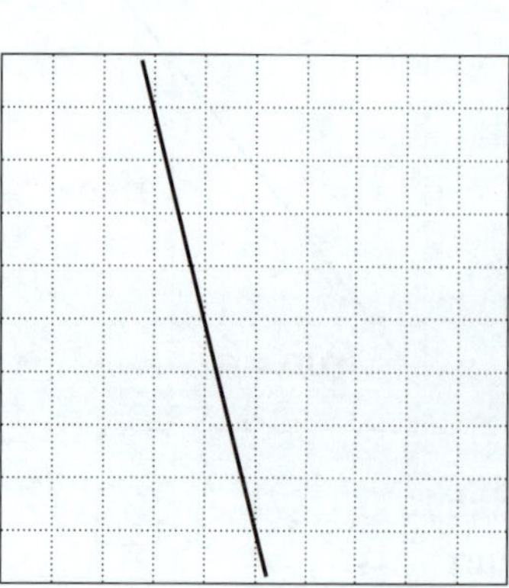

m = ________

8

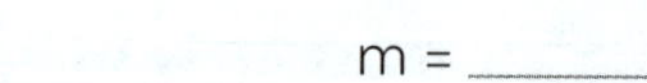

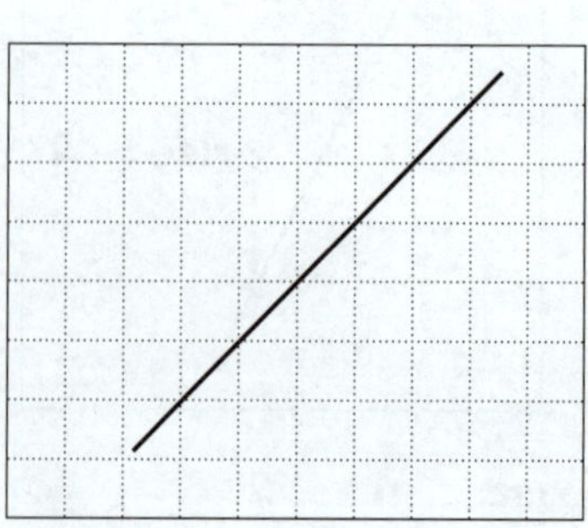

m = ________

 ISBN: 9780170497978

Draw line segments to show these gradients.

9 $m = 2 \left(\text{or } \frac{2}{1}\right)$

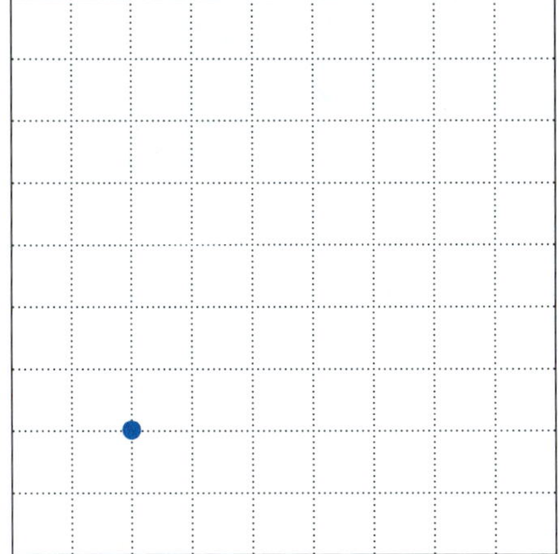

10 $m = \frac{5}{6}$

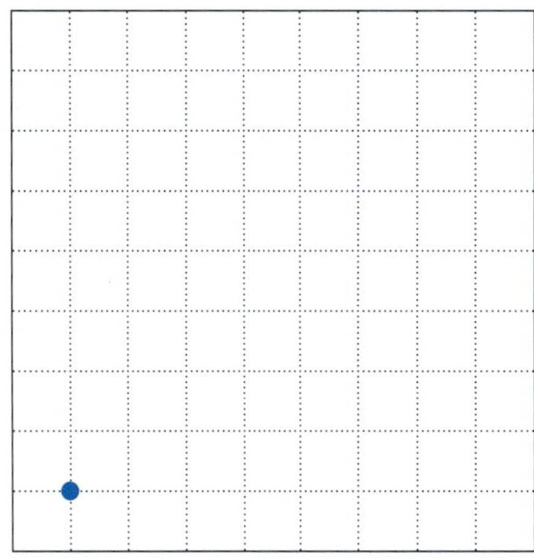

11 $m = -\frac{2}{3}$

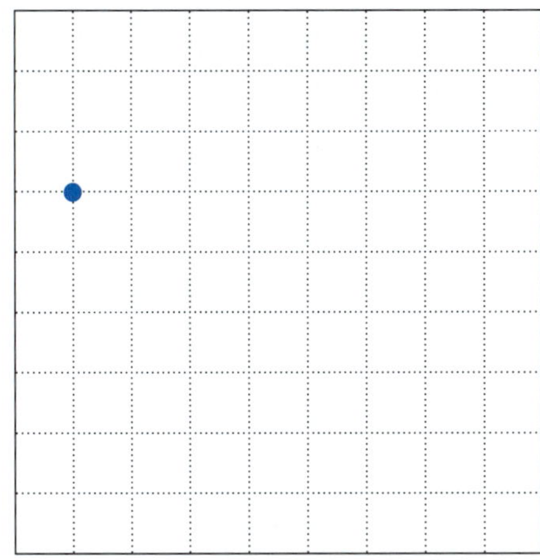

12 $m = -\frac{4}{5}$

13 $m = -4$

14 $m = 0.25$

Find the gradients of these lines. Write your answers as fractions or whole numbers.

15

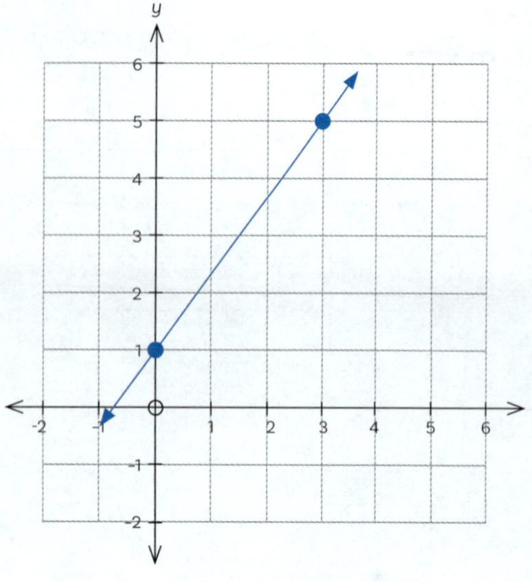

m = ________

16

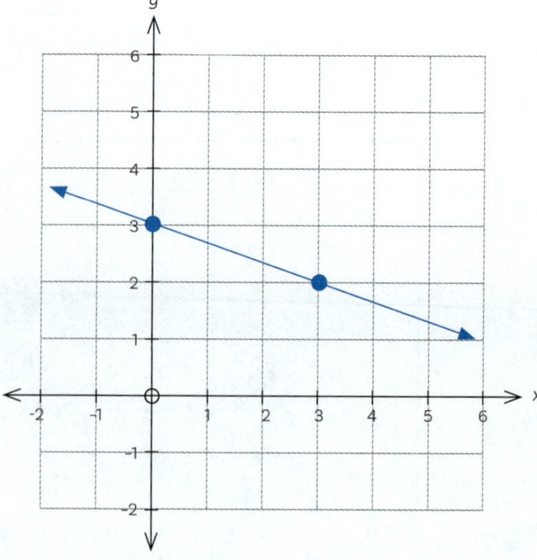

m = ________

17

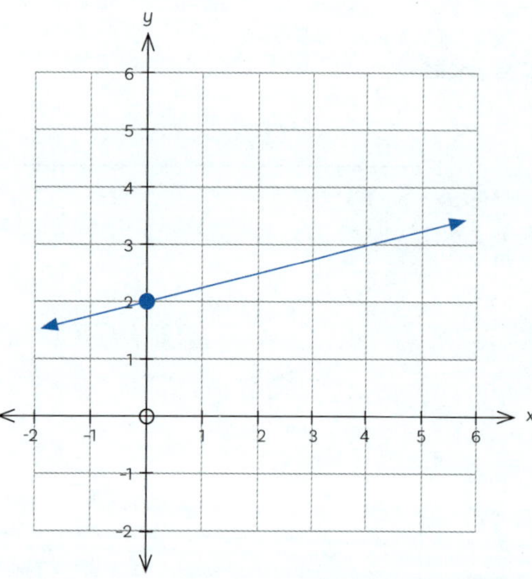

m = ________

18

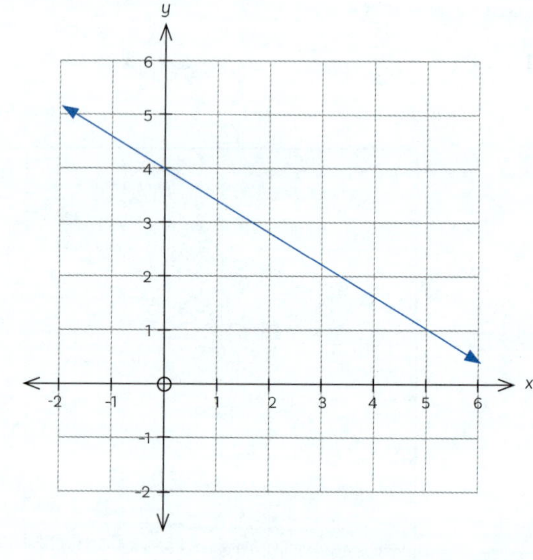

m = ________

19

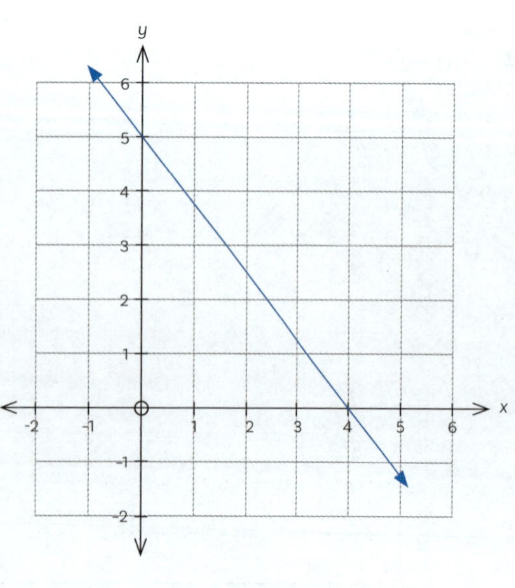

m = ________

20

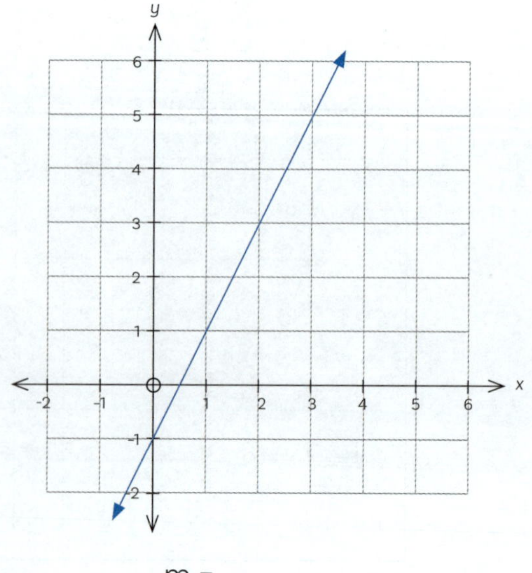

m = ________

ISBN: 9780170497978

Drawing straight lines — continuous data

- Continuous data is unrounded **measured** data.
- It is shown as a **line** on a graph, not just points.

1 Plotting points using the equation

- There are several ways of plotting graphs, but this method will work with **any** type of graph – lines and curves.

Example: Plot the line given by the equation $y = 3x - 2$.

Step 1: Create a table for values of x and y.

Substitute the value of x into the equation.

x	3x – 2	y	Coordinates
0	3(0) – 2	-2	**(0, -2)**
1	3(1) – 2	1	**(1, 1)**
2	3(2) – 2	4	**(2, 4)**
3	3(3) – 2	7	**(3, 7)**
4	3(4) – 2	10	**(4, 10)**

Step 2: Plot the points on a graph.

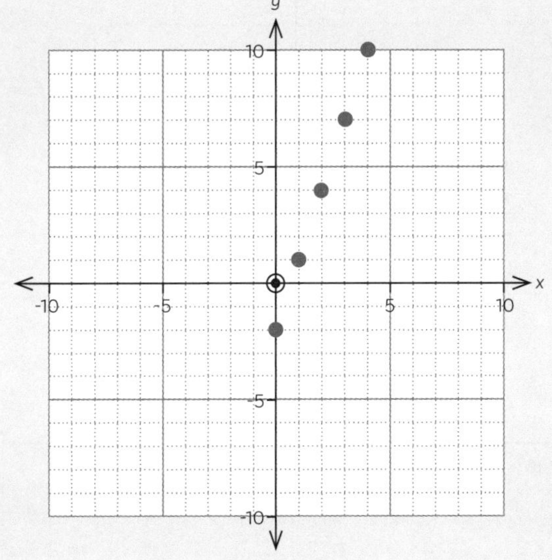

Step 3: Join the points with a **ruled** line, extend the line to the edge of the graph and add an arrow to each end.

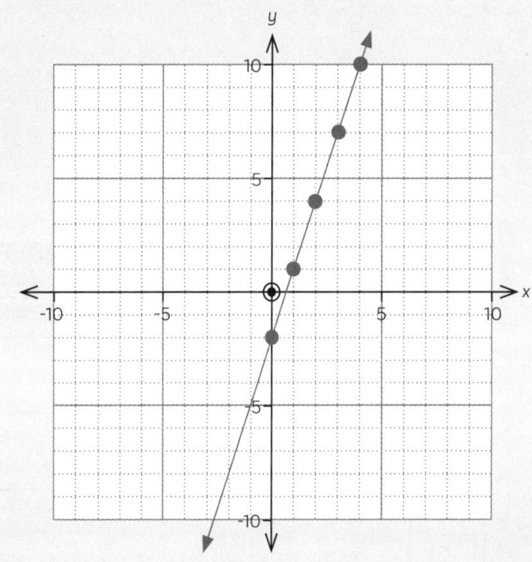

ISBN: 9780170497978

Complete the tables and draw the graph for each of the following.

1 $y = x + 4$

x	x + 4	y	Coordinates
0	0 + 4	4	(0, 4)
1	1 + 4	5	(1, 5)
2	___ + 4		
3			
4			

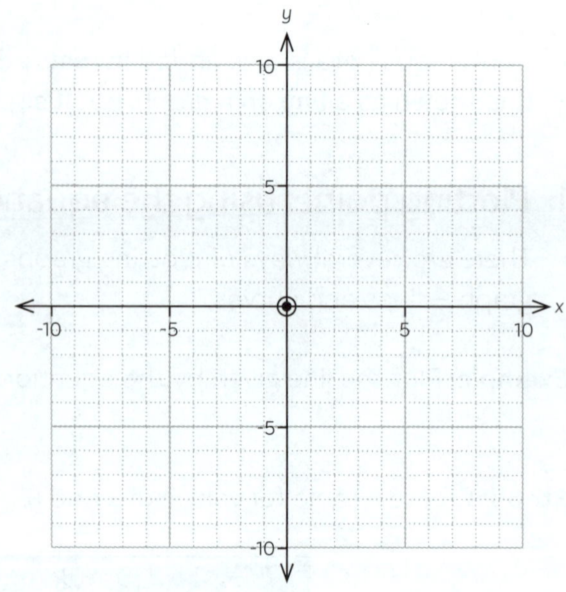

2 $y = 3x + 1$

x	3x + 1	y	Coordinates
0	3(0) + 1	1	(0, 1)
1			
2			
3			
4			

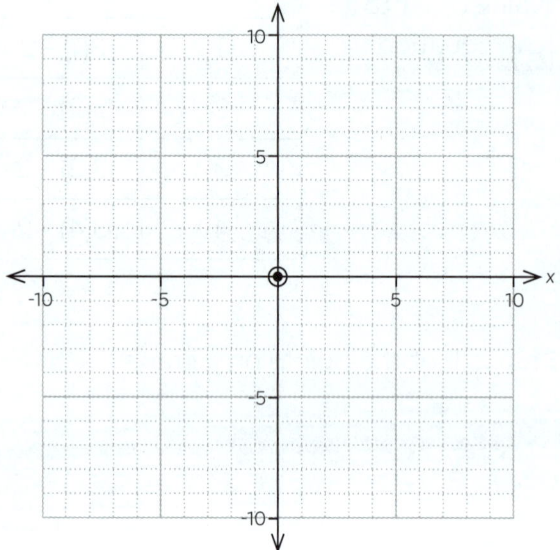

3 $y = \frac{1}{2}x + 3$

x	$\frac{1}{2}x + 3$	y	Coordinates
0			
1			
2			
3			
4			

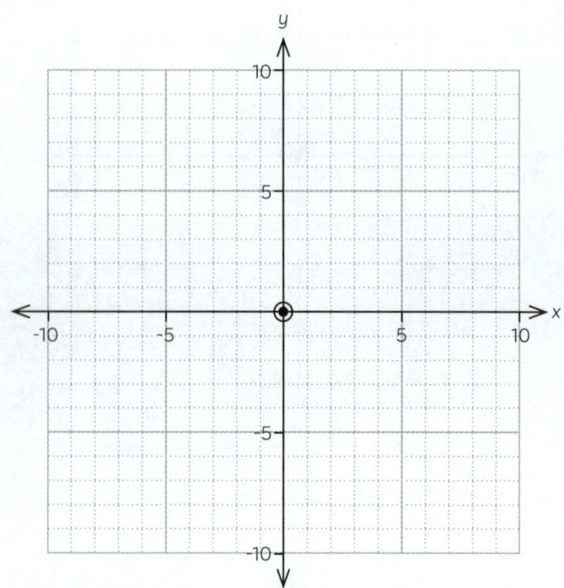

ISBN: 9780170497978

4 $y = -x + 5$

x	-x + 5	y	Coordinates
0			
1			
2			
3			
4			

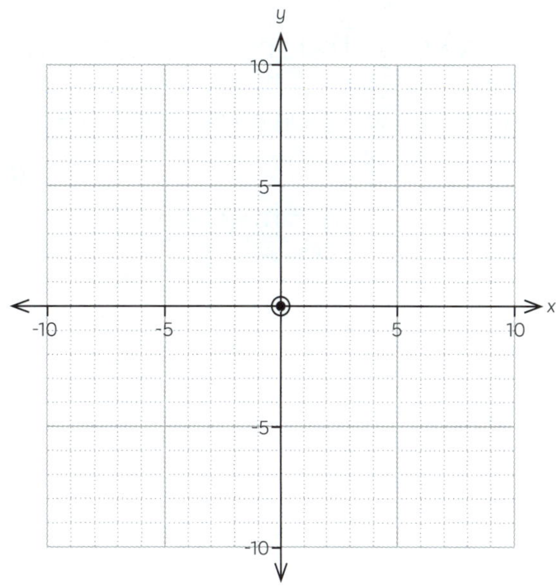

5 $y = 2x + 3$

x	2x + 3	y	Coordinates
0			
1			
2			
3			
4			

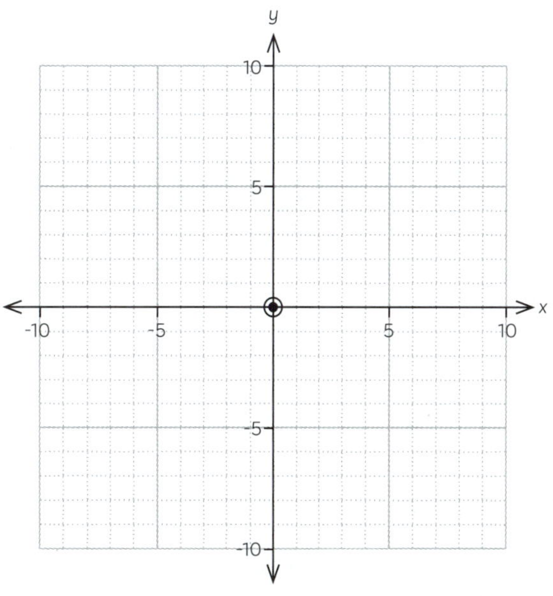

6 $y = -2x - 1$

x	-2x - 1	y	Coordinates
0			
1			
2			
3			
4			

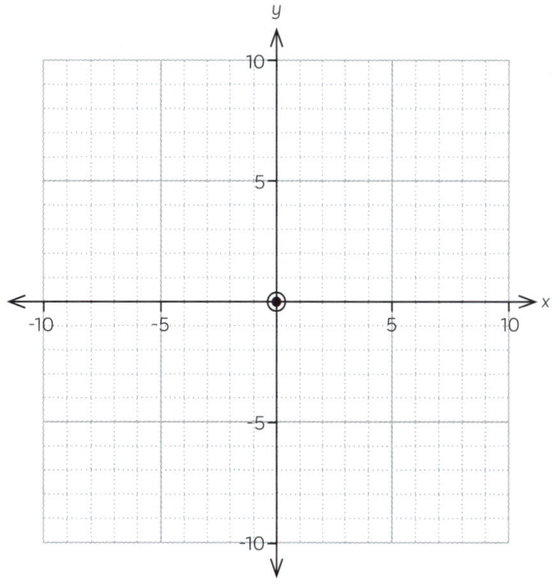

2 Drawing straight lines using the gradient and intercept

- When you are given an equation of a line, use the format $y = mx + c$.

$y = mx + c$

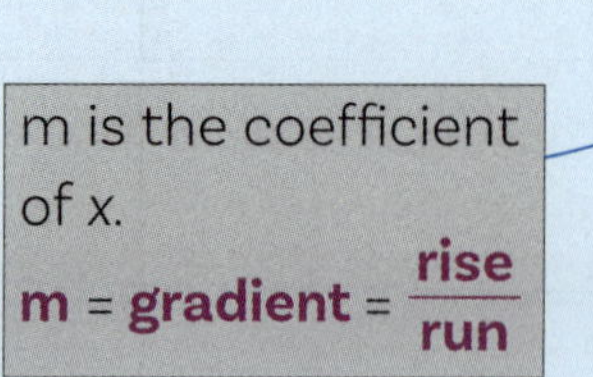

c = the y intercept.
It is the point where the line cuts the y-axis, and the value for y when we substitute $x = 0$ into the equation.

Example 1: Draw the graph of $y = \frac{3}{4}x - 1$

Step 1: Plot the y intercept.

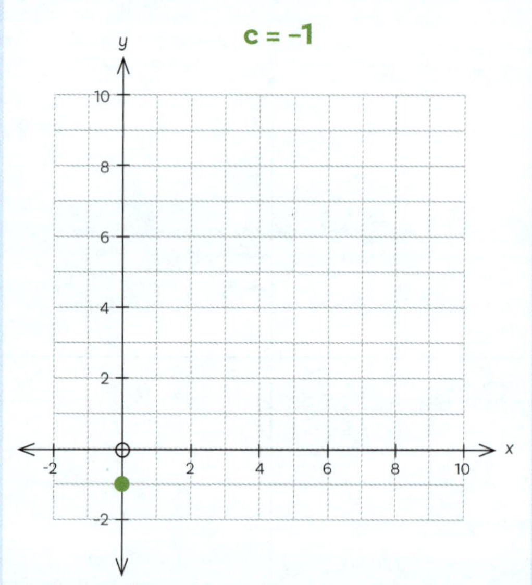

Step 2: From the intercept, use the gradient to plot at least two more points.

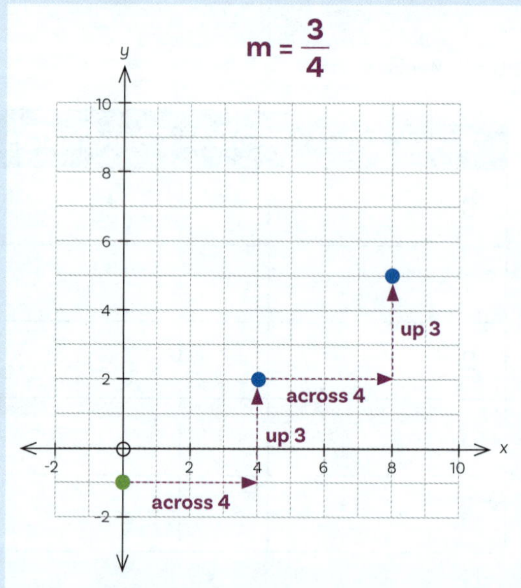

Step 3: Draw a ruled line through the points, extend the line to the edges of the graph and add an arrow to each end.

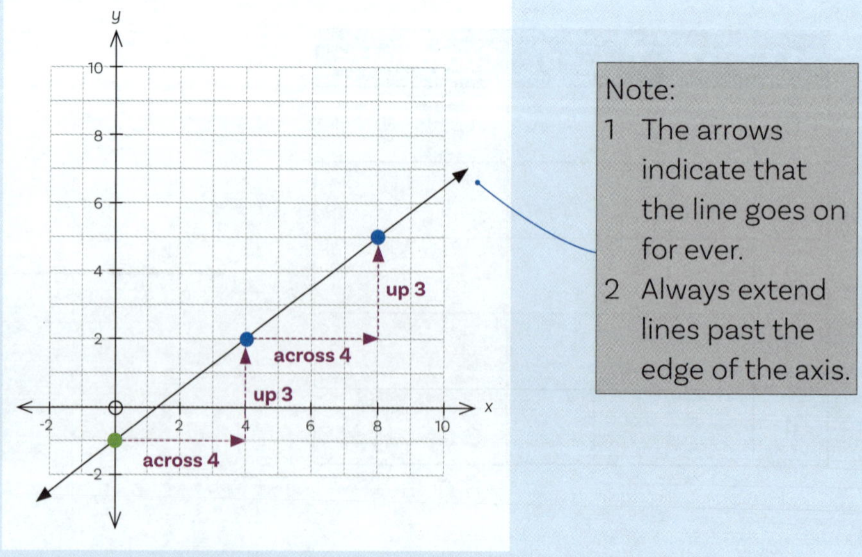

Note:
1. The arrows indicate that the line goes on for ever.
2. Always extend lines past the edge of the axis.

Note: Always plot a **minimum of three points**.

ISBN: 9780170497978

Example 2: Draw the graph of $y = -\frac{2}{3}x + 7$

Step 1: Plot the y intercept.

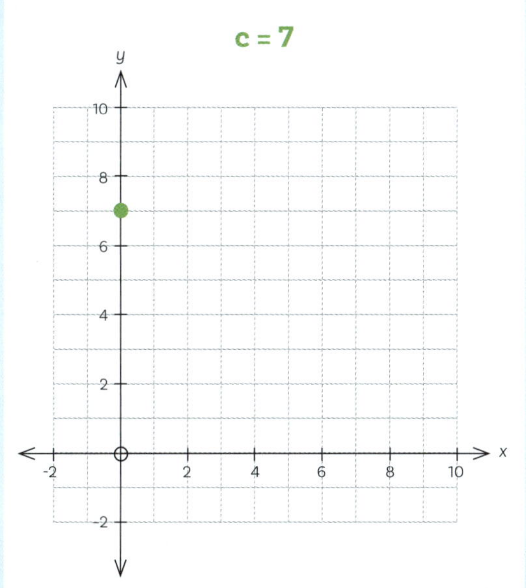

Step 2: From the intercept, use the gradient to plot at least two more points.

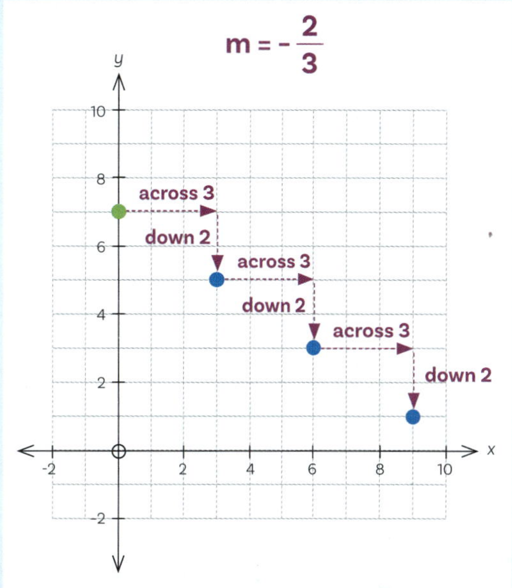

Step 3: Draw a ruled line through the points, extend the line to the edges of the graph and add an arrow to each end.

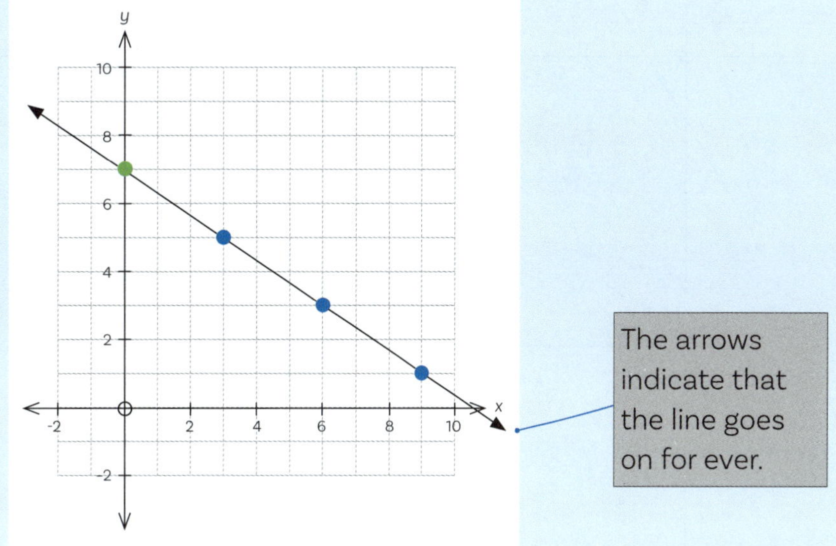

The arrows indicate that the line goes on for ever.

Match the equations with the graphs.

$y = \frac{3}{5}x + 2$	$y = \frac{3}{5}x - 2$	$y = -\frac{3}{5}x + 2$	$y = -\frac{5}{3}x + 2$	$y = -\frac{3}{5}x - 2$	$y = \frac{5}{3}x - 2$

7

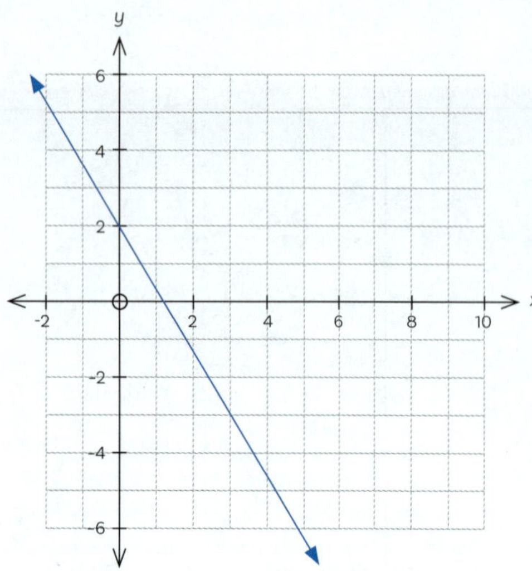

8

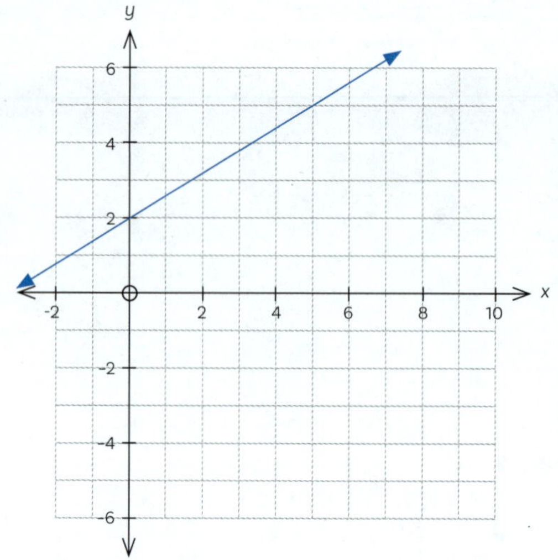

9

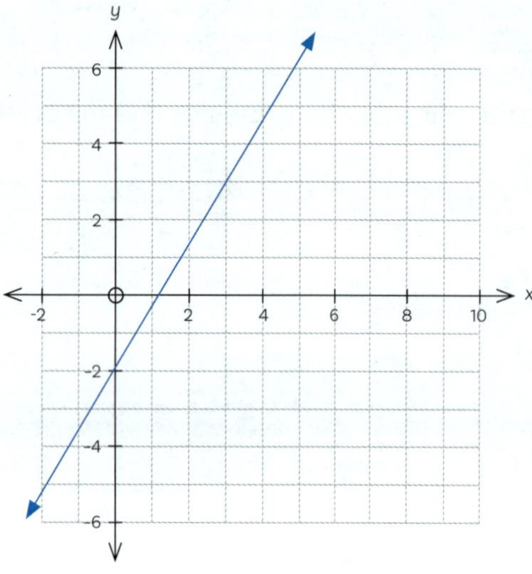

10

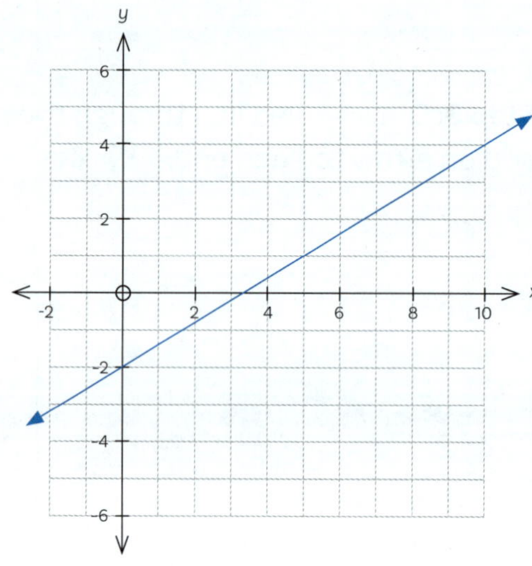

11

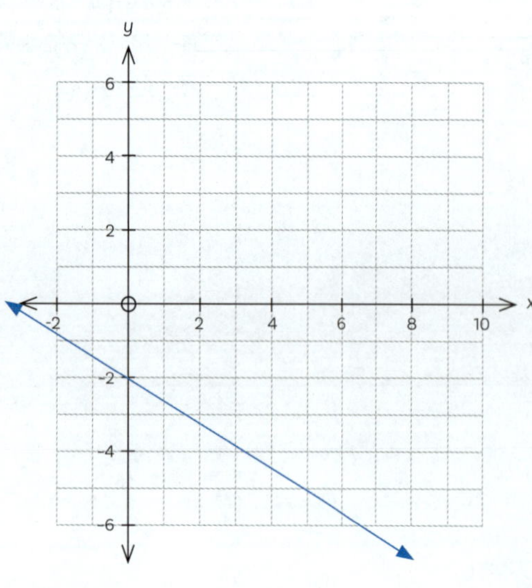

12

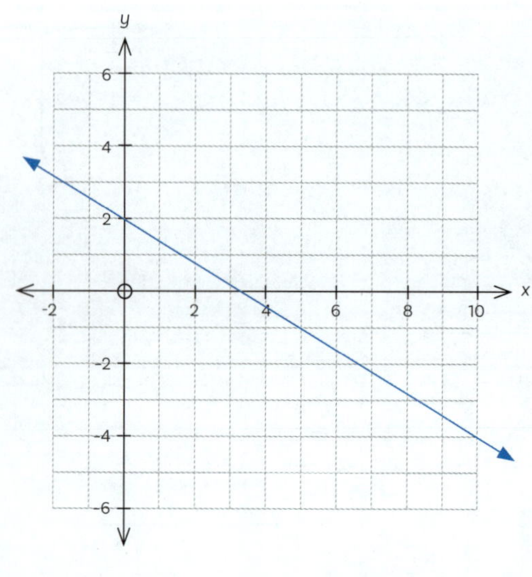

 ISBN: 9780170497978

Plot these lines on the axis using the intercept and gradient.

13 $y = 2x + 1$ **c = 1** **m = 2 = $\frac{2}{1}$**

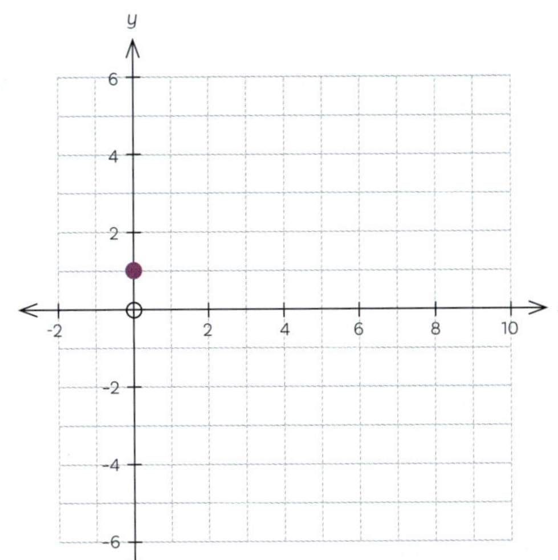

14 $y = -x + 3$ **c =** ______ **m =** ______

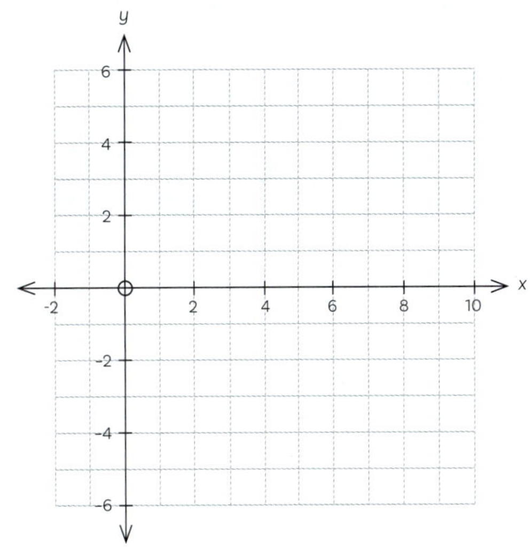

15 $y = \frac{1}{2}x - 4$ **c =** ______ **m =** ______

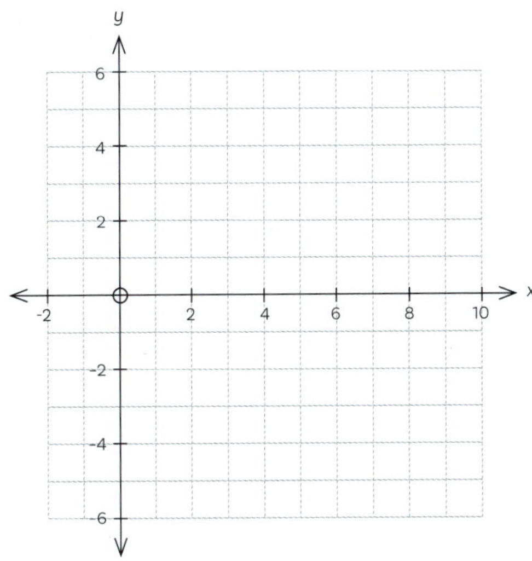

16 $y = -\frac{2}{3}x + 2$ **c =** ______ **m =** ______

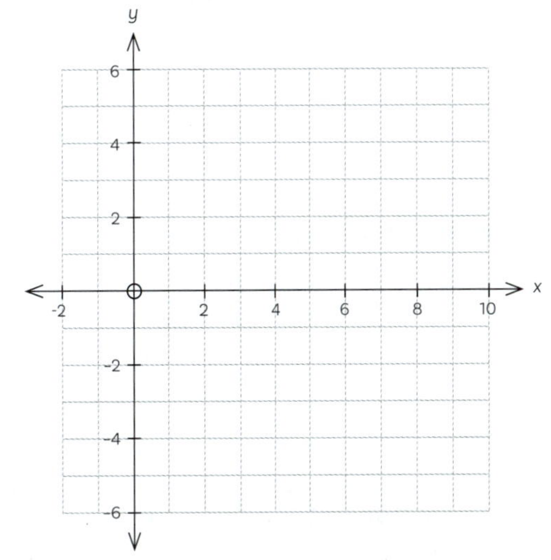

17 $y = 3x - 5$ **c =** ______ **m =** ______

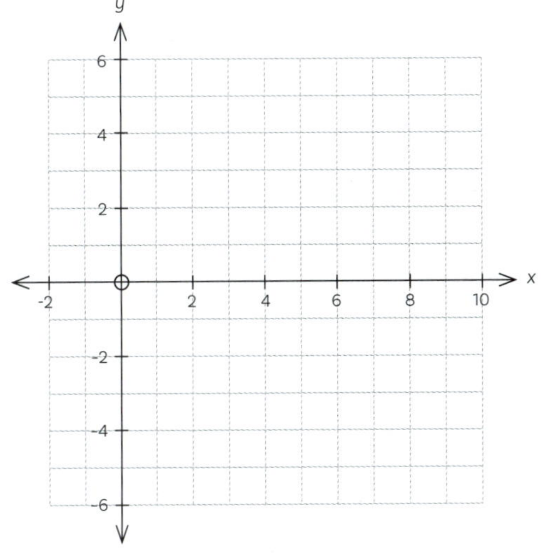

18 $y = -\frac{1}{4}x$ **c =** ______ **m =** ______

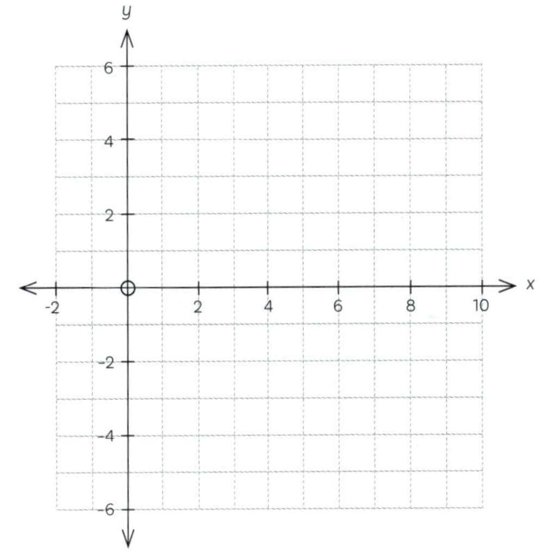

ISBN: 9780170497978

3 Drawing horizontal and vertical lines

Example 1: Draw the graph of $y = 2$.

Step 1: Create a table.

x	y	Coordinates
0	**2**	(0, **2**)
1	**2**	(1, **2**)
2	**2**	(2, **2**)
3	**2**	(3, **2**)

It doesn't matter what the x value is, y will **always be 2** so the line cannot move up or down.

Step 2: Plot at least three points, then join the points.

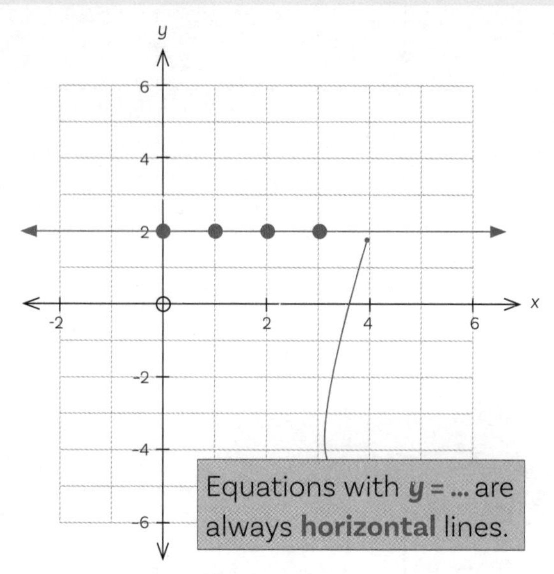

Equations with **y = ...** are always **horizontal** lines.

Example 2: Draw the graph of $x = 3$.

Step 1: List at least three points where $x = 3$, e.g. (3, 0), (3, 1), (3, 2), (3, 3).

It doesn't matter what the y value is, x will **always be 3** so the line cannot move sideways.

Step 2: Plot these points, then join the points.

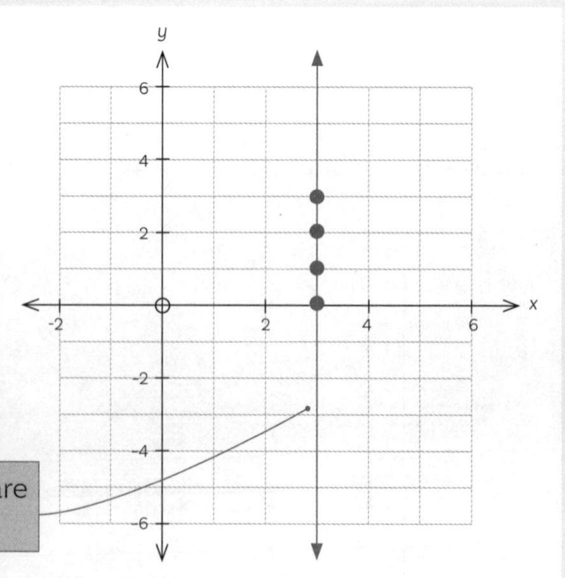

Equations with **x = ...** are always **vertical** lines.

This means the **x-axis** is the line **y = 0** and the **y-axis** is the line **x = 0**.

ISBN: 9780170497978

Write the correct equation for each graph.

19

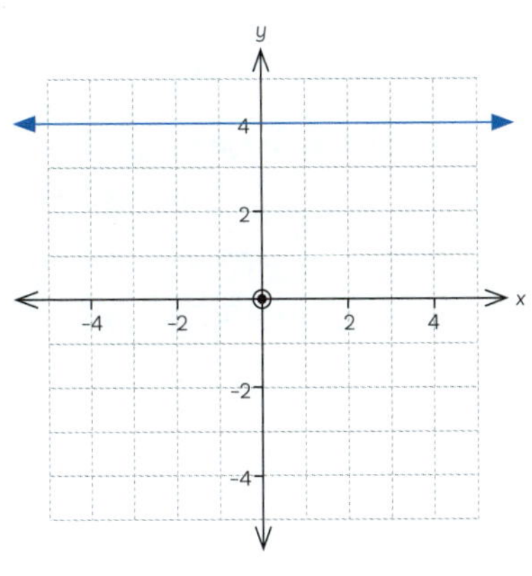

20

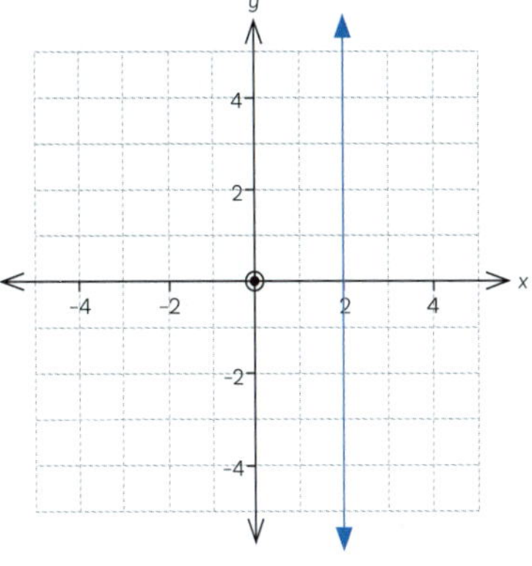

21

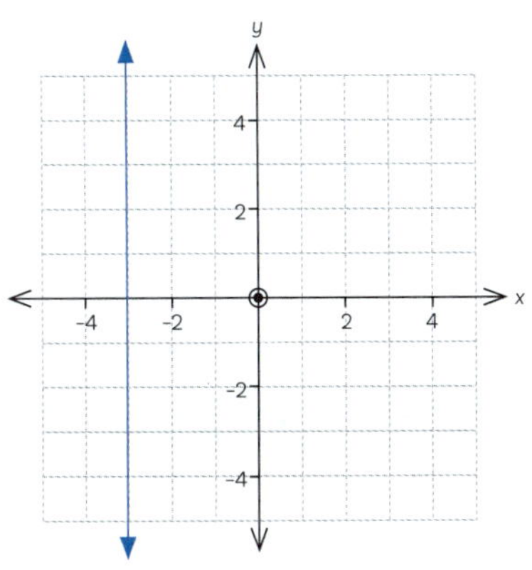

22

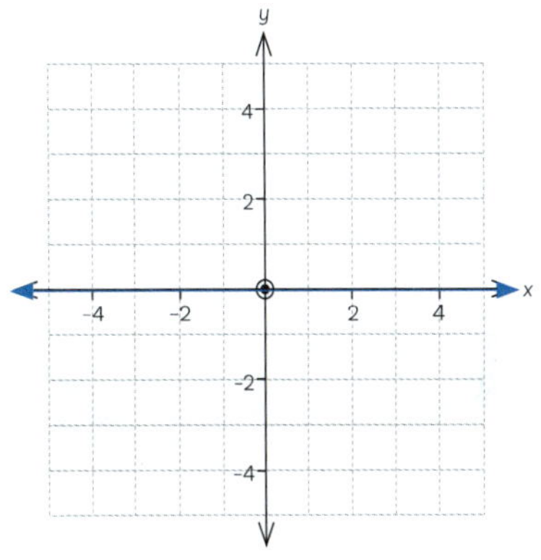

Draw these lines on the graphs.

23 $y = 1$

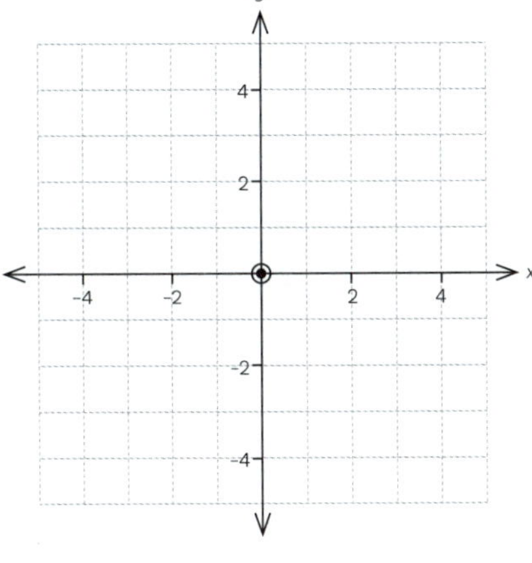

24 $x = 4$

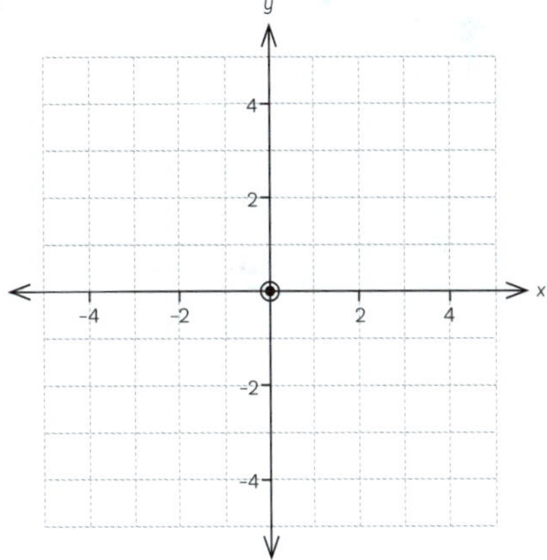

25 $y = -2$

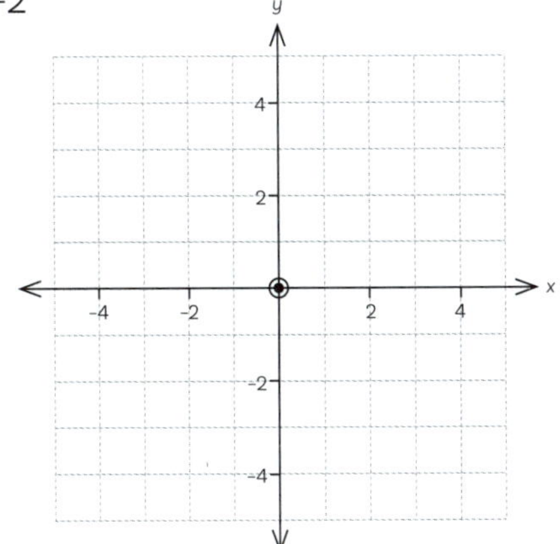

26 $y = 3$

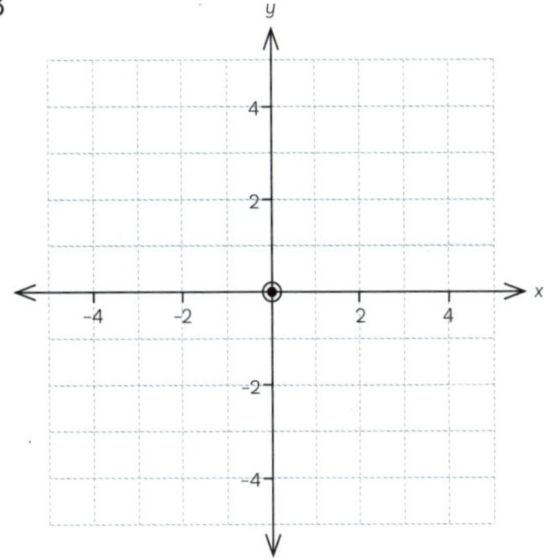

ISBN: 9780170497978

Writing equations from graphs

- Use $y = mx + c$ as a template for your equation.
- Remember: $y = mx + c$

m is the coefficient of x.

$m = \text{gradient} = \dfrac{\text{rise}}{\text{run}}$

c = the y intercept. It is the point where the line cuts the y-axis, and the value for y when we substitute $x = 0$ into the equation.

Example 1:

Step 1: Find the y intercept (c).

$c = -3$

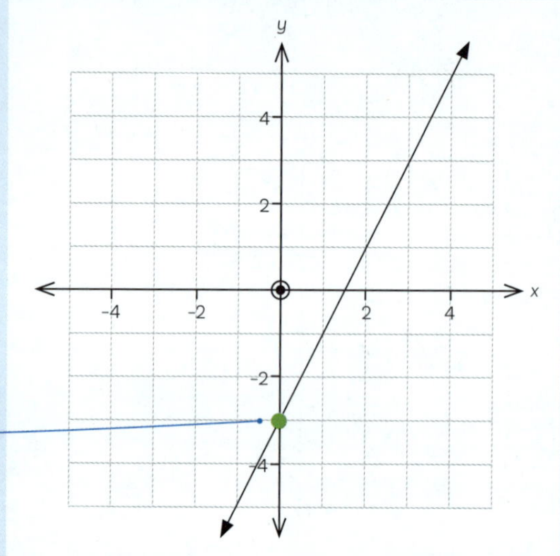

Step 2: Work out the gradient (m).

Draw a right-angled triangle through any two points through which the line passes.

$m = \text{gradient} = \dfrac{\text{rise}}{\text{run}} = \dfrac{6}{3} = 2$

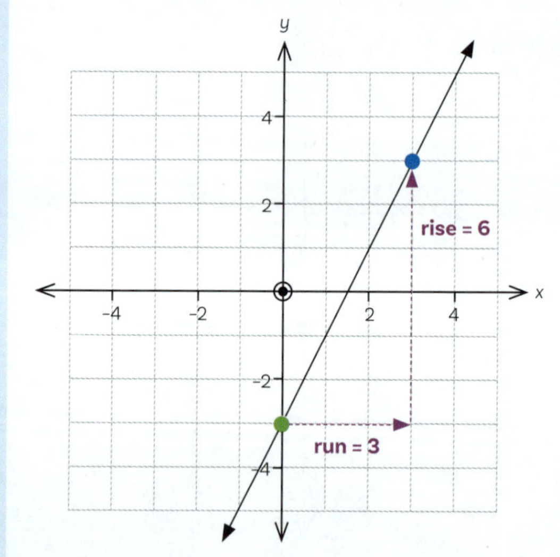

Step 3: Substitute into $y = mx + c$.

$y = mx + c$ So $y = 2x - 3$

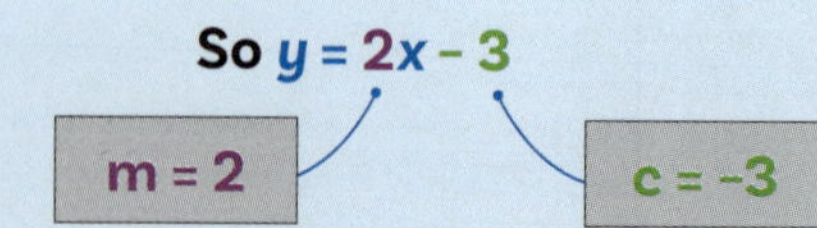

Step 4: Check: Substitute at least one point on the line into the equation.

At (4, 5): $y = 2(4) - 3 = 5$ ✓

match

 ISBN: 9780170497978

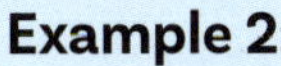

Example 2:

Step 1: Find the y intercept (c).

$c = 1$

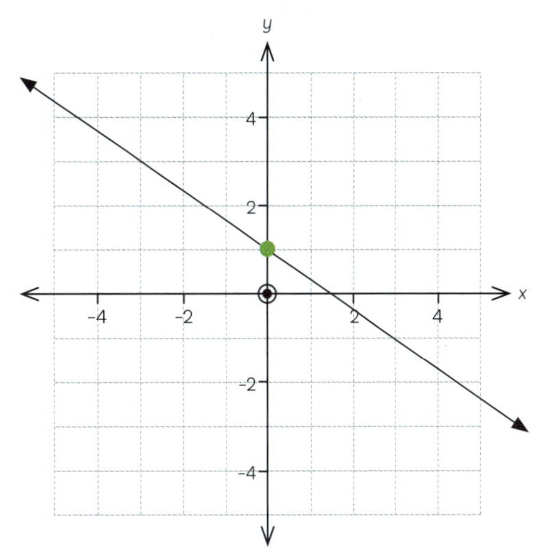

Step 2: Work out the gradient (m).

Draw a right-angled triangle through any two points through which the line passes.

$$m = \text{gradient} = \frac{\text{rise}}{\text{run}} = \frac{4}{-6} = -\frac{2}{3}$$

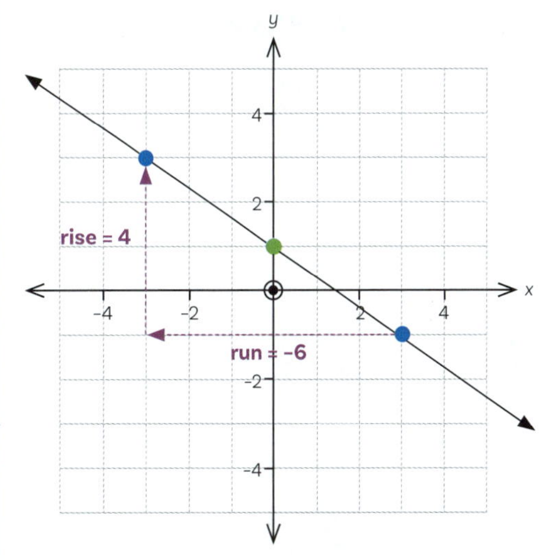

Step 3: Substitute into $y = mx + c$.

$y = mx + c$

$m = -\frac{2}{3}$ $c = 1$

So $y = -\frac{2}{3}x + 1$

Step 4: Check: Substitute at least one point on the line into the equation.

At $(3, -1)$: $y = -\frac{2}{3}(3) + 1 = -2 + 1 = -1$ ✓

match

Highlight/circle the correction equation for each graph.

1

$y = \frac{1}{2}x + 3$

$y = -\frac{1}{2}x + 3$

$y = 2x - 3$

$y = -2x + 3$

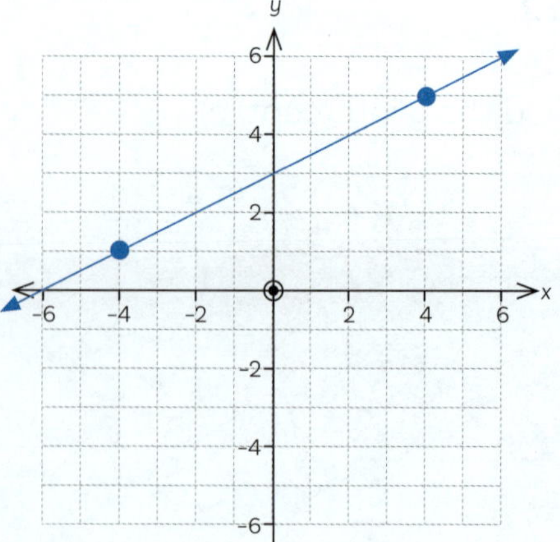

2

$y = -3x - 5$

$y = 5x + 3$

$y = 3x - 5$

$y = 5x - 3$

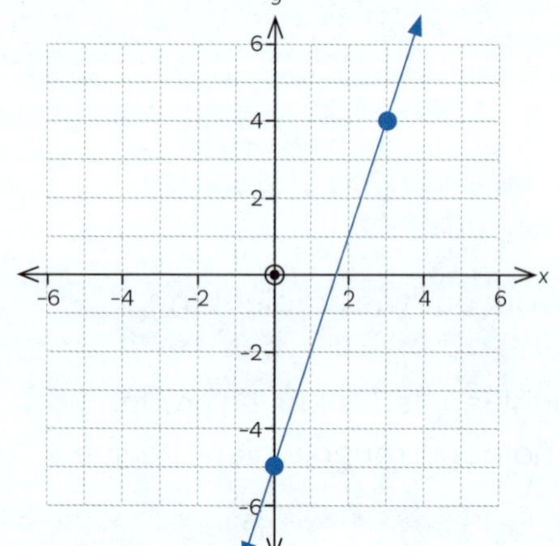

3

$y = \frac{3}{4}x + 2$

$y = -\frac{3}{4}x + 2$

$y = -\frac{4}{3}x + 2$

$y = \frac{4}{3}x + 2$

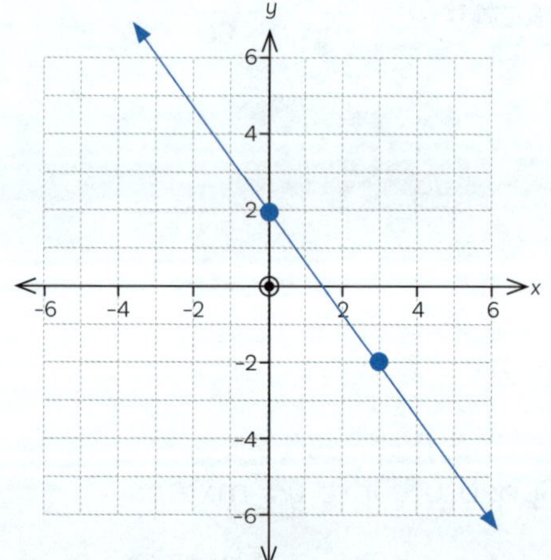

4

$y = \frac{3}{5}x - 1$

$y = -\frac{3}{5}x - 1$

$y = -\frac{5}{3}x - 1$

$y = \frac{5}{3}x - 1$

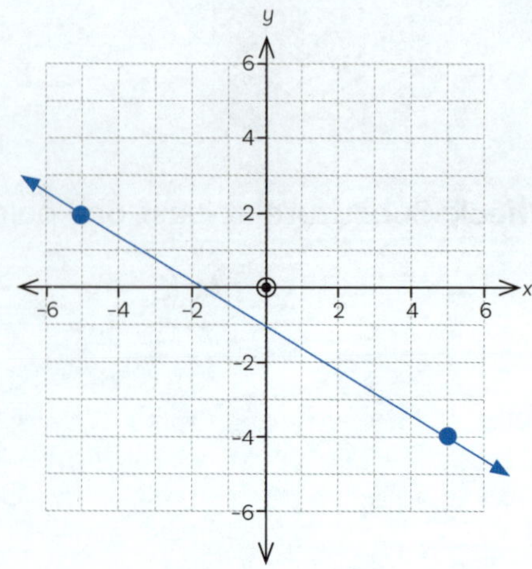

 ISBN: 9780170497978

Write the equations of these graphs lines.

5

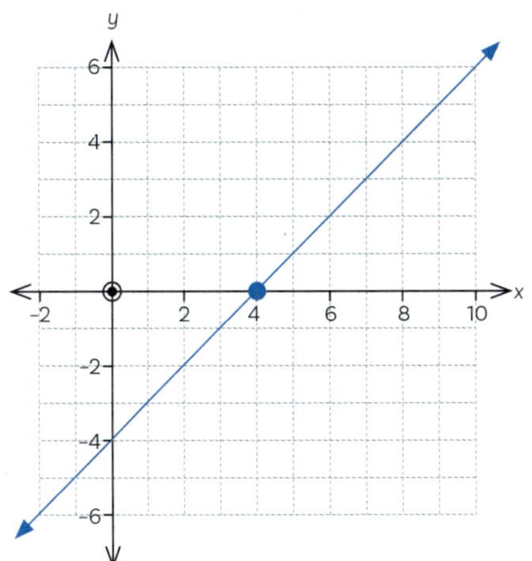

Gradient = ____ y intercept = ____

y = ____ x ____ ______

↑
sign

6

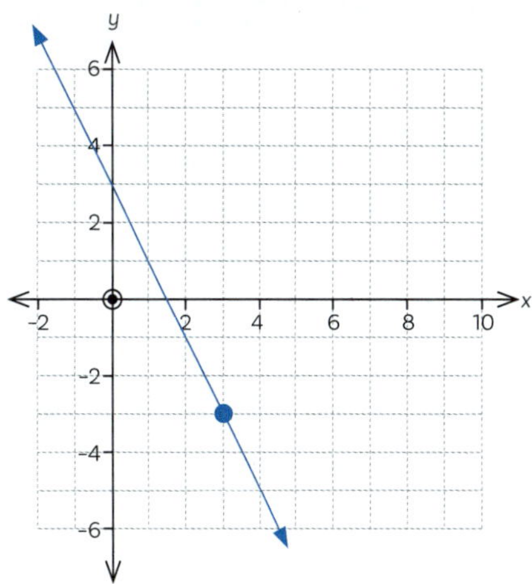

Gradient = ____ y intercept = ____

y = ____ x ____ ______

↑
sign

7

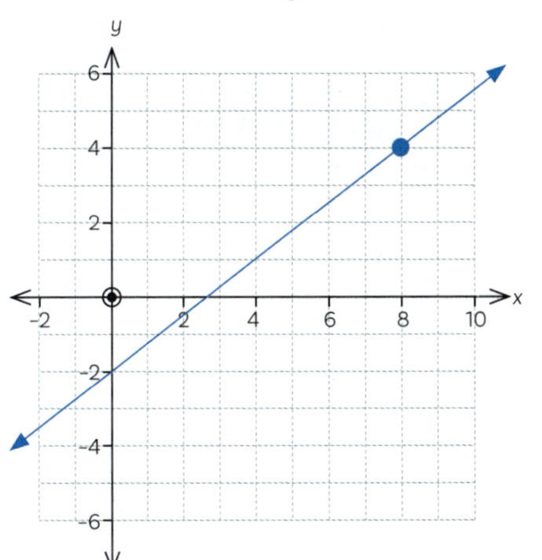

Gradient = ____ y intercept = ____

y = ____ x ____ ______

8

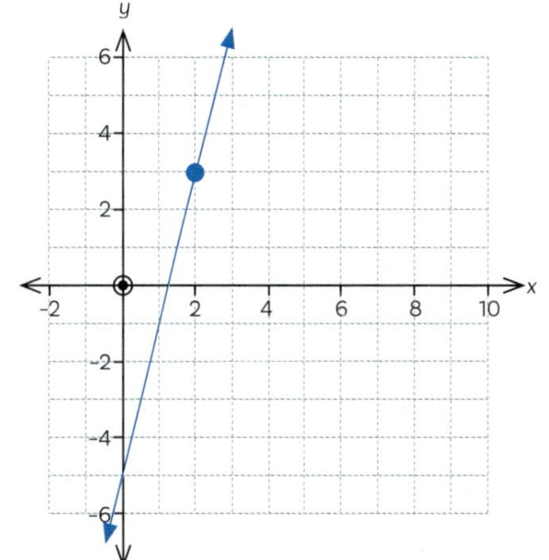

Gradient = ____ y intercept = ____

y = ____ x ____ ______

9

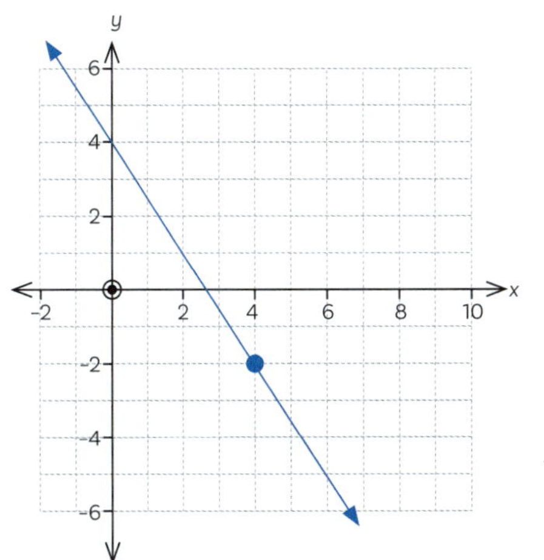

Gradient = ____ y intercept = ____

y = ____ x ____ ______

10

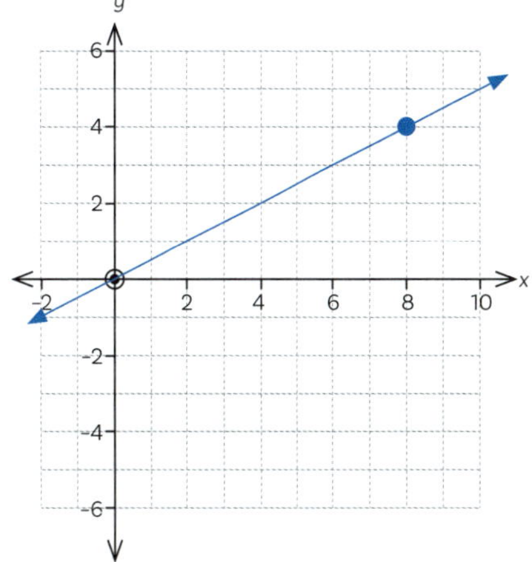

Gradient = ____ y intercept = ____

y = ____ x ____ ______

ISBN: 9780170497978

Solving linear equations

- 'Solve' means '**find the value for x**'.

Rules:
1. You can do anything you like to an equation as long as you do the **same to both sides**.
2. There should be only **one equals sign** per line.
3. Collect all the variables on one side and numbers on the other side.
4. When you want to get rid of something, perform the **opposite** operation.
5. Your aim is to get **x = ...**

One-step equations

Examples:

1

$y + 5 = 17$ — We need to get rid of the **+ 5** from the left side.

$y + 5 - 5 = 17 - 5$ — Do the **opposite** of **+ 5. Subtract 5** from **both** sides.

$y = 12$ — This is our aim: to have the variable on the left and its value on the right.

Notice that there should be just **one** '=' sign per line, and they are **lined up** under each other.

We can always **check** that the solution works: **12** + 5 = 17 ✓

2

$p - 11 = 4$ — We need to get rid of the **– 11** from the left side.

$p - 11 + 11 = 4 + 11$ — Do the **opposite** of **– 11. Add 11** to **both** sides.

$p = 15$

Check that the solution works: **15** – 11 = 4 ✓

3

$\frac{d}{3} = -7$ — We need to get rid of the **÷ 3** from the left side.

$\frac{d}{3} \times \frac{3}{1} = -7 \times \frac{3}{1}$ — Do the **opposite** of **÷ 3. Multiply both** sides by **3** (or $\frac{3}{1}$ if you are dealing with fractions).

$d = -21$

Check that the solution works: $\frac{-21}{3} = -7$ ✓

4

$-8z = 54$ — Remember, $-8z$ means **$-8 \times z$**. We need to get rid of the **multiply by –8** from the left side.

$\frac{-8z}{-8} = \frac{54}{-8}$ — Do the **opposite** of **multiply by –8. Divide both** sides by **–8**.

$z = -6.75$

Check that the solution works: $-8 \times$ **–6.75** = 54 ✓

 ISBN: 9780170497978

Solve the following, showing all the steps in the working.

1 $y + 7 = 8$

$y + 7 - 7 = 8 - 7$

$y =$ ______

2 $q - 3 = 15$

______ = ______

$q =$ ______

3 $11m = 44$

______ = ______

$m =$ ______

4 $\frac{a}{5} = 6$

______ = ______

$a =$ ______

5 $g - 19 = 81$

______ = ______

$g =$ ______

6 $h + 13 = 8$

______ = ______

$h =$ ______

7 $\frac{s}{4} = 13$

______ = ______

$s =$ ______

8 $-2x = 27$

______ = ______

$x =$ ______

9 $d - 3.5 = 21$

10 $p + 7.2 = 20$

11 $-5e = -91$

12 $9 + b = 6$

13 $\frac{v}{25} = 7.2$

14 $y - 0.25 = 3.5$

ISBN: 9780170497978

An extra trick:

Sometimes the **variable** is on the **right**-hand side, e.g. $39 = 12y$.

Because both sides must be equal to each other, you can **flip** them around.

$39 = 12y$ so

$$12y = 39$$

$$y = \frac{39}{12}$$

$$y = 3.25$$

Check that the solution works: $39 = 12 \times$ **3.25** ✓

15 $11 = p + 9$

16 $91 = -14a$

17 $5 = z - 17$

18 $-1 = b + 13$

19 $45d = 18$

20 $8 = \frac{s}{15}$

21 $-14 = g + 23$

22 $9 = m - 14$

23 $12 = 31 + e$

24 $-2 = \frac{x}{17}$

ISBN: 9780170497978

Forming and solving linear equations

- **Define your variable**. It can help to use first letter of the word whose value you need to find.
- Often it is useful to draw a diagram.
- Words used for the four basic operations:

+	plus, total, more, and, add(ed), increased by, at least, greater than	−	subtract(ed), less, decreased by, smaller than
x	of, times, multiplied by, product	÷	divided by, shared between, out of, per

- 'Double' and 'twice' both mean multiply by two.
- 'Triple' and 'treble' mean multiply by three.

Examples: For the following, define the variable, write an equation and solve it in order to find a solution.

1 A regular hexagon has a perimeter of 39 cm. Find the length of each side.

Let s represent the length of each side.

$6s = 39$ Divide by 6.

$s = 6.5$ cm

Each side is 6.5 cm.

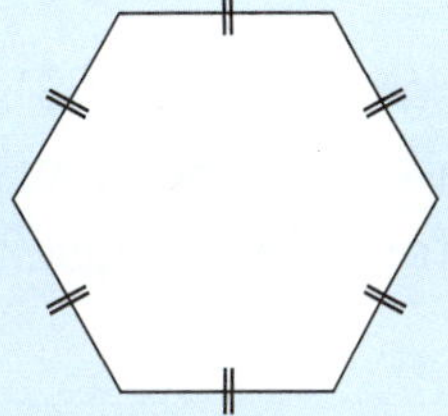

2 Half a number is 23. Find the number.

Let n represent the number. $\frac{n}{2} = 23$ Multiply by 2.

$n = 46$

The number is 46.

Define the variable (x), write an equation and solve it in order to find a solution.

1 A square has a perimeter of 26 cm. Find the length of one side.

Let x represent ______

Equation: ______

______

The length of one side = ______

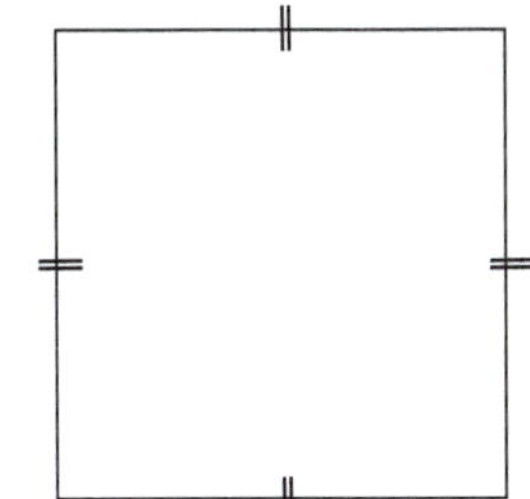

2 A tree which is 7.2 m high grew 1.3 m in the last year. How high was it a year ago?

Let x represent ______

Equation: ______

______

Height a year ago = ______

ISBN: 9780170497978

3 Double a number is nineteen. Find the number.

Let x represent ______________________

Equation: ______________________

____

The number = ______________________

4 A number reduced by ten is eight. Find the number.

Let x represent ______________________

Equation: ______________________

____

The number = ______________________

5 The sum of a number and two is fourteen. Find the number.

Let x represent ______________________

Equation: ______________________

____

The number = ______________________

6 A tenth of a number is fifty. Find the number.

Let x represent ______________________

Equation: ______________________

____

The number = ______________________

7 Ellie gets a pay increase of $1.80 per hour. If her new rate is $19.50, how much did she earn before the increase?

____

____

____

____

8 One hundred dollars is shared equally between eight students. How much does each student get?

____

____

____

____

9 A regular pentagon has a perimeter of 42 cm. Find the length of each side.

____

____

____

____

10 The length of a car is 5.6 m. The total length of the car and the trailer is 13.1 m. How much longer is the car plus the trailer compared with the car alone?

____

____

____

____

 ISBN: 9780170497978

Two-step equations

1 **Rearrange:** add or subtract the terms so the **variable** (e.g. x) is on the **left** and all the **numbers** are on the **right**.

2 **Multiply or divide:** multiply or divide so **one of the variable = number**.

Remember: To get rid of something, **do the opposite operation**.

Examples:

1
$$9x - 4 = 23$$
$$9x - 4 + 4 = 23 + 4$$
Rearrange: add 4 to both sides.
$$9x = 27$$
$$\frac{9x}{9} = \frac{27}{9}$$
Multiply or divide: divide both sides by 9.
$$x = 3$$

2 Notice that in this example, the variable is on the right.
$$21 = 7 - 4x$$
Rearrange: add 4x to both sides.
$$21 + 4x = 7 - 4x + 4x$$
$$4x + 21 = 7$$
Rearrange: subtract 21 from both sides.
$$4x + 21 - 21 = 7 - 21$$
$$4x = -14$$
Multiply or divide: divide both sides by 4.
$$\frac{4x}{4} = \frac{-14}{4}$$
$$x = -3.5$$

Solve the following.

1 $9x - 7 = 65$

2 $6x + 11 = 71$

3 $5x + 1 = 56$

4 $7x - 12 = 30$

5 $2x + 19 = 7$

6 $10x + 9 = -25$

ISBN: 9780170497978

7 $9x - 7 = 20$

8 $4x + 34 = 100$

9 $20x - 14 = 6$

10 $\frac{x}{5} - 7 = 6$

11 $11x - 132 = 0$

12 $41 = 7x - 1$

13 $16 = 9 + \frac{x}{12}$

14 $19 = -6x + 1$

15 $11 = 2x - 29$

16 $81 = 6 - 15x$

17 $0 = 9x + 72$

18 $10 + \frac{x}{4} = 16$

ISBN: 9780170497978

Define the variable (x), write an equation and solve it in order to find a solution.

19 A number is multiplied by five, and four is added to it. The answer is 39.

Let x represent ______________________

Equation: ______________________

____

____

The number is ______________________

20 A number is multiplied by three, and then one is subtracted. The answer is 11.

21 If a number is doubled, and then 11 is subtracted, the answer is zero.

22 The sum of a third of a number and four is one.

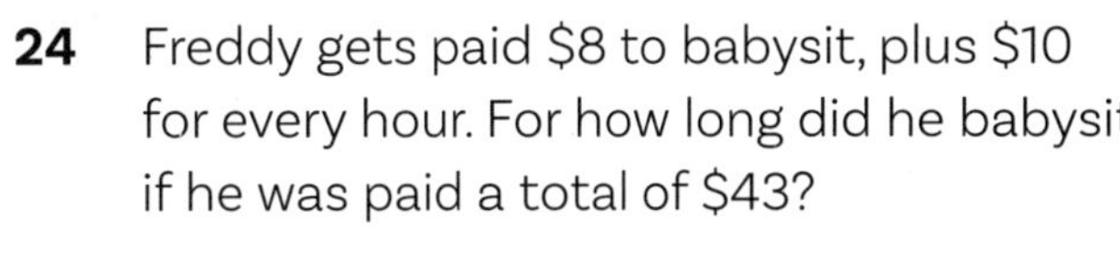

23 Jess earns \$5 an hour for picking raspberries plus \$2 for every punnet. If she can earn \$19 in an hour, how many punnets does she pick each hour?

24 Freddy gets paid \$8 to babysit, plus \$10 for every hour. For how long did he babysit if he was paid a total of \$43?

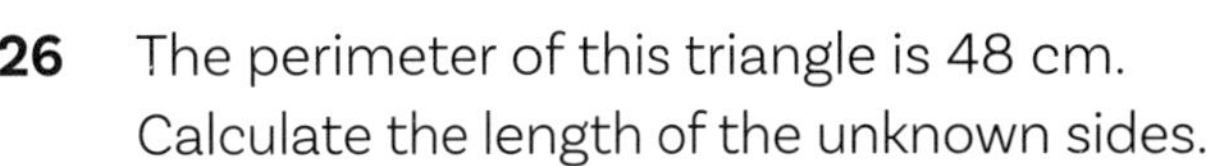

25 The perimeter of this rectangle is 30 cm. Calculate the length of the unknown sides.

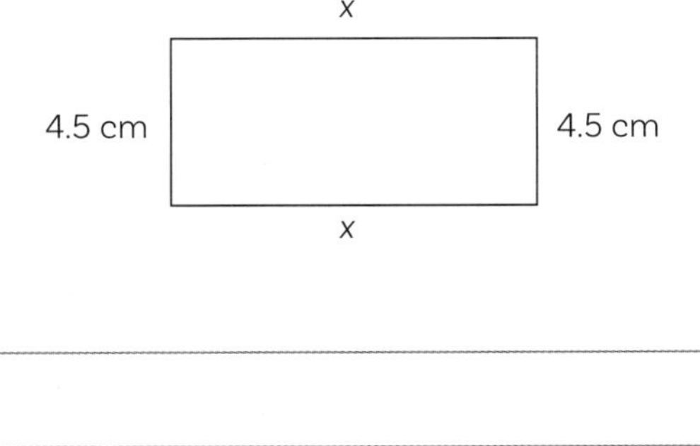

26 The perimeter of this triangle is 48 cm. Calculate the length of the unknown sides.

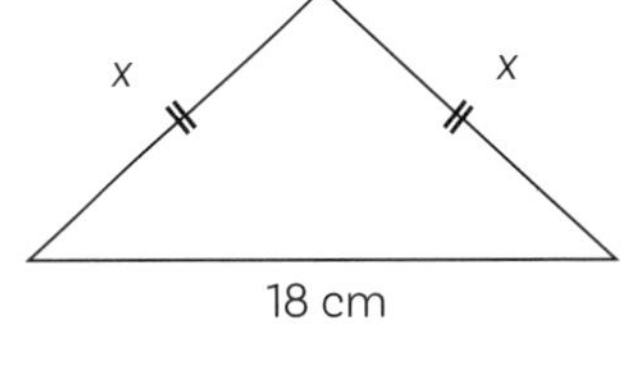

ISBN: 9780170497978

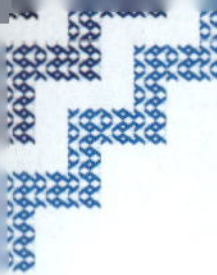

Equations with variables on both sides

1 **Rearrange:** add or subtract the terms so the **variable** (e.g. x) is on the **left** and all the **numbers** are on the **right**.

2 **Multiply or divide:** multiply or divide so **one of the variable = number**.

Examples:

1

$4x = 40 - x$ — **Rearrange:** **add x** to both sides.

$4x + x = 40 - x + x$

$5x = 40$ — **Multiply or divide:** **divide** both sides by **5**.

$\frac{5x}{5} = \frac{40}{5}$

$x = 8$

2

$13 + 2x = 5x + 1$ — **Rearrange:** **subtract 5x** from both sides.

$13 + 2x - 5x = 5x + 1 - 5x$

$13 - 3x = 1$ — **Rearrange:** **subtract 13** from both sides.

$13 - 3x - 13 = 1 - 13$

$-3x = -12$ — **Multiply or divide:** **divide** both sides by **-3**.

$\frac{-3x}{-3} = \frac{-12}{-3}$

$x = 4$

Solve the following.

1 $6x = 12 + 2x$

2 $9x = x + 16$

3 $5x = 28 - 2x$

4 $3x + 11 = 7 - x$

 ISBN: 9780170497978

5 $10x - 6 = 5x + 9$

6 $4 + 3x - 1 = 2x - 8$

7 $x - 12 = 7 - x$

8 $18 + 5x = 6 - x$

9 $4 + 7x = 49 - 2x$

10 $3x + 4 + 4x = -24 - 7x$

Hint: For numbers **11** to **14**, use the trick mentioned on page 132.

11 $8x + 6 = 13x - 15$

12 $19 - 12x = x - 7$

13 $13 - 20x = 4x + 37$

14 $x + 11 = 9x + 14$

Define the variable (x), write an equation and solve it in order to find a solution.

15 Doubling a number gives the same answer as subtracting the number from nine.

Let x represent ______________________

Equation: ______________________

The number is ______________________

16 Tripling a number and subtracting ten gives the same answer as adding four to it.

17 Adding five to half a number gives the same answer as adding one to the number.

18 Adding seven to quadruple a number gives the same answer as multiplying it by eight and adding eleven.

Write an equation using x as the variable. Then solve it in order to answer the question.

19 The triangle and the regular hexagon have equal perimeters. Calculate their dimensions.

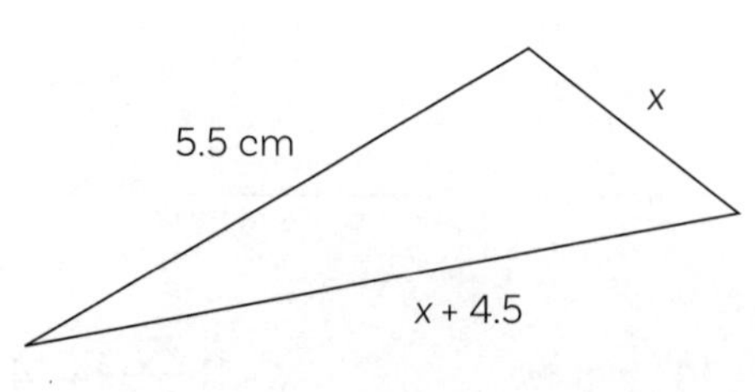

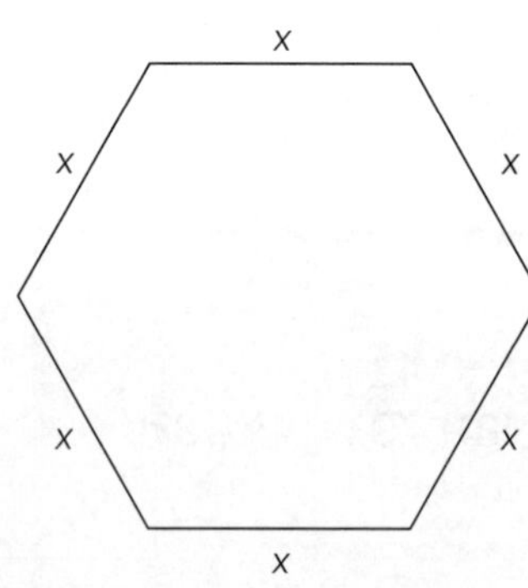

 ISBN: 9780170497978

Find the errors

Some of the following equations are solved correctly. If so, put a tick in the '✓ or ×' column. Some are incorrect. If so, put a cross in the '✓ or ×' column, highlight the mistake and write the correct solution in the right column.

		✓ or ×	Correct solution
1	$5x - 2 = x - 4$ $4x - 2 = -4$ $4x = -6$ $x = -1\frac{1}{2}$		
2	$7x - 14 = 1 + x$ $8x - 14 = 1$ $8x = 15$ $x = 1.875$		
3	$x - 10 = 16 - 12x$ $13x - 10 = 16$ $13x = 26$ $x = 2$		
4	$1 - x = 6x + 1$ $1 - 7x = 1$ $-7x = 0$ $x = 0$		
5	$2x - 21 = 11x + 33$ $-9x - 21 = 33$ $-9x = 54$ $x = -\frac{1}{6}$		
6	$7 - x = 11x - 23$ $7 + 10x = -23$ $10x = -30$ $x = -3$		

Equations with brackets

1 **Expand:** expand the brackets.
2 **Rearrange:** add or subtract the terms so the **variable** (e.g. x) on the **left**, and all the **numbers** on the **right**.
3 **Multiply or divide:** multiply or divide so **one of the variable = number**.

Examples:

1

$$4(x - 3) = 18$$
Expand: expand the brackets.

$$4x - 12 = 18$$
$$4x - 12 + 12 = 18 + 12$$
Rearrange: add 12 to both sides.

$$4x = 30$$
$$\frac{4x}{4} = \frac{30}{4}$$
Multiply or divide: divide both sides by 4.

$$x = 7.5$$

2

$$-5(3x - 4) = 76 + x$$
Expand: expand the brackets.

$$-15x + 20 = 76 + x$$
Rearrange: subtract x from both sides.

$$-15x + 20 - x = 76 + x - x$$
$$-16x + 20 = 76$$
Rearrange: subtract 20 from both sides.

$$-16x + 20 - 20 = 76 - 20$$
$$-16x = 56$$
$$\frac{-16x}{-16} = \frac{56}{-16}$$
Multiply or divide: divide both sides by -16.

$$x = -3.5$$

Solve the following.

1 $2(x + 3) = 11$

2 $6(x - 1) = 48$

3 $10(x - 3) = 25$

4 $7(6 + x) = 77$

 ISBN: 9780170497978

5 $3(5x + 7) = 6$

6 $8(x + 5) = 12$

7 $14 = 5(2 + x)$

8 $-3 = -1(7x - 4)$

9 $-2(x - 3) = 14 - x$

10 $-10(13 - x) = 24 + 2x$

11 $-(9 + 5x) = x - 3$

12 $-4(5x - 8) = 10 + 2x$

13 $5(x + 1) = 2(7x - 11)$

14 $6(4x - 1) = 11 - 7(1 - 4x)$

ISBN: 9780170497978

Mixing it up

Do the working needed to complete the cross-number in your exercise book.

Across	
1	$4x + 1 = 49$
3	$3x + 1 = 76$
6	$1 + \frac{x}{3} = 9$
8	$45 = 2x - 9$
9	$3 + \frac{x}{4} = 38$
10	$5(x - 2) = 7x - 34$
11	$3x + 8 = 100 - x$
15	$\frac{x}{14} - 2 = 1.5$
16	$2(x - 9) - 1 = 23 + x$

Down	
2	$\frac{x}{2} = 14$
3	$99 = 5x - 11$
4	$126 - x = 2x$
5	$89 - x = 3(x + 7)$
7	$2(x - 50) = x + 46$
10	$10 - x = -3$
12	$5x - 4 = 101 + 2x$
13	$\frac{x}{4} = 4\frac{3}{4}$
14	$\frac{3x}{2} - 5 = 16$

ISBN: 9780170497978

Inequations

Symbols you need to know:

> means '**is greater than**'   ≥ means '**is greater than or equal to**'

< means '**is less than**'   ≤ means '**is less than or equal to**'

Inequations with integers

Insert a > or < sign in order to create true statements.

1 3 ☐ 5   **2** 8 ☐ 7   **3** 0 ☐ 1

4 0 ☐ -1   **5** -5 ☐ -4   **6** 3 ☐ -3

7 Complete the table for the range of integers shown. The first three rows have been done for you.

Symbols	Possible values of x	Words
$x > 2$	-6 -5 -4 -3 -2 -1 0 1 2 **3 4 5 6**	*x is greater than two*
$x = 4$	-6 -5 -4 -3 -2 -1 0 1 2 3 **4** 5 6	*x equals four*
$x \leq 3$	**-6 -5 -4 -3 -2 -1 0 1 2 3** 4 5 6	*x is less than or equal to three*
$x < 5$	-6 -5 -4 -3 -2 -1 0 1 2 3 4 5 6	
	-6 -5 -4 -3 -2 -1 0 1 2 3 4 5 6	x is equal to -1
$x > 5$	-6 -5 -4 -3 -2 -1 0 1 2 3 4 5 6	
	-6 -5 -4 -3 -2 -1 0 1 2 3 4 5 6	x is greater than or equal to 1
	-6 -5 -4 -3 -2 -1 0 1 2 3 4 5 6	
$x < -2$	-6 -5 -4 -3 -2 -1 0 1 2 3 4 5 6	
	-6 -5 -4 -3 -2 -1 0 1 2 3 4 5 6	x is greater than or equal to 3
	-6 -5 -4 -3 -2 -1 **0 1 2 3 4 5 6**	
$x \leq 1$	-6 -5 -4 -3 -2 -1 0 1 2 3 4 5 6	
$x \geq -4$	-6 -5 -4 -3 -2 -1 0 1 2 3 4 5 6	
	-6 -5 -4 -3 -2 -1 0 1 2 3 4 5 6	

ISBN: 9780170497978

Inequations on a number line

- When drawing inequations on a number line, we need to consider **all** numbers, not just integers.
- For instance: $x > 2$ means x cannot be exactly 2, but it can be 2.000...01 or anything greater.
  $x < 2$ means x cannot be exactly 2, but it can be less than 2.
  $x \geq 2$ means x can be exactly 2 or anything greater.
  $x \leq 2$ means x can be exactly 2 or anything smaller.

We use symbols on a number line to show each of these situations.

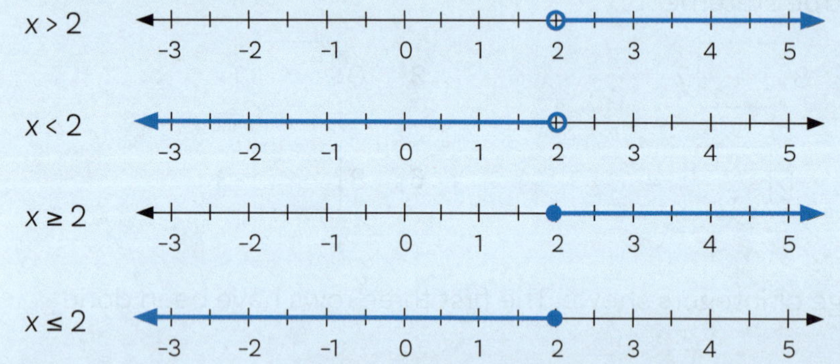

x can be any number greater than 2.

x can be any number less than 2.

x can be 2 or any number greater than 2.

x can be 2 or any number less than 2.

Notice:
If the point is **ex**cluded (> or <), we use a hollow dot (○).
If the point is **in**cluded (≥ or ≤), we use a solid dot (●).

Complete the table for the range of numbers shown.

Symbols	Possible values of x	Words
	-3 -2 -1 0 1 2 3 4 5	
	-3 -2 -1 0 1 2 3 4 5	
$x \leq 3$	-3 -2 -1 0 1 2 3 4 5	
	-3 -2 -1 0 1 2 3 4 5	x is greater than or equal to 1
$x < -1.5$	-3 -2 -1 0 1 2 3 4 5	
	-3 -2 -1 0 1 2 3 4 5	
	-3 -2 -1 0 1 2 3 4 5	x is less than or equal to 0

ISBN: 9780170497978

Solving inequations

Inequations have **<**, **≤**, **>** or **≥** signs.

You solve an inequation in **exactly** the same way as you solve an equation except:

- if you need to **multiply or divide** the equation by a **negative number**, you must **reverse the sign**.
- if you **swap sides**, you must **reverse the sign**.

Examples:

1

$7x < 21$

$\frac{7x}{7} < \frac{21}{7}$ — Divide by **7**.

$x < 3$

2

$-4x > 30$

$\frac{-4x}{-4} < \frac{30}{-4}$ — Divide by **-4** ⇒ **change sign direction**.

$x < -7.5$

3

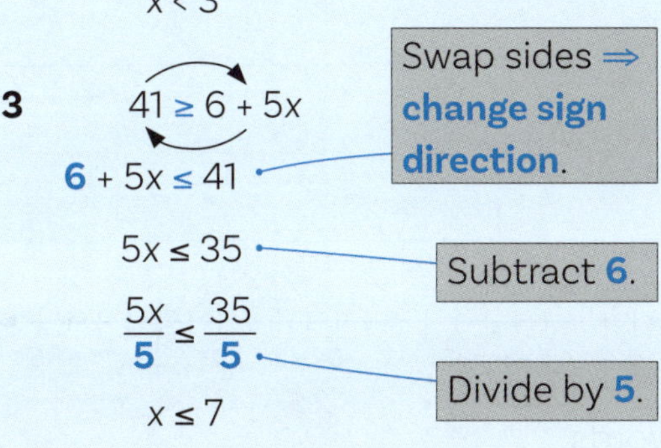

$41 \geq 6 + 5x$ — Swap sides ⇒ **change sign direction**.

$6 + 5x \leq 41$

$5x \leq 35$ — Subtract **6**.

$\frac{5x}{5} \leq \frac{35}{5}$ — Divide by **5**.

$x \leq 7$

4

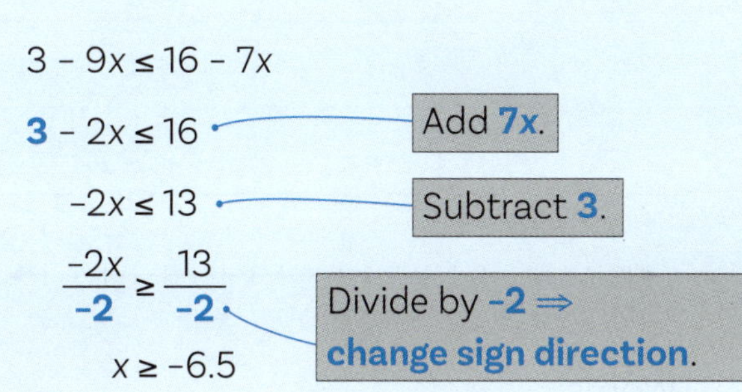

$3 - 9x \leq 16 - 7x$

$3 - 2x \leq 16$ — Add **7x**.

$-2x \leq 13$ — Subtract **3**.

$\frac{-2x}{-2} \geq \frac{13}{-2}$ — Divide by **-2** ⇒ **change sign direction**.

$x \geq -6.5$

Solve the following, highlight the solution for the range of integers shown and write the solution using words.

1 $3x \geq 12$

____

____

-5 -4 -3 -2 -1 0 1 2 3 4 5

Words: ______________________

2 $9x \leq -18$

____

____

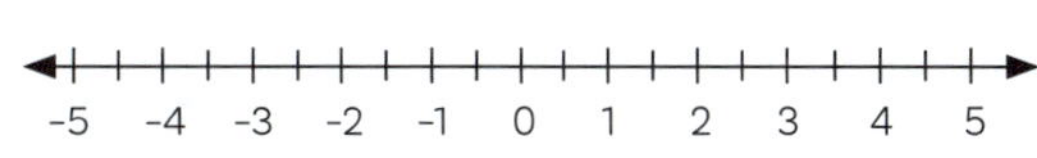

-5 -4 -3 -2 -1 0 1 2 3 4 5

Words: ______________________

3 $30 < 10x$

____

____

____

-5 -4 -3 -2 -1 0 1 2 3 4 5

Words: ______________________

4 $5x - 3 < 7$

____

____

____

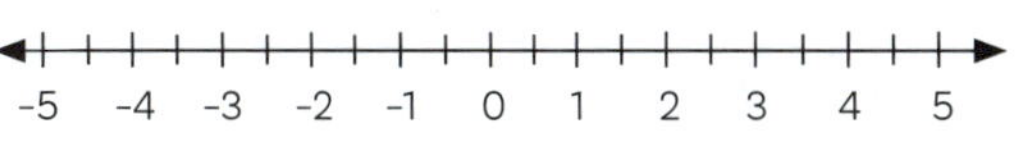

-5 -4 -3 -2 -1 0 1 2 3 4 5

Words: ______________________

ISBN: 9780170497978

5 $3x - 2 \leq -11$

-5 -4 -3 -2 -1 0 1 2 3 4 5

Words: ______

6 $4x \geq x - 12$

-5 -4 -3 -2 -1 0 1 2 3 4 5

Words: ______

7 $3x - 8 < 1$

-5 -4 -3 -2 -1 0 1 2 3 4 5

Words: ______

8 $5 < x + 7$

-5 -4 -3 -2 -1 0 1 2 3 4 5

Words: ______

9 $2x + 1 < -5$

-5 -4 -3 -2 -1 0 1 2 3 4 5

Words: ______

10 $10 \geq 11 + x$

-5 -4 -3 -2 -1 0 1 2 3 4 5

Words: ______

11 $-1 \geq x + 3$

-5 -4 -3 -2 -1 0 1 2 3 4 5

Words: ______

12 $6x - 1 \leq 11$

-5 -4 -3 -2 -1 0 1 2 3 4 5

Words: ______

 ISBN: 9780170497978

Substitution and formulae

Substitution with one variable

- When substituting into an expression, you replace the variables with numbers.
- It is very important to remember **BEDMAS** or **GEMA** when doing this.

Examples:

1 Let $b = 5$.

$A = b^2 - 2$
$= 5^2 - 2$
$= 25 - 2$
$= 23$

Replace **b** with **5**.

2 Let $c = -2$.

$A = \frac{10 - 3c}{4}$
$= \frac{10 - 3 \times -2}{4}$
$= \frac{10 + 6}{4}$
$= 4$

Remember, the divide line acts like brackets, so find the value of the numerator first.

Answer the following questions.

1 Complete the following table.

Formula	$b = 3$	$b = 5$	$b = 0$	$b = -2$
$A = 4b$	$A = 4 \times 3$ $= 12$	A = ______ = ______	A = ______ = ______	A = ______ = ______
$A = b + 2$	A = ______ = ______	A = ______ = ______	A = ______ = ______	A = ______ = ______
$A = 6b - 5$	A = ______ = ______	A = ______ = ______	A = ______ = ______	A = ______ = ______
$A = 1 + b^2$	A = ______ = ______ = ______	A = ______ = ______ = ______	A = ______ = ______ = ______	A = ______ = ______ = ______
$A = \frac{1 + b}{2}$	A = ______ = ______ = ______	A = ______ = ______ = ______	A = ______ = ______ = ______	A = ______ = ______ = ______

2 If $c = -3$, find the values of the following.

a $5c$ = ______
= ______

b $10 + c$ = ______
= ______

c $c - 2$ = ______
= ______

d $2(c - 1)$ = ______
= ______

e c^2 = ______
= ______

f $\frac{c + 8}{5}$ = ______ = ______

ISBN: 9780170497978

Formulae with one variable

- A **formula** is an **algebraic expression** of a **rule**.

Example:
This is an equilateral triangle:

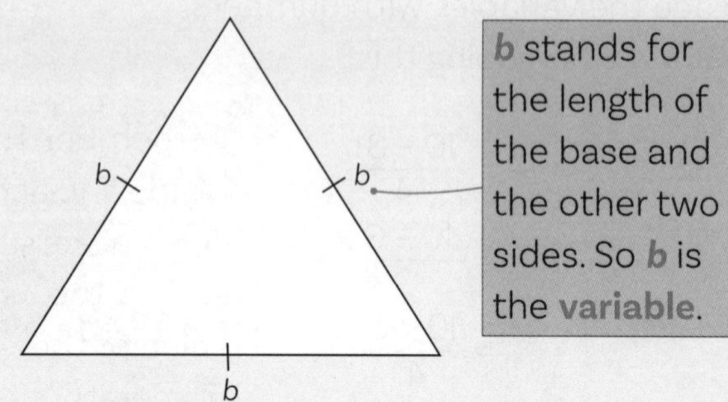

Perimeter $= b + b + b$ — Simplify.

$= 3b$

$P = 3b$ — This is the **formula** for finding the perimeter of this triangle.

Using the formula:

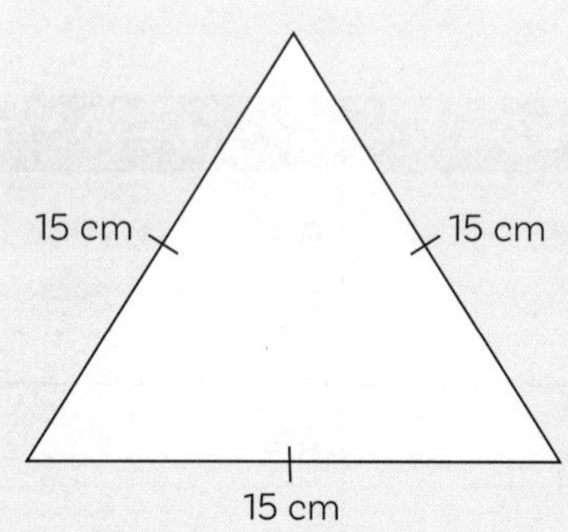

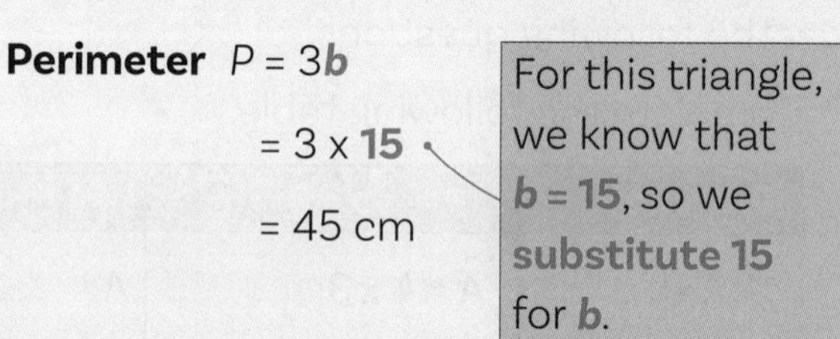

Some more examples:

1 Archie is making lemon cordial. The recipe states that he should use equal volumes of water, sugar and lemon juice. The total volume of cordial is given by $\mathbf{V = 3c}$, where **c** stands for the **number of cups of lemon juice**. Calculate the total volume (**V**) of cordial if he has four cups of lemon juice.

$V = 3\mathbf{c}$ — Replace **c** with the number of cups of lemon juice.

$= 3 \times \mathbf{4}$

$= 12$ cups

Notice that there should be just **one** '=' sign per line, and they are **lined up** under each other.

2 Sally Spade is a gardener. She charges \$35 per hour plus \$20 for her travel time. The formula for her total charge is $\mathbf{C = 20 + 35h}$, where ***h*** stands for the **number of hours** that she works. Calculate her charge if she works for five hours.

$C = 20 + 35\mathbf{h}$

$= 20 + 35 \times \mathbf{5}$ — Replace **h** with the number of hours.

$= \$195$

 ISBN: 9780170497978

Answer the following questions.

1 The amount of tartaric acid needed for Archie's cordial recipe is half a tablespoon (T) per cup of juice.

a Write down the formula for the total number of tablespoons of tartaric acid needed for c cups of juice. T = ____________

b Calculate the quantity of tartaric acid needed for five cups of juice. T = ____________

= ____________

= ____________

2 One side of an isosceles triangle is 4 cm longer than each of the other two sides (s). (It might help if you sketch the triangle.)

a Write down the formula for calculating the perimeter (P) of the isosceles triangle. P = ____________

b Calculate its perimeter if the short sides are 12 cm long. P = ____________

= ____________

= ____________

3 Huia earns $15 per hour for helping to clean her parents' motels.

a Write the formula for the amount she gets paid, where h stands for the number of hours she has worked. A = ____________

b How much would she get paid for working five and a half hours? A = ____________

= ____________

= ____________

c She also gets paid $17.50 per hour for helping her uncle in the milking shed. Write a formula for the amount that she is paid for this work. A = ____________

d She has the choice of doing six hours of motel cleaning or five hours working in the milking shed. Which would earn her the most money? Show your calculations. Write a formula for the amount that she is paid.

____

____

____

e It's a 20-minute bike ride to her uncle's dairy farm, so her uncle decides he will pay Huia an extra $10 each time she comes to work. He also feels that she is working so hard that he will increase her pay to $19 per hour. Write a formula for the amount that she will be paid for each working day. A = ____________

f The following Saturday she worked for six hours at the dairy farm. Calculate the amount she should be paid. A = ____________

ISBN: 9780170497978

4 Hemi babysits his neighbours' children. They pay him \$20 for the first hour, and \$16 dollars per hour for each extra hour.

a A formula for calculating his pay is $P = 20 + 16(h - 1)$, where P stands for his total pay and h stands for the total number of hours that he babysat. Calculate his pay if he babysits for five hours.

$P =$ ____________

$=$ ____________

b His neighbour uses the formula $P = 4 + 16h$ to calculate his pay. Show by expanding and simplifying that this formula gives the same result as the formula in part **a**.

$P = 20 + 16(h - 1)$

$=$ ____________

$=$ ____________

c When Grace babysits, she is paid \$22 for the first hour and 15 dollars per hour for each extra hour. Write two different formulae for calculating her pay.

$P =$ ____________

$P =$ ____________

d Both babysit for four hours. Calculate the pay for each person.

Hemi: $P =$ ____________ Grace: $P =$ ____________

$=$ ____________ $=$ ____________

$=$ ____________ $=$ ____________

Who gets paid more and by how much?

____

e Georgia also babysits. A formula for calculating her pay is $P = 24 + 14(h - 1)$. Explain what this formula means.

____

____

____

f Rewrite the formula for Georgia's pay if, in addition, she is paid \$3 each way to cover her bus fare.

$P =$ ____________

g The formula for calculating her pay (without bus fare) changes to $P = 48 + 14(h - 2)$. Explain what this change means, compared with the formula in **f**.

____

____

____

ISBN: 9780170497978

Substitution with several variables

Examples: Let $b = 4$, $c = 6$ and $d = -3$.

1

$A = b^2 + d$

$= 4^2 + (-3)$

$= 16 - 3$

$= 13$

Replace b with 4.

2

$A = \frac{5b - c}{d}$

$= \frac{5 \times 4 - 6}{-3}$

$= \frac{14}{-3}$

$= -4\frac{2}{3}$

Remember, the divide line acts like brackets, so find the value of the numerator first.

Answer the following questions.

1 Complete the following table.

Formula	$b = 2, c = 5$	$b = 9, c = 4$	$b = 6, c = -2$
$A = 20 - 2bc$	$A = 20 - 2 \times 2 \times 5$ = ______ = ______	A = ______ = ______ = ______	A = ______ = ______ = ______
$A = c(b - 1)$	A = ______ = ______ = ______	A = ______ = ______ = ______	A = ______ = ______ = ______
$A = (c - b)^2$	A = ______ = ______ = ______	A = ______ = ______ = ______	A = ______ = ______ = ______
$A = \frac{b^2 - 3c}{2}$	A = ______ = ______ = ______	A = ______ = ______ = ______	A = ______ = ______ = ______

2 If $d = -2$, $e = 6$ and $f = -4$, find the values of the following.

a $e - f + 2d =$ ______
= ______
= ______

b $12 - ef + 3d =$ ______
= ______
= ______

c $4def - 11 =$ ______
= ______
= ______

d $-d + 2f =$ ______
= ______
= ______

e $f^2 - 3de =$ ______
= ______
= ______

f $2e^2 + 5df =$ ______
= ______
= ______

ISBN: 9780170497978

Formulae with two or more variables

Example:

This is an equilateral triangle:

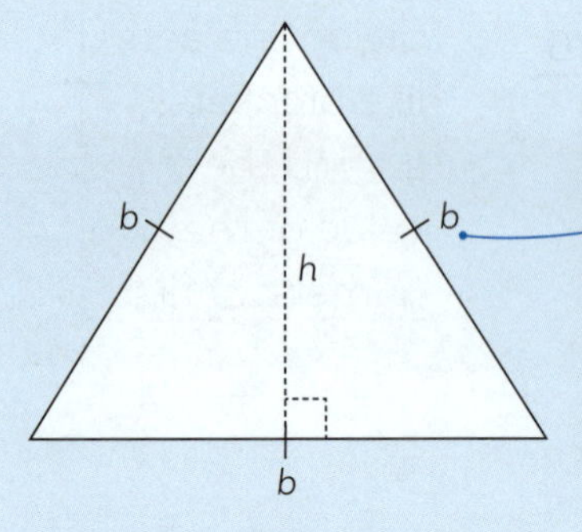

b stands for the length of the base and the other two sides. ***h*** is the perpendicular height. So ***b*** and ***h*** are **variables**.

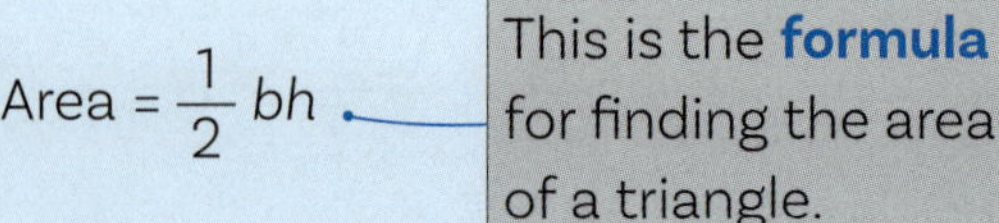

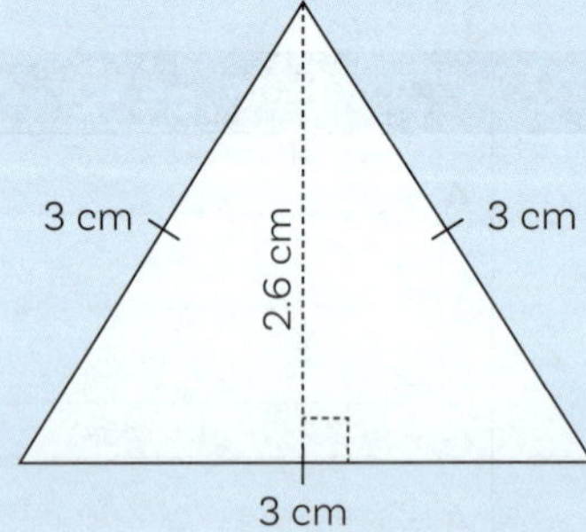

Area = $\frac{1}{2}bh$

$= \frac{1}{2} \times 3 \times 2.6$

$= 3.9 \text{ cm}^2$

For this triangle, we know that **$b = 3$ and $h = 2.6$**, so we substitute **3** for ***b*** and **2.6** for ***h***.

Answer the following questions.

1 Cooper is paid \$21.50 per hour for a 40-hour week (h) as a plumbing apprentice. If he works overtime (more than 40 hours in a week), he is paid \$30 for every extra hour (e).

a Write down the formula for calculating how much he is paid in any week (P). P = ______________

b Calculate how much he would get paid if he worked for 47 hours in a week. P = ______________

= ______________

= ______________

c Maria is an apprentice electrician and her basic pay is also based on a 40-hour week, and she also gets paid an hourly rate for any extra hours she works. The formula for calculating her weekly pay is $P = 910 + 28h$. Explain what this formula means.

____

____

d Jacob is training to be a builder. He is paid \$23 per hour (h), however long he works during a week. His boss also pays him \$8 for every day (d) he works, to cover his travel to and from a site which is some distance away. Write a formula for calculating his weekly pay. P = ______________

ISBN: 9780170497978

2 Driver reaction time is the time it takes for the brain to process information such as a cat running in front of the car. It is the length of time between the event and the **start** of braking. During this time, the vehicle continues to travel at its current speed, so it can cover a considerable distance. The formula for calculating this distance is:

$$D = vt$$

- D stands for the distance travelled in metres.
- v stands for velocity in metres per second.
- t stands for the reaction time in seconds.

a The average reaction time for an adult is 0.75 seconds. Eli is driving at 50 kph, which means that he is travelling at a velocity of 14 m/s. A dog runs out in front of his car. Show that the car will travel slightly less than the average length of a classroom (10.8 m) **before** he begins to brake.

$D = vt$

= ____________

= ____________

b Reaction times can be much longer if a person has been drinking or is sleepy. Maia is driving home after working a night shift. Her reaction time is 1.5 seconds. Calculate how far she will travel **before** braking if she is travelling at 60 kph (17 m/s).

$D = vt$

= ____________

= ____________

c How much **further** would she have travelled before braking if she had been travelling at 80 kph (22 m/s)?

____

____

3 Liam needs to hire a concrete mixer for a few days. Harry's Hire will charge him $40 per day plus $22 for every hour of use. (It has a meter to record use time.) Let d stand for the number of days and h stand for the number of hours of actual use.

a Write down a formula for calculating the cost (C) of hiring the concrete mixer for d days and using it for h hours. C = ____________

b Calculate the cost if he uses it for five hours over a period of three days. C = ____________

= ____________

c Mike's Machines' formula for calculating the charge for hiring a concrete mixer for d days and using it for h hours is $C = 70d + 8h$. Explain in words what this means.

____

____

d Calculate the cost of hiring a concrete mixer from Mike's Machines if it is used for five hours over a period of three days.

C = ____________

e Which hire company was the cheapest and by how much? ____________

ISBN: 9780170497978

Rearrangement of formulae

1 **Rearrange**: Put the term which contains the required subject on the **left**.
2 **Fractions**: Get rid of fractions by **multiplying by the denominator**.
3 Use **normal equation-solving rules** to isolate the subject.

Examples:

1 In physics, the force of a moving object is calculated using the formula $F = ma$, where m is the mass of the object and a is its acceleration. Make m the subject of this formula.

$$F = ma$$
$$ma = F$$
$$\frac{m\not{a}}{\not{a}} = \frac{F}{a}$$
$$m = \frac{F}{a}$$

Swap sides so m is on the left.

Divide both sides by a.

2 The area of a triangle is found by using the formula $A = \frac{1}{2}bh$, where b is the length of the base and h is the perpendicular height. Make b the subject of this formula.

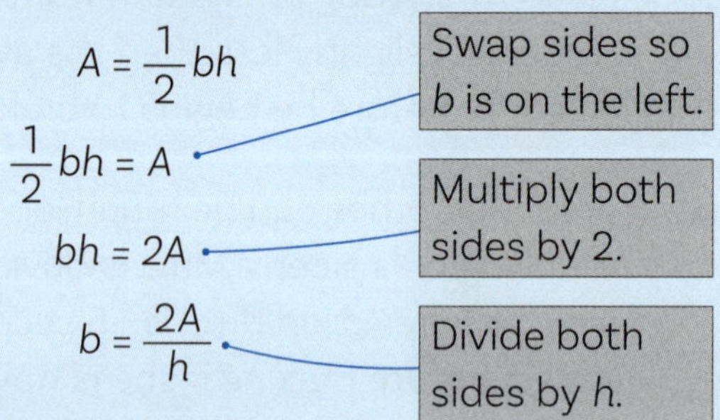

3 The volume of a cylinder is found by using the formula $V = \pi r^2 h$, where r is the radius and h is its height. Rewrite this expression making h the subject.

$$V = \pi r^2 h$$
$$\pi r^2 h = V$$
$$\frac{\not{\pi}\not{r^2}h}{\not{\pi}\not{r^2}} = \frac{V}{\pi r^2}$$
$$h = \frac{V}{\pi r^2}$$

Swap sides so h is on the left.

Divide both sides by πr^2.

4 Rewrite the formula making r the subject.

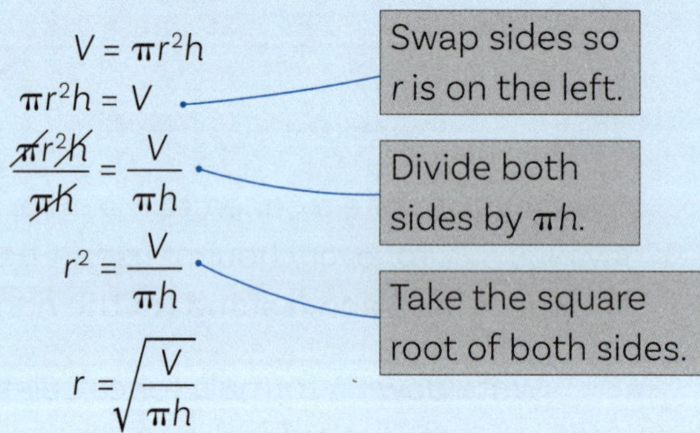

Answer the following questions.

1 The perimeter of a square is given by the formula $P = 4d$, where d is the distance along one side. Make d the subject of this formula.

2 Ohm's Law states that the voltage in a circuit is the product of the current flowing through it (I) and the resistance in the circuit (R): $V = IR$. Make I the subject of this formula.

ISBN: 9780170497978

3 The area of a square is given by the formula $A = d^2$. Make d the subject of this formula.

4 The circumference of a circle is given by the equation $C = 2\pi r$. Make r the subject of this formula.

5 The speed (s) of an object is calculated by the formula $s = \frac{d}{t}$, where d stands for the distance travelled and t is the time taken.

a Make d the subject of this formula.

b Make t the subject of this formula.

6 The area of a circle is given by the formula $A = \pi r^2$, where r stands for the radius of the circle. Make r the subject of this formula.

7 The amount of interest earned (I) can be calculated using the formula $I = \frac{PRT}{100}$, where P stands for the principal (amount invested), R for the rate of interest and T for the length of time the money has been invested. Make P the subject of this formula.

8 In physics, the kinetic energy (E) of an object is given by the formula $E = \frac{1}{2}mv^2$, where m is the mass of the object and v is its velocity.

a Make m the subject of this formula.

b Make v the subject of this formula.

ISBN: 9780170497978

Understanding instructions in algebra

Instruction	Example	What do I do?	What should the answer look like?
Solve	$5x - 1 = 9$ Contains an '=' sign.	Shift terms with variables to the left, and terms with constants to the right. $5x - 1 = 9$ (+ 1) $5x = 10$ (÷ 5) $x = 2$	variable = constant $x = 2$
Evaluate	$5x - 1$ when $x = 9$ You are told the **value** of the variable.	Substitute the value for the variable. $5x - 1 = 5(9) - 1$ $= 45 - 1$ $= 44$	expression = constant $5x - 1 = 44$
Expand	$3a(4a + b - 2)$ Contains **brackets**.	Multiply every term inside the brackets by the term outside. $3a(4a + b - 2)$ $= 12a^2 + 3ab - 6a$	An expression with no brackets. $12a^2 + 3ab - 6a$
Simplify	Adding/subtracting $5a + b + 2a^2 - 2a - 3b$ Contains a mixture of **like and unlike** terms.	Combine like terms. $5a + b + 2a^2 - 2a - 3b$ $= 3a + 2a^2 - 2b$	An expression containing no like terms. $3a + 2a^2 - 2b$
	Multiplying/dividing $\frac{15a^3b}{5a^2b^4c}$ The same variable occurs in **more than one place**.	Add or subtract indices for each variable that occurs more than once. $\frac{15a^3b}{5a^2b^4c} = \frac{3a}{b^3c}$ You 'cancel out' the HCF: $5a^2b$.	An expression in which each variable occurs no more than once. $\frac{3a}{b^3c}$
Factorise	$24ab^3 - 6a^2b$ Several terms containing **common factors**. The terms are added and/or subtracted.	Put the common factor outside the bracket. Divide each term by the common factor to find what goes inside the brackets. $24ab^3 - 6a^2b = 6ab(4b^2 - a)$	An expression with brackets. **No common factors inside the brackets.** $6ab(4b^2 - a)$

ISBN: 9780170497978

Write the most appropriate instruction (**Solve**, **Evaluate**, **Expand**, **Simplify** or **Factorise**) for each question. Then follow your chosen instruction in order to answer the question.

	Question	Instruction	Answer
1	$2x(x - 3y)$		
2	$4x - 5y + 2y - x$		
3	$5x - 9 = 21$		
4	$\frac{x^3y}{xy^2}$		
5	$6xy^3 + 2x^2y$		
6	$\frac{x}{2} - 7 = 15$		
7	$7x + 2x^2$ where $x = 3$		
8	$10x^2 - 6x - x - 1 + x^2$		
9	$20 - 3(2x - 1)$		
10	$A = \pi r^2h$ where $r = 2$ and $h = 3$		

ISBN: 9780170497978

Non-linear relationships

Linear or not?

- **Linear** pattern are patterns that increase or decrease by the **same amount** each time.
- Anything that increases by **varying numbers** is **not a linear pattern**.

Examples:

1 Consider the number of triangles.

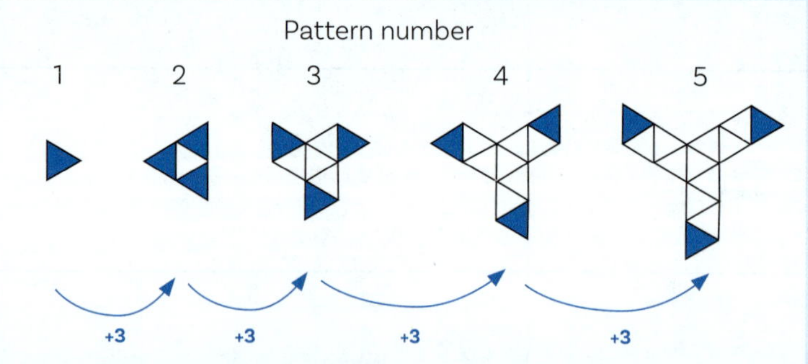

This pattern **increases** by the **same number** of triangles (**3**) each time, therefore it **is** linear.

You can see this if you draw a graph.

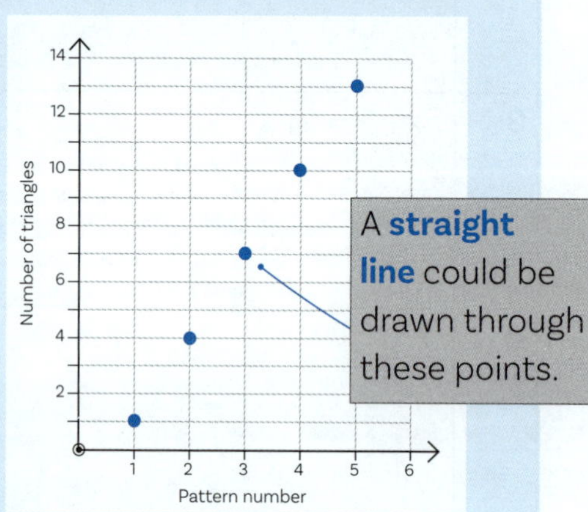

2 Consider the number of dots.

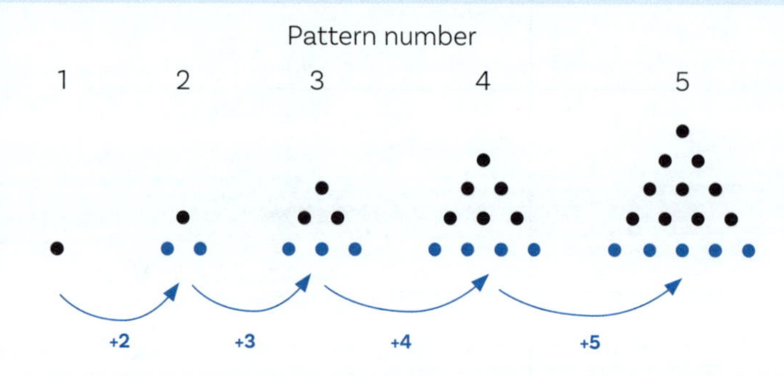

This pattern increases by **different numbers** of dots each time, therefore it is **not** linear.

You can see this if you draw a graph.

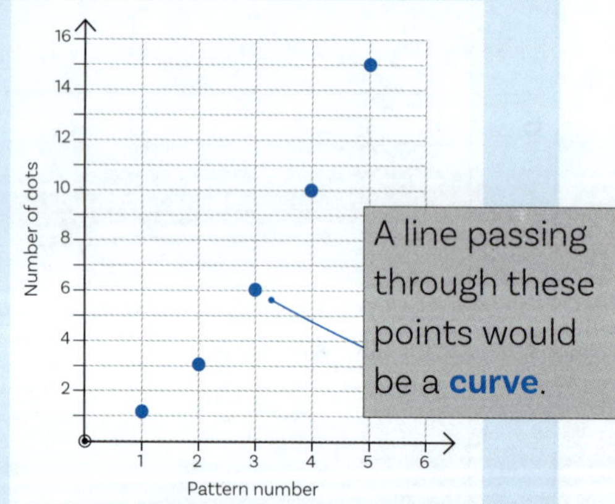

3 Consider these numbers.

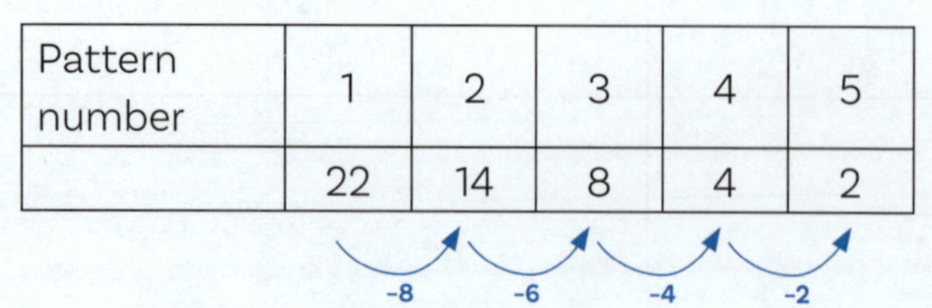

Pattern number	1	2	3	4	5
	22	14	8	4	2

This pattern decreases by **different numbers** of dots each time, therefore it is **not** linear.

You can see this if you draw a graph.

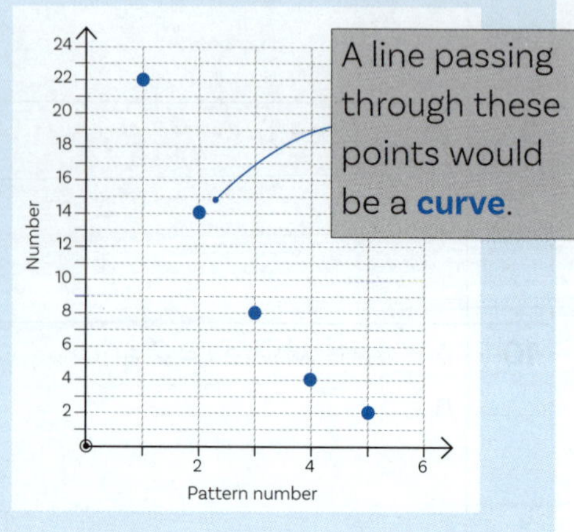

ISBN: 9780170497978

Indicate whether the following patterns are linear or non-linear.

1 Write down the number of dots on each figure.

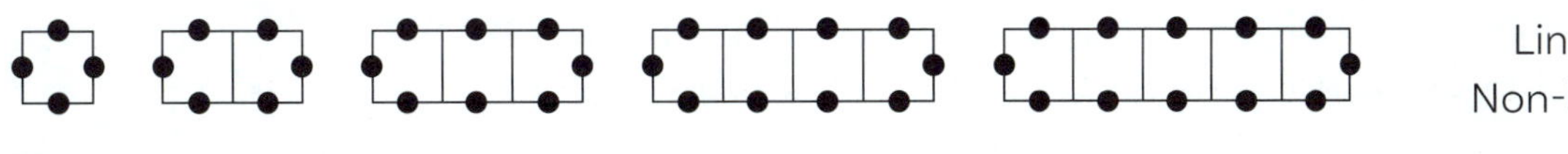

Linear
Non-linear

2 Write down the number of boxes in each figure.

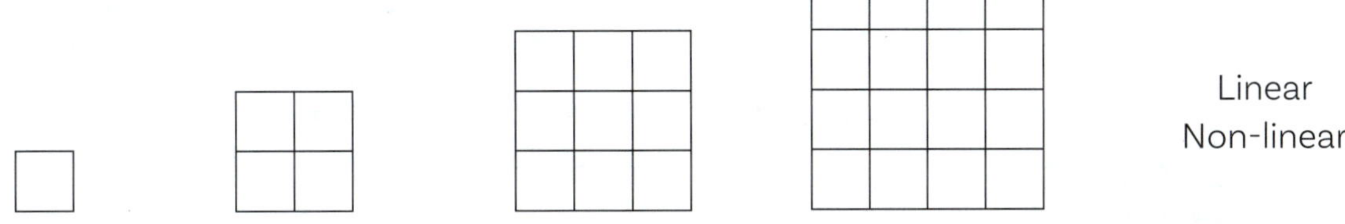

Linear
Non-linear

3 Write down the number of hexagons in each figure.

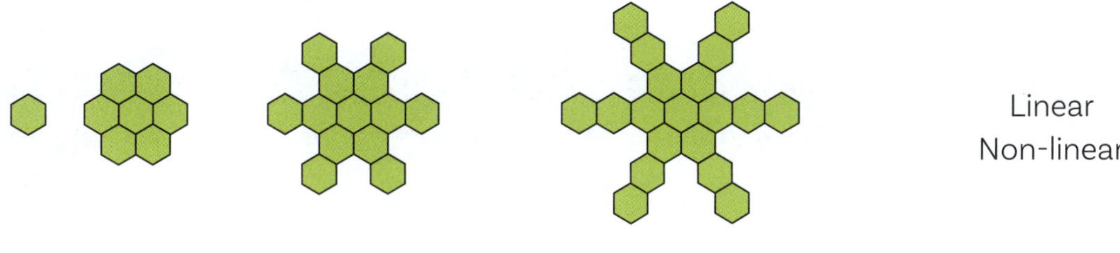

Linear
Non-linear

4 Write down the numbers represented by these tallies.

Linear
Non-linear

Consider these sequences of numbers.

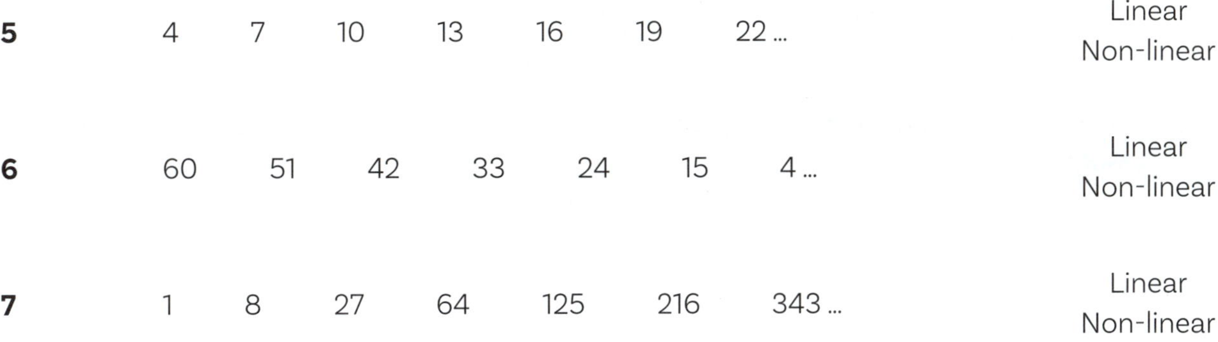

5	4	7	10	13	16	19	22 ...	Linear Non-linear
6	60	51	42	33	24	15	4 ...	Linear Non-linear
7	1	8	27	64	125	216	343 ...	Linear Non-linear

ISBN: 9780170497978

Quadratic patterns

- The **parabola** is the shape of the graph obtained when any **quadratic equation** is plotted.
- A **quadratic equation** is an equation in which the **highest power of x is 2**.
- In this book, we will consider quadratics in the following forms: $y = x^2$, $y = x^2 \pm b$, $y = -x^2$

Example:

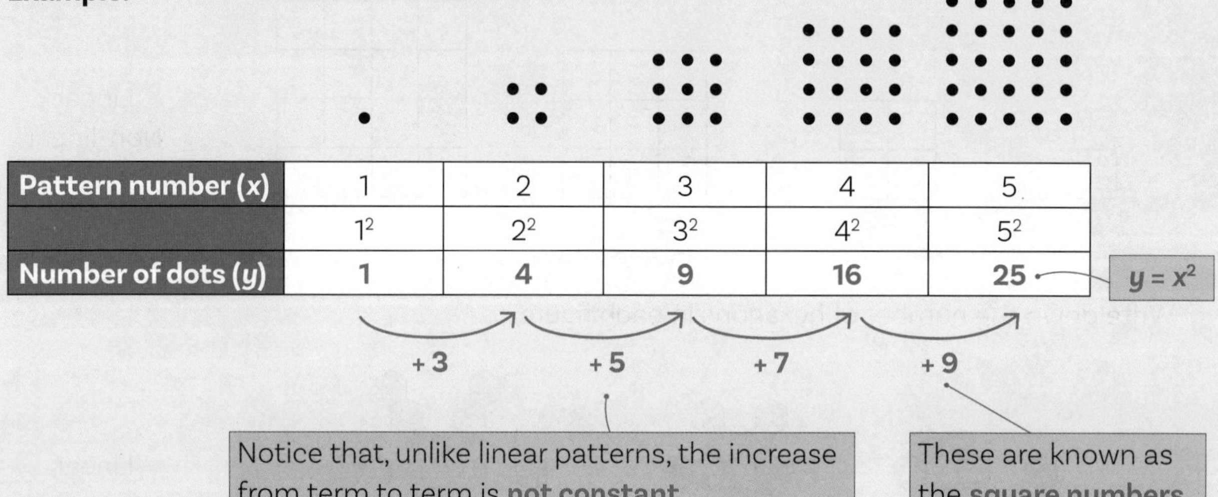

Pattern number (x)	1	2	3	4	5
	1^2	2^2	3^2	4^2	5^2
Number of dots (y)	1	4	9	16	25

Plotting these points on a graph

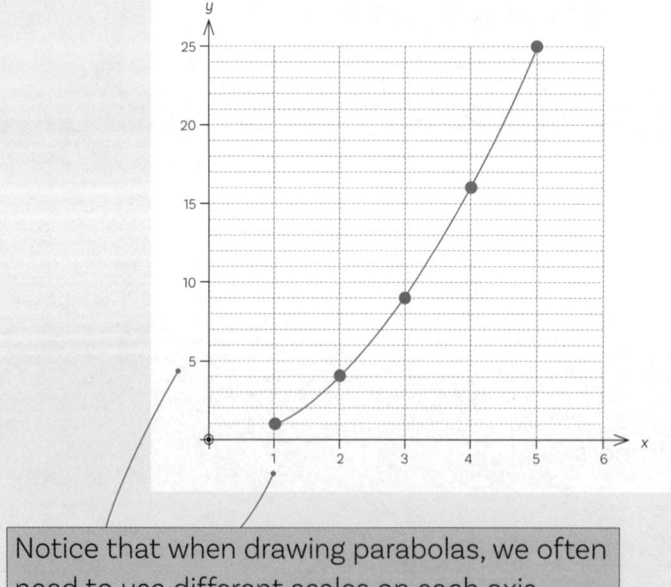

If we consider that x can take any value, not just integers, then we can connect these points with a **smooth** curve.

ISBN: 9780170497978

Extending the graph

You can't just rule a longer line, as you can for linear graphs. Sometimes you need to **extend** the table and calculate more values.

x	-5	-4	-3	-2	-1	0	1	2	3	4	5
x^2	$(-5)^2$	$(-4)^2$	$(-3)^2$	$(-2)^2$	$(-1)^2$	0^2	1^2	2^2	3^2	4^2	5^2
y	25	16	9	4	1	0	1	4	9	16	25

Plotting all these points produces a curve called a **parabola**. Again, we connect the points with a **smooth** curve and add **arrows** to each end to indicate that the curve goes beyond the axes.

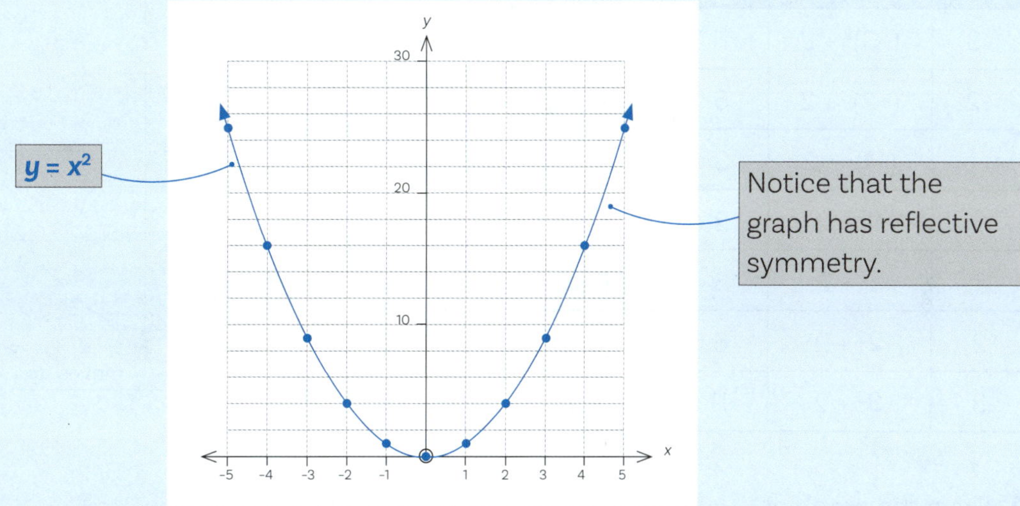

Parabolas have many practical applications

Trajectories of thrown objects

Cross-sections of satellite dishes, headlight reflectors, heater reflectors, etc.

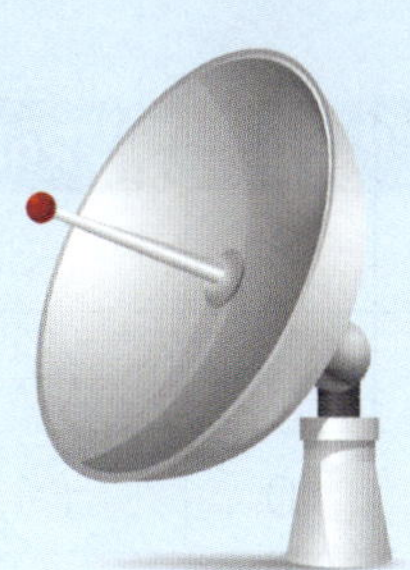

Areas of squares

1 cm

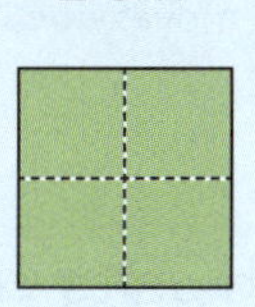

2 cm

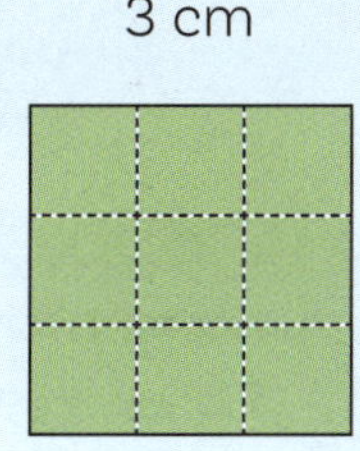

3 cm

The shapes of suspension bridges

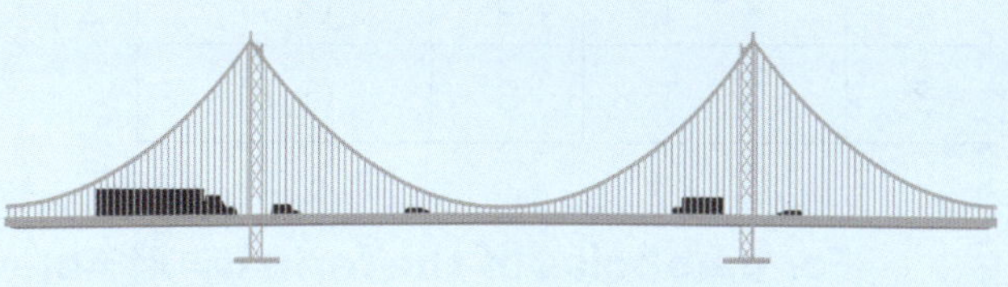

Drawing parabolas

1 In the form $y = x^2 \pm b$

Examples:

1 Draw the graph of $y = x^2 + 2$.

The large grey squares (x^2) each have two small white squares added (+ 2).

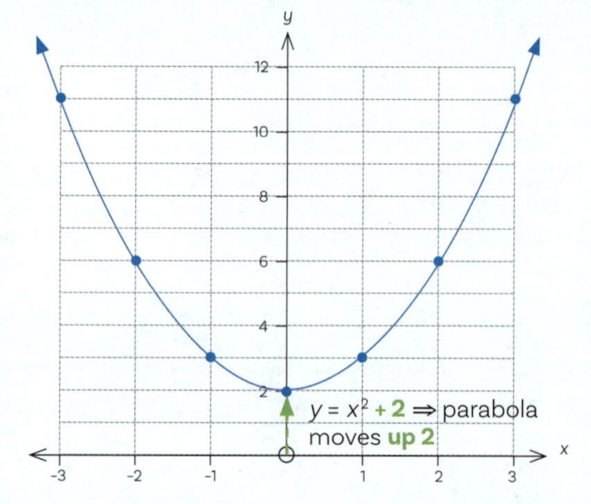

Step 1: Make a table.

x	$x^2 + 2$	y	Point
-3	$(-3)^2 + 2$	11	(-3, 11)
-2	$(-2)^2 + 2$	6	(-2, 6)
-1	$(-1)^2 + 2$	3	(-1, 3)
0	$0^2 + 2$	2	(0, 2)
1	$1^2 + 2$	3	(1, 3)
2	$2^2 + 2$	6	(2, 6)
3	$3^2 + 2$	11	(3, 11)

Step 2: Plot the points and join with a smooth curve.

2 Draw the graph of $y = x^2 - 1$.

The large grey squares (x^2) each have one small square removed (– 1).

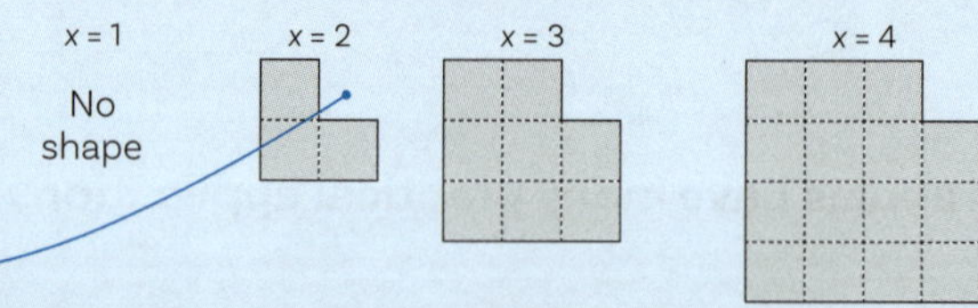

Step 1: Make a table.

x	$x^2 - 1$	y	Point
-3	$(-3)^2 - 1$	8	(-3, 8)
-2	$(-2)^2 - 1$	3	(-2, 3)
-1	$(-1)^2 - 1$	0	(-1, 0)
0	$0^2 - 1$	-1	(0, -1)
1	$1^2 - 1$	0	(1, 0)
2	$2^2 - 1$	3	(2, 3)
3	$3^2 - 1$	8	(3, 8)

Step 2: Plot the points and join with a smooth curve.

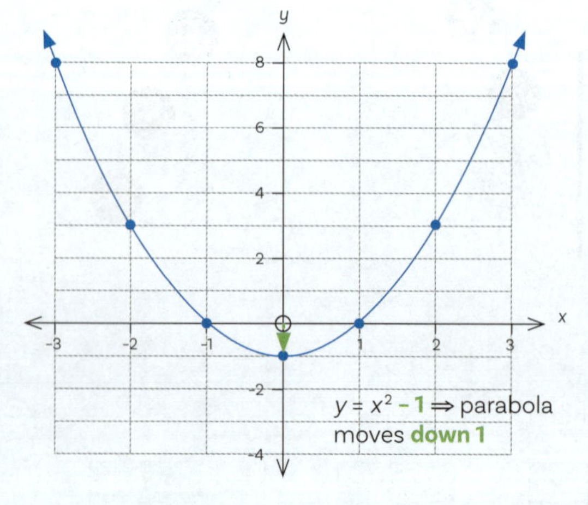

For parabolas of the form $y = x^2 \pm b$:

+ b ⇒ move b units **up**

– b ⇒ move b units **down**

ISBN: 9780170497978

Complete the tables, plot the points, and join them to form a smooth curve.

Note: **1** The maximum or minimum should be a smooth curve, **not** a point.
2 It is much eaiser to draw a smooth curve if you turn the page sideways.

1 $y = x^2 + 3$

x	$x^2 + 3$	y	Point
-3	$(-3)^2 + 3$	12	(–3, 12)
-2	$(-2)^2 + 3$		(–2, ____)
-1			(____, ____)
0			(____, ____)
1			(____, ____)
2			(____, ____)
3			(____, ____)

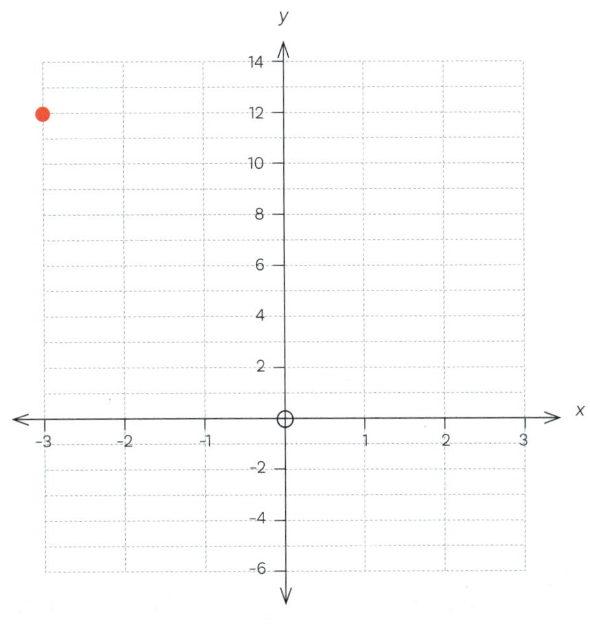

Compared with the graph of $y = x^2$, the parabola $y = x^2 + 3$ has moved up/down ______.

2 $y = x^2 - 4$

x	$x^2 - 4$	y	Point
-3	$(-3)^2 - 4$	2	(–3, 5)
-2	$(-3)^2 - 4$		(–2, ____)
-1			(____, ____)
0			(____, ____)
1			(____, ____)
2			(____, ____)
3			(____, ____)

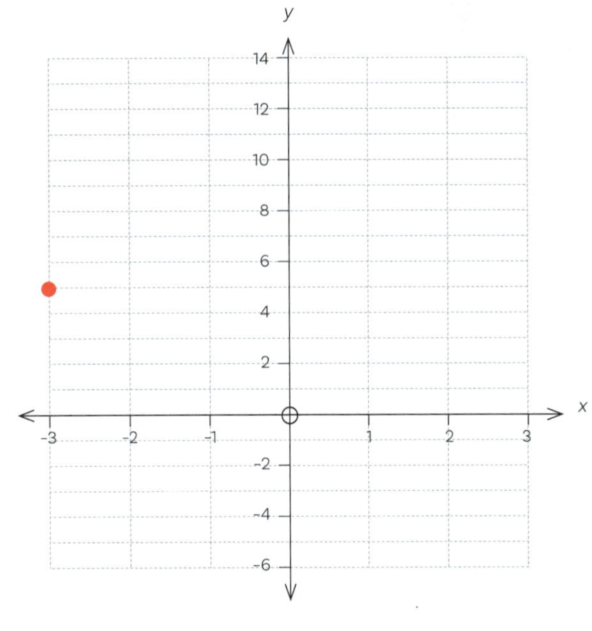

Compared with the graph of $y = x^2$, the parabola $y = x^2 - 4$ has moved up/down ______.

3 $y = x^2 + 5$

x	$x^2 + 5$	y	Point
-3			(_____, _____)
-2			(_____, _____)
-1			(_____, _____)
0			(_____, _____)
1			(_____, _____)
2			(_____, _____)
3			(_____, _____)

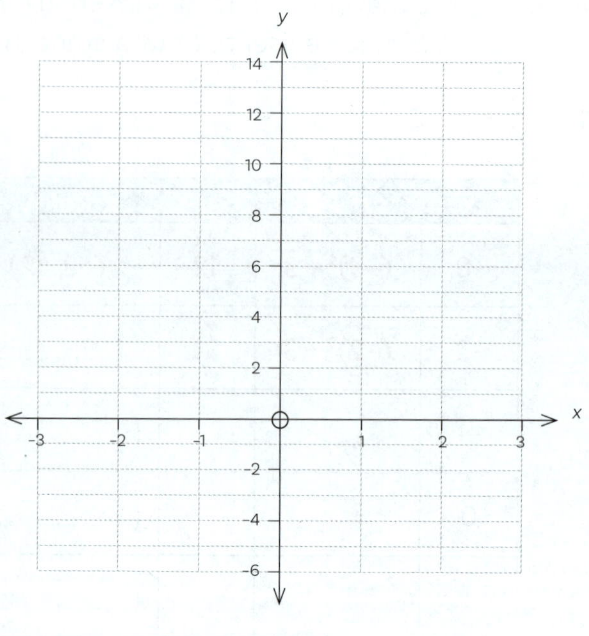

Compared with the graph of $y = x^2$, the parabola $y = x^2 + 5$ has moved up/down _____.

4 $y = x^2 - 2$

x	$x^2 - 2$	y	Point
-3			(_____, _____)
-2			(_____, _____)
-1			(_____, _____)
0			(_____, _____)
1			(_____, _____)
2			(_____, _____)
3			(_____, _____)

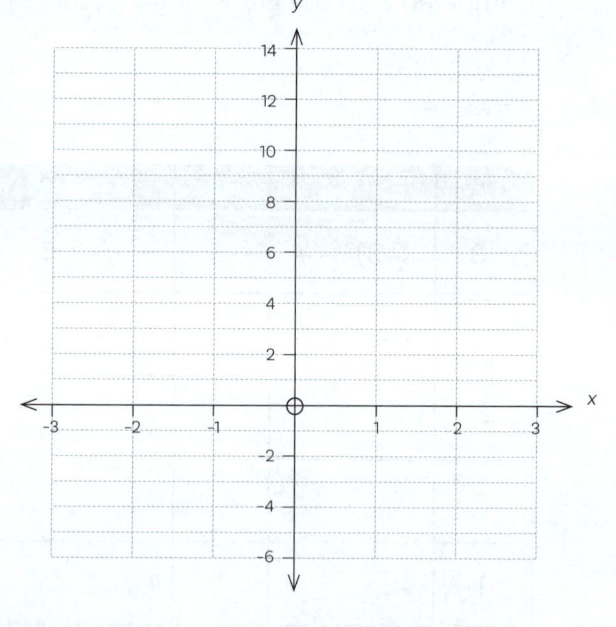

Compared with the graph of $y = x^2$, the parabola $y = x^2 - 2$ has moved up/down _____.

ISBN: 9780170497978

2 In the form $y = -x^2 \pm b$

Examples:

1 Draw the graph of $y = -x^2$.

Step 1: Make a table.

x	$-x^2$	y	Point
-3	$-(-3)^2$	-9	(-3, -9)
-2	$-(-2)^2$	-4	(-2, -4)
-1	$-(-1)^2$	-1	(-1, -1)
0	$-(0)^2$	0	(0, 0)
1	$-(1)^2$	-1	(1, -1)
2	$-(2)^2$	-4	(2, -4)
3	$-(3)^2$	-9	(3, -9)

Step 2: Plot the points and join with a smooth curve.

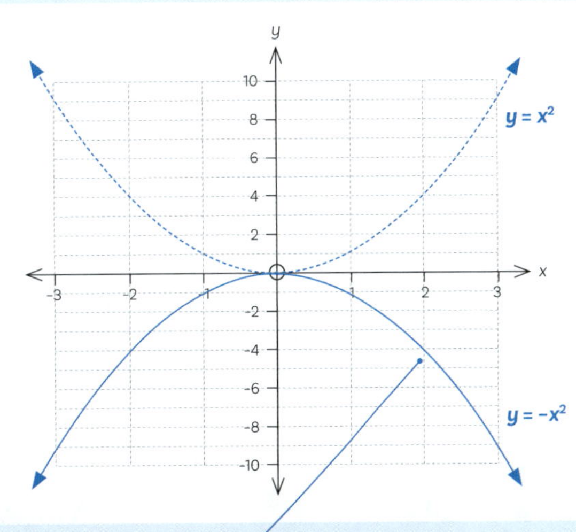

Notice that $y = -x^2$ is the reflection of $y = x^2$ in the x-axis.

2 Draw the graph of $y = -x^2 - 2$.

Step 1: Make a table.

x	$-x^2 - 2$	y	Point
-3	$-(-3)^2 - 2$	-11	(-3, -11)
-2	$-(-2)^2 - 2$	-6	(-2, -6)
-1	$-(-1)^2 - 2$	-3	(-1, -3)
0	$-(0)^2 - 2$	-2	(0, -2)
1	$-(1)^2 - 2$	-3	(1, -3)
2	$-(2)^2 - 2$	-6	(2, -6)
3	$-(3)^2 - 2$	-11	(3, -11)

Step 2: Plot the points and join with a smooth curve.

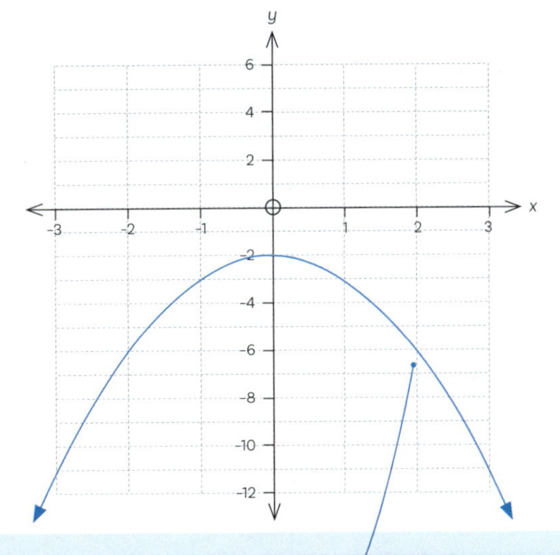

Notice that $y = -x^2 - 2$ is the same shape as $y = -x^2$, but it has been shifted **down 2**.

For parabolas of the form $y = -x^2 \pm b$: the parabola is **upside down**
+ b ⇒ move b units **up**
– b ⇒ move b units **down**

Complete the tables, plot the points, and join them to form a smooth curve.

5 $y = -x^2 + 3$

x	$-x^2 + 3$	y	Point
-3	$-(-3)^2 + 3$	-6	$(-3, -6)$
-2	$-(-2)^2 + 3$	-1	(_____, _____)
-1			(_____, _____)
0			(_____, _____)
1			(_____, _____)
2			(_____, _____)
3			(_____, _____)

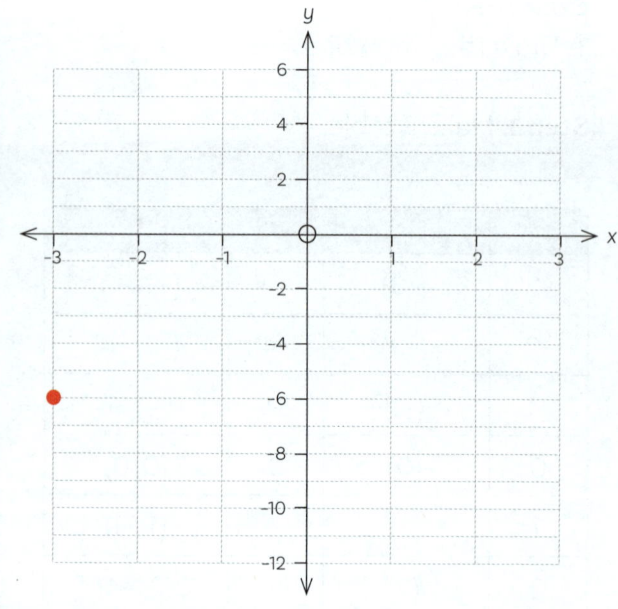

Compared with the graph of $y = -x^2$, the parabola $y = -x^2 + 3$ has moved up/down _____.

6 $y = -x^2 - 4$

x	$-x^2 - 4$	y	Point
-3			(_____, _____)
-2			(_____, _____)
-1			(_____, _____)
0			(_____, _____)
1			(_____, _____)
2			(_____, _____)
3			(_____, _____)

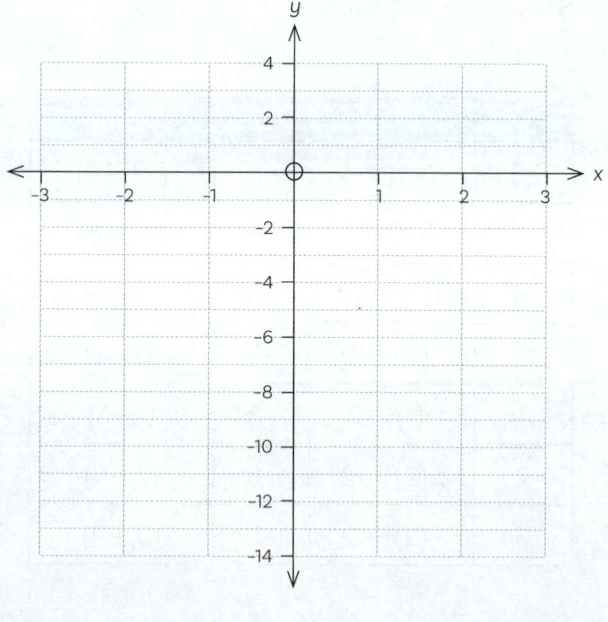

Compared with the graph of $y = -x^2$, the parabola $y = -x^2 - 4$ has moved up/down _____.

 ISBN: 9780170497978

Putting it together

The following graphs all take the form $y = \pm x^2 \pm b$, where b represents an integer. Match the graphs to their equations.

$y = x^2 + 1$	$y = -x^2 - 1$	$y = x^2 + 3$	$y = x^2 - 1$
$y = x^2 - 3$	$y = -x^2 - 3$	$y = -x^2 + 1$	$y = -x^2 + 3$

1

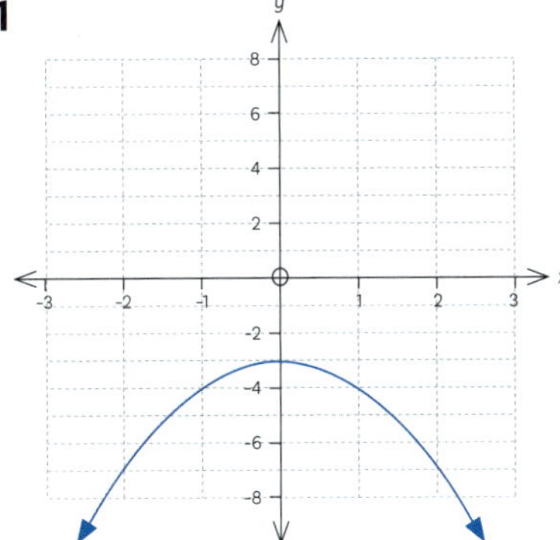

____

2

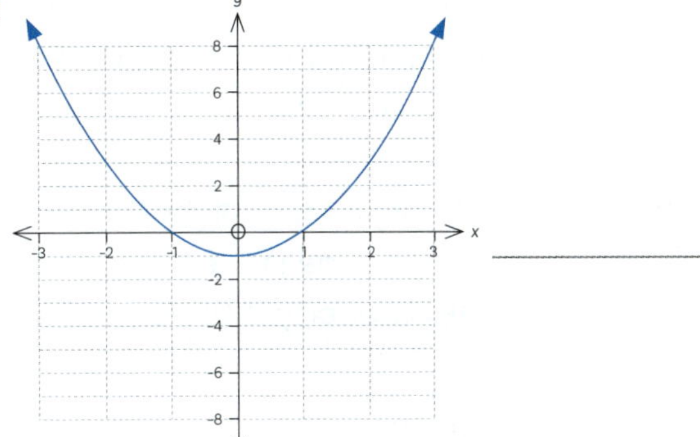

____

3

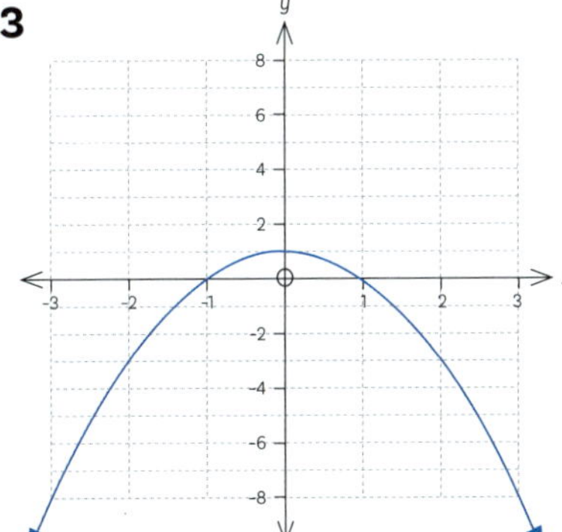

____

4

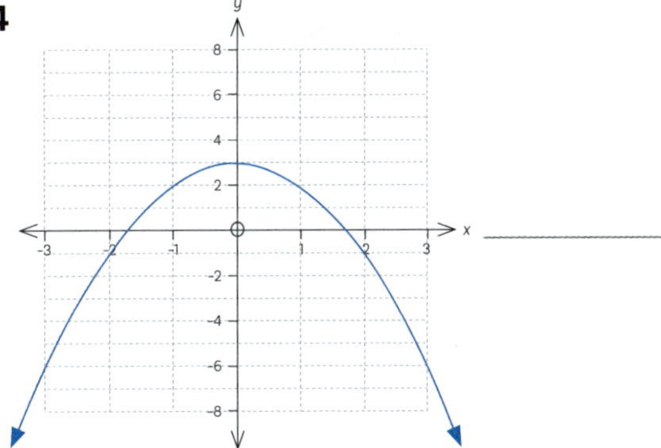

____

5

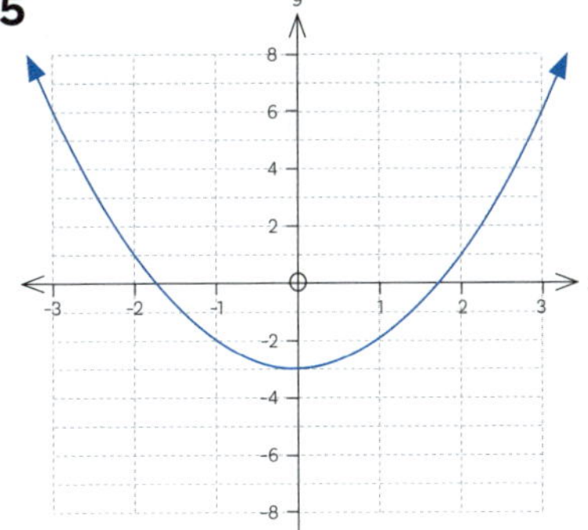

____

6

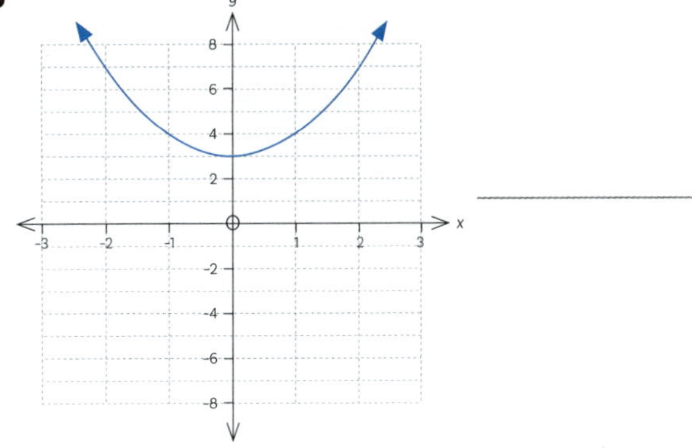

____

7

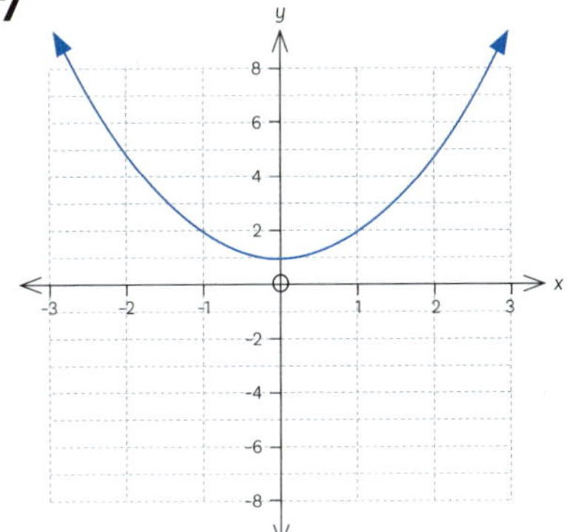

____

8

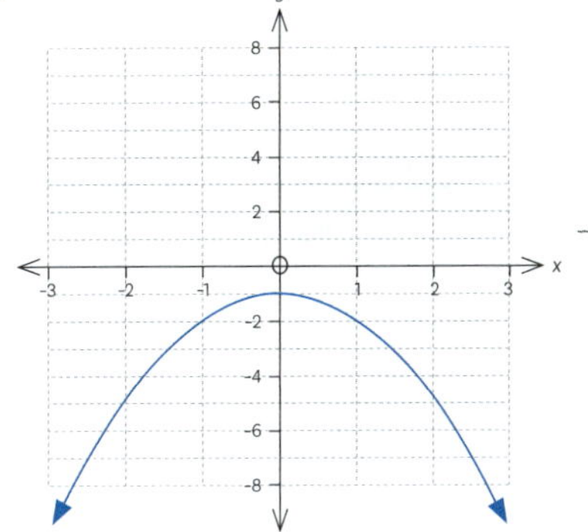

____

ISBN: 9780170497978

MEASUREMENT

The language of measurement

Volume and capacity

- **Volume** measures how much **space** is taken up by an object. Units: mm^3, cm^3, m^3.
- **Capacity** measures the **amount that an object can hold**. Units: mL, L.
- Sometimes these terms are used interchangeably.

Example: Consider a drink bottle.
Its volume is the amount of space taken up by the bottle.
Its capacity is the amount of water that the bottle can hold.

Match these words to measurement ideas below.

long	warm	cold	gradient	fever	era
hot	wide	stretch	heat	steep	pitch
heavy	decline	long	space	load	icy
incline	far	bulk	room	age	light
slant	slope	distance	period	reach	flat

Length ______ ______ ______ ______ ______ ______

Temperature ______ ______ ______ ______ ______ ______

Volume/capacity ______ ______ ______

Angle ______ ______ ______ ______ ______ ______ ______ ______

Time ______ ______ ______ ______

Mass ______ ______ ______

 ISBN: 9780170497978

Measuring devices

Match these measuring devices to what they would be used to measure.

tape measure	syringe	scales	stopwatch	protractor
clinometer	ruler	compass	cup	measuring cup
tablespoon	pedometer	clock	measuring cylinder	pipette
timer	teaspoon	thermometer	odometer	spring balance

Length ____________________

____

____

____

Mass ____________________

____

Time ____________________

____

____

Temperature ____________________

Capacity ____________________

____

____

____

____

____

____

Angle ____________________

____

____

These pictures might help if you are not familiar with some of the devices.

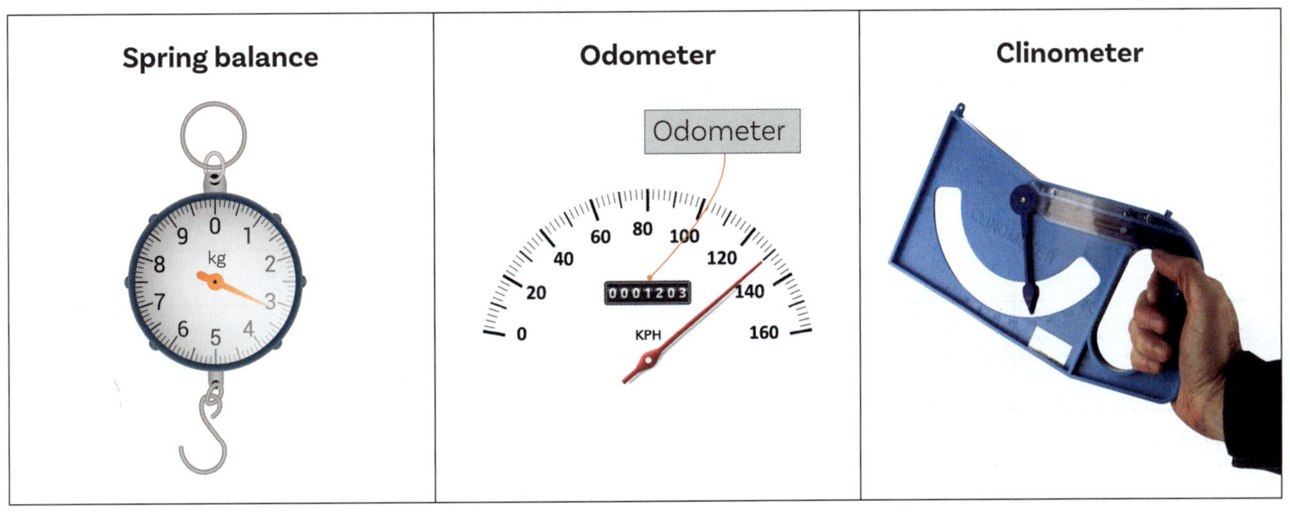

ISBN: 9780170497978

Units

Abbreviations (shortened versions) for units

s	cm	m	c	ha	L
kg	cc	min	mg	MB	cal
m^2	g	t	mL	m^3	Tbsp
mm	tsp	°C	km	kJ	GB

Complete the table by matching the abbreviations to the units, and write what each is used for.

Unit of measurement	Shortened version	Used to measure (length, mass, volume, capacity, time, temperature, area, energy or data)
minute		
metre	*m*	*length*
milligram		
kilometre		
tablespoon		
kilogram		
cup		
hectare		
gram		
millimetre		
litre		
calorie		
gigabyte		
tonne		
centimetre		
degrees Celsius		
second		
megabyte		
millilitre		
teaspoon		
kilojoule		
cubic metre		
square metre		
cubic centimetre		

ISBN: 9780170497978

Length

- The basic unit for measuring length is the **metre**.
- All other units of length in the metric system are based on the metre.

Use the following chart to help you convert lengths.

µ is the Greek letter *mu* (pronounced 'mew'), and in this context it means **one millionth** (of a metre).

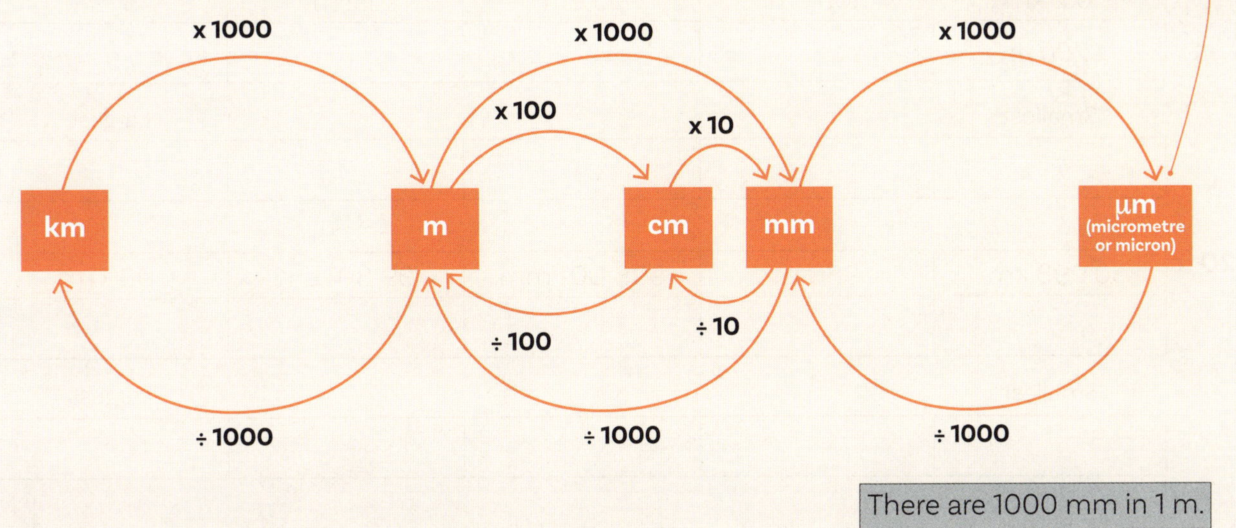

Example: How many millimetres are in 3.7 metres?

3.7 m = 3.7 x 1000
= 3700 mm

Highlight the correct conversion for each of the following.

1	231 mm	0.231 m	23.1 m
		2.31 cm	23 100 µm
3	150 m	1.5 km	1500 cm
		15 000 mm	15 000 cm
5	4.3 km	430 000 mm	430 000 cm
		43 m	430 m

2	21 cm	21 000 µm	2.1 mm
		210 mm	0.0021 m
4	3.01 m	0.0301 km	310 cm
		301 00 mm	3010 mm
6	9.888 km	98 880 mm	98 888 m
		988.8 m	988 800 cm

Convert the following.

7 16 m = ______________ cm

8 9 mm = ______________ µm

9 3 km = ______________ m

10 21 cm = ______________ m

11 4000 m = ______________ km

12 5.5 cm = ______________ mm

13 2 m = ______________ mm

14 1800 µm = ______________ cm

ISBN: 9780170497978

Highlight the greater length.

15 13 cm 140 mm

16 2230 m 2.32 km

17 32 m 325 cm

18 742 mm 0.74 m

19 Put these lengths in order from smallest to largest. Hint: Rewrite them using the same units.

0.2 km	105 cm	15 cm	1.2 m	25 mm
200 m				

Smallest / Largest

Smallest				Largest

20

0.998 km	980 m	998 001 mm	99 801 cm	989 m

Smallest				Largest

Circle or highlight the most likely unit of length for the following.

21 The length of a bedroom.

km m cm mm

22 The thickness of a finger.

km m cm mm

23 The length of a shoelace.

km m cm mm

24 The distance from Taupō to Whanganui.

km m cm mm

25 The width of this book.

km m cm mm

26 The thickness of a plate.

km m cm mm

Estimating length

From the column on the right, select the most likely length for the following.

27 The height of a coffee mug. ______________ 12 m

28 The height of a drink bottle. ______________ 4.9 cm

29 The length of a basketball court. ______________ 21.1 km

30 The distance for a half marathon. ______________ 80 mm

31 The height of a fridge. ______________ 16.5 cm

32 The height of a street light. ______________ 28.65 m

33 The width of a human tongue. ______________ 1.8 m

ISBN: 9780170497978

Mass

- The basic unit for measuring mass is the **gram**.
- All other units of mass in the metric system are based on the gram.
- Mass is often mistakenly called weight.
  Weight is a measure of the pull of gravity on an object and is measured in **newtons**.
  Mass is the amount of matter an object contains and is measured in **grams**.

Use the following chart to help you convert mass.

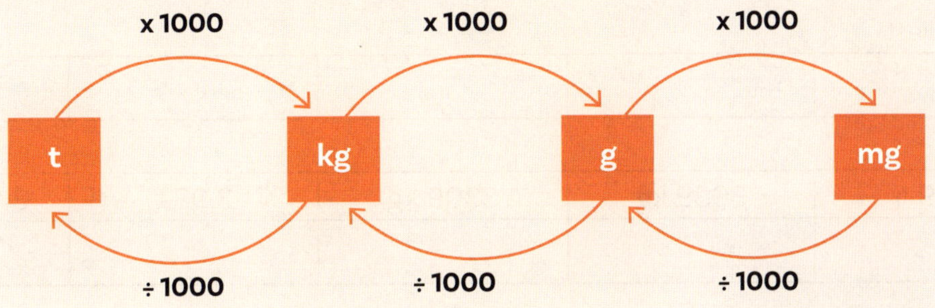

There are 1000 g in 1 kg.

Example: How many grams are there in 2.6 kilograms?

2.6 kg = 2.6 x 1000
= 2600 g

Highlight the correct conversion for each of the following.

1	0.15 kg	150 000 mg	0.0015 t
		150 g	0.015 t
3	7600 mg	0.076 kg	7.6 g
		0.076 g	76 g
5	3.4 t	34 000 kg	3400 kg
		34 000 g	340 000 mg

2	2100 g	0.21 kg	210 000 g
		2.1 kg	0.021 t
4	5.34 g	5430 mg	534 mg
		0.00534 kg	0.00543 kg
6	0.0087 t	8070 g	8.77 kg
		8700 g	870 000 mg

Convert the following.

7 520 mg = ______________ g

8 0.7 t = ______________ kg

9 931 kg = ______________ t

10 81 g = ______________ mg

11 655 g = ______________ kg

12 23 kg = ______________ g

13 5392 g = ______________ kg

14 2.6 kg = ______________ mg

Highlight the greater mass.

15 0.81 kg 801 g

16 92 g 90 000 mg

17 0.05 t 53 kg

18 0.00787 t 7780 g

19 Put these masses in order from smallest to largest. Hint: Rewrite them using the same units.

81 100 g	0.080 t	81 kg	8100 g	810 000 mg

Smallest				Largest

20

3.39 t	3039 kg	3309 kg	3.93 t	3 039 000 g

Smallest				Largest

Circle or highlight the most likely unit of mass for the following.

21 The mass of a cat.

t kg g mg

22 The amount of butter in a biscuit recipe.

t kg g mg

23 The mass of a banana.

t kg g mg

24 The mass of a ladybird.

t kg g mg

25 The mass of a bus.

t kg g mg

26 The mass of a bowling ball.

t kg g mg

Estimating mass

From the column on the right, select the most likely mass of the following.

27 A cellphone. ______________ 3490 kg

28 An orca. ______________ 800 g

29 A small dog. ______________ 10.5 kg

30 A large potato. ______________ 19 g

31 This book. ______________ 245 g

32 A pebble. ______________ 145 g

 ISBN: 9780170497978

Capacity (volume)

- The basic unit for measuring capacity is the **litre**.
- All other units of capacity in the metric system are based on the litre.

Use the following chart to help you convert capacity.

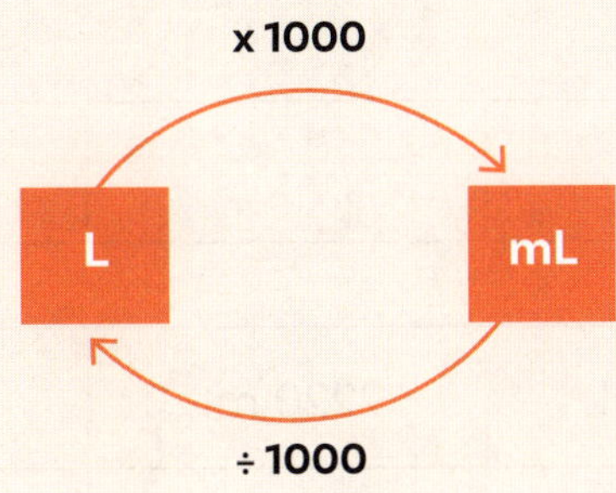

There are 1000 mL in 1 L.

Example: How many millilitres are there in 8.6 litres?

8.6 L = 8.6 x 1000
= 8600 mL

Highlight the correct conversion for each of the following.

1	0.27 L	2700 mL	270 mL
		27 mL	0.00027 mL
2	540 mL	5 430 000 L	0.054 L
		0.54 L	0.5 L
3	1119 mL	11.19 L	1.199 L
		1.119 L	0.1119 L
4	0.0093 L	8.9 mL	0.93 mL
		0.00093 mL	9.3 mL

Convert the following.

5 2 L = ____________ mL

6 5700 mL = ____________ L

7 183 mL = ____________ L

8 72 L = ____________ mL

9 3.1 L = ____________ mL

10 20 600 mL = ____________ L

11 5 mL = ____________ L

12 1.99 L = ____________ mL

ISBN: 9780170497978

13 Put these capacities in order from smallest to largest. Hint: Rewrite them using the same units.

0.908 L	809 mL	0.89 L	1.9 L	900 mL

Smallest Largest

14

2.02 L	2002 mL	2220 mL	2.202 L	2.2 L

Smallest Largest

Estimating capacity

From the column on the right, select the most likely capacity of the following.

15 A coffee mug. ____________ 1.6 L

16 A wheelie bin. ____________ 5 L

17 A shampoo bottle. ____________ 6.5 mL

18 A fridge. ____________ 500 mL

19 A swimming pool. ____________ 240 L

20 A kettle. ____________ 450 L

21 A watering can. ____________ 108 000 L

22 A human eyeball. ____________ 350 mL

 ISBN: 9780170497978

Appropriate units

- Length is measured in mm, cm, m or km.
- Mass is measured in mg, g, kg or t.
- Capacity is measured in mL or L.

Example: The mass of this tūī would be measured in which of the following units?

L kg cm g

The most appropriate answer is g (grams).

Circle or highlight the most appropriate unit of measurement for the following.

1 The amount of detergent in a bottle.

mL kg m g

2 The mass of a fly.

t L mm mg

3 The length of a gymnasium.

m mL cm g

4 The mass of a cat.

t kg g L

5 The mass of a school bag.

cm kg t mg

6 The amount of milk in a bottle.

g m mg mL

7 The amount of flour in a cake recipe.

mL m L g

8 The width of a swimming pool.

km kg L m

9 The amount of mayonnaise in a sandwich.

kg mL g cm

10 The length of a rabbit.

km kg cm L

11 The capacity of a bath.

mL t L kg

12 The mass of a car.

L kg g t

13 The mass of an elephant.

mL kg g t

14 The length of a classroom.

cm g mm m

15 The amount of baking soda in a teaspoon.

mL L g mg

16 The mass of a sofa.

mL kg g mg

ISBN: 9780170497978

Estimating quantities

Use the most appropriate quantities from the right column to complete the following sentences.

1	The weight of a hippo is most likely to be	________	8849 m
2	The length of the Auckland Harbour Bridge is most likely to be	________	6 L
3	The capacity of an average human stomach is most likely to be	________	196 cm
4	The mass of a watermelon is most likely to be	________	91.4 m
5	The length of a cricket pitch is most likely to be	________	12 000 kg
6	The height of the Auckland Sky Tower is most likely to be	________	50 L
7	The mass of a kiwi is most likely to be	________	150 L
8	The length of a hockey field is most likely to be	________	57 g
9	The height of a basketball hoop is most likely to be	________	39.47 m
10	The amount of air in a balloon is most likely to be	________	5.5 kg
11	The mass of a bus is most likely to be	________	1.5 L
12	The length of a standard surfboard is most likely to be	________	3500 kg
13	The length of a 737 aeroplane is most likely to be	________	1020 m
14	The mass of a loaf of bread is most likely to be	________	328 m
15	The capacity of a fish tank is most likely to be	________	3.05 m
16	The height of Mt Everest is most likely to be	________	650 g
17	The capacity of a car's fuel tank is most likely to be	________	1.8 m
18	The height of a garden fence is most likely to be	________	2.5 kg
19	The mass of a laptop charger is most likely to be	________	400 g
20	The mass of a tennis ball is most likely to be	________	20.12 m

 ISBN: 9780170497978

Time

Converting units

- Time can be measured in seconds (s), minutes (min), hours (h), days (d), etc.

Use the following chart to help you convert times.

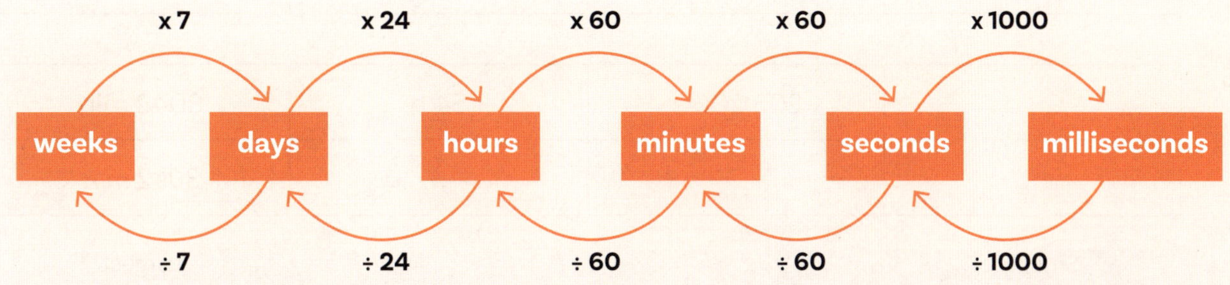

You also need to know: 1 that there are about four weeks in a month.
2 the names and order of the 12 months in a year.

There are 60 s in 1 min.

Example: How many seconds are in 12 minutes?

12 min = 12 x 60
= 720 s

Highlight the correct conversion for each of the following.

1	180 seconds	3 hours	3 min
		7.5 days	2 min
3	4 weeks	4100 min	4032 min
		672 hours	241 000 min

2	25 hours	150 min	1 day
		5 days	1500 min
4	3 days	4320 hours	48 hours
		21 hours	259 000 min

Convert the following.

5 360 s = ____________ min

6 4 d = ____________ h

7 240 min = ____________ h

8 1.5 h = ____________ min

9 150 min = ____________ s

10 132 h = ____________ d

Highlight the longer period of time.

11 80 min 1.5 h

12 61 h 2.5 d

13 250 s 4 min

14 110 min 5 h

15 9 h 545 min

16 1.5 min 100 s

17 Put these times in order from smallest to largest. Hint: Rewrite them using the same units.

299 min	0.2 d	16 800 s	4.9 h
299 min			

Smallest | | | Largest

18

2.1 d	205 200 s	54 h	3042 min
			3042 min

Smallest | | | Largest

Circle or highlight the most likely unit of time for the following.

19 The time it takes to walk to school.

months weeks minutes days

20 The time it takes to grow vegetables.

minutes months years seconds

21 The time it takes to tie your shoelaces.

milliseconds days seconds hours

22 The time it takes to boil water.

seconds days milliseconds minutes

23 The time it takes a valley to form.

years months hours days

24 The time it takes to recover from a cold.

years milliseconds minutes days

Estimating time

From the column on the right, select the most likely length of time for the following.

25	The time it takes to run 100 m.	______________	2 hours
26	The time it takes to brush your teeth.	______________	45 min
27	The time it takes to cook a meal.	______________	1 year
28	The time it takes Earth to orbit the sun.	______________	19 s
29	The time it takes a plastic bag to decompose.	______________	2 min
30	The time it takes to watch a movie.	______________	20 years

 ISBN: 9780170497978

Stopwatches

- When using a stopwatch, the time is displayed from left to right.

When timing a period shorter than one hour, a digital stopwatch will look something like this:

This reads 8 minutes, 16 seconds and 40 one hundredths of a second.

Some screens look a little different:

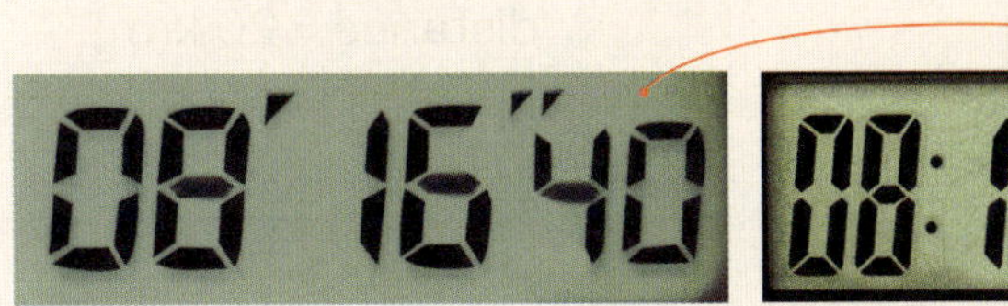

The last two digits might be smaller or the digits might be separated by different symbols.

Highlight the shorter times.

1	00:58.42	00:59.10	**2**	1:10.65	01:09.65
3	12:14.35	14:12.35	**4**	3:12.50	03:12.05

5 Put these times in order from quickest to slowest.

01:25.99	01:52.99	02:09.99	00:26.90	00:25.99

Quickest				Slowest

6 Pieter and Hazel completed a puzzle. Below are their times.

Pieter 02:28.14 Hazel 01:47.87

a Who was faster at the puzzle? ______________________

b Write Pieter's time in words. ______________________

c How much faster was Hazel at the puzzle? ______________________

7 John's 200 m race time was 08:06:40 and Leon's was 08:07:42.
How much quicker would Leon have to be to equal John's time? ______________________

ISBN: 9780170497978

Speed

- Speed is a **derived measure** because it is calculated using two other measures: distance and time.
- Any of the three variables can be calculated if the other two are known.
- Common units for speed are metres per second (m/s) and kilometres per hour (km/h). However, other units for distances and time can be used.

Formula for calculating each	Triangles showing relationship between the three variables	Examples
speed = $\frac{\text{distance}}{\text{time}}$	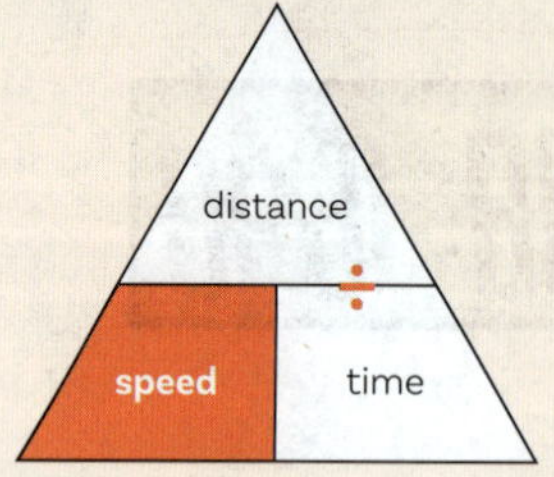	distance = 20 km time = 4 h speed = $\frac{\text{distance}}{\text{time}}$ = $\frac{20}{4}$ = 5 km/h
distance = speed x time	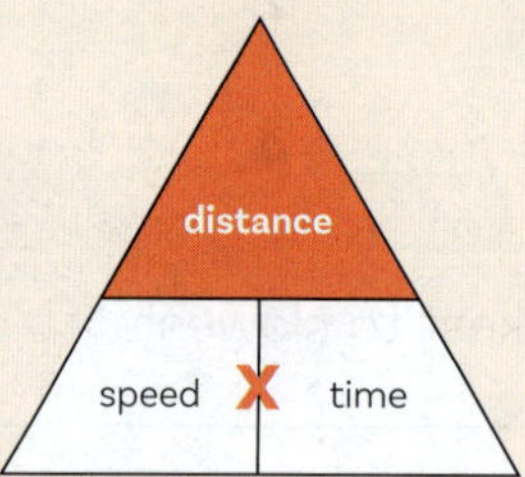	speed = 3 m/s time = 40 s distance = speed x time = 3 x 40 = 120 m
time = $\frac{\text{distance}}{\text{speed}}$	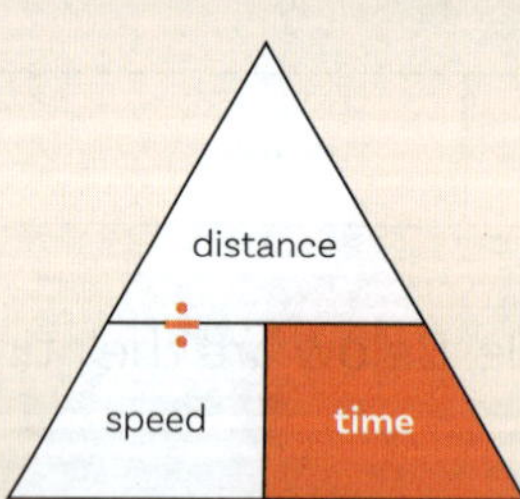	distance = 45 km speed = 30 km/h time = $\frac{\text{distance}}{\text{speed}}$ = $\frac{45}{30}$ = 1.5 h

Highlight the correct speed, distance or time for these situations.

1	distance = 20 m time = 5 s	0.4 m/s	4 km/s
		4 m/h	4 m/s
3	speed = 80 km/h time = 1.5 h	120 m	12 km
		1.2 km	120 km

2	distance = 350 km time = 5 h	70 m/s	70 km/h
		7 km/h	70 km/s
4	distance = 200 m speed = 40 m/s	5 min	0.5 s
		5 s	50 s

ISBN: 9780170497978

Calculate the following speeds.

5 A car travels 120 kilometres in 2 hours. Calculate its average speed.

____

6 A ball rolls 75 metres in 15 seconds. Calculate its speed.

____

7 A high-speed train covers 820 km in 2 hours and 30 minutes. Calculate its average speed.

____

8 A cyclist travels 1200 metres in 2 minutes. Calculate his average speed in m/s.

____

Calculate the following distances.

9 A dog runs at 6 m/s for 20 seconds. How far does it run?

____

10 A car travels at a speed of 90 km/h for 3 hours. How far does it travel?

____

11 Emma tramps at a steady speed of 4 km/h for 3.5 hours. How far does she tramp?

____

12 A bus travels at 45 km/h. How many kilometres does it cover in 20 minutes?

____

Calculate the following times.

13 A boat travels 150 kilometres at 30 km/h. How long does the trip take?

____

14 A drone flies 2400 metres at 20 m/s. How long does the flight take?

____

15 A food delivery scooter travels 12 km at a constant speed of 24 km/h. How long does it take to deliver the food?

____

16 A rollercoaster covers 1200 metres of track at an average speed of 20 m/s. How long does the ride last?

____

Answer the following questions.

17 Angela walks for 1.5 hours at a speed of 5 km/h. How far did she travel?

____

18 A cyclist rides for 3 hours and travels 60 kilometres. What is the average speed of the cyclist?

____

19 A runner completes a 10 km race in 50 minutes. What is the runner's average speed in km/h?

____

20 A 500 MB file is transferred at a speed of 5 MB/s. How long does the transfer take?

____

ISBN: 9780170497978

Scales

Reading scales

- Find **zero** on the scale to make sure that you read in the **correct direction**.
- If zero is not on the scale, make sure you read from smaller values to bigger values.
- Include **units** in your answer.
- Think about your answer. Does it seem reasonable?

Example:

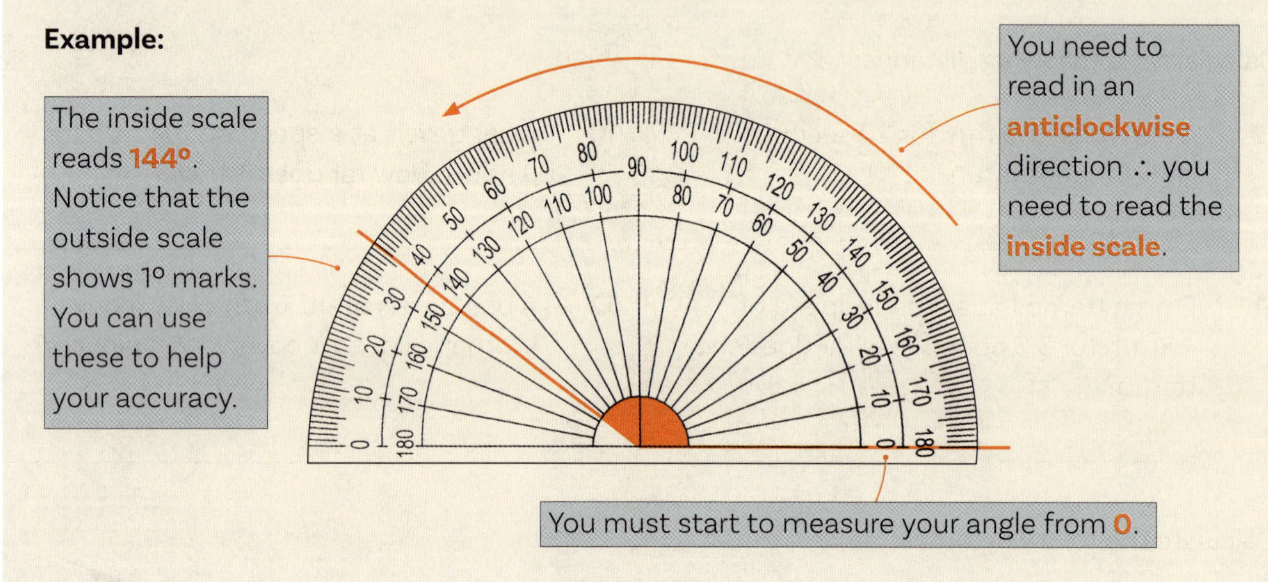

Write the measurements given by the pointers.

1

A B C

0 1 2 3 4 5 6 7
cm

A = ____________________

B = ____________________

C = ____________________

2

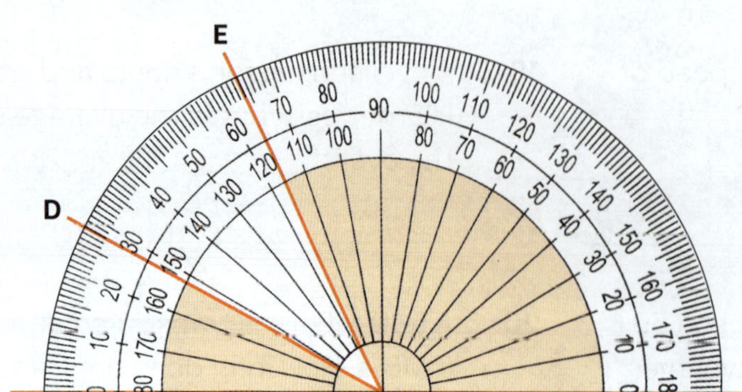

D = ____________________

E = ____________________

ISBN: 9780170497978

3

500 mL
300 mL
100 mL

____

4

____

5

__________ tank

6

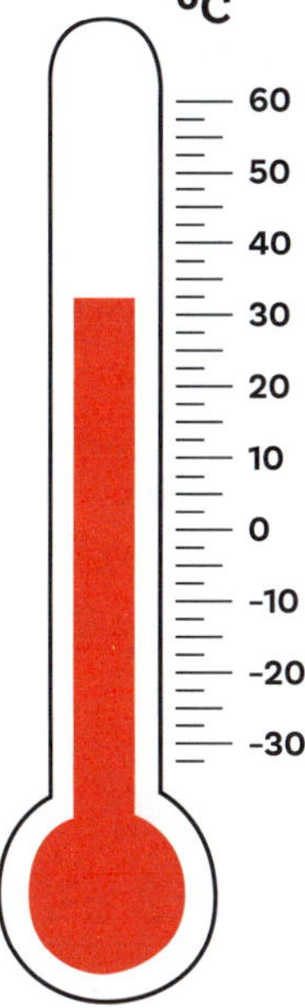

____

7

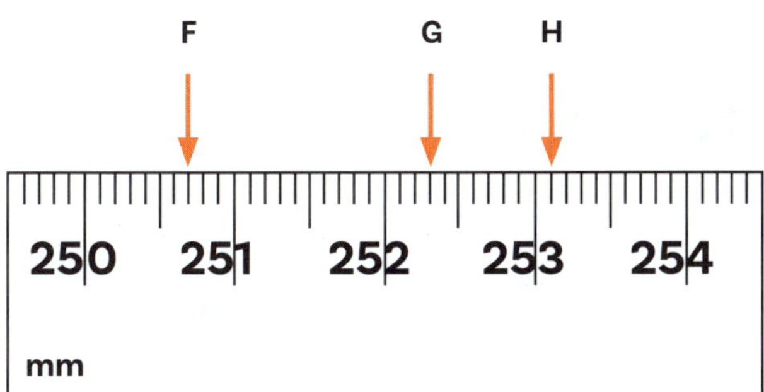

F = ____________________

G = ____________________

H = ____________________

8

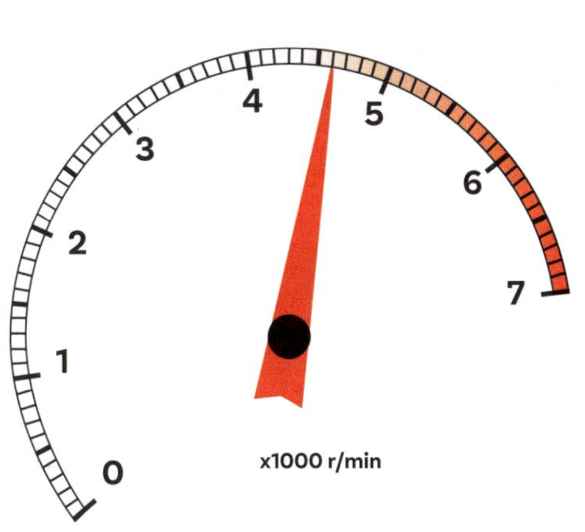

Speed = ____________________

9

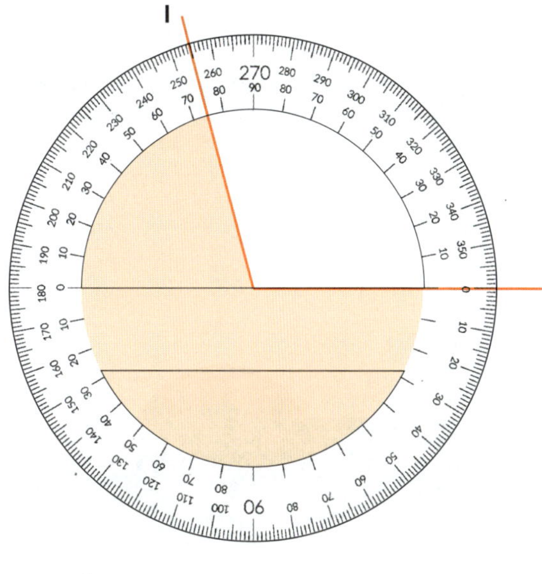

I = ____________________

ISBN: 9780170497978

Showing values on scales

Colour or add an arrow to show the given measurements.

1 134°

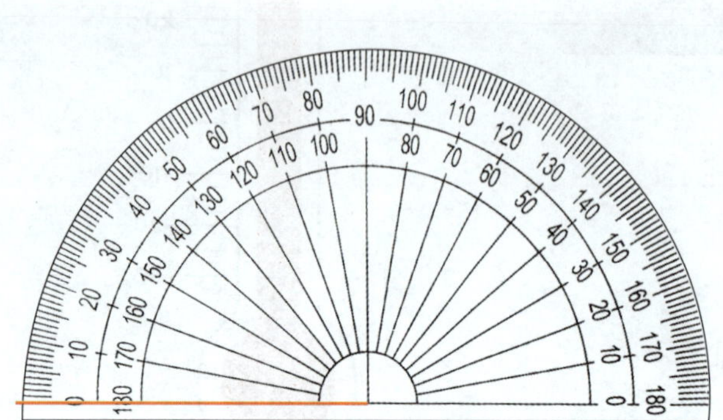

2 85 km/h

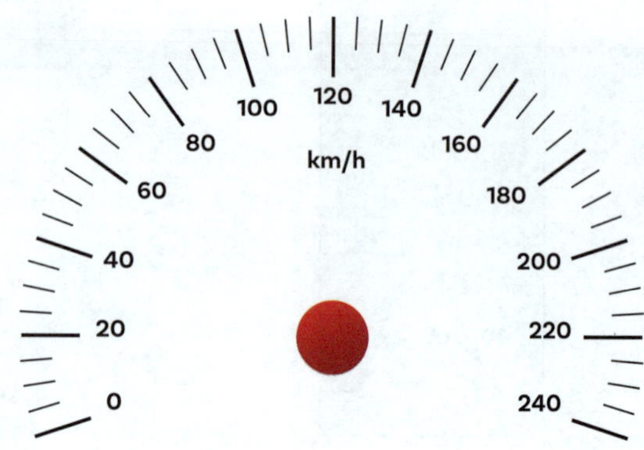

3

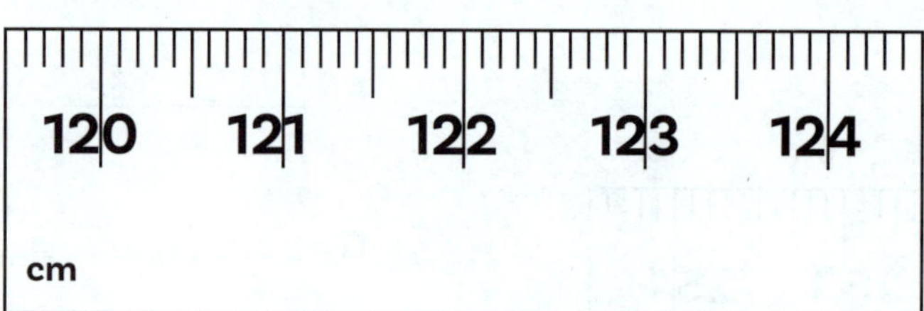

A = 123.1 cm

B = 120.4 cm

C = 121.9 cm

4 38 V

5 140 mL

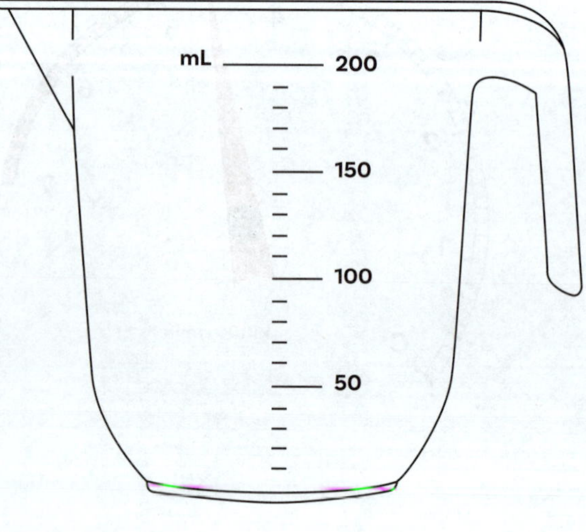

 ISBN: 9780170497978

6 295°

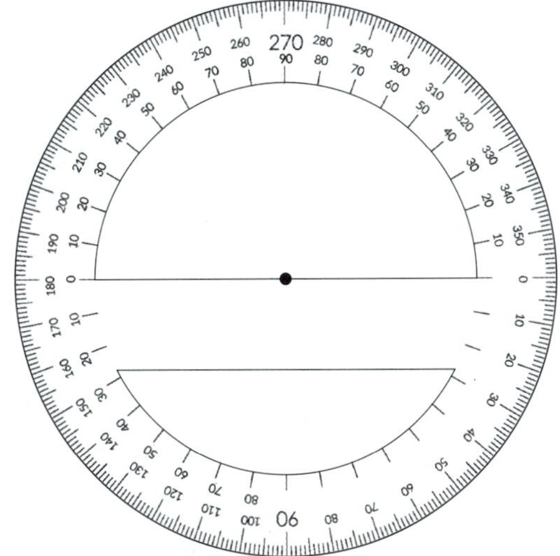

7 32.5°

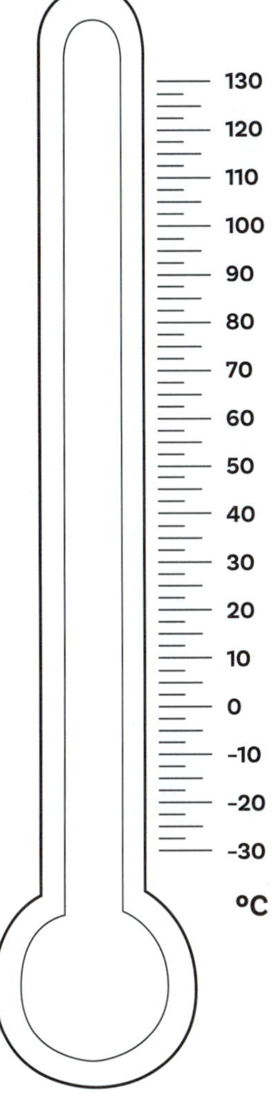

8 48 km/h

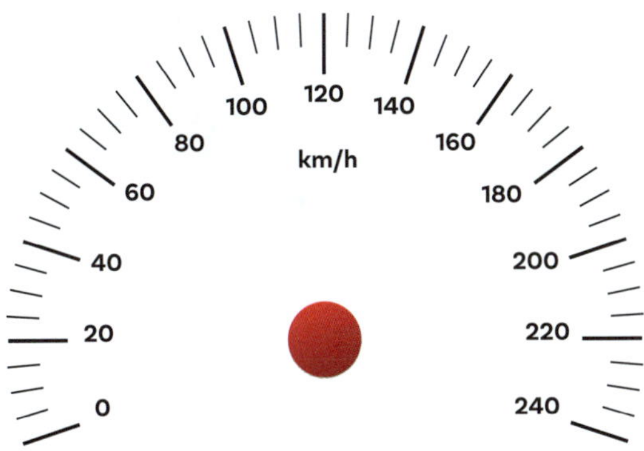

9 850 mL

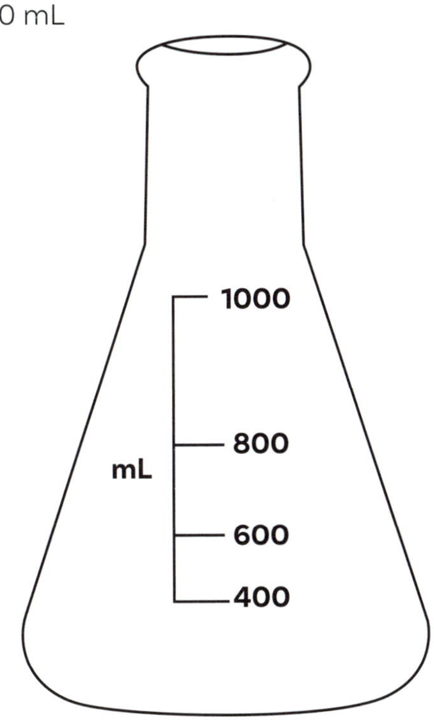

10 Five eighths of the tank.

Perimeter

Shapes with linear sides

- The perimeter is the **distance around the outside** of a two-dimensional (2D) shape.
- To find the perimeter, you need to **start at one corner** and **add** the distances around the outside of a shape.
- You can add lengths only if they are in the **same units**, so you may need to do some conversions.
- '**Regular**' means all the sides and angles in a figure are the **same**.

These symbols tell you that all the sides are equal.

Here you have the height, but it's not needed to calculate the perimeter.

Examples:

1

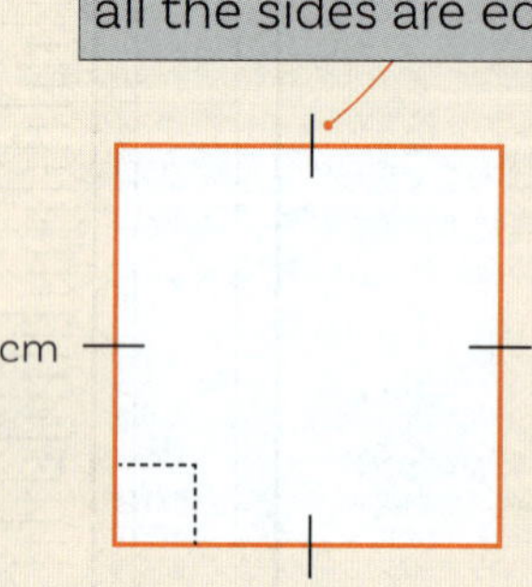

Perimeter = 3 + 3 + 3 + 3
= 12 cm

2

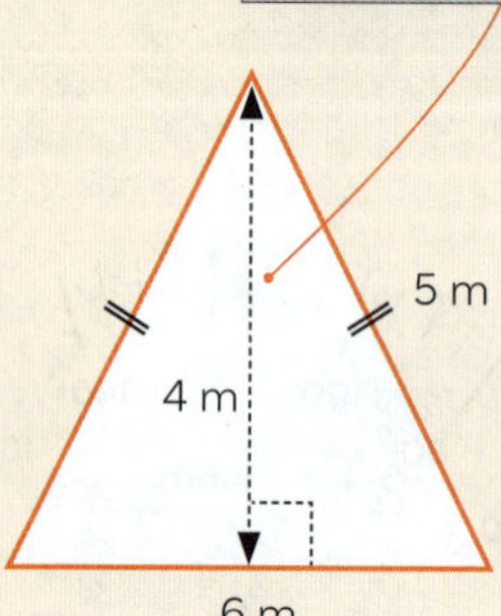

Perimeter = 5 + 5 + 6
= 16 m

Calculate the perimeters of these shapes.

1

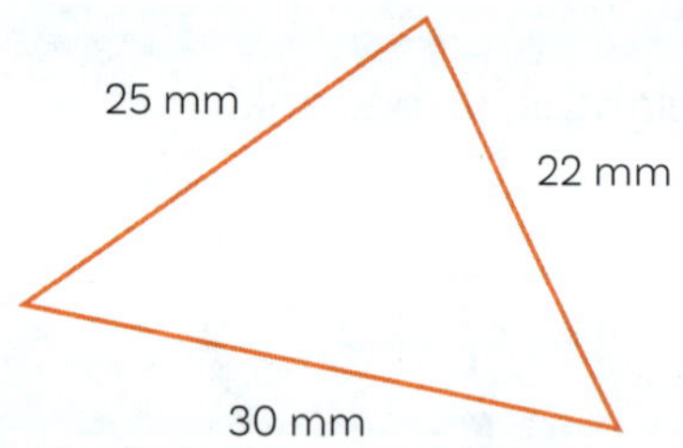

____

____

2

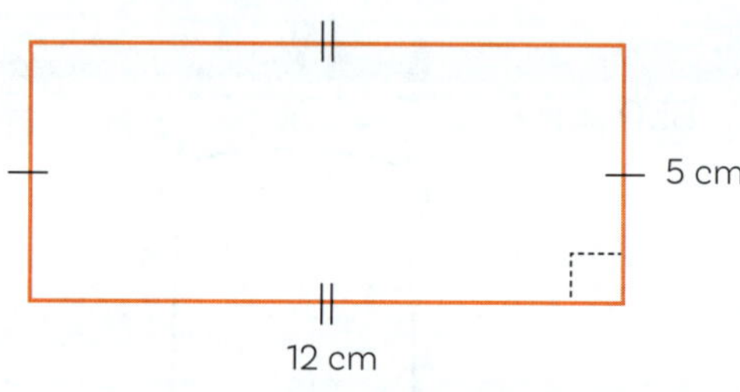

____

____

3

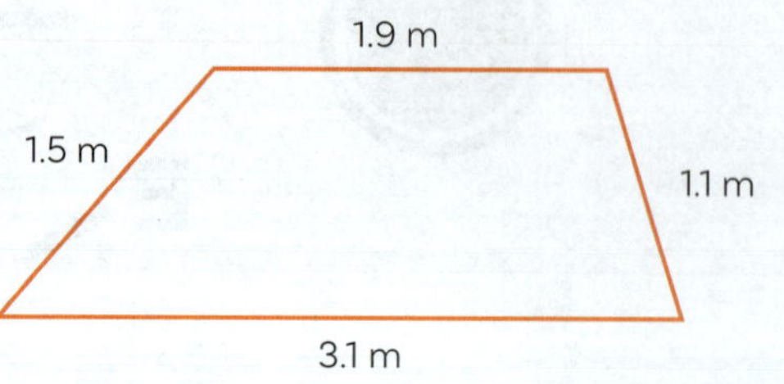

____

____

4

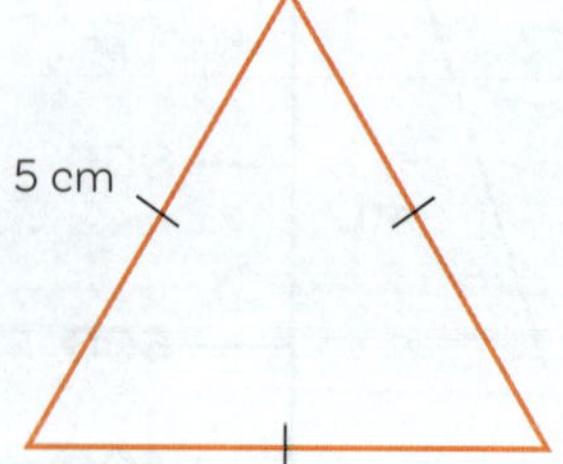

____

____

ISBN: 9780170497978

5

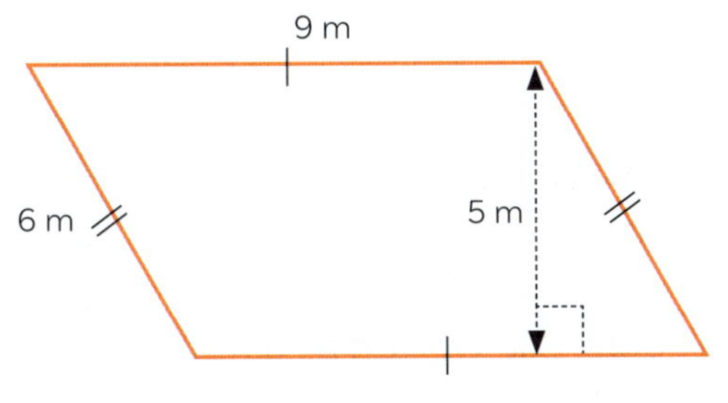

6

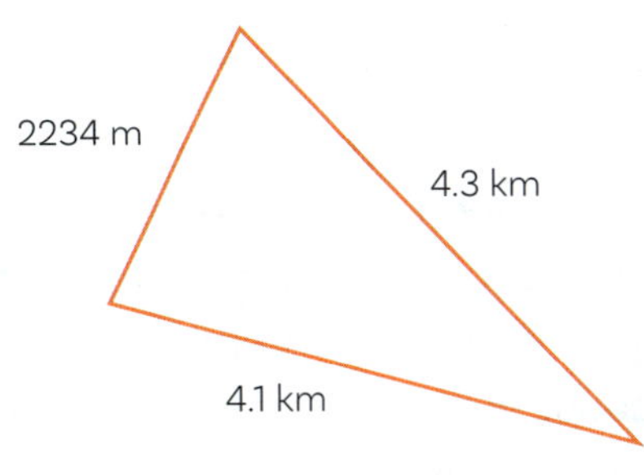

7 This is a regular hexagon.

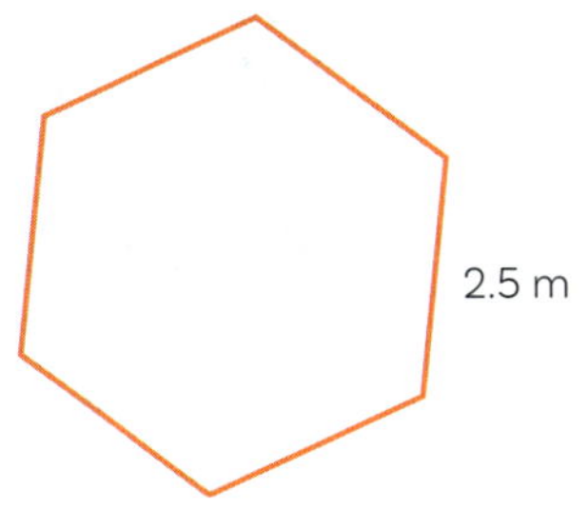

Answer the following questions.

8 The perimeter of this equilateral triangle is 36 km. How long is each side?

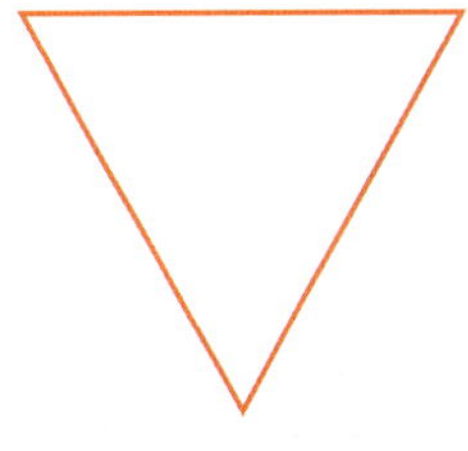

9 The perimeter of this rectangle is 160 cm. Calculate the length of side w.

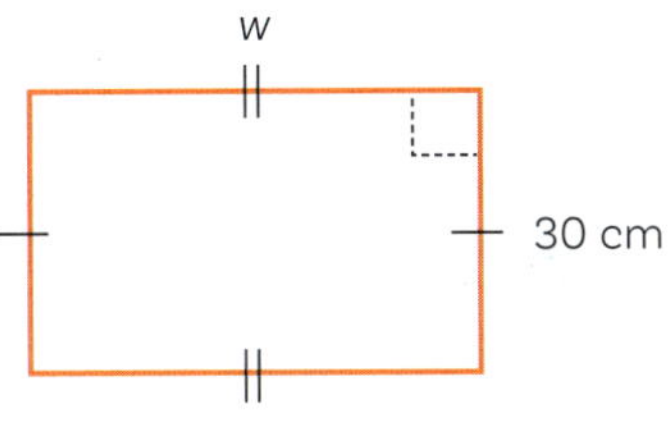

10 Javier needs to build a fence around his rectangular garden. The garden is 180 m long and 150 m wide. How much fencing will Javier need in total?

11 At the start of her workout, Eva had to jog three times around the outside of a basketball court. If the court measured 29 m by 15 m, how far did she jog?

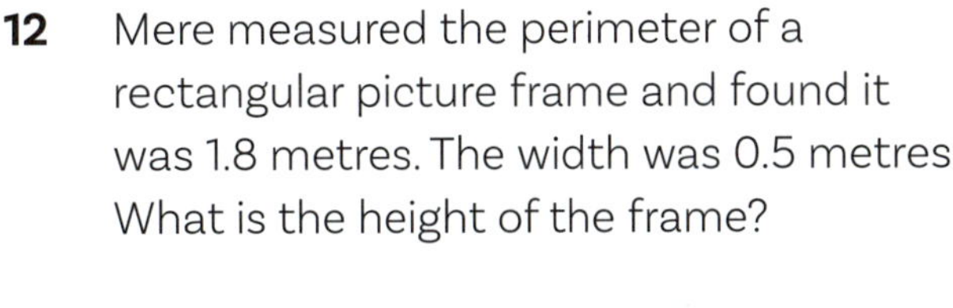

12 Mere measured the perimeter of a rectangular picture frame and found it was 1.8 metres. The width was 0.5 metres. What is the height of the frame?

ISBN: 9780170497978

Circles

- The perimeter of a circle has a special term: **circumference**.
- π (pi) is about **3.14**, and represents the number of diameters needed to make up the length of the circumference.
- Because π is an irrational number (a number which cannot be written as a fraction), you will always need to **round your answers** appropriately, and indicate the number of decimal places.

circumference = π x d

π can be found on your calculator:  SHIFT $\times 10^x$
(Do **not** use 3.14.)

d stands for **diameter** and is the distance across the circle through the centre.

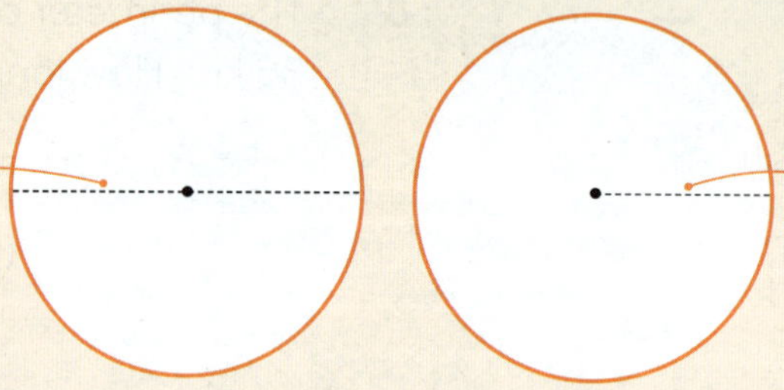

r stands for **radius** and is the distance from the centre to the perimeter of the circle.

Examples:

1

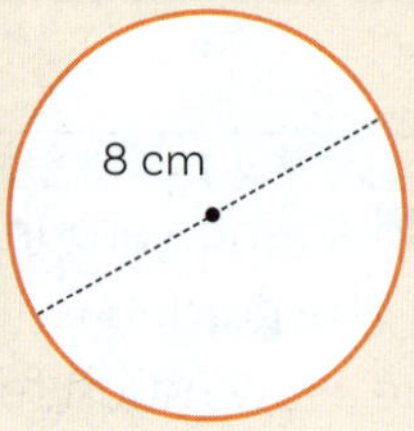

8 cm

Circumference = $\pi \times d$
= $\pi \times 8$
= 25.13 cm (2 dp)

2

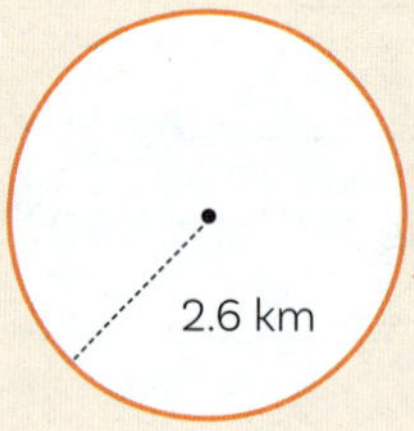

2.6 km

Circumference = $\pi \times d$
= $\pi \times (2 \times 2.6)$
= 16.34 km (2 dp)

3

Calculate the perimeter of half a circle, then add the diameter.

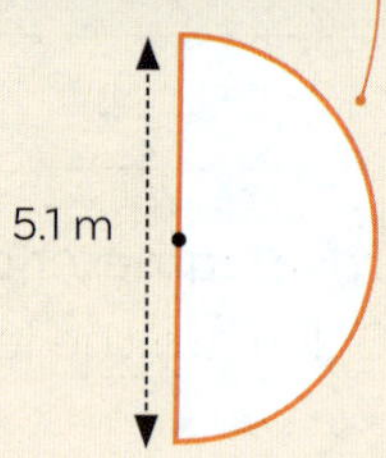

5.1 m

Perimeter = $\dfrac{\pi \times d}{2} + 5.1$
= $\dfrac{\pi \times 5.1}{2} + 5.1$
= 13.11 m (2 dp)

Calculate the perimeters of these shapes. Round your answers to 4 sf.

1

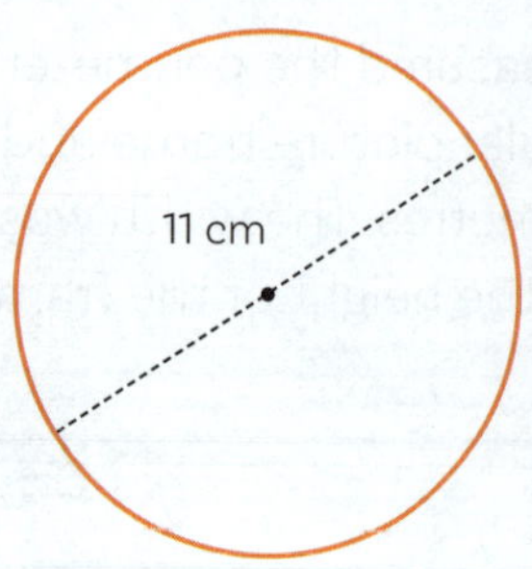

2

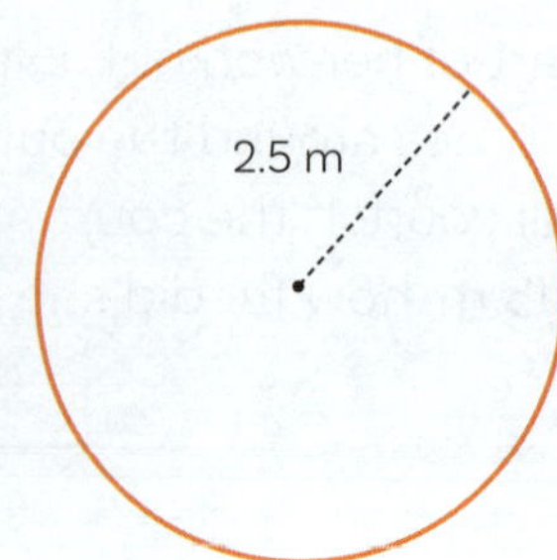

ISBN: 9780170497978

3

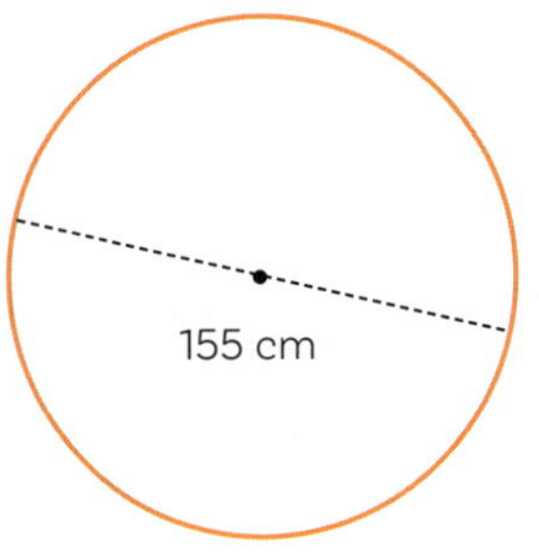

4

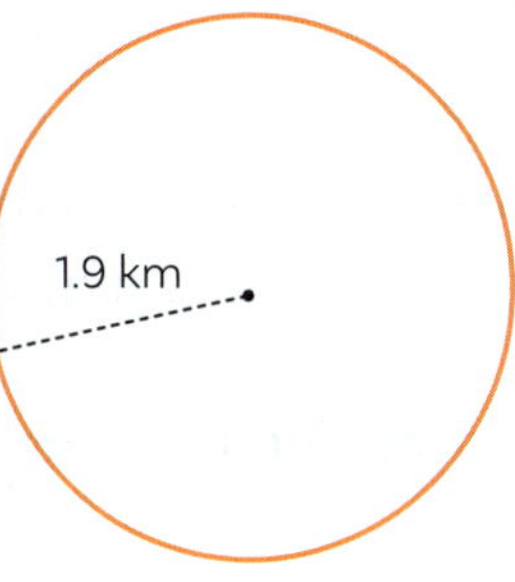

5

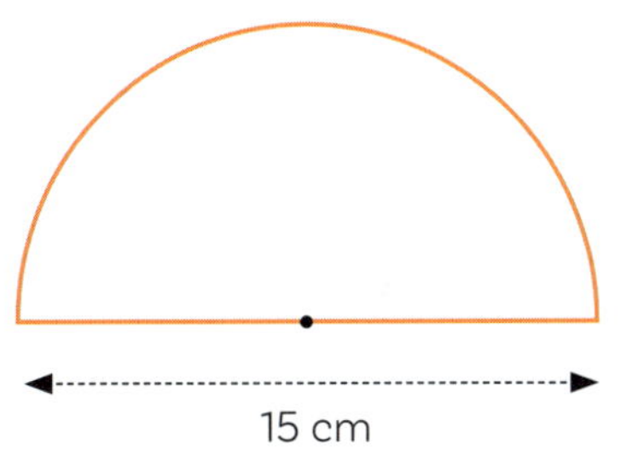

6

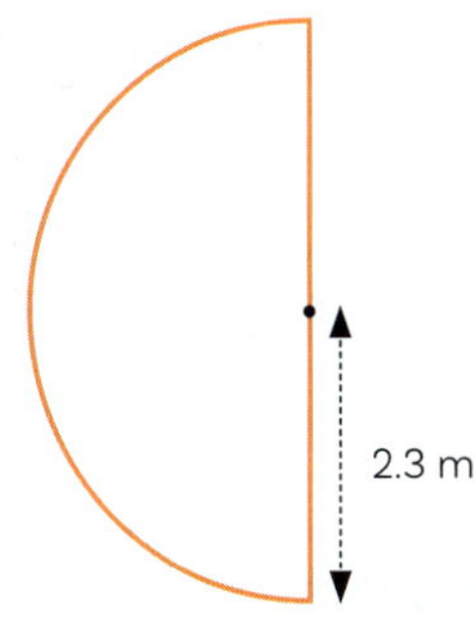

7

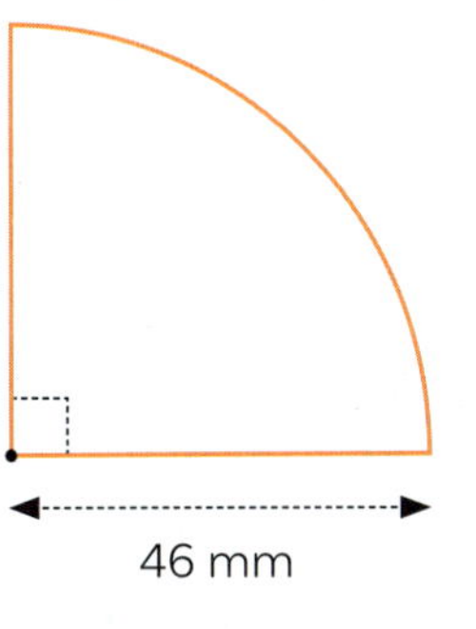

8

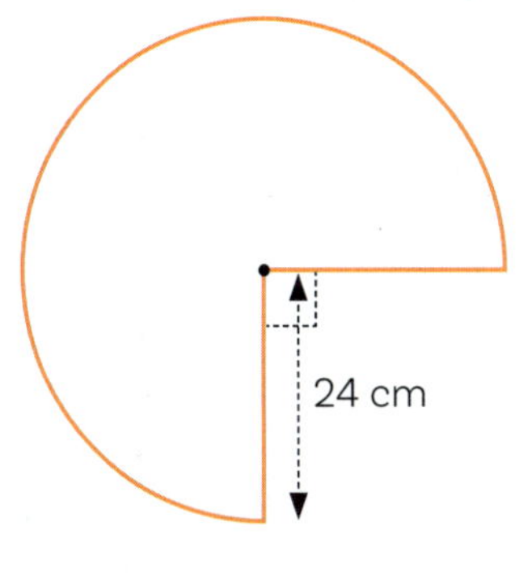

Answer the following questions.

9 A circle has a diameter of 3.1 km. Calculate its circumference.

10 A circle has a radius of 19 m. Calculate its circumference.

ISBN: 9780170497978

Compound shapes

- A compound shape is one made up of **several 'basic' shapes**.
- Not all measurements may be written on diagrams, so you might need to calculate some.
- Watch out for lengths being given in different units.

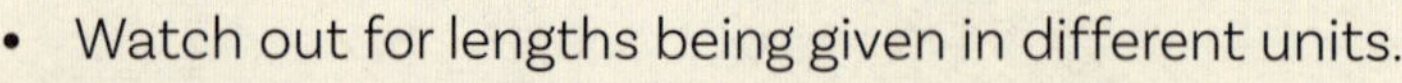

Examples:

1

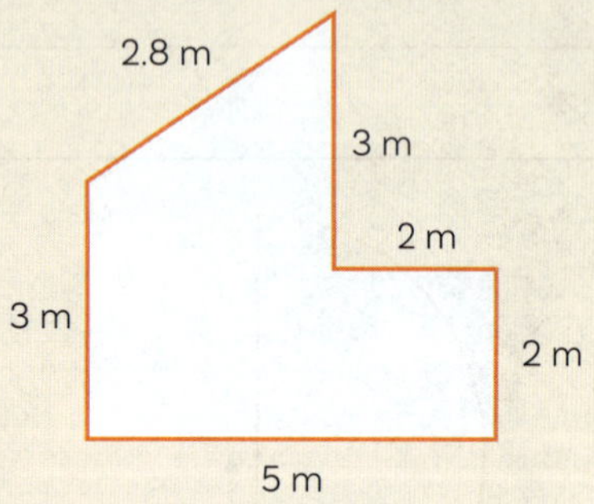

Perimeter = 2.8 + 3 + 2 + 2 + 5 + 3
= 17.8 m

2

There are two values missing here which you need to calculate.
70 - 40 = 30 cm
40 - 20 = 20 cm

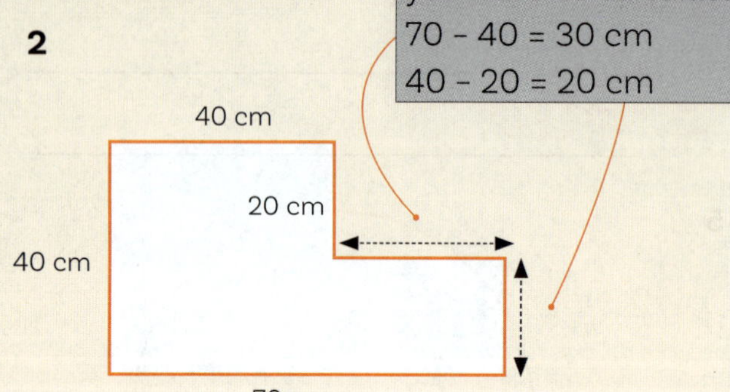

Perimeter = 40 + 20 + 30 + 20 + 70 + 40
= 220 cm

Calculate the perimeters of these compound shapes. For questions with circles, round your answer to 4 sf. For this exercise assume that angles that look like right angles are right angles.

1

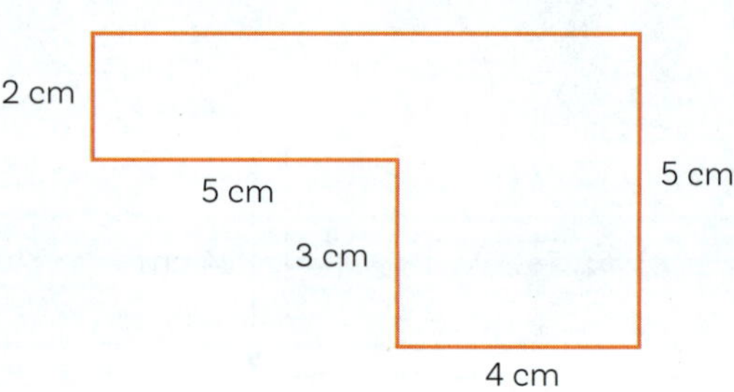

2

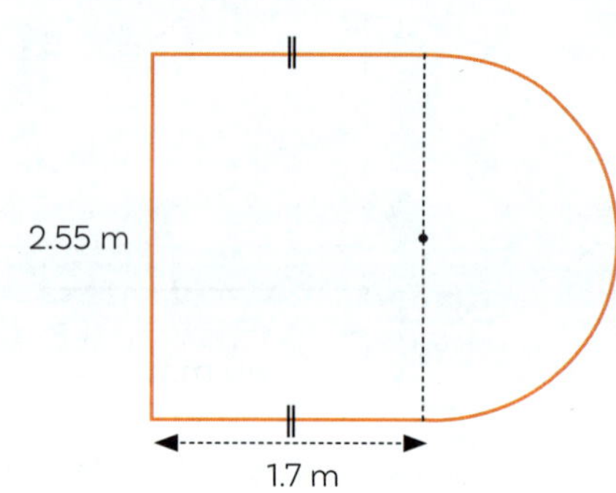

3

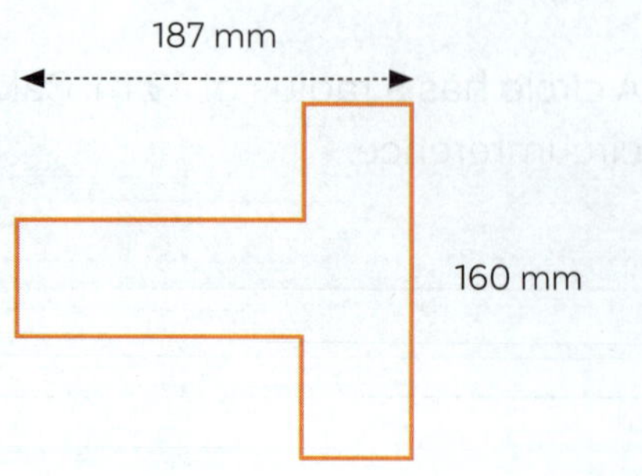

4

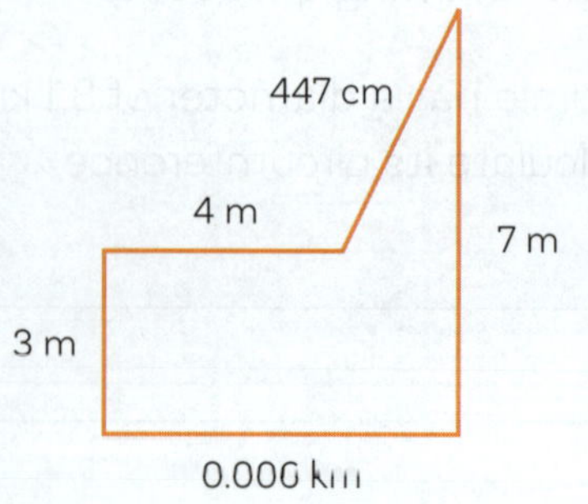

 ISBN: 9780170497978

5

2.2 m
1.3 m

6

76 cm
380 mm
19 cm

7

48 cm
63 cm
21 cm
90 cm

8

8 cm
32 cm

9

3.8 km
6.08 km

10

0.4 m
0.4 m

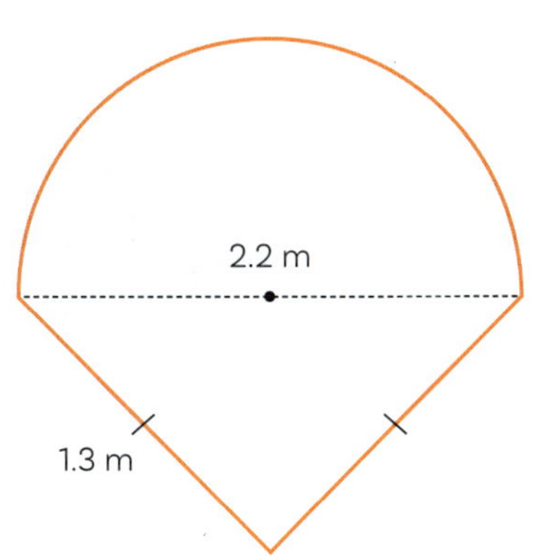

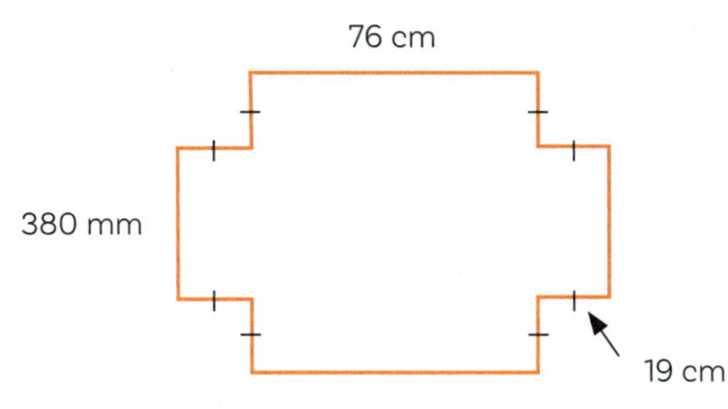

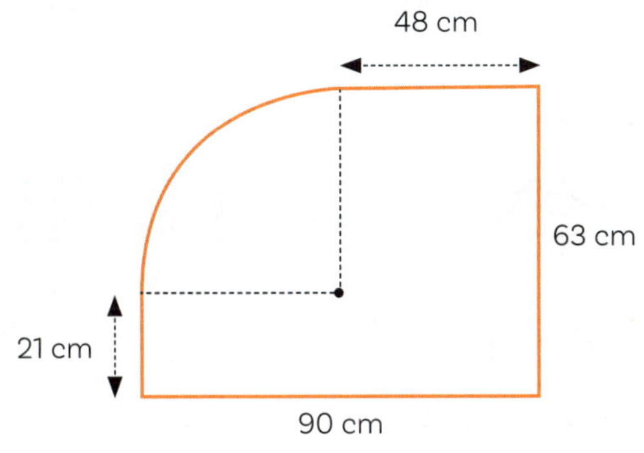

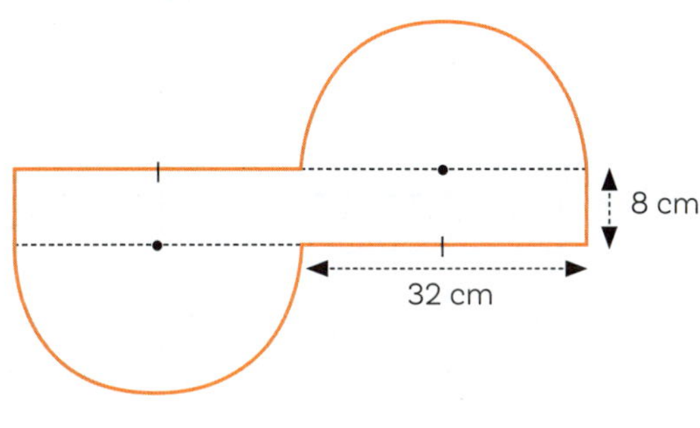

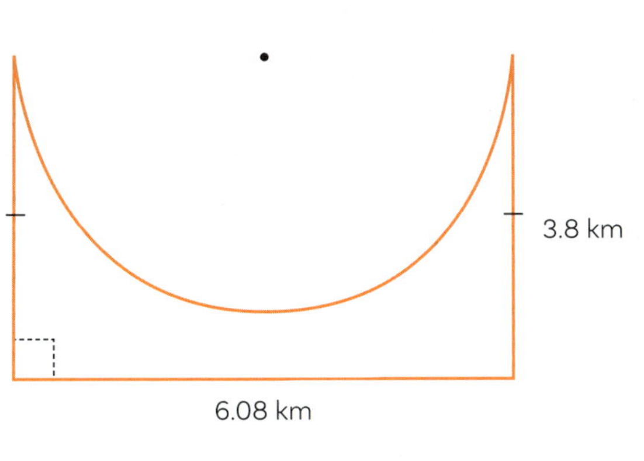

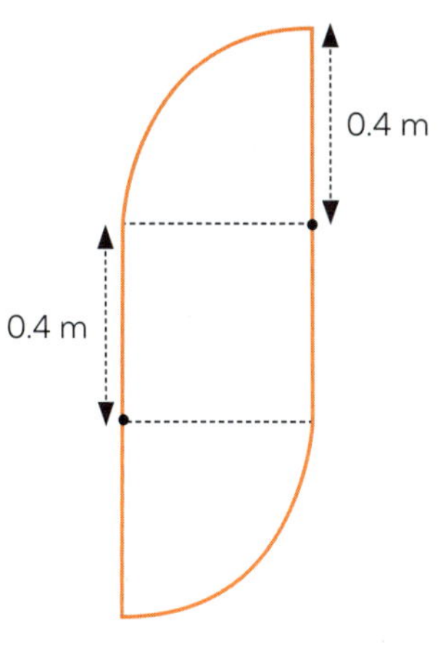

Area

Units of area

- Length is measured in mm, cm, m or km.
- Area is measured in mm², cm², m², ha (hectares) or km².
- Two-dimensional (2D) shapes have units that are squared.
- The area of a shape is a **flat surface** inside a 2D shape.

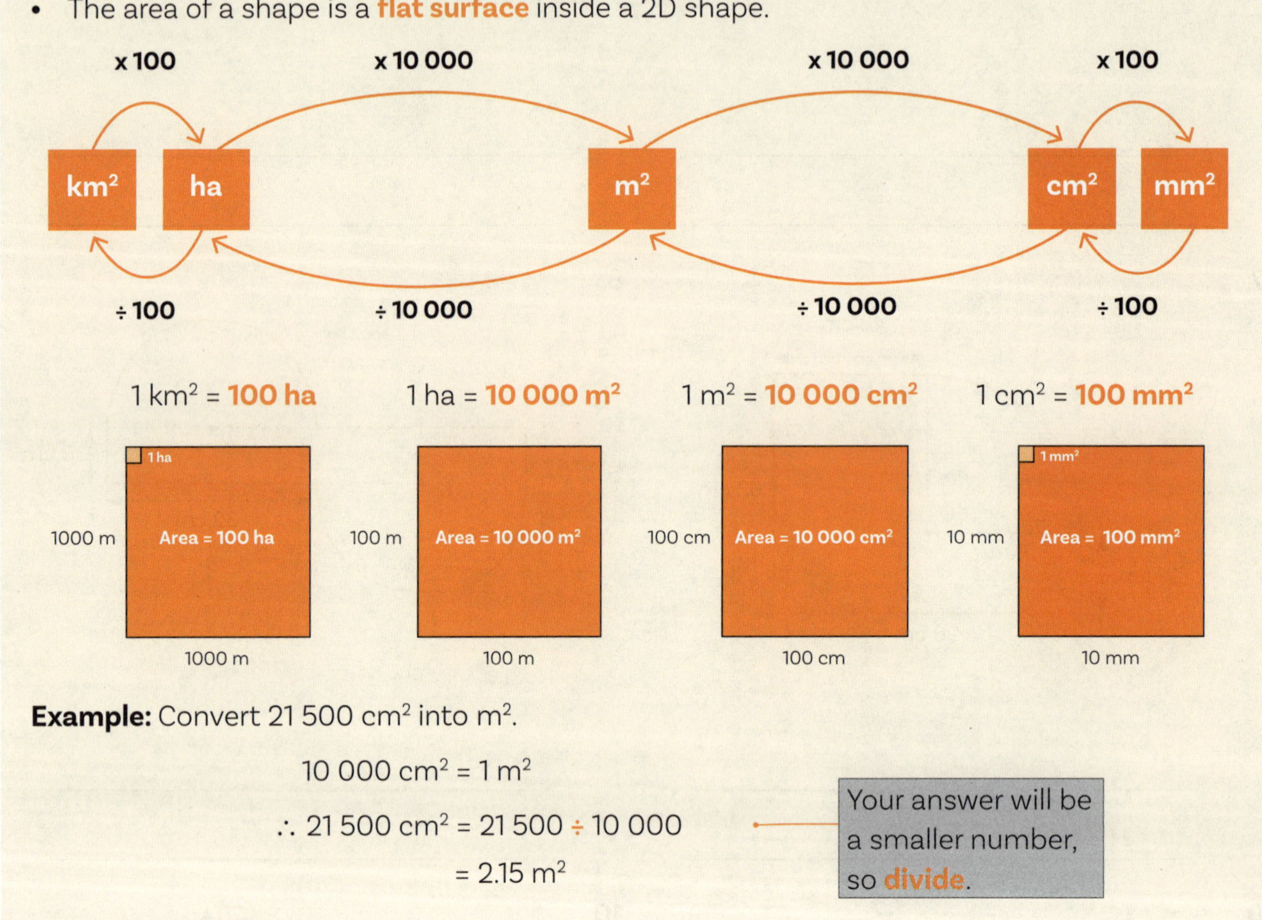

Example: Convert 21 500 cm² into m².

$10\,000 \text{ cm}^2 = 1 \text{ m}^2$

$\therefore 21\,500 \text{ cm}^2 = 21\,500 \div 10\,000$

$= 2.15 \text{ m}^2$

Your answer will be a smaller number, so **divide**.

Highlight the correct conversion for each of the following.

1	8000 m²	0.08 ha	8 ha
		0.008 ha	0.8 ha
3	15 000 cm²	15 m²	0.15 m²
		0.015 m²	1.5 m²
5	250 ha	25 km²	0.25 km²
		2.5 km²	250 km²
7	99 900 cm²	9.990 m²	99.90 m²
		9990 m²	999.0 m²

2	5 ha	0.5 km²	0.005 km²
		0.05 km²	5 km²
4	9800 mm²	0.0098 m²	0.98 m²
		0.098 m²	9.8 m²
6	359 000 m²	3.95 ha	35.9 ha
		0.395 ha	359 ha
8	104 ha	104 000 m²	140 000 m²
		1 040 000 m²	10 400 m²

ISBN: 9780170497978

Quadrilaterals

Square and rectangle

Area = base x vertical height

A* = *b* x *h

Examples:

1 Calculate the area of this square.

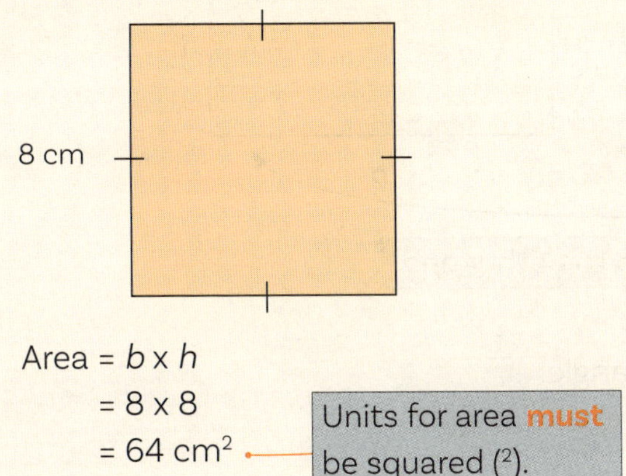

Area = $b \times h$
= 8 x 8
= 64 cm^2

Units for area **must** be squared (^{2}).

2 The area of this rectangle is 15 m^2.
Calculate its height.

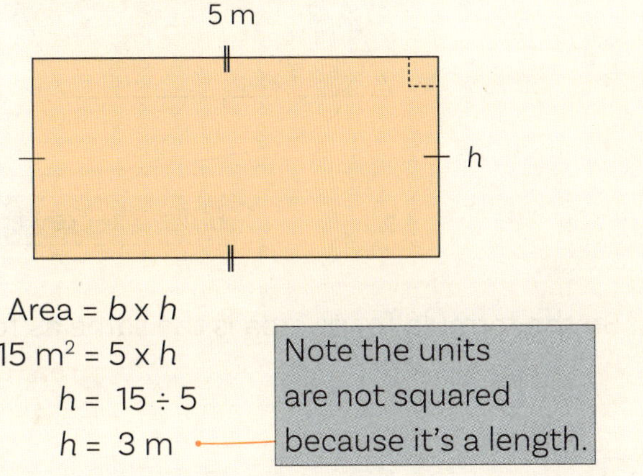

Area = $b \times h$
15 m^2 = 5 x h
h = 15 ÷ 5
h = 3 m

Note the units are not squared because it's a length.

Answer the following questions.

1 Calculate the area of this rectangle.

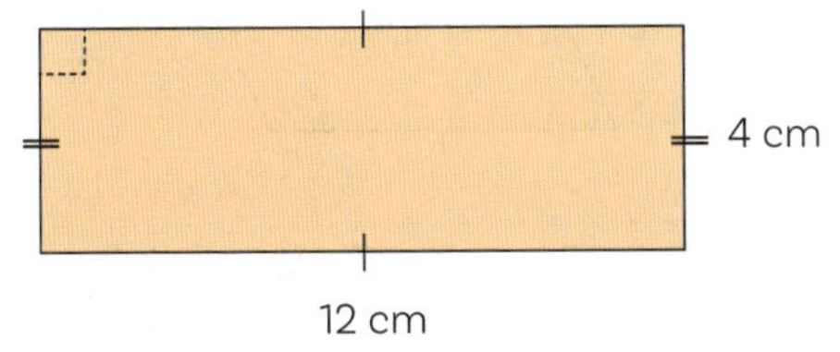

2 Calculate the area of this square.

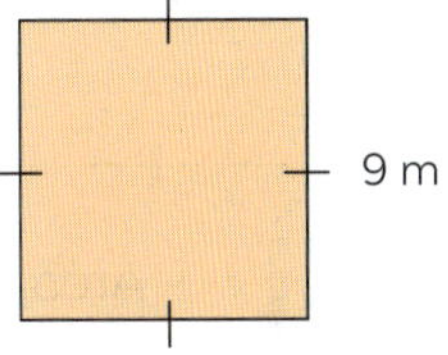

3 The area of this rectangle is 42 km^2.
Calculate the length of side x.

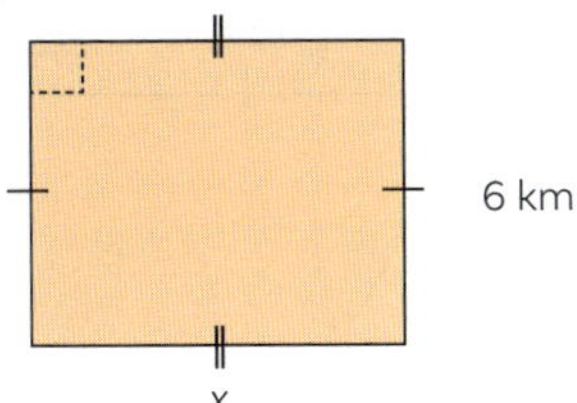

4 The area of this square is 49 cm^2
Calculate the length of the sides.

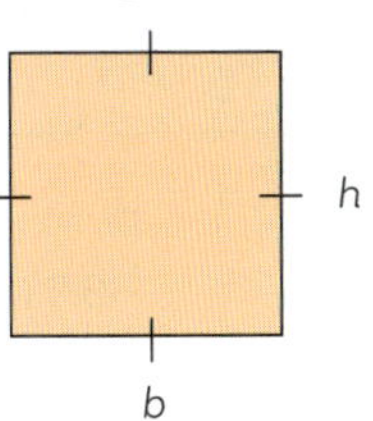

5 Sketch a rectangle and label it as if it has an area of 28 m^2.

6 Sketch a square and label it as if it has an area of 144 cm^2.

ISBN: 9780170497978

Parallelogram and rhombus

- A **parallelogram** has opposite pairs of sides that are parallel and equal.
- A **rhombus** has four equal sides, and two pairs of opposite parallel sides.

You can rearrange a parallelogram to look like a rectangle.

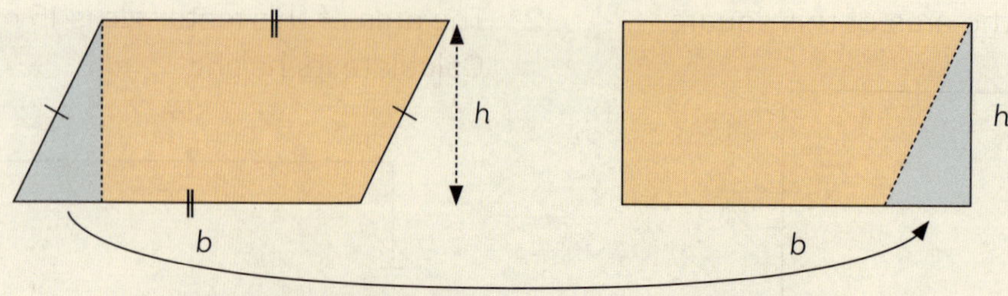

Shift the grey triangle to the other end.

So the formula for its area is the same as for a rectangle.

Area = base x vertical height

A* = *b* x *h

Examples :

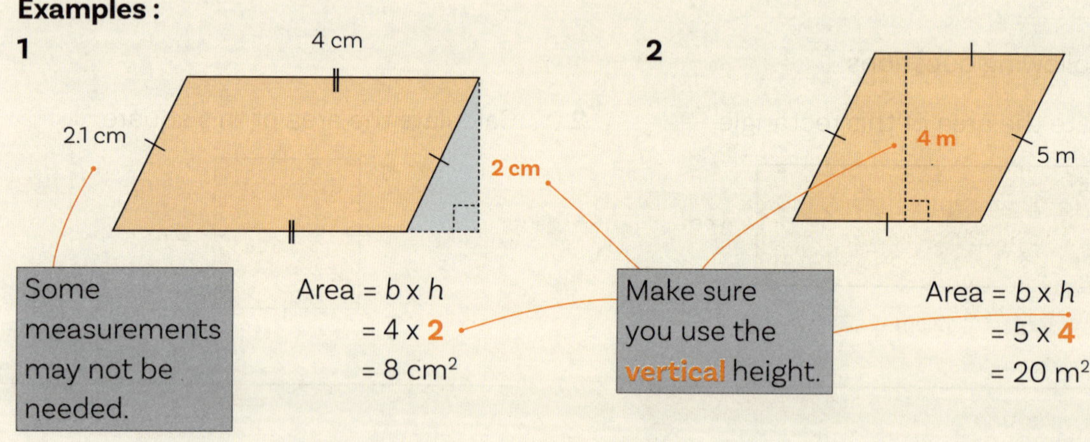

Calculate the areas of these shapes.

7

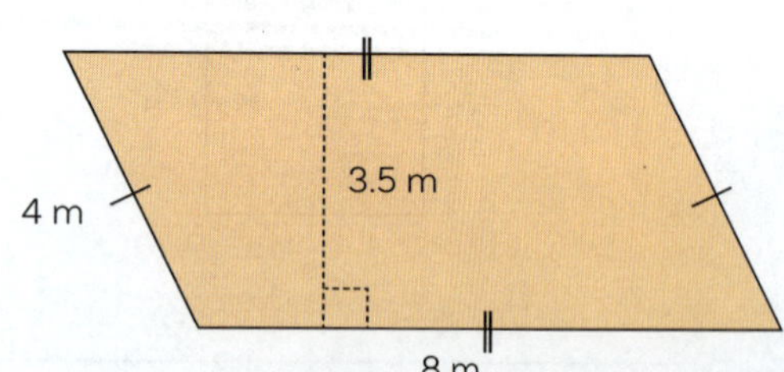

8

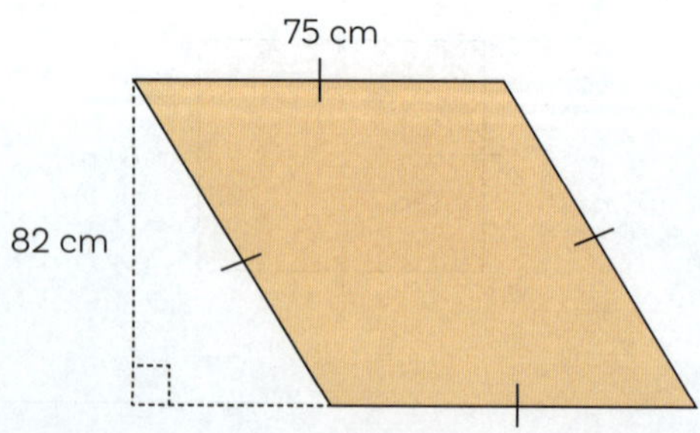

ISBN: 9780170497978

9

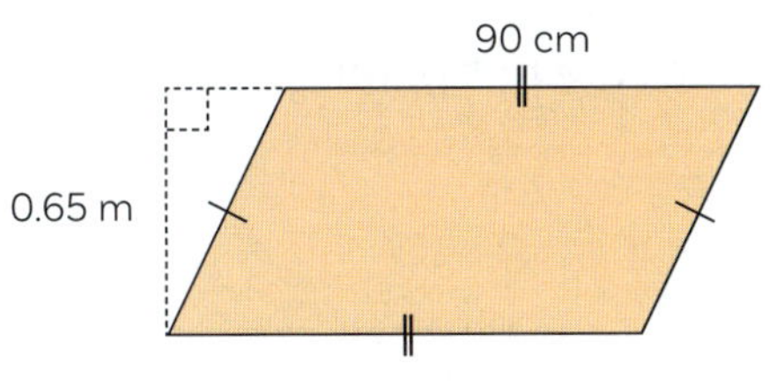

10

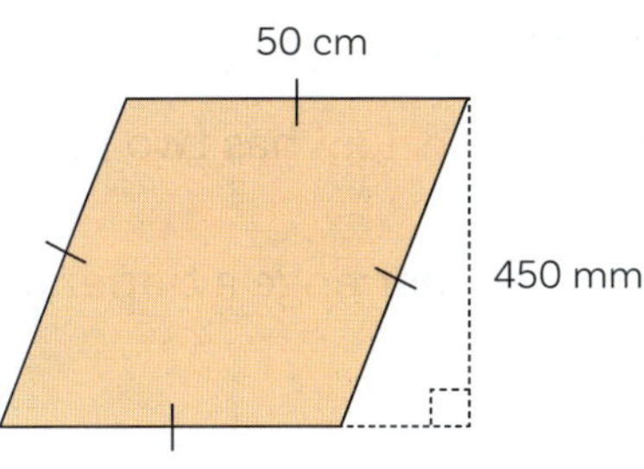

11

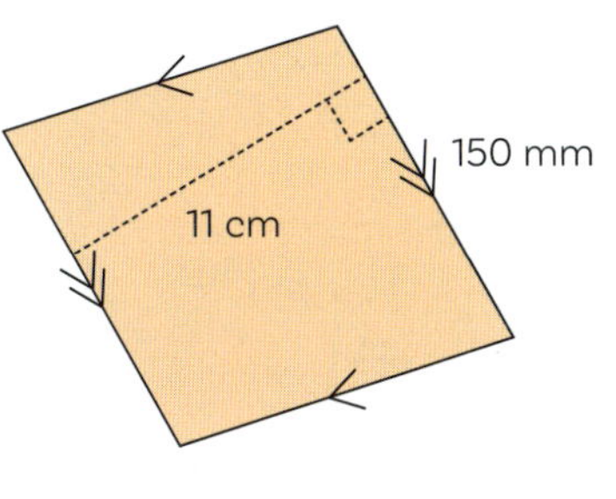

12

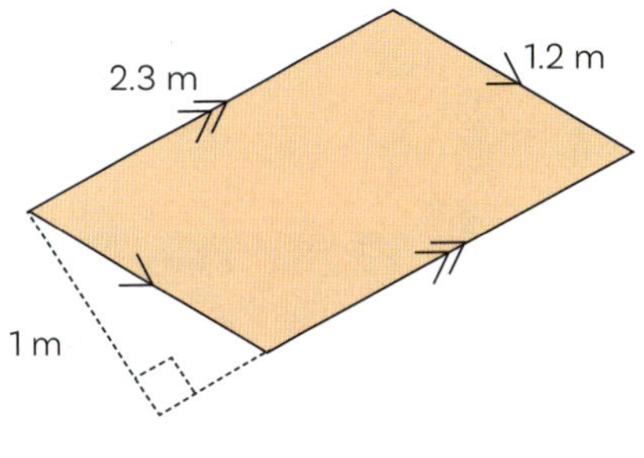

Answer the following questions.

13 The area of this parallelogram is 40 km^2. Calculate the vertical height h.

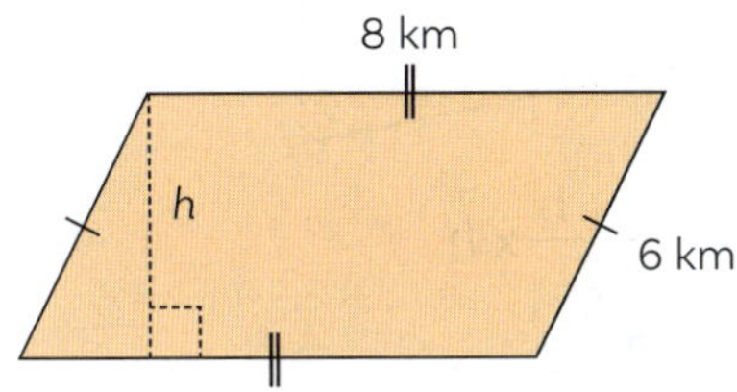

14 The area of this rhombus is 132 m^2. Calculate the length of the sides.

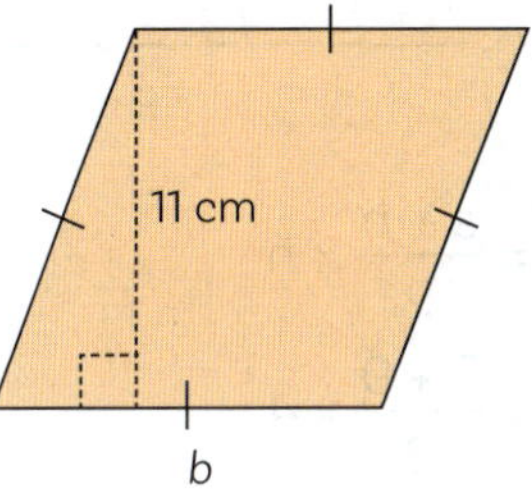

15 Sketch a rhombus and label it as if it has an area of 56 cm^2.

16 Sketch a parallelogram and label it as if it has an area of 35 m^2.

ISBN: 9780170497978

Trapezium

- A **trapezium** has two parallel sides; the other two sides are not parallel.

You can rearrange a trapezium to look like a rectangle.

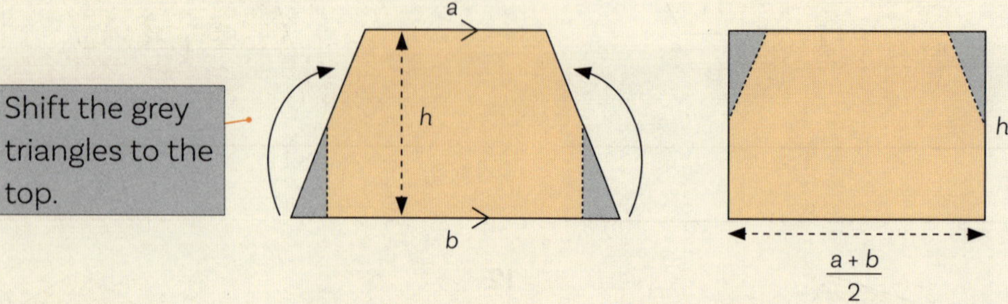

Area = (average of a and *b*) x height

$$A = \frac{a+b}{2} \times h$$

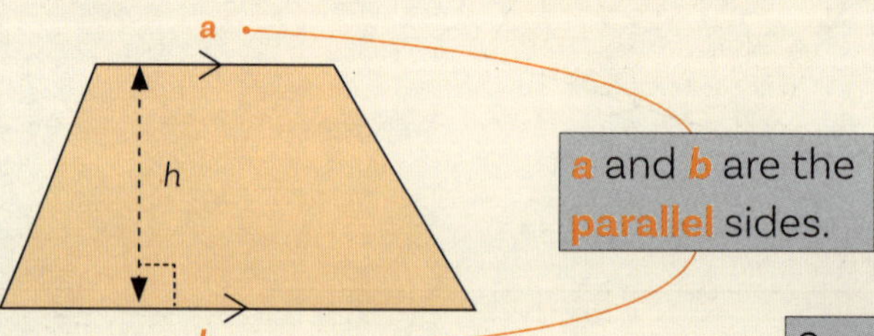

Examples:

1

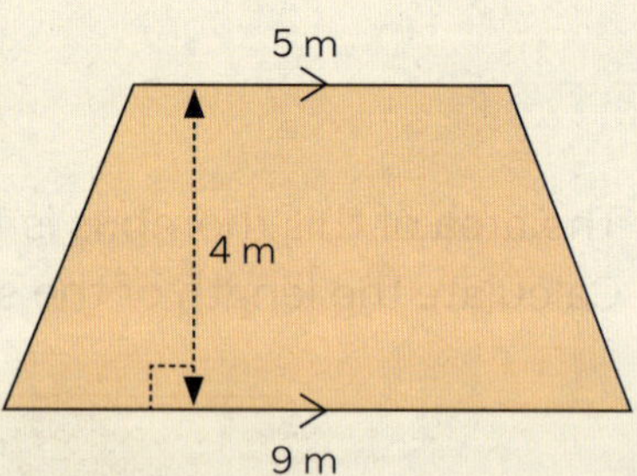

$A = \frac{a+b}{2} \times h$

$= \frac{5+9}{2} \times 4$

$= 28 \text{ m}^2$

2

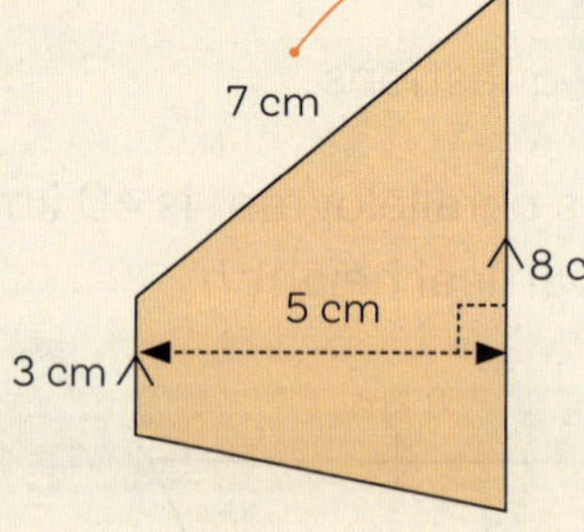

$A = \frac{a+b}{2} \times h$

$= \frac{3+8}{2} \times 5$

$= 27.5 \text{ cm}^2$

Calculate the areas of these shapes.

17

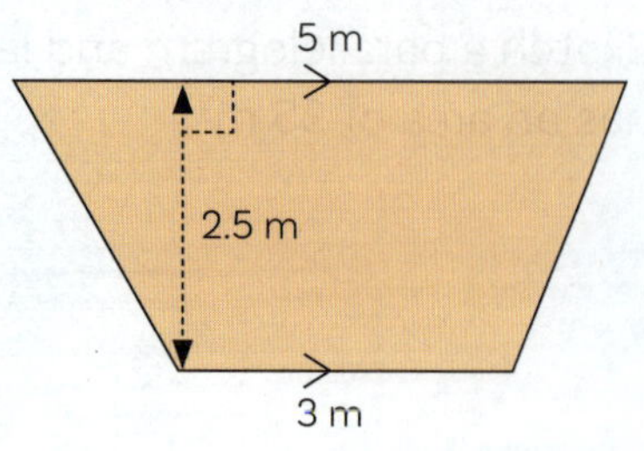

18

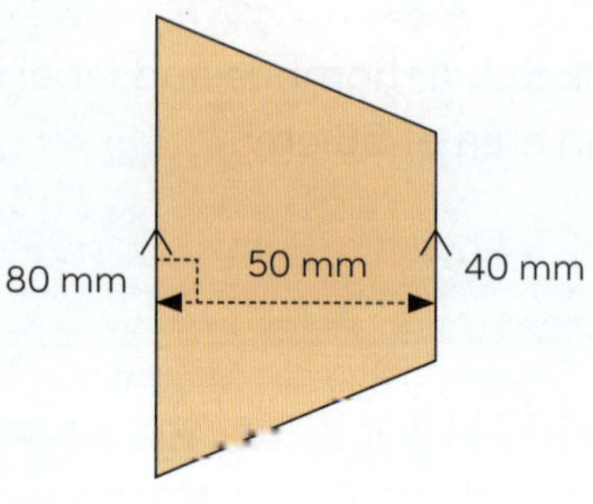

ISBN: 9780170497978

19

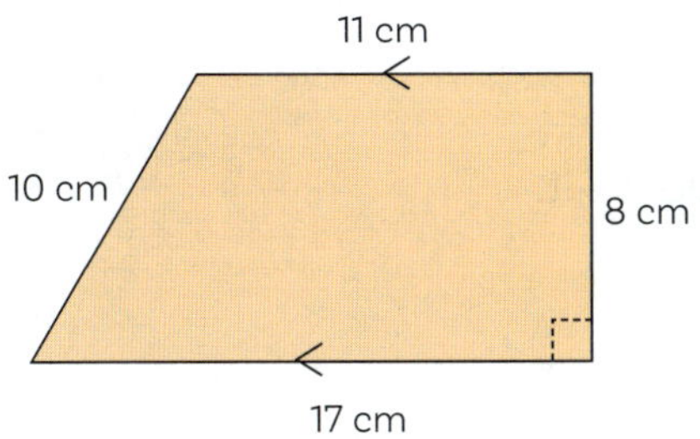

20

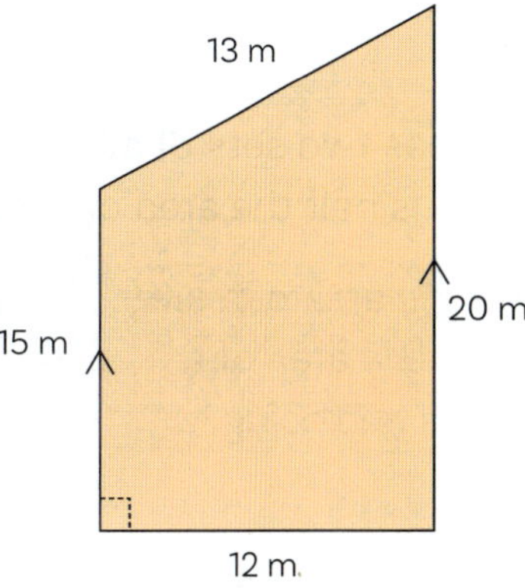

21

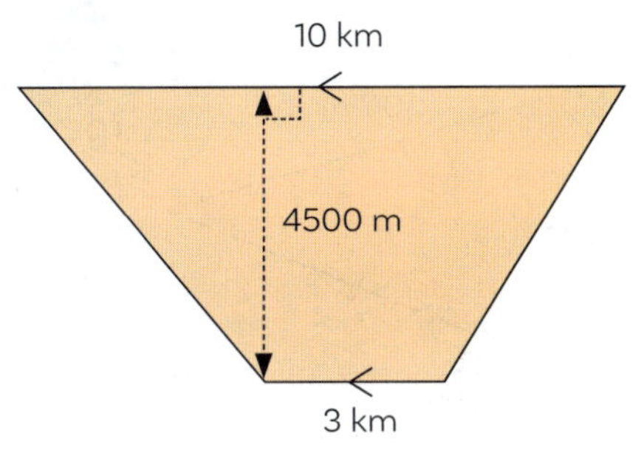

22

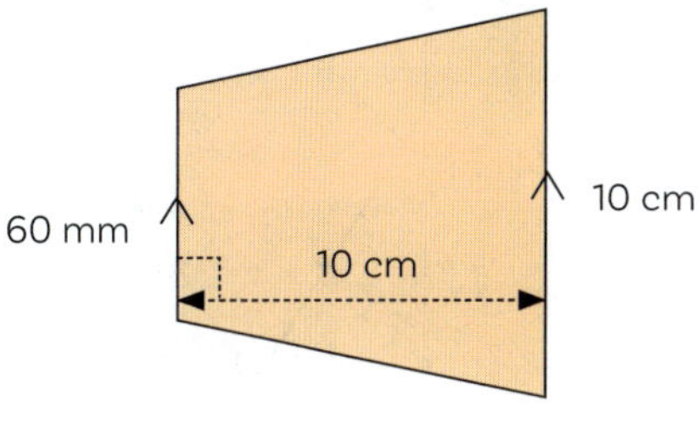

Answer the following questions.

23 The area of this trapezium is 56 km^2. Calculate the length of side x.

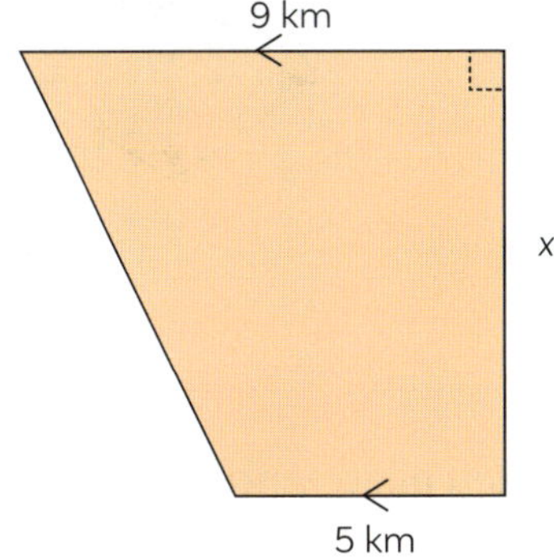

24 The area of this trapezium is 8.52 cm^2. Calculate the length of side y.

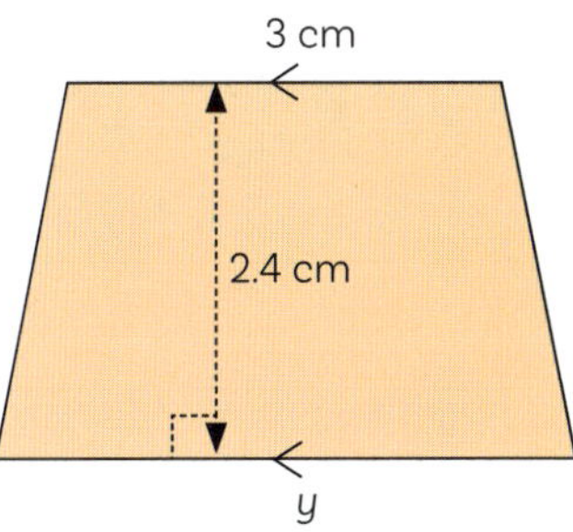

ISBN: 9780170497978

Kite

- A **kite** has two sets of adjacent equal sides.
- Its area is half the area of the rectangle which encloses it.

Notice the area of a kite is half of the area of a rectangle enclosing it.

Area = $\frac{1}{2}$ x base x height

$$A = \frac{1}{2} \times b \times h$$

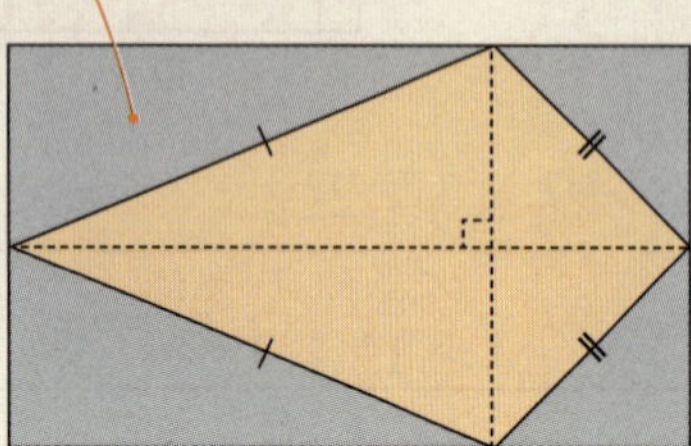

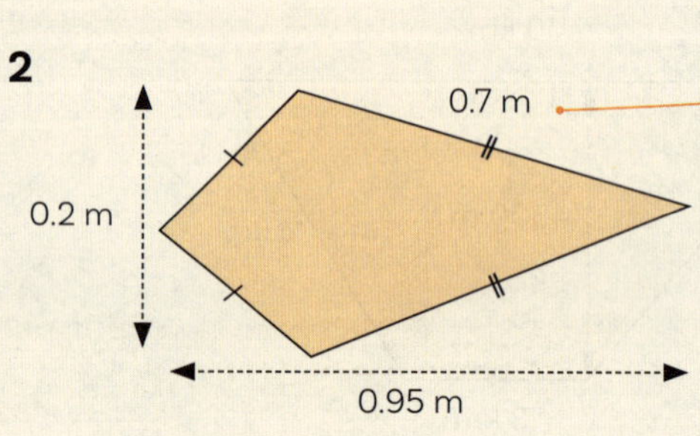

Examples:

1

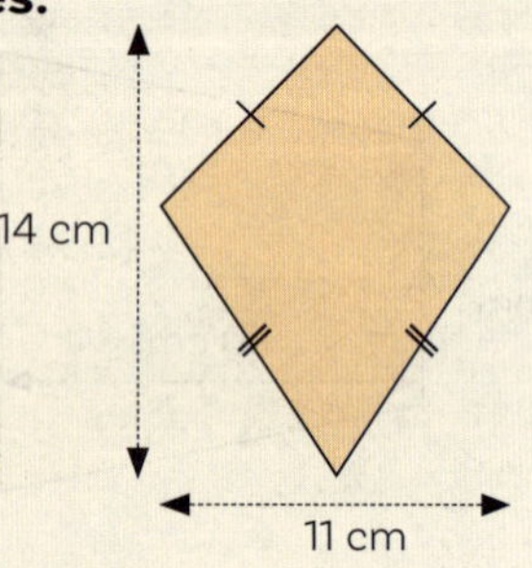

$$A = \frac{1}{2} \times b \times h$$
$$= \frac{1}{2} \times 11 \times 14$$
$$= 77 \text{ cm}^2$$

2

Some measurements may not be needed.

$$A = \frac{1}{2} \times b \times h$$
$$= \frac{1}{2} \times 0.2 \times 0.95$$
$$= 0.095 \text{ m}^2$$

Calculate the areas of these kites.

25

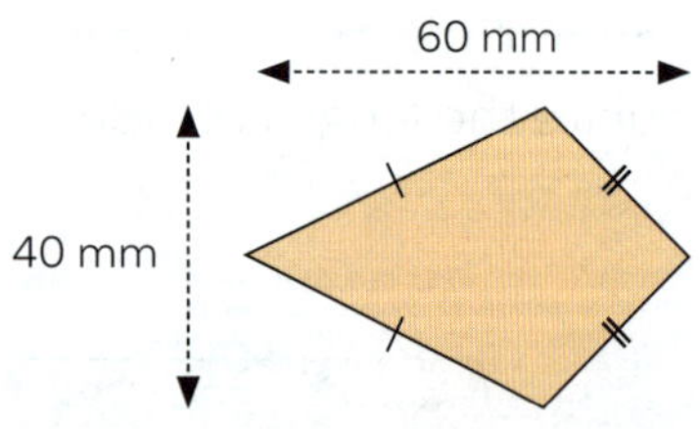

____

____

26

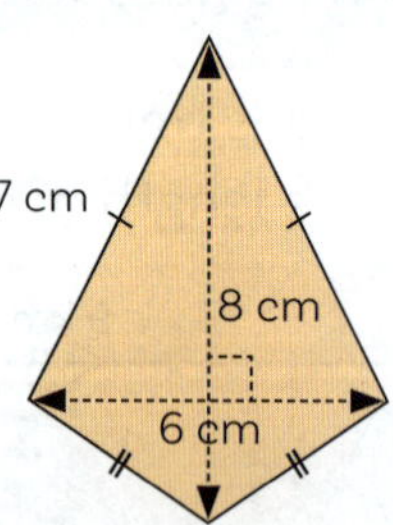

____

____

27 This kite has an area of 8.1 m^2. Calculate the length of x.

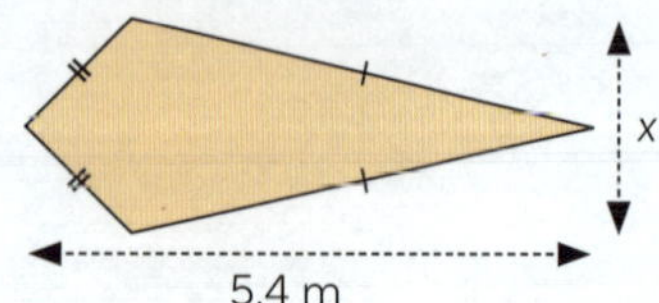

____

____

28 Sketch a kite and label it as if it has an area of 20 cm^2.

 ISBN: 9780170497978

Triangles

- A **triangle** has three sides, and its area is half the area of a rectangle or square.

$$\textbf{Area} = \frac{1}{2} \times \textbf{base} \times \textbf{vertical height}$$

$$A = \frac{1}{2} \times b \times h$$

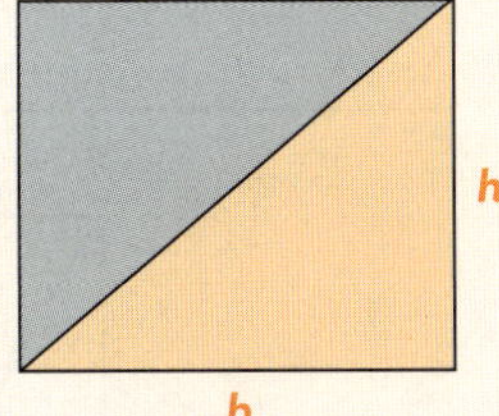

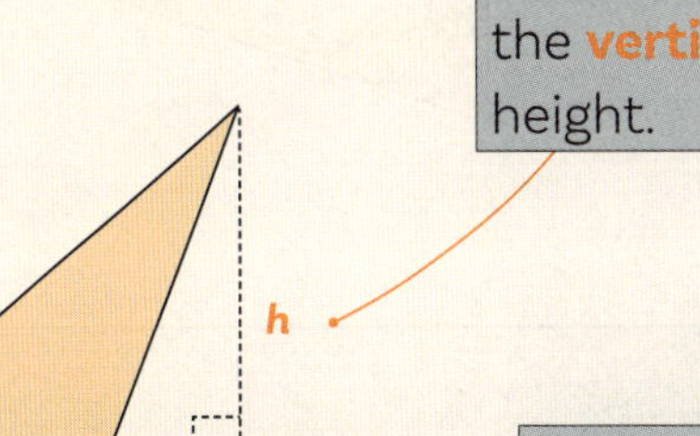

You must use the **vertical** height.

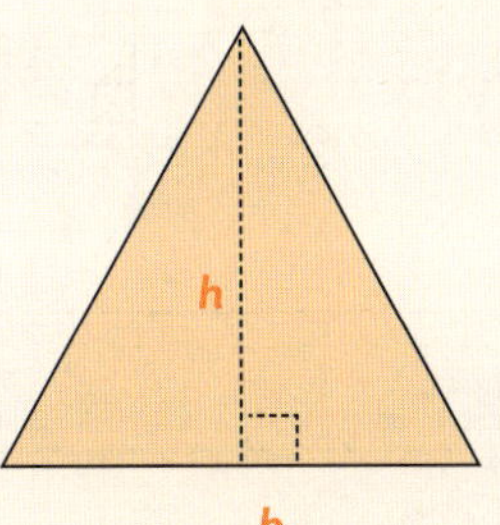

Some measurements may not be needed.

Examples:

1

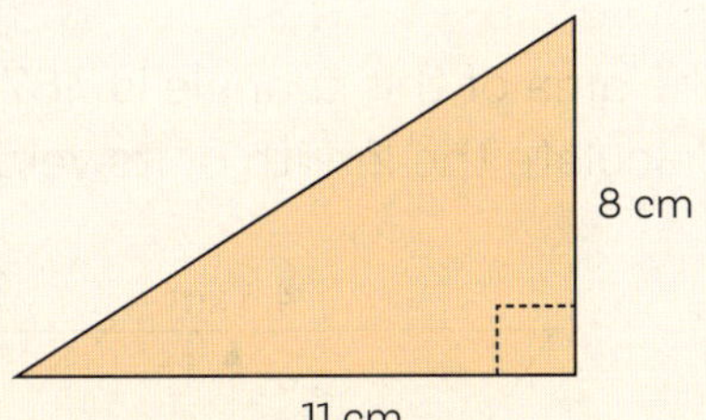

$$A = \frac{1}{2} \times b \times h$$
$$= \frac{1}{2} \times 11 \times 8$$
$$= 44 \text{ cm}^2$$

2

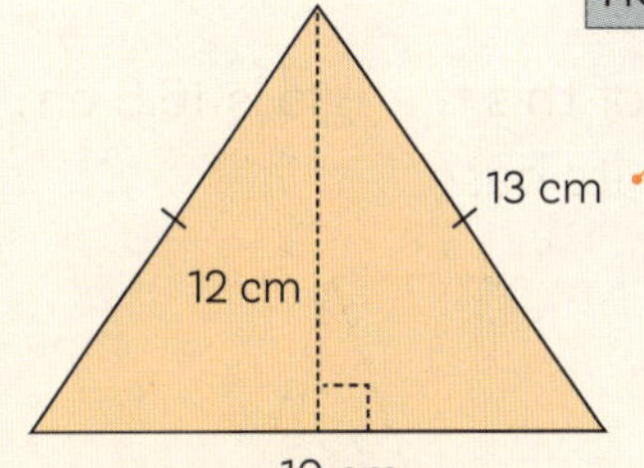

$$A = \frac{1}{2} \times b \times h$$
$$= \frac{1}{2} \times 10 \times 12$$
$$= 60 \text{ cm}^2$$

Calculate the areas of these shapes.

1

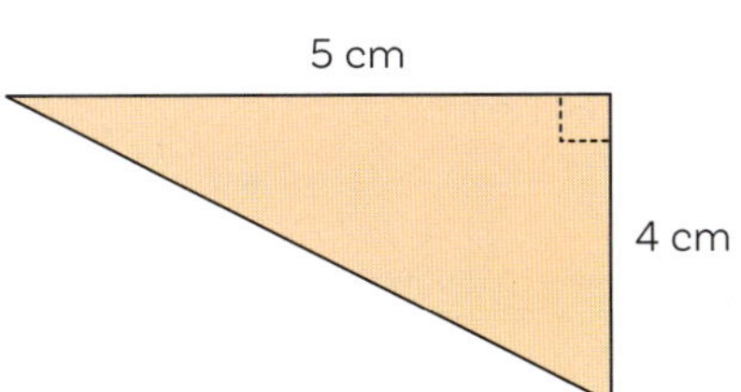

____

____

2

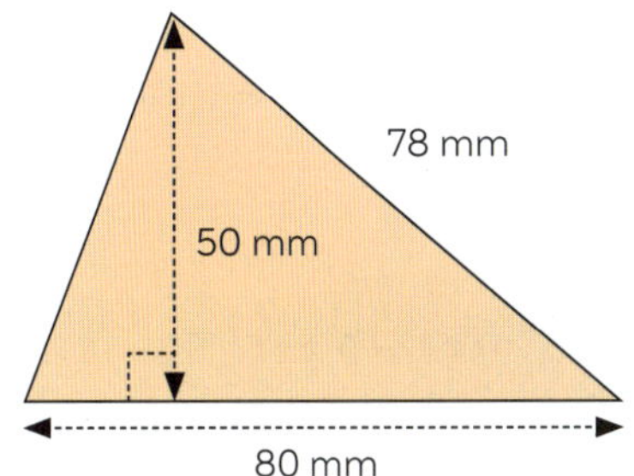

____

____

ISBN: 9780170497978

3

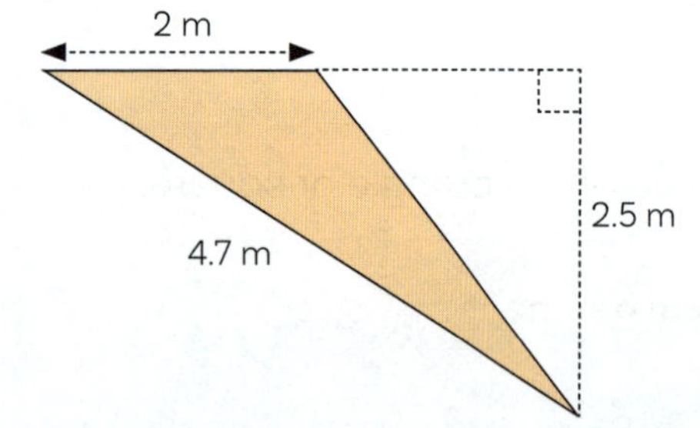

4

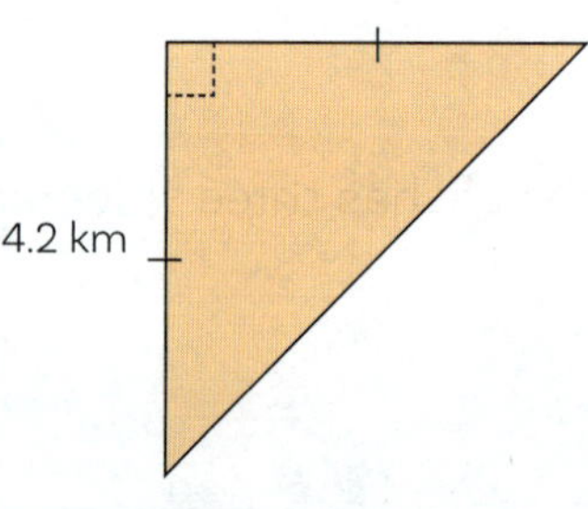

5

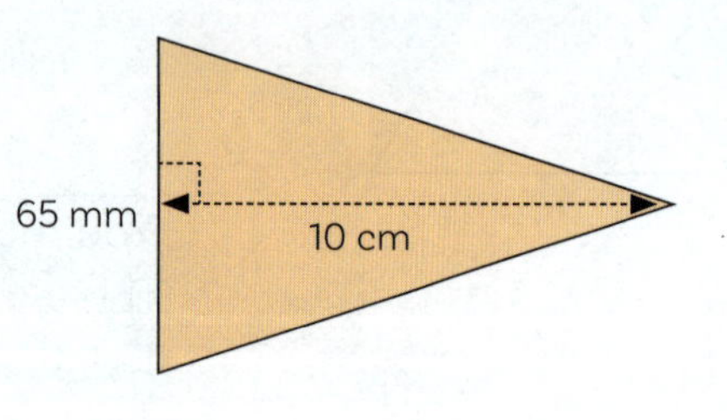

6

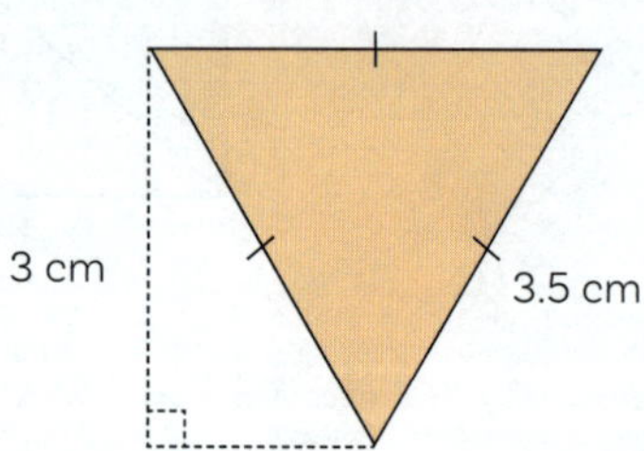

Answer the following questions.

7 The area of this triangle is 16.5 cm^2. Calculate its base.

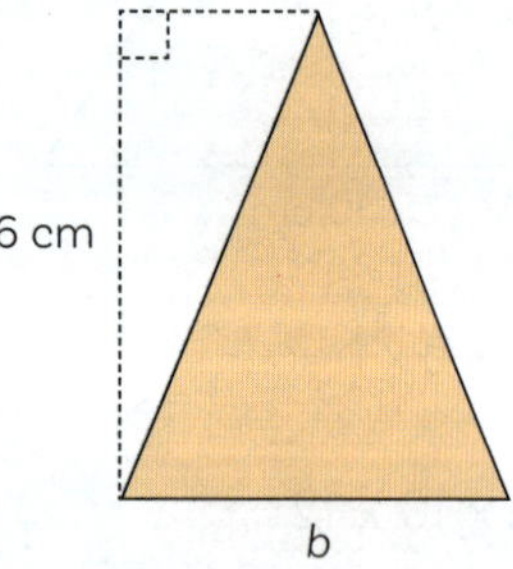

8 The area of this triangle is 7.875 km^2. Calculate the length of its vertical height.

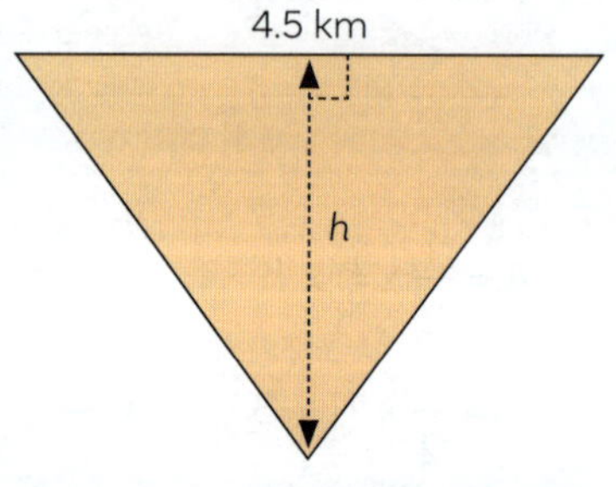

9 Sketch and label a triangle with an area of 18 m^2.

10 Sketch and label a triangle with an area of 60 mm^2.

ISBN: 9780170497978

Circles

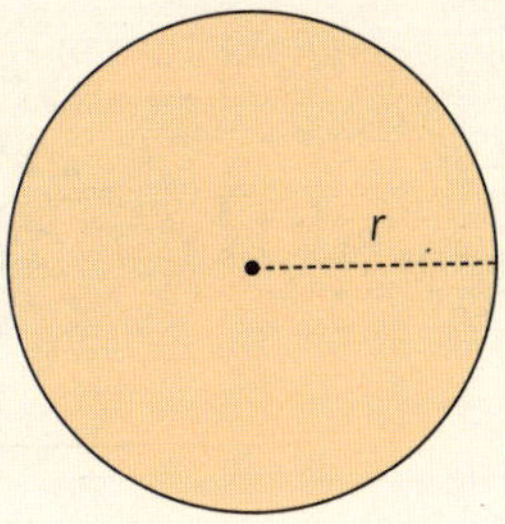

$$\text{Area} = \pi \times \text{radius}^2$$

$$A = \pi r^2$$

Examples:

1

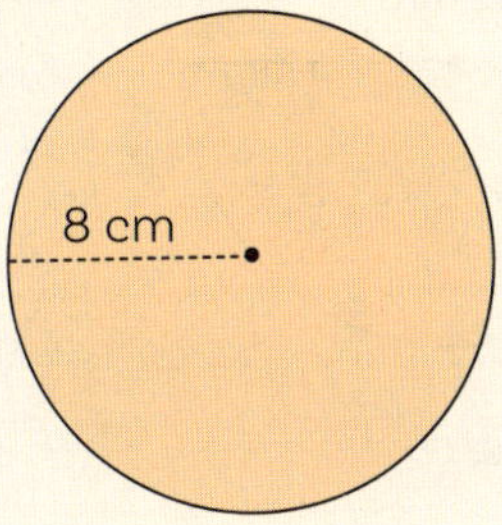

$A = \pi r^2$

$= \pi \times 8^2$

$= 201.06\ \text{cm}^2$ (2 dp)

2

If you have the diameter, then halve it to get the radius.

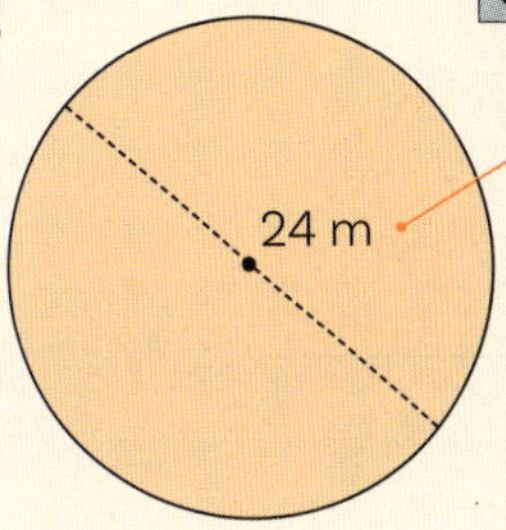

$A = \pi r^2$

$= \pi \times 12^2$

$= 452.39\ \text{m}^2$ (2 dp)

3

For a semicircle, you must halve the area of a circle ($\div 2$ or $\times \frac{1}{2}$).

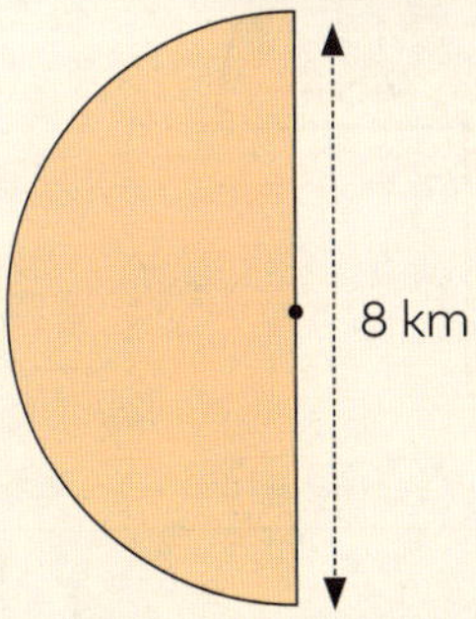

$A = \frac{1}{2} \times \pi r^2$

$= \frac{1}{2} \times \pi \times 4^2$

$= 25.13\ \text{km}^2$ (2 dp)

4

For this shape you must find three quarters the area of a circle ($\times 0.75$ or $\times \frac{3}{4}$).

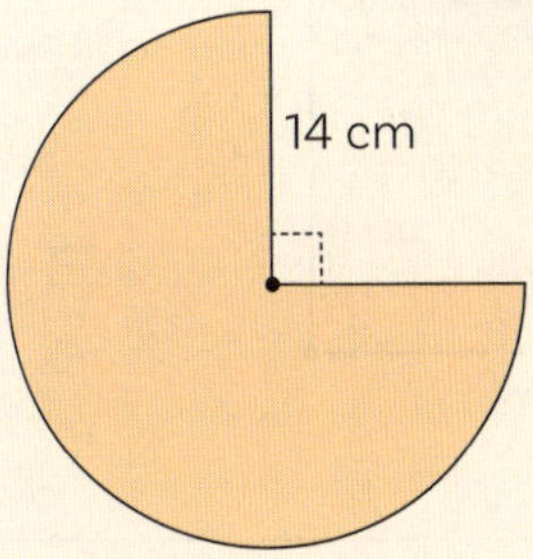

$A = \frac{3}{4} \times \pi r^2$

$= \frac{3}{4} \times \pi \times (14)^2$

$= 461.81\ \text{cm}^2$ (2 dp)

Calculate the areas of these shapes. Round your answers to 4 sf.

1

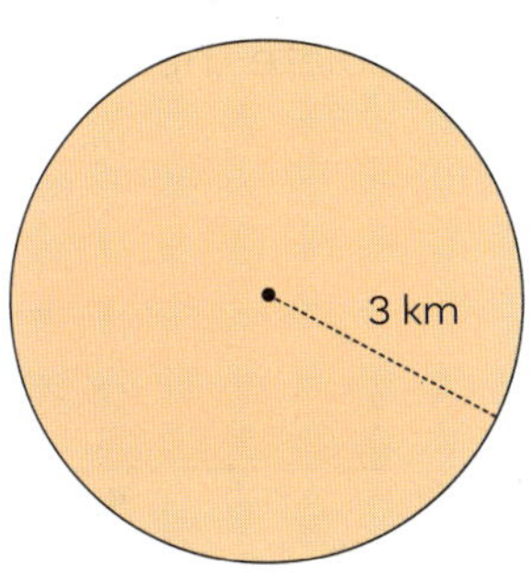

2

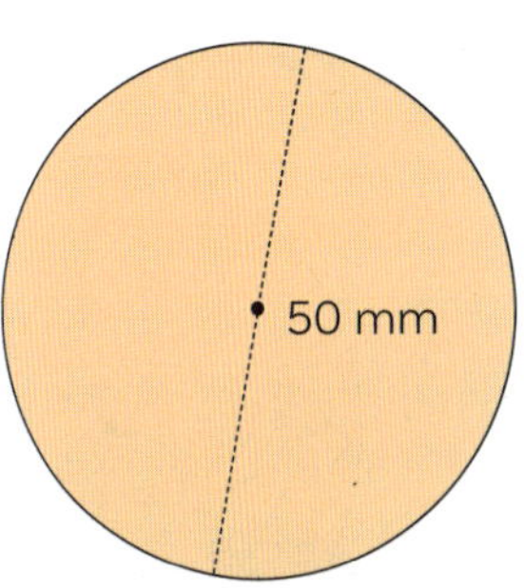

3

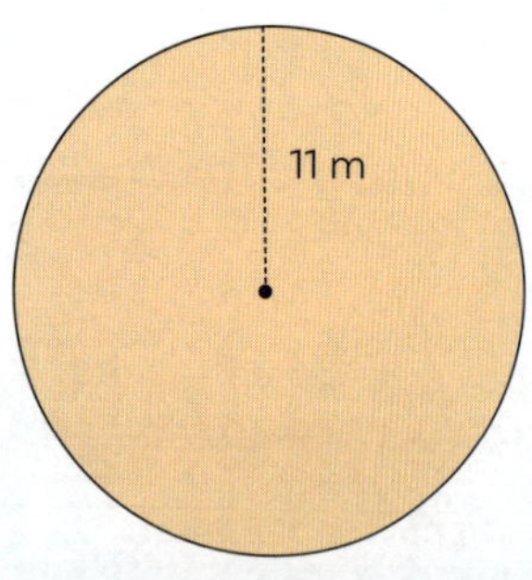

4

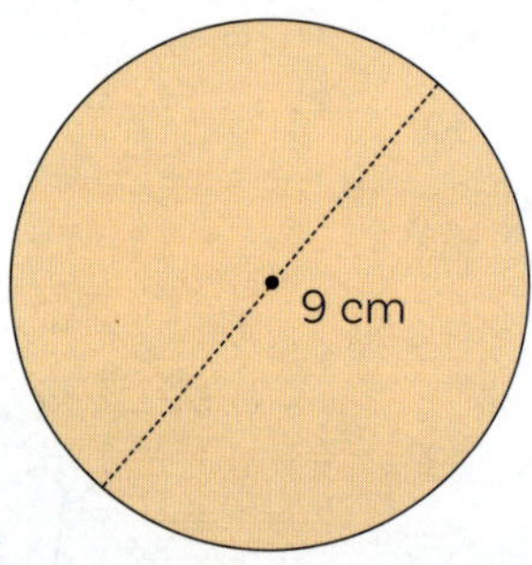

5

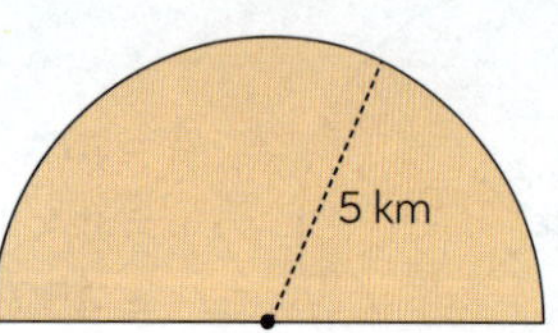

6

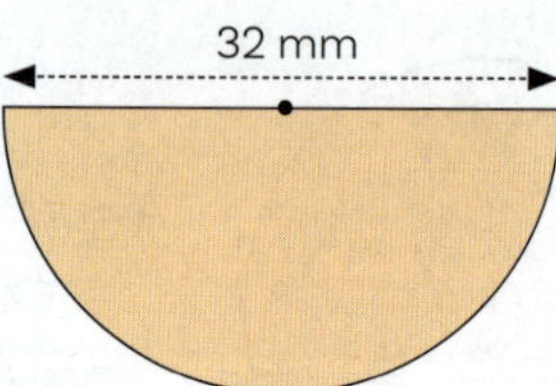

7

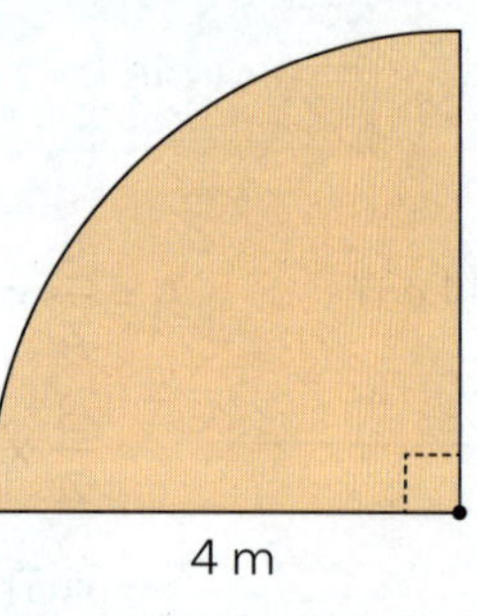

8

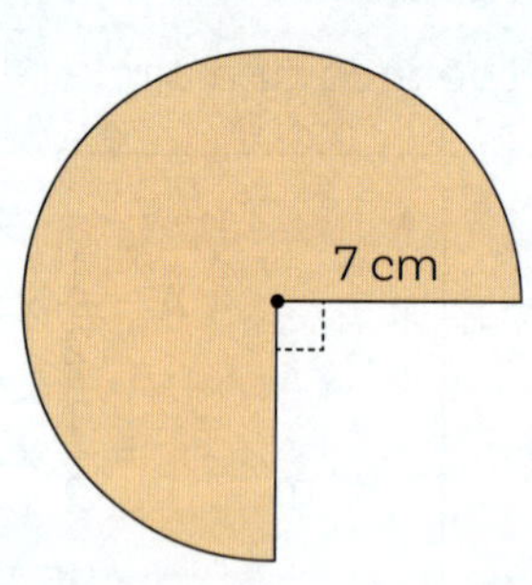

Answer the following questions.

9 The area of this circle is 113.10 km^2 (2 dp). Calculate the length of its radius.

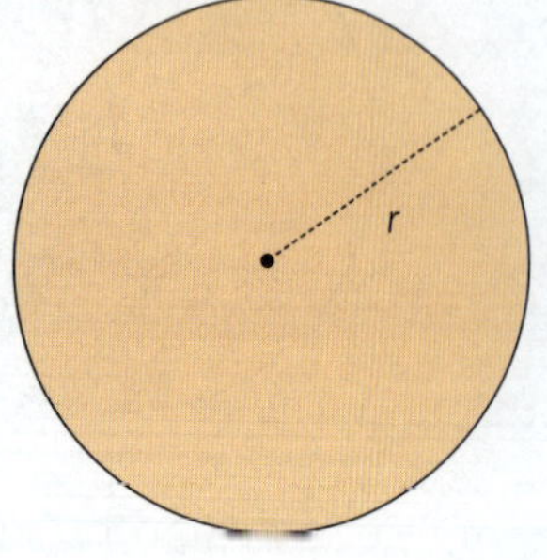

10 The area of the semicircle is 190.07 cm^2 (2 dp). Calculate the length of its radius.

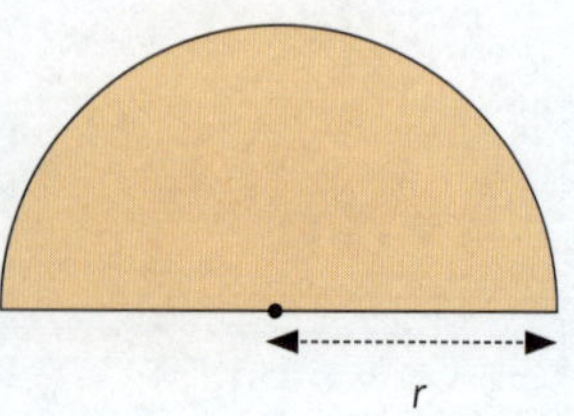

 ISBN: 9780170497978

Compound shapes

- Remember, compound shapes are shapes that are made up of **other simple shapes**.
- You need to find the areas of the simple shapes and then **add** them together.

Example:

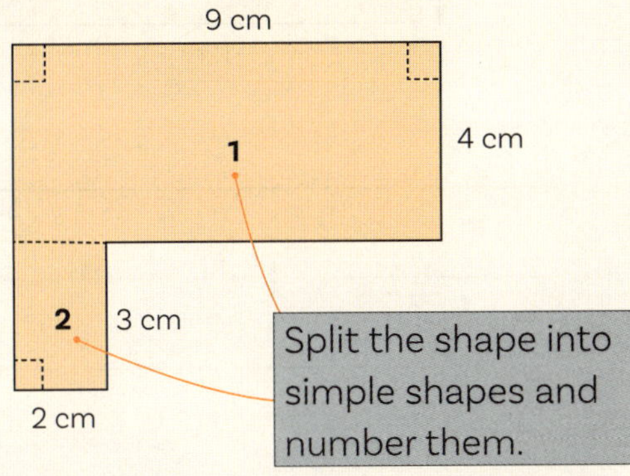

Area = $(b_1 \times h_1) + (b_2 \times h_2)$

= (9 x 4) + (2 x 3)

= 36 + 6

= 42 cm^2

Calculate the two areas and add them together.

Shapes with holes

- You need to find the areas of the simple shapes and then **subtract** one from the other.

Example:

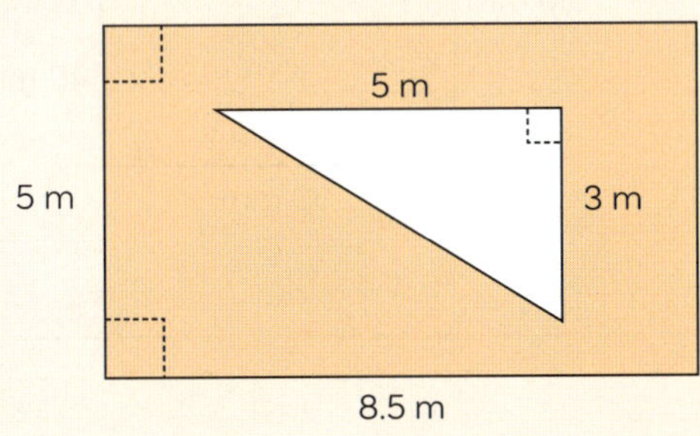

Shaded area = rectangle – triangle

= (8.5 x 5) – ($\frac{1}{2}$ x 5 x 3)

= 42.5 – 7.5

= 35 m^2

Calculate the two areas and subtract one from the other.

Calculate the areas of these shapes.

1

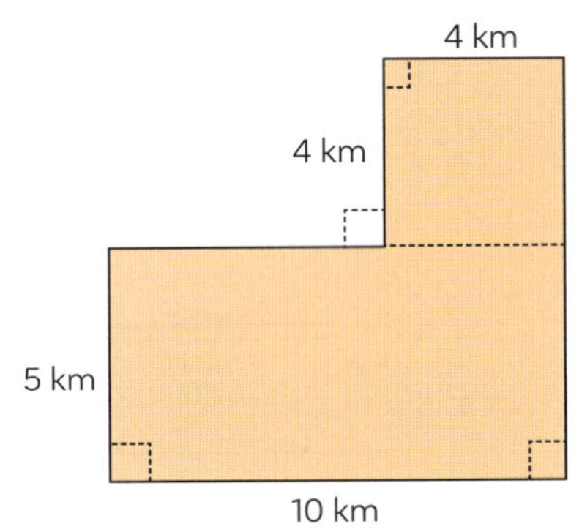

____

____

____

2

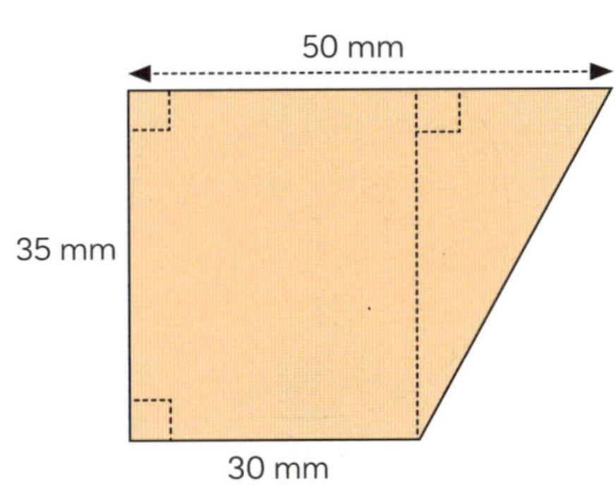

____

____

____

3

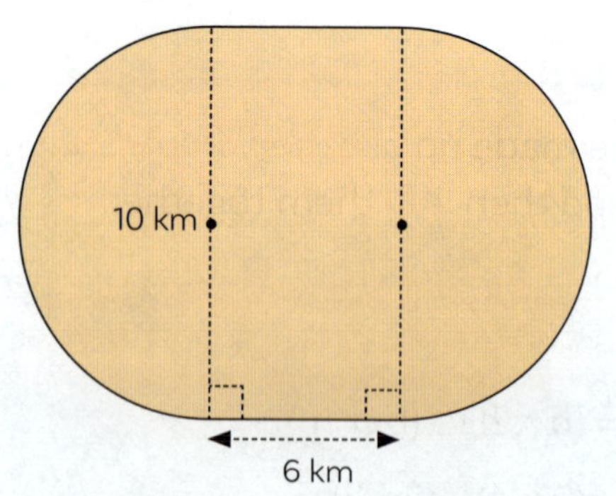

4

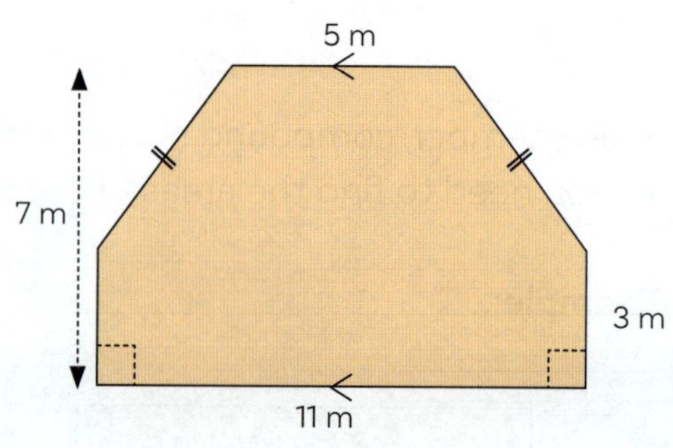

5

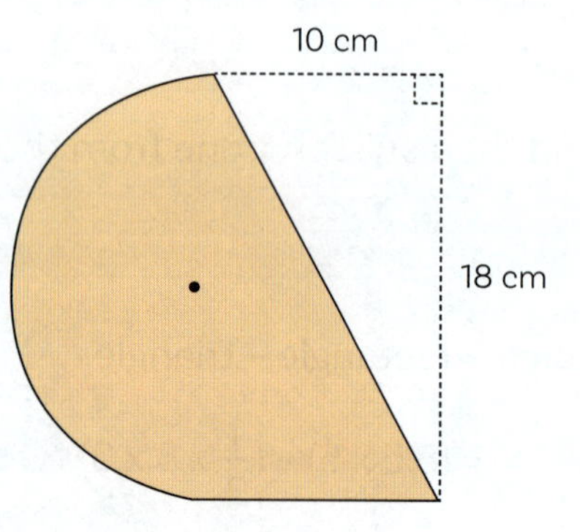

6

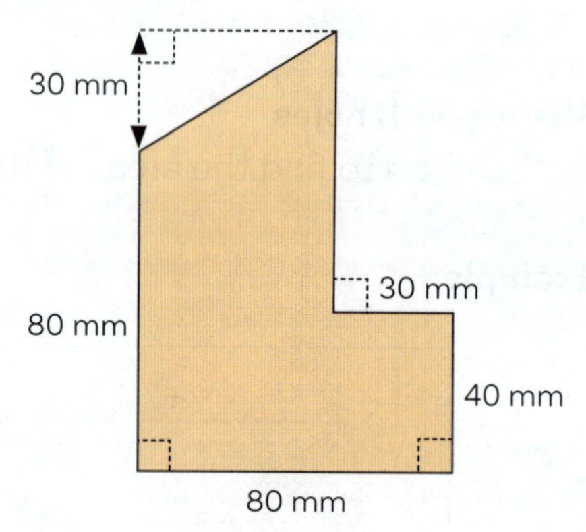

7

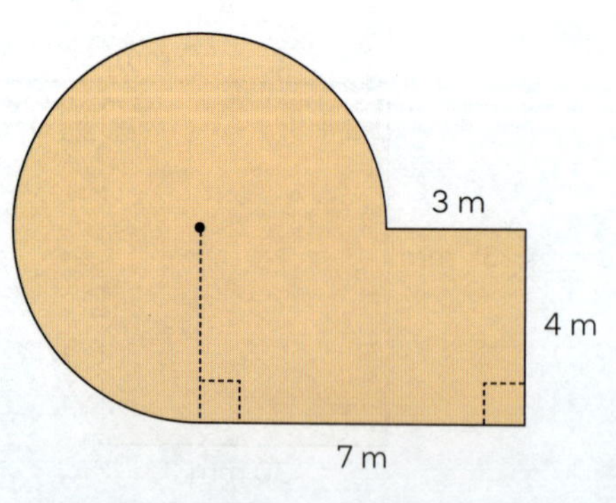

8

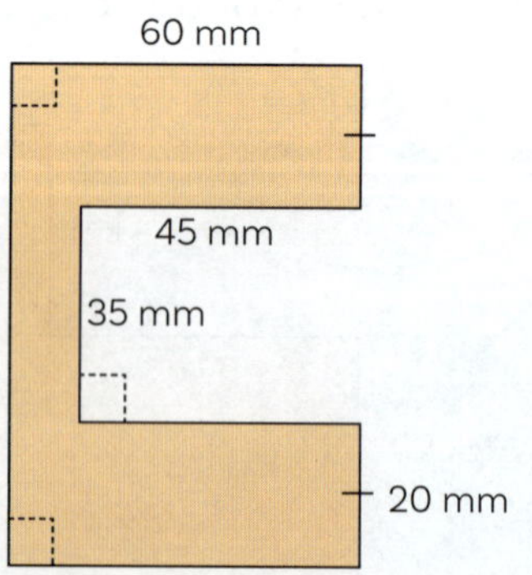

ISBN: 9780170497978

9

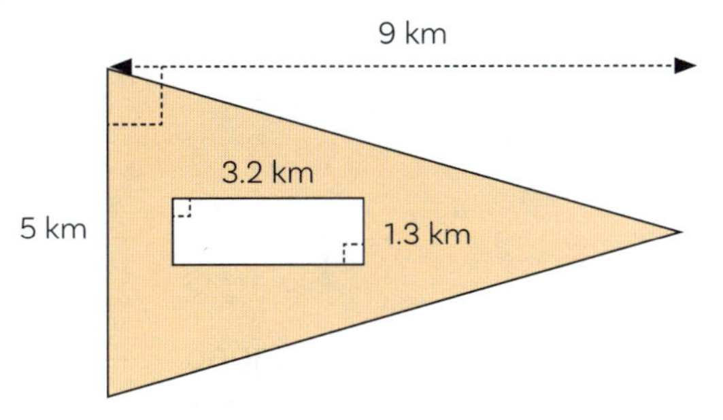

10

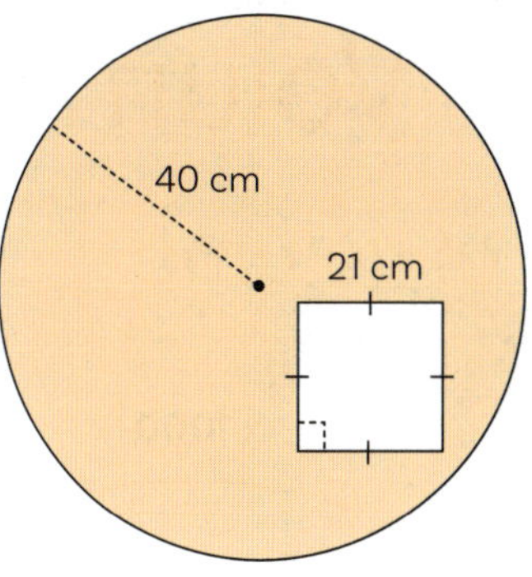

11

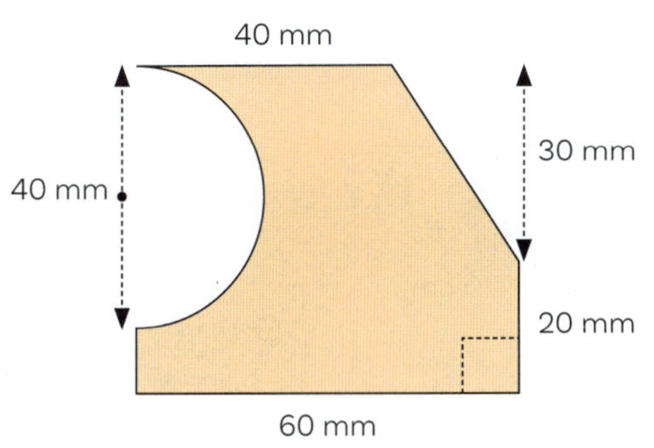

12

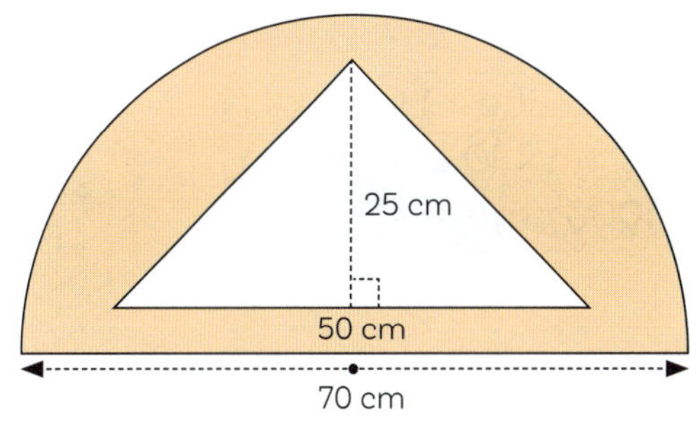

13

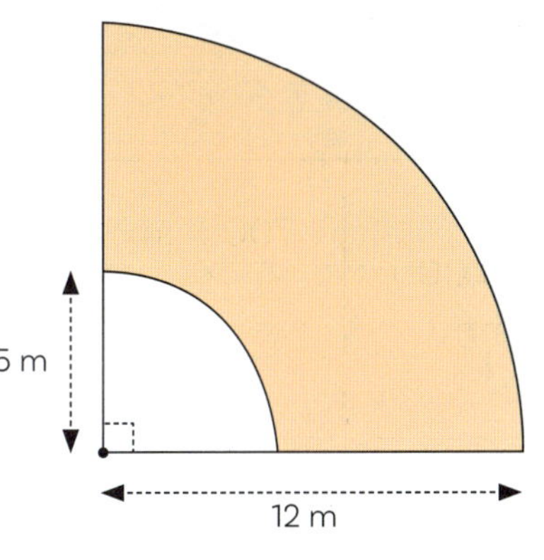

14

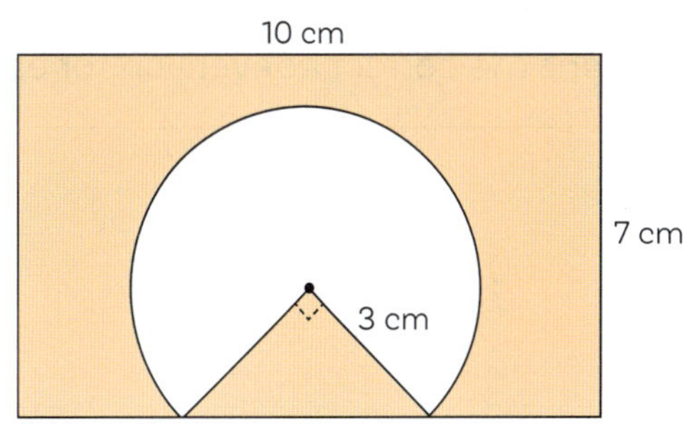

Volume

Units of volume

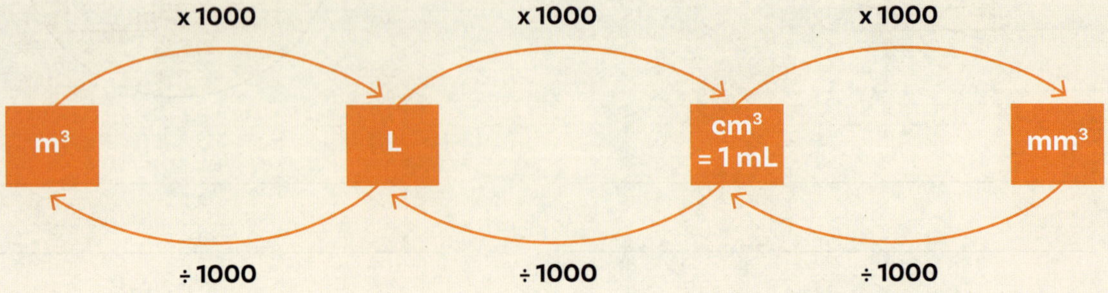

m^3 → ×1000 → L → ×1000 → cm^3 = 1 mL → ×1000 → mm^3

mm^3 → ÷1000 → cm^3 = 1 mL → ÷1000 → L → ÷1000 → m^3

Reminder: Relationship between volume (m^3, cm^3, mm^3) and capacity (L, mL):

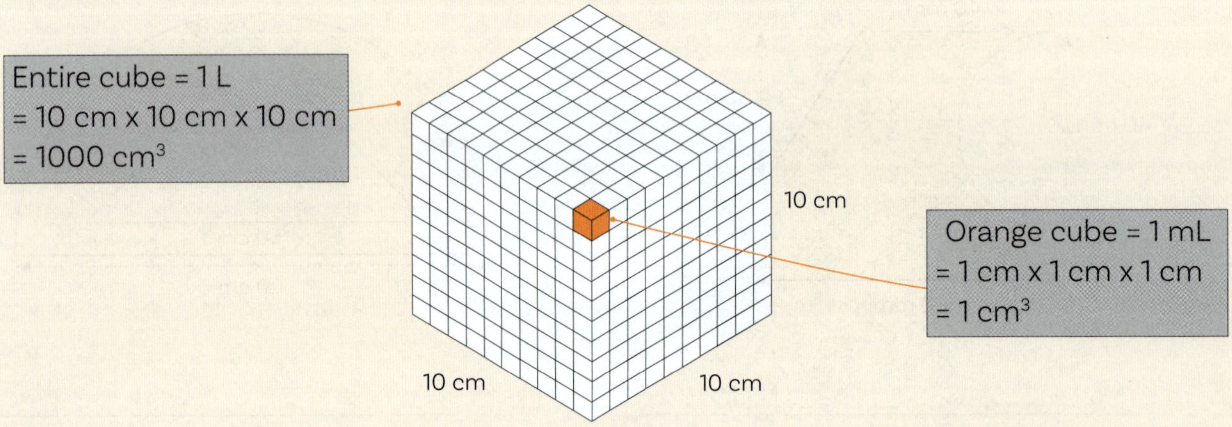

Entire cube = 1 L
= 10 cm x 10 cm x 10 cm
= 1000 cm^3

Orange cube = 1 mL
= 1 cm x 1 cm x 1 cm
= 1 cm^3

10 cm, 10 cm, 10 cm

Also: 1 m^3 = 100 cm x 100 cm x 100 cm
= 1000 L

Highlight the correct conversion for each of the following.

1	3000 cm^3	300 000 mm^3	0.003 m^3
		30 L	0.03 m^3
2	700 000 mm^3	7000 cm^3	0.7 L
		70 cm^3	7 L
3	4.1 m^3	410 000 cm^3	4100 cm^3
		4 100 000 cm^3	41 000 cm^3
4	8000 cm^3	0.8 L	800 000 mm^3
		8 L	80 000 mm^3
5	0.022 m^3	220 000 cm^3	2200 cm^3
		2 200 000 mm^3	22 000 cm^3
6	0.0099 m^3	99 000 mm^3	9900 cm^3
		990 000 mm^3	990 cm^3

ISBN: 9780170497978

Cuboids

- The volume of a three-dimensional (3D) shape is the amount of **space** the shape occupies.
- A **cuboid** is a box shape, e.g. a shoebox.
- A **cube** is a box shape where all the dimensions are equal, e.g. a Rubik's cube.

Examples:

1

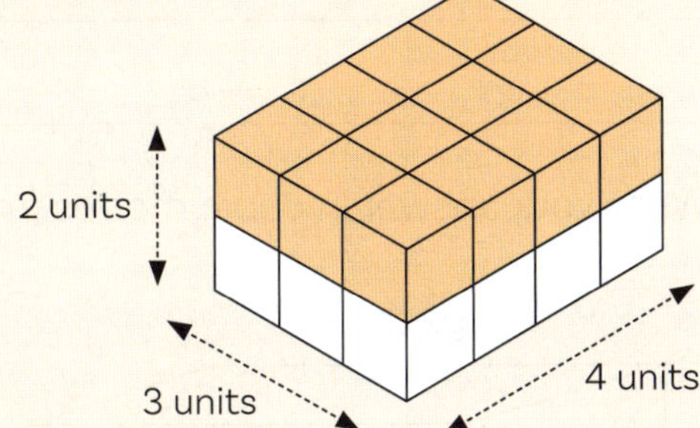

Count the cubes:
Each layer has 3 x 4 = 12 units

Total volume = 2 layers of **12 units**
= 24 units

Using the formula:
Volume = height x width x depth
= 2 x 4 x 3
= 24 units

2

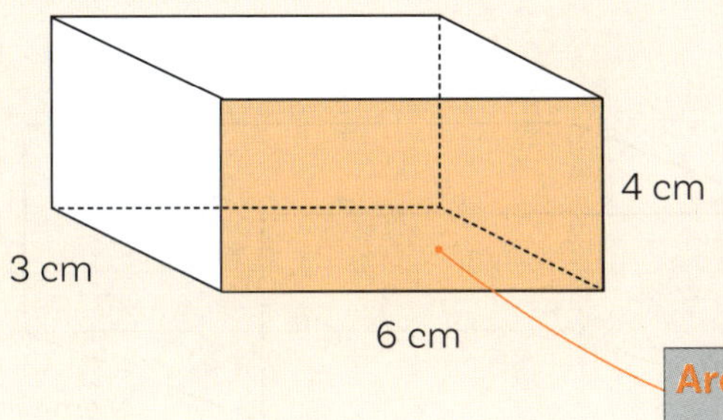

Volume = $h \times w \times d$
= 4 x 6 x 3
= 72 cm^3

3 Another way to think about it is to find the area of the 'face' and multiply it by the depth.

Volume = **area of face** x d
= **(4 x 6)** x 3
= **(24)** x 3
= 72 cm^3

3 cm
4 cm
6 cm

Area of the face is **24 cm^2**. Then multiply it by the depth (3 cm).

Calculate the volumes of these cuboids.

1

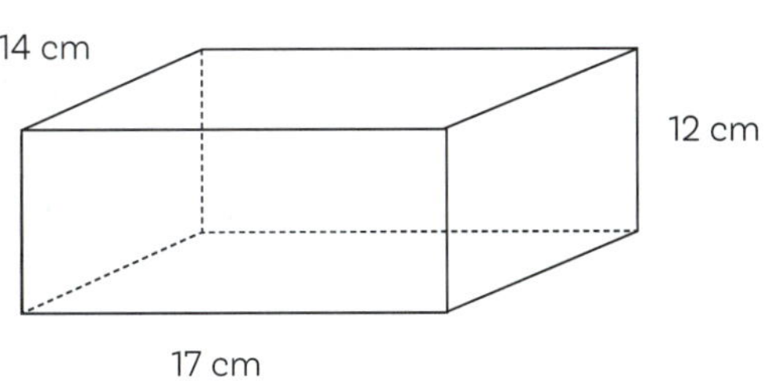

____

____

2

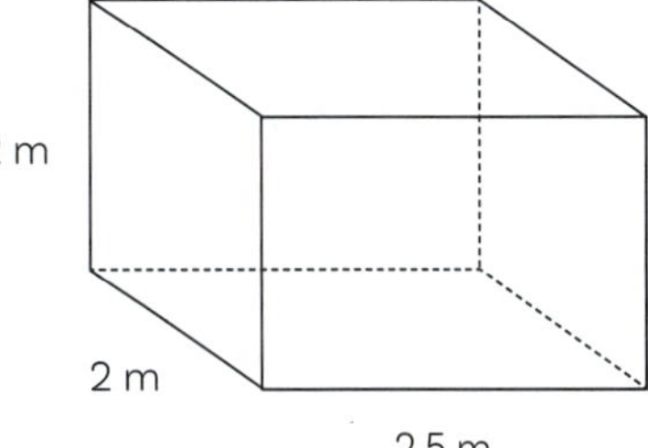

____

____

ISBN: 9780170497978

3

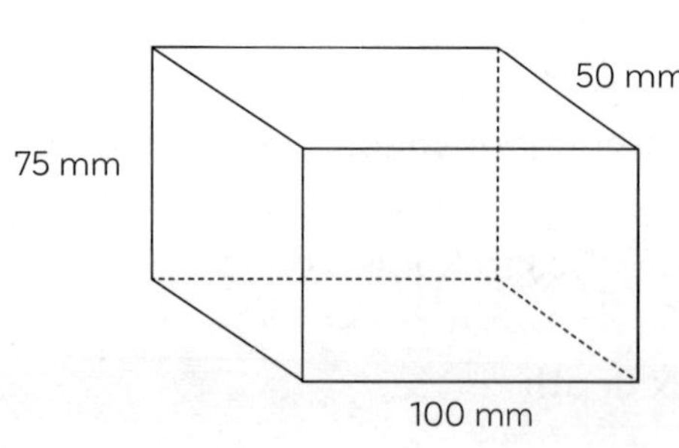

4

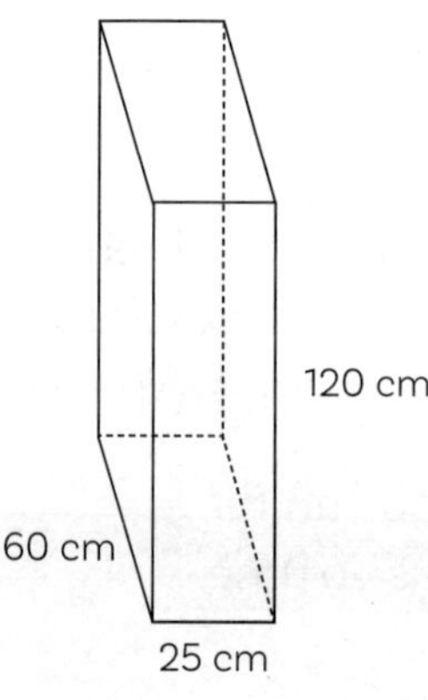

5 Write your answer in cubic centimetres (cm³).

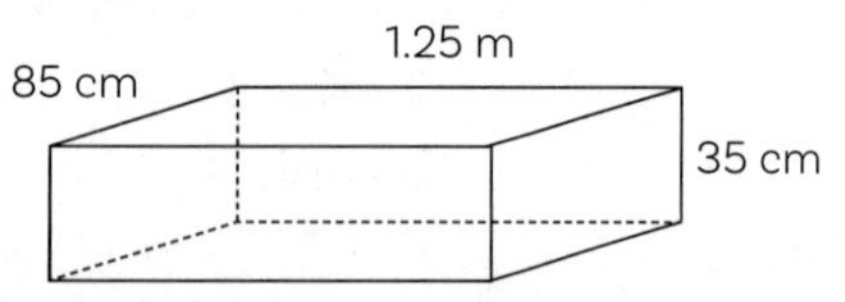

6 Write your answer in cubic metres (m³).

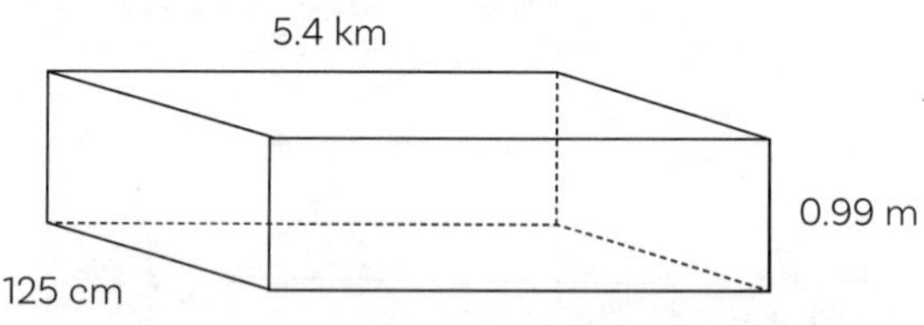

Answer these questions.

7 This cube and cuboid have the same volume. What are the dimensions of the cube? Write the dimensions on the diagram.

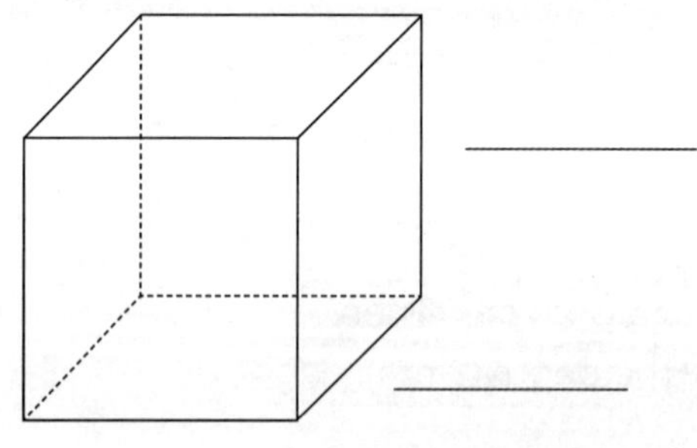

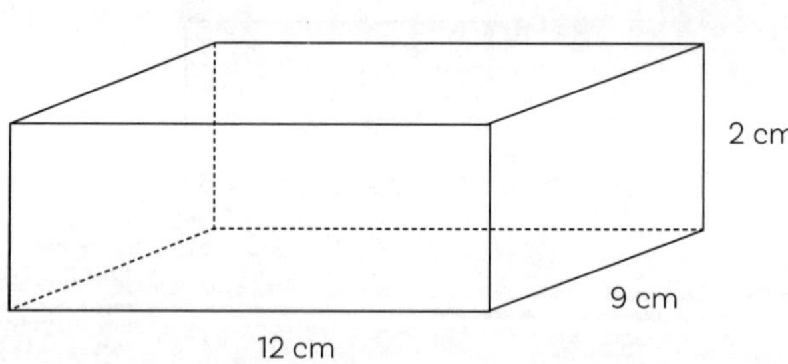

8 The volume of a cuboid is 132 cm³. It has dimensions of 4 cm and 3 cm. What is the third dimension of the cuboid?

9 A storage container measures 150 cm by 90 cm by 60 cm. Small cartons, each measuring 5 cm by 6 cm by 10 cm, are to be packed tightly inside the container. How many cartons can fit inside the container?

 ISBN: 9780170497978

Compound cuboids

- The volume of a compound cuboid can be found by finding the area of the face and multiplying by the depth.

Volume = area of face x depth

Example:

Split the face into rectangles and then multiply by the depth.

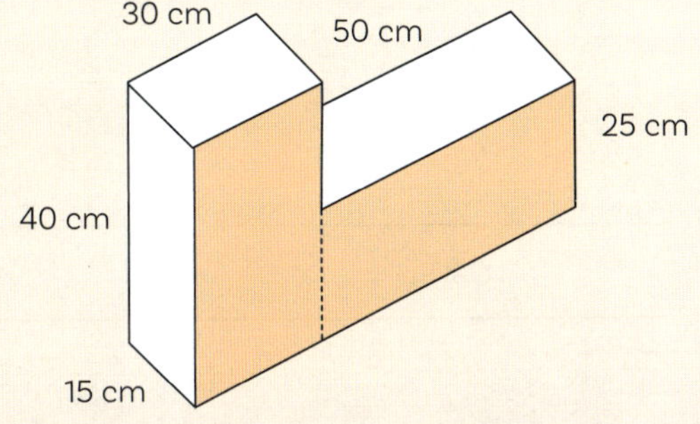

Volume = **area of face** x *d*

= **((25 x 50) + (30 x 40))** x *d*

= **(1250 + 1200)** x d

= **(2450)** x 15

= 36 750 cm^3

Or split the shape into cuboids.

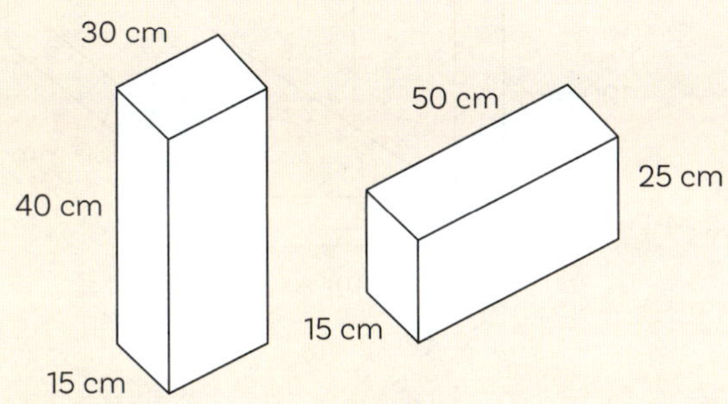

Volume = **cuboid 1** + **cuboid 2**

= (40 x 30 x 15) + (50 x 25 x 15)

= 18 000 + 18 750

= 36 750 cm^3

Calculate the volumes of these compound cuboids.

1

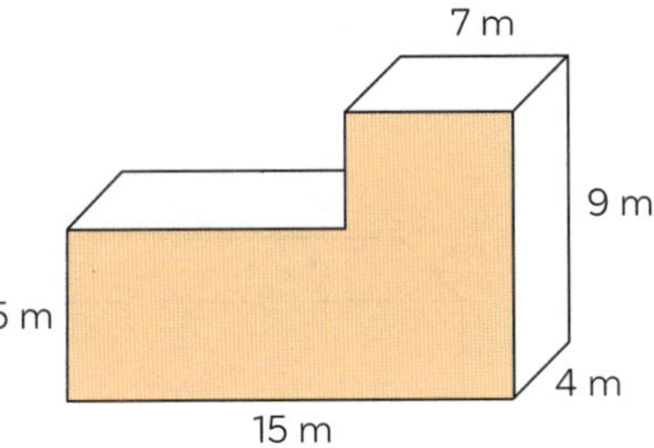

____

____

2

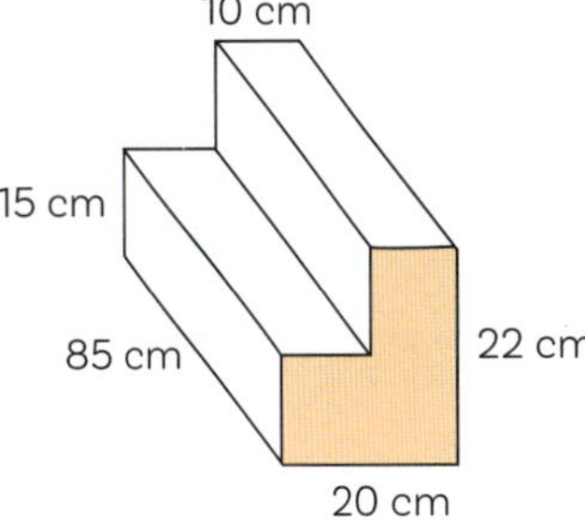

____

____

3

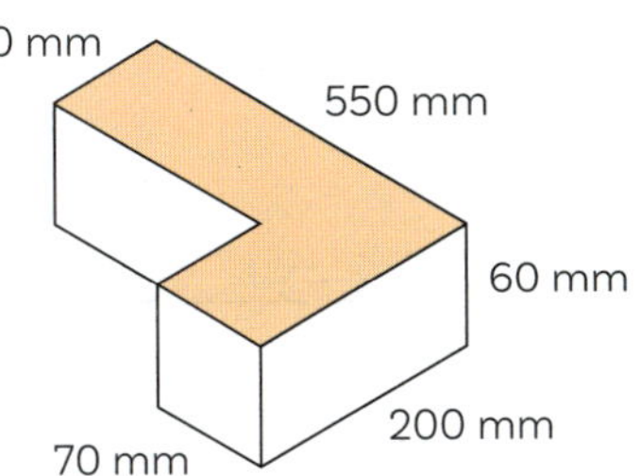

____

____

4

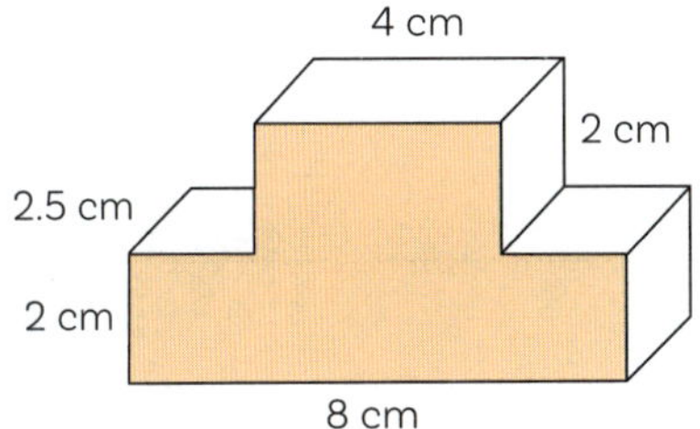

____

____

ISBN: 9780170497978

5

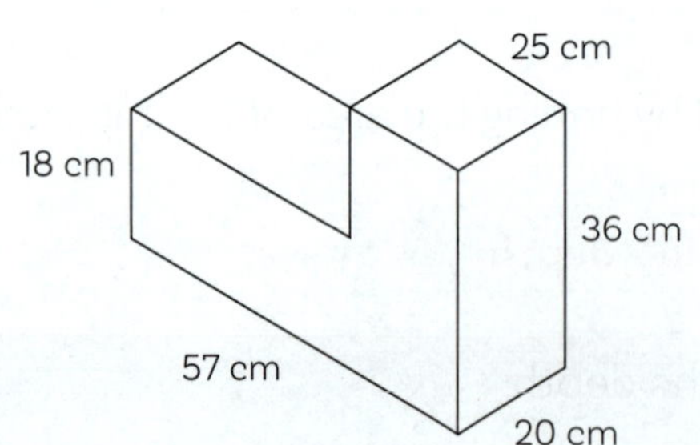

6

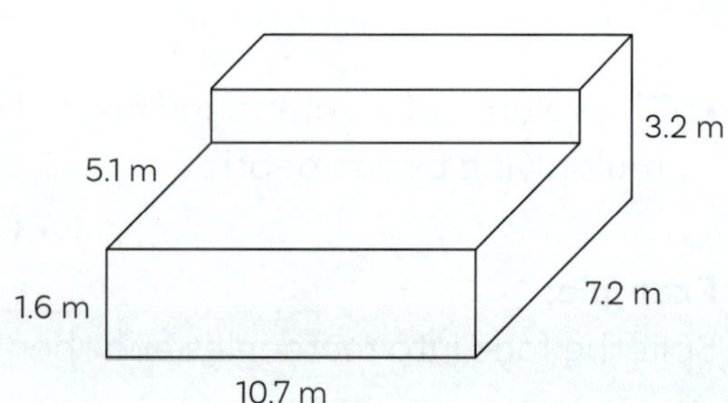

7

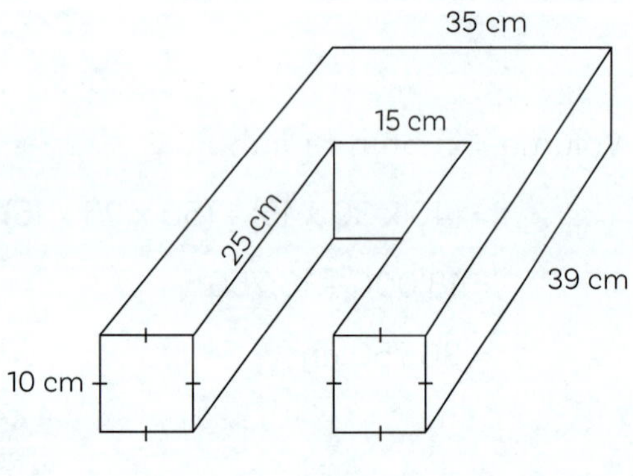

8

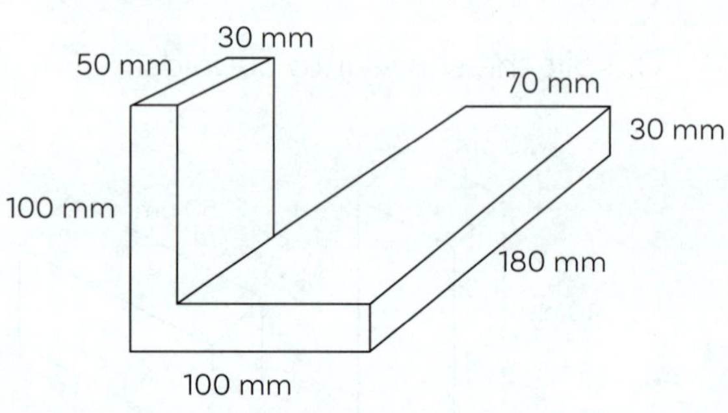

9

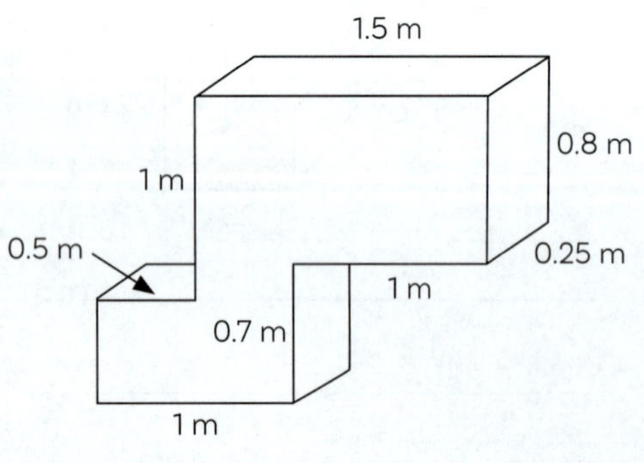

10

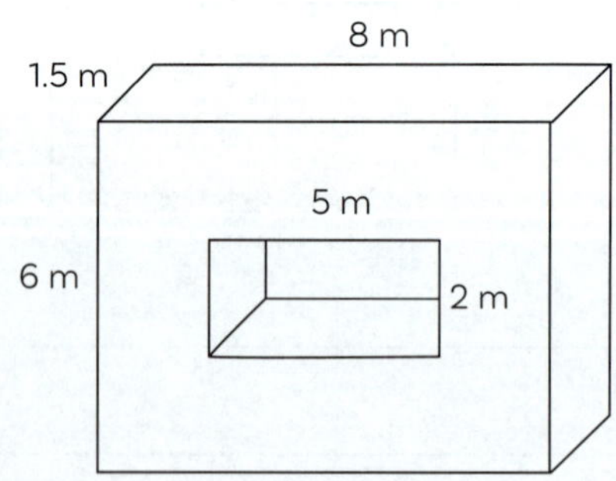

ISBN: 9780170497978

Scaling

Scale factor

- When scaling shapes, the figure gets **larger** or **smaller**.
- The **scale factor** tells us how much larger or smaller the shape becomes.

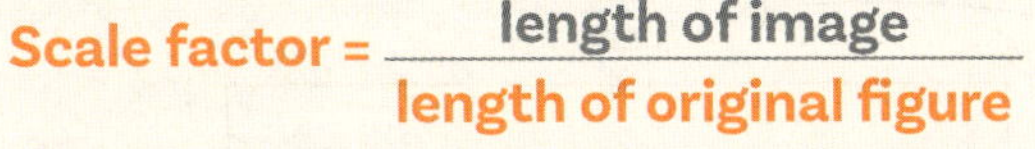

$$\text{Scale factor} = \frac{\text{length of image}}{\text{length of original figure}}$$

Examples:

1 Original figure — Image

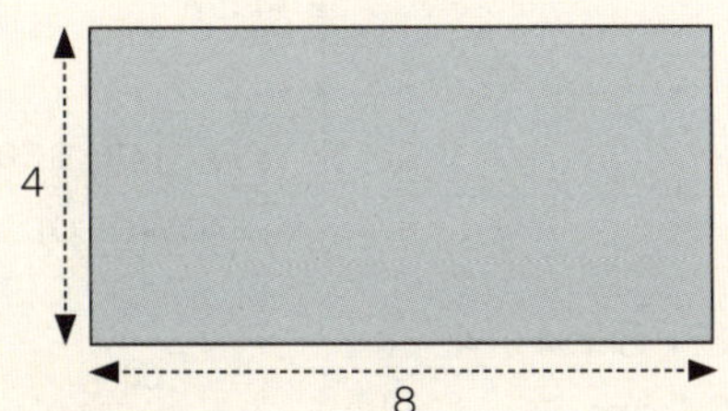

$$\text{Scale factor} = \frac{\text{length of image}}{\text{length of original figure}}$$

$$= \frac{8}{4}$$

$$= 2$$

2 Original figure — Image

6 m

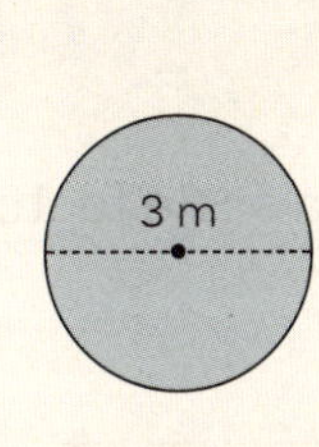

$$\text{Scale factor} = \frac{\text{length of image}}{\text{length of original figure}}$$

$$= \frac{3}{6}$$

$$= \frac{1}{2} \text{ or } 0.5$$

Write the scale factor for these enlargements

1

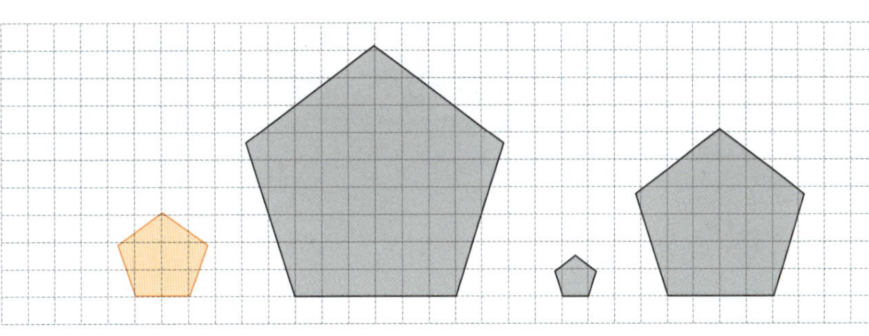

scale factor = ______ scale factor = ______ scale factor = ______

2

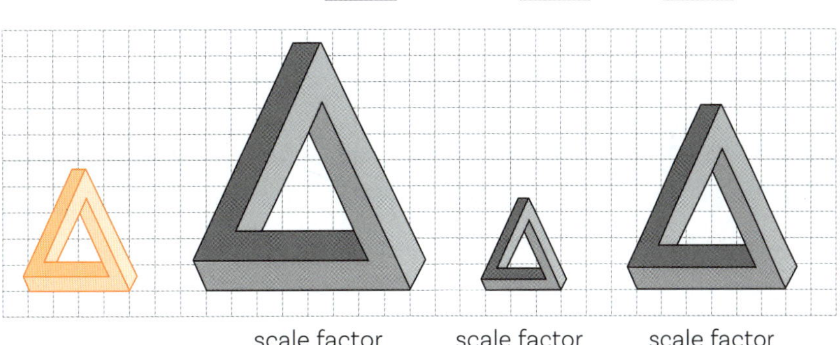

scale factor = ______ scale factor = ______ scale factor = ______

ISBN: 9780170497978

Scale factors for perimeter, area and volume

- Notice the scale factor applies to the **dimensions** and **not area or volume**.

Examples:

Perimeter

This rectangle's dimensions have been quadrupled (x 4): a scale factor of 4.

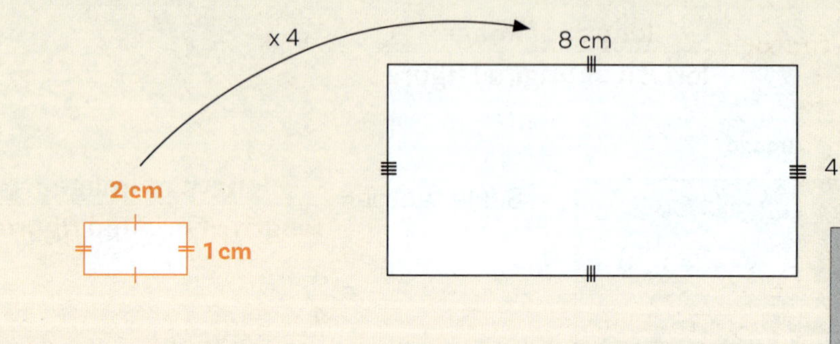

Perimeter = 2 + 2 + 1 + 1
= 6 cm

Perimeter = 8 + 8 + 4 + 4
= 24 cm

x 4

The scale factor to the power of **one**, (scale factor)^1:
$4^1 = 4$
For **perimeter**, the scale factor stays the **same**.

Area

This triangle's dimensions have been tripled (x 3): a scale factor of 3.

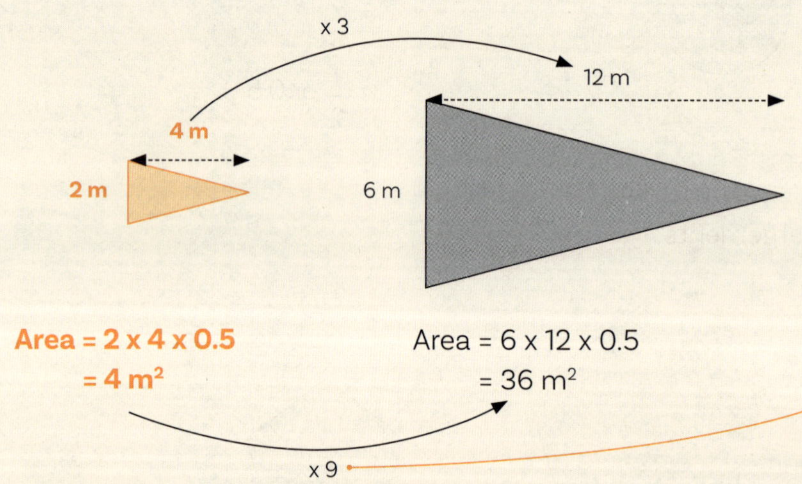

The scale factor to the power of **two**, (scale factor)^2:
$3^2 = 9$
For **area**, the scale factor must be **squared**.

Volume

This cuboid's dimensions have been doubled: a scale factor of 2.

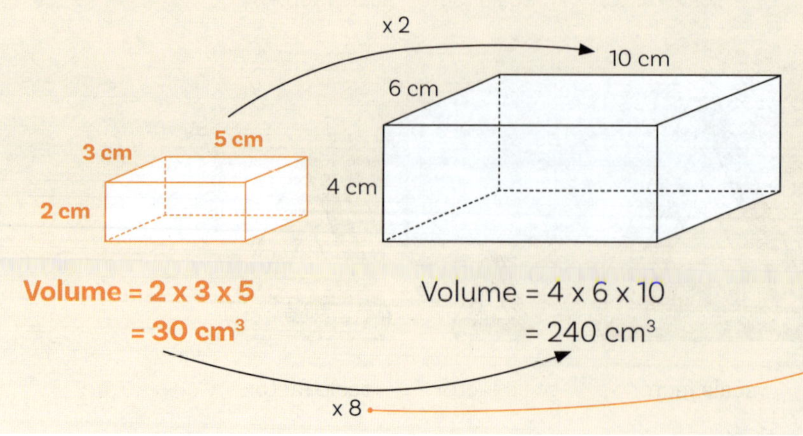

The scale factor to the power of **three**, (scale factor)^3:
$2^3 = 8$
For **volume**, the scale factor must be **cubed**.

ISBN: 9780170497978

1 This image of this square has a scale factor of 3. Calculate the perimeter and area of both shapes.

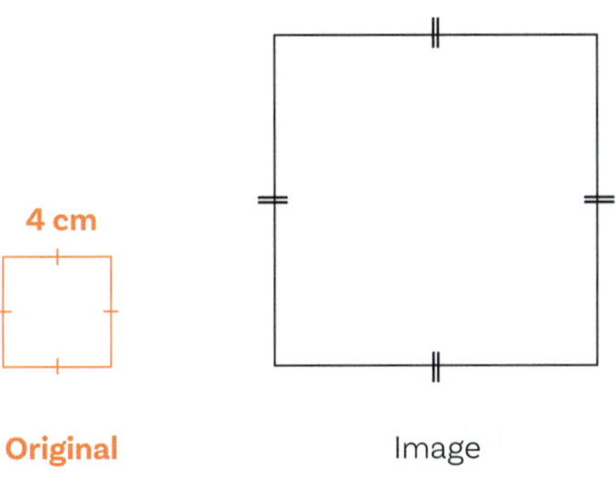

Perimeter original ________________

Perimeter image ________________

Area of original ________________

Area of image ________________

2 This cuboid is enlarged by a scale factor of 3. Calculate the volume of the enlarged cuboid.

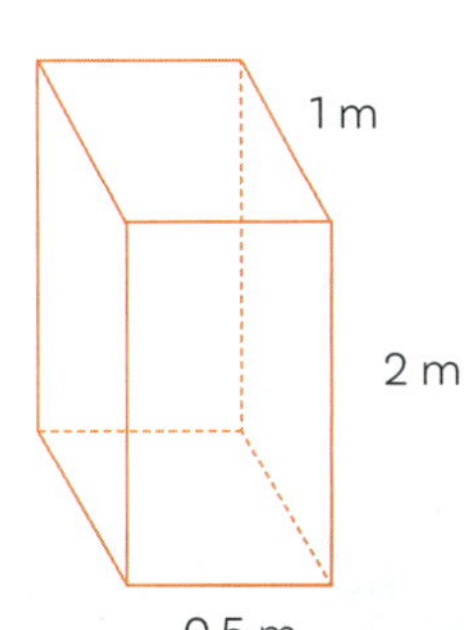

____

____

3 This triangle has been increased by a scale factor of 2. Calculate the perimeter of the enlarged shape.

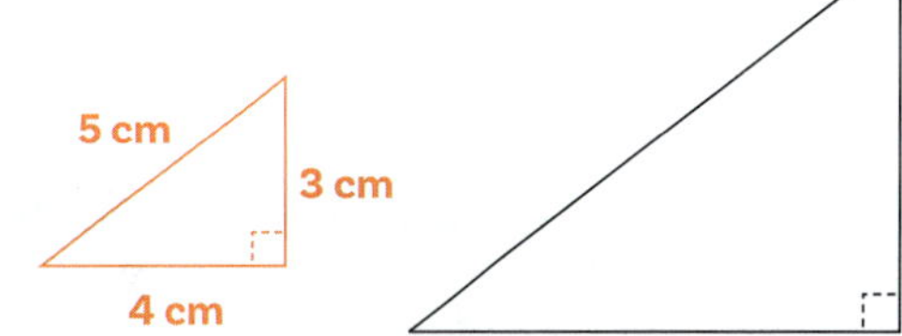

____

____

4 What scale factor has this shape been increased by?

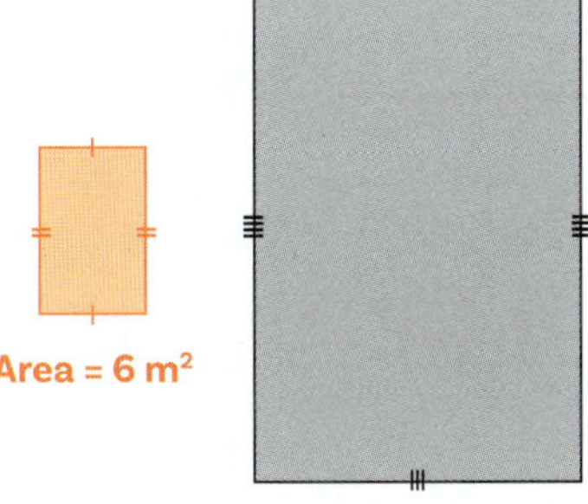

____

5 Calculate the perimeter of the enlarged parallelogram.

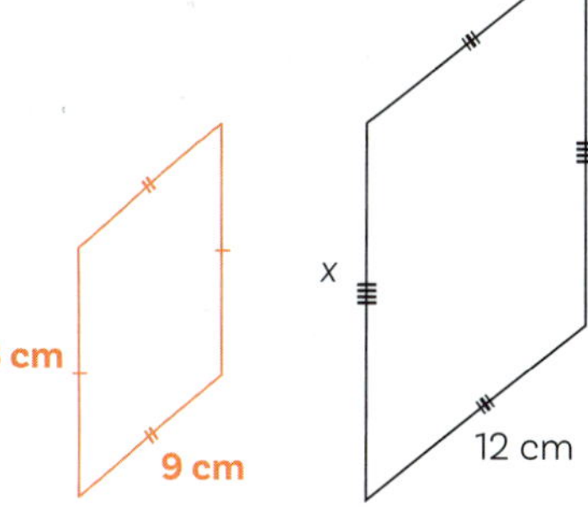

____

6 This cube has been increased by a scale factor of 2.5. Find the dimensions of the enlarged cube and its volume.

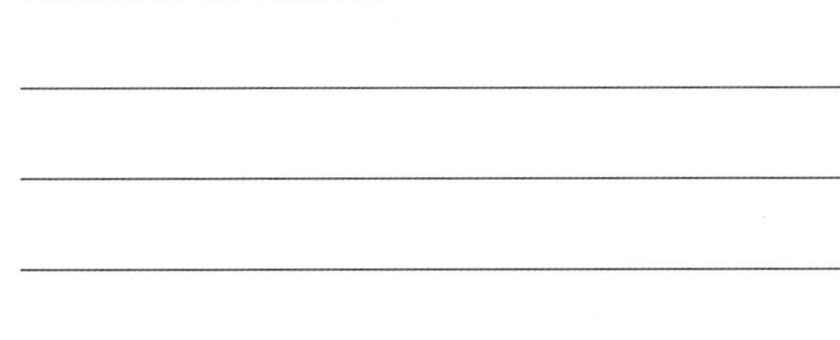

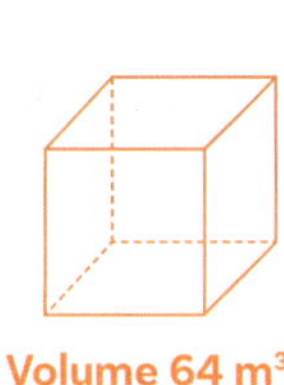

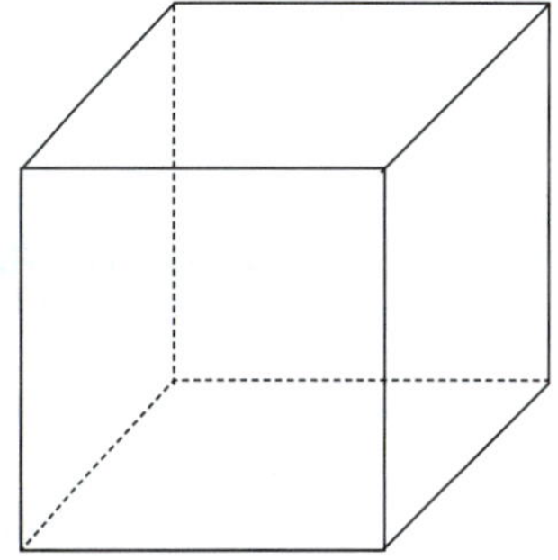

ISBN: 9780170497978

The Theorem of Pythagoras

Activity

1 Trace the two blue squares containing the numbers 1 to 5 onto a piece of paper.

2 Cut out your copies of these squares.

3 Cut along the dotted lines on the bigger blue square.

4 Like a jigsaw, fit pieces 1 to 5 onto the large orange square, and stick them down.

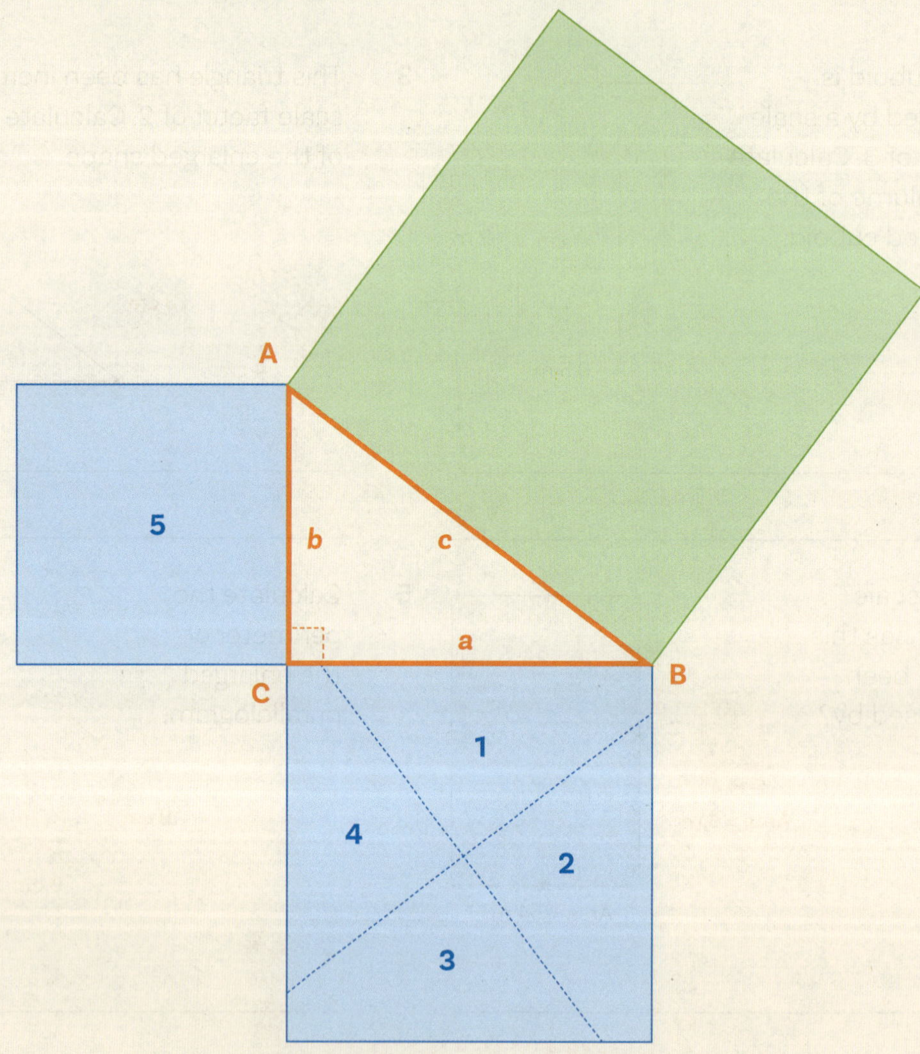

Complete:

- The area of the **green** square = c^2
- The area of the **bottom** square (containing 1, 2, 3 and 4) = ____________
- The area of the **smallest** square (5) = ________

So: c^2 = ________ + ________

You have just illustrated the Theorem of Pythagoras.

 ISBN: 9780170497978

The Theorem of Pythagoras:

- It applies to **right-angled** triangles only.
- It is used for finding **lengths** of sides.
- The longest side is the **hypotenuse**.
- The hypotenuse is always **opposite the right angle**.

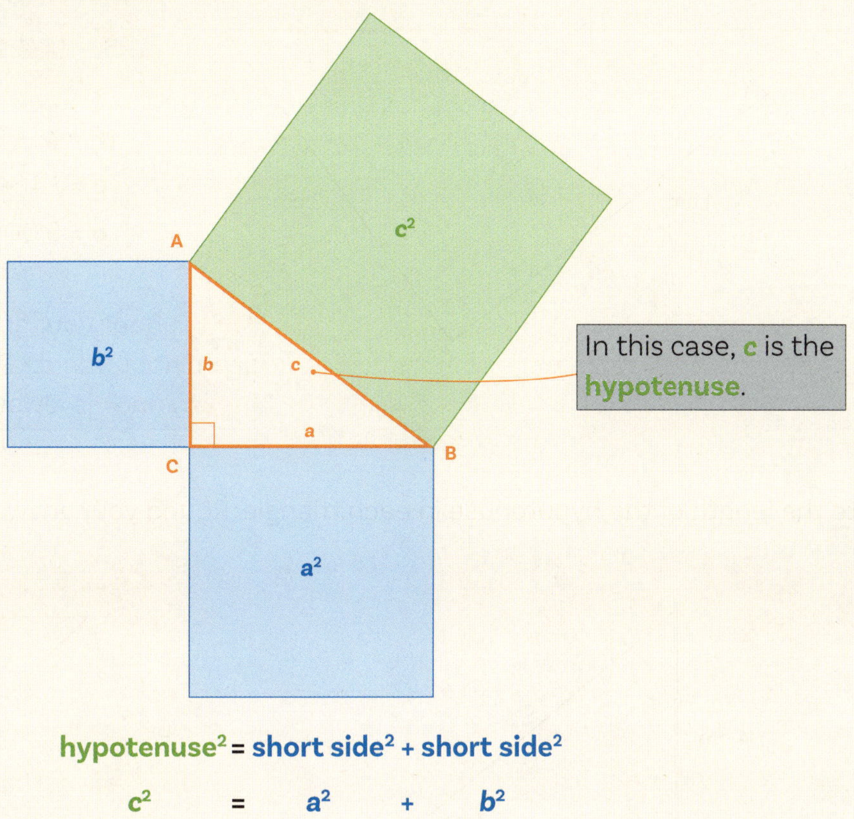

hypotenuse^2 = short side^2 + short side^2

$$c^2 = a^2 + b^2$$

Finding the length of the hypotenuse

Examples:

1 Calculate the length of c.

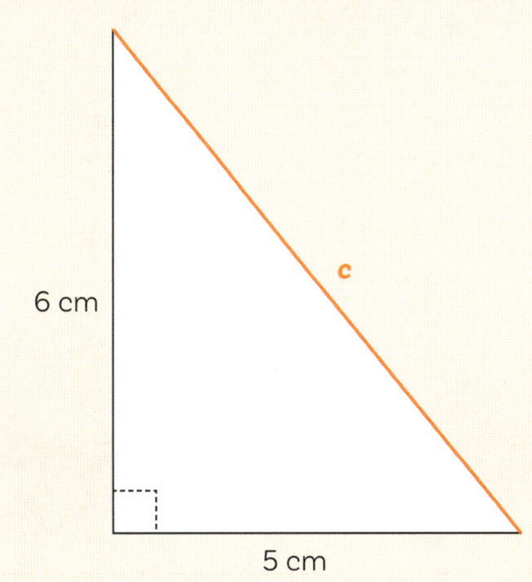

$$c^2 = a^2 + b^2$$
$$= 6^2 + 5^2$$
$$c = \sqrt{6^2 + 5^2}$$
$$c = 7.81 \text{ cm (2 dp)}$$

Make sure you use **brackets** on your calculator: $\sqrt{(6^2 + 5^2)}$

Don't forget to:

1 include **units** in your answer

2 **round** your answer appropriately.

2 Sometimes:

- the letters may **not** be *a*, *b* and *c*
- the triangle might be **orientated differently**.

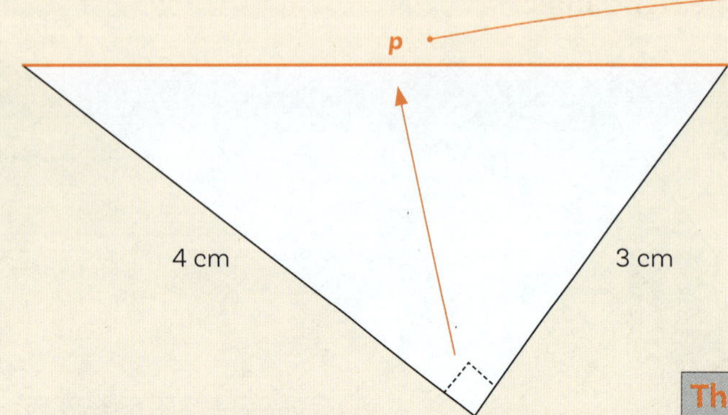

p is opposite the right angle, so **p is the hypotenuse**.
This means that p^2 must be **on its own** on one side of the = sign.

$p^2 = 4^2 + 3^2$

$p = \sqrt{4^2 + 3^2}$

$p = 5.00$ cm (2 dp)

Think about your answer. Does it seem about right? Remember, the **hypotenuse** is always the **longest** side.

Calculate the length of the hypotenuse in each triangle. Round your answers to 2 dp.

1

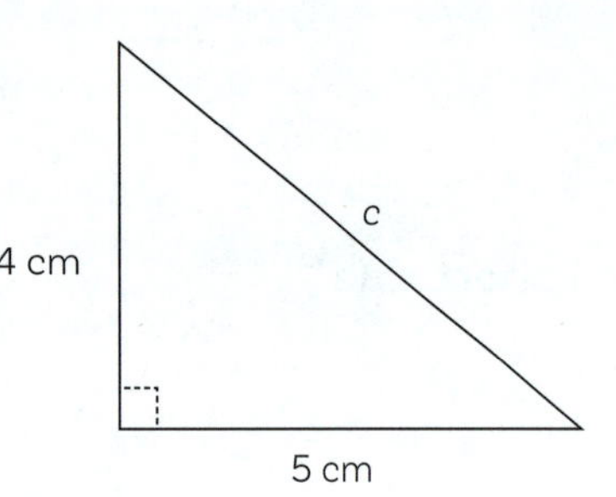

2

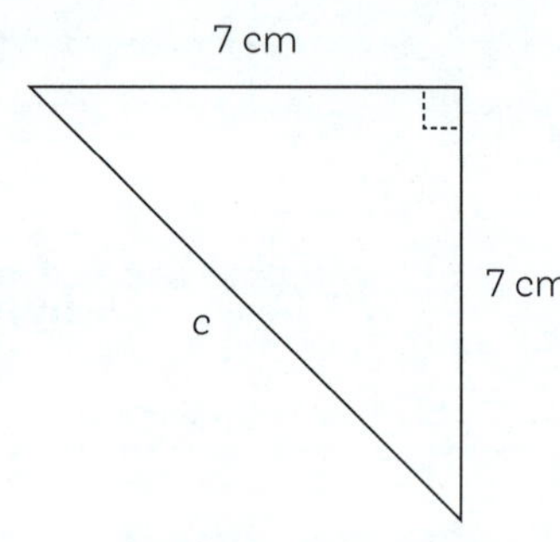

3

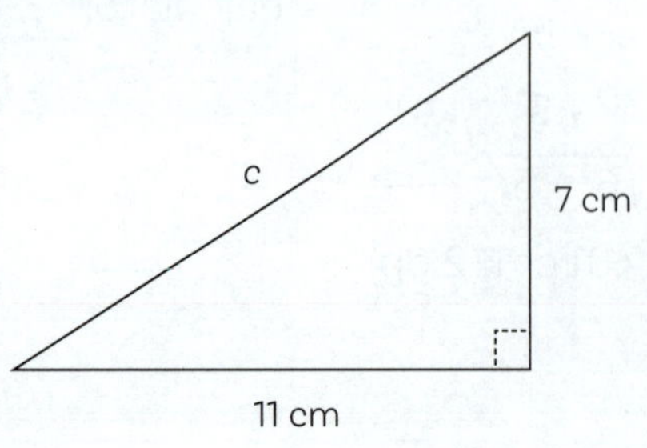

4

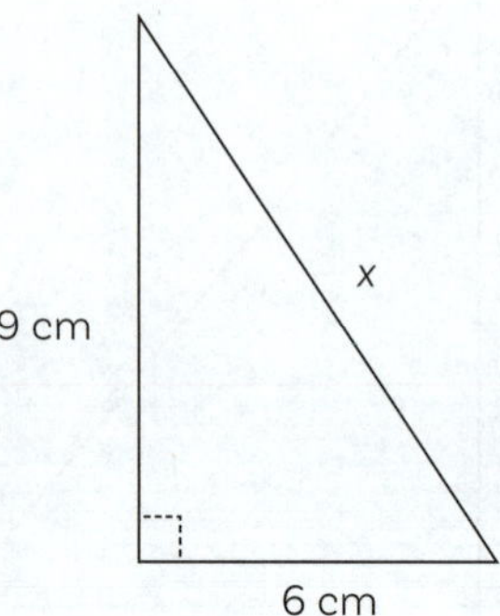

ISBN: 9780170497978

5

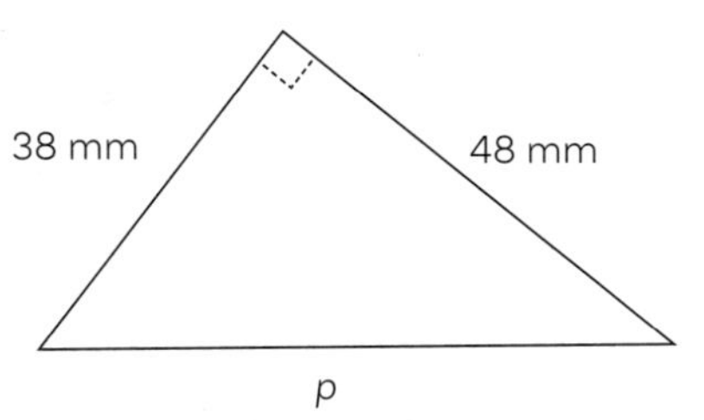

6

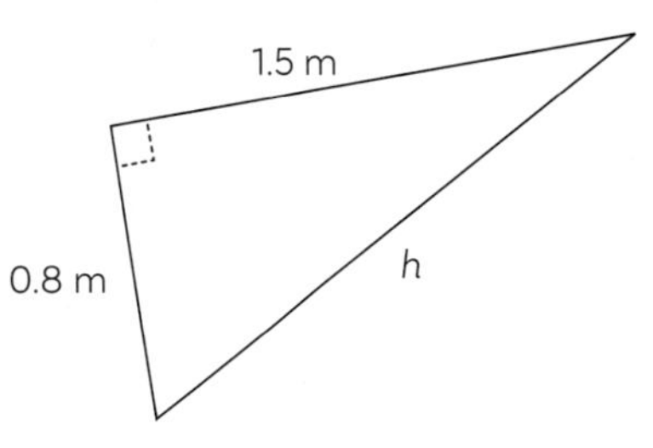

7

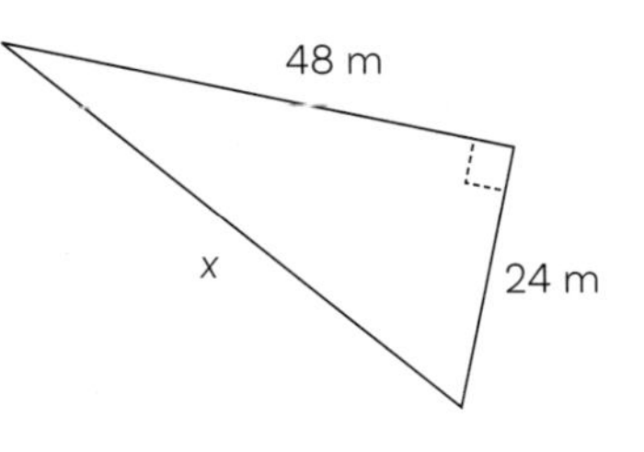

8

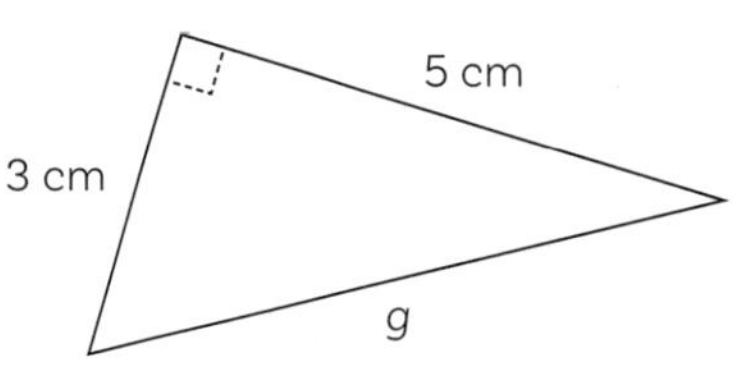

9

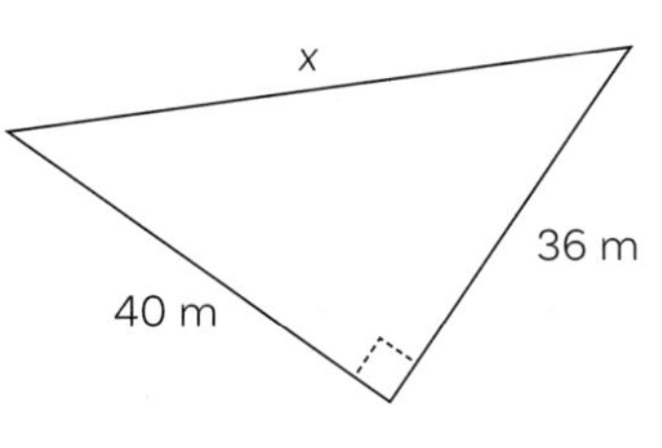

10

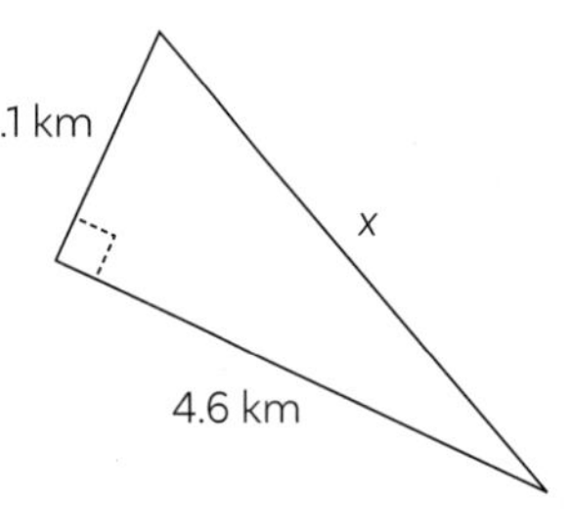

11

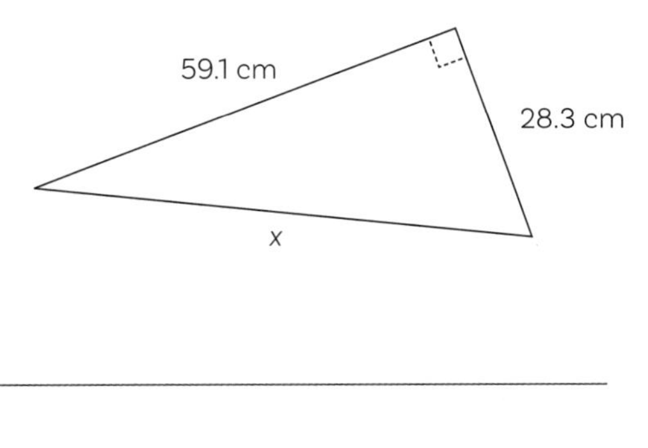

12

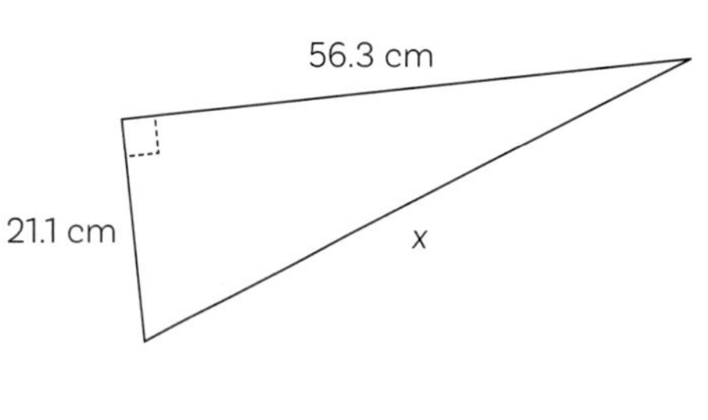

ISBN: 9780170497978

Finding the lengths of short sides

Example: Calculate the length of a.

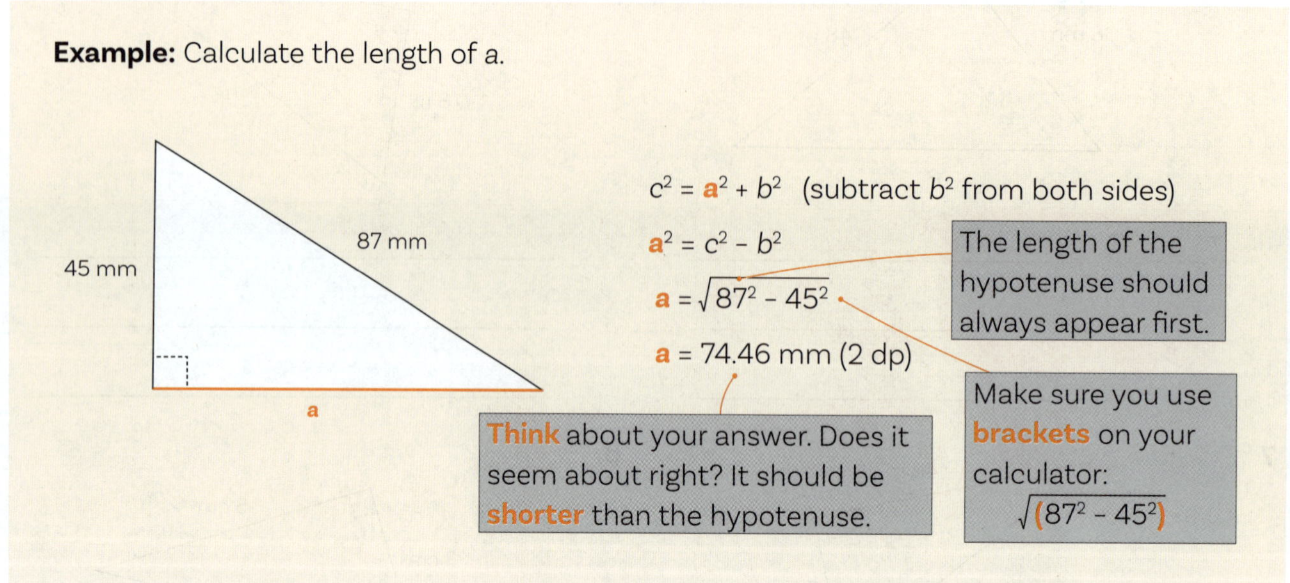

Calculate the unknown length in each triangle. Round your answers to 2 dp.

1

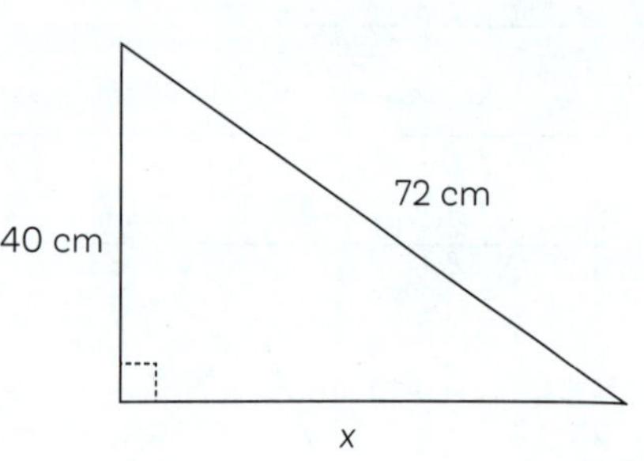

2

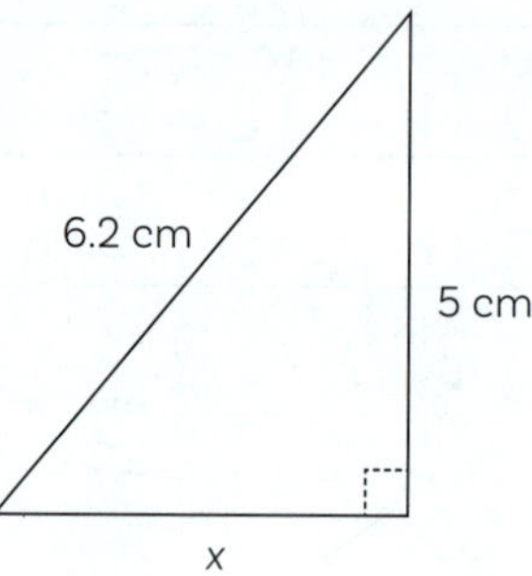

3

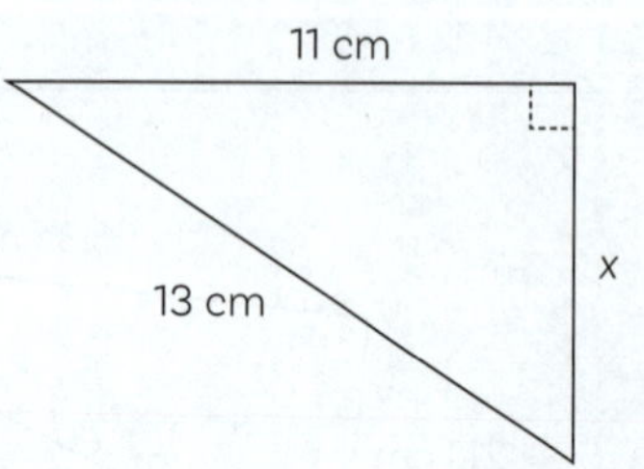

4

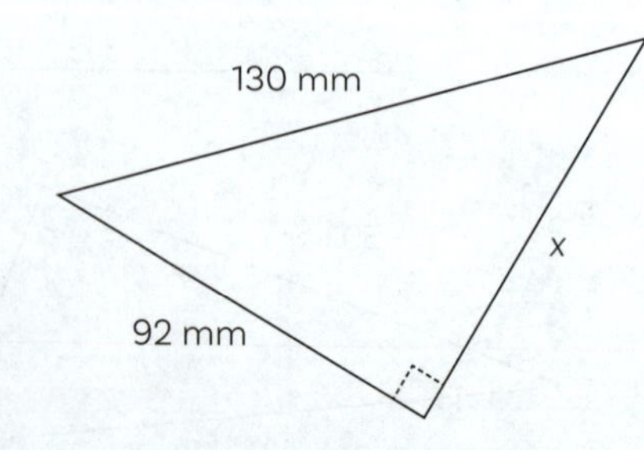

 ISBN: 9780170497978

5

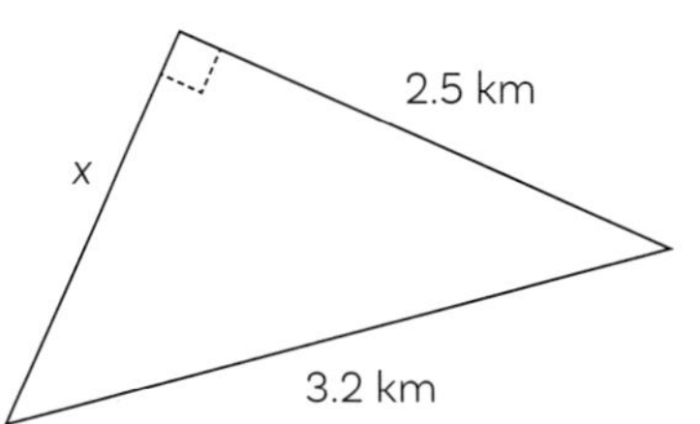

6

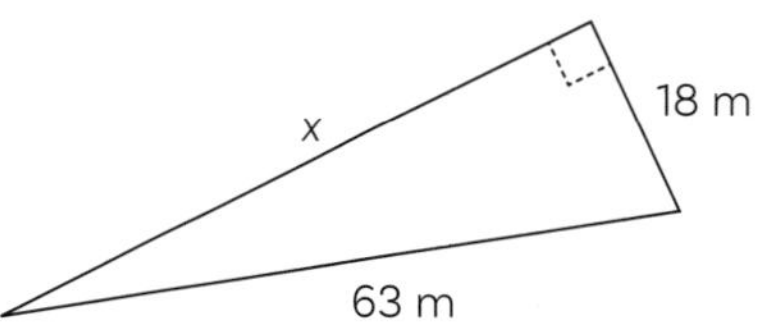

7

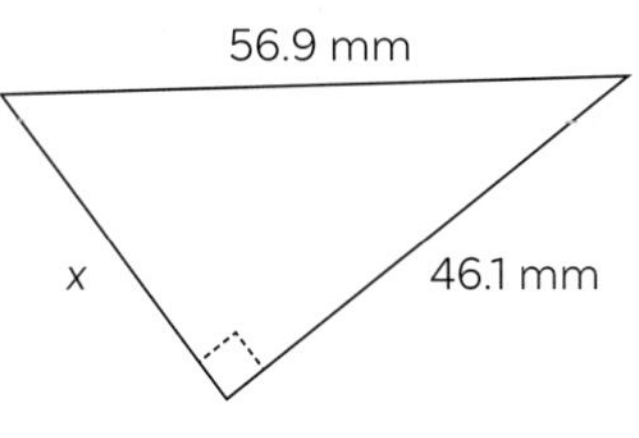

8

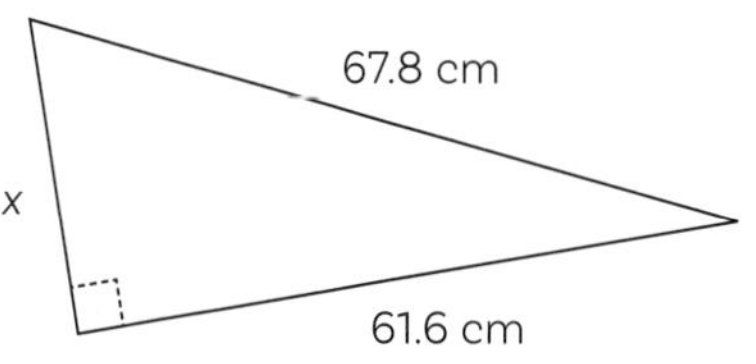

9

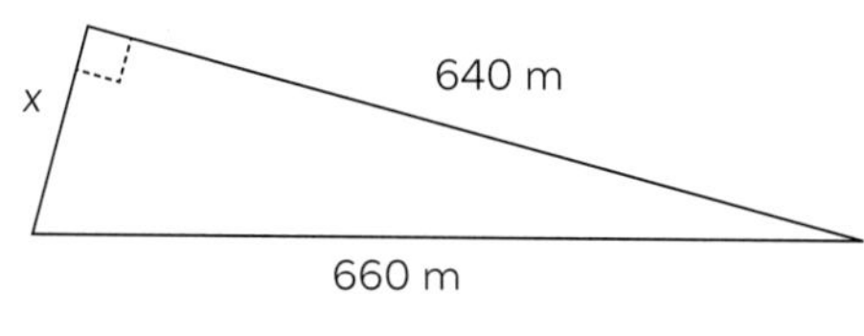

10

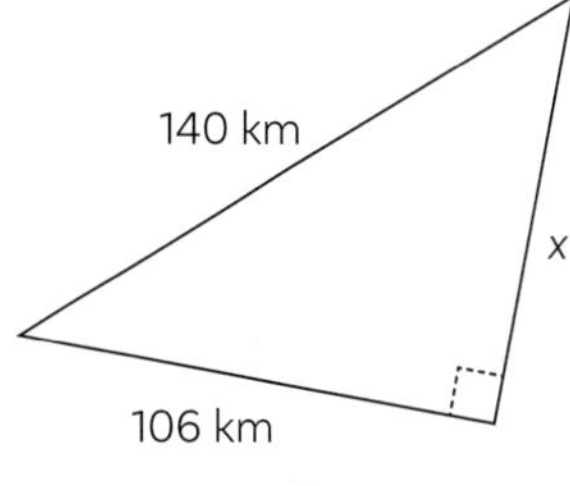

11

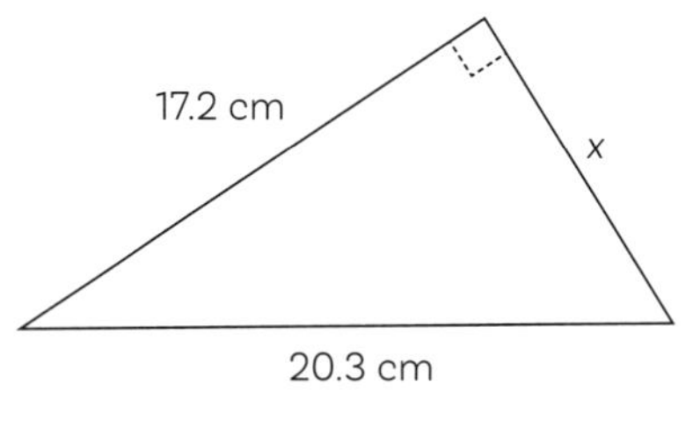

12

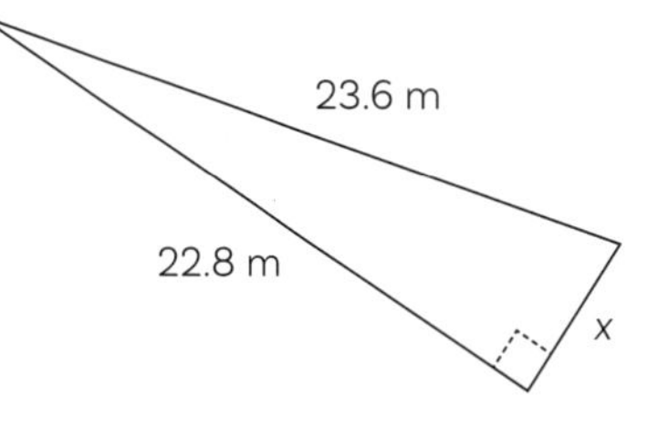

ISBN: 9780170497978

Mixing it up

Calculate the unknown length in each triangle. Round your answers to 2 dp.

1

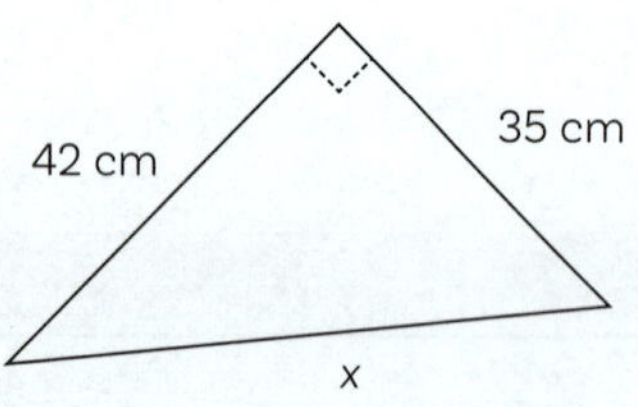

2

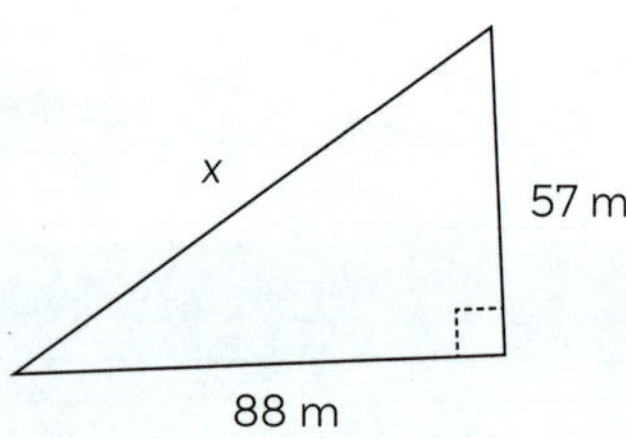

3

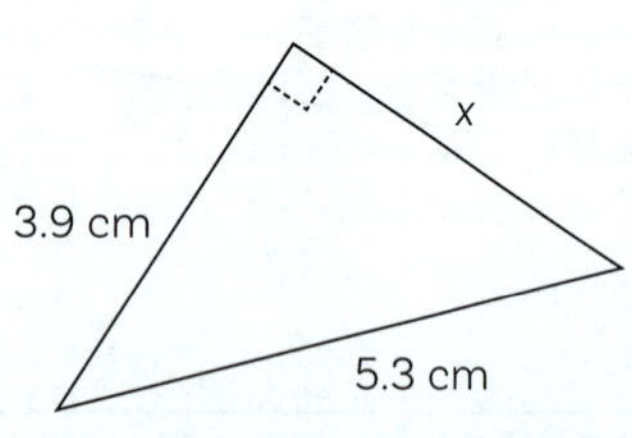

4

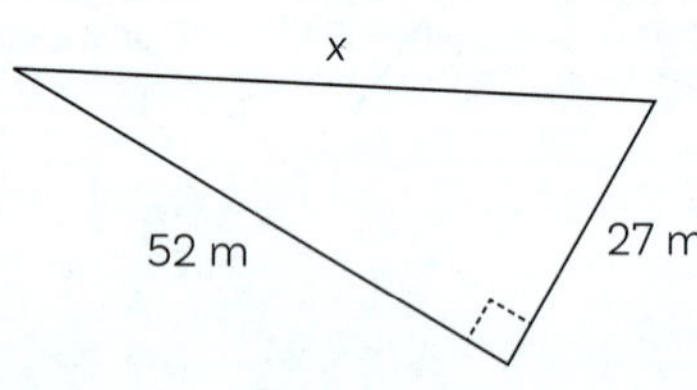

5

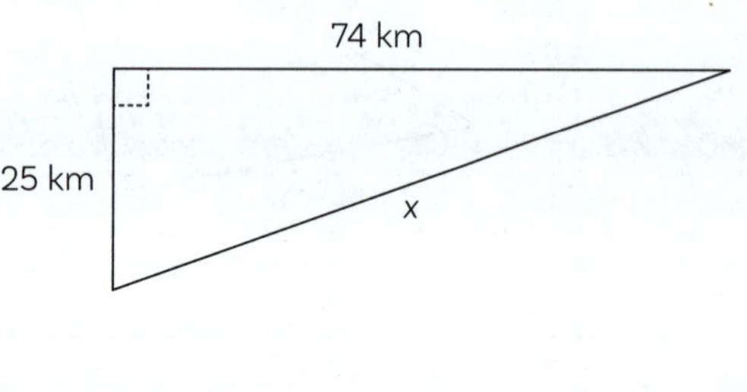

6

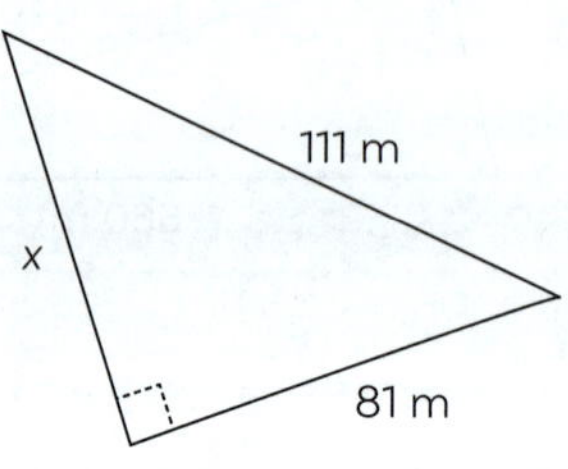

7

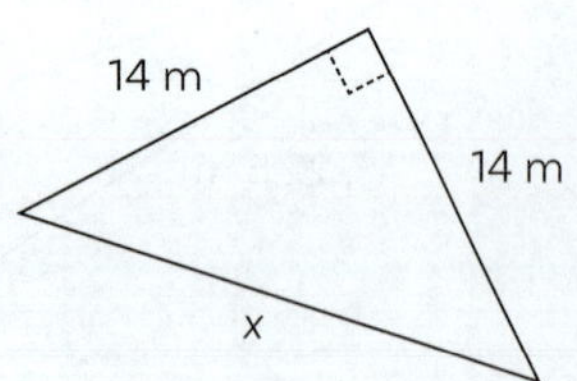

8

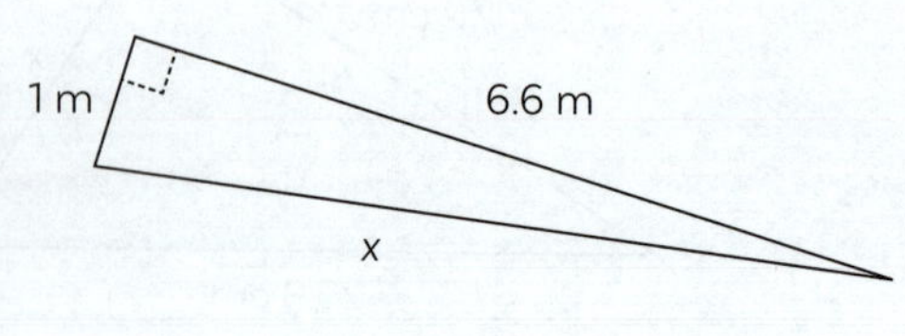

 ISBN: 9780170497978

GEOMETRY

The language of geometry

Use the terms in the box and match them to the most appropriate image below. Each term can be used once only.

Obtuse angle	Bisector	Diagonal	Right angle
Quadrilateral	Supplementary angles	Vertex	Acute angle
Parallel lines	Adjacent angles	Reflex angle	Complementary angles

1

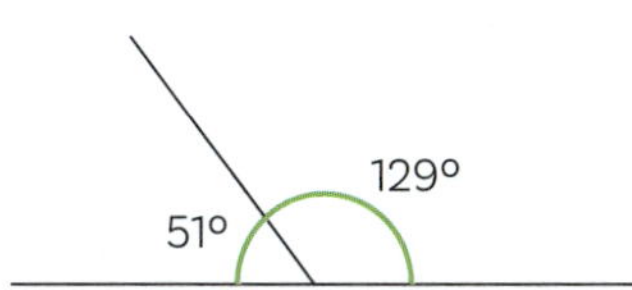

____

2

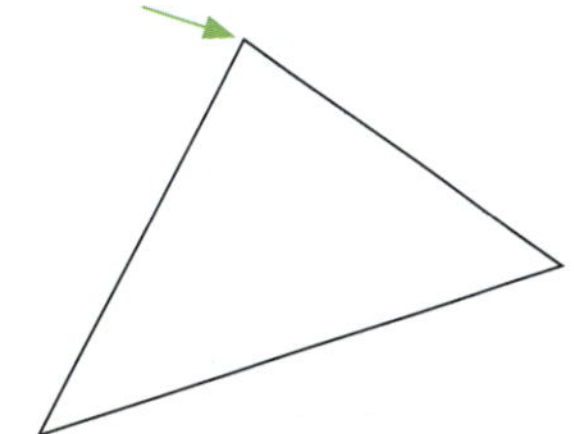

____

3

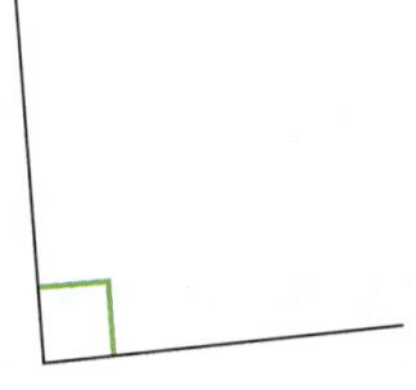

____

4

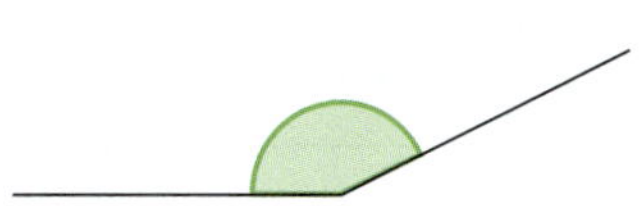

____

5

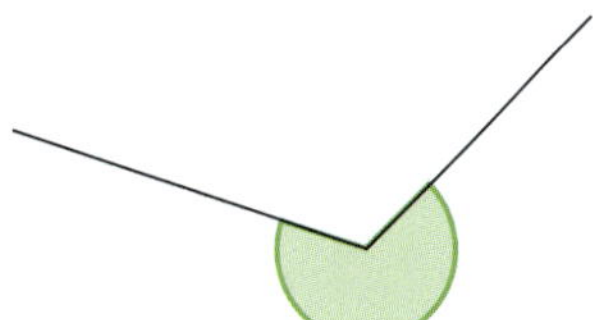

____

6

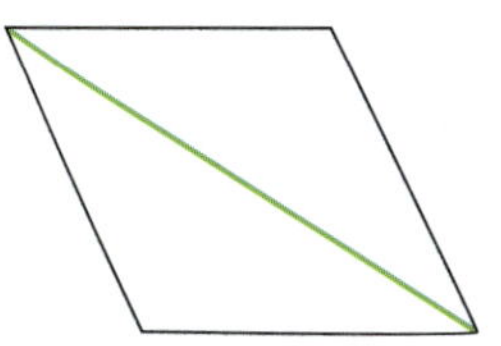

____

7

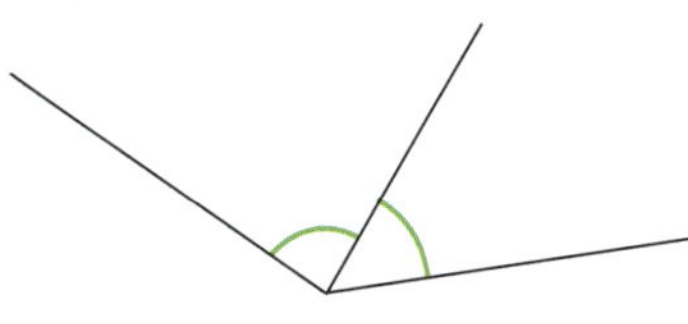

____

8

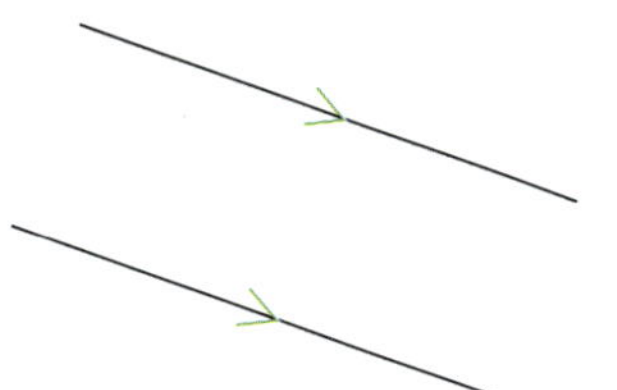

____

9

____

10

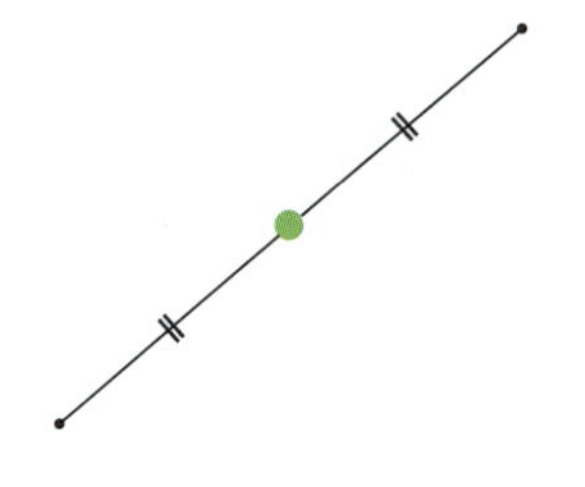

____

11

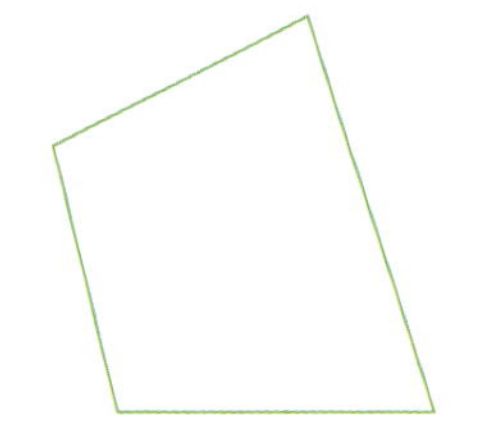

____

12

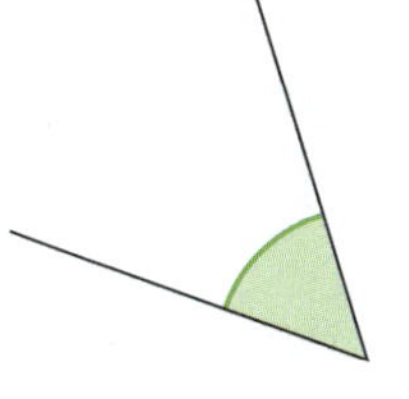

____

ISBN: 9780170497978

Angles

Angle revision

Angles at a point

- Angles at a point, or angles in a full rotation, **add to 360°**.

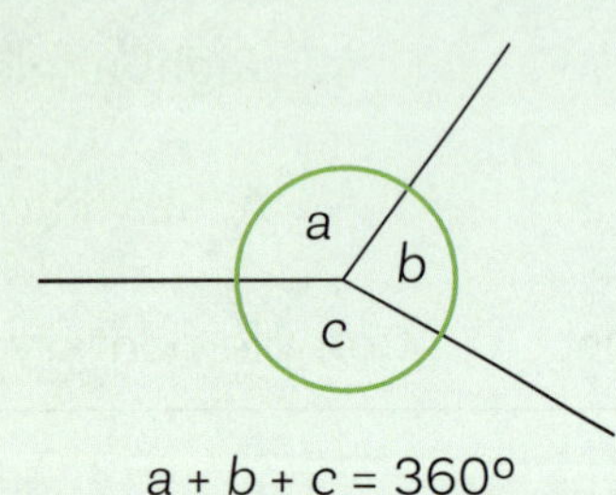

$a + b + c = 360°$

Example:

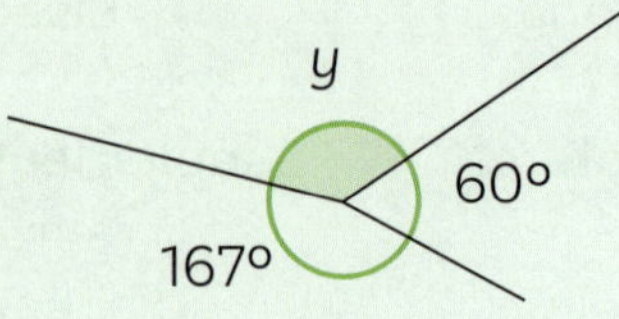

$y = 360° - 167° - 60°$

$y = 133°$

Angles at a point add to 360°.

Reason: $\angle$s at a point = 360°

Angles on a line

- Angles on a line **add to 180°**.
- These are also known as **supplementary** angles.

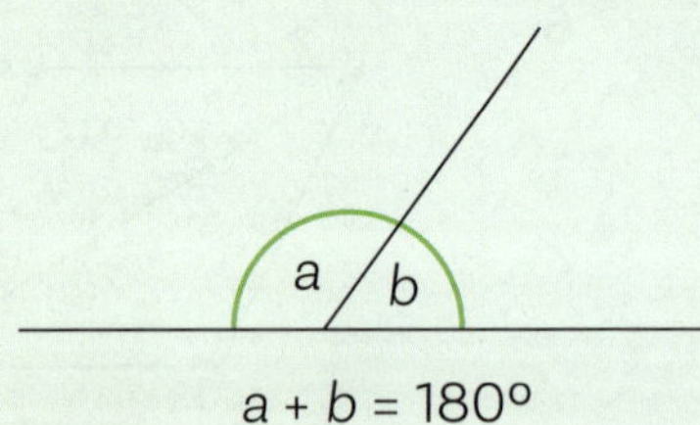

$a + b = 180°$

Example:

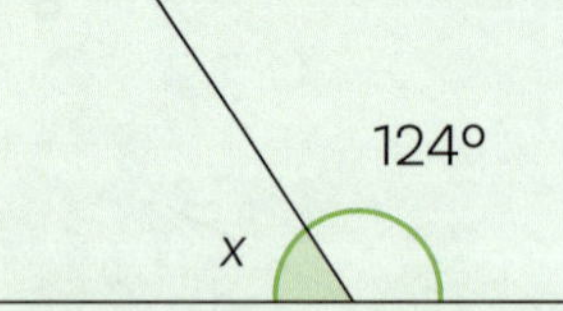

$x = 180° - 124°$

$x = 56°$

You are allowed to shorten 'angles on a line add to 180°' to this:

Reason: $\angle$s on a line = 180°

When you are asked for a reason, you must include **detail**.

Vertically opposite angles

- Vertically opposite angles **are equal**.

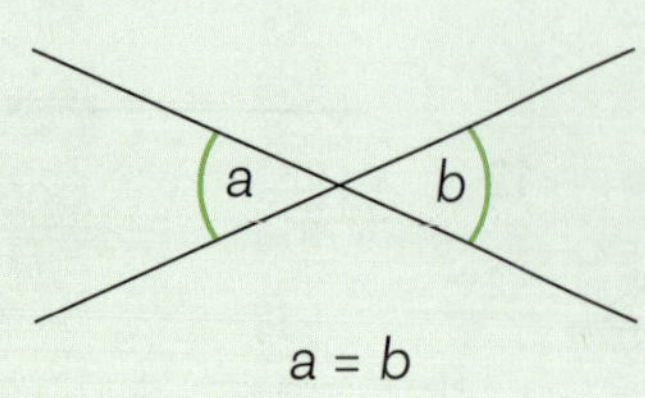

$a = b$

Example:

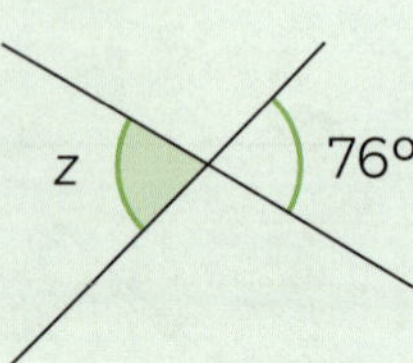

$z = 76°$

Vertically opposite angles are equal.

Reason: Vert opp $\angle$s =

 ISBN: 9780170497978

Calculate the missing angles and write the reason(s) used. If your reasons are different from those in the answers, check them with your teacher.

1

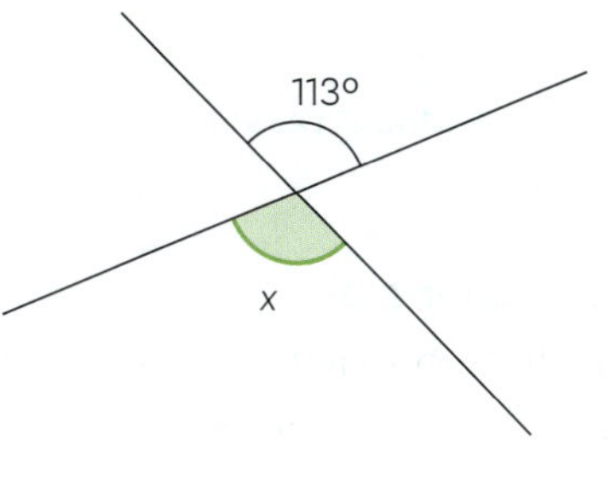

Reason(s):

2

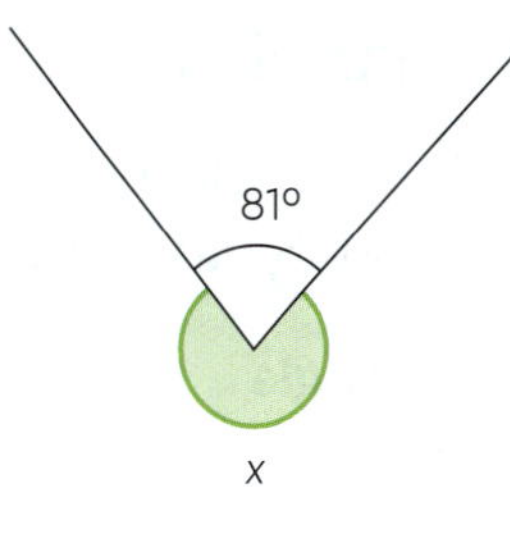

Reason(s):

3

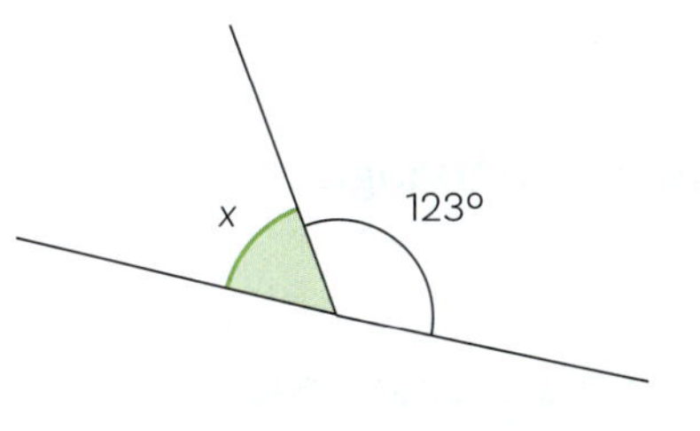

Reason(s):

4

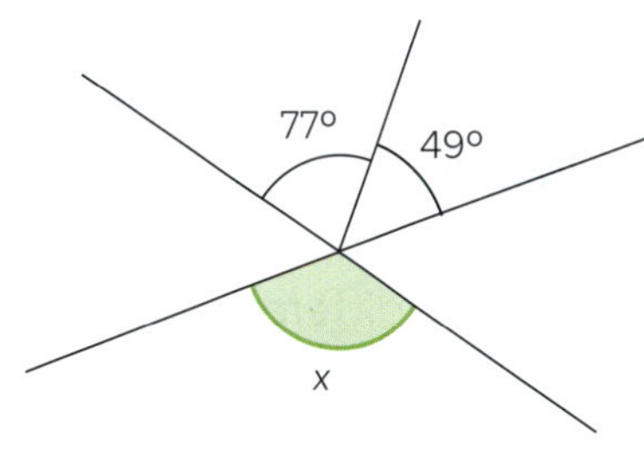

Reason(s):

5

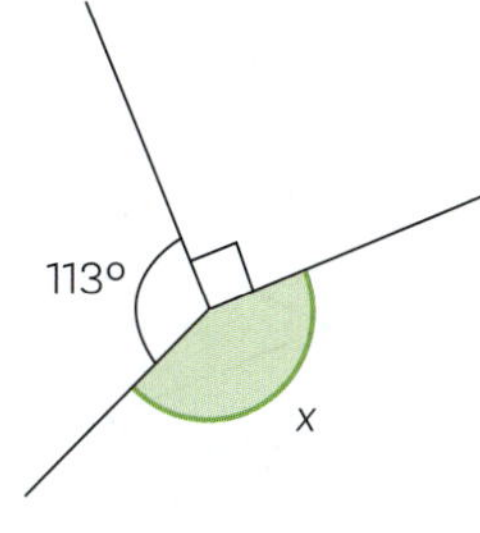

Reason(s):

6

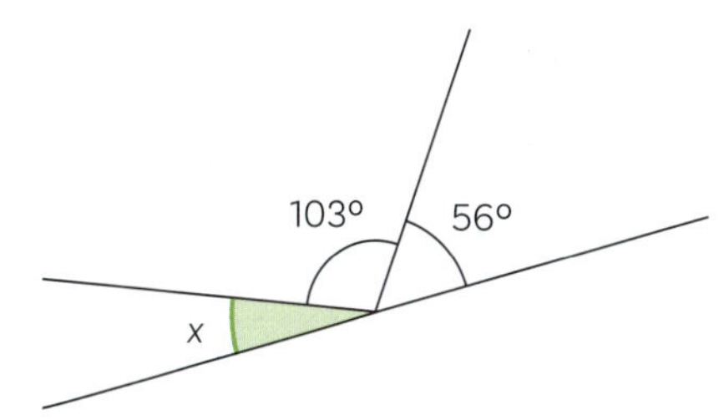

Reason(s):

7

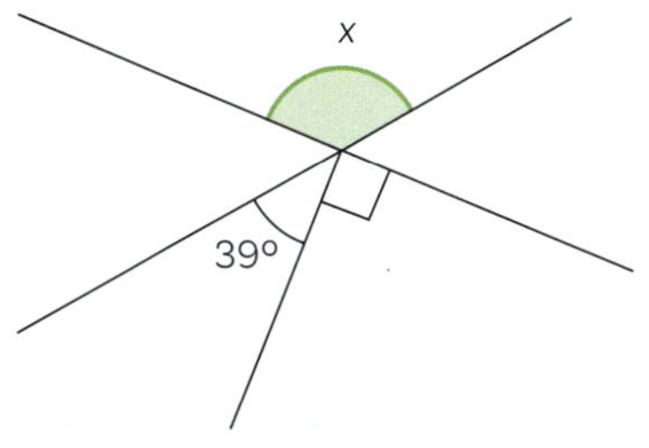

Reason(s):

8

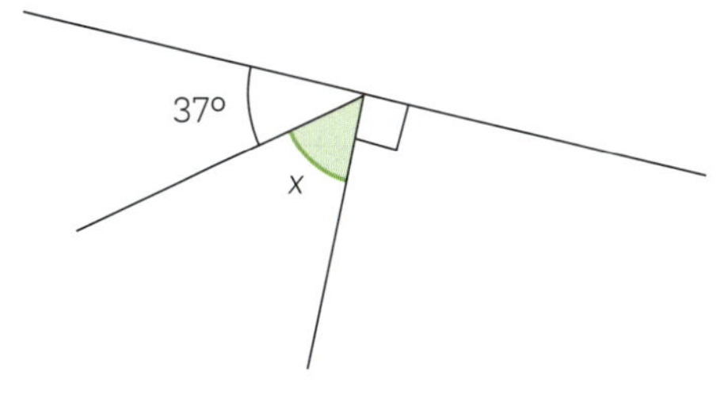

Reason(s):

ISBN: 9780170497978

Triangles

Naming triangles

- A **triangle** is any closed shape (no gaps) with exactly **three straight sides**.
- There are four types of triangles.

Equilateral triangle

- All three sides are exactly the same length.
- All three angles are the same size.

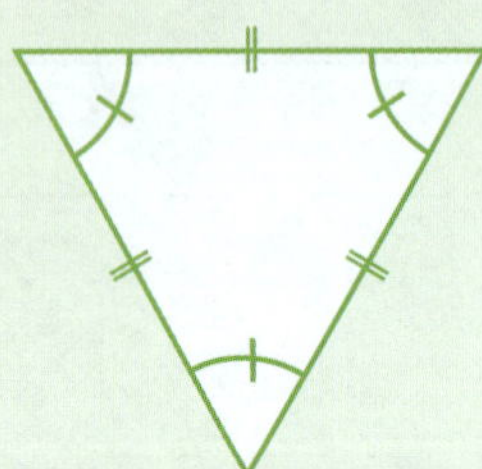

Isosceles triangle

- Exactly two sides are the same length.
- Two angles are the same size. We call these base angles.

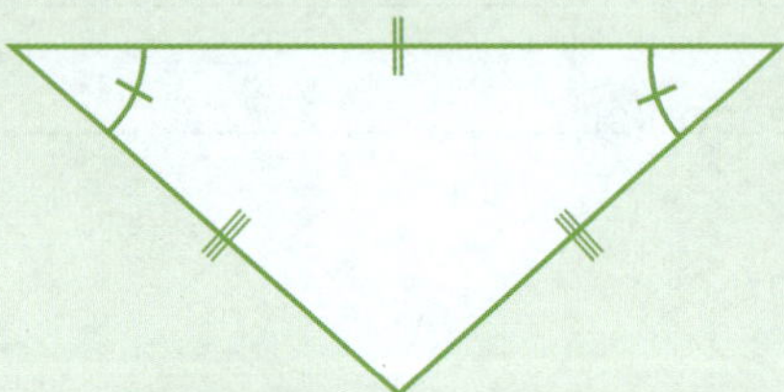

Scalene triangle

- All sides have different lengths.
- All angles have different sizes.

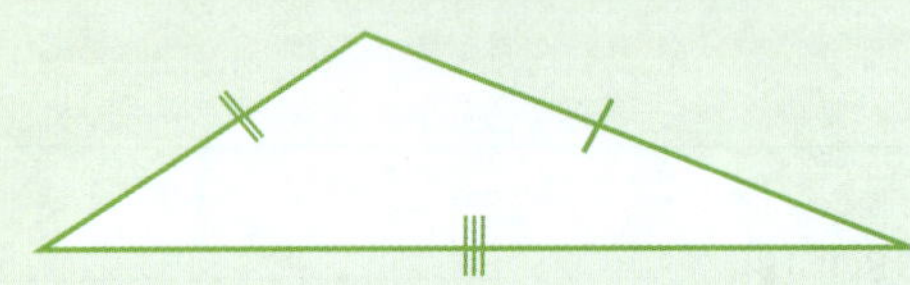

Right-angle triangle

- One angle is 90°.
- Most right-angled triangles are scalene.
- Some are isosceles.

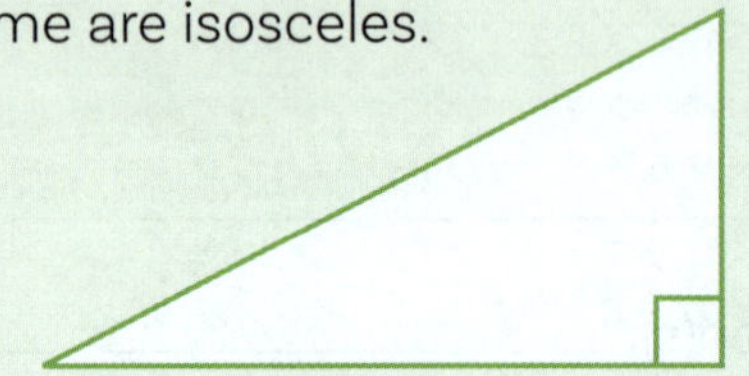

Choose one or two phrases to describe each triangle.

1

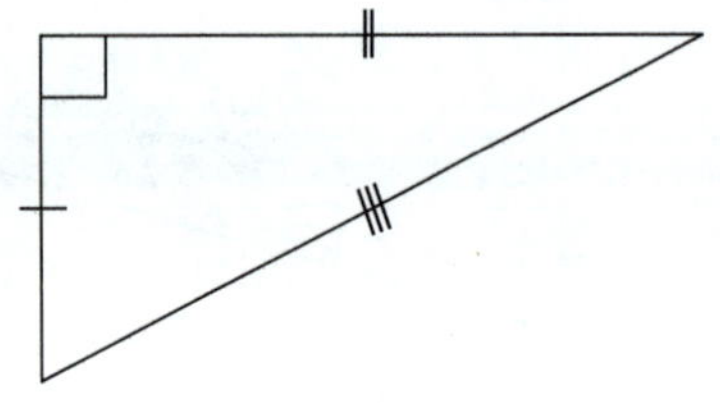

__________ and __________

2

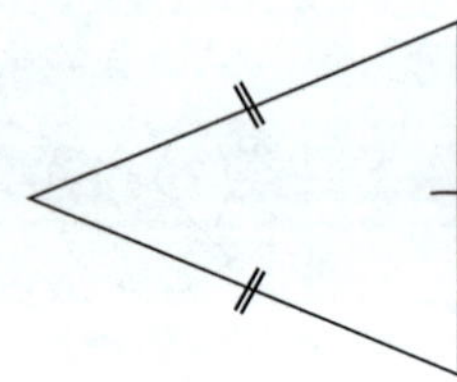

____

3

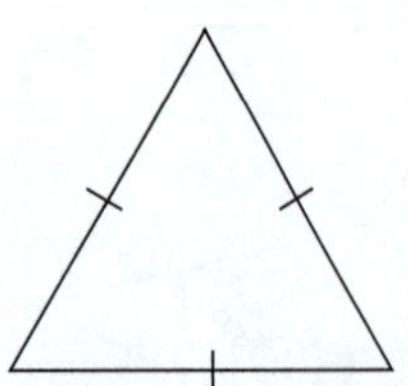

____

4

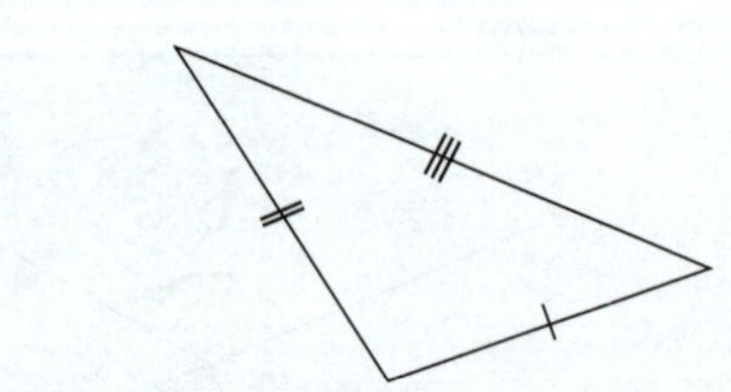

____

5

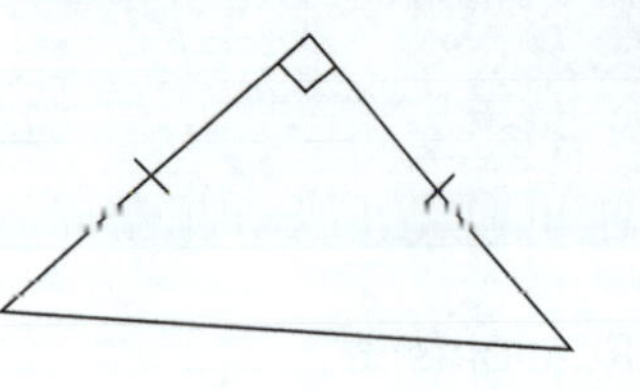

__________ and __________

6

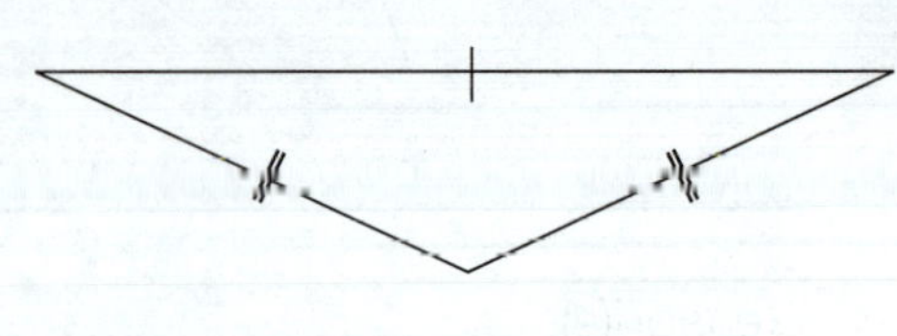

____

 ISBN: 9780170497978

Angles in a triangle

Interior angles

Remember:

For all triangles

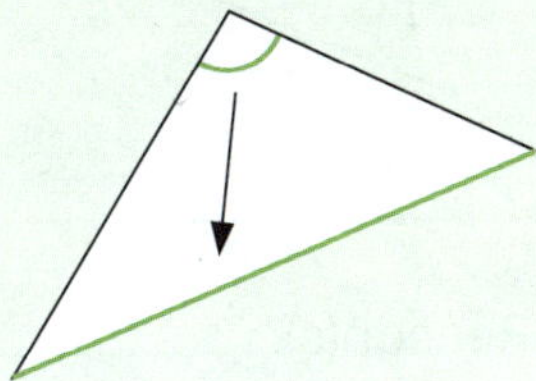

The longest side is opposite the biggest angle.

and

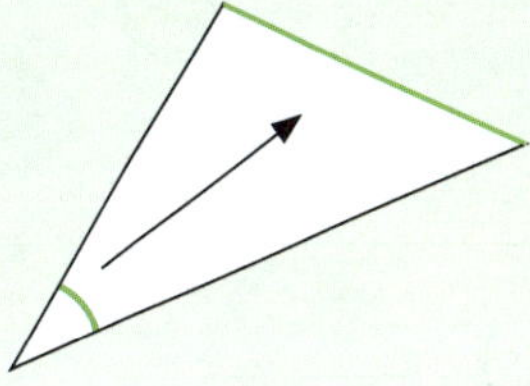

The shortest side is opposite the smallest angle.

- The angles in a triangle **add to 180°**.

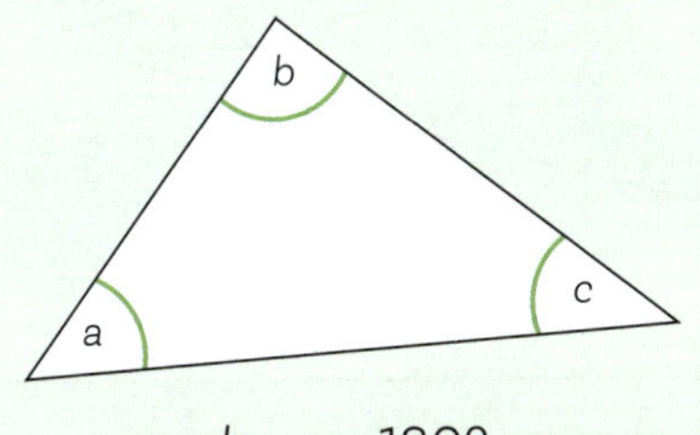

$a + b + c = 180°$

Example:

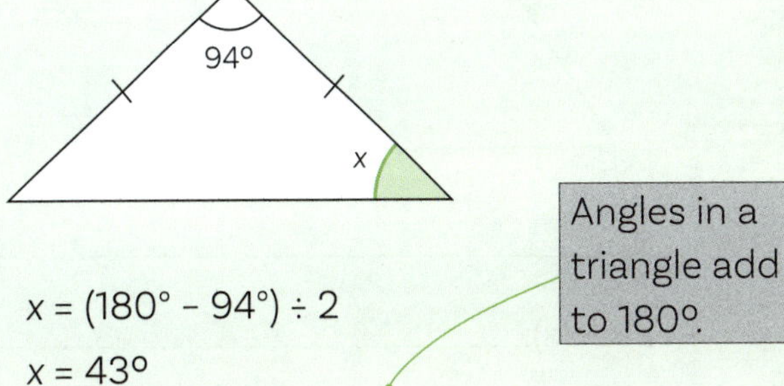

$x = (180° - 94°) \div 2$

$x = 43°$

Angles in a triangle add to 180°.

Reasons: Isosceles $\triangle$ and $\angle$s in a $\triangle$ = 180°

Exterior angles

The exterior angle of a triangle = sum of the interior opposite angles.

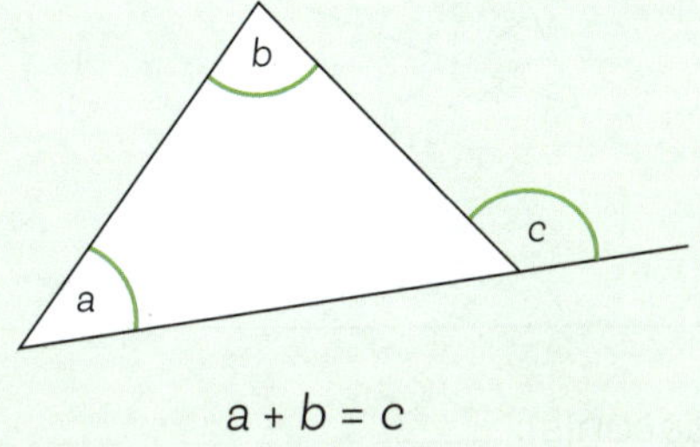

$a + b = c$

Example:

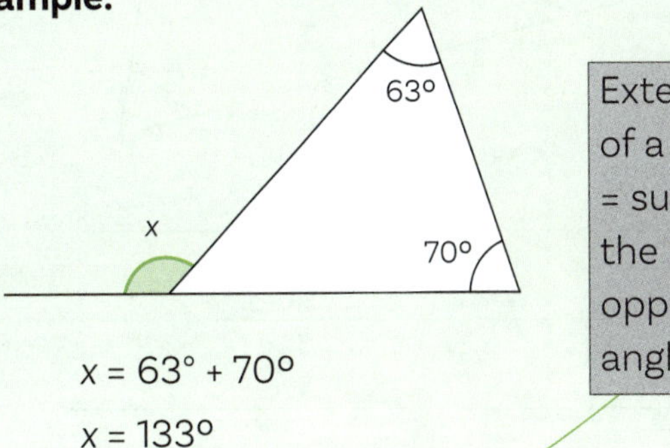

$x = 63° + 70°$

$x = 133°$

Exterior angle of a triangle = sum of the interior opposite angles.

Reason: Ext $\angle$ of a $\triangle$ = sum of int opp $\angle$s

Calculate the missing angles and give reason(s).

7

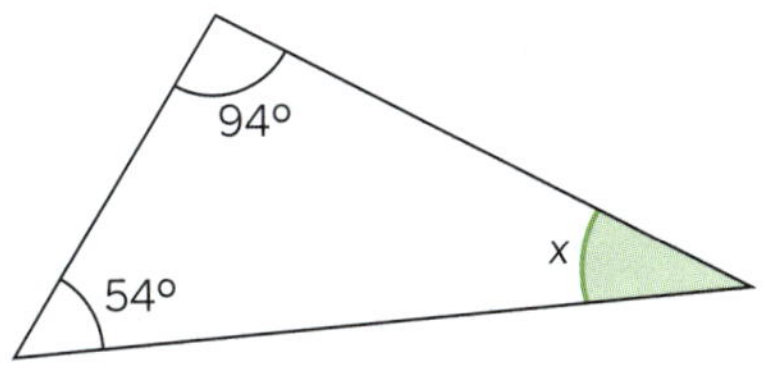

____

Reason(s): ______________________

8

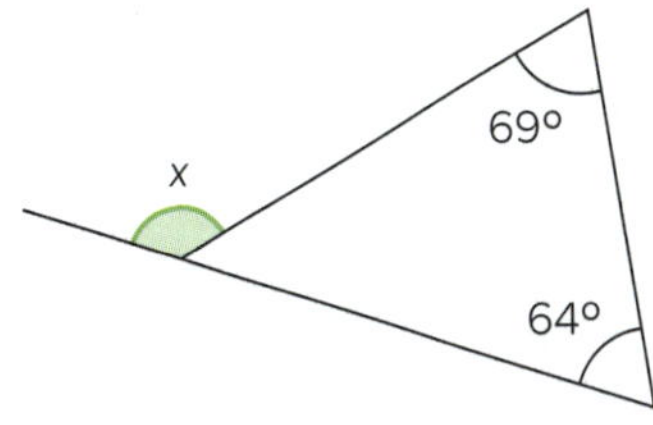

____

Reason(s): ______________________

ISBN: 9780170497978

9

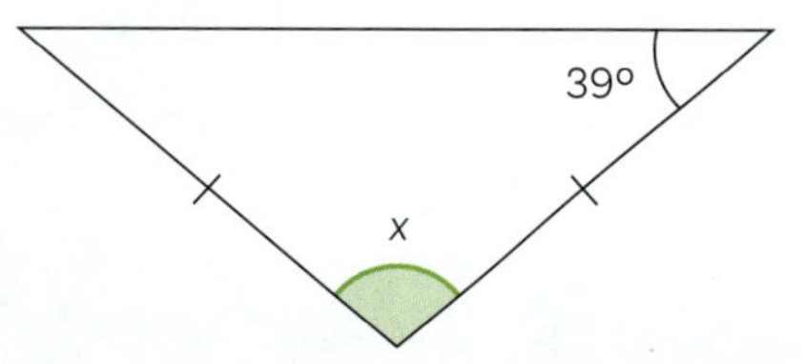

Reason(s):

10

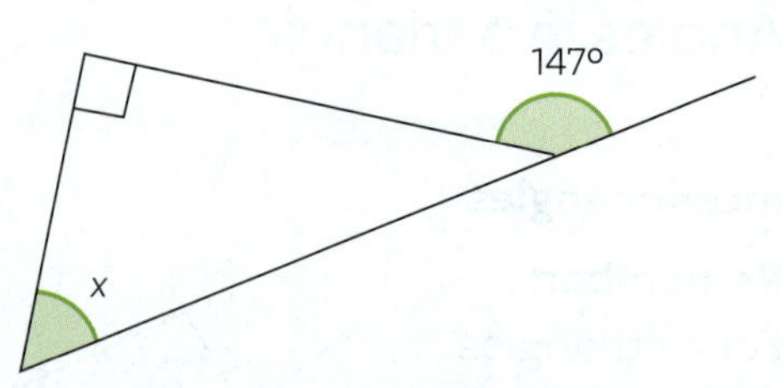

Reason(s):

11

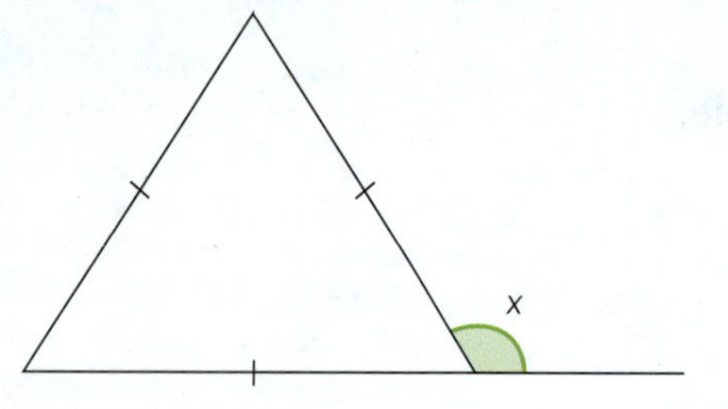

Reason(s):

12

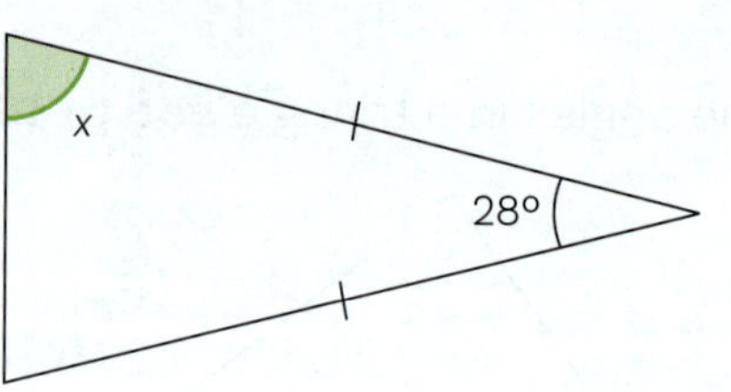

Reason(s):

13

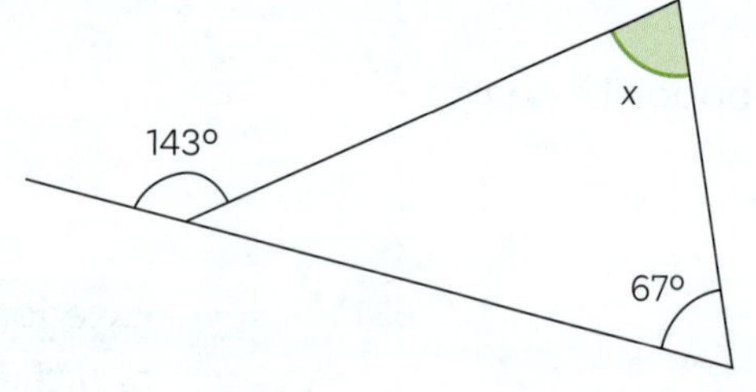

Reason(s):

14

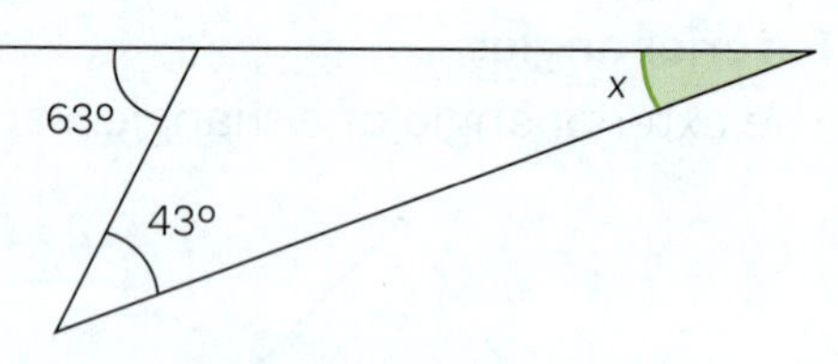

Reason(s):

15

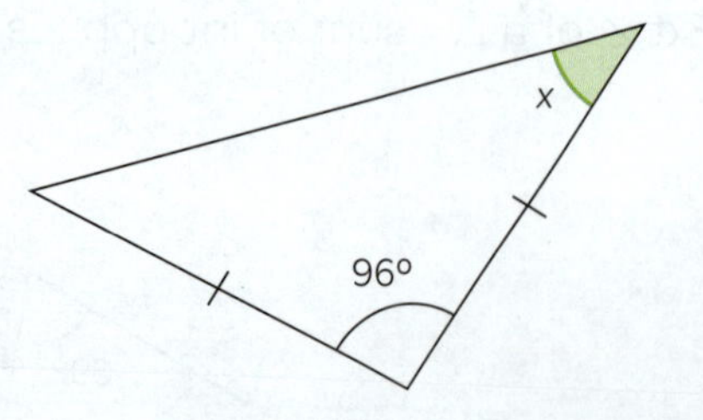

Reason(s):

16

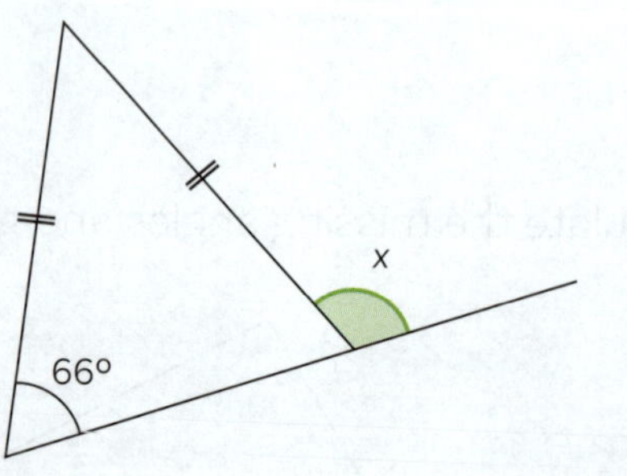

Reason(s):

ISBN: 9780170497978

Quadrilaterals

Angles in a quadrilateral

- A **quadrilateral** is any closed shape (no gaps) with exactly **four straight sides**.
- The four angles in a quadrilateral **add to 360°**.

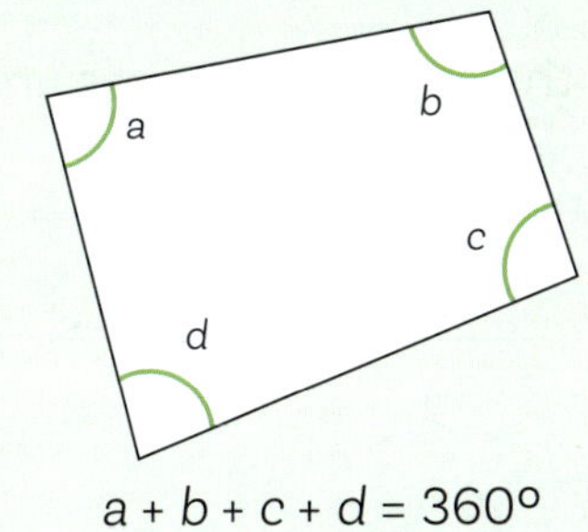

$a + b + c + d = 360°$

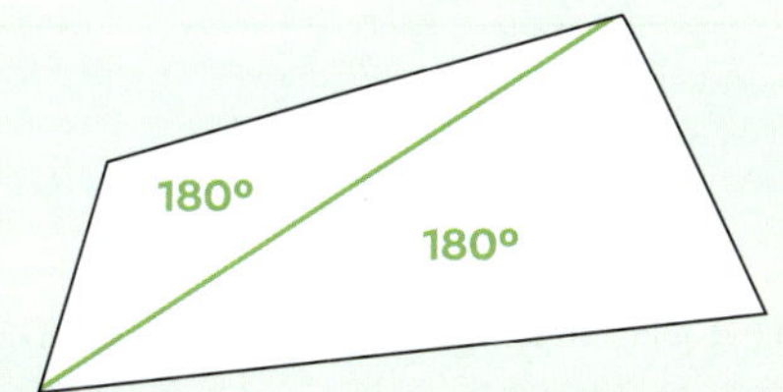

You could think of it as two triangles
$180° + 180° = 360°$

Example:

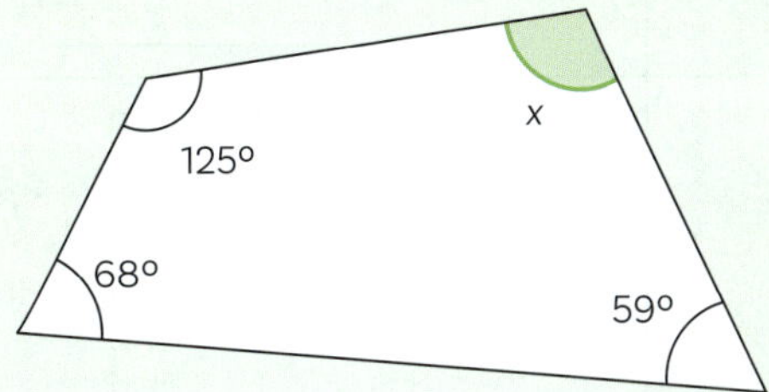

$125° + 68° + 59° + x = 360°$
$x = 360° - 125° - 68° - 59°$
$x = 108°$

Reason: $\angle$s in quad = 360°

Angles in a quadrilateral add to 360°.

Calculate the size of the missing angle and write the reason(s).

1

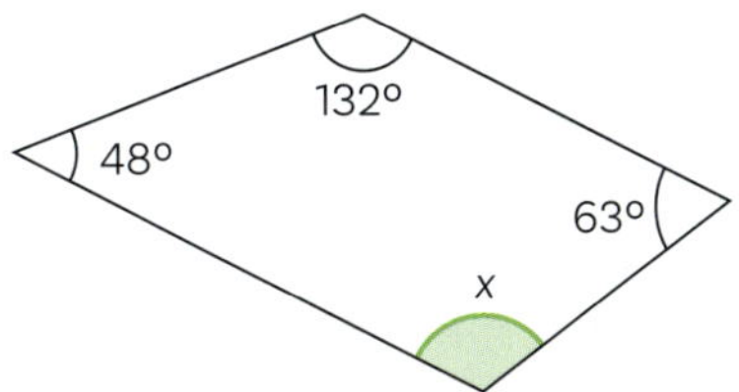

____

____

Reason(s): ____________________

2

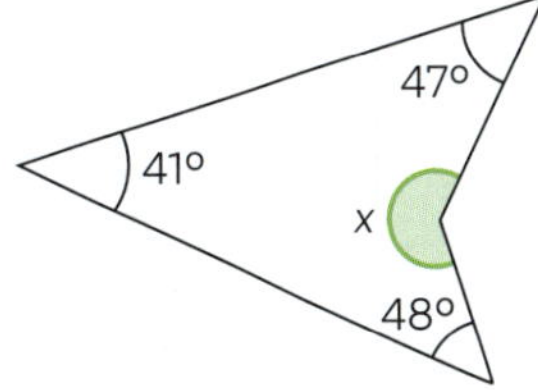

____

____

Reason(s): ____________________

3

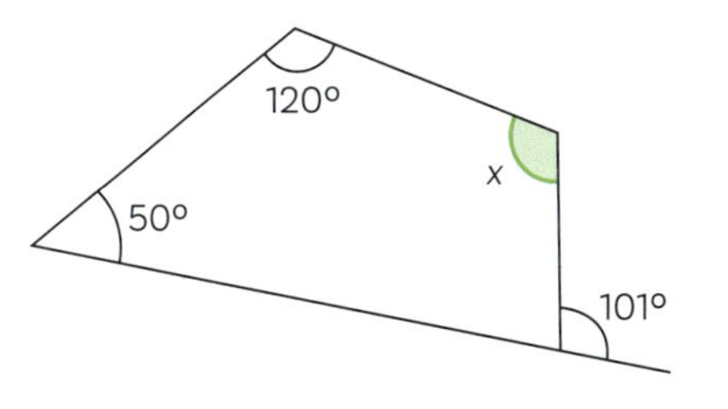

____

____

Reason(s): ____________________

____

4

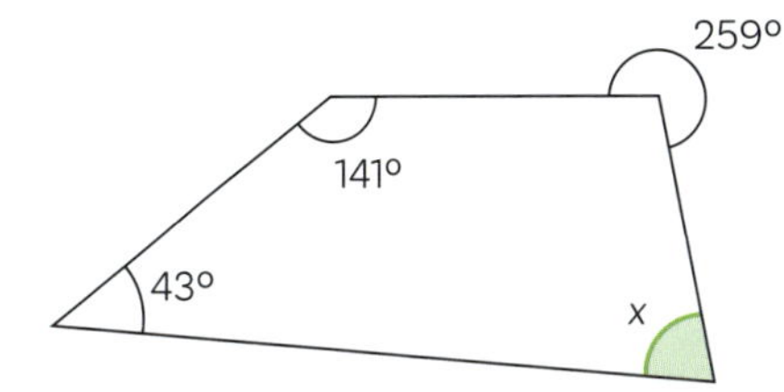

____

____

Reason(s): ____________________

____

ISBN: 9780170497978

Angles in special quadrilaterals

Name	Diagram	Angle properties
Rectangle		All the angles in squares and rectangles are __________ and __________ angles.
Square		
Parallelogram		In a parallelogram or a rhombus, there are two opposite pairs of __________ angles.
Rhombus		
Trapezium		In an ordinary trapezium, there are ______ equal angles.
Isosceles trapezium		An isosceles trapezium has ______ pairs of __________ angles.
Right trapezium		A right trapezium has ______ right angles and ______ other angles which are ______ equal.
Kite		In a kite, there is ______ pair of equal angles and the other two angles are ______ equal.

 ISBN: 9780170497978

Calculate the size of the missing angle.

5

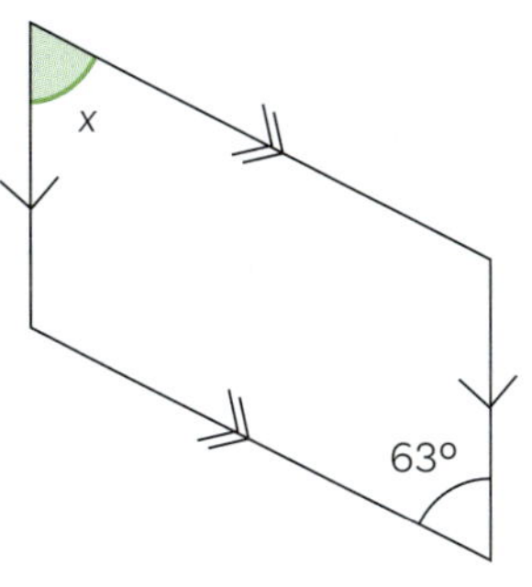

6

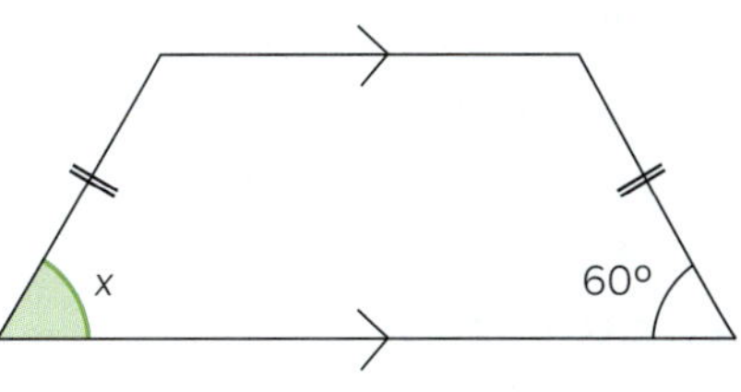

7

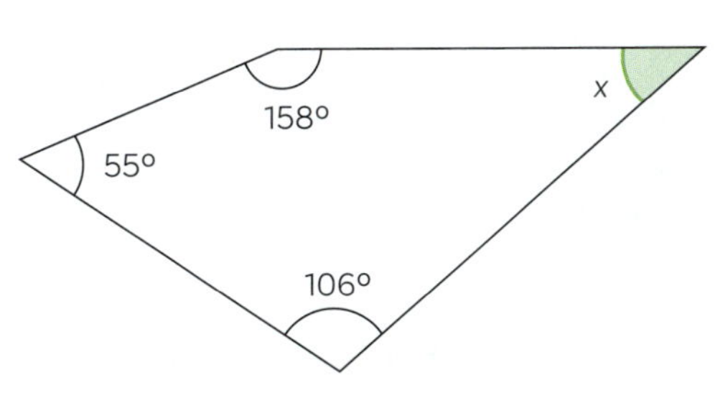

8

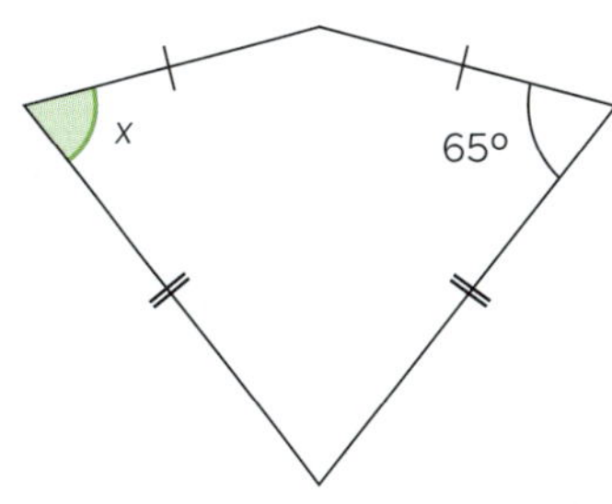

9

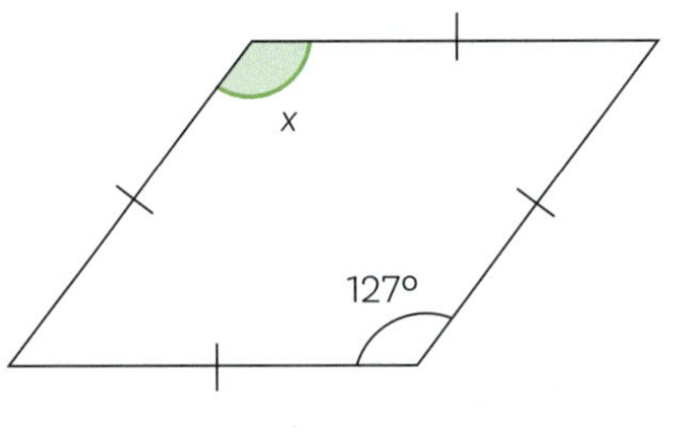

10

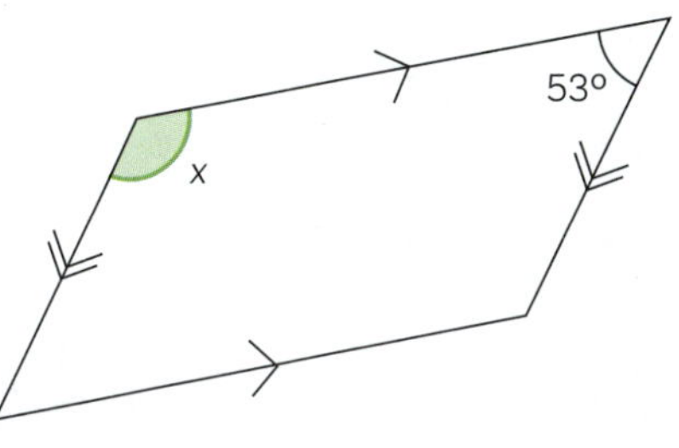

11

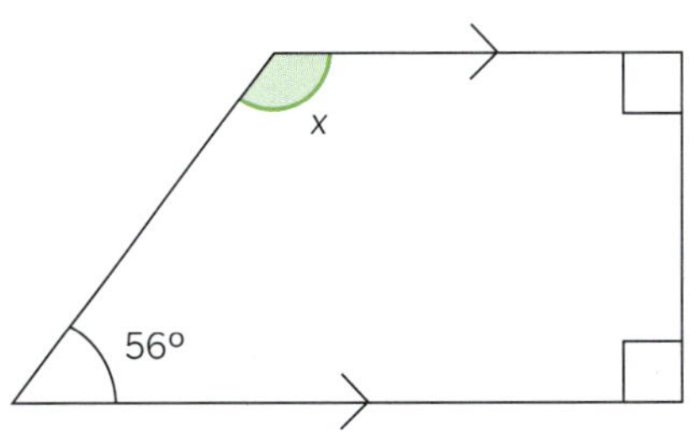

12

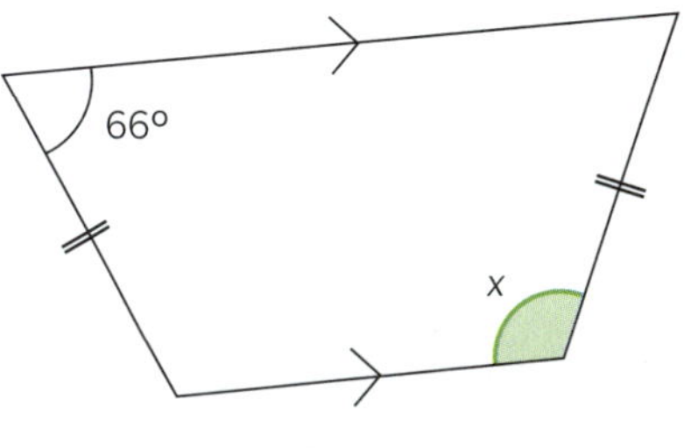

ISBN: 9780170497978

Parallel lines

- Parallel lines are always the **same distance** from each other and they **never meet** (never intersect each other). They have the same gradient.
- You will usually need to **give reasons** for answers involving parallel lines.

Alternate angles

- Alternate angles on parallel lines are **equal**.
- These form a **Z** or **N** shape.

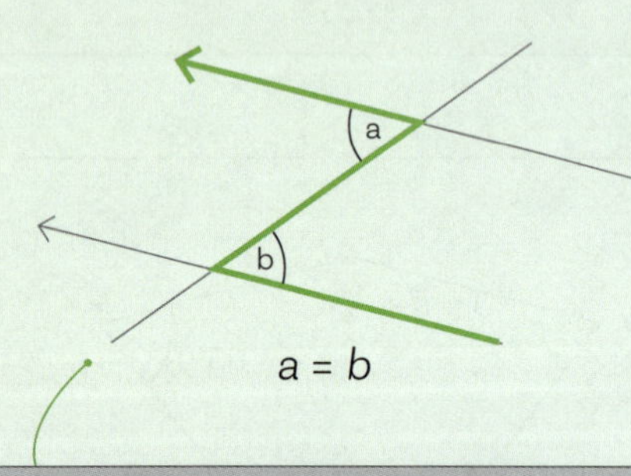

$a = b$

A line which crosses parallel lines like this is called a **transversal**.

Example: Find the value of x.

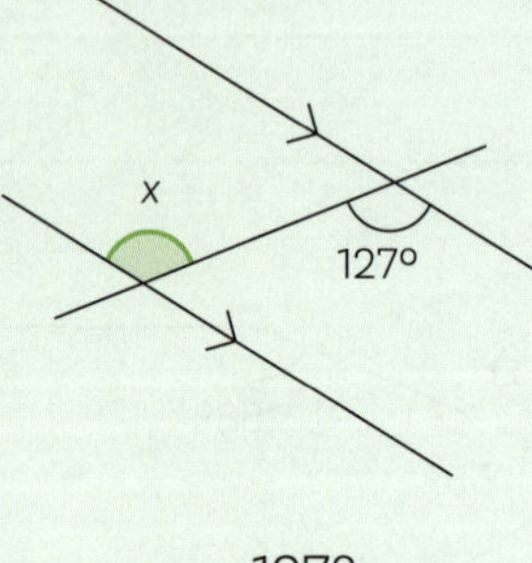

You are allowed to shorten 'Alternate angles are equal, parallel lines' to this.

$x = 127°$

Reason: Alt ∠s =, ∥ lines

Corresponding angles

- Corresponding angles on parallel lines are **equal**.
- These form an **F** shape.

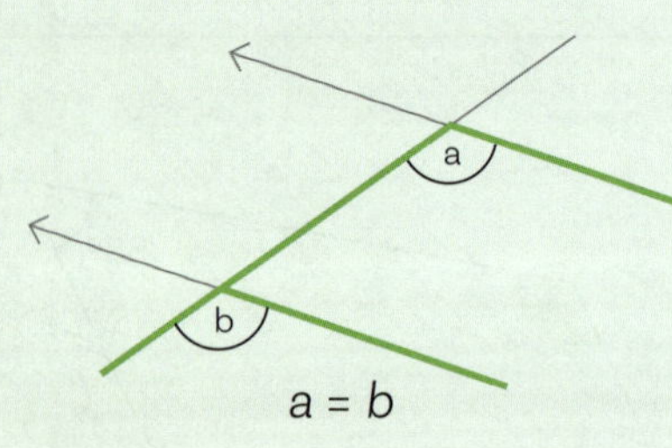

$a = b$

Example: Find the value of y.

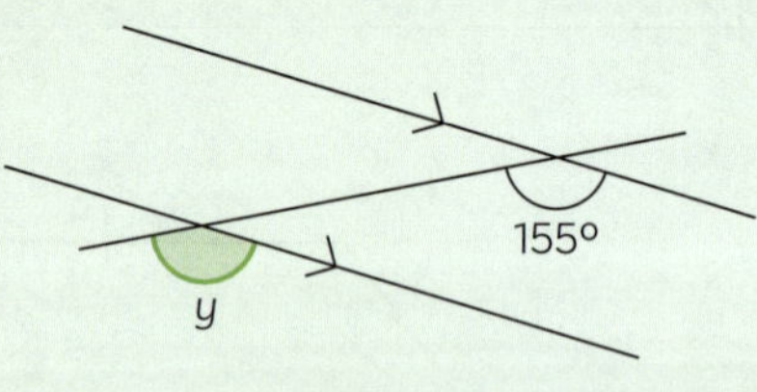

$y = 155°$

'Corresponding angles are equal, parallel lines'.

Reason: Corr ∠s =, ∥ lines

Co-interior angles

- Co-interior angles on parallel lines **add to 180°**.
- These form a **C** or **U** shape.

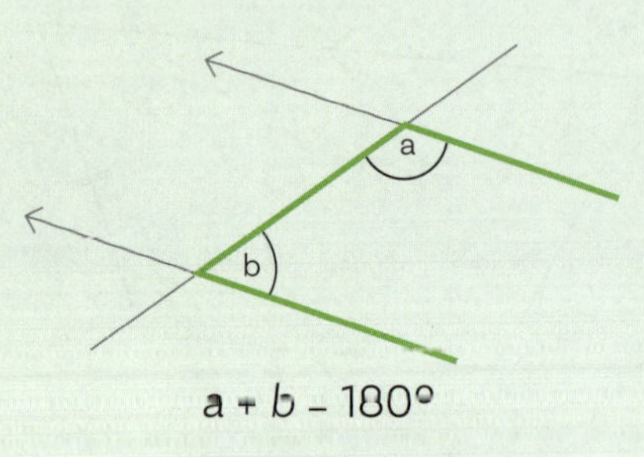

$a + b = 180°$

Example: Find the value of z.

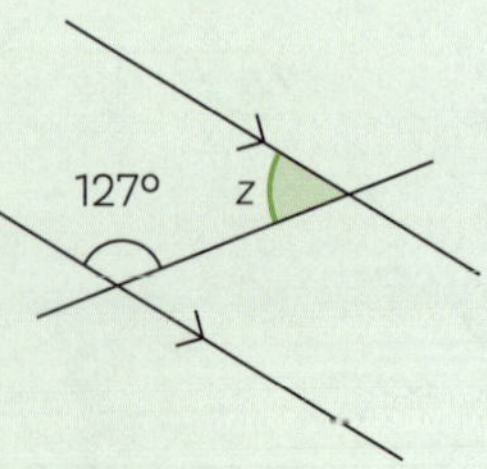

$z = 180° - 127°$

$z = 53°$

'Co-interior angles add to 180°, parallel lines'.

Reason: Co-int ∠s add to 180°, ∥ lines

 ISBN: 9780170497978

State whether these angles are alternate, corresponding or co-interior.

1

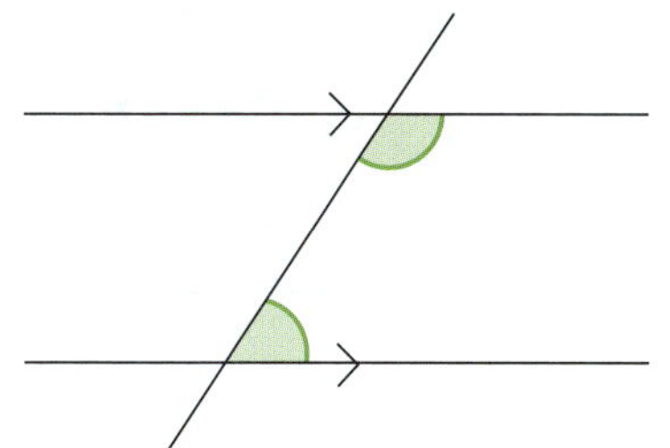

____

2

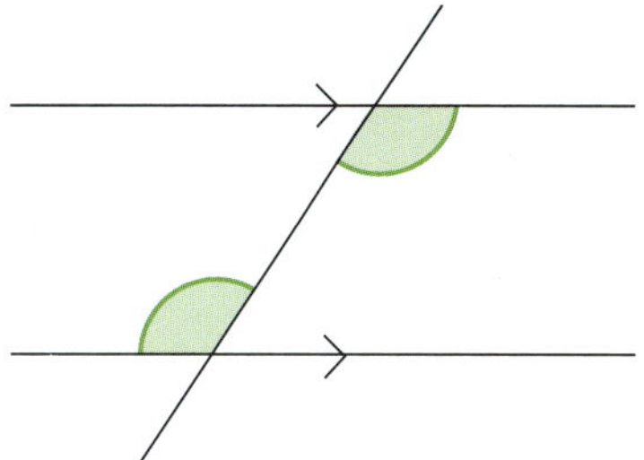

____

3

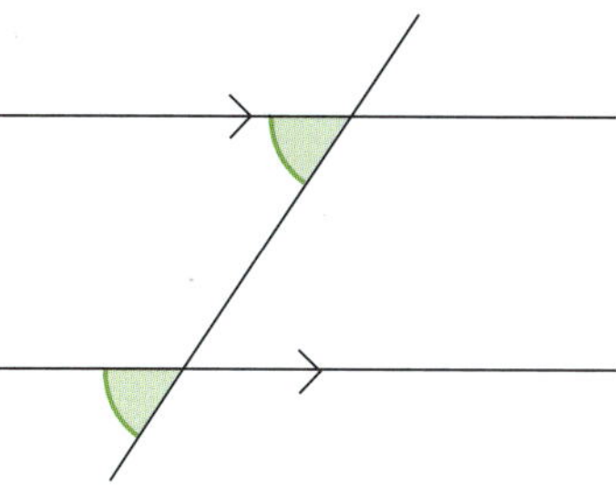

____

4

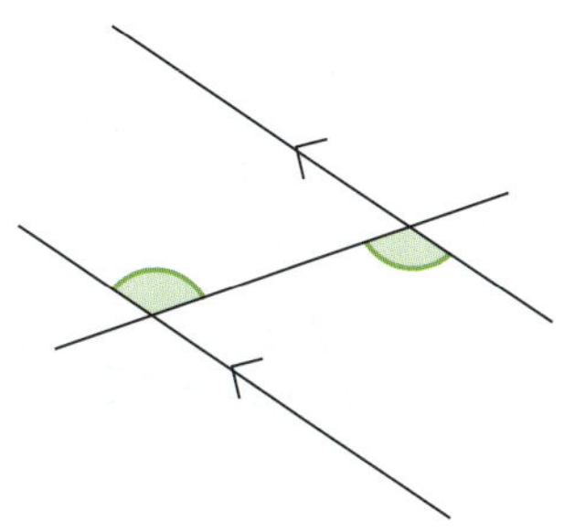

____

5

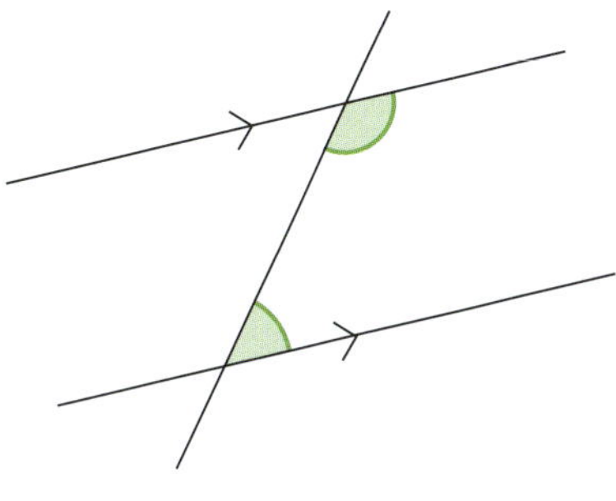

____

6

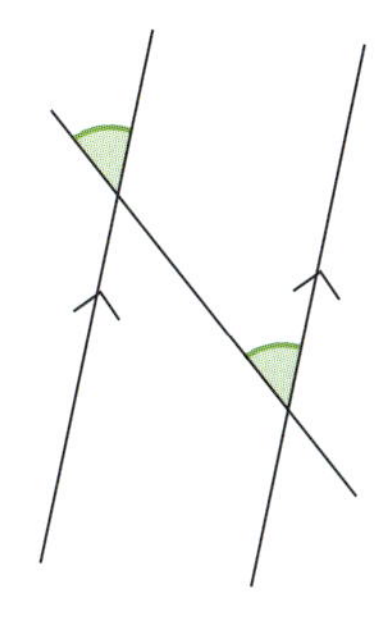

____

Calculate the missing angles and give the reason for your answer.

7

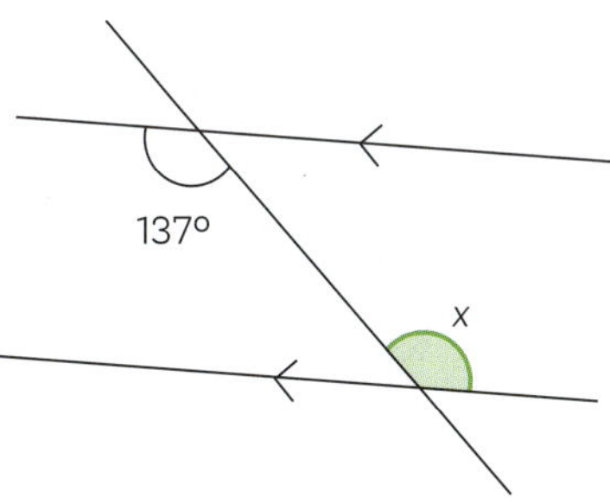

____

Reason: ______________________

8

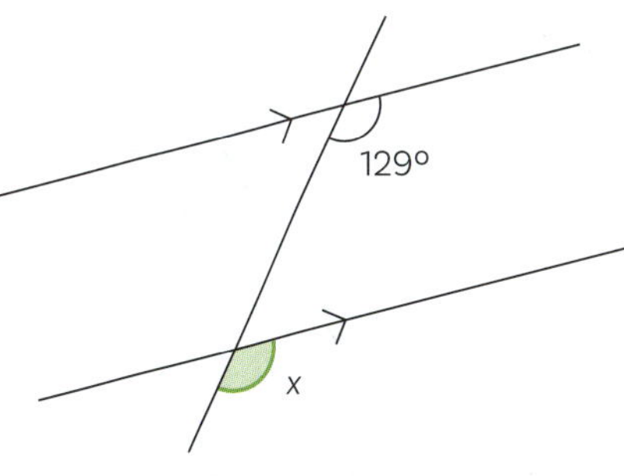

____

Reason: ______________________

9

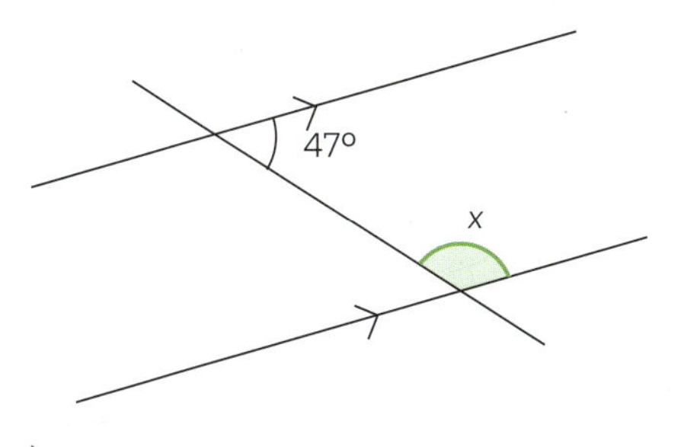

____

Reason: ______________________

10

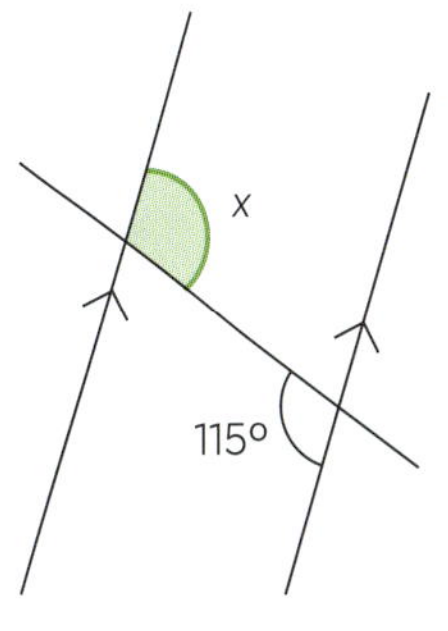

____

Reason: ______________________

ISBN: 9780170497978

11

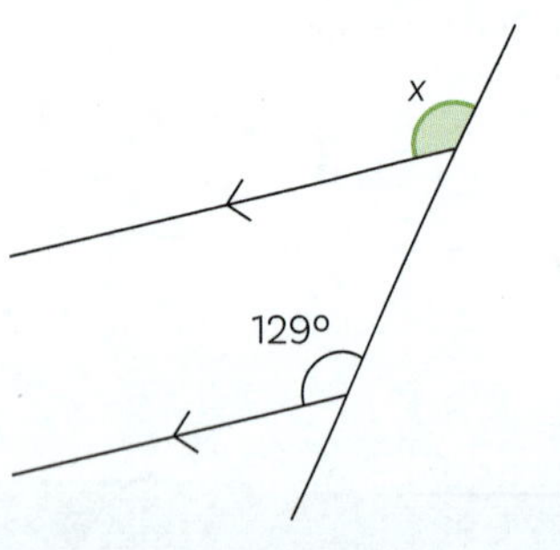

Reason:

12

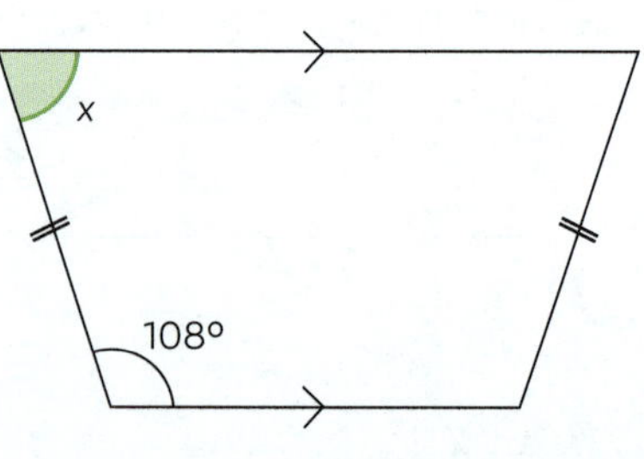

Reason:

13

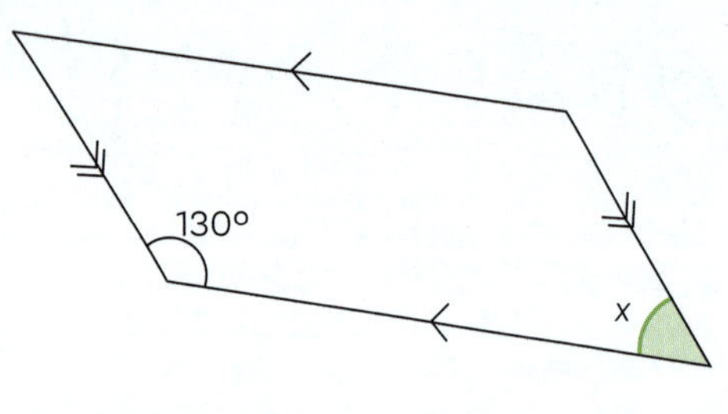

Reason:

14

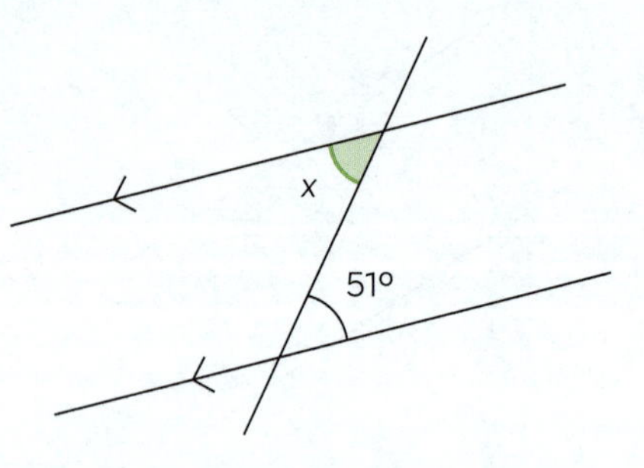

Reason:

Calculate the missing angles.

15

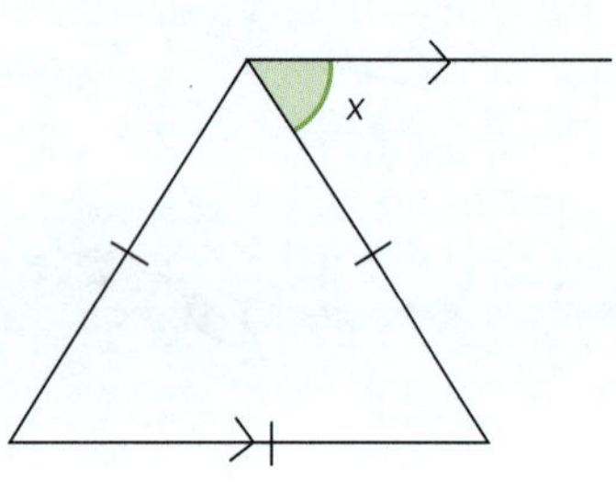

16

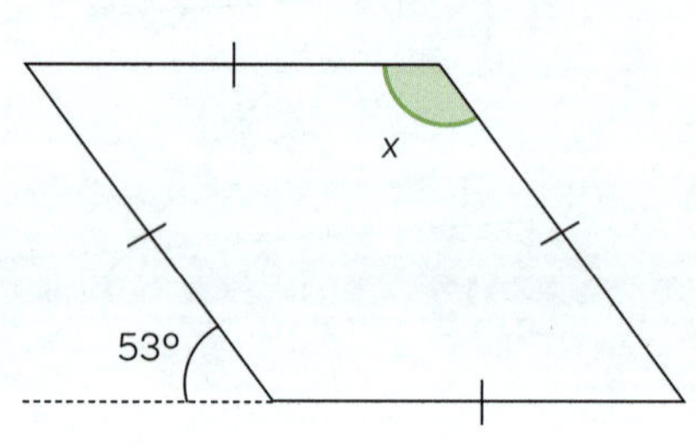

17

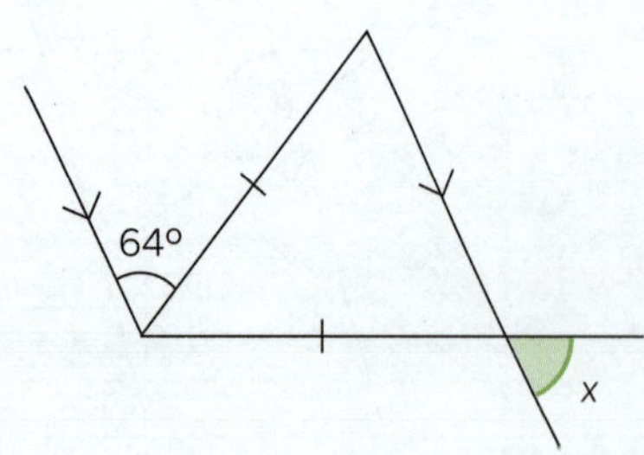

18

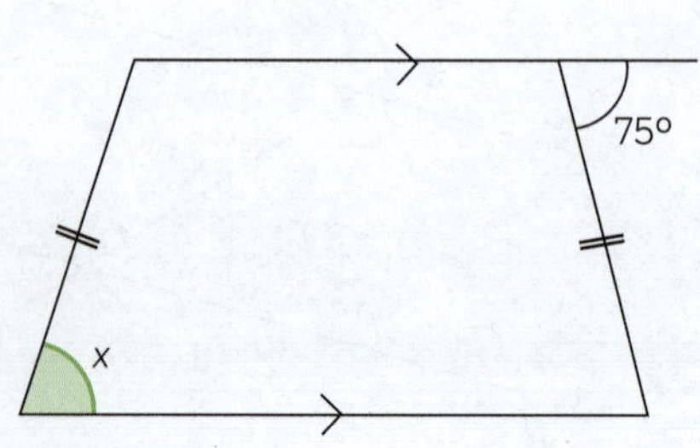

 ISBN: 9780170497978

2D and 3D shapes

2D and 3D language

Dimensions

1D (one-dimensional) shapes	**2D (two-dimensional) shapes**	**3D (three-dimensional) shapes**
• have **1** measurement: length.	• have **2** measurements: height and width.	• have **3** measurements: height, width and depth.
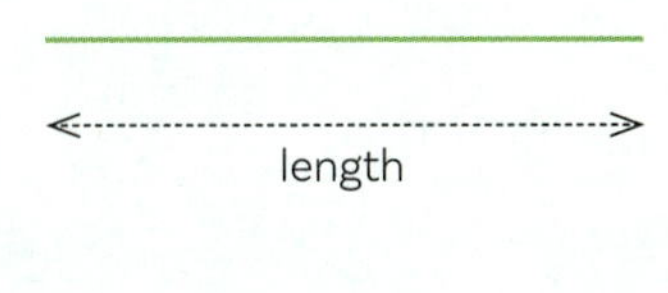	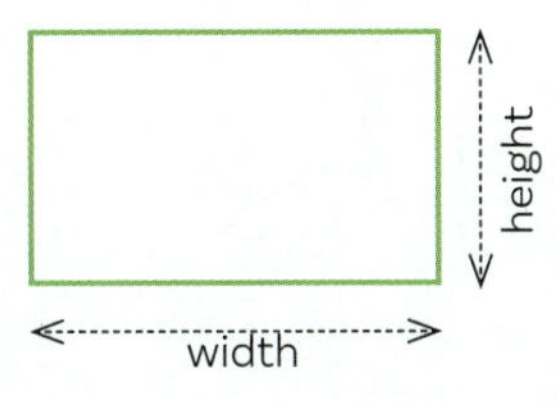	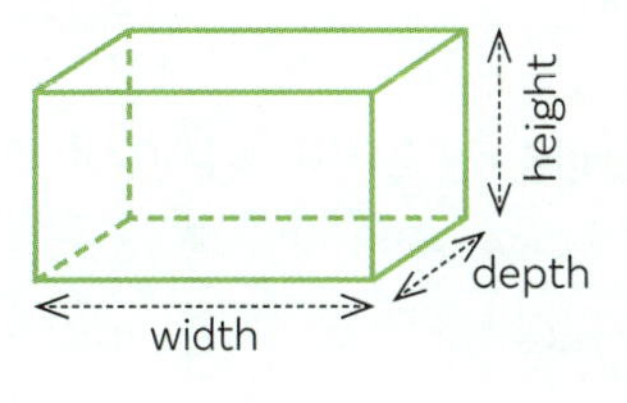

Vertices, faces, sides and edges

- We talk about **one vertex** or **several vertices**.

2D shapes have vertices, one face and sides.

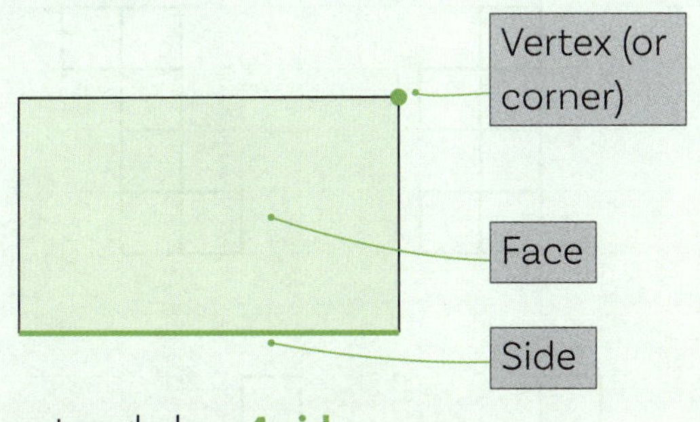

A rectangle has **4 sides**, **4 vertices** and **1 face**.

3D shapes have vertices, faces and edges.

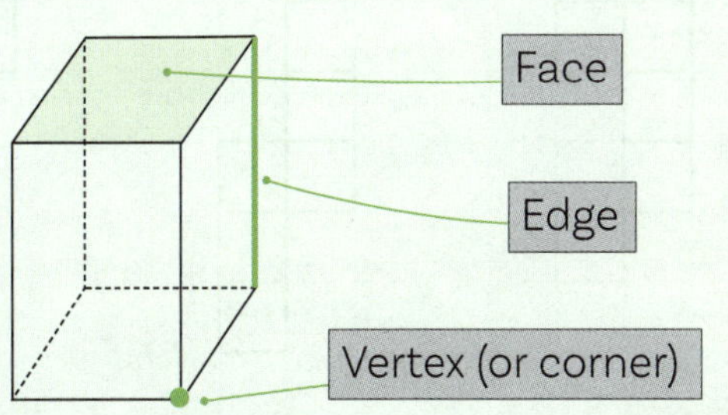

A cube has **6 faces**, **8 vertices** and **12 edges**.

Write down the numbers of vertices, edges and faces these 3D shapes have.

1

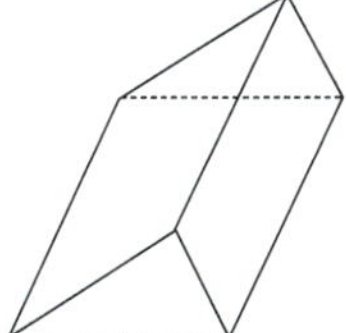

Vertices ________

Edges ________

Faces ________

2

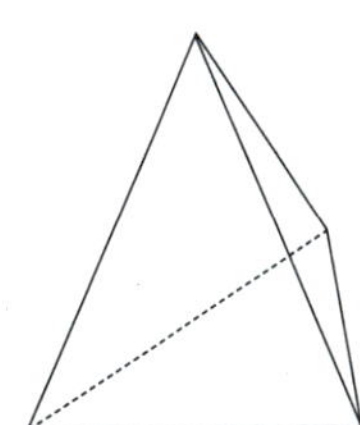

Vertices ________

Edges ________

Faces ________

3

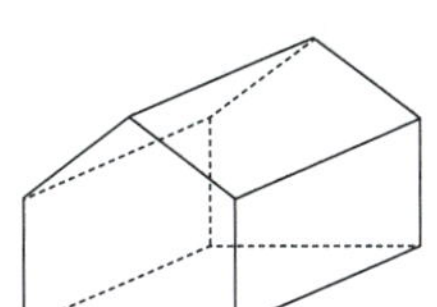

Vertices ________

Edges ________

Faces ________

4

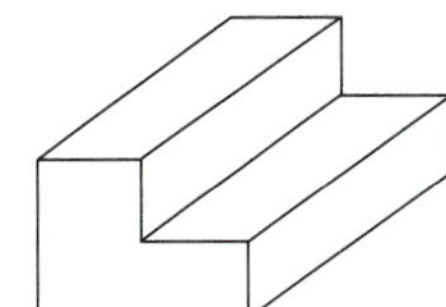

Vertices ________

Edges ________

Faces ________

ISBN: 9780170497978

Nets

- Nets are the two-dimensional versions of three-dimensional shapes. When cut out and folded correctly, they form a solid.

Example: This solid is a cube and can be constructed from a net like below.

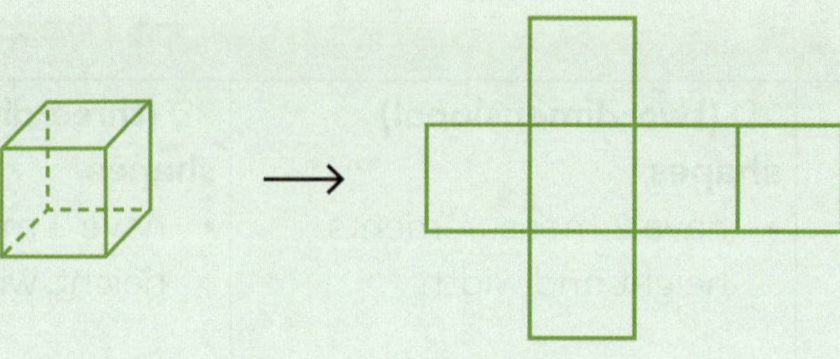

1 Highlight or shade the nets that could form a closed cube. You should find 11.

ISBN: 9780170497978

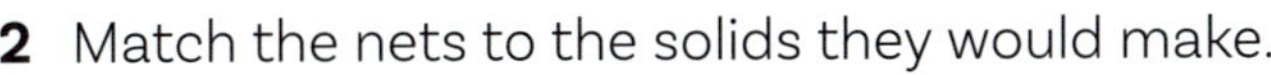

2 Match the nets to the solids they would make.

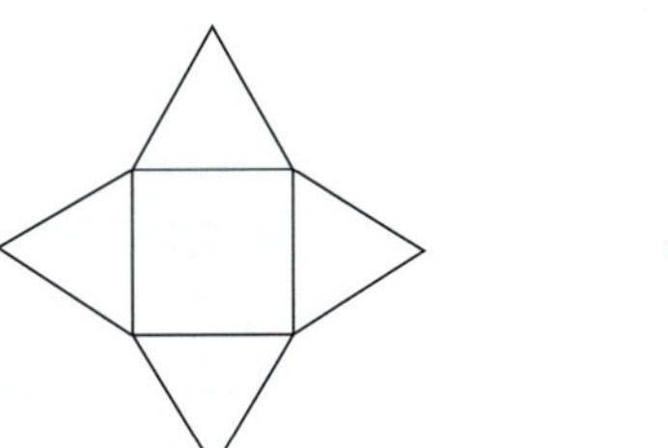

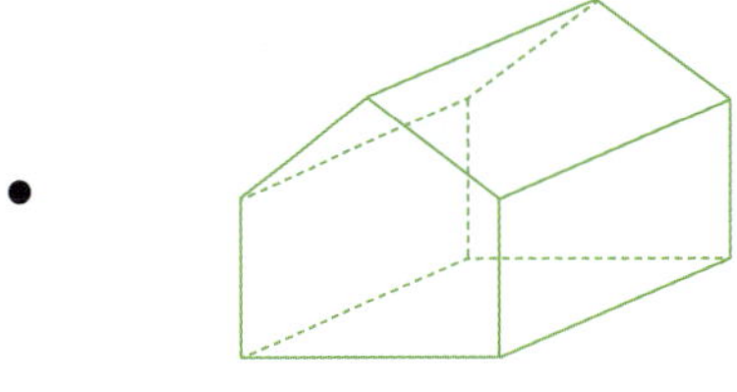

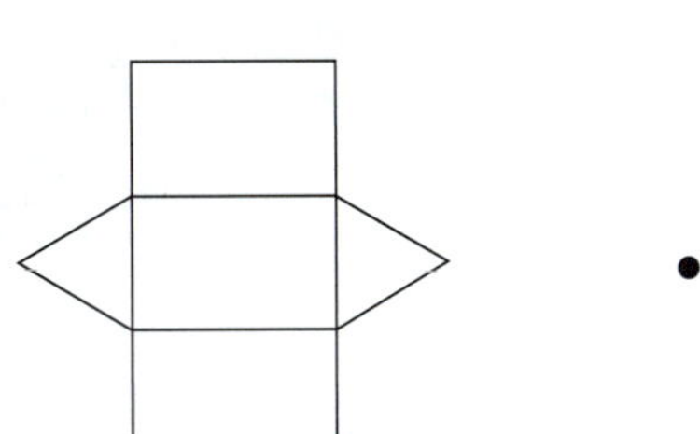

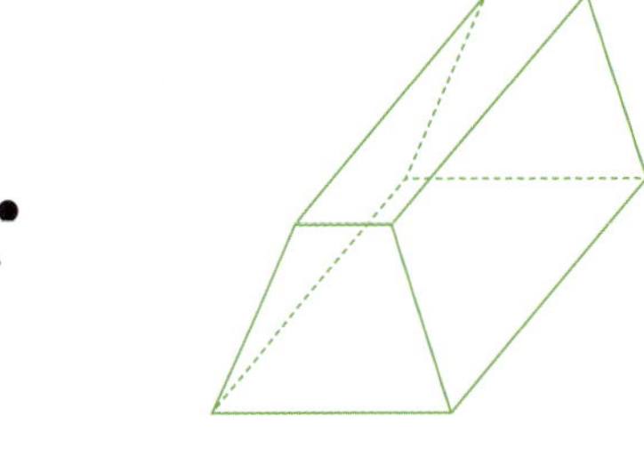

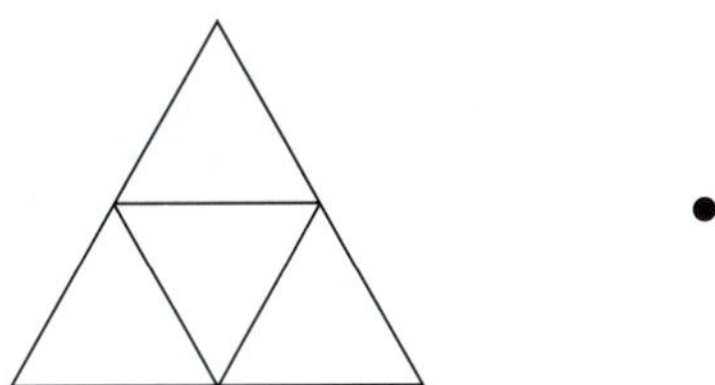

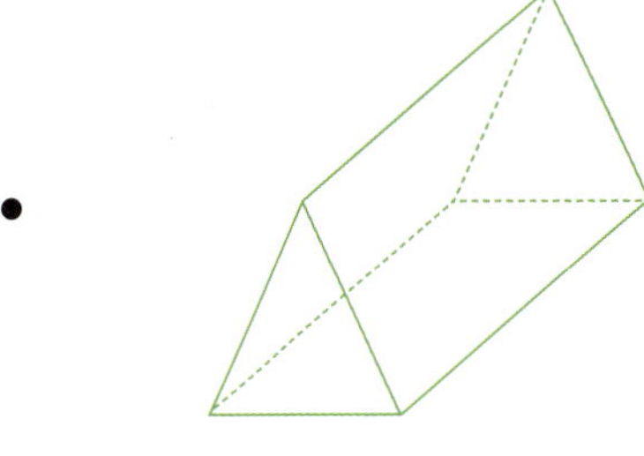

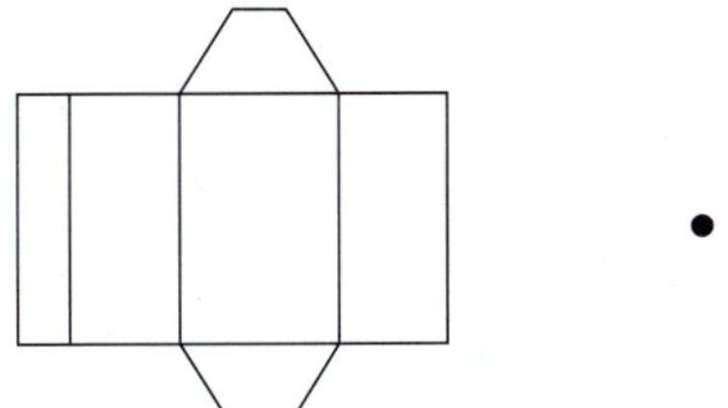

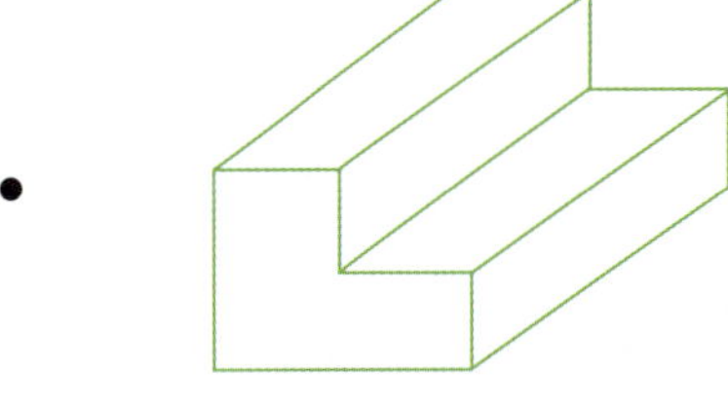

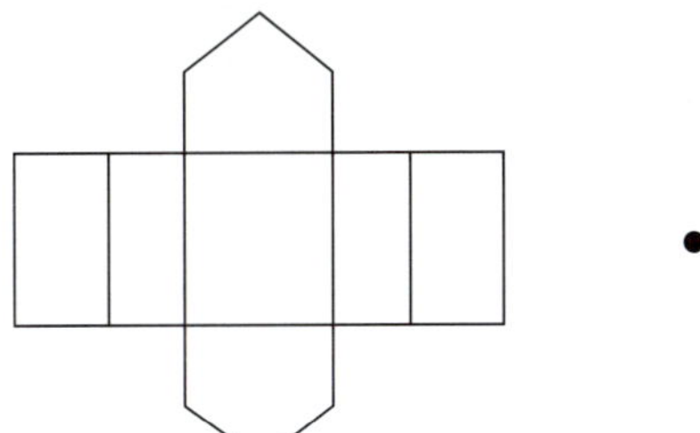

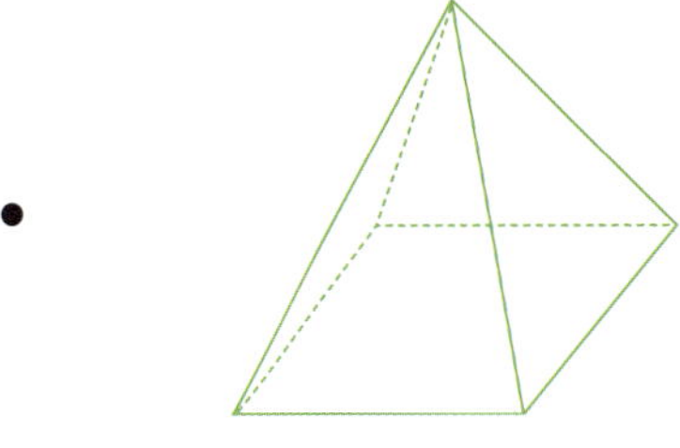

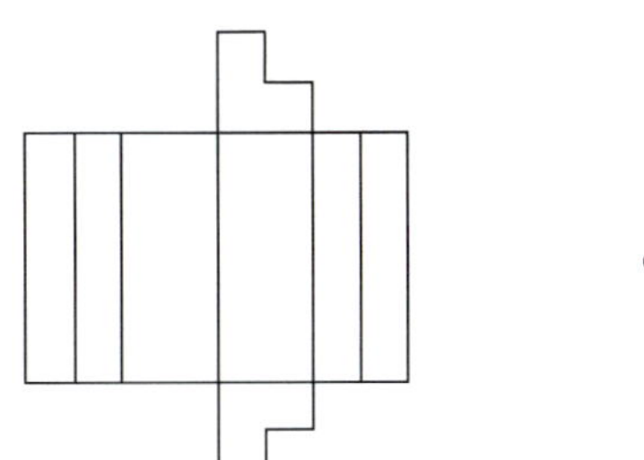

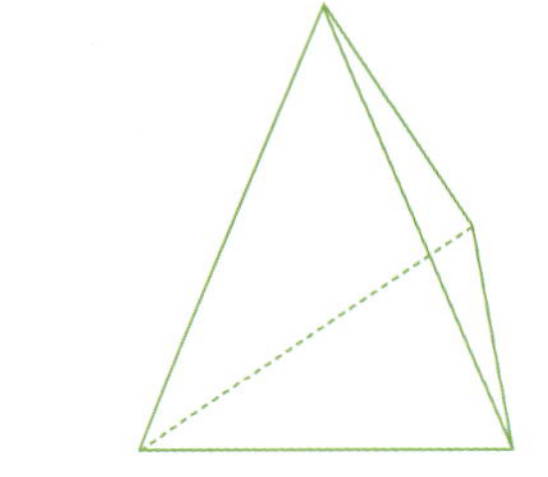

ISBN: 9780170497978

Isometrics

Copying isometric shapes

- The dots on isometric paper make it easier to draw 3D shapes.

  One cube would look like this:

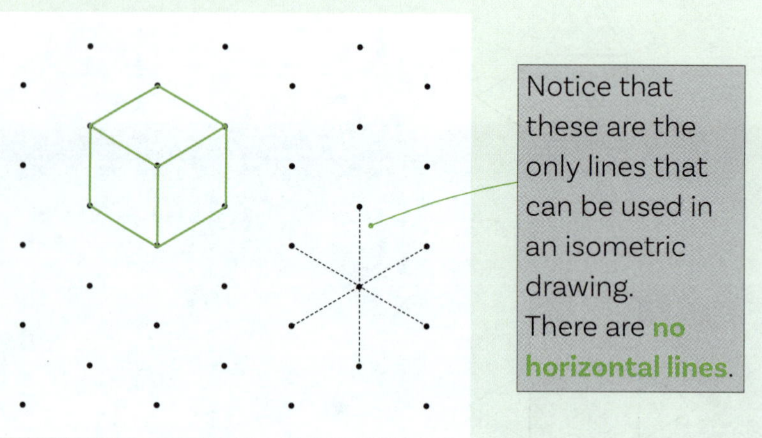

Copy these shapes, showing the junctions between each block. The first one has been started for you. Use a ruler.

1

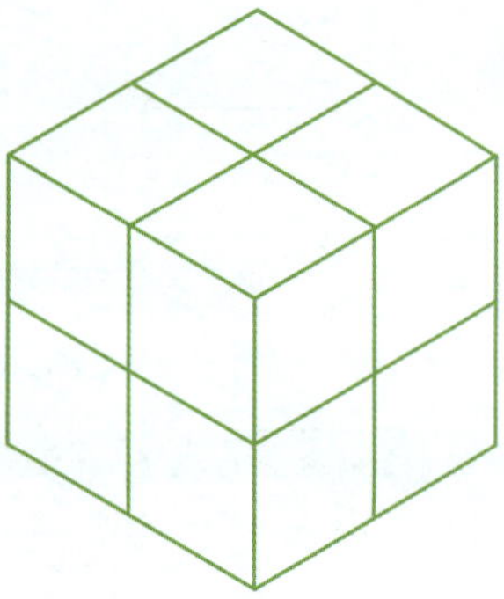

2

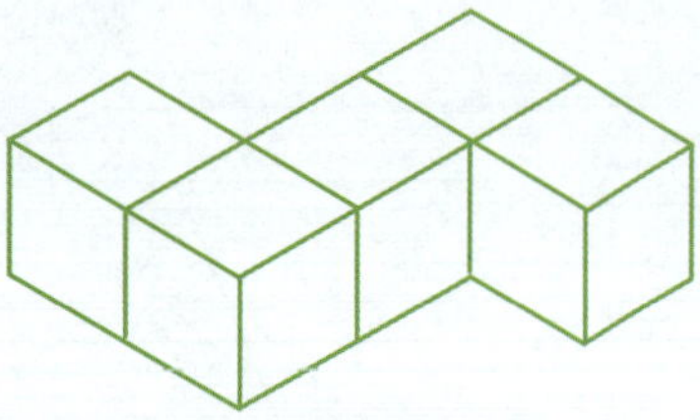

 ISBN: 9780170497978

3

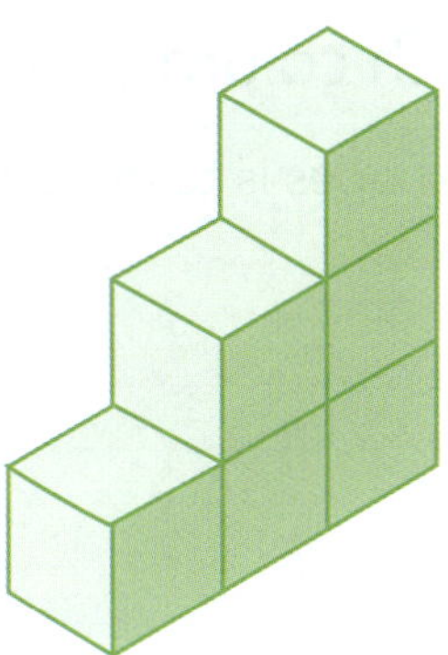

Draw outlines of these shapes without showing the junctions between the blocks. The first lines have been done for you.

4

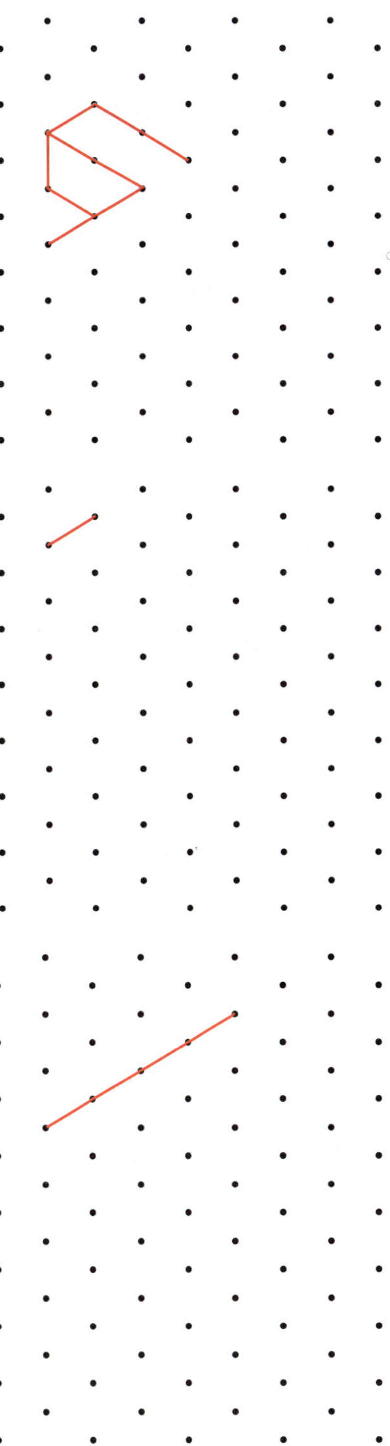

5

6

ISBN: 9780170497978

Drawing isometric shapes from numbers in each column

- Another way of showing the numbers of blocks in some shapes is to draw it from the top, and write in the number of blocks in each column.

Example:

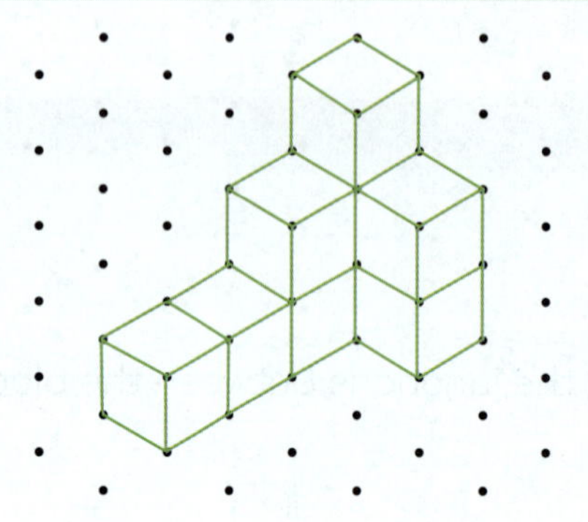

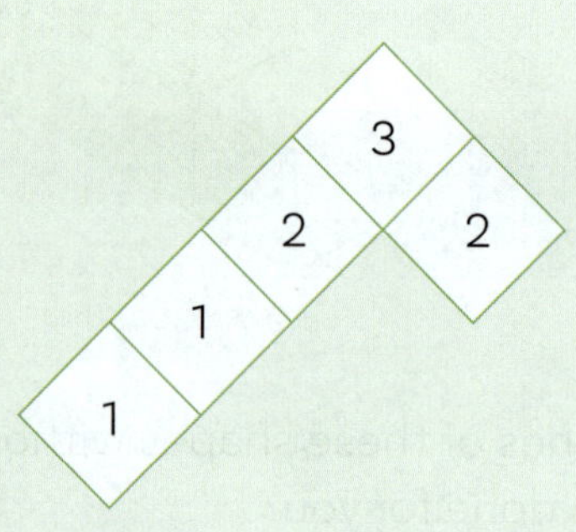

Write down the number of blocks in each column of these shapes.

7

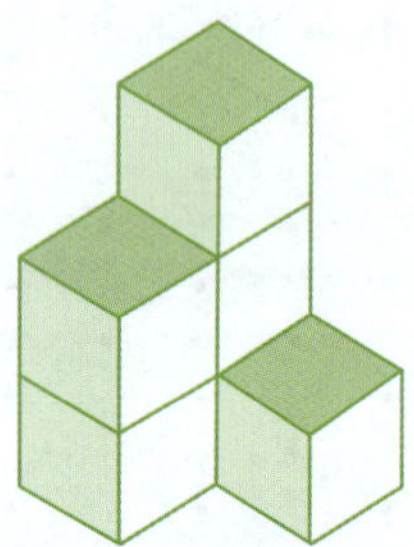

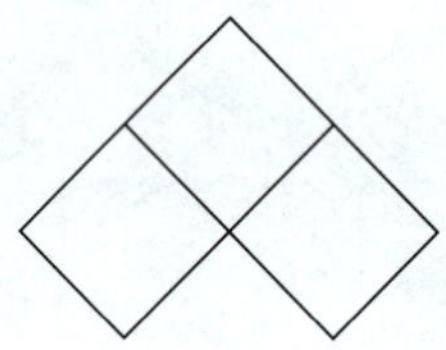

8

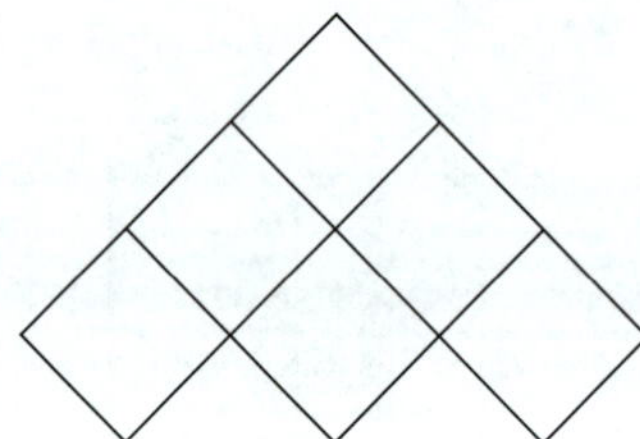

9

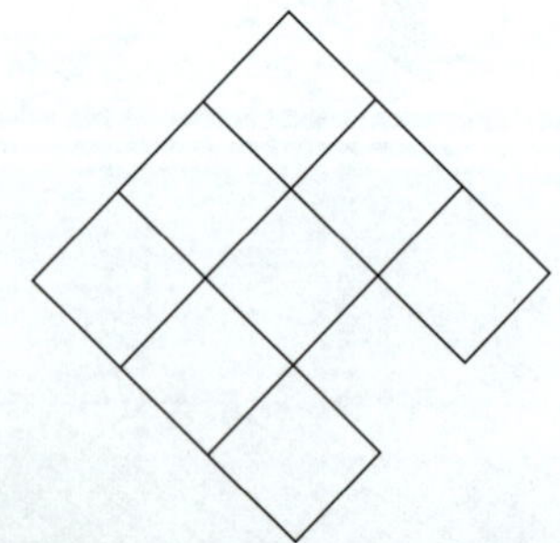

10

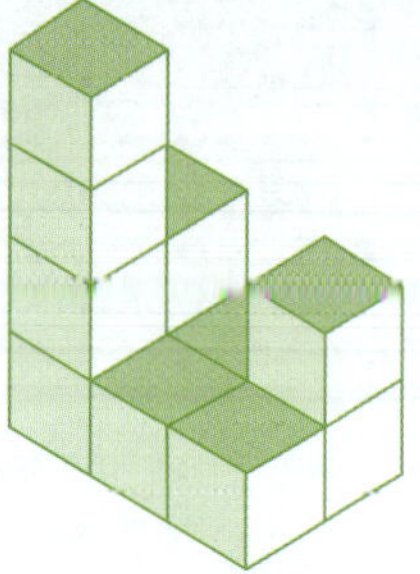

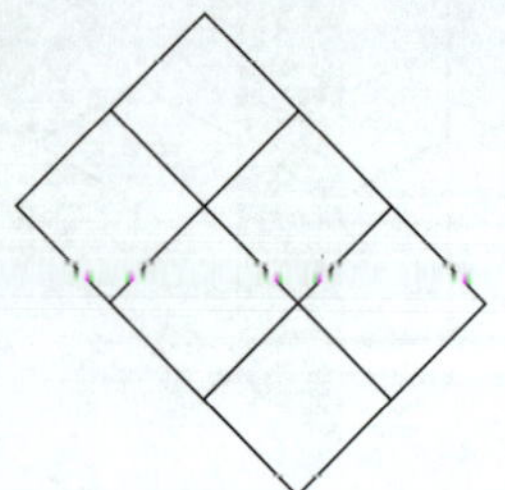

 ISBN: 9780170497978

11

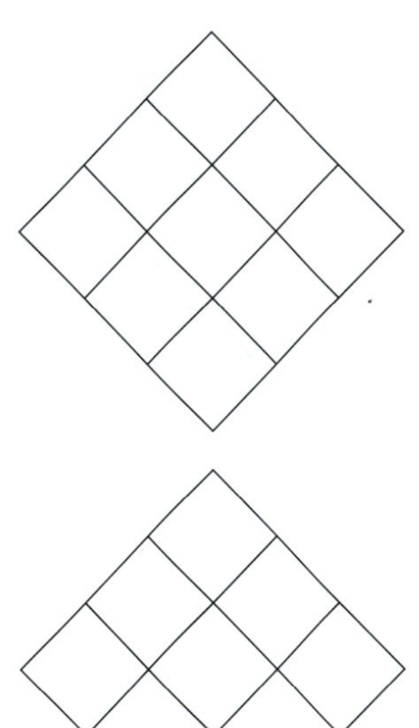

12

Draw these structures on the isometric grids. Hint: Building them with blocks first may help.

13

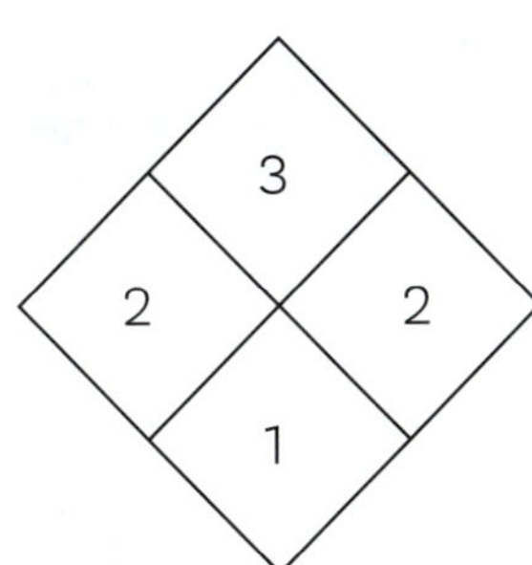

14

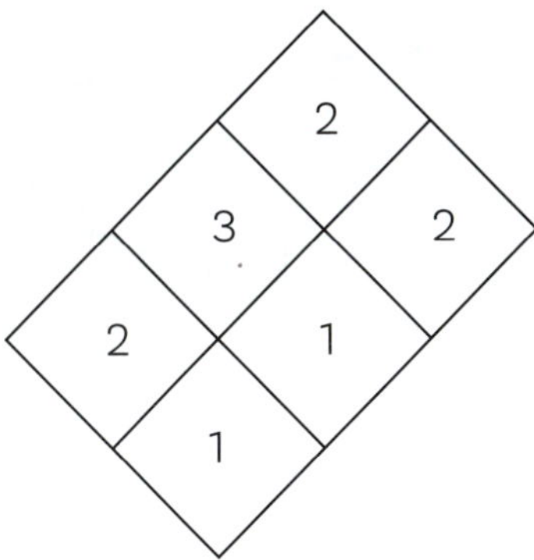

15

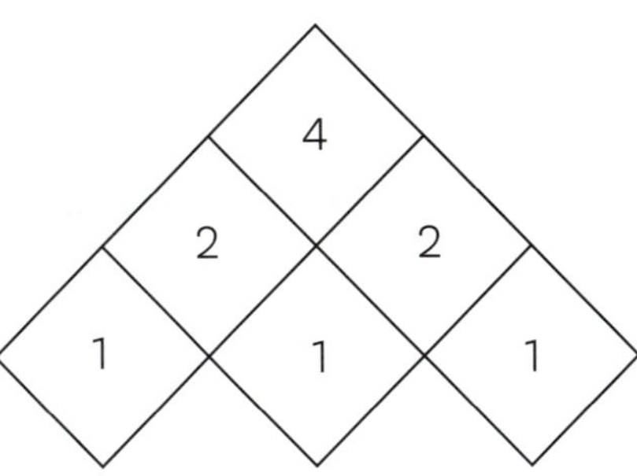

ISBN: 9780170497978

Different views of isometric diagrams

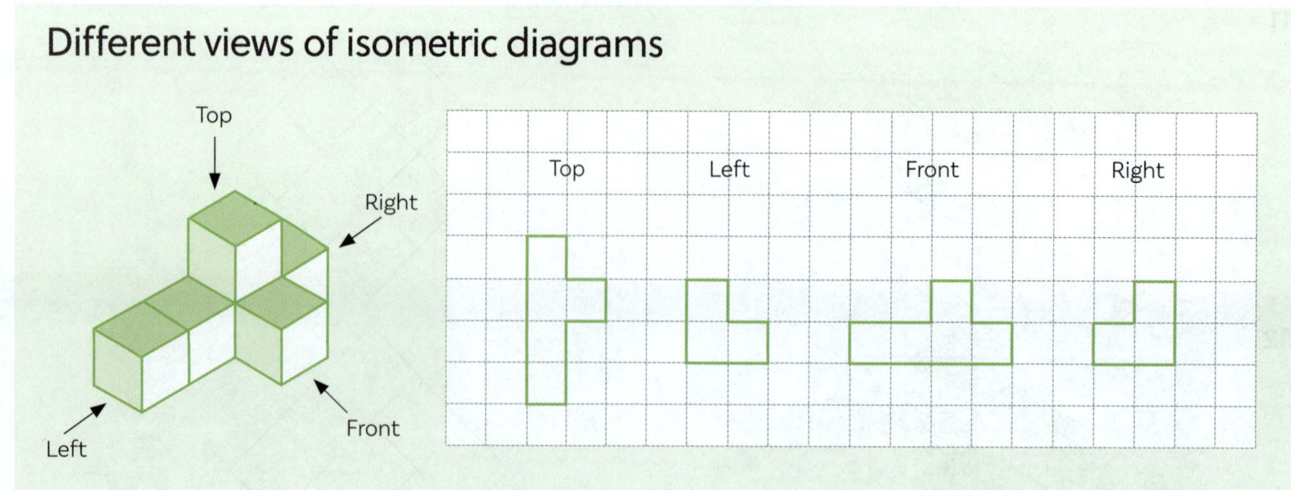

Match these shapes with their 2D views. There are no blocks hidden in behind.

A B C D

16 __________

Top Left Front Right

17 __________

Top Left Front Right

18 __________

Top Left Front Right

19 __________

Top Left Front Right

 ISBN: 9780170497978

Transformation geometry

- A transformation is changing or moving a figure by following certain rules.
- The transformed figure is called the **image**.
- A transformation may change the position, size, shape or orientation of the object.

Translation	Reflection
The figure is **shifted**.	The figure is **reflected in a mirror** line.
Rotation	**Enlargement**
The figure **rotates around a point**.	The figure **gets bigger or smaller**.

ISBN: 9780170497978

Translation

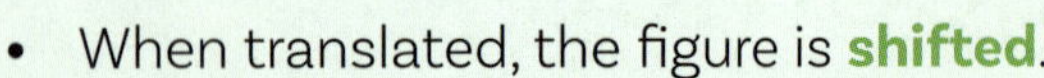

- When translated, the figure is **shifted**.

The **direction** and **distance** are often described using **vectors**:

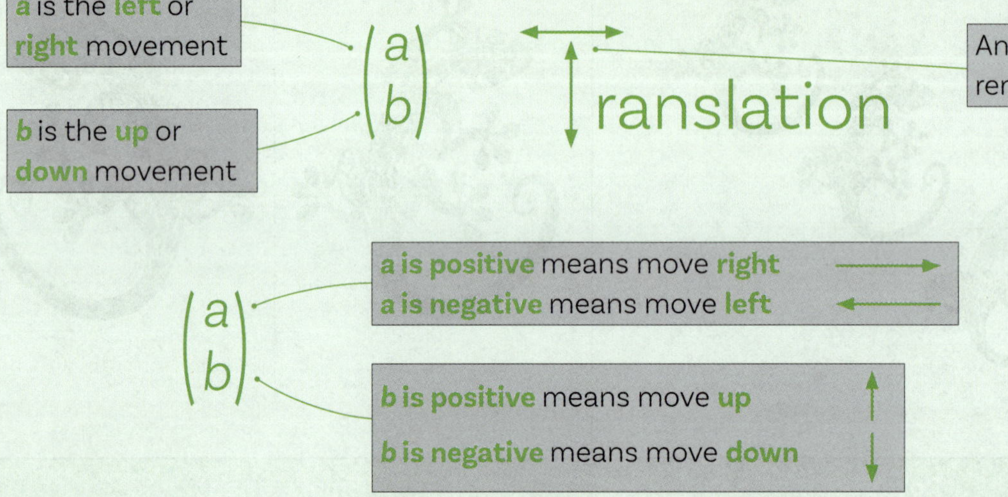

Examples:

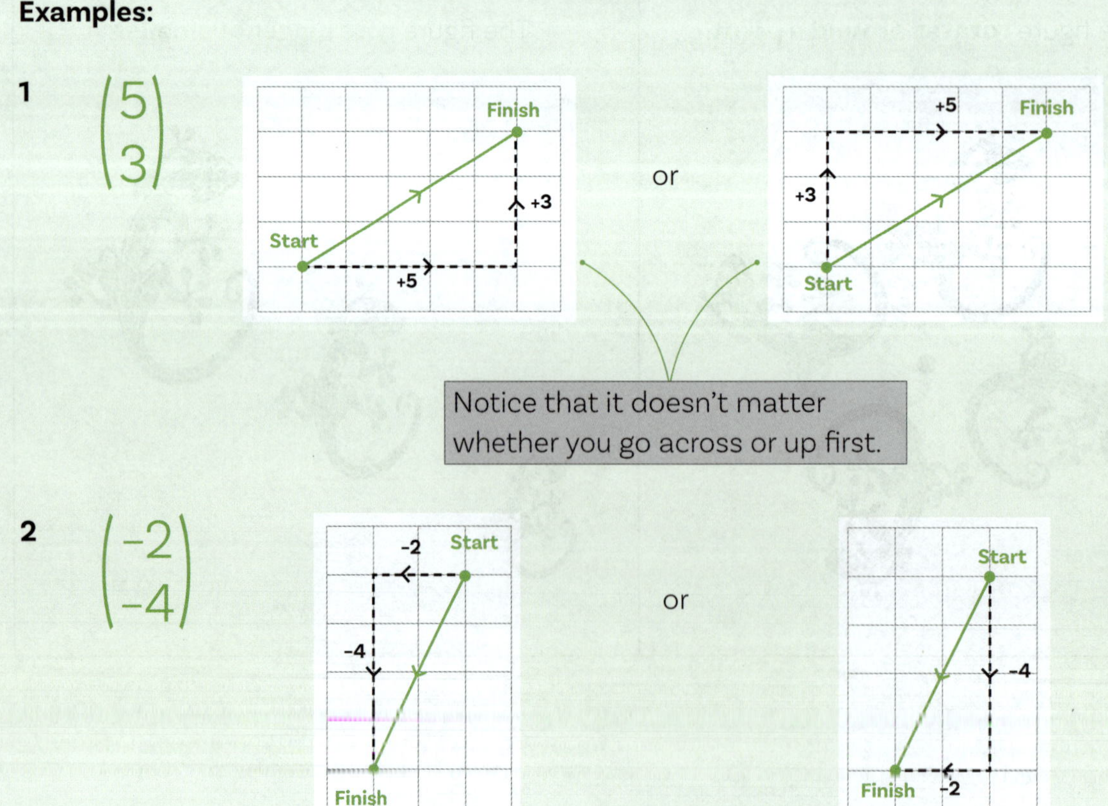

 ISBN: 9780170497978

Match these vectors to one of the descriptions below.

$\begin{pmatrix}-1\\2\end{pmatrix}$	$\begin{pmatrix}-2\\4\end{pmatrix}$	$\begin{pmatrix}-4\\-2\end{pmatrix}$	$\begin{pmatrix}1\\-2\end{pmatrix}$	$\begin{pmatrix}2\\-4\end{pmatrix}$	$\begin{pmatrix}4\\2\end{pmatrix}$

1 Right four and up two $\begin{pmatrix}\quad\\\quad\end{pmatrix}$

2 Left two and up four $\begin{pmatrix}\quad\\\quad\end{pmatrix}$

3 Right two and down four $\begin{pmatrix}\quad\\\quad\end{pmatrix}$

4 Left one and up two $\begin{pmatrix}\quad\\\quad\end{pmatrix}$

5 Left four and down two $\begin{pmatrix}\quad\\\quad\end{pmatrix}$

6 Right one and down two $\begin{pmatrix}\quad\\\quad\end{pmatrix}$

Describe in words what these vectors mean.

7 $\begin{pmatrix}1\\5\end{pmatrix}$ ________ one and ________ five

8 $\begin{pmatrix}3\\-6\end{pmatrix}$ ________ three and ________ six

9 $\begin{pmatrix}-7\\8\end{pmatrix}$ ________ seven and ________ eight

10 $\begin{pmatrix}-10\\-4\end{pmatrix}$ ________ ten and ________ four

11 $\begin{pmatrix}-5\\2\end{pmatrix}$ ____________________

____

12 $\begin{pmatrix}9\\-11\end{pmatrix}$ ____________________

____

13 Write vectors for each of those on the grid.

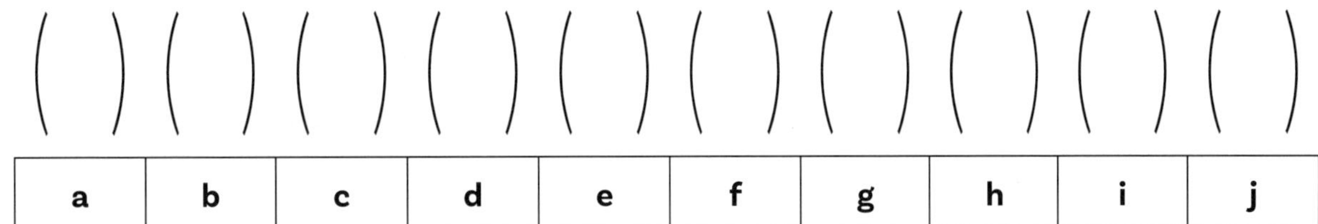

a	b	c	d	e	f	g	h	i	j

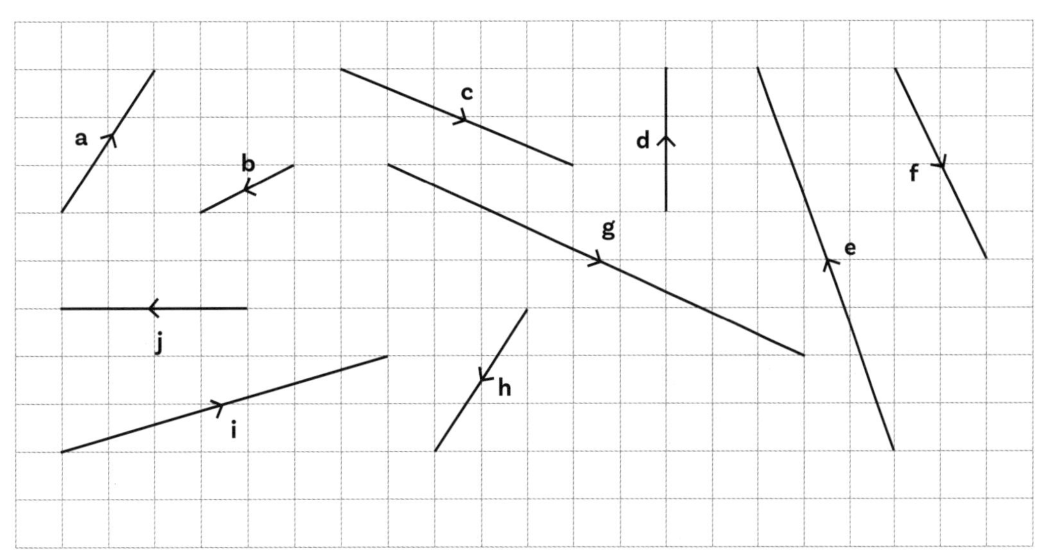

ISBN: 9780170497978

Drawing vectors for translated figures

- When drawing vectors for translated figures, you must draw the vector from a point on the original to the **equivalent** point on the image.

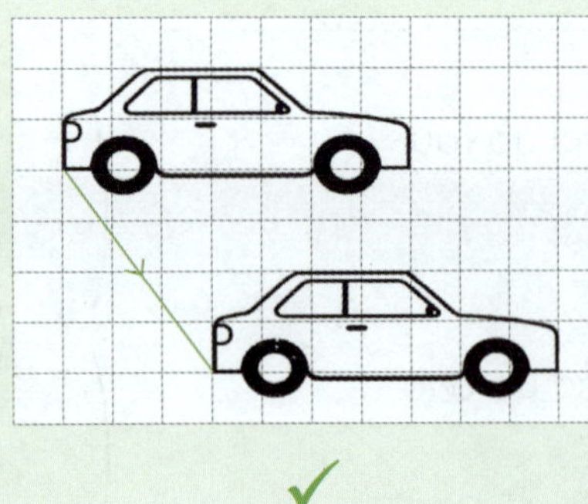
✓

✗

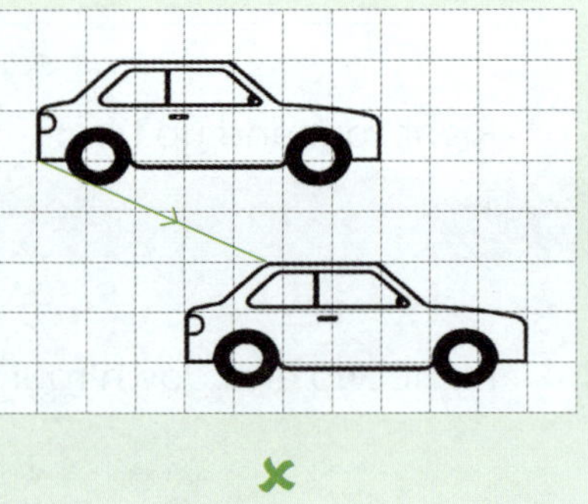
✗

Write the vector for the translation of each figure. The green shape is the original.

14

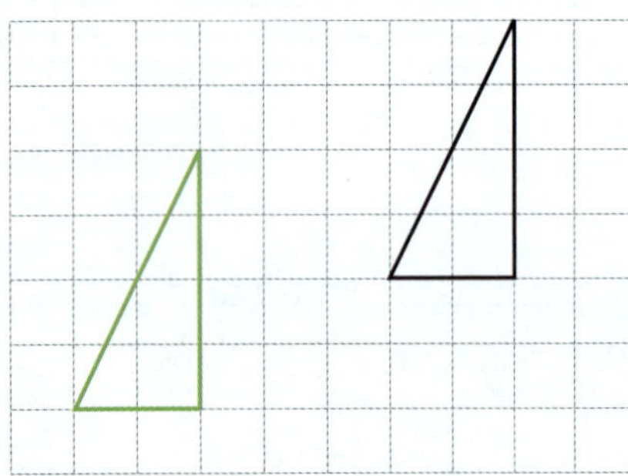

$\begin{pmatrix} \\ \end{pmatrix}$

15

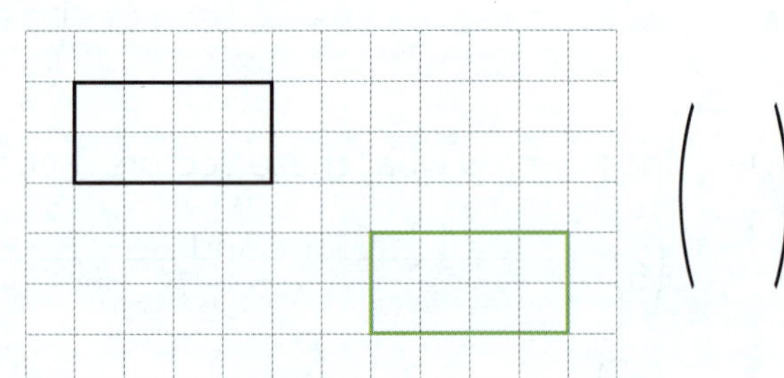

$\begin{pmatrix} \\ \end{pmatrix}$

16

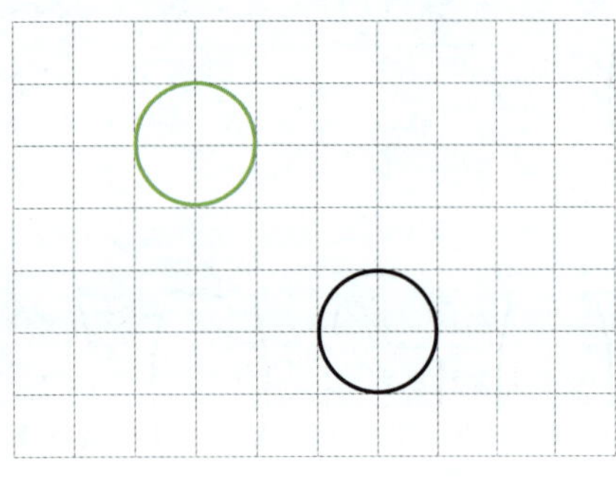

$\begin{pmatrix} \\ \end{pmatrix}$

17

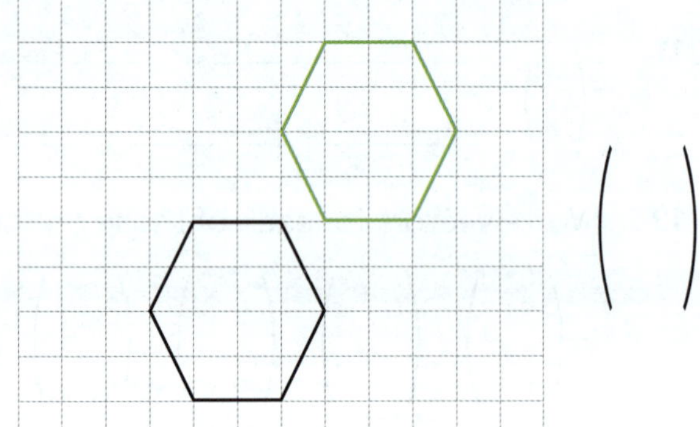

$\begin{pmatrix} \\ \end{pmatrix}$

18

$\begin{pmatrix} \\ \end{pmatrix}$

19

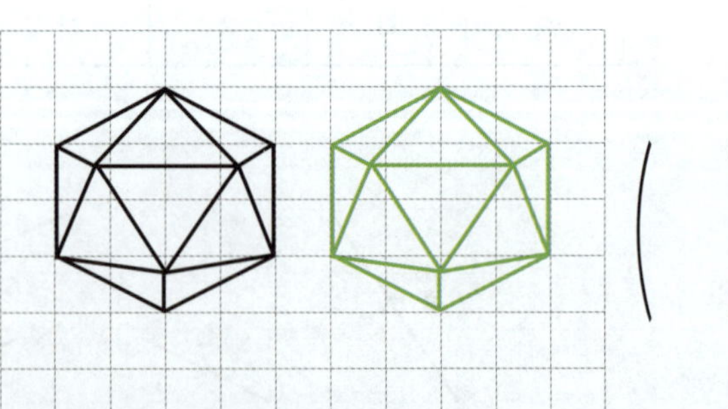

$\begin{pmatrix} \\ \end{pmatrix}$

20

$\begin{pmatrix} \\ \end{pmatrix}$

21

$\begin{pmatrix} \\ \end{pmatrix}$

ISBN: 9780170497978

Reflection

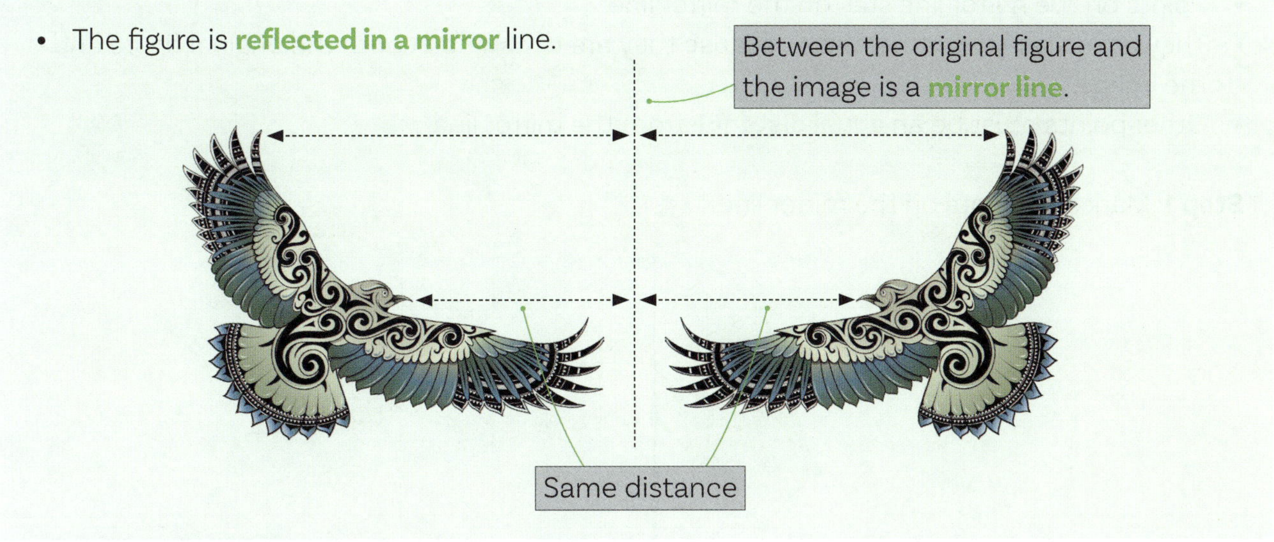

Rule mirror lines for the following reflections.

1

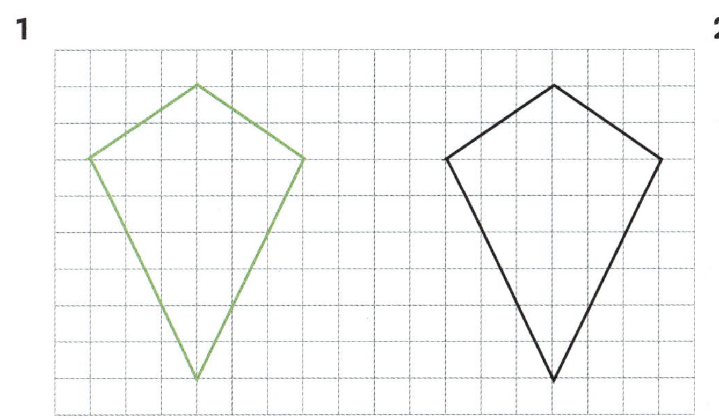

2

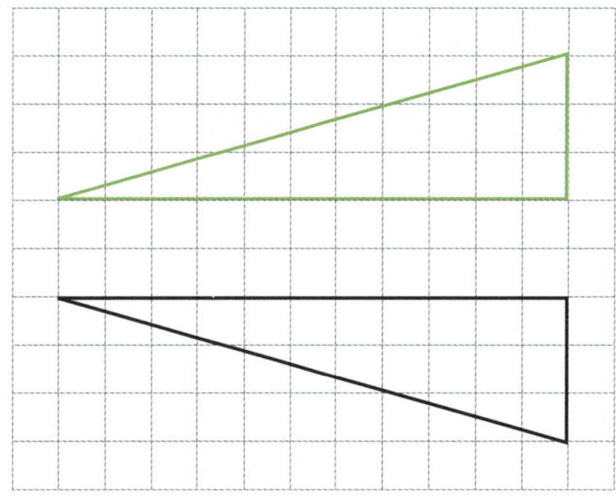

3

4

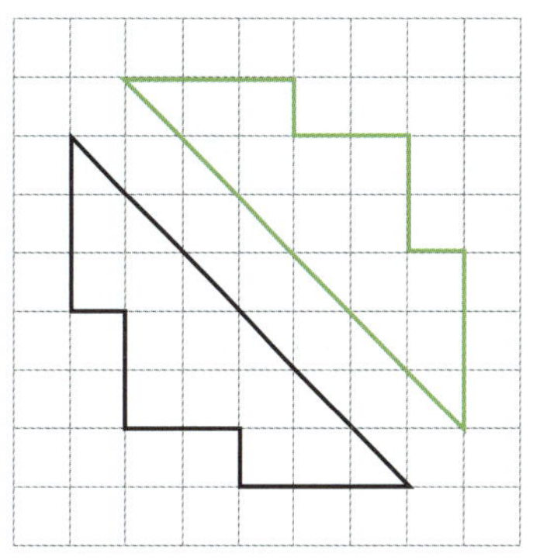

5

6

ISBN: 9780170497978

Drawing reflections

- Points on the mirror line stay on the mirror line.
- They are called **invariant points** because they are **the same** in both the original figure and the image.
- Other points must be an **equal distance** from the mirror line.

Step 1: Mark any points on the mirror line.

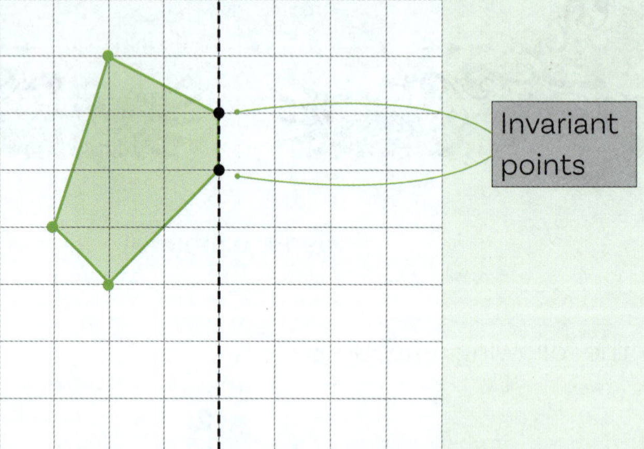

Step 2: Using lines at right angles to the mirror line, mark points that are the same distance from it, but on the opposite side.

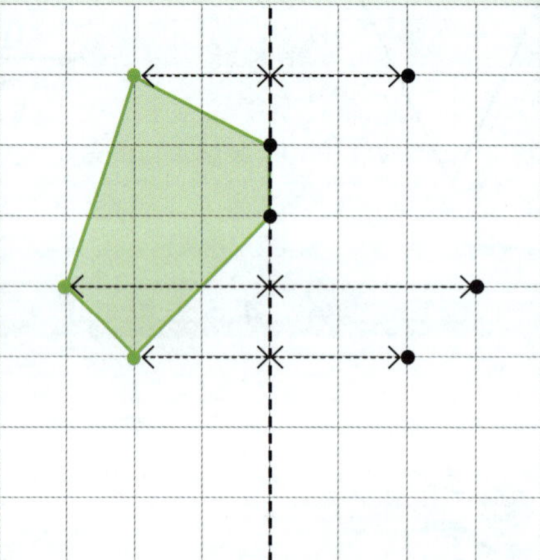

Step 3: Connect the points.

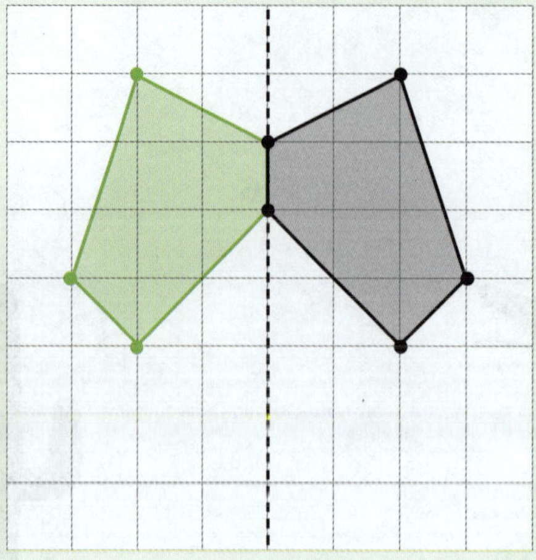

ISBN: 9780170497978

Draw reflections of the following figures.

Hint: You may find this easier if you turn the page so the mirror line is vertical.

7

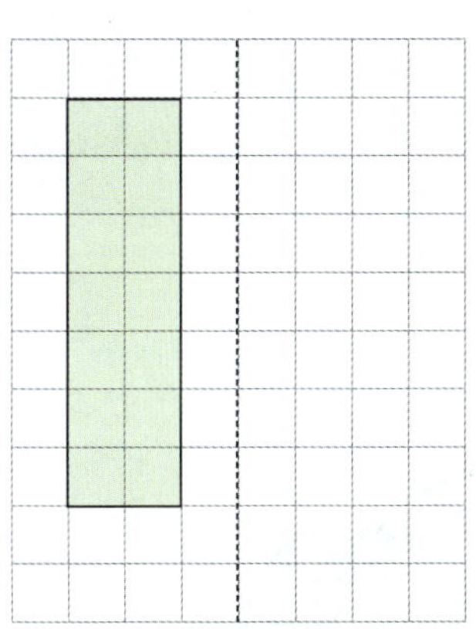

8

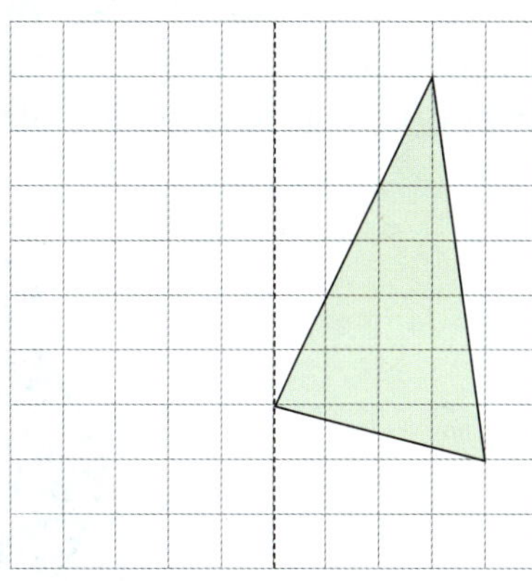

9

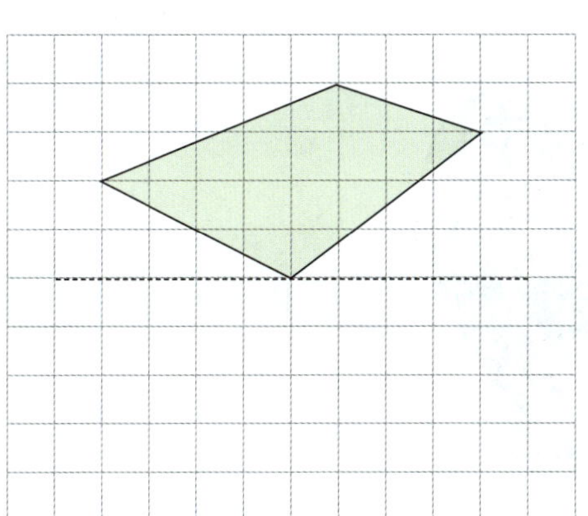

10

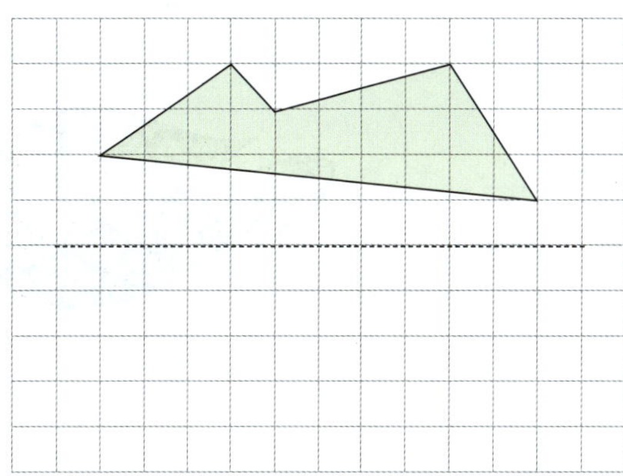

11 The first point has been found for you.

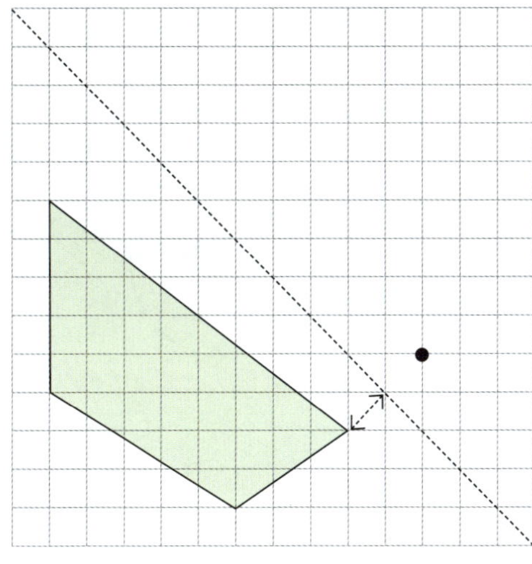

12 The first point has been found for you.

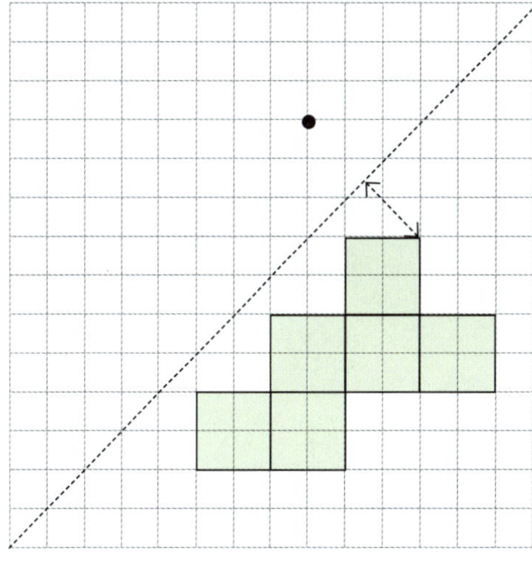

13

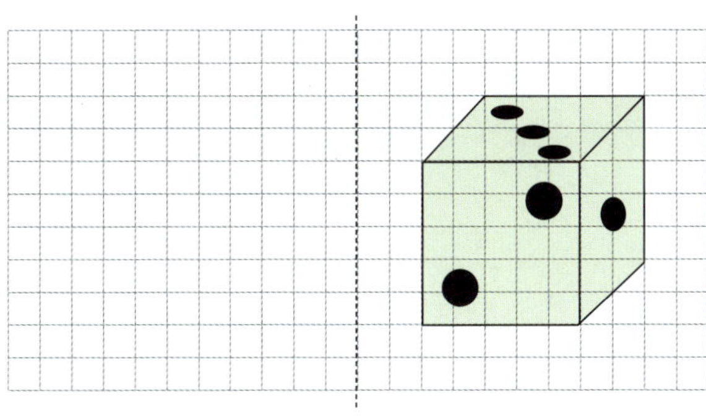

14

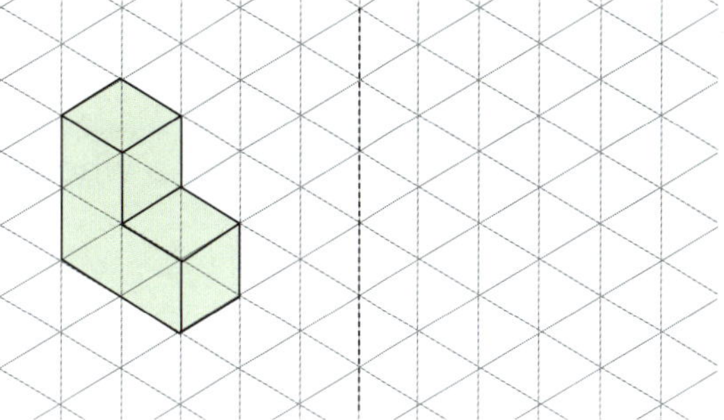

ISBN: 9780170497978

Rotation

- The figure **rotates around a point**.
- The **point** is known as the **centre of rotation**.
- Rotations, unless specified otherwise, are always measured in a **clockwise direction**.

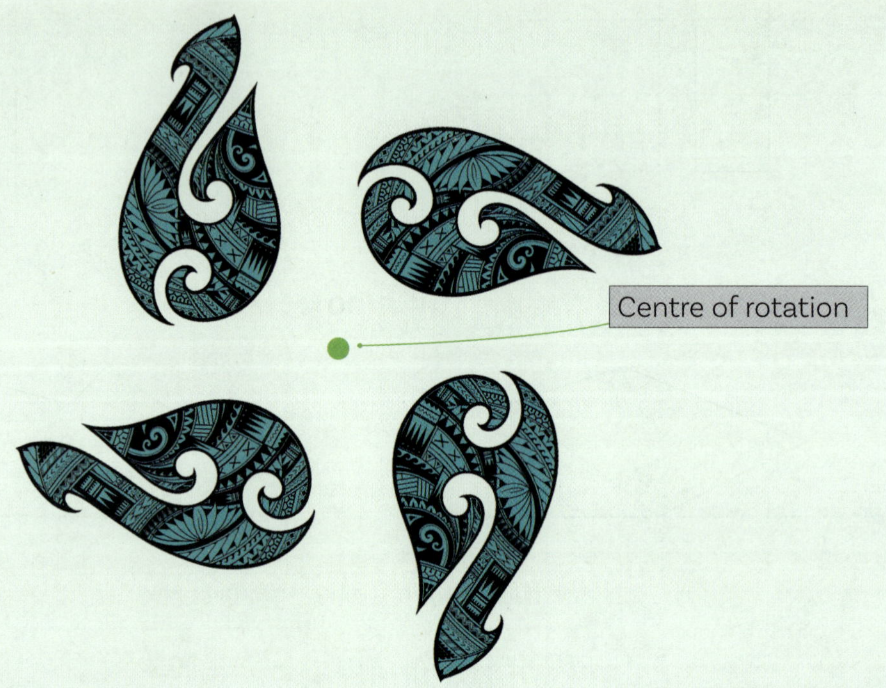

We will use only these angles:

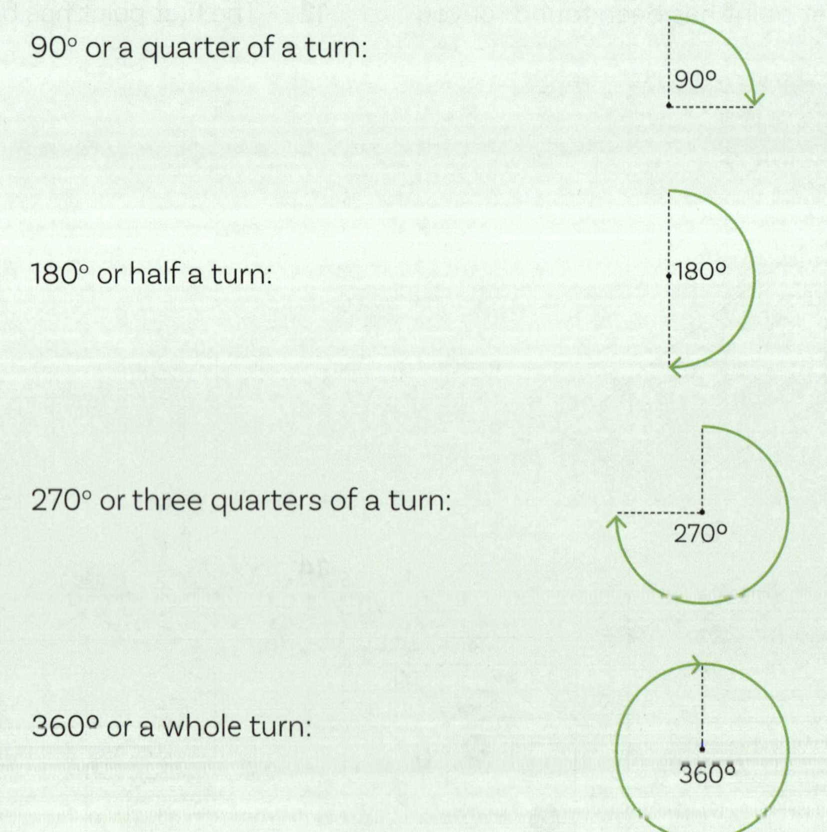

ISBN: 9780170497978

Using angles of rotation

Examples: Write the angle of rotation for each of the following.

Remember: 1 The **green** figure is the **original**, so start your angle there.
2 The **blue** figure is the **image**.

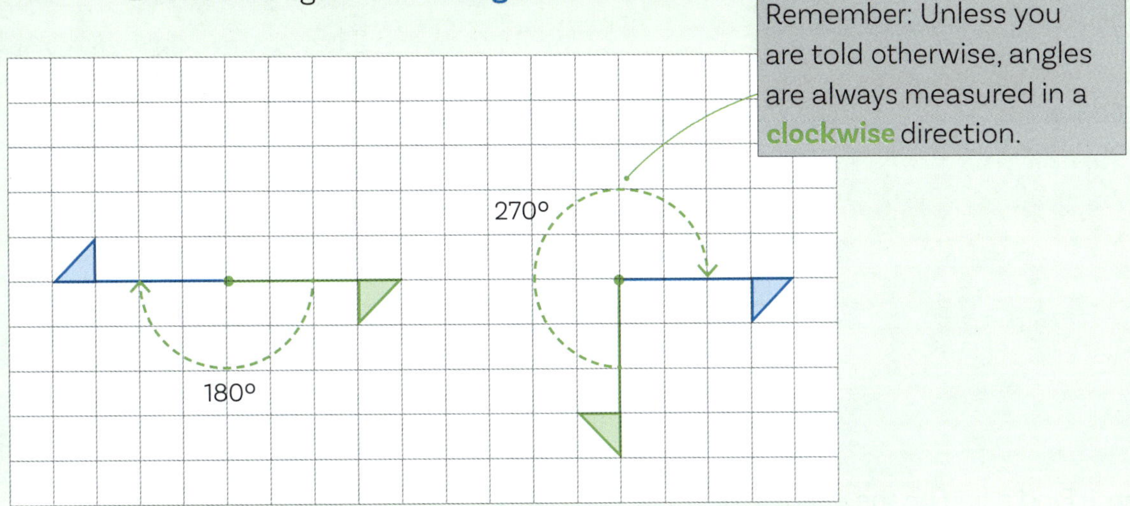

Write the angle of rotation for each of the following. Remember: The green figure is the original.

1

Angle = __________°

2

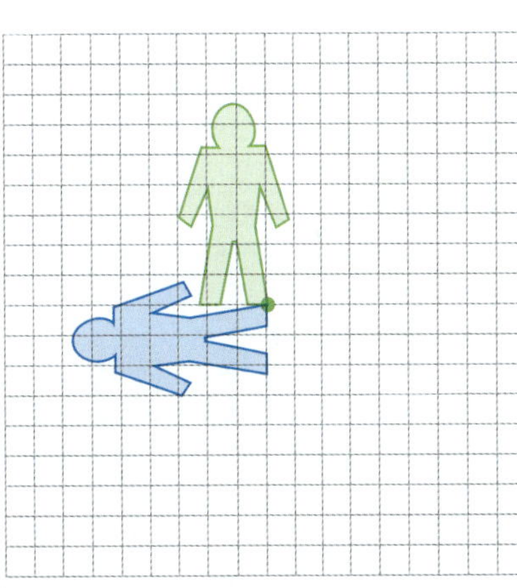

Angle = __________°

3

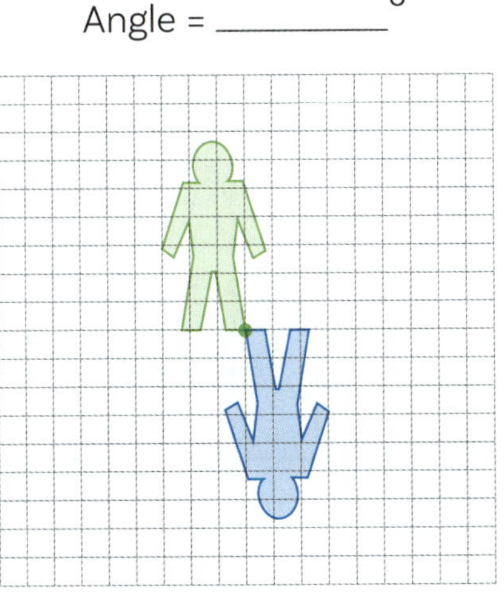

Angle = __________°

4

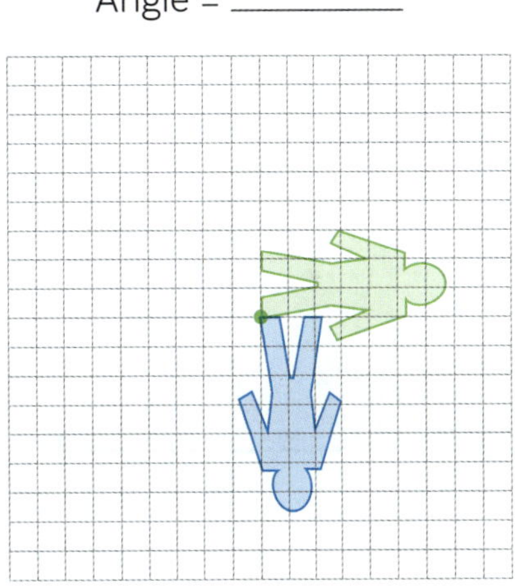

Angle = __________°

ISBN: 9780170497978

Drawing rotations

- Remember that unless you are told otherwise, rotations are always **clockwise**.
- It is really helpful to have a pin and tracing paper for this.

Example: Rotate this figure 90° clockwise around the point.

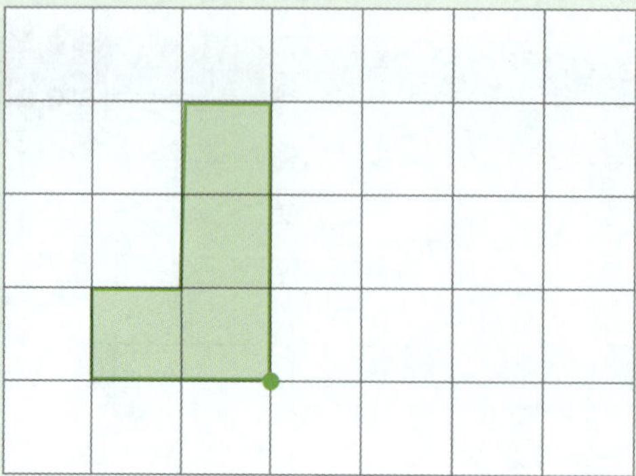

Step 1: Find a line on the shape which passes through the centre of rotation.

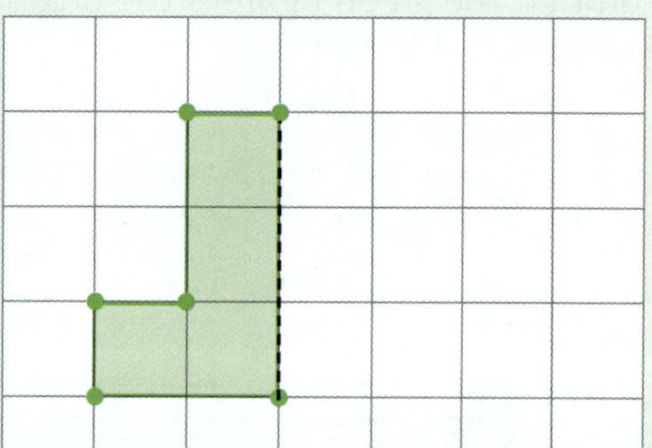

Step 2: Rotate the line by the required amount.

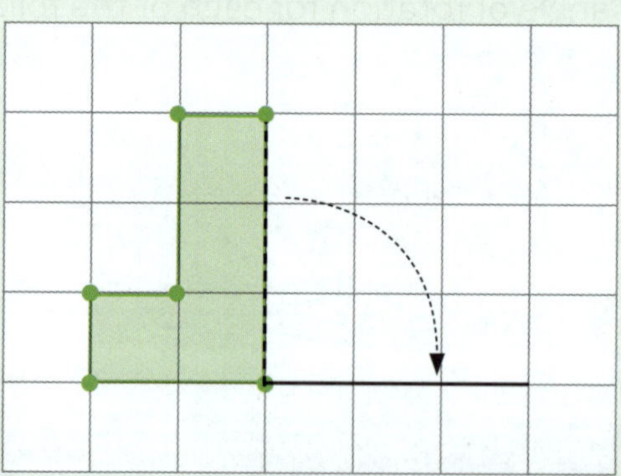

Step 3: Plot the remaining points in relation to this line.

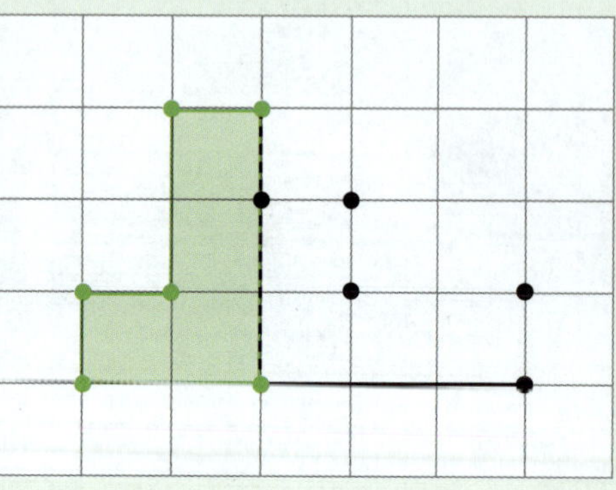

Step 4: Join the points.

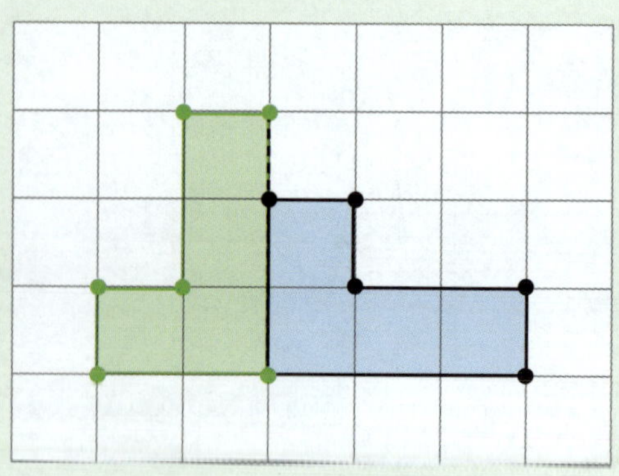

 ISBN: 9780170497978

Draw the images of these figures after they have been rotated.

5 Rotate this figure 180° clockwise about the point.

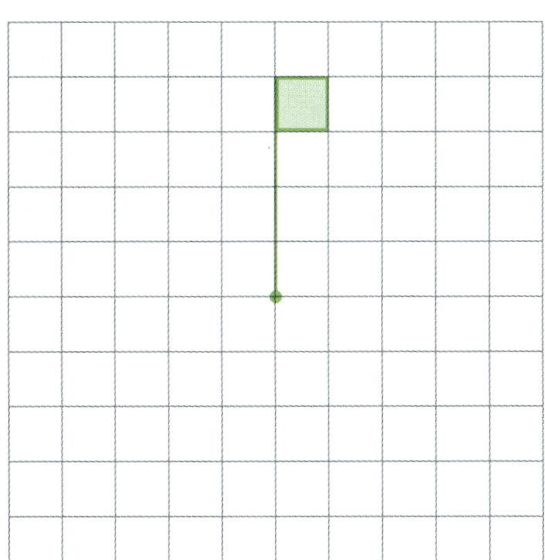

6 Rotate this figure 90° clockwise about the point.

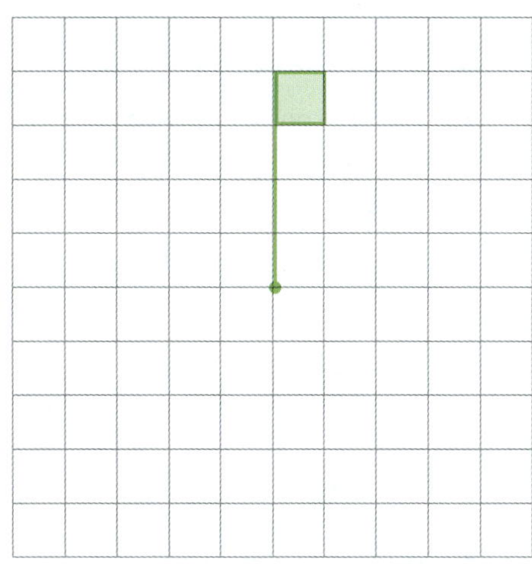

7 Rotate this figure 90° clockwise about the point.

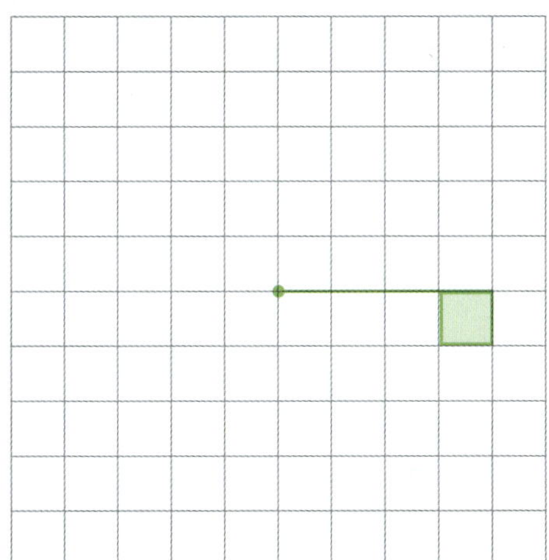

8 Rotate this figure 270° clockwise about the point.

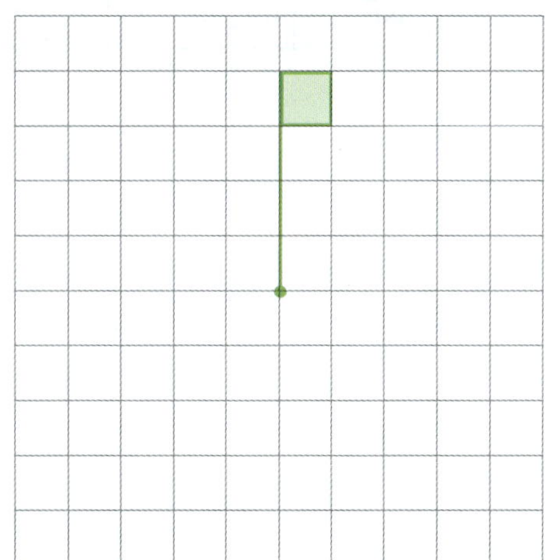

9 Rotate this figure 270° clockwise about the point.

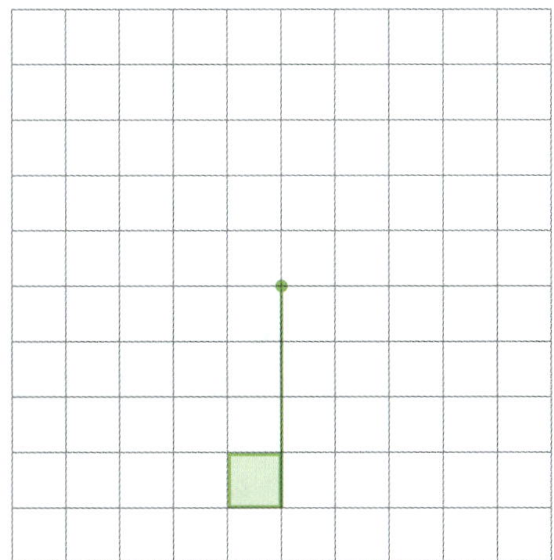

10 Rotate this figure 90° **anti**clockwise about the point.

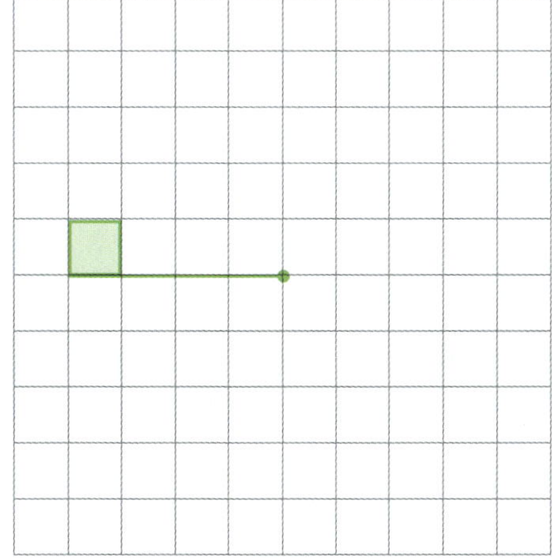

Position and orientation

Directions

- Direction can be given in terms of north, south, east and west.
- To help you remember:

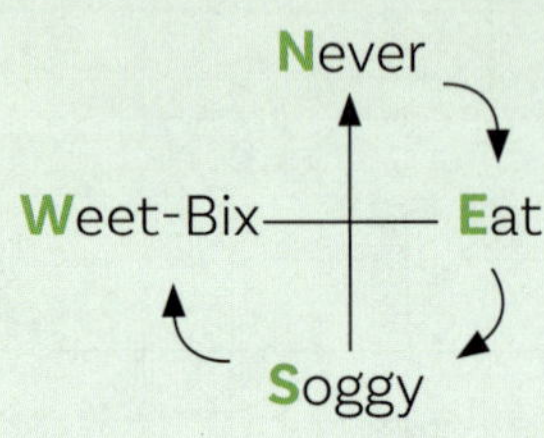

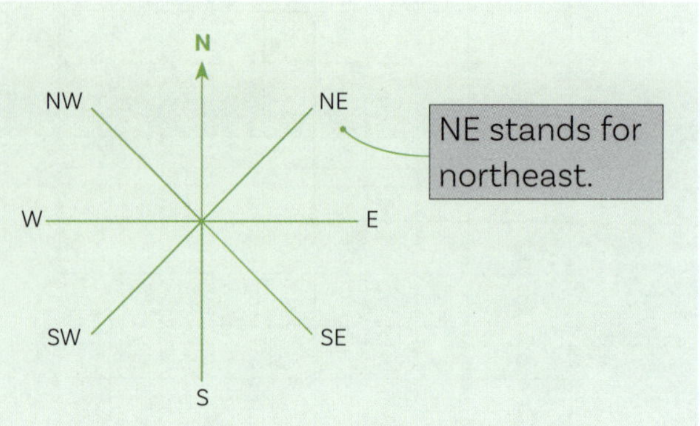

Answer the following questions.

Match the directions of the green lines in the diagrams to those in the list. The lines are either in the direction of the arrow or from A to B.

W	NE	S	E	NW	SE	SW	N

1 __________ **2** __________ **3** __________ **4** __________

5 __________ **6** __________ **7** __________ **8** __________

9 Anton walks in a clockwise direction around this circuit. Write the directions in which he is walking on the lines provided.

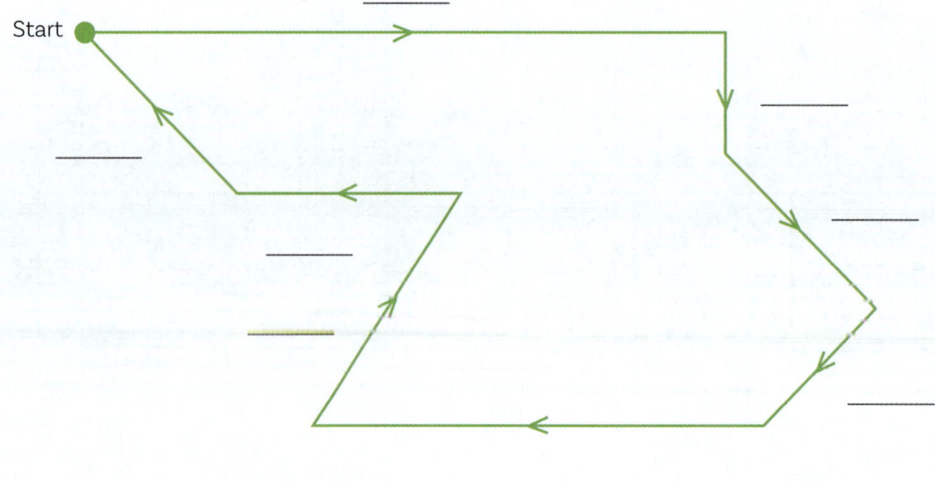

 ISBN: 9780170497978

10 Aroha is looking at plans for a tiny home. Answer the following questions.

a Against which wall of the house is the kitchen bench? ____________

b What is located in the southwest corner of the house? ____________

c There is a small sunroom containing three chairs, a table and some plants. In which corner of the house is this located? ____________

11 This section of a map shows part of Canterbury.

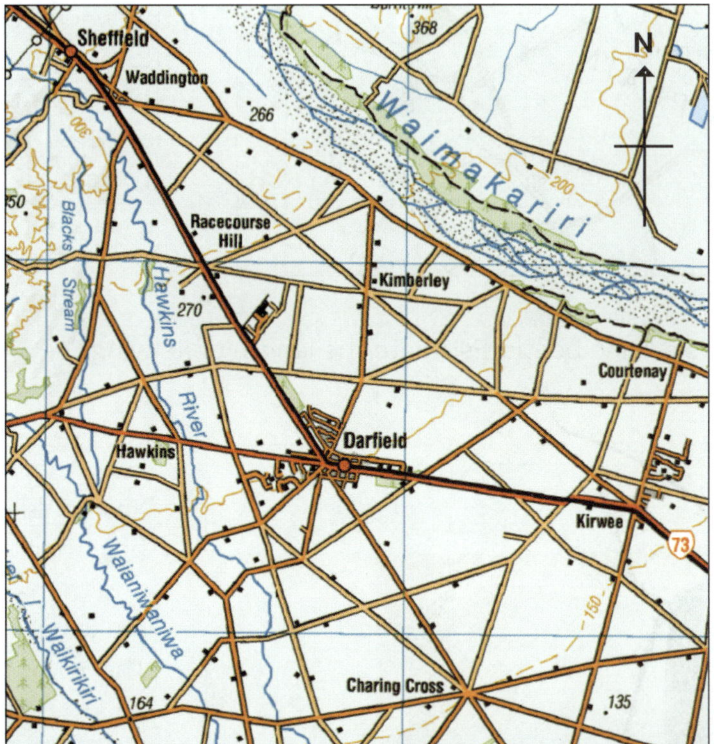

In which direction would you be driving if you were going

a from Darfield to Kirwee? ________ **b** from Sheffield to Darfield? ________

c from Kimberley to Darfield? ________ **d** from Charing Cross to Darfield? ________

ISBN: 9780170497978

Scales

- A scale gives a measure of **distance** on a map or diagram.
- You will not be able to determine exact distances, but you need to be able to **estimate** distances.
- Estimations should be made to no more than **two significant figures**.

Examples:

1 The distance between the gridlines is 10 km.
Estimate the distance between Culverden and Rotherham.

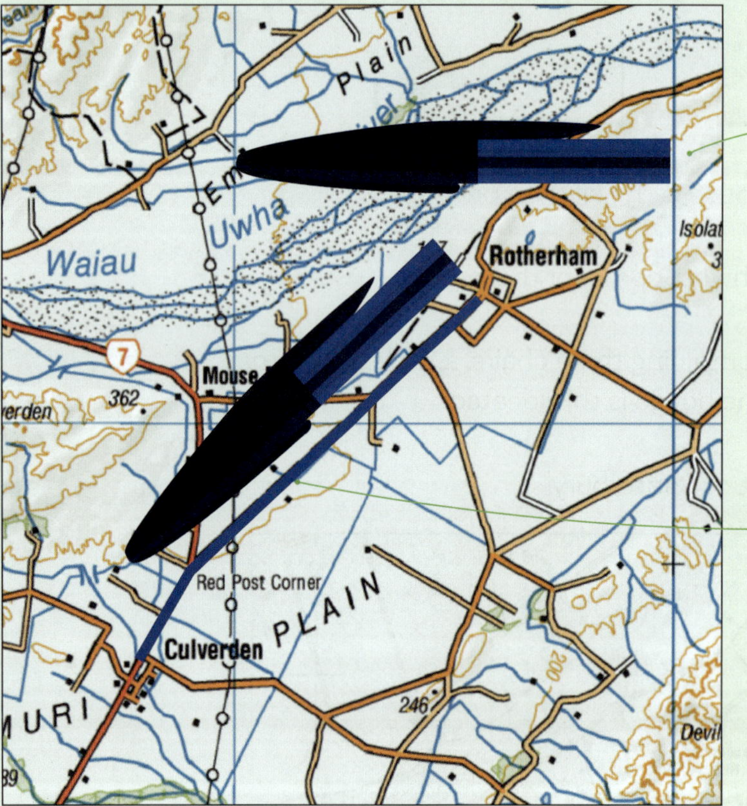

Use part of a pen or your finger to measure the distance between the gridlines.

Then use the pen to estimate the distance needed.
In this case the distance between Culverden and Rotherham is a little more than one part of a pen length, so a good estimate would be 12 km.

2 The diagram hows a huhu beetle. Estimate the length of its wings.

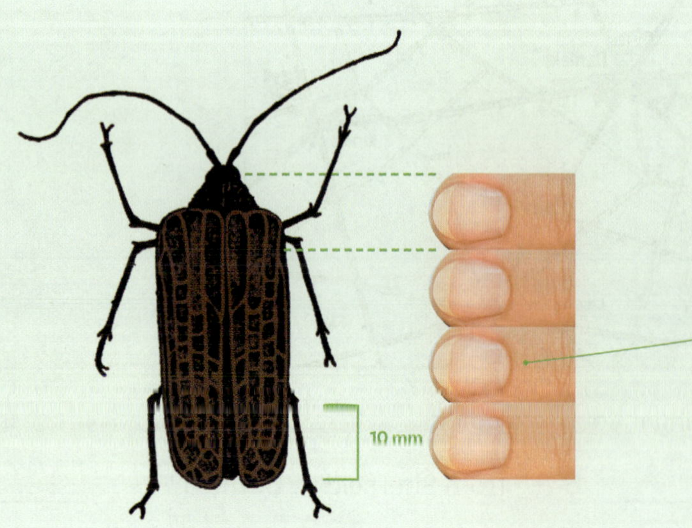

You could use the width of a fingernail to estimate 10 mm, and then count how many make up the length of a wing. The wings are between three and four fingernails long (30–40 mm), so a good estimate would be 35 mm.

ISBN: 9780170497978

Answer the following questions.

1 This is the plan for a house. The lines on the grid are 1 metre apart. Estimate the following distances.

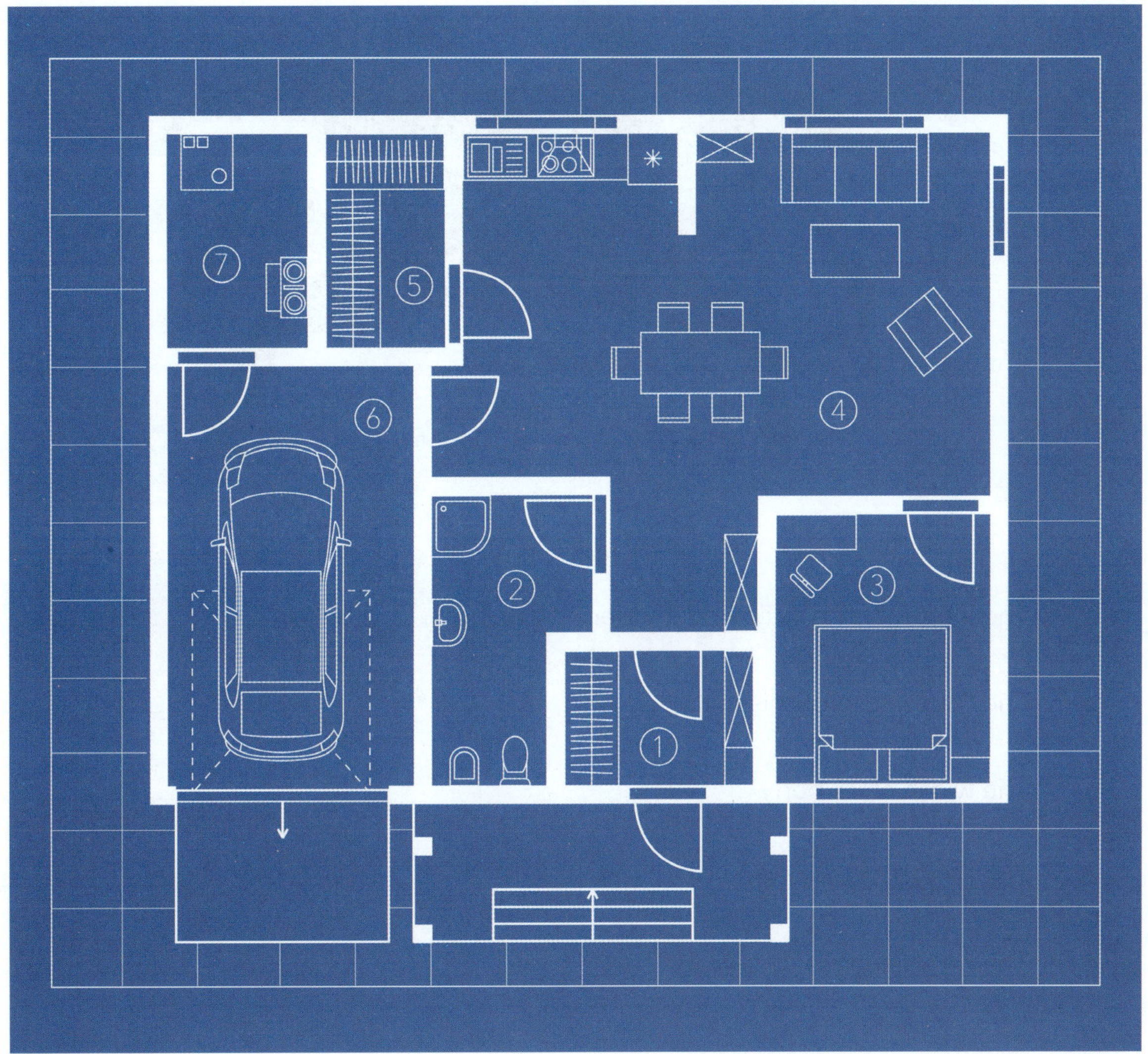

a The length of the car. ____________ m

b The internal length of the garage. ____________ m

c The internal width of the garage. ____________ m

d The width of the double bed. ____________ m

e The length of the dining table ____________ m

f The external width of the front of the house (side with the front door). ____________ m

2 This photograph shows a red rock crab. Estimate the following lengths to the nearest half centimetre.

a The length of the indicated section of the leg. ______________ cm

b The total width of this crab ______________ cm

c The width of its body. ______________ cm

d The length of a pincer. ______________ cm

e The total length of this crab. ______________ cm

3 Estimate the widths of these seeds if 1 cm on the picture = 2 mm on the real object.

Mustard seed	**Peppercorn**	**Cumin seed**	**Red kidney bean**
____________ mm	____________ mm	____________ mm	____________ mm

  ISBN: 9780170497978

4 This map shows an area in Taranaki. The distance between the gridlines is 10 km. Estimate the following distances to the nearest half kilometre.

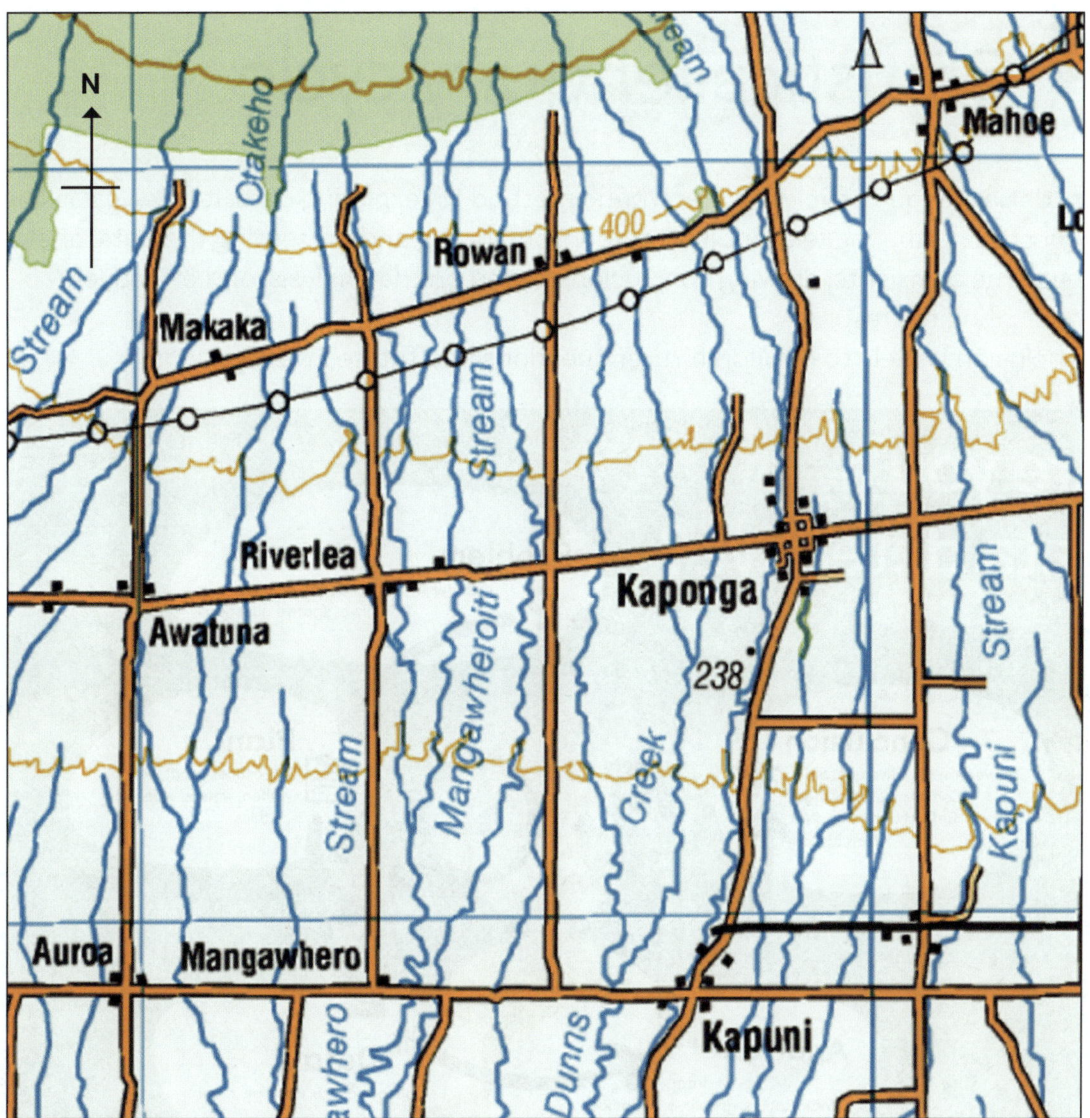

		Overall direction	Distance
a	Awatuna to Makaka	North	________ km
b	Riverlea to Mangawhero	________	________ km
c	Makaka to Mahoe	________	________ km
d	Kaponga to Riverlea	________	________ km
e	Auroa to Kapuni	________	________ km
f	Makaka to Kapuni via Auroa	________	________ km

ISBN: 9780170497978

STATISTICS

Statistical enquiry cycle

The **statistical enquiry cycle** is a systematic method for exploring data. It involves asking a clear question, gathering relevant information, organising and presenting the data, analysing it for patterns or insights, drawing conclusions based on the analysis, and effectively communicating the results.
The conclusion is likely to result in further questions and future investigations.

Some useful definitions

Types of data

Primary data: this is data that you collect yourself.

Secondary data: this is data that you are given or that you find. You have not collected it yourself.

Data information

Data dictionary: this is the information about primary data – data you collect yourself. This should include:

- a general description of the data
- a definition of each column heading, including the question asked (if applicable)
- any codes (e.g. f for female, m for male) used as values in the data.

Metadata: this is the information that you are given with secondary data.

ISBN: 9780170497978

Problem, plan and data

Thinking about the data

This is some of the data that you collected from a survey of all 128 dogs from the small town of Wai-iti.

Sex	Breed	Age (years)	Mass (kg)	Sleeps	???	Cost of feed per week
Female	Dalmatian	3.5	23.9	Inside	Y	$21
Male	Bichon frise	2.5	7.1	Outside	N	$18
Male	Labrador	1.0	19.1	Outside	N	$24
Female	German shepherd	1.0	33.4	Inside	Y	$23
Male	Labrador	105	28.9	Outside	N	$22
Female	Golden retriever	5.5	21.7	Outside	M	$22
Female	Fox terrier	4.0	4.8	Inside	Y	$20
Male	Mixture	7.0	14.8	Outside	Y	$17
Female	Chihuahua	8.5	1.6	Inside	N	$49
Male	Schnauzer	12.0	7.2	Inside	Y	$21

Consider the following.

1 Highlight any values which seem unreasonable.

Explain why you think they're unreasonable.

____

____

____

____

____

____

____

2 There is a missing heading for one of the columns. Write two possible questions that could have been asked that would result in Yes/No answers.

1 ____

____

2 ____

____

ISBN: 9780170497978

Investigative questions

The sample you have been given is for just some of the dogs in Wai-iti. Do the results of this sample suggest that the following questions could be answered using the full set of data?

1 What is the most common breed of dog in Wai-iti? Yes/No Justify your answer.

____

____

2 Which breed of dog is the best behaved in Wai-iti? Yes/No Justify your answer.

____

____

3 Are there more male than female dogs in Wai-iti? Yes/No Justify your answer.

____

____

4 Are big dogs in Wai-iti fed more than small dogs? Yes/No Justify your answer.

____

____

5 Are Wai-iti female dogs heavier than male dogs? Yes/No Justify your answer.

____

____

6 Write another question that could be answered with this data set.

____

Some possible conclusions

Hana looks at the sample and comes to these conclusions about all 128 dogs from Wai-iti. Decide whether you think her conclusions are reasonable. Circle Yes, No or Maybe. Give your reasons.

7 All female dogs in Wai-iti sleep inside. Agree/Disagree/Maybe

Reason: ______________________

8 Most Wai-iti dogs have a mass of less than 35 kg. Agree/Disagree/Maybe

Reason: ______________________

9 Labradors are the most common dog breed in Wai-iti. Agree/Disagree/Maybe

Reason: ______________________

10 Labradors in Wai-iti are mostly male. Agree/Disagree/Maybe

Reason: ______________________

 ISBN: 9780170497978

Types of questions and identifying variables and groups of interest

There are four different types of statistical questions:

Summary questions – these investigate **one** variable for **one** group. This could be a word or a number.

Examples: What is your favourite food? — **One** variable – type of food

How many hats do you own? — **One** variable – number of hats

Comparative questions – these investigate **one** variable for **two** groups.

Example: Did the Year 9 boys get higher scores than the girls in the English test at Paradise High School?

One variable – English score
Two groups – girls and boys

Relationship questions – compare **two** variables for **one** group.

Example: Is there a relationship between height and foot length in my class?

Two variables – height and foot length
One group – class

Time series questions – **one** variable over a period of **time**.

Example: How does the number of absences at our school change over the term?

One variable – absences
One time period – a term

For each of these, highlight the type of question.

	Question	Type of question
1	What colour are your eyes?	Summary Comparative Relationship Time series
2	Are left-handed students absent from school more than right-handed students?	Summary Comparative Relationship Time series
3	How much money did you spend on clothes last month?	Summary Comparative Relationship Time series
4	Do Year 10 students have a faster reaction time than Year 9 students?	Summary Comparative Relationship Time series
5	Are Maths teachers cooler than Science teachers?	Summary Comparative Relationship Time series
6	How does the minimum daily temperature change over the month?	Summary Comparative Relationship Time series

ISBN: 9780170497978

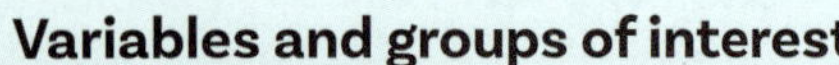

Variables and groups of interest

- The **variable** is the piece of information or measurement that you are collecting.
- The **group of interest** is the group from which you collect data.

Example:

The variable is grades.

Do Year 9 students who play sports get better grades than students who don't play sports at Paradise High School?

The group of interest is Year 9 students at Paradise High School.

Write down the variable and group of interest for these questions.

	Question	Variable	Group of interest
7	What is the average number of electric cars are in the school car park each day?	*Number of electric cars*	*Cars in the school car park*
8	What is the average time it takes for students in my class to get to school?		
9	Are male cats in Wai-iti heavier than female cats?		
10	Does sitting at the front of the classroom affect test scores of Year 9 students at Paradise High School?		
11	Does the area of paper in a paper plane affect how far it flies?		
12	What is the average number of books borrowed from the library by its members during each visit?		
13	Is there a relationship between age and resting heart rate in the members of a football team?		

ISBN: 9780170497978

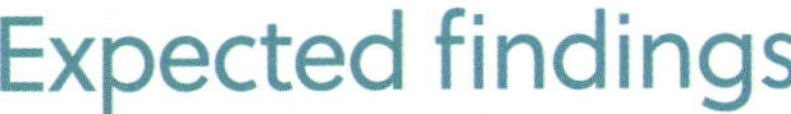

Expected findings

- Expected findings are opinions or thoughts about what you might find from an investigation.
- Different people are likely to have different opinions about expected outcomes.
- For that reason, it is important to **justify** your opinions and thoughts.

Example:

Question
Should our school have a school uniform?

Yes

Reasons
Adds to school spirit. Students don't have to think about what to wear. Removes competition to look cool.

No

Reasons
Would allow students to express their personality. Cheaper.

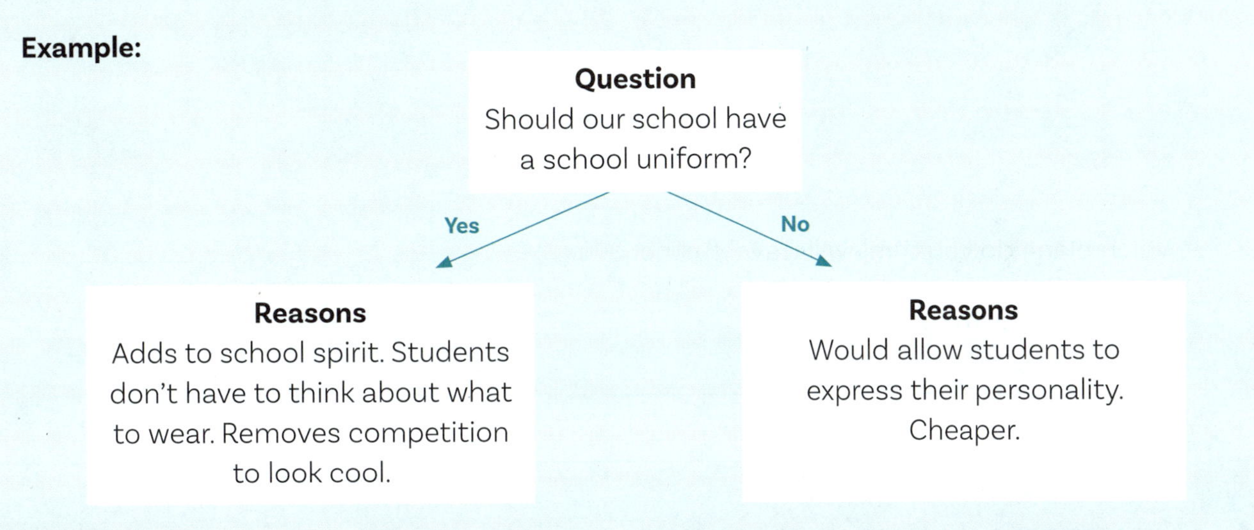

Come up with reasons that someone might agree or disagree with these expected findings.

1

Question
Are dogs that sleep inside heavier?

Expected finding

Yes

Reasons

No

Reasons

2

Question
Are school uniform fleeces better than wool jerseys?

Expected finding

Yes

Reasons

No

Reasons

ISBN: 9780170497978

Answer the following questions.

3 These two paper planes are thrown by the same person in the same conditions. The distance they travelled is measured.

Plane A

Plane B

Which plane do you think will travel further? ____________

Explain your answer.

____

____

4 Does the angle of a ramp affect how far the marble travels? Yes/No

Explain your answer.

____

____

5 **a** Do you think that students would get better marks if cellphones were banned from the school? Yes/No

b Explain your answer.

____

____

6 **a** Are taller people able to stand on one foot for longer than shorter people? Yes/No

b Explain your answer.

____

____

 ISBN: 9780170497978

Collection of data

Primary data

- Primary data is data that **you collect yourself**.
- Before you collect and analyse the data, it is important to consider the **purpose** of your investigation.
- You need to develop a **detailed plan** of how you are going to collect it.

When collecting data, measurements should be:

1 **Accurate** – the data values are close to the true value.
If the Plunket nurse is weighing a baby, the scales should calibrated (checked that they are not weighing consistently too high or low), and the baby should be lying still.

2 **Valid** – the data values actually represent what they claim to.
When the mass of just the baby is wanted, then the baby should not be wearing anything.

3 **Reliable** – means making sure your results are correct by measuring and recording carefully, using the right tools, and doing it the same way each time.

4 **Collected ethically** – means gathering information in a fair, respectful way where people or parents choose to take part and their answers are kept private.

Secondary data

- Secondary data is data **someone else collected**.
- It is important to learn as much as you can about how it was gathered, e.g. who collected it, when, where and for what purpose. Sometimes this is difficult.
- This information will help you to judge how reliable the data is.

Answer the following questions.

1 When collecting people's heights, indicate (✓or ×) which of these factors should be considered.

	Is the student wearing shoes?
	Is the student wearing a jersey?
	Has the student's hair been flattened?
	Were people's heights measured inside or outside?
	Was the data including student names left on the whiteboard after class?
	Was all the data collected on the same day?
	Was the same measuring device used for all students?
	When the heights were recorded, were they double-checked?
	Had the student eaten lunch?
	Did the same person do all the measuring?

ISBN: 9780170497978

2 Mary is carrying out a statistical investigation. This is the start of her report:

Stats investigation

Question
Does a person's height affect the length of time they can stand on one foot?

Expected outcome
Shorter people will be able to stand on one foot for longer.

Plan
Get any Year 9 or 10 student who walks past me at interval and tell them they have to stand on one foot for as long as possible. Then measure their height.

a What variable(s) is she investigating? ______

b Who is the group of interest? ______

c Is her plan thorough enough? Suggest some things she should be more specific about or any changes she should make.

______

______

______

______

______

______

d Which of these questions should you ask Mary to make sure she has collected the data **ethically**?

	Did you explain what the data was going to be used for?
	Did you collect the data inside or outside?
	Were they wearing correct uniform?
	Did you ask people if they would take part?
	Were their answers kept private?
	Did you use the same stopwatch each time?
	Was anyone forced or tricked into participating?
	Could they say no or stop at any time?

ISBN: 9780170497978

Data display

- There are different ways of displaying data. Which is most appropriate depends on the **type** of data.

Descriptive data	Discrete data	Continuous data
Tally chart	Tally chart	Histogram
Pictograph	Pictograph	Line graph/time series
Dot plot	Dot plot	Scatter plot
Bar graph	Bar graph	Box plot
Strip graph	Strip graph	
Pie graph	Line graph/time series	**If rounded**
	Scatter plot	Dot plot
	Box plot	

Write the names of each graph, and the types of data for which each is appropriate.

1

Pie graph

Descriptive

2

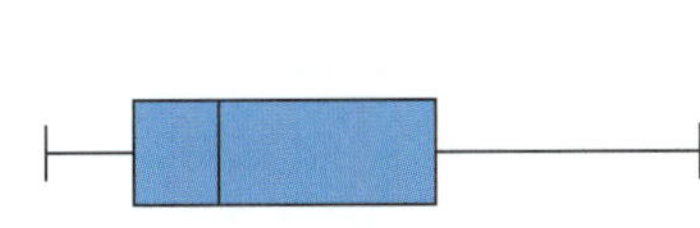

3

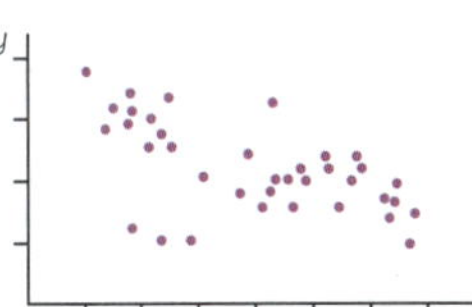

4

French	||||
German	~~||||~~ ||||
Latin	||
Spanish	~~||||~~

5

6

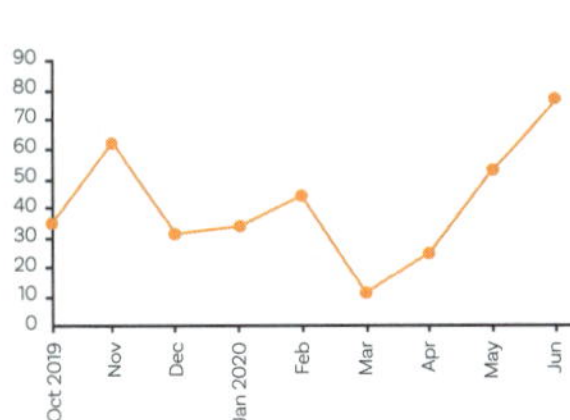

7

8

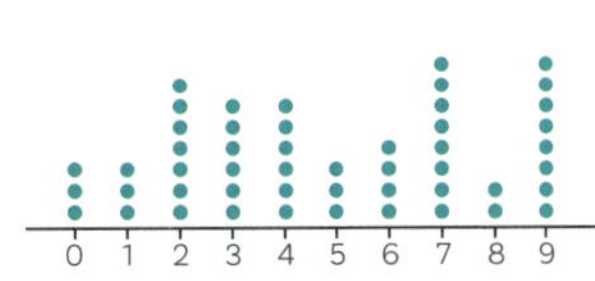

9

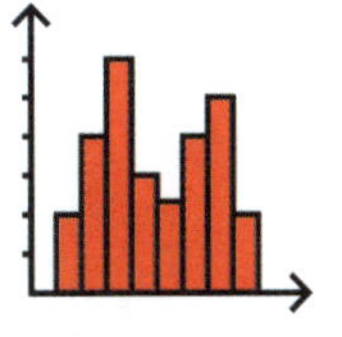

All sorts of other graphs are used, but remember, fancy doesn't necessarily mean better or easier to understand.

ISBN: 9780170497978

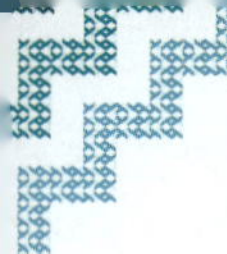

Reading axes

- **Axes** are the horizontal and vertical lines which show the scale.
- The **vertical** axis is the ***y***-axis, the **horizontal** is the ***x***-axis.

We speak of **one** axis or **several** axes.

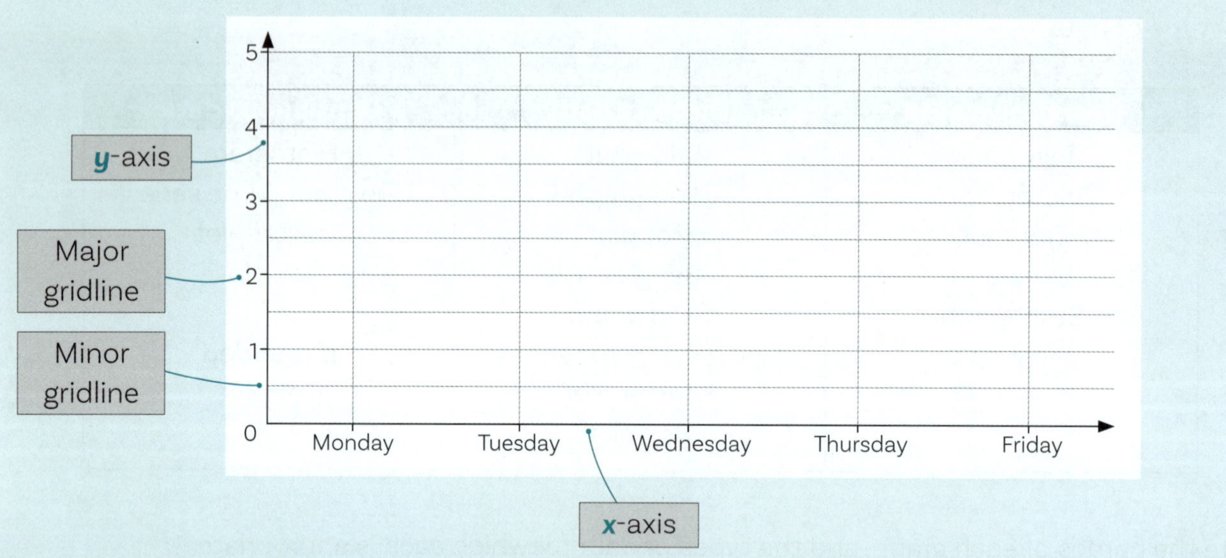

- The gridlines **with numbers** are called **major** gridlines.
- The gridlines **without numbers** are called **minor** gridlines.
- Look out for multipliers. The axis label may read, for example, '(x 1000)' or '(thousands)'.

Examples:

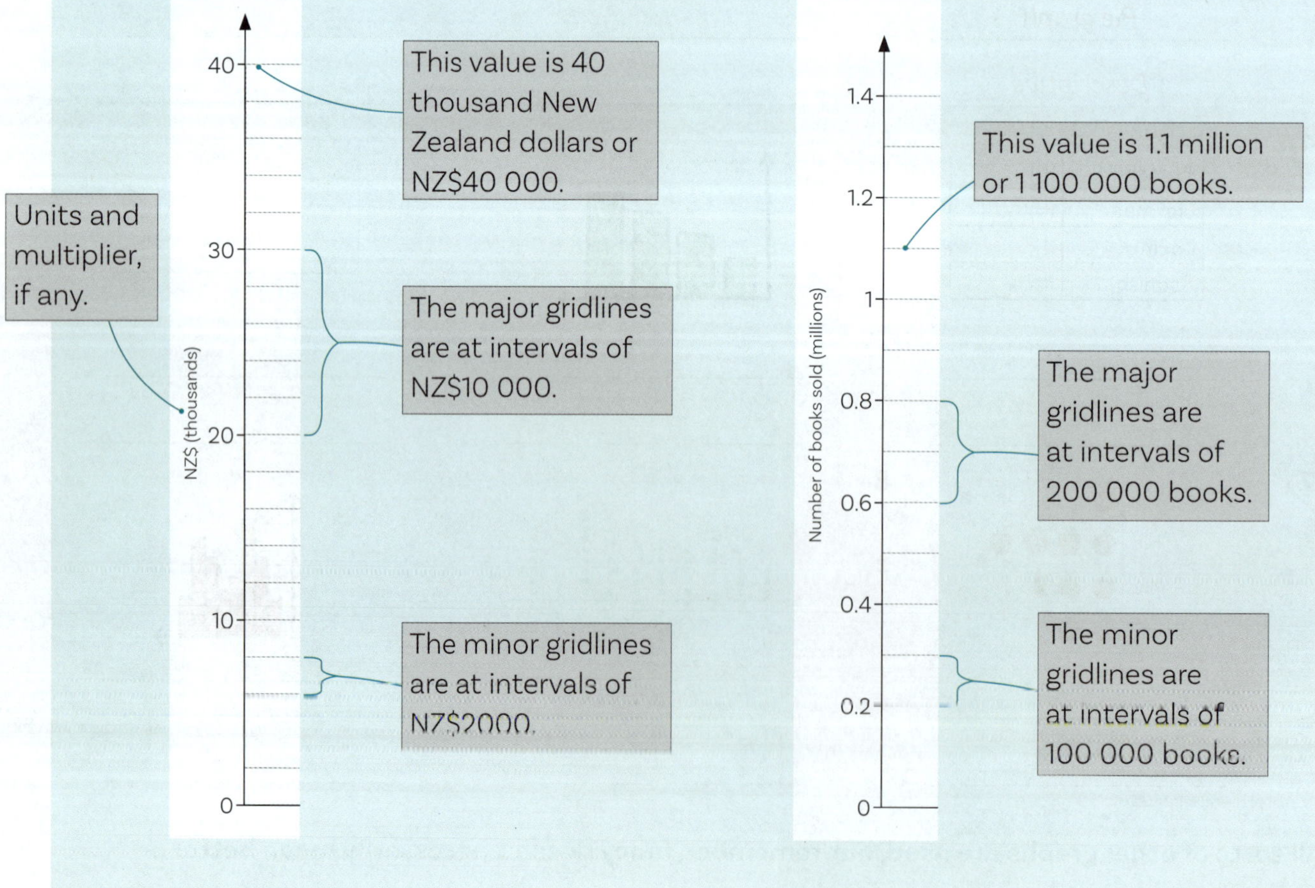

ISBN: 9780170497978

Write down the major and minor intervals, and then fill in the missing values from these axes.

1 Major ________ Minor ________

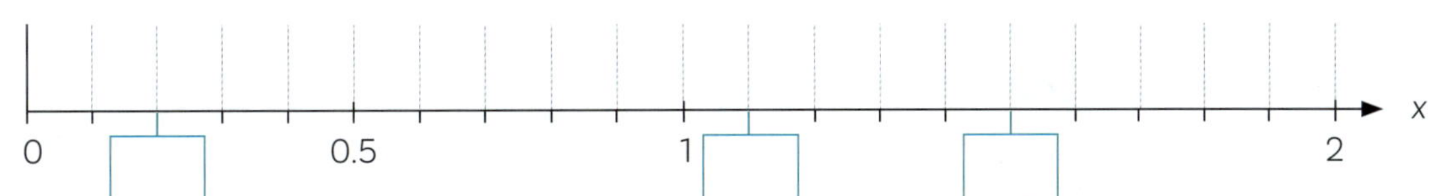

2 Major ________ Minor ________

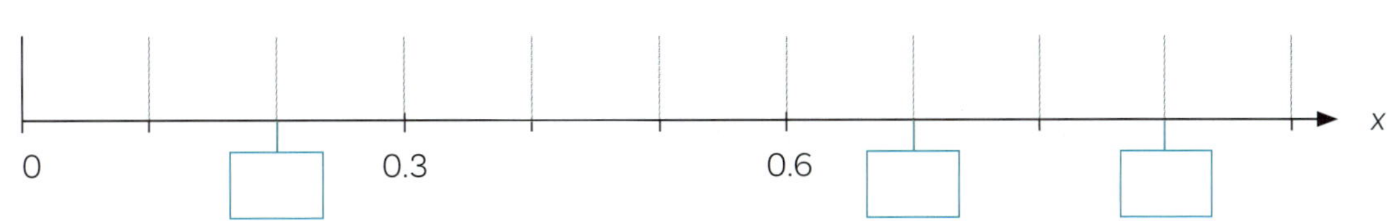

Write down the values and units represented by each of these points.

3

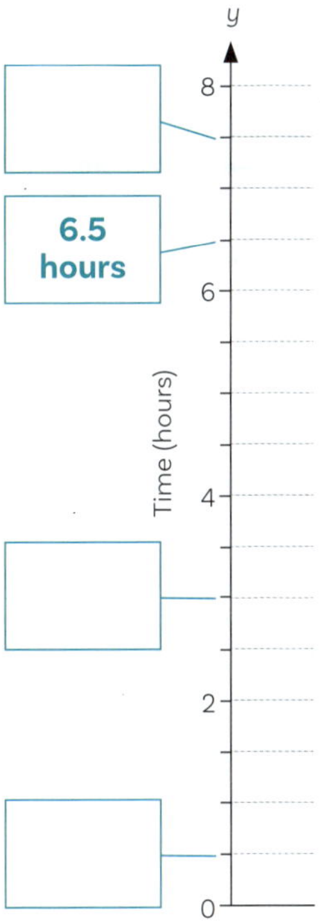

y
8
6
4
2
0
Time (hours)
6.5 hours

4

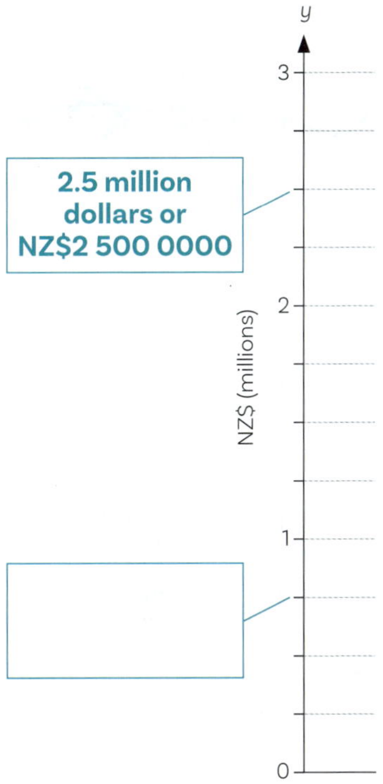

y
3
2
1
0
NZ$ (millions)
2.5 million dollars or NZ$2 500 0000

5

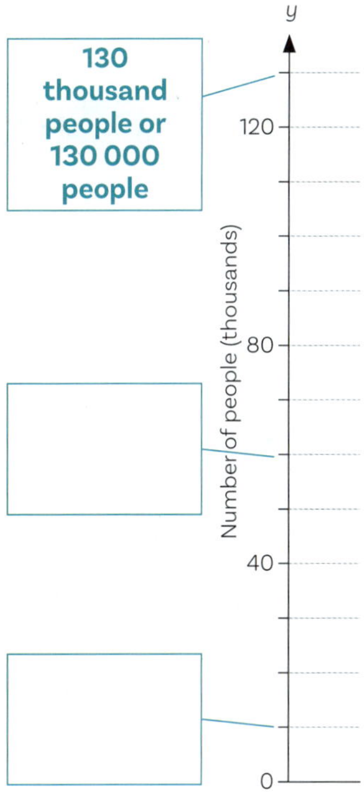

y
120
80
40
0
Number of people (thousands)
130 thousand people or 130 000 people

6

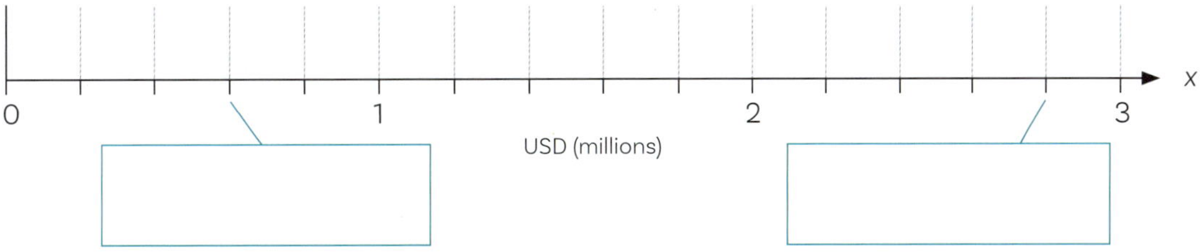

0
1
2
3
x
USD (millions)

7

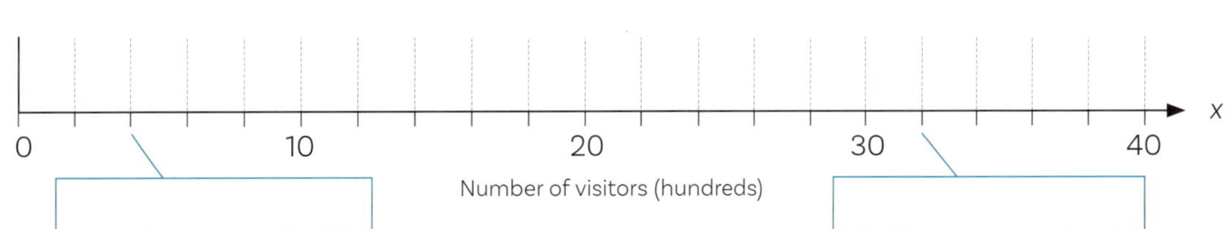

ISBN: 9780170497978

Data interpretation

- When reading information off graphs, you might be asked to:
  - read values
  - calculate fractions, percentages or proportions
  - agree or disagree with a statement about the graph – there could be more than one correct response, so you **must justify** your answer
  - identify similarities or differences
  - identify misleading features or information.

1 The graph shows the number of babies born in New Zealand with the names Theodore, Mason and Elijah.

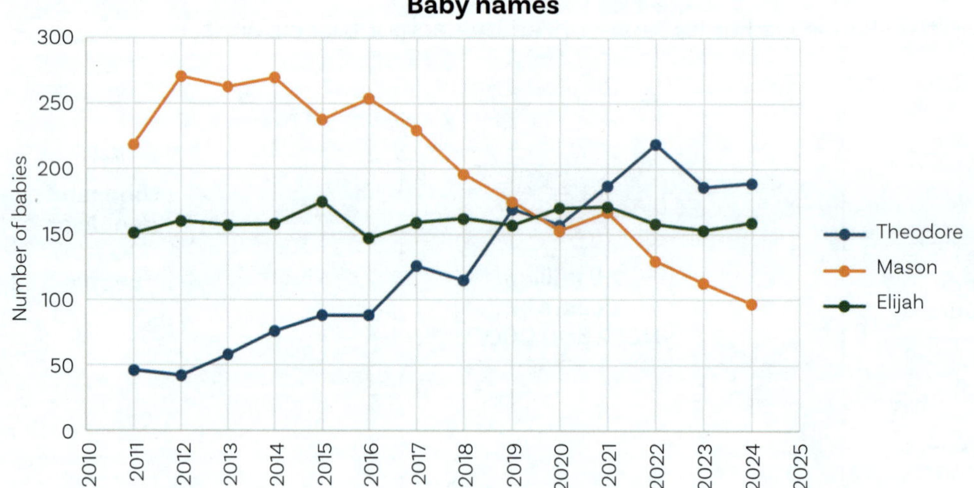

a Which of the three names was most popular in 2018? ______________________

b How many babies were named Elijah in 2016? ______________________

c Which name has increased most in popularity over the past 15 years? ______________________

d Which name hasn't changed much in popularity? ______________________

e Similar numbers of babies have been called ______________________ each year.

f A baby born in 2025 is more likely to be called Theodore than either Mason or Elijah.

☐ Agree ☐ Disagree ☐ Can't tell for sure

Explain your answer.

____

____

 ISBN: 9780170497978

2 This graph shows the medal hauls for the four most successful countries at the Paris Olympics.

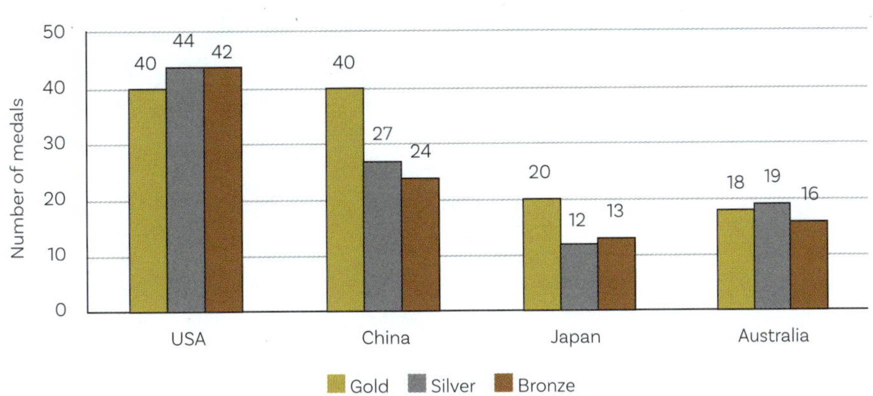

a How many medals did China win in total? __________

b Which countries won more silver than gold medals? __________

c What percentage of Australia's medals were gold? __________

d Which country was the most successful at the Paris Olympics? __________

Explain your answer.

____

____

3 This graph shows the origins of Te Papa visitors.

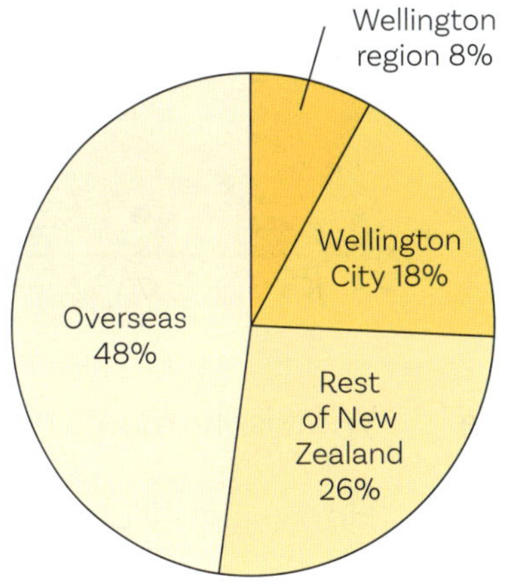

a Suggest a question that visitors could be asked in order to obtain this data.

____

____

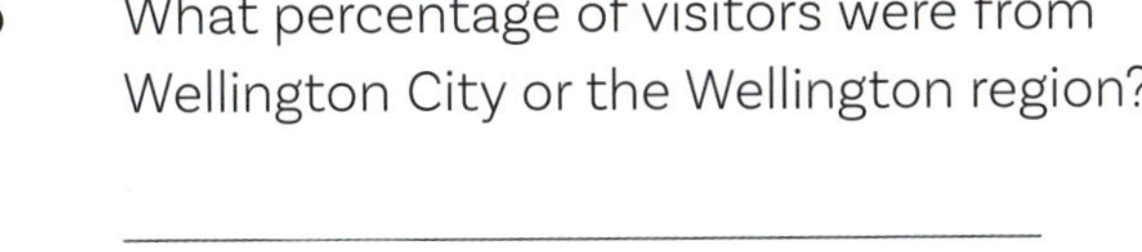

b What percentage of visitors were from Wellington City or the Wellington region?

____

c Most visitors are from New Zealand.

☐ Agree ☐ Disagree ☐ Can't tell for sure

Explain your answer.

____

____

ISBN: 9780170497978

4 The Coast to Coast is a race across the South Island of New Zealand. Below are the individual times for the 222 athletes who finished the race in the one-day event.

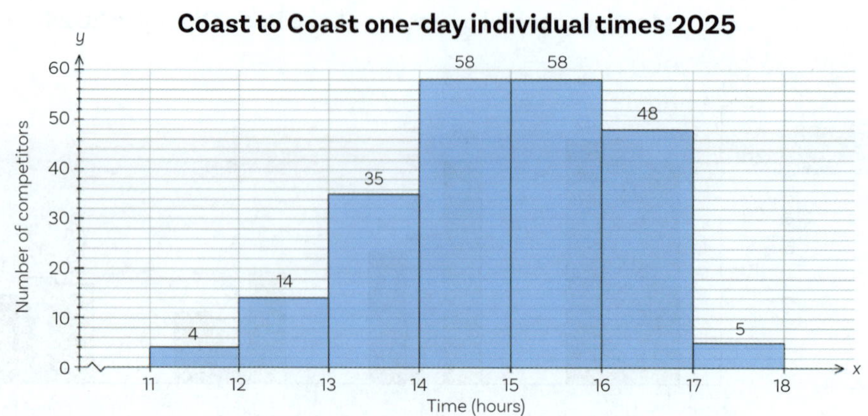

a How many athletes took more than 16 hours to finish? ______

b What percentage of athletes took between 11 and 12 hours? ______

c Next year, the winning time will be less than 11 hours.

☐ Agree ☐ Disagree ☐ Can't tell for sure

Explain your answer.

______

______

5 This dot plot shows the heights (cm) of 42 All Blacks.

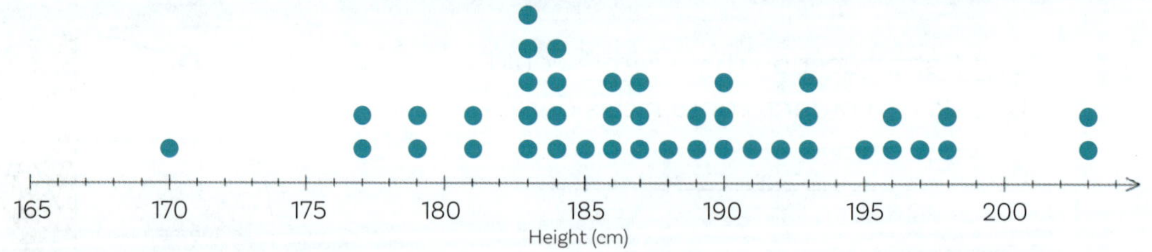

a What is the most common height? ______

b How many All Blacks have heights between 194 and 200 cm? ______

c What percentage of All Blacks are shorter than 182 cm? ______

d You have to be tall to play rugby professionally.

☐ Agree ☐ Disagree ☐ Can't tell for sure

Explain your answer.

______

______

 ISBN: 9780170497978

Scatter plots

- A scatter plot is used to show the **relationship** between **two variables**.
- These variables can be **continuous** or **discrete**.
- Each dot represents two pieces of data about one object, e.g. the height and mass of a person.

Coordinates revision

- A positive ***x*** coordinate tells you how far to move to the **right**.
- A positive ***y*** coordinate tells you how far to move **up**.
- Coordinates are written in brackets, in alphabetical order: **(*x*, *y*)**.

Understanding scatter plots

Examples:

1

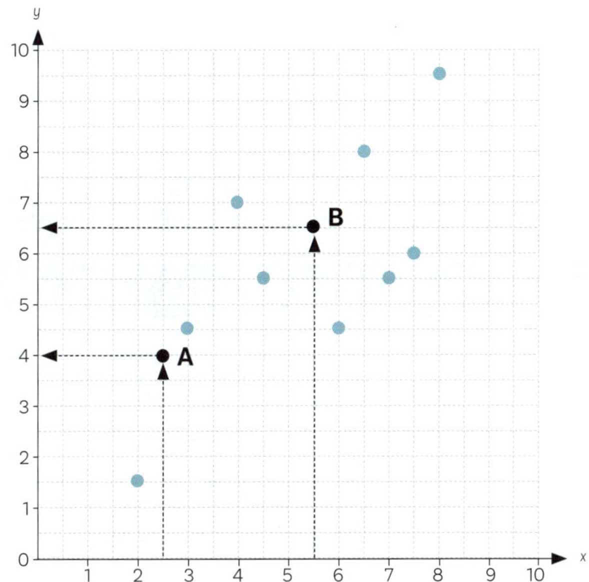

A (2.5, 4)

B (5.5, 6.5)

2 For a group of students, this graph shows how long each spent practising for sport each week and the time it took for them to run 400 m.

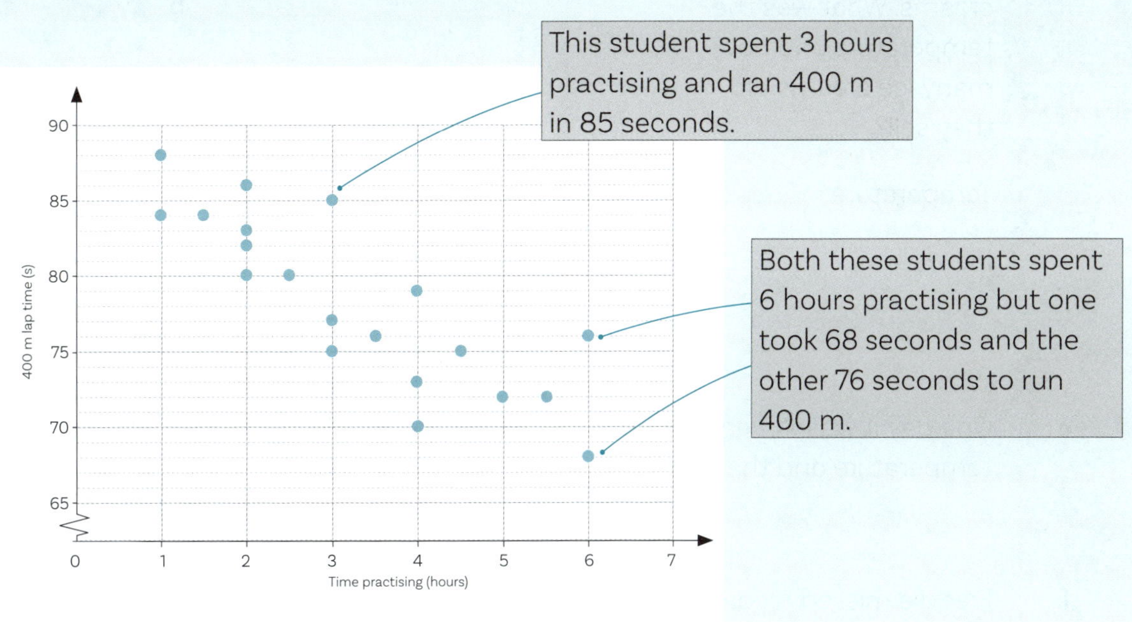

ISBN: 9780170497978

3 Scatter plots can also be interpreted without numbers on their axes.

Who is the tallest?
April

Who is the youngest?
Celidh

Compare these two people.
They are similar in height but Felix is older than Henri.

Height

Age

April

Lucy

Henri

Felix

Celidh

Eruera

Answer the following questions.

1 Every day, the owner of an ice cream stall recorded the highest temperature and the number of ice creams they sold (see graph). Give the coordinates and description of the following.

Day	Coordinates	Description
a	(_____, _____)	It was _______ °C and they sold _______ ice creams.
b	(_____, _____)	It was _______ °C and they sold _______ ice creams.

c One day it was only 17°C. How many ice creams did they sell? __________

d On another day it was quite hot, but they didn't sell many ice creams. What was the temperature and how many ice creams did they sell?

Temperature _______

Ice creams _______

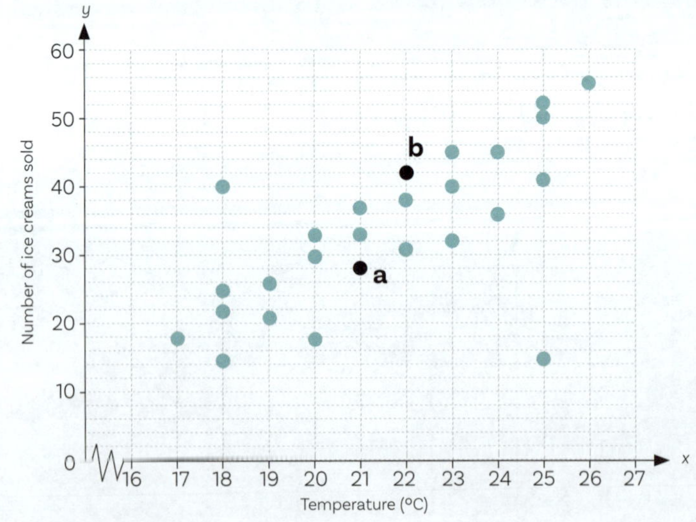

e One day it wasn't very hot but sales were surprisingly high. What was the temperature and the sales?

Temperature _______

Ice creams _______

f Freddie missed recording one day where it was 19 °C and they sold 14 ice creams. Add this point to the graph.

  ISBN: 9780170497978

2 This graph shows how long each student spent studying and grades each received.

Are these statements true or false?

a Freya's grade was higher than Kaia's. True/False

b Maisey spent the most time studying. True/False

c Asher spent more time studying than Elsie, but got a lower grade. True/False

3 Teachers recorded the number of cups of coffee they drank and the number of hours of sleep they got that night (see graph).

Teacher	Coordinates	Description
a	(_____, _____)	They drank _____ cup(s) of coffee and slept for _____ hours.
b	(_____, _____)	They drank _____ cup(s) of coffee and slept for _____ hours.

c Highlight and label the points for a teacher who:

i Drank 4 cups of coffee and slept for 7 hours.

ii Drank no coffee and slept for 8 hours.

d How many teachers drank more than 3 cups of coffee?

____

e In general, teachers who drank more coffee tended to sleep more/less?

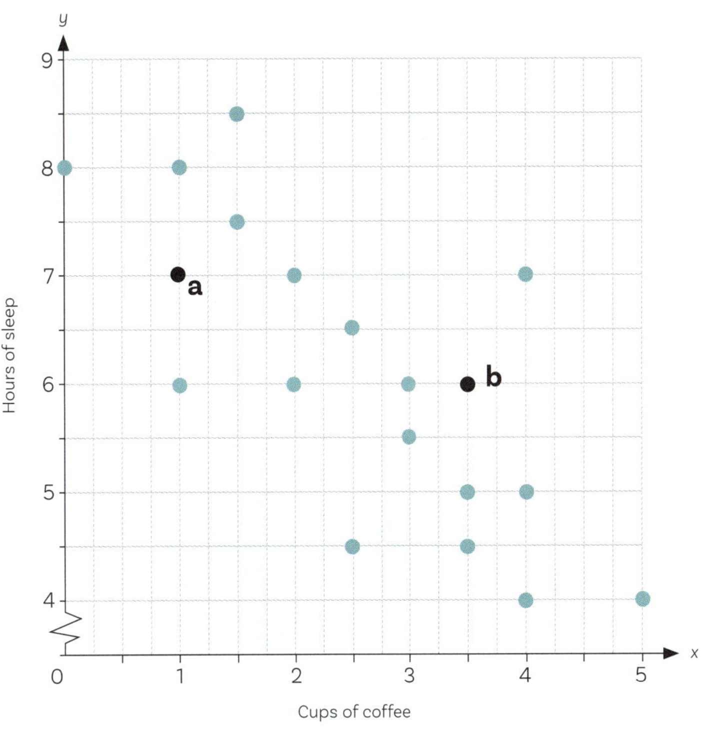

ISBN: 9780170497978

Describing and comparing features of scatter plots

Direction

Positive:

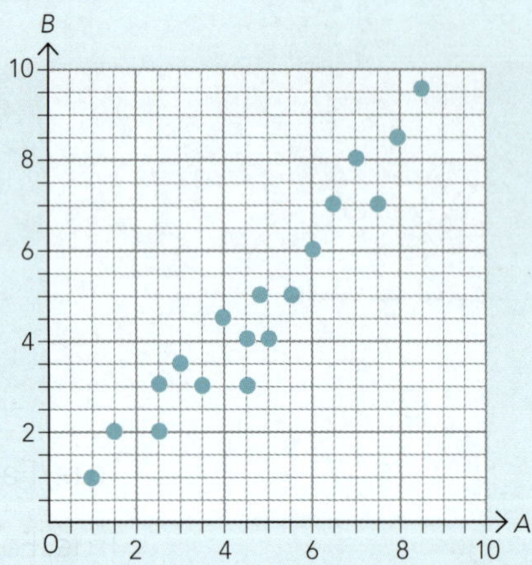

As A gets bigger, B gets **bigger**.

Negative:

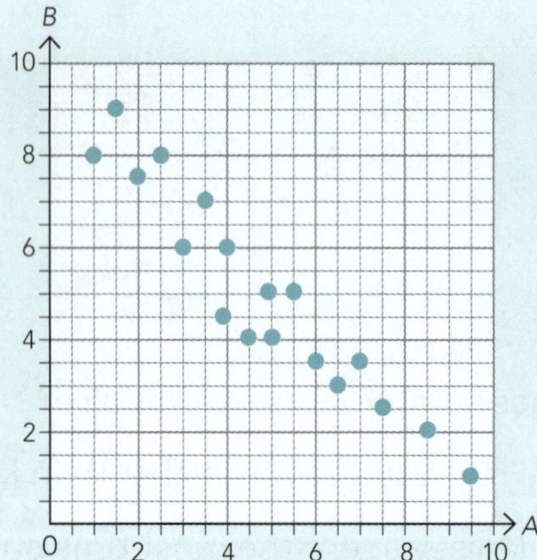

As A gets bigger, B gets **smaller**.

Strength

Strong:

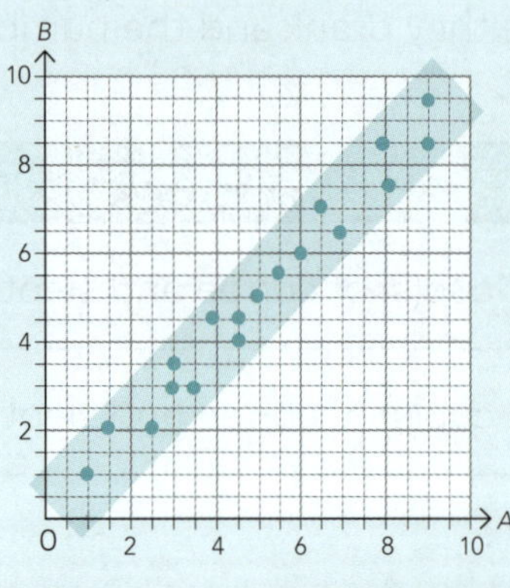

If the scatter band is narrow:

- You can have confidence that the relationship is strong.

Moderate:

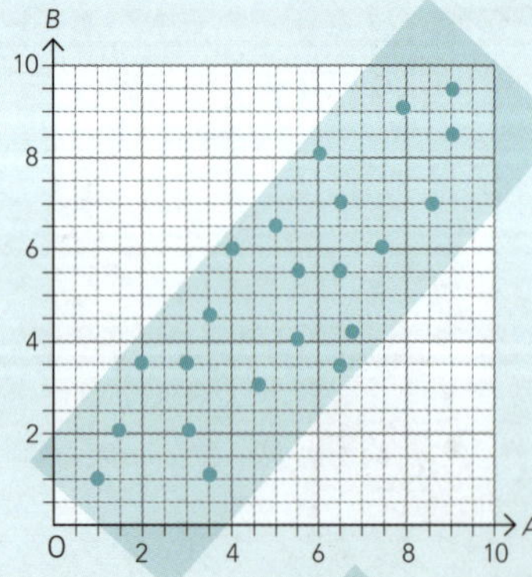

If the scatter band is similar to this:

- The relationship is moderately strong.

Weak:

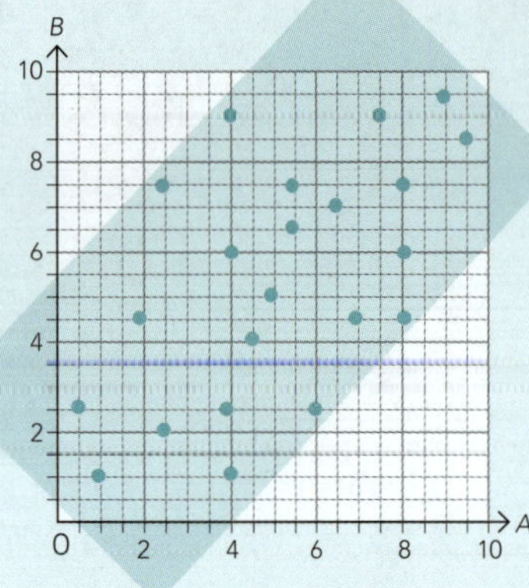

If the scatter band is wide:

- The relationship is weak.

 ISBN: 9780170497978

Highlight the appropriate descriptors for these graphs.

4

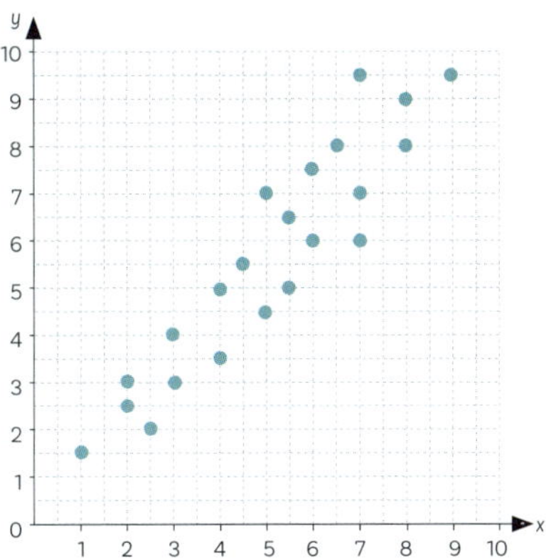

Direction: Positive/Negative
Strength: Strong/Moderate/Weak

5

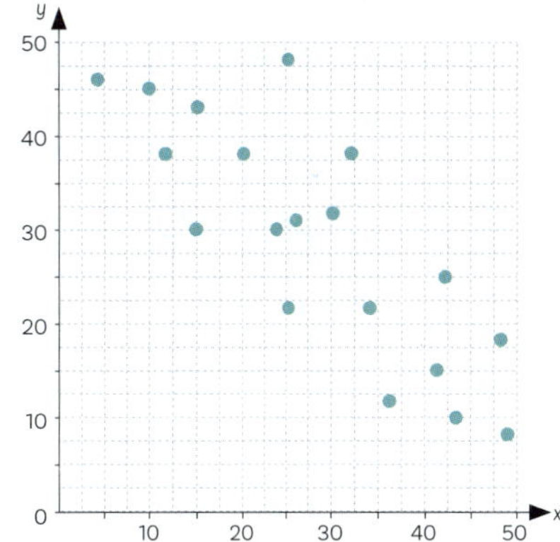

Direction: Positive/Negative
Strength: Strong/Moderate/Weak

6

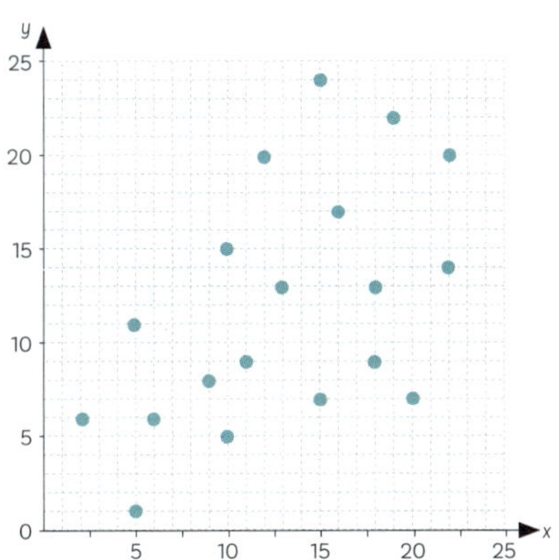

Direction: Positive/Negative
Strength: Strong/Moderate/Weak

7

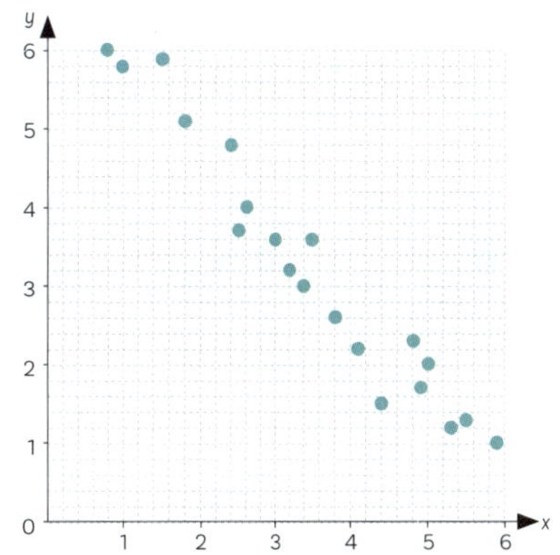

Direction: Positive/Negative
Strength: Strong/Moderate/Weak

8 The graph shows the relationship between the length of a footprint and the height of the person who made it.

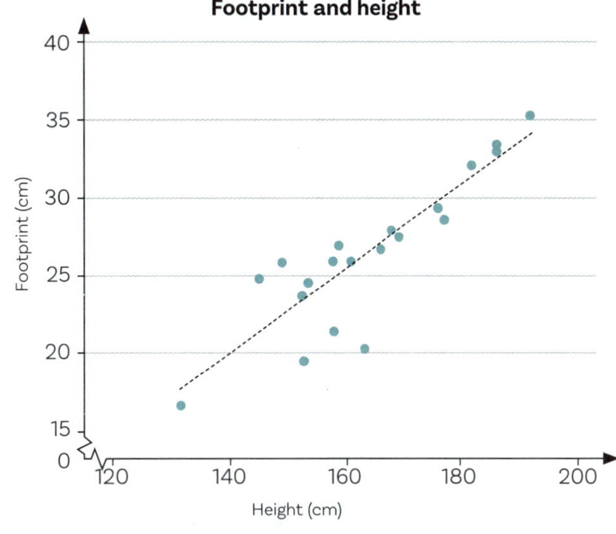

The graph shows a positive/negative relationship between a person's height and the length of their footprint. This means that taller people tend to have ______________ footprints.

ISBN: 9780170497978

Line of best fit

- It is useful to add a line of best fit to a linear scatter plot. Most computer programs will do this for you.
- The line
  - should be **ruled** if it's a straight line
  - should have about the same number of points above and below it
  - should pass through the middle of the data at each end.

Examples:

A good straight line of best fit:

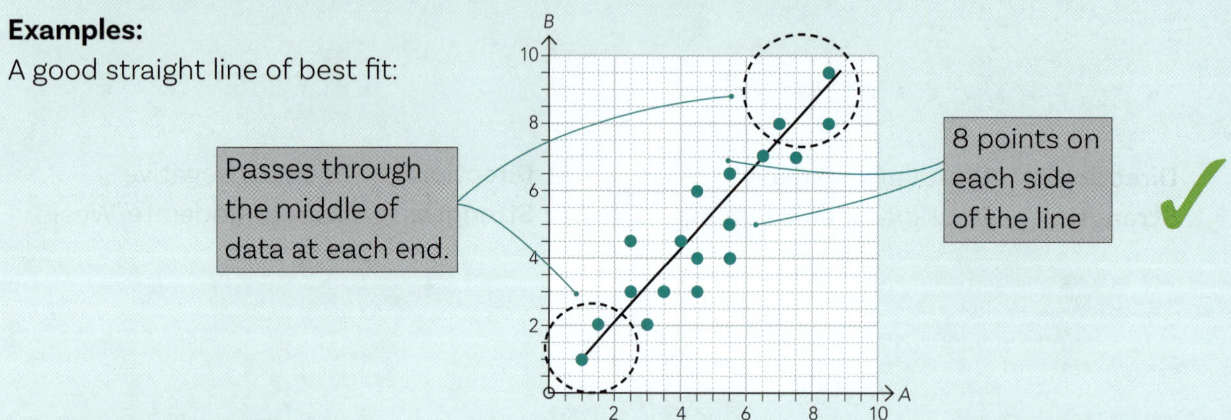

Poor lines of best fit:

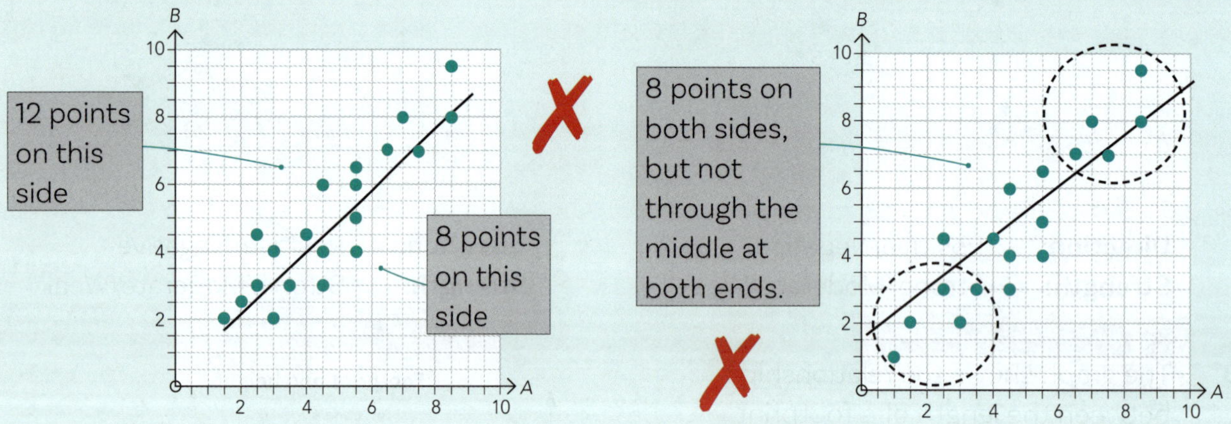

Sometimes a curve might be more appropriate than a straight line.

Examples:

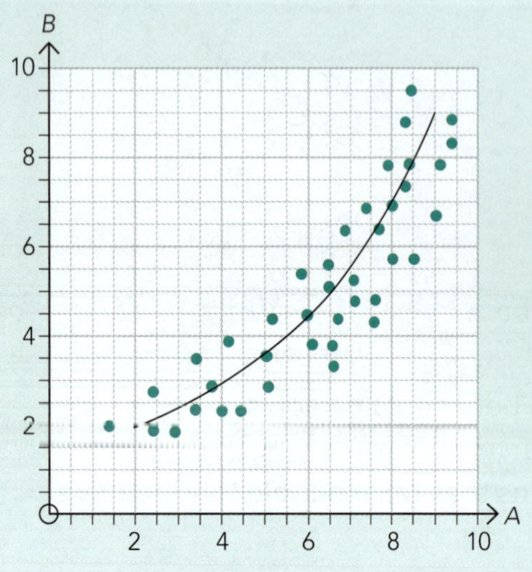
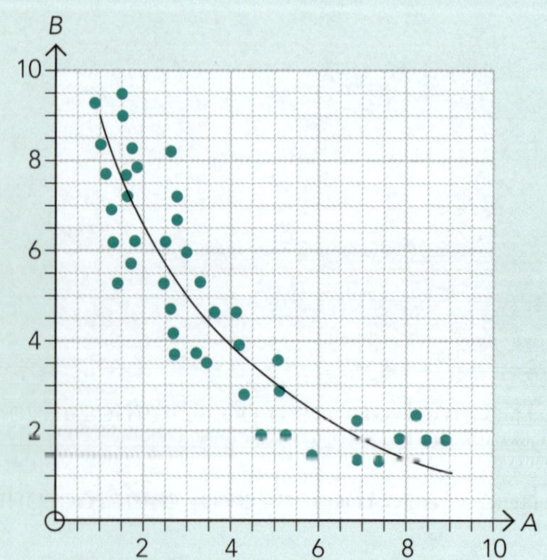

ISBN: 9780170497978

Sketch a line or curve of best fit on the following graphs.

9

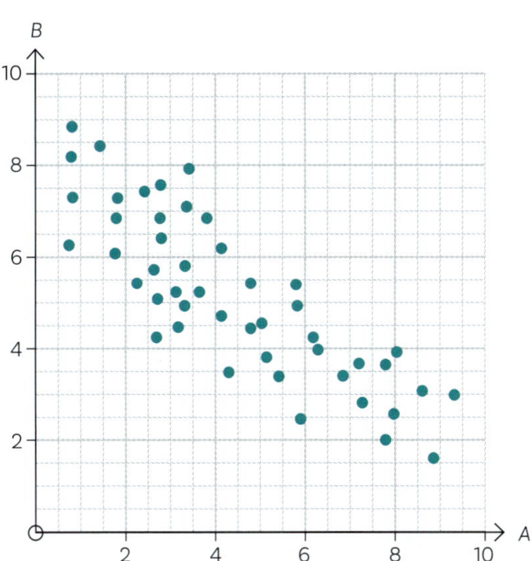

10

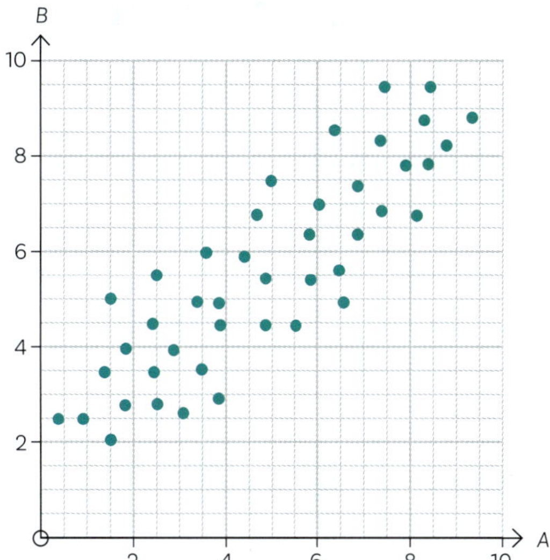

11

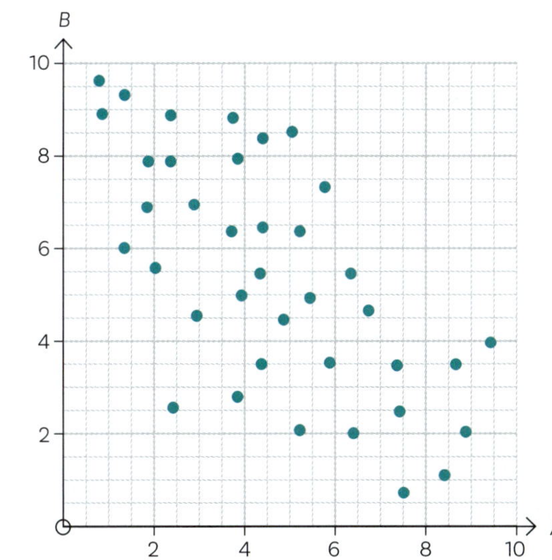

12

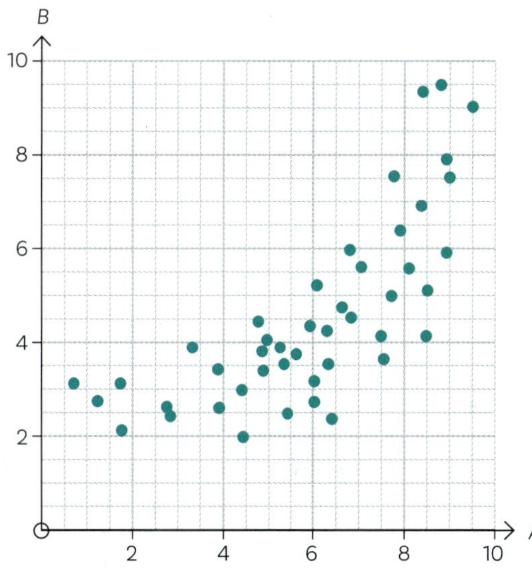

13

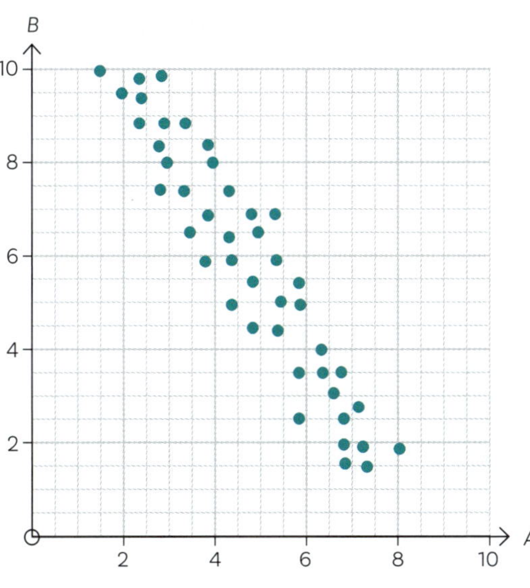

14

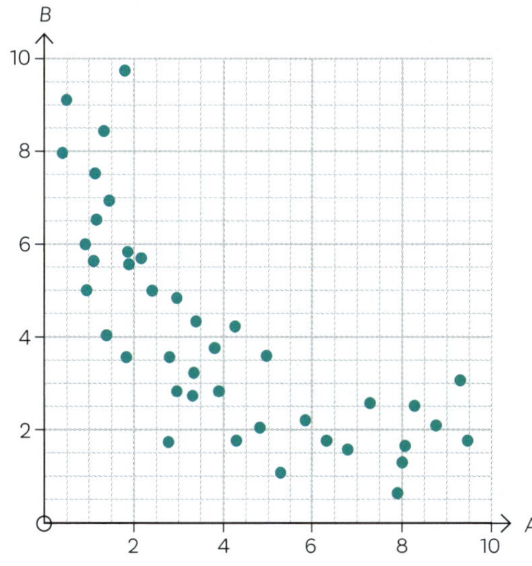

ISBN: 9780170497978

Data analysis

- There are three things that we need to know in order to be able to discuss and compare distributions:

  1 Where is the **centre** of the data?
  2 How widely is the data **spread**?
  3 Are there any **unusual features**?

Measures of centre (averages)

- There are **three** measures for the centre of data.

Name	Calculation	Advantages	Disadvantages
Mean	$\frac{\text{the sum of all the data values}}{\text{the number of data values}}$	• Easy to calculate	• Distorted by very big or small values
Median	middle value	• Usually a good measure of centre	• Data must be put in order
Mode	value that occurs most frequently	• Very easy to find	• Very unreliable as measure of centre • Often there are two or none

Mean

- The numbers do not need to be in order for this calculation.
- Means are not always whole numbers, so sensible rounding may be needed.
- The mean is influenced by unusually large or small values.

$$\textbf{Mean} = \frac{\textbf{sum of all the data values}}{\textbf{number of data values}}$$

Notice that 0 must be included in the calculation.

Example:

0 3 9 5 1 3 5 72

$$\text{Mean} = \frac{0+3+9+5+1+3+5+72}{8}$$

$$= 12.25$$

There are 8 numbers in the data set.

The mean of this data set is 12.25.

Notice what happens to the mean if the 72 is removed.

0 3 9 5 1 3 5

$$\text{Mean} = \frac{0+3+9+5+1+3+5}{7}$$

$$= 3.71 \text{ (2 dp)}$$

There are now 7 numbers in the data set.

The mean of this data set is now 3.71 (2 dp).

The 72 was so much larger than the other values that it influenced the mean.

ISBN: 9780170497978

For these data sets, estimate the mean and then calculate it.

1 **a** 5 42 45 49 50 51

Estimate = ________ Mean = $\frac{5 + \qquad\qquad}{6}$

= ____________________

b 42 45 49 50 51

Estimate = ________ Mean = ____________________________

= ____________________

c The mean for set **b** is bigger/smaller than that for set **a** because ____________________

____

Median

- If there is an **odd number of values** in a data set, the median is the **middle number**.
- If there is an **even number of values**, the median is **halfway between the two middle numbers** in the data set.
- Before you can calculate the median, you must **put the data in order**.

Examples:

1 A data set with an odd number of values

30, 23, 13, 32, 17, 10, 21, 26, 9

Cross them off as you go, to make sure you don't miss any.

Put them **in order** before finding the median: 9, 10, 13, 17, **21**, 23, 26, 30, 32

This is the middle number.

The median of this data set = 21.

2 A data set with an even number of values

52, 55, 56, **58, 61**, 61, 64, 98

These are the middle numbers. Add them together and divide by 2.

The median for this data set = $\frac{\mathbf{58 + 61}}{\mathbf{2}}$ **= 59.5.**

Notice that the median is not influenced by the unusually large value (98).

2 For these data sets, estimate the median and then put the data in order and find the median.

a 49, 3, 18, 45, 7, 12, 36, 27, 31, 22, 41

Estimate = ____________

____

Median = ____________

b 30, 43, 5, 21, 9, 47, 17, 13, 26, 34, 2, 38

Estimate = ____________

____

Median = ____________

Mode

- The mode is the **most common value**.
- Sometimes there are **several modes**.
- If there are **three or more** numbers that occur equally, we say that the data is **polymodal**.
- If there are no repeated numbers, then there is **no mode**.

Examples:

1 **(14) 3 20 8 21 (14) 6 17 24 8 (14) 3 12**

The most common number is **14**: there are three of them.

The mode of this data set is 14.

2 **(9) 5 19 (7) 13 (9) 17 8 15 (7) 11 3 14**

Both **7** and **9** occur twice.

The modes are 7 and 9.

3 **36 (40) (42) 46 (45) 47 (40) (42) 49 36 (45)**

There are three numbers that occur equally often: **40**, **42** and **45**.

We say that the data is **polymodal**.

3 Find the mode(s), if any, of these data sets.

a 3 5 7 9 11 14 14 18 21 27 Mode(s) = ____________

b 20 21 22 25 28 31 33 36 38 43 Mode(s) = ____________

c 12 12 14 16 17 17 22 24 26 27 Mode(s) = ____________

ISBN: 9780170497978

Measures of spread

Range

- The range is the **maximum value minus the minimum value** in the data set.
- Note: the range is a **single number**.
- Like the mean, the range is affected by unusually large or small values.
- The data does not need to be in order to calculate the range.
- The range is a measure of the **variability** of the data.

Range = maximum – minimum

Quartiles

- The upper quartile (UQ) is the **median** of the **top half** of the data.
- The lower quartile (LQ) is the **median** of the **bottom half** of the data.
- The quartiles and the median divide the data into **quarters**.

Interquartile range (IQR) = upper quartile (UQ) – lower quartile (LQ)

Examples:

1 If the number of pieces of data is **odd**, **exclude** the median from the top and bottom halves of the data.

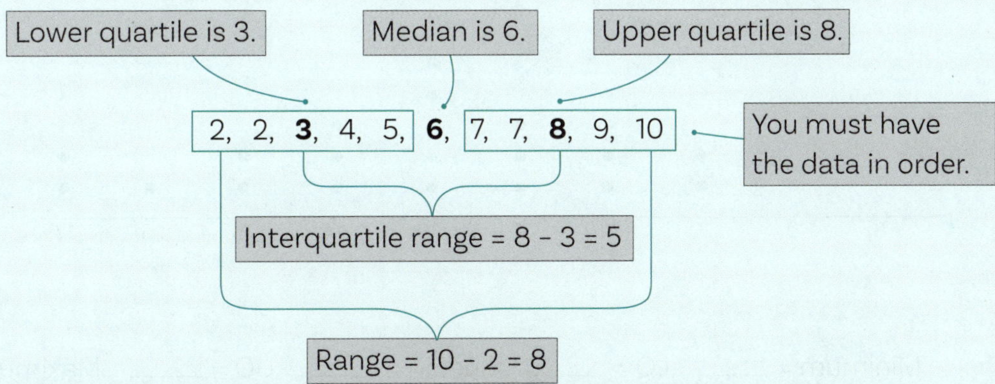

2 If the number of pieces of data is **even**, find the median of the top and bottom halves of the data.

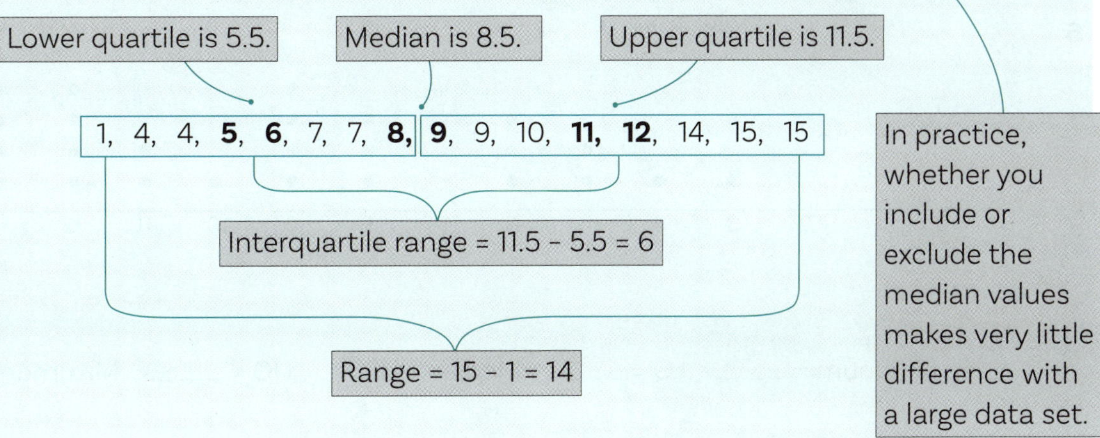

In practice, whether you include or exclude the median values makes very little difference with a large data set.

Ranges and interquartile ranges are used to measure the variability of groups of data.

ISBN: 9780170497978

Calculate the statistics for the following data sets.

1 2, 4, 6, 7, 9, 10, 12, 12, 16, 18, 20

Minimum = ______ LQ = ______ Median = ______ UQ = ______ Maximum = ______

Range = ________________ Interquartile range = ________________

2 1, 3, 3, 5, 7, 8, 9, 10, 10, 12, 13, 19, 22, 23

Minimum = ______ LQ = ______ Median = ______ UQ = ______ Maximum = ______

Range = ________________ Interquartile range = ________________

3 2.0, 2.1, 2.1, 2.3, 2.5, 2.7, 2.9, 3.0, 3.2, 3.4, 3.4, 3.7, 3.9, 4.0

Minimum = ______ LQ = ______ Median = ______ UQ = ______ Maximum = ______

Range = ________________ Interquartile range = ________________

4

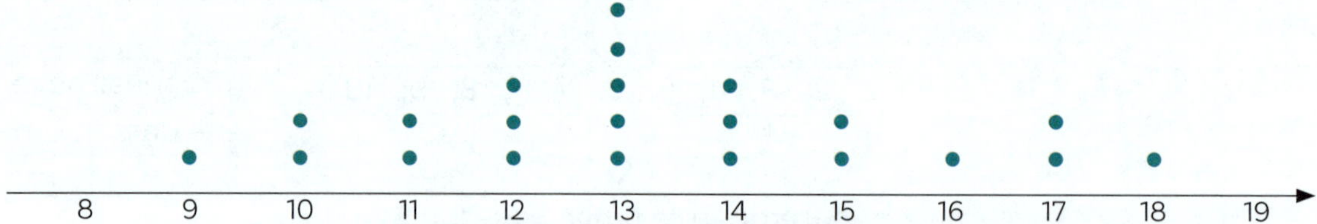

Minimum = ______ LQ = ______ Median = ______ UQ = ______ Maximum = ______

Range = ________________ Interquartile range = ________________

5

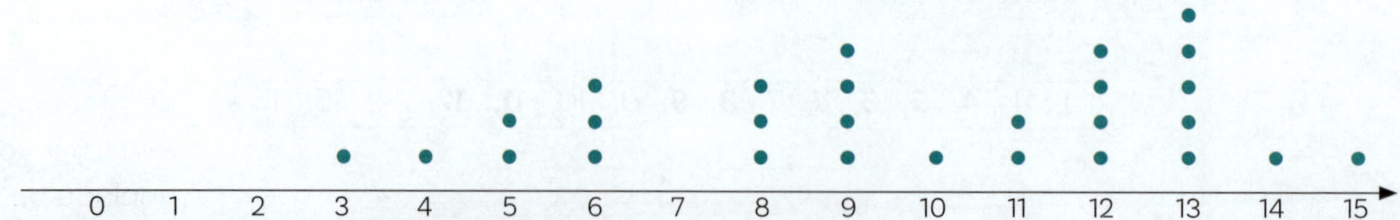

Minimum = ______ LQ = ______ Median = ______ UQ = ______ Maximum = ______

Range = ________________ Interquartile range = ________________

ISBN: 9780170497978

Unusual features

- These could be an **unusual point** or **clusters**.
- An unusual point is one that is separate from the rest of the data.
- A cluster is a group of data that is away from the rest of the data.

How many makes a cluster?
Don't get hung up on labels and definitions. It's best to write what you see. If there are any points that are away from the rest, then say that!

Examples:

1 An unusual point

Height of Year 9 students in cm: 149, 161, 155, 172, 170, **201**, 141, 158

This student's height is unusual because it's 29 cm larger than the next tallest height.

2 An unusual cluster

It is often easiest to see unusual points and clusters when the data is graphed.

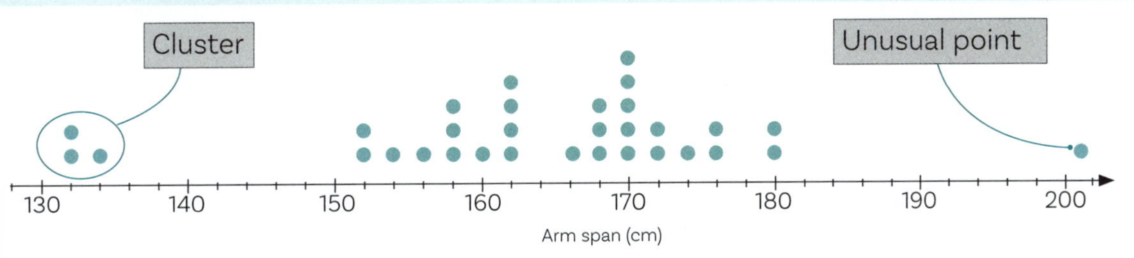

Note:
1. Check that unusual points are not mistakes in measurement, counting or recording.
2. Include them when you graph and analyse your data. Think about whether the unusual feature is possible and state your thoughts when you discuss the data.

Circle or highlight any unusual features in these data sets and state whether they are clusters or unusual points.

1

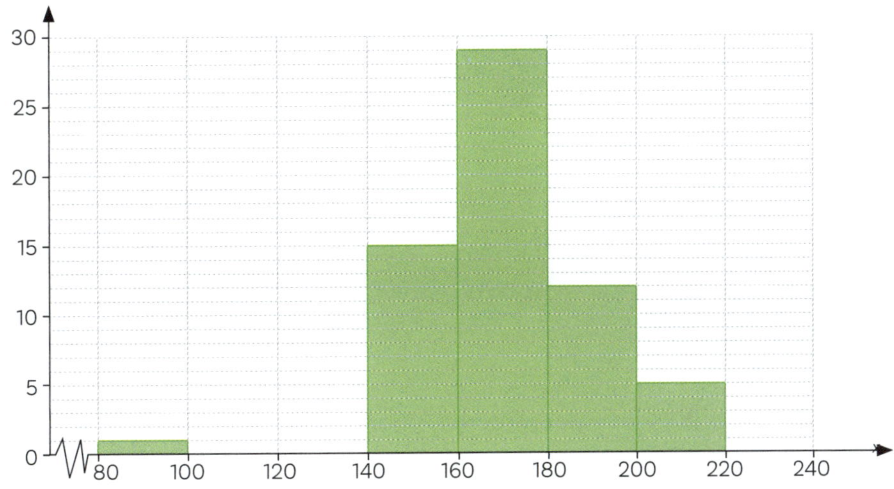

ISBN: 9780170497978

2

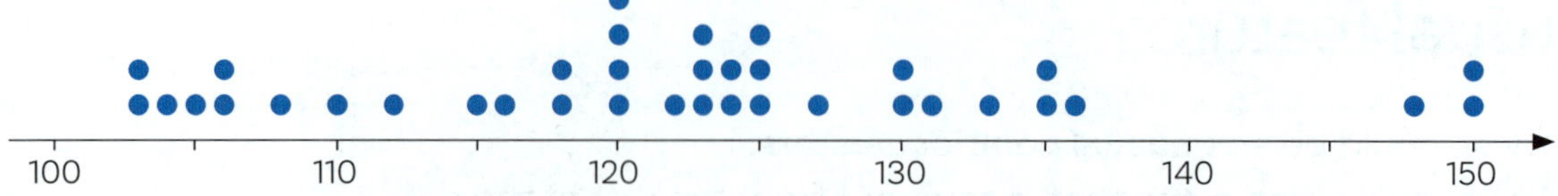

3

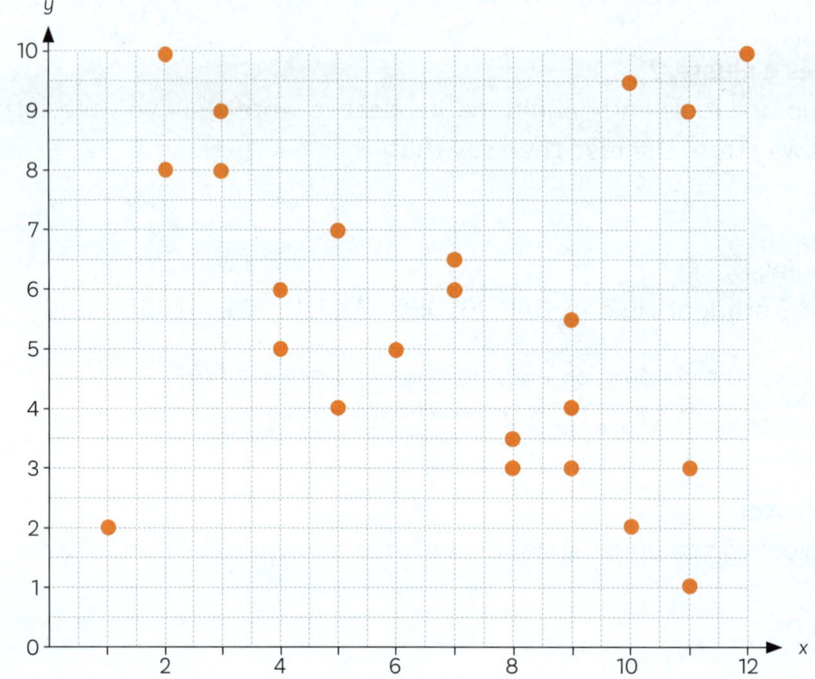

4

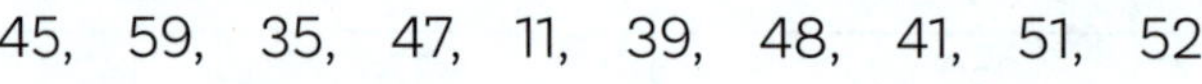
45, 59, 35, 47, 11, 39, 48, 41, 51, 52

5

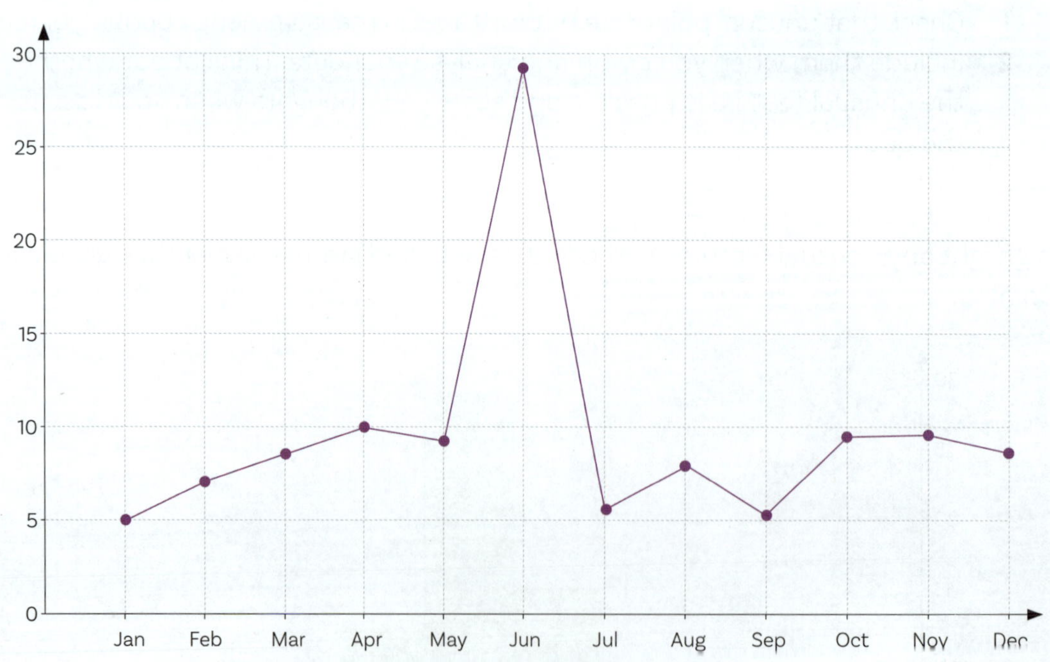

What makes the point unusual? ______________________________

____

ISBN: 9780170497978

Decision trees

- Decision trees are a method of classifying data.
- Decision trees are used in areas such as finance, marketing, retail and healthcare.

Cassie went into the forest and recorded the details of the monsters she saw. There are five types of monsters in the forest, although no one is quite sure what a Gloamwither looks like.

Details of the monsters she saw:

Horns	Furry	Number of eyes	Type
Yes	No	3	
No	Yes	1	
No	No	3	
No	Yes	1	
Yes	Yes	3	
No	Yes	1	

Decision tree:

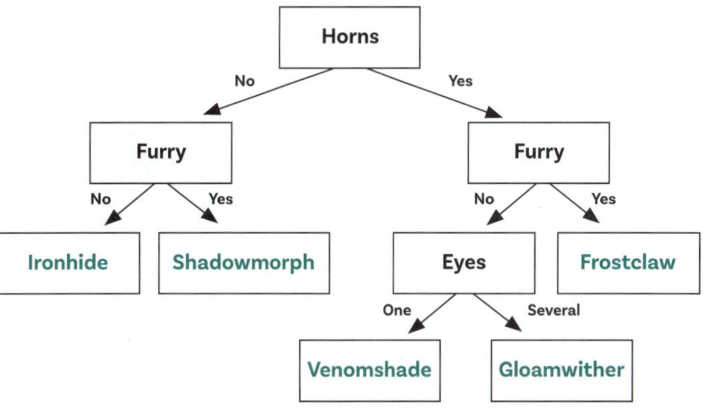

1 Use the decision tree to help you do the following.

a Name the pictures above.

b Fill in the last column of the table.

c Sketch what you think a Gloamwither looks like.

2 She saw three monsters of the same type. What kind were they? ____________________

3 She didn't see one of the monsters above. Which one was it? ____________________

4 Cassie's friend saw a furry monster with three eyes, and horns.

Which monster did she see? ____________________

ISBN: 9780170497978

5 Lucy's mother is trying to understand what vegetables Lucy will eat. So far she has worked out some preferences which are shown on the decision tree below.

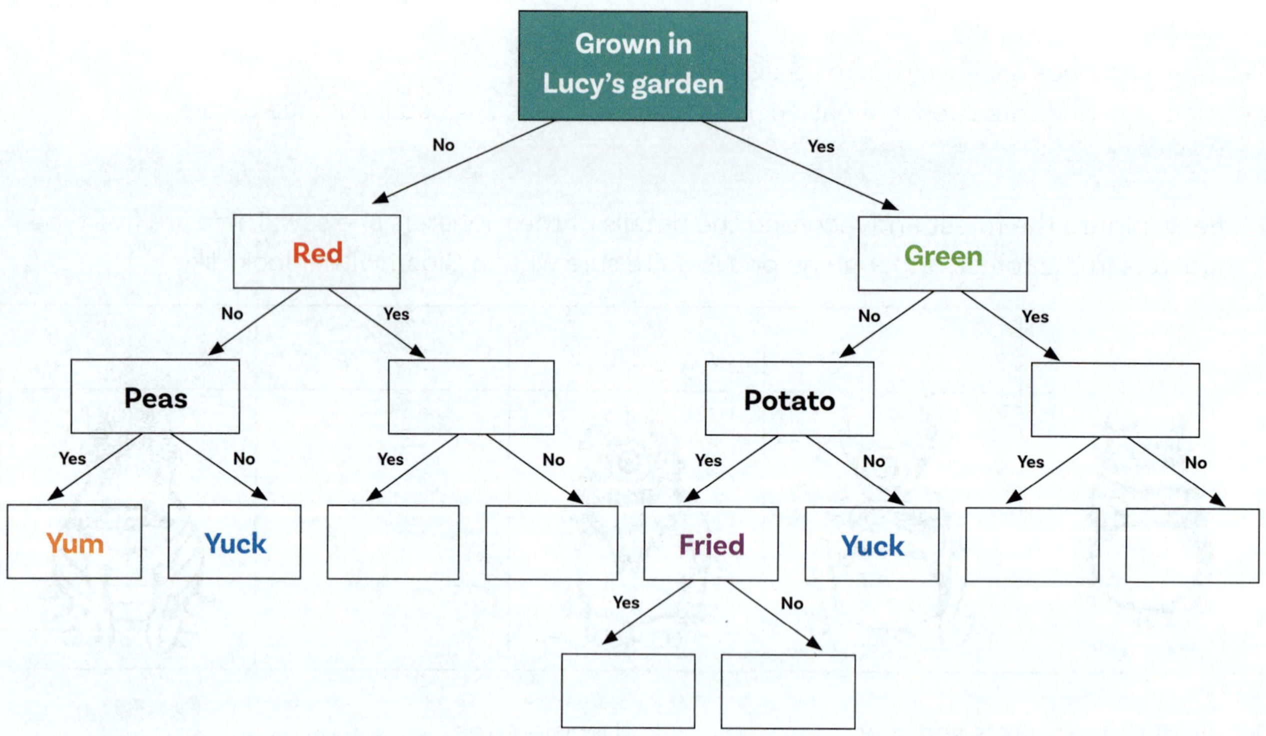

a Using these facts, complete the decision tree.

- Lucy will eat a tomato that wasn't grown in her garden.
- Lucy will not eat a potato unless it's fried.
- The only green vegetable she will eat out of her garden is broccoli.

Use your completed decision tree to answer these questions.

b How does Lucy prefer her potato to be cooked? ______________________

c Will Lucy eat a carrot that has been grown in her garden? Yes/No

d What kind of vegetables will Lucy eat that are not grown in her garden?

______________________ and ______________________

e What kind of vegetables will Lucy eat that are grown in her garden?

______________________ and ______________________

f Explain how the decision tree shows you that Lucy will not eat parsnips grown in her garden.

____

____

____

  ISBN: 9780170497978

Conclusions

- Once you have analysed the data, you must write a conclusion.
- In this, you should:
  - Answer your investigative question.
  - Communicate your findings in context and with evidence.
  - Provide possible explanations for your findings.
  - Reflect on your expected findings.
  - Reflect on how you carried out your investigation. Suggest improvements.

1 ***Alex's investigation***

Question: *What pet would Paradise High School students most like to own?*

Expected finding: *I think that most students would prefer to have a dog, because my favourite animal is a dog.*

Plan: *I will ask all 61 students in my year group.*

Results:

a Highlight the best conclusion for this data and give reasons for your choice.

i	Lots of Paradise High School students want to own a dog, with 23% of students selecting it.
ii	The majority of students want to own a cat.
iii	The preferred pet in my year group was a cat, with 44% of students selecting it.

Reasons: ______________________________

____

b Do the results support Alex's expected finding?

Yes ☐ No ☐ Can't tell for sure ☐

c Was Alex's expected finding reasonable? Why/why not?

____

d How could his plan be improved?

____

____

ISBN: 9780170497978

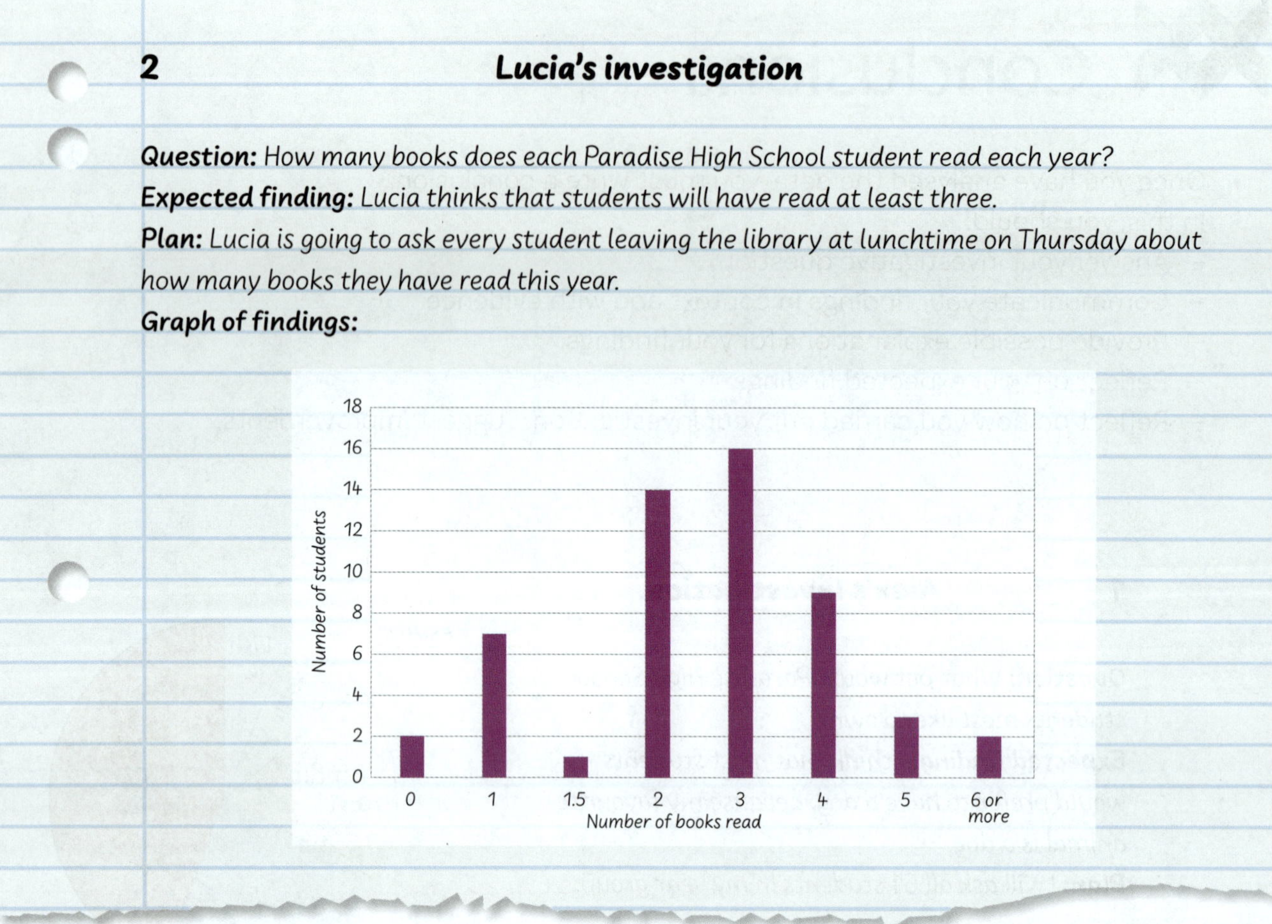

a What is wrong with this graph? ____________________

b Highlight the best conclusion for this data and give reasons for your choice.

i	Only two Paradise High School students have read six or more books this year.
ii	Most Paradise High School students have read fewer than three books this year.
iii	Most Paradise High School students have read two or three books this year.

Reasons: ____________________

____

c Do the results support Lucia's expected finding?

Yes ☐ No ☐ Can't tell for sure ☐

d Was Lucia's expected finding reasonable? Why/why not?

____

e How could her plan be improved?

____

____

ISBN: 9780170497978

3 **Finley's investigation**

Question: *How does the temperature in my Science classroom compare with that in my Maths classroom?*
Expected finding: *I think that the Maths classroom is on average warmer because it has carpet.*
Plan: *I will measure the temperature on each day for a week during the periods when I have Science and Maths.*
Graph of findings:

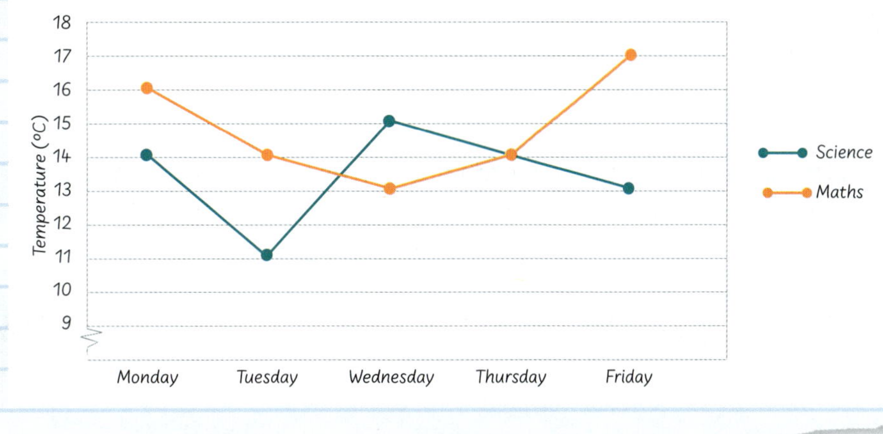

a What conclusion can Finley come to?

b Do the results support Finley's expected findings?

c Can you see anything wrong with his plan?

ISBN: 9780170497978

PROBABILITY

The probability scale

- A probability value tells us **how likely** it is that an event will occur.
- We use numbers between **0** and **1** to describe probability.

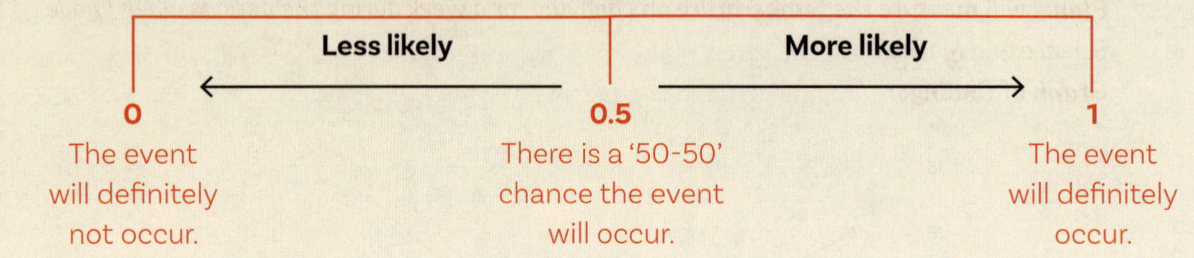

1 Discuss the meanings of these words and terms with your neighbours, and match them to their appropriate probability value. Some words may fit in several places. If you have different answers, discuss them with your teacher.

~~very likely~~	~~impossible~~	certain	slight chance	very unlikely	probable
almost certain	no way	a sure thing	definite	no chance	maybe
good chance	guaranteed	likely	even chance	unlikely	fifty-fifty

1 ____________________

0.9 *very likely*

0.7 ____________________

0.5 ____________________

0.3 ____________________

0.1 ____________________

0 *impossible*

ISBN: 9780170497978

Events, outcomes and sample space

- An **event** is what we do in an experiment, e.g. tossing a coin.
- An **outcome** is a result of the experiment, e.g. getting a head.
- The **sample space** is a **list of the outcomes that can occur** when we do a probability experiment.
- You can find the sample space by drawing a **probability tree** or making a **table**.

When one event occurs, make a list.

For example:

1. If you toss a coin, there are only two outcomes: head, tail.
   ∴ Sample space contains two items: head, tail.

2. If you pull a marble out of this bag, there are only three outcomes: red, black, white.
   ∴ Sample space contains three items: red, black, white.

When two events occur, draw a probability tree or make a table.

For example: Toss a coin and then pull a marble from the bag.

Draw a probability tree.

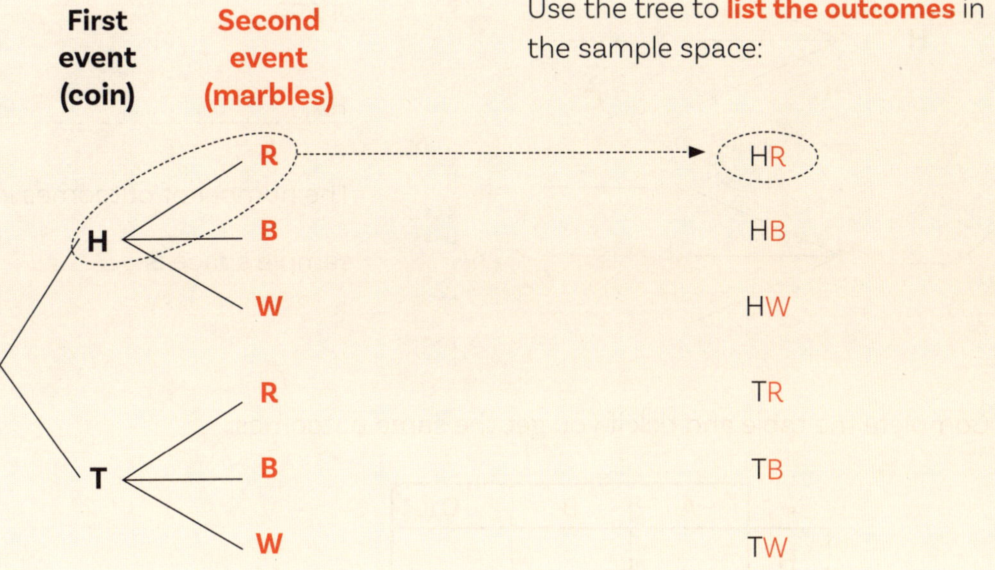

The **number of outcomes** in the sample space is **6**.

Another way of calculating the number of outcomes in the sample space:

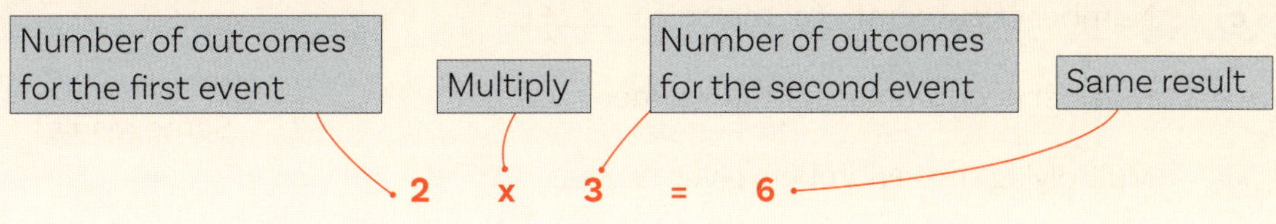

ISBN: 9780170497978

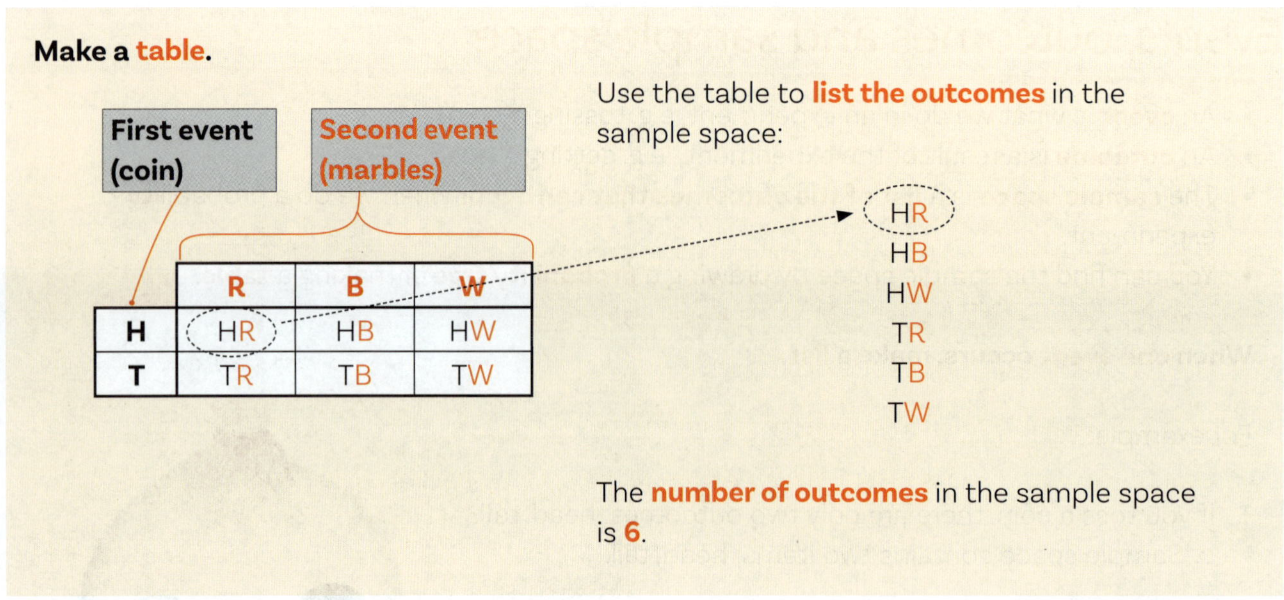

Answer the following.

1 One coin is tossed, then this spinner is spun.

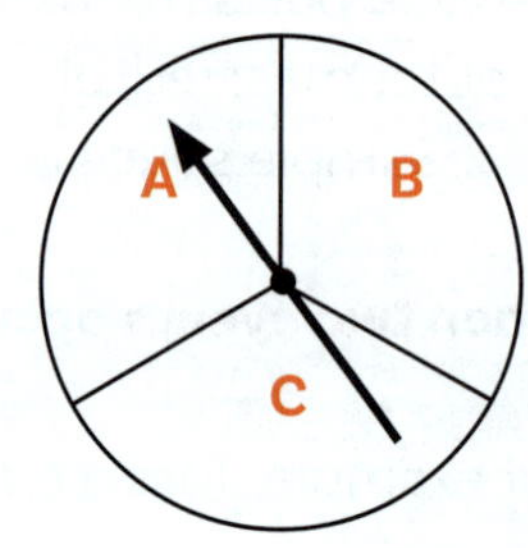

a Complete the probability tree, list the outcomes and write the number of outcomes in the sample space.

Coin | **Spinner**

H → _____, _____, *C*

_____ → _____, _____, _____

List the outcomes in the sample space:

HA, ____________________

The number of outcomes in the sample space is _______.

b Complete the table and tick if you get the same outcomes.

	A	B	C
H			
T			

Same result? ☐

c Number of outcomes for the coin = *2*

Number of outcomes for the spinner = _______

Multiplying these numbers gives _______

Same result? ☐

ISBN: 9780170497978

2 Some friends need to choose what to eat for dinner. The choices are burgers, Thai or pizza, and then after dinner go to minigolf or go skating.

a Complete the probability tree and write the outcome at the end of each branch.

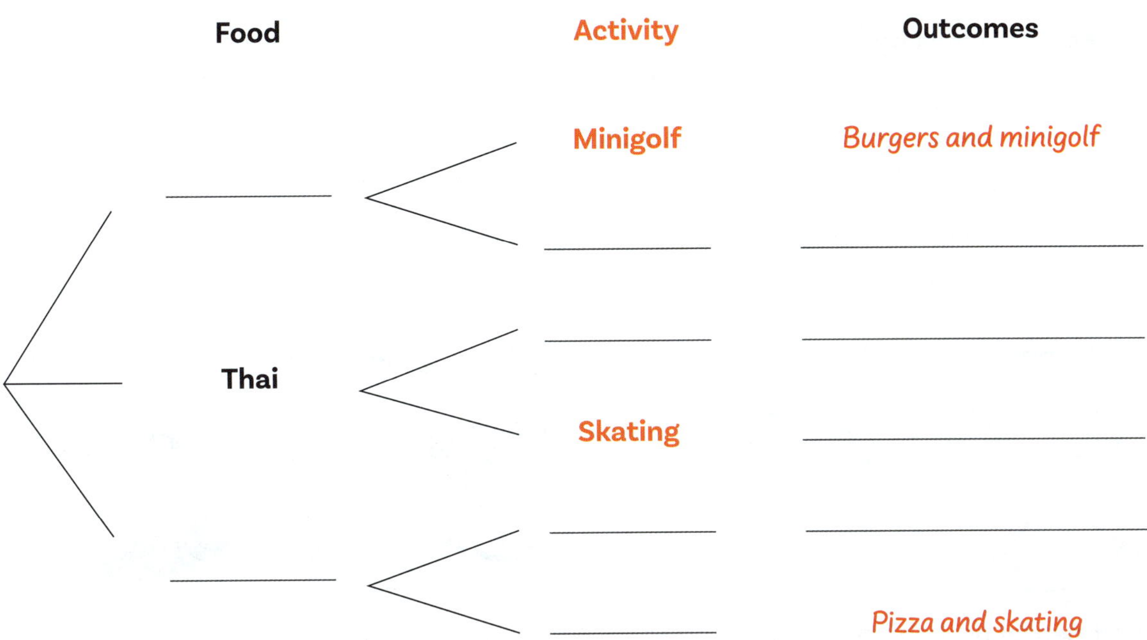

b The number of outcomes in the sample space is ________.

c Complete the table and tick if you get the same result.

		Skating
Burgers		

Same result? ☐

d Number of food options x Number of activities = ______ x ______

= ______

Same result? ☐

ISBN: 9780170497978

Ways of calculating probabilities

- There are three types of probability: **theoretical**, **experimental** and **actual**.

Theoretical probability – is the probability obtained from a probability model
– can be calculated where there are **equally likely outcomes**.

Note: Unless told otherwise, assume dice, coins, etc. are **fair**: they produce **equally likely outcomes**.

e.g. The probability of tossing a coin and getting a head.

Some tools for theoretical probability:

Spinners

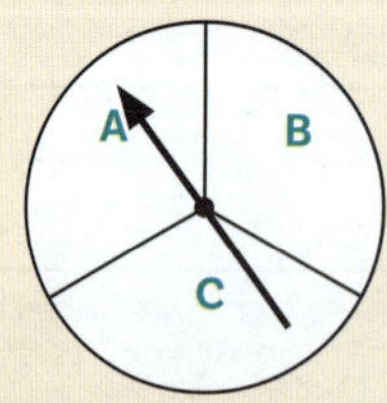

Coins

Dice or die (singular)

Bags of marbles, etc.

Experimental probability – is the probability obtained from an **experiment** or an **observational study (survey)**
– is calculated using **long run relative frequency**.

e.g. The probability of a red car passing in the next five minutes.

For both of these types:

$$\textbf{Probability} = \frac{\text{number of 'favourable' outcomes}}{\text{number of outcomes in the sample space}}$$

The number of outcomes we are interested in. (number of 'favourable' outcomes)

The total number of possible outcomes. (number of outcomes in the sample space)

Actual probability – is almost always unknown. It is the actual probability that an event occurs.

e.g. The probability of the bus being late this morning.

Highlight which type of probability applies to these situations.

1	Rolling a 4 on a die.	Theoretical	Experimental
2	Surveying the class to see who has been on a plane.	Theoretical	Experimental
3	Dropping a piece of toast to see if it lands butter-side down.	Theoretical	Experimental
4	Picking a red lolly out of a mixed bag of lollies.	Theoretical	Experimental
5	Tossing a coin at the start of a game.	Theoretical	Experimental

  ISBN: 9780170497978

Calculating theoretical probability

- When we use devices such as coins, dice and spinners, we **know** the probabilities of single events. We have **equally likely outcomes**.
- We can use these probabilities to calculate the probabilities of combined events.

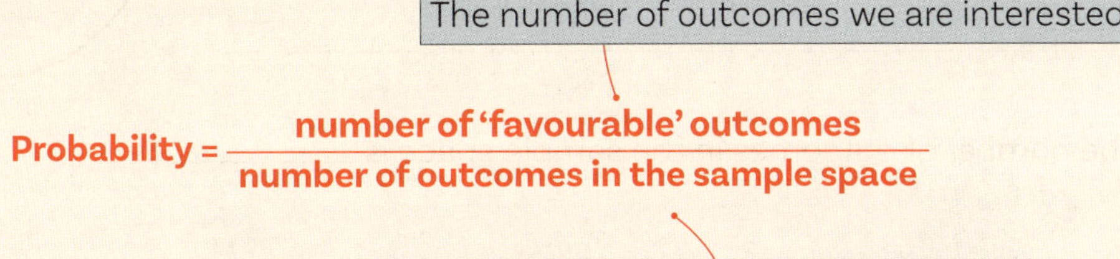

The number of outcomes we are interested in.

Probability = $\dfrac{\textbf{number of ‘favourable’ outcomes}}{\textbf{number of outcomes in the sample space}}$

The total number of possible outcomes.

Examples:

1 One event: write a **list** of all the outcomes and use it to **calculate probabilities**.

e.g. Rolling a die (dice).

a List the outcomes (sample space): **1, 2, 3, 4, 5, 6**

b Write down the number of outcomes: **6**

There are **3** even numbers: 2, 4 and 6.

c Calculate the probability of rolling a 5: $\frac{1}{6}$

d Calculate the probability of rolling an even number: $\frac{3}{6} = \frac{1}{2}$

There are **4** numbers less than 5: 1, 2, 3 and 4.

e Calculate the probability of rolling a number less than 5: $\frac{4}{6} = \frac{2}{3}$

2 More than one event: draw **probability trees** or make **probability tables** and use them to **calculate probabilities**.

e.g. Picking a marble out of the bag, then spinning the spinner.

a Calculate the probability of getting a red marble and a 3.

b Calculate the probability of getting a black marble and an even number.

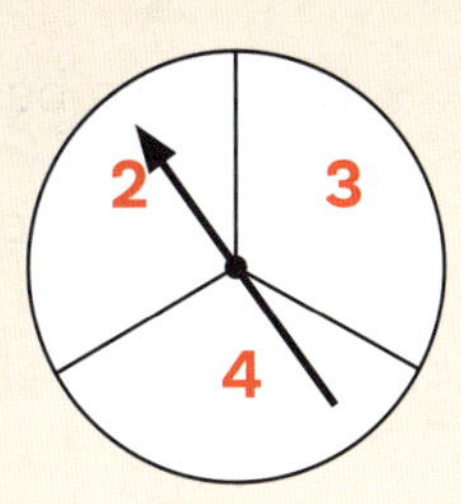

Using a **table**:

	2	3	4
R	R2	R3	R4
B	B2	B3	B4

This means ‘The probability of getting a red (marble) and a 3’.

a P(red and 3) = $\frac{1}{6}$

b P(black and even) = $\frac{2}{6} = \frac{1}{3}$

ISBN: 9780170497978

Answer the following.

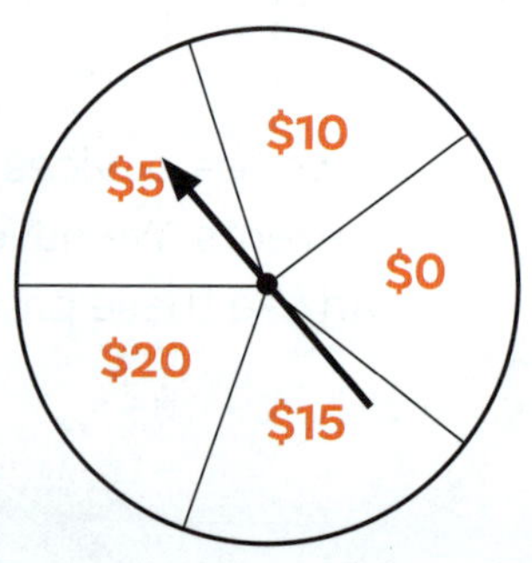

1 It costs $5 to spin this spinner. You win the amount the pointer lands on.

a List the outcomes (sample space).

____

____

b The number of outcomes in the sample space is ________

c What's the probability of getting no money back? ________

d What's the probability of getting at least your money back? ________

e What's the probability of making a profit? ________

f What's the probability of making a profit of $20? ________

2 A marble is selected from the bag and a die is rolled.

a Complete the table.

				4		
R		R2				
B						
W						

b Number of possibilities in the sample space = ________

c Use the table to help you calculate the following probabilities.

i The probability of getting a black marble and a 5. P = ________

ii The probability of getting a red marble and a 1 or 2. P = ________

iii The probability of getting an odd number. P = ________

iv The probability of getting a black marble and an odd number. P = ________

v The probability of getting a white marble and a 7. P = ________

 ISBN: 9780170497978

3 A spinner is spun and a coin is tossed.

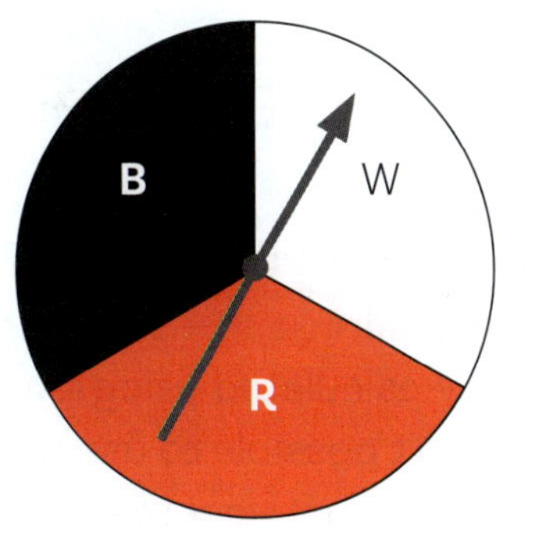

a Complete the tree diagram.

Spinner	Coin	Outcome	Probability
______	H	______	______
	______	RT	P(RT) = ______
B	______	______	______
	T	______	______
______	______	WH	______
	______	______	______

b Number of possibilities in the sample space = ______

c Use the tree to calculate the following probabilities.

i The probability of getting a black and a head. P = ______

ii The probability of getting a red and a head or tail. P = ______

iii The probability of getting a tail. P = ______

iv The probability of landing on white. P = ______

v The probability of getting a green and a head. P = ______

vi The probability of getting a tail and red or a tail and a black. P = ______

ISBN: 9780170497978

Calculating probabilities from observations

- Where we do not know the probabilities of events, we can do an **observational study (survey)** (or an **experiment** – see next section).
- Probabilities are calculated using **long run relative frequency**.
- Sometimes it isn't possible to use theoretical probabilities.
  e.g. The probability that your teacher will be late to class.
- In situations like this, we have to **estimate** probabilities based on **surveys**.

$$\textbf{Probability} = \frac{\textbf{number of 'favourable' outcomes}}{\textbf{number of outcomes in the sample space}}$$

Examples:

1 Here are the observations of the teacher's lateness for the last 20 periods.

On time	14
Late	6

The teacher has been late six times. Based on this data:

P(being late to next class) $= \frac{6}{20} = 0.3$ **(2 dp)**

2 80 students at a school were asked what activity they would like to do.

Rugby	Kī-o-rahi	Badminton	Weaving
17	28	21	14

P(kī-o-rahi) $= \frac{28}{80} = 0.35$

P(kī-o-rahi or badminton) $= \frac{28}{80} + \frac{21}{80} = \frac{49}{80}$

$= 0.6125$

3 A class of students had the demographics below.

	Blond hair	Not blond hair	Totals
Year 9	4	16	**20**
Year 10	2	10	**12**
Totals	**6**	**26**	**32**

P(blond hair) $= \frac{6}{32} = 0.1874$

P(Year 10 and blond hair) $= \frac{2}{32}$

$= 0.0625$ (2 dp)

ISBN: 9780170497978

Answer the following questions.

1 These are the results for the school basketball team so far this season.

Win	2
Draw	1
Loss	5

a How many games have they played? _______________

b Based on these results, what is the probability they will win their next game?

P(win) = _______________

c Based on these results, what is the probability they draw or lose their next game?

P(draw or lose) = _______________

2 A survey was done on what students would like for dinner.

Lasagne	Roast	Fish	Kebabs
14	17	8	21

a How many students were asked? _______________

If a student was picked at random, calculate the following probabilities.

b P(fish) _______________

c P(not roast) _______________

d P(kebabs or roast) _______________

3 Students went on a school trip. The students chose to either snowboard or ski.

a Complete the table.

	Experienced	First time	Totals
Snowboarding	12		
Skiing	18	46	
Totals			**120**

b What is the probability that a student went skiing? _______________

c What is the probability that a student was experienced? _______________

d What is the probability that a student was a first-time snowboarder? _______________

e Which sport had a great proportion of experienced students? Justify your answer.

____

____

____

ISBN: 9780170497978

Experimental probability investigation

- Sometimes it isn't possible to calculate probabilities, so we need to carry out **experiments** in order to estimate them.

Dice experiment

Henry thinks that a die is more likely to land on a 6 because it's opposite the 1. He thinks that because there is just one hole drilled into the side with a 1 on it, it is heavier and will land down more often than the other sides. Scarlett disagrees with him. In order to test this they both decide to do experiments.

Investigative question: Is a die more likely to land on a 6 than a 1?

Sample space: 1, 2, 3, 4, 5, 6

Number of trials: 10

These are Henry's results: **2, 1, 1, 6, 2, 6, 6, 5, 3, 3**

Here is how he recorded his results.

We call the probability calculated from the results of an experiment the **experimental probability**.

Die roll	Total	Probability	
1	2	$\frac{2}{10}$	0.2
2	2		
3			
4			
5			
6			

a Complete the table.

b Do you think Henry's results prove that the probability of landing on a 6 is greater than the probability of landing on a 1? Yes/No

Explain why or why not.

____

c What do you think Henry needs to do in order to find out whether his idea is true?

____

d Scarlett did her own experiment. She rolled a die 50 times. Complete her table of results.

	1	2	3	4	5	6
Frequency	卌 卌	卌 |||	卌	卌 卌 |	卌 ||||	卌 ||
Probability	$\frac{10}{50} = 0.2$					

 ISBN: 9780170497978

e Do you think Scarlett's results prove that Henry's idea was wrong? Yes/No

Explain why or why not.

Their teacher decided that it would be good to test Henry's idea with the whole class. She organised for all 29 students to each roll a die 50 times. Their combined results are shown in this table.

	Total	Probability (2 dp)
6	231	$\frac{231}{1450}$ =
Not 6	1219	=

f Complete the table.

g Do you think the class's results prove that Henry's idea was wrong? Yes/No

Explain why or why not.

---

h Complete the table below to show the probabilities of throwing sixes and not sixes in each of the experiments.

	Henry	Scarlett	Class
Number of tosses	10	50	1450
P(6)			
P(not 6)			

What happens to the probabilities as the number of throws increases?

In fact, it has been shown that normally dice are 'fair', so the probabilities of throwing 1, 2, 3, 4, 5 or 6 are the same.

i How many sixes would you expect if you rolled a die a million times?

---

j When Henry did his experiment, he rolled a die 10 times and these were his results.

2, 1, 1, 6, 2, 6, 6, 5, 3, 3

His last two rolls produced threes.
Tama was watching him and said that if he rolled the die an eleventh time, it probably wouldn't be a 3.

Do you agree with him? Yes/No

Explain why or why not.

ISBN: 9780170497978

Simulations

- To simulate means to pretend, to imitate, or to mimic.
- In a simulation, we imitate a probability situation using devices such as cards, random numbers, dice, coins, etc.

Cereal card experiment

A cereal promotion involves collecting cards which have New Zealand native birds on them. There is one card inside each box. Alex wants to collect one of each of the cards and wonders how many boxes she will need to buy to collect them all.

She decided to use a die for her simulation.

If she rolls a 1 or 2, this will represent the kiwi.
If she rolls a 3 or 4, this will represent the kea.
If she rolls a 5 or 6, this will represent the ruru.

For each trial, she rolled the die until she had a complete set of cards.
Then she recorded the number of throws it took to collect each set.

Kiwi	Kea	Ruru

These were her results.

Trial number	Results from die	Number of rolls to get the set of three
1	2, 5, 5, 1, 4	5
2	4, 5, 4, 1	4
3	3, 5, 4, 4, 4, 5, 6, 5, 6, 2	10
4	3, 3, 3, 2, 4, 1, 5	7
5	5, 3, 4, 1	4
6	2, 4, 2, 6	4
7	5, 4, 2	3
8	3, 3, 3, 2, 4, 4, 3, 5	8
9	6, 3, 6, 1	4
10	3, 6, 3, 3, 3, 2	6
	Total	**55**

For this trial, it took **five** rolls of the die before she had collected the set of three cards.

Then she calculated the average number of throws needed in order to collect the full set.

$$\text{Average number of throws needed for a full set} = \frac{\text{total number of throws}}{\text{total number of trials}} = \frac{55}{10} = 5.5$$

This means that her simulation has shown that she is likely to have to buy five or six packets in order to get the full set of birds.

 ISBN: 9780170497978

a What assumptions has Alex made about the cards?

____

____

Now, you do the same simulation to see if you get similar results.

Roll the die as many times as it takes to get the full set of three cards.
Once you have the full set of all three birds, record the number of rolls it took in the right-hand column and start the next trial.

Trial number	Results from die	Number of rolls to get the set of three
1		
2		
3		
4		
5		
6		
7		
8		
9		
10		
	Total	

Average number of throws needed for a full set = $\dfrac{\text{total number of throws}}{\text{total number of trials}} = \dfrac{\quad}{\quad} =$

This means that your simulation has shown that it is likely that you would have to buy

______________________ packets in order to get the full set of birds.

b What do you think you could do to make the estimate of the number of boxes needed more accurate?

____

c Describe how you could use a die to simulate a similar situation, but there were just two birds on cards: either a kiwi or a fantail.

____

____

ISBN: 9780170497978

Answers

NUMBER (pp. 6–88)

The language of mathematics (pp. 6)

Words to operations (p. 6)

1	÷	**2**	+
3	–	**4**	x
5	–	**6**	+
7	+	**8**	+
9	÷	**10**	x
11	–	**12**	x
13	–	**14**	+
15	+	**16**	–
17	x	**18**	–
19	–	**20**	+

Integers (pp. 7–11)

Adding and subtracting (pp. 7–8)

1 7

2 -5

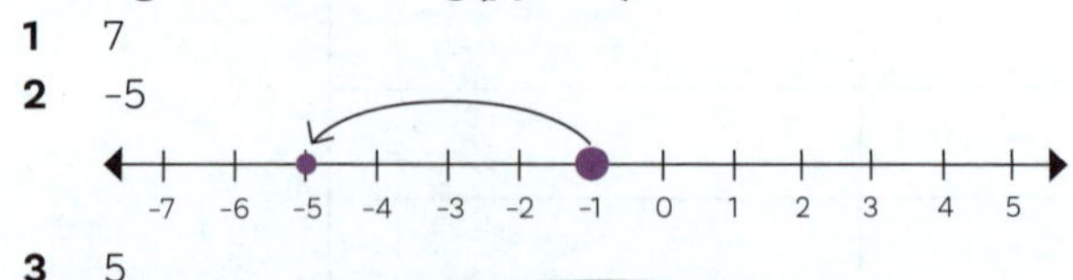

3 5

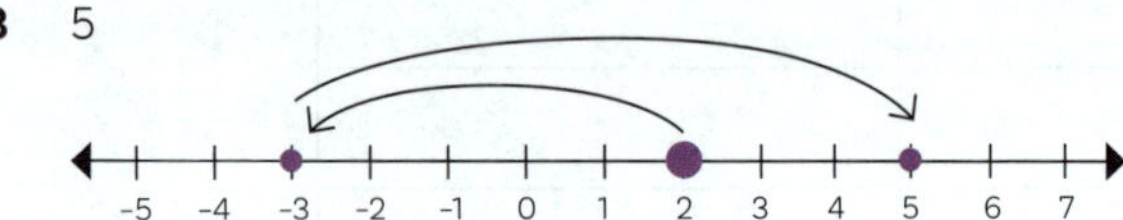

4 -1

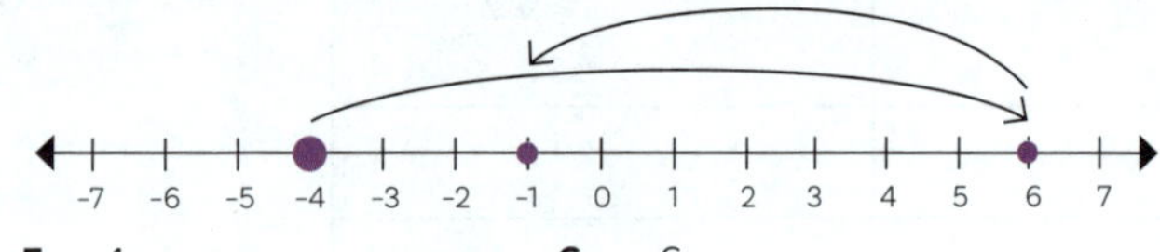

5	4	**6**	-6
7	-7	**8**	-12
9	11	**10**	14
11	+10 + 2 - 5 = 7	**12**	-2 + 5 - 4 = -1
13	-7 - 2 - 1 = -10	**14**	-3 + 9 + 2 = 8
15	+9 - 1 - 8 = 0	**16**	-2 + 8 - 12 = -6
17	+6 - 2 + 7 - 4 = 7	**18**	-13 - 7 + 9 - 1 = -12

19 +5 - 4 - 3 + 2 - 1= -1
-5 + 4 + 3 - 2 - 1= -1
-5 + 4 - 3 + 2 + 1= -1

20 -2 - 4 + 6 + 8 - 10 = -2
-2 + 4 - 6 - 8 + 10 = -2
+2 + 4 - 6 + 8 - 10 = -2

21	3 - 4 - 5 + 14 = 8	**22**	-4 + 5 - 7 + 9 = 3
23	0 - 8 + 3 + 9 = 4	**24**	-7 - 2 + 15 - 8 + 3 = 1

Multiplying and dividing (pp. 9–11)

1 5 x 4 = +5 + 5 + 5 + 5
= 20

2 7 x 5 = +7 + 7 + 7 + 7 + 7
= 35

3 4 x -7 = -7 - 7 - 7 - 7
= -28

4 -6 x 3 = -6 - 6 - 6
= -18

5 4 x 2 = 8
2 x 4 = 8

6 -5 x -3 = 15
-3 x -5 = 15

7 8 x -3 = -24
-3 x 8 = -24

8 6 x 5 = 30
5 x -6 = 30

9 -10 ÷ 5 = -2 because 5 x -2 = -10

10 -27 ÷ -3 = 9 because -3 x 9 = -27

11 30 ÷ -5 = -6 because -5 x -6 = 30

12 $\frac{-12}{4}$ = -3 because 4 x -3 = -12

13	4 x 9 = 36	9 x 4 = 36	36 ÷ 9 = 4	36 ÷ 4 = 9
14	7 x -6 = -42	-7 x 6 = -42	-42 ÷ 7 = -6	-42 ÷ -6 = 7
15	-2 x -8 = 16	-8 x -2 = 16	16 ÷ -2 = -8	16 ÷ -8 = 2
16	$8 \times \frac{1}{4} = 2$	$\frac{1}{4} \times 8 = 2$	$2 \div \frac{1}{4} = 8$	$2 \div 8 = \frac{1}{4}$
17	10, $\frac{1}{5}$ and 50	$50 \times \frac{1}{5} = 10$	$10 \div \frac{1}{5} = 50$	$10 \div 50 = \frac{1}{5}$

18	16	**19**	-5
20	-24	**21**	7
22	-28	**23**	-2
24	18	**25**	3
26	36	**27**	-18
28	2	**29**	-6
30	7 x -5 = -35	**31**	-11 x 6 = -66
32	-24 ÷ 6 = -4	**33**	-72 ÷ 8 x -1 = 9
34	8 x 3 x -2 = -48	**35**	-4 ÷ -2 x -13 = -26

Types of numbers (12–19)

Multiples (p. 12)

1

Number	First five multiples
3	3, 6, 9, 12, 15
5	5, 10, 15, 20, 25
7	7, 14, 21, 28, 35
6	6, 12, 18, 24, 30
9	9, 18, 27, 36, 45

2

True or False
True
True
False
True
False

3 5, 10, 15, 20, 25, 30, 35 LCM is 35
7, 14, 21, 28, 35

4 6, 12, 18, 24, 30 LCM is 30
10, 20, 30

5 8, 16, 24, 32, 40 LCM is 24
12, 24

6 4, 8, 12, 16, 20, 24, 28
7, 14, 21, 28
It will take 28 minutes.

Factors (p. 13)

1

Number	Factors
8	1, 2, 4, 8
15	1, 3, 5, 10, 15
10	1, 2, 5, 10
14	1, 2, 7, 14
38	1, 2, 19, 38

2

True or False
False
True
True
True
False

 ISBN: 9780170497978

3 1, 3, 5, 15 HCF is 3
1, 3, 7, 21

4 1, 2, 7, 14 HCF is 2
1, 2, 4, 8, 16

5 1, 2, 3, 5, 6, 10, 15, 30 HCF is 6
1, 2, 3, 4, 6, 8, 12, 24

6 1, 2, 3, 6, 9, 18
1, 2, 3, 6
She could have **2** groups with **9** right-handers and **3** left-handers in each group.
She could have **3** groups with **6** right-handers and **2** left-handers in each group.
She could have **6** groups with **3** right-handers and **1** left-hander in each group.

Prime numbers (pp. 14–17)

1

1	**2**	**3**	4	**5**	6	**7**	8	9	10
11	12	**13**	14	15	16	**17**	18	**19**	20
21	22	**23**	24	25	26	27	28	**29**	30
31	32	33	34	35	36	**37**	38	39	40
41	42	**43**	44	45	46	**47**	48	49	50

2 Other than 2, yes.

3 53

4 **Odd** **Even**

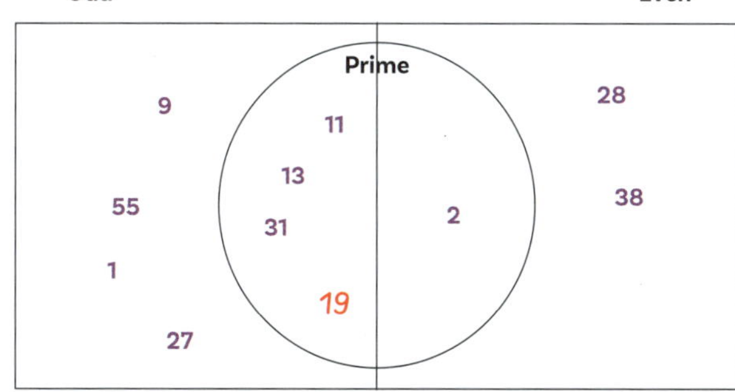

5

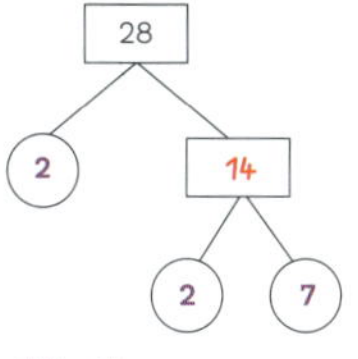

28 = **2^2 x 7**

6

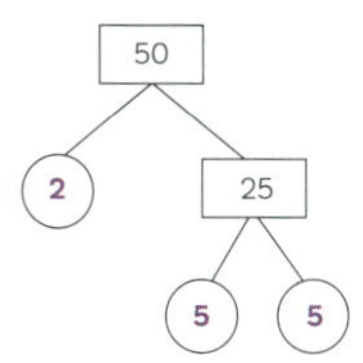

50 = **2 x 5^2**

7

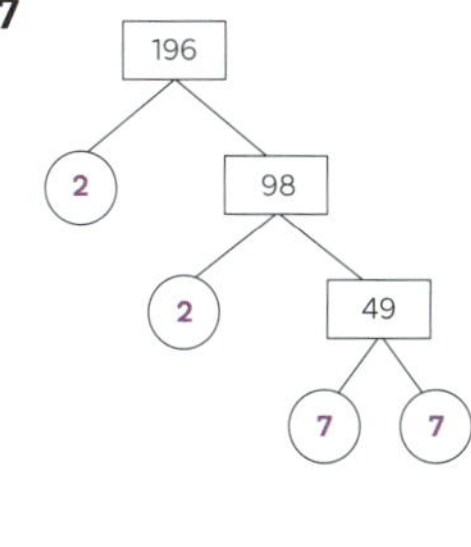

196 = **2^2 x 7^2**

8

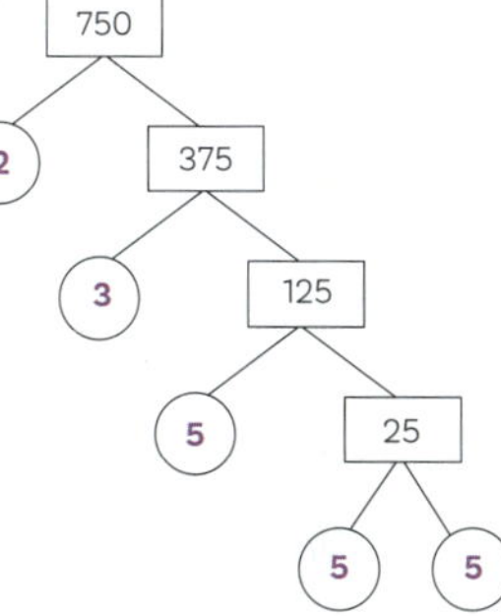

750 = **2 x 3 x 5^3**

9

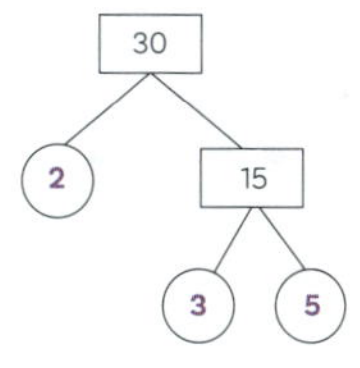

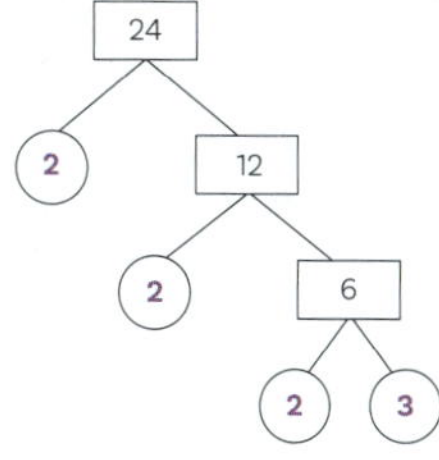

30 = **2 x 3 x 5**
24 = **2 x 2 x 2 x 3**

HCF = **2 x 3** = **6**
LCM = **6 x 5 x 2 x 2** = **120**

10

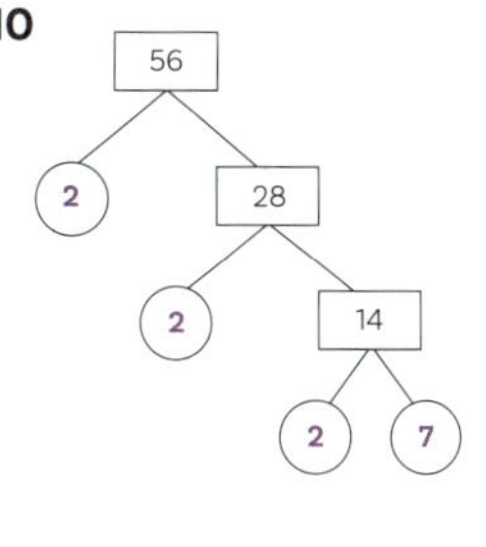

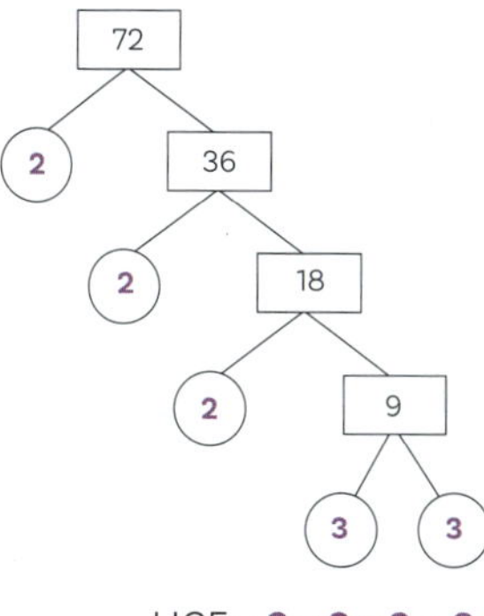

56 = **2 x 2 x 2 x 7**
72 = **2 x 2 x 2 x 3 x 3**

HCF = **2 x 2 x 2** = **8**
LCM = **8 x 7 x 3 x 3** = **504**

11

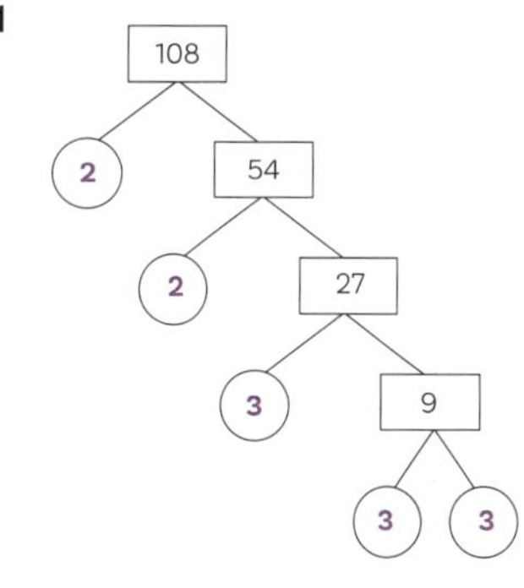

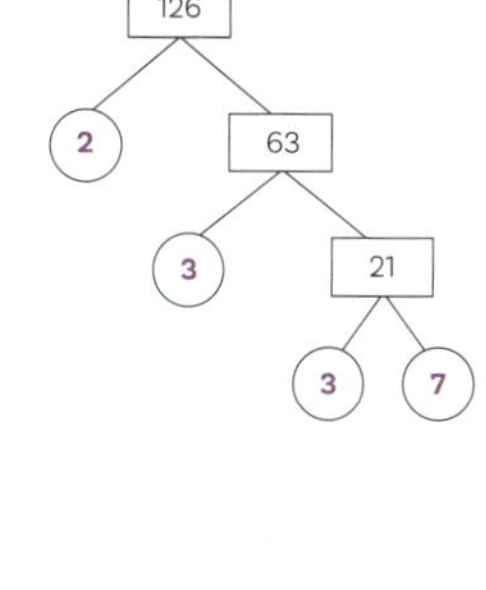

108 = **2 x 2 x 3 x 3 x 3**
126 = **2 x 3 x 3 x 7**

HCF = **2 x 3 x 3** = **18**
LCM = **18 x 2 x 3 x 7** = **756**

12

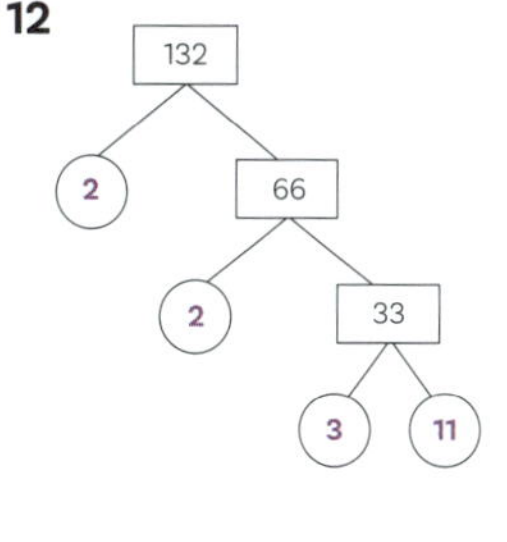

420
2
210
2
105
3
35
5
7

132 = **2 x 2 x 3 x 11**
420 = **2 x 2 x 3 x 5 x 7**

HCF = **2 x 2 x 3** = **12**
LCM = **12 x 11 x 5 x 7**
= **4620**

ISBN: 9780170497978

Square numbers (p. 18)

1

1	4	9	16	25
1^2	2^2	3^2	4^2	5^2

2 1, 4, 9, 16, 25, 36, 49, 64, 81, 100
3 36, 81, 144, 225, 324, 441
4 16 + 9 = 25
5 64 + 36 = 100
6 4 + 9 + 36 = 49
7 **a**

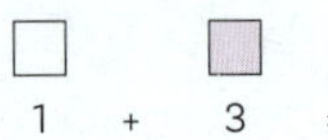

1 + 3 = 4

1 + 3 + 5 = 9

1 + 3 + 5 + 7 = 16

1 + 3 + 5 + 7 + 9 = 25

b They are all square numbers.
c 1 + 3 + 5 + 7 + 9 + 11 = 36

Mixing it up (p. 19)

1 **a** 109°C
b 23°C (not -23°C)
2 **a** The HCF of 78, 104 and 143 is 13 ∴ 13 bags.
b 6 apples, 8 pears and 11 feijoas
3 **a** The LCM of 20, 12 and 5 is 60 ∴ 60 bags.
b She will need 3 packs of pens, 5 packs of pencils and 12 packs of highlighters.
4 **a** False
b Prime numbers must have two factors. One has only one factor.
c 41
d 109
5 **a** 11 tiles
b 8 tiles

Powers (pp. 20–21)

1	3^4	**2**	12^3
3	$(-7)^2$	**4**	$(-2)^5$
5	4^2	**6**	10^3
7	3^3	**8**	-3^3 or $(-3)^3$
9	2^5	**10**	-2^5 or $(-2)^5$
11	-2^2	**12**	-10^4 or -100^2
13	64	**14**	64
15	81	**16**	-64
17	-100	**18**	1
19	100 000	**20**	19
21	32	**22**	4 × 8 = 32
23	Yes 5		
24	4	**25**	3
26	6	**27**	2
28	11	**29**	1
30	-2	**31**	-1
32	512	**33**	20 736
34	9261	**35**	-169
36	-759 375	**37**	24.389
38	-0.008	**39**	0.00004096

40

$10^3 \times 10^2$	100 000
$10^8 \div 10^2$	1 000 000
$-10^3 \times 10^1$	-10 000
$(-10)^4 \times 10^0$	10 000
$10^0 \div 10^3$	0.001

Roots (pp. 22–23)

1	$\sqrt[3]{8} = 2 \Rightarrow 2^3 = 8$	**2**	$\sqrt[2]{81} = 9 \Rightarrow 9^2 = 81$
3	$1^5 = 1 \Rightarrow \sqrt[5]{1} = 1$		
4	$4^2 = 16 \Rightarrow \sqrt[2]{16} = 4$ or $2^4 = 16 \Rightarrow \sqrt[4]{16} = 2$		
5	8	**6**	5
7	-3	**8**	10
9	3	**10**	1
11	8.5	**12**	218
13	0.9	**14**	-15
15	6	**16**	0.6

Mixing it up (p. 23)

1	1^0	=	1
2	$(-10)^2$	>	-10^2
3	$(-2)^3$	=	-2^3
4	0.9^3	<	0.9^2
5	10^{-1}	>	-1
6	$10^3 \times 10^0$	=	10^3
7	$\left(\frac{1}{2}\right)^2$	<	$\frac{1}{2}$
8	10^0	<	10
9	$\sqrt{200}$	>	14
10	$\sqrt{64}$	>	$\sqrt[3]{64}$
11	$\sqrt{25} + \sqrt{4}$	>	$\sqrt{29}$
12	$\sqrt{25} - 1$	>	$\sqrt{24} - 1$
13	$\sqrt{9+16}$	<	$\sqrt{9} + 16$
14	$\sqrt{10\,000}$	=	$\sqrt[3]{1\,000\,000}$

 ISBN: 9780170497978

15

Square root	Square numbers on either side	Lower and upper limits for square root	Value
$\sqrt{12}$	*9 and 16*	*3 and 4*	*3.464*
$\sqrt{6}$	4 and 9	2 and 3	2.449
$\sqrt{90}$	81 and 100	9 and 10	9.487
$\sqrt{60}$	49 and 64	7 and 8	7.746
$\sqrt{18}$	16 and 25	4 and 5	4.243
$\sqrt{30}$	25 and 36	5 and 6	5.477

Order of operations (pp. 24–25)

B	Brackets	( ) { } [ ]
E	Exponents	2^3 or $\sqrt{\ }$
D	Division	÷
M	Multiplication	x
A	Addition	+
S	Subtraction	−

G	Grouping	( ) { } [ ]
E	Exponents	2^3 or $\sqrt{\ }$
M	Multiplication and Division	x ÷
A	Addition and Subtraction	+ −

1 14
2 8
3 16
4 17
5 19
6 12
7 14
8 3
9 −11
10 −15
11 −3.5
12 9
13 9
14 −18
15 17
16 2
17 −5
18 −13

Words to calculations (p. 25)

1 (16 x 2) − 12 x 3 = −4 — $4
2 $\frac{16}{2}$ − 12 ÷ 3 = 4 — $4 more
3 (16 ÷ 2) − 12 − 3 = −7 — $7 less
4 −16 + 2 x 12 − 3 = 5 — $5 more
5 16 x 2 − 12 ÷ 3 = 28 — $28 more
6 $\frac{16}{2}$ + 12 x 3 = 44 — $44
7 (16 + 2 + 12) ÷ 3 = 10 — $10

Fractions (pp. 26–45)

Numerators and denominators (p. 26)

1

a $\frac{1}{3}$ $\frac{2}{3}$

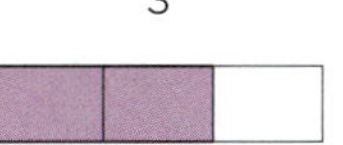

When the numerator increases, the size of the shaded section **increases**.

b $\frac{1}{4}$ $\frac{1}{5}$

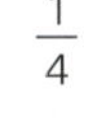

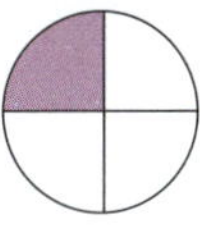

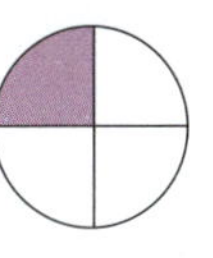

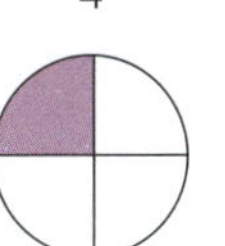

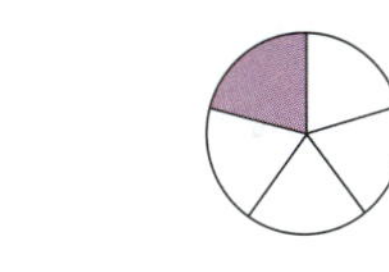

When the denominator increases, the size of the shaded section **decreases**.

2

$\frac{1}{25}$	$\frac{2}{25}$	$\frac{7}{25}$	$\frac{11}{25}$	$\frac{12}{25}$	$\frac{16}{25}$	$\frac{25}{25}$

3

$\frac{1}{10}$	$\frac{1}{8}$	$\frac{1}{5}$	$\frac{1}{4}$	$\frac{1}{3}$	$\frac{1}{2}$	$\frac{1}{1}$

Equivalent fractions (pp. 27–28)

1

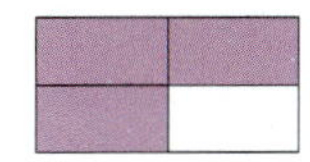

$\frac{6}{8} = \frac{3}{4}$

2

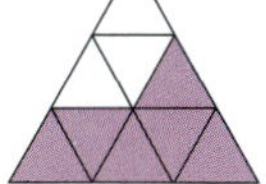

$\frac{2}{3} = \frac{6}{9}$

3

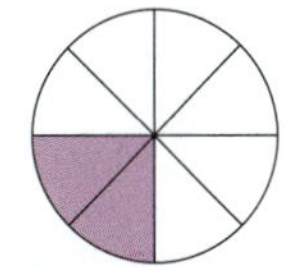

$\frac{1}{4} = \frac{2}{8}$

4

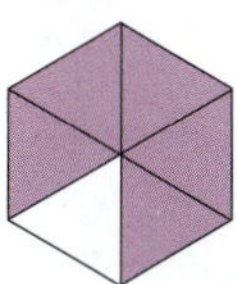

$\frac{10}{12} = \frac{5}{6}$

5

$\frac{4}{8} = \frac{1}{2}$

6 5
7 3
8 12
9 24
10 $\frac{1}{3}$
11 $\frac{5}{7}$
12 $\frac{3}{5}$
13 $\frac{4}{13}$
14

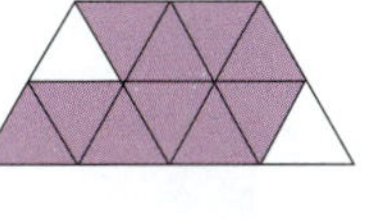

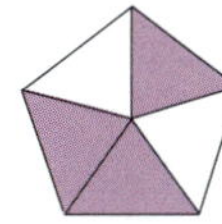

15 $\frac{1}{3} = \frac{2}{6} = \frac{3}{9} = \frac{4}{12} = \frac{5}{15} = \frac{6}{18} = \frac{10}{30}$

16 $\frac{4}{6} = \frac{12}{18} = \frac{2}{3} = \frac{72}{108} = \frac{8}{12} = \frac{24}{36}$

17 $\frac{12}{15} = \frac{36}{45} = \frac{20}{25} = \frac{16}{20} = \frac{24}{30} = \frac{28}{35} = \frac{4}{5}$

ISBN: 9780170497978

Converting between improper and mixed fractions (pp. 29–30)

	Improper fraction	Mixed fraction
1	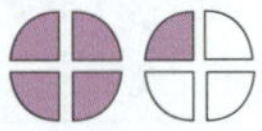 $\frac{5}{4}$ *Five quarters*	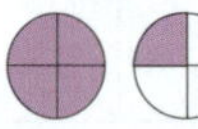 $1\frac{1}{4}$ *One and one quarter*
2	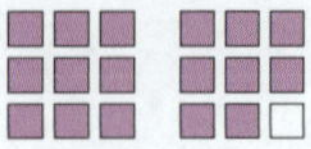 $\frac{17}{9}$ Seventeen ninths	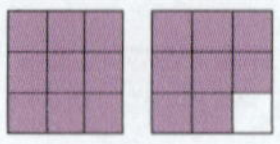 $1\frac{8}{9}$ One and eight ninths
3	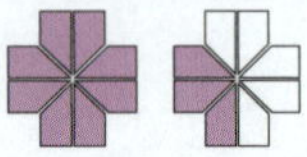 $\frac{11}{8}$ Eleven eighths	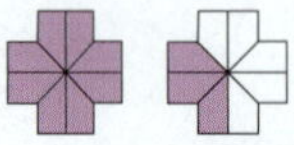 $1\frac{3}{8}$ One and three eighths
4	 $\frac{13}{5}$ *Thirteen fifths*	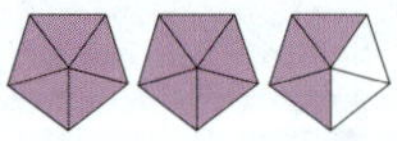 $2\frac{3}{5}$ Two and three fifths

5 $\frac{23}{6} = \frac{6}{6} + \frac{6}{6} + \frac{6}{6} + \frac{5}{6} = 3\frac{5}{6}$

6 $\frac{14}{3} = \frac{3}{3} + \frac{3}{3} + \frac{3}{3} + \frac{3}{3} + \frac{2}{3} = 3\frac{2}{3}$

7 $\frac{21}{2} = 10\frac{1}{2}$

8 $\frac{31}{7} = 4\frac{3}{7}$

9 $5\frac{1}{3}$

10 $4\frac{4}{5}$

11 $7\frac{2}{7}$

12 $3\frac{7}{8}$

13 $4\frac{3}{6}$ or $4\frac{1}{2}$

14 $2\frac{6}{9}$ or $2\frac{2}{3}$

15 $4\frac{1}{5} = \frac{5}{5} + \frac{5}{5} + \frac{5}{5} + \frac{5}{5} + \frac{1}{5} = \frac{21}{5}$

16 $2\frac{4}{9} = \frac{9}{9} + \frac{9}{9} + \frac{4}{9} = \frac{22}{9}$

17 $1\frac{1}{6} = \frac{7}{6}$

18 $3\frac{2}{7} = \frac{23}{7}$

19 $\frac{17}{2}$

20 $\frac{18}{5}$

21 $\frac{43}{4}$

22 $\frac{67}{6}$

23 $\frac{41}{7}$

24 $\frac{55}{12}$

Adding and subtracting fractions (pp. 31–33)

1 $\frac{4}{5}$

2 $\frac{1}{6}$

3 $\frac{5}{8}$

4 $\frac{3}{7}$

5 $\frac{9}{10}$

6 $\frac{1}{4}$

7 $\frac{1}{6} + \frac{3}{6} = \frac{4}{6}$

8 $\frac{6}{7} - \frac{2}{7} = \frac{4}{7}$

9 $\frac{5}{7} - \frac{4}{7} = \frac{1}{7}$

10 $\frac{5}{7} + \frac{2}{7} = \frac{7}{7}$

11 $\frac{5}{6} - \frac{1}{6} = \frac{4}{6}$

12 $\frac{1}{6} + \frac{2}{3} = \frac{1}{6} + \frac{4}{6} = \frac{5}{6}$

13 $\frac{3}{4} - \frac{1}{2} = \frac{3}{4} - \frac{2}{4} = \frac{1}{4}$

14 $\frac{5}{8} + \frac{1}{4} = \frac{5}{8} + \frac{2}{8} = \frac{7}{8}$

15 $\frac{7}{9} - \frac{1}{3} = \frac{7}{9} - \frac{3}{9} = \frac{4}{9}$

16 $\frac{9}{10} - \frac{3}{5} = \frac{9}{10} - \frac{6}{10} = \frac{3}{10}$

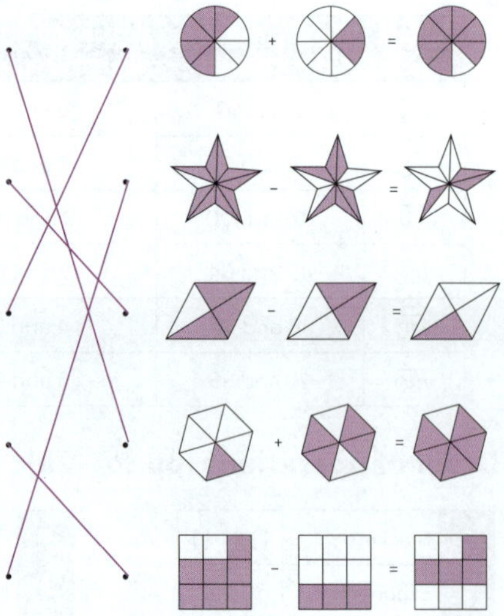

17 $\frac{5}{6}$

18 $\frac{5}{8}$

19 $\frac{1}{14}$

20 $\frac{1}{9}$

21 $\frac{26}{63}$

22 $\frac{13}{24}$

23 $\frac{27}{35}$

24 $\frac{6}{55}$

25 $1\frac{1}{6}$

26 $1\frac{17}{20}$

27 $1\frac{5}{8}$

28 $1\frac{9}{40}$

Multiplying fractions (p. 34)

1 $\frac{1}{15}$

2 $\frac{1}{6}$

3 $\frac{30}{49}$

4 $\frac{4}{30} = \frac{2}{15}$

5 $\frac{3}{40}$

6 $\frac{15}{6} = \frac{5}{2} = 2\frac{1}{2}$

7 $\frac{2}{3}$

8 $6\frac{1}{20}$

9 $\frac{3}{4} \times \frac{4}{5} = \frac{12}{20}$

10 $\frac{6}{5} \times \frac{3}{4} = \frac{18}{20} = \frac{9}{10}$

11 $\frac{2}{5} \times 4 = \frac{8}{5}$

12 $\frac{5}{6} \times \frac{3}{7} = \frac{15}{42} = \frac{5}{14}$

13 $\frac{3}{2} \times \frac{5}{3} = \frac{15}{6} = \frac{5}{2} = 2\frac{1}{2}$

14 $\frac{9}{10} \times \frac{8}{6} = \frac{72}{60} = \frac{6}{5} = 1\frac{1}{5}$

Dividing fractions (pp. 35–37)

1 $\frac{15}{6}$

2 $\frac{3}{11}$

3 $\frac{3}{13}$

4 $\frac{4}{23}$

5 $\frac{1}{21}$

6 $\frac{5}{603}$

7 $2 \div \frac{1}{6} = 2 \times 6 = 12$

$2 \div \frac{1}{6}$ means 'How many **sixths** are there in **two**?'

8 $3 \div \frac{1}{4} = 3 \times 4 = 12$

$3 \div \frac{1}{4}$ means 'How many **quarters** are there in **three**?'

9 $2 \div \frac{1}{3} = \frac{2}{1} \times \frac{3}{1} = \frac{6}{1} = 6$

$2 \div \frac{1}{3} = 6$ means 'There are **six** ***thirds*** in **two**.'

 ISBN: 9780170497978

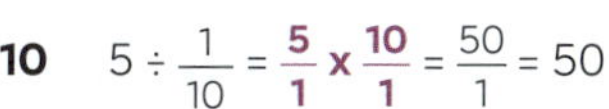

10 $5 \div \frac{1}{10} = \mathbf{\frac{5}{1}} \times \mathbf{\frac{10}{1}} = \frac{50}{1} = 50$

$5 \div \frac{1}{10} =$ **50** means 'There are **fifty tenths** in **five**.'

11 6

$\frac{3}{4} \div \frac{1}{8} =$ **6** means 'There are **six eighths** in **three quarters**.'

12 $\frac{1}{2}$

$\frac{1}{3} \div \frac{2}{3} = \mathbf{\frac{1}{2}}$ means 'There is **half** of **two thirds** in **one third**.'

13 $\frac{12}{15} = \frac{4}{5}$ **14** $\frac{8}{21}$

15 $\frac{45}{16} = 2\frac{13}{16}$ **16** $\frac{14}{10} = \frac{7}{5} = 1\frac{2}{5}$

17 $\frac{8}{45}$ **18** $\frac{9}{16}$

19 $\frac{15}{24} = \frac{5}{8}$ **20** $\frac{9}{45} = \frac{1}{5}$

21 $\frac{3}{5} \div \frac{1}{4} = \mathbf{\frac{3}{5}} \times \mathbf{\frac{4}{1}} = \mathbf{\frac{12}{5}}$ **22** $\frac{7}{9} \div \frac{4}{\mathbf{7}} = \frac{7}{9} \times \frac{\mathbf{7}}{4} = \frac{49}{36}$

23 $\frac{2}{7} \div \frac{1}{2} = \mathbf{\frac{4}{7}}$ **24** $\frac{5}{6} \div \frac{2}{3} = \frac{15}{\mathbf{12}} = \frac{5}{\mathbf{4}}$

25 $\mathbf{\frac{3}{8}} \div 2 = \frac{3}{\mathbf{16}}$ **26** $\frac{7}{9} \div \frac{1}{\mathbf{6}} = 4\frac{2}{3}$

Ordering fractions (p. 38)

1

~~$\frac{3}{5}$~~	$\frac{7}{20}$	$\frac{1}{4}$	$\frac{1}{2}$	$\frac{9}{10}$	$\frac{3}{10}$	$\frac{4}{5}$	$\frac{13}{20}$
$\frac{12}{20}$	$\frac{7}{20}$	$\frac{5}{20}$	$\frac{10}{20}$	$\frac{18}{20}$	$\frac{6}{20}$	$\frac{16}{20}$	$\frac{13}{20}$

Smallest Biggest

$\frac{1}{4}$	$\frac{3}{10}$	$\frac{7}{20}$	$\frac{1}{2}$	$\frac{3}{5}$	$\frac{13}{20}$	$\frac{4}{5}$	$\frac{9}{10}$

2

$\frac{5}{25}$	$\frac{4}{50}$	$\frac{7}{10}$	$\frac{2}{5}$	$\frac{12}{25}$	$\frac{1}{2}$	$\frac{4}{5}$	$\frac{3}{10}$
$\frac{10}{50}$	$\frac{4}{50}$	$\frac{35}{50}$	$\frac{20}{50}$	$\frac{24}{50}$	$\frac{25}{50}$	$\frac{40}{50}$	$\frac{15}{50}$

Smallest Biggest

$\frac{4}{50}$	$\frac{5}{25}$	$\frac{3}{10}$	$\frac{2}{5}$	$\frac{12}{25}$	$\frac{1}{2}$	$\frac{7}{10}$	$\frac{4}{5}$

3

~~$\frac{1}{4}$~~	$\frac{2}{3}$	$\frac{7}{12}$	$\frac{1}{2}$	$\frac{5}{6}$	$\frac{3}{4}$	$\frac{1}{6}$	$\frac{5}{12}$
$\frac{3}{12}$	$\frac{8}{12}$	$\frac{7}{12}$	$\frac{6}{12}$	$\frac{10}{12}$	$\frac{9}{12}$	$\frac{2}{12}$	$\frac{5}{12}$

0 $\frac{1}{6}$ $\frac{1}{4}$ $\frac{5}{12}$ $\frac{1}{2}$ $\frac{7}{12}$ $\frac{2}{3}$ $\frac{3}{4}$ $\frac{5}{6}$ 1

Comparing fractions (pp. 39–40)

1 > **2** < **3** >

4 < **5** > **6** <

7 $\frac{2}{3}$ < $\frac{3}{4}$ **8** $\frac{2}{5}$ > $\frac{1}{4}$

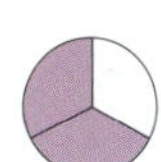
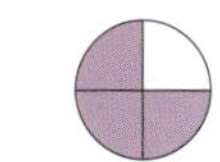
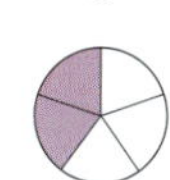
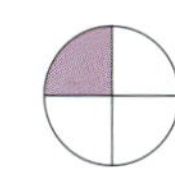

9 $\frac{4}{5}$ < $\frac{7}{8}$ **10** $\frac{1}{3}$ < $\frac{3}{7}$

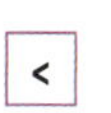

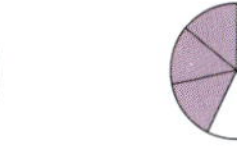

11 $\frac{5}{7}$ > $\frac{4}{6}$ **12** $\frac{5}{9}$ < $\frac{3}{5}$

13 $\frac{2}{3}$ > $\frac{6}{10}$; $= \frac{20}{30}$, $= \frac{18}{30}$ **14** $\frac{3}{4}$ > $\frac{2}{5}$; $= \frac{15}{20}$, $= \frac{8}{20}$

15 $\frac{5}{8}$ < $\frac{2}{3}$; $= \frac{15}{24}$, $= \frac{16}{24}$ **16** $\frac{2}{7}$ < $\frac{1}{3}$; $= \frac{6}{21}$, $= \frac{7}{21}$

17 $\frac{5}{6}$ < $\frac{7}{8}$; $= \frac{20}{24}$, $= \frac{21}{24}$ **18** $\frac{4}{5}$ > $\frac{5}{7}$; $= \frac{28}{35}$, $= \frac{25}{35}$

19 $\frac{7}{10}$ < $\frac{5}{7}$; $= \frac{49}{70}$, $= \frac{50}{70}$ **20** $\frac{8}{11}$ > $\frac{25}{35}$; $= \frac{200}{275}$, $= \frac{198}{275}$

Fraction of a quantity (p. 41)

1 14 **2** 21
3 33 **4** 9
5 40 **6** 54
7 36 **8** $39
9 $\frac{1}{5}$ **10** $318.20

Increasing and decreasing by a fraction (pp. 42–43)

1 28 **2** 45
3 594 **4** 108
5 365 **6** 140
7 110 **8** 105
9 $387.20 **10** 1215 g or 1.215 kg
11 20 **12** 450
13 155 **14** 128
15 390 **16** 168
17 375 **18** 324
19 348 m^2 **20** 4.23 kg

Given a fraction, find the whole amount (pp. 44–45)

1 80 **2** 192
3 273 **4** 1224
5 112 **6** 3270
7 150 **8** 60
9 318 **10** 68
11 756 **12** 180
13 1230 people **14** 108 lollies
15 684 people

ISBN: 9780170497978

Decimals (pp. 46–54)

Place value (pp. 46–48)

		Number	Words
1	7 254	200	Two hundred
2	265 971	5000	*Five thousand*
3	79	70	Seventy
4	4 365 194	60 000	Sixty thousand
5	801 035	800 000	Eight hundred thousand
6	329 247 840	9 000 000	Nine million
7	51 241	40	Forty
8	306 128 324	300 000 000	Three hundred million
9	20 199	100	One hundred
10	982 105 075	80 000 000	Eighty million

		Decimal	Fraction	Words
11	0.712	0.7	$\frac{7}{10}$	*Seven tenths*
12	0.564	0.004	$\frac{4}{1000}$	Four thousandths
13	14.127	0.020	$\frac{2}{100}$	Two hundredths
14	98.501	0.5	$\frac{5}{10}$	Five tenths
15	19.832	0.03	$\frac{3}{100}$	Three hundredths
16	600.020	0.000	$\frac{0}{1000}$	Zero thousandths
17	1.009	0.009	$\frac{9}{1000}$	Nine thousandths
18	0.075	0.07	$\frac{7}{100}$	Seven hundredths

19 Eight hundred and twenty-six
20 Twelve thousand four hundred and forty-one
21 Three thousand five hundred and seven
22 Eighty-two and six tenths (or point six)
23 Seven hundred and fifteen thousand, six hundred and twenty-four and five tenths (or point five)
24 Two hundred and three million, four hundred and seventy-three thousand, six hundred and fourteen
25 Zero and sixty-three hundredths (or point six three)
26 Three hundred thousand and sixty and two tenths (or point two)
27 Nine hundred and eighty thousand and ten and forty-seven hundredths (or point four seven)

28	9 015	**29**	43.5
30	2 000 731	**31**	600 004
32	3.022	**33**	1 830 004
34	5.009	**35**	0.86
36	43 000 191.02		

Decimals on number lines (pp. 49–50)

1

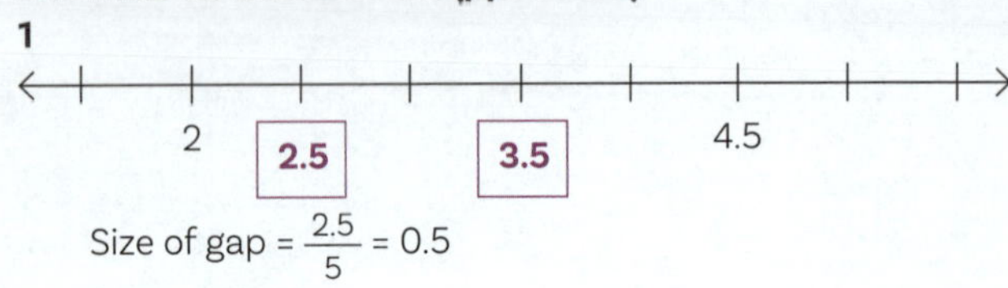

Size of gap = $\frac{2.5}{5}$ = 0.5

2

0.4, 0.8, 1.4, 1.8

Size of gap = $\frac{0.6}{3}$ = 0.2

3

4.5, 5.1, 6.0, 6.3

Size of gap = $\frac{1.2}{4}$ = 0.3

4

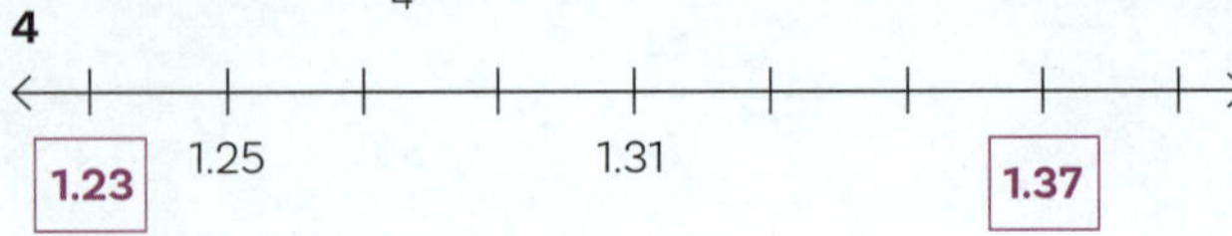

Size of gap = $\frac{0.06}{3}$ = 0.02

5

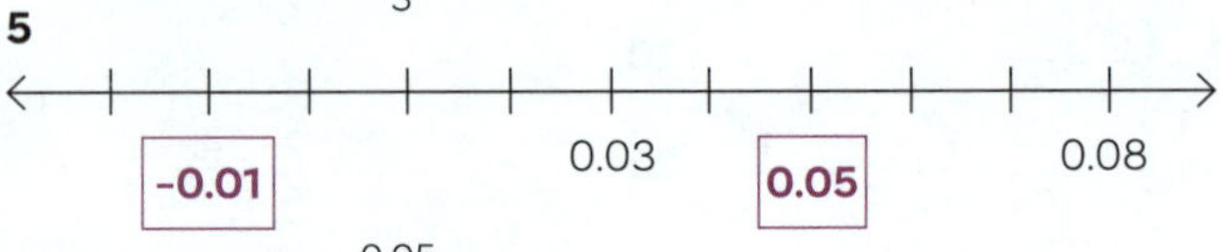

Size of gap = $\frac{0.05}{5}$ = 0.1

6

Challenge (p. 50)

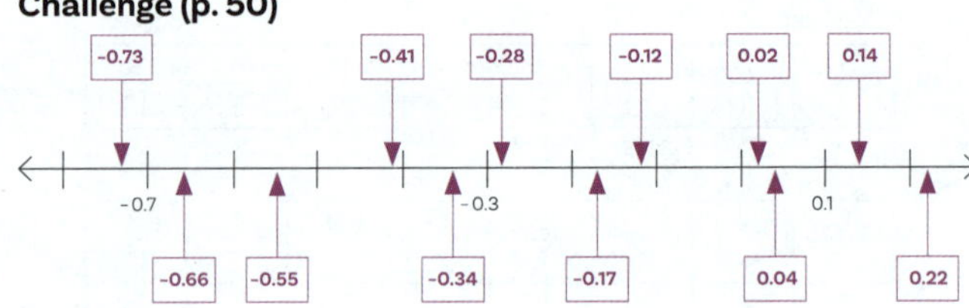

Comparing decimals (pp. 51–52)

1	24.42	**6**	0.9 = 0.90
2	1 798	**7**	864.03 > 863.40
3	5.42	**8**	9.603 < 9.630
4	3.167	**9**	4.011 < 4.110
5	10.10	**10**	0.759 > 0.75
11	*0.41*	**12**	5.118
13	61.053	**14**	100.720
15	4.184	**16**	9.183
17	0.912	**18**	85.127

19

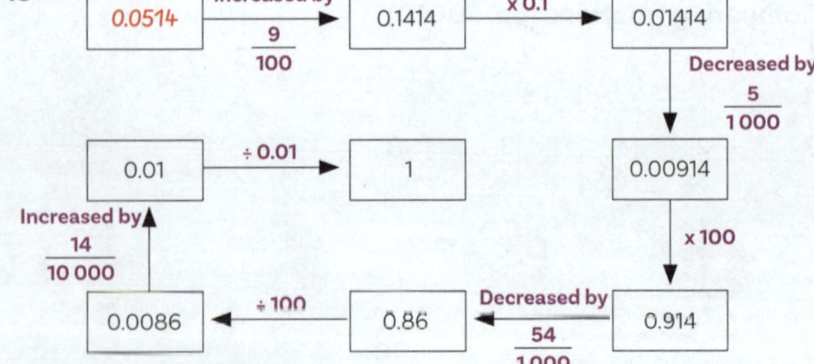

20 7.007, 7.077, 7.707, 7.770
21 0.011, 0.101, 0.110, 0.111
22 4.043, 4.304, 4.340, 4.403

ISBN: 9780170497978

23 0.889, 0.898, 0.989, 0.998
24 0.050, 0.055, 0.505, 0.550

Recurring decimals (p. 53)

1 0.77777…
2 0.23232323…
3 0.718718718…
4 0.64326432…
5 $0.\dot{1}\dot{9}$
6 $0.\dot{1}4\dot{3}$
7 $0.0\dot{9}6\dot{7}$
8 $0.00\dot{8}$
9 $0.\dot{3}$
10 $0.\dot{1}\dot{8}$
11 $0.\dot{7}0\dot{3}$
12 $1.4\dot{6}$
13 $0.\dot{4}\dot{5}$
14 $7.\dot{3}\dot{6}$

Using decimals to compare fractions (p. 54)

1 $0.\dot{3}$ = 0.3333… / 0.34 $\frac{1}{3}$ < $\frac{17}{50}$

2 0.25 / $0.\dot{2}\dot{7}$ $\frac{1}{4}$ < $\frac{3}{11}$

3 0.5714 / $0.\dot{5}$ $\frac{4}{7}$ > $\frac{5}{9}$

4 $0.4\dot{6}$ / $0.\dot{4}\dot{5}$ $\frac{7}{15}$ > $\frac{5}{11}$

5 $0.8\dot{3}$ / $0.\dot{8}\dot{1}$ $\frac{5}{6}$ > $\frac{9}{11}$

6 0.1428 / 0.1875 $\frac{1}{7}$ < $\frac{3}{16}$

7 $0.1\dot{3}$ / 0.125 $\frac{2}{15}$ > $\frac{1}{8}$

8 $0.\dot{7}\dot{2}$ / $0.\dot{7}$ $\frac{8}{11}$ < $\frac{7}{9}$

9 $0.\dot{1}$ / 0.1176 $\frac{1}{9}$ < $\frac{2}{17}$

10 $2.\dot{3}$ / 2.2857 $\frac{21}{9}$ > $\frac{16}{7}$

11 $1.\dot{4}$ / 1.428 $1\frac{4}{9}$ > $1\frac{3}{7}$

12 $0.\dot{6}\dot{3}$ / $0.\dot{6}2\dot{9}$ $\frac{7}{11}$ > $\frac{17}{27}$

Percentages (pp. 55–66)

1 Percentage green 67%
Percentage white 33%
2 Percentage purple 25%
Percentage white 75%
3 Percentage red 8%
Percentage white 92%
4 Percentage blue 15%
Percentage yellow 21%
Percentage white 64%
5 87%
6 31%

Converting between decimals and percentages (pp. 56)

1 85%
2 13%
3 4%
4 84.5%
5 90%
6 2.7%
7 700%
8 130%
9 0.36
10 0.08
11 0.98
12 1.2
13 0.4
14 0.003
15 1.02
16 0.9999
17 2
18 0.0001

Converting between fractions and percentages (pp. 57–58)

	Fraction	Fraction out of 100	Percentage
1	$\frac{7}{10}$	$\frac{70}{100}$	70%
2	$\frac{3}{4}$	$\frac{75}{100}$	75%
3	$\frac{2}{5}$	$\frac{40}{100}$	40%
4	$\frac{60}{400}$	$\frac{15}{100}$	15%
5	$\frac{4}{25}$	$\frac{16}{100}$	16%
6	$\frac{17}{25}$	$\frac{85}{100}$	85%
7	$\frac{3}{50}$	$\frac{6}{100}$	6%
8	$\frac{6}{5}$	$\frac{120}{100}$	120%

9

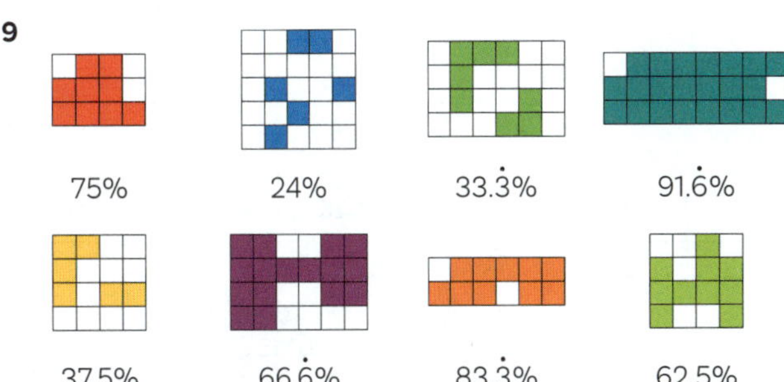

Converting between fraction, decimals and percentages (p. 58)

	Fraction	Fraction out of 100	Decimal	Percentage
1	$\frac{1}{4}$	$\frac{25}{100}$	0.25	25%
2	$\frac{7}{100}$	$\frac{7}{100}$	0.07	7%
3	$\frac{3}{5}$	$\frac{60}{100}$	0.6	60%
4	$\frac{2}{3}$	$\frac{66.\dot{6}}{100}$	$0.\dot{6}$	$66.\dot{6}$%
5	$\frac{19}{20}$	$\frac{95}{100}$	0.95	95%
6	$\frac{7}{8}$	$\frac{87.5}{100}$	0.875	87.5%
7	$\frac{9}{50}$	$\frac{18}{100}$	0.18	18%
8	$1\frac{1}{10}$	$\frac{110}{100}$	1.10	110%

ISBN: 9780170497978

Challenges (p. 59)

1

42%	$\frac{2}{5}$	0.45	~~39%~~	$\frac{5}{8}$	50%	$\frac{7}{20}$	0.36
0.42	0.4	0.45	*0.39*	0.625	0.5	0.35	0.36

Smallest → Largest

$\frac{7}{20}$	0.36	*39%*	$\frac{2}{5}$	42%	0.45	50%	$\frac{5}{8}$

2

82%	0.89	$\frac{16}{20}$	84.5%	$\frac{8}{9}$	0.81	$\frac{7}{8}$	85%
0.82	0.89	0.8	0.845	$0.\dot{8}$	0.81	0.875	0.85

Smallest → Largest

$\frac{16}{20}$	0.81	82%	84.5%	85%	$\frac{7}{8}$	$\frac{8}{9}$	0.89

3

$\frac{4}{21}$	0.102	12%	$\frac{27}{200}$	0.21	$\frac{19}{110}$	0.151	11.2%
0.190	0.102	0.12	0.135	0.21	$0.1\dot{7}\dot{2}$	0.151	0.112

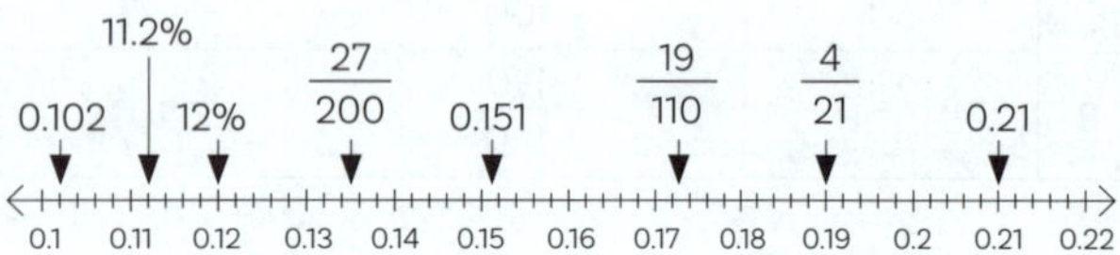

4

1.01	$\frac{27}{25}$	107%	$1\frac{1}{25}$	102.8%	1.10	$\frac{21}{20}$	1.065
1.01	1.08	1.07	1.04	1.028	1.10	1.05	1.065

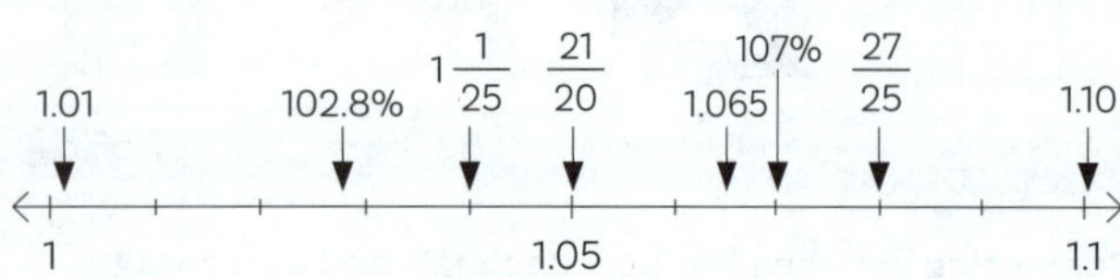

Calculating percentages (p. 60)

1	80%	**2**	60%
3	25%	**4**	75.5%
5	7.5%	**6**	12.5%
7	$66.\dot{6}\%$	**8**	87.5%
9	94%	**10**	$4.1\dot{6}\%$
11	20%		

Finding percentages of amounts (pp. 61–62)

1	9.4	**2**	9
3	30	**4**	4.4
5	210	**6**	0.08
7	480	**8**	1250
9	129	**10**	208
11	29.04	**12**	1331
13	139.2	**14**	60.5
15	252	**16**	9500
17	90 mL	**18**	9000 books
19	270 toys	**20**	28 kg
21	**a** $17	**b**	$68
22	**a** $17.50	**b**	$32.50

Increasing by a percentage (p. 63)

1	150	**2**	56
3	322	**4**	529 g
5	67.6 km	**6**	62.7 kg
7	44.157	**8**	99.84
9	12 960	**10**	$2.73
11	$5175	**12**	$6608

Decreasing by a percentage (p. 64)

1	52	**2**	66
3	144 g	**4**	$527
5	54.6 km	**6**	29.4 kg
7	$82.25	**8**	118.08 cm
9	$29 760		
10	**a** $34.70	**b**	$63.00
11	$1275.00		

Given a percentage, find the whole amount (pp. 65–66)

1

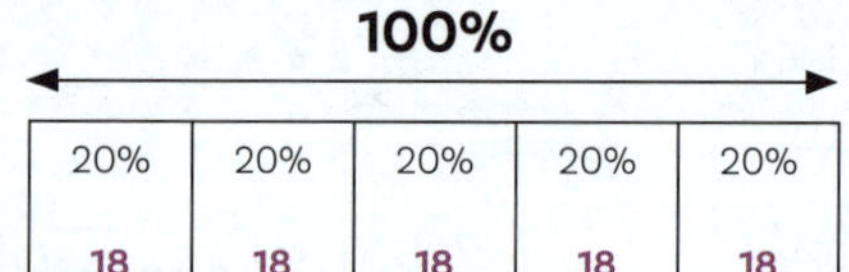

Original amount is 90

2

100%

10%	10%	10%	10%	10%	10%	10%	10%	10%	10%
13	13	13	13	13	13	13	13	13	13

Original amount is 130

3

100%

25%	25%	25%	25%
32	32	32	32

Original amount is 128

4 Original amount is 120

5	200	**6**	37.5
7	160	**8**	80
9	525	**10**	400
11	7500	**12**	13 600
13	30	**14**	$90
15	2750	**16**	20

Rounding (pp. 67–74)

Rounding to whole numbers (pp. 67–68)

1	20	**2**	2130
3	20190	**4**	14
5	300	**6**	76 500
7	23 514 300	**8**	4 142 000
9	199 000	**10**	47 000
11	1000	**12**	100 000
13	1 000 000	**14**	592 000 000
15	2 317 000 000	**16**	790 000 000

17 **a** The nearest ten
b 29 400
c The nearest thousand
d 10 597 (not 10 596.9 – you cannot sell 0.9 of a pie!)
e Need 10 600 pies, so 530 boxes

ISBN: 9780170497978

Rounding decimals (p. 69)

	0 dp	1 dp	2 dp
4.2564	4	4.3	4.26
23.8888	24	23.9	23.89
7.6019	8	7.6	7.60
0.28364	0	0.3	0.28
9.0951	9	9.1	9.10
0.0647	0	0.1	0.06

Significant figures (p. 70)

1 288 **2** 280
3 2880 **4** 2.08
5 280.0 **6** 2.800
7 4 **8** 3
9 2 **10** 7
11 5 **12** 3
13 2 **14** 3
15 1 **16** 5
17 4 **18** 3
19 2 **20** 5

Rounding to significant figures (pp. 71–72)

1 500 **2** 1000
3 10 **4** 0.1
5 2900 **6** 19 000
7 0.21 **8** 7 300 000
9 284 000 **10** 194 000
11 2.02 **12** 0.0189
13 9.003 **14** 946 200 000
15 0.02076 **16** 8.001
17 False
7 could mean 7.0, but if it had been rounded to 0 dp or 1 sf, it could also mean anything between 6.5 and $7.4\dot{9}$. And 7.0, if it had been rounded to 1 dp or 2 sf, could mean anything between 6.95 and $7.04\dot{9}$. This is a much narrower band of values.

18

	Reported	Lowest number	Highest number
Ferris wheel	6600	6550	6649
Rollercoaster	13 000	12 500	13 499
Carousel	8100	8050	8149
Bumper cars	16 000	15 500	16 499

Appropriate rounding (p. 73)

1

	Little or no rounding	Rounding okay	Reason
Dose of a medicine	✓		Too little or too much might endanger patient.
Buying wood for making a deck		✓	Need to round because lengths supplied and lengths used will vary.
Savings goal for a new bike		✓	An approximate goal is okay because models and prices change.
Time allowed for sitting an NCEA examination	✓		To be fair, every student should have the same length of time.
Time needed to drive to a holiday destination		✓	Exact times can't be predicted because of variable road and traffic conditions, etc.
Strength of steel needed for a bridge	✓		If the steel is not strong enough, the bridge might collapse.

2

	Appropriately rounded or not? (✓ or ×)	If not, a more appropriate figure or expression
I have saved five thousand three hundred and nineteen dollars and 42 cents.	×	About \$5300 or \$5000
I am 156.3 cm tall.	×	156 cm tall
A car tyre pressure should be 28 psi.	✓	
Canterbury godwits migrate 10 875 km.	×	About 11 000 km
In New Zealand, 90% of the 96 species of seabird are threatened with extinction. So 86.4 species are threatened.	×	86 species

Estimations/approximations (p. 74)

1 18 **2** 12
3 16 **4** 5
5 37 **6** 19
7 600 **8** 480
9 3 **10** 32
11 \$85 **12** \$30

Scientific notation (pp. 75–79)

Powers of 10 (pp. 75–76)

1 4.56 **2** 5 130 000
3 92.6 **4** 0.00763
5 1.2493 **6** 0.0006
7 34 000 **8** 100 000

Converting numbers from scientific notation to ordinary form (p. 76)

1 130 **2** 85
3 60 000 **4** 2.47
5 28 000 **6** 1267.5
7 133 000 **8** 3.71
9 86 823 **10** 40 020.1
11 5 500 000 **12** 7620.7
13 80 000 **14** 1 110 000

Converting numbers from ordinary form to scientific notation (pp. 77–78)

1 8.1×10^3 **2** 1.235×10^1
3 5.5×10^4 **4** 1.6930×10^2
5 4.6×10^4 **6** 8.9×10^1
7 1.642×10^2 **8** 7×10^0
9 8.99×10^5 **10** 3.5×10^0
11 1.541×10^7 **12** 9.045×10^1
13 3.6×10^4 **14** 9000
15 24 999 **16** 1.7×10^3
17 5.2×10^6 **18** 0.01×10^0
19 8.19×10^4 **20** 4.5×10^2
21 1.25×10^8 **22** 0.8

23

2.45×10^5	5.42×10^1	4.25×10^3	5.24×10^2	2.54×10^4	4.52×10^0
245 000	54.2	4250	524	25 400	4.52

Smallest Biggest

4.52×10^0	5.42×10^1	5.24×10^2	4.25×10^3	2.54×10^4	2.45×10^5

24

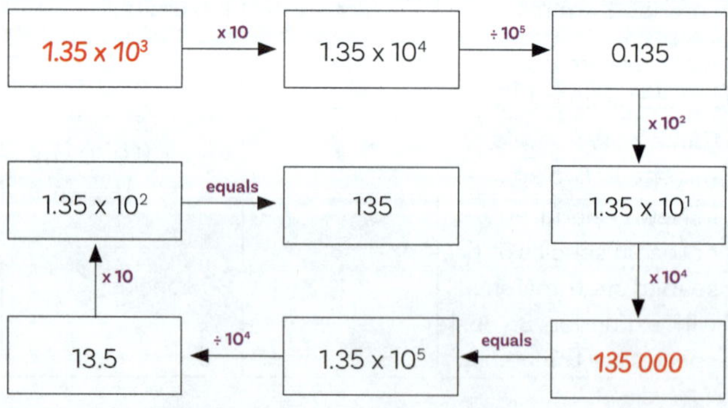

Scientific notation on your calculator (p. 79)

1 3860 **2** 205 900
3 130.2 **4** 0.3364
5 130.8 **6** 99 370
7 475 800 **8** 107.4
9 20 740 **10** 24 780

11

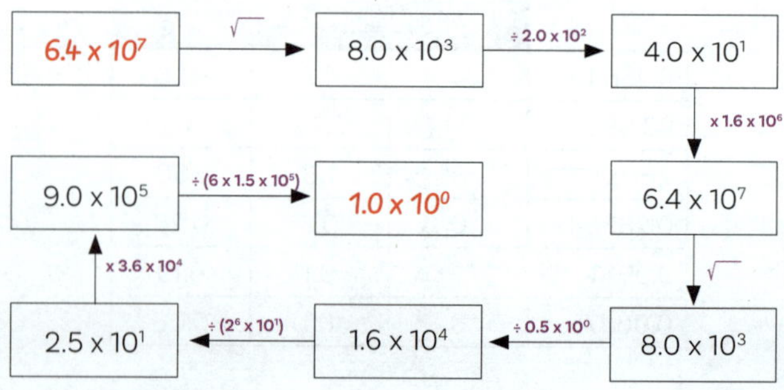

Rates (pp. 80–81)

1 \$40.50 **2** \$9.95
3 10 minutes
4 Sunny Rice costs \$2.50 per kg.
Budget Rice costs \$2.80 per kg.
So Sunny Rice is cheaper per kg.
5 500 g bag costs \$6.98 per kg.
1.5 kg bag costs \$5.99 per kg.
3 kg bag costs \$5.50 per kg.
So the 3 kg bag is cheapest per kg.
6 The cost of a single ticket purchase for the week is
2 x 2.70 x 5 = \$27.00
The weekly bus pass is only \$15.50 for the week.
So the weekly pass is cheaper.
7 15 hours **8** 4.5 km

Ratios (pp. 82–84)

Simplifying ratios (p. 82)

1 3:2 **2** 2:5
3 4:13 **4** 2:3
5 40:3 **6** 1:28
7 1:40 **8** 36:3
9 4:1 **10** 5:9
11 3:40 **12** 1:240

Using ratios where the total is given (pp. 83–84)

1 \$36:\$54 **2** \$25:\$35
3 680 g:170 g **4** 75 mL:375 mL
5 450 m:150 m **6** \$4.50:\$11.25
7 6 cups of sugar and 18 cups of flour
8 420 students
9 \$33:\$22 **10** 38 400 own electric cars
11 80 **12** 1:10
13 70 000 kg or 70 tonnes

Financial mathematics (pp. 85–88)

Calculations with money (p. 85)

Total price (digital price)	Swedish rounding (paying by cash)	Cheaper with cash or digital payment?
\$97.18	\$97.20	Digital
\$26.31	\$26.30	Cash
\$5.49	\$5.50	Digital
\$2359.96	\$2360.00	Digital
\$990.81	\$990.80	Cash
\$37.54	\$37.50	Cash

ISBN: 9780170497978

GST (p. 86)

1 \$105.80 2 \$28.18 3 \$11.44
4 \$118.82 5 \$3625.94 6 \$105.51
7 \$0.41 8 \$64.29 9 \$828.00
10 a \$78.13 b \$599.00
11 a \$0.78 b \$6.00
12 a \$825 b \$6325

Interest (p. 87)

Value of loan	Rate of interest	Interest per year	Number of years	Total to be paid back
\$2000	4%	\$80	3	\$2000 + (\$80 x 3) = \$2240
\$500	3%	\$15	5	\$500 + (\$15 x 5) = \$575
\$14 000	6.5%	\$910	4	\$14 000 + (\$910 x 4) = \$17 640
\$158 000	8.2%	\$12 956	6	\$158 000 + (\$12 956 x 6) = \$235 736

Profit and loss (p. 88)

1

Buying price	Selling price	Profit	Loss	%
\$90	\$108	\$18	–	20%
\$16	\$12	–	\$4	25%
\$225	\$270	\$45	–	20%
\$1280	\$768	–	\$512	40%
\$150	\$145.50	–	\$4.50	3%
\$50	\$115	65	–	130%

2 a \$225 b 15%
3 a \$180 b \$3720
c \$720 d 38%

ALGEBRA (pp. 89–169)

The language of algebra (pp. 89–91)

Phrases to expressions (pp. 89–90)

1 $7b$ 2 b^3
3 $\frac{7}{b}$ 4 $7 - b$
5 $\sqrt{b}$ 6 $b - 7$
7 $\frac{b}{7}$ 8 $7 + b$
9 $\sqrt[3]{b}$ 10 b^7
11 $\frac{y}{2}$ or $y \div 2$ 12 y^2
13 $y - 4$ 14 $\sqrt[3]{y}$
15 $2y$ 16 $\frac{8}{y}$
17 The square root of p
18 p divided by 5 or a fifth of p
19 p to the fourth or p to the power of 4
20 Triple p, treble p or three p

More about variables (p. 91)

1 a The variable is p and it stands for the number of papers Kahu delivered.
b Total = $0.08p$
= 0.08×240
= \$19.20
2 a The variable is c and it stands for the total number of cactus plants that Angus buys.
b Total = $c + 13$
= $8 + 13$
= 21 cacti
3 a The variable is d and it stands for the distance along the side of the paddock.
b 121 posts

Simplifying expressions (pp. 92–96)

Multiplying (p. 92)

1 p^3 2 $5w$
3 $6d$ 4 $8cd$
5 $12m^2$ 6 $15abc$
7 $7n$ 8 $20ab$
9 y^2 10 $9hj$
11 bfp 12 $-5y$

Dividing (p. 93)

1 $\frac{m}{3}$ 2 $\frac{7}{c}$
3 $\frac{a}{3}$ 4 $\frac{5}{y}$
5 $\frac{p}{2}$ 6 $\frac{3d}{e}$
7 $\frac{3}{z}$ 8 $\frac{5bc}{e}$
9 $5h$ 10 $\frac{1}{4c}$

Like terms (p. 94)

1 unlike 2 like
3 like 4 unlike
5 unlike 6 like
7 like 8 like
9 like 10 like
11 unlike 12 unlike
13

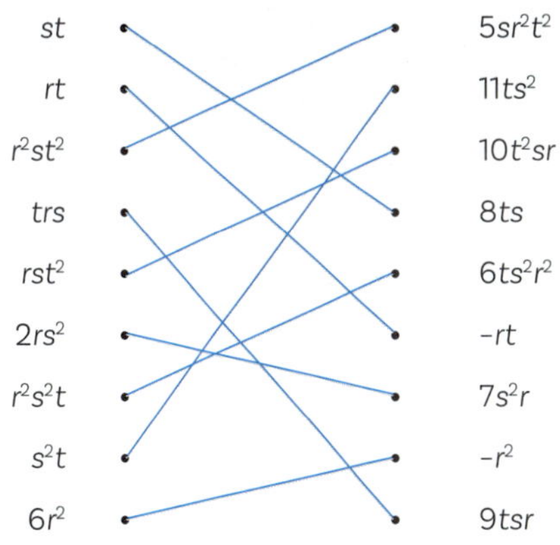

st	$5sr^2t^2$
rt	$11ts^2$
r^2st^2	$10t^2sr$
trs	$8ts$
rst^2	$6ts^2r^2$
$2rs^2$	$-rt$
r^2s^2t	$7s^2r$
s^2t	$-r^2$
$6r^2$	$9tsr$

Adding and subtracting (p. 95)

1 $5p$ 2 $7a$
3 $-f$ 4 5
5 $3b$ 6 $8c$
7 $6e^2 - 4f$ 8 $5y^2 - 7y$
9 $2x^2 - 7$ 10 $2p^2 - 6p + 1$
11 $6a + b$ 12 $14 - c$
13 $9d + 4e$ 14 $10f + g - 5$

15 $-j + 4k + 4$ 16 $6m - n - 9$
17 $2p + 3q$ 18 $2a + 6ab - 2b$
19 $c - 4d$ 20 $g^2 - 2gh$
21 $4y^2 + 5 - 2y - xy^2$ 22 $c^2 - d^2 - 4$

Mixing it up (p. 96)

1 $\frac{2}{a}$ 2 $a + b$
3 $3a^2 - 2a$ 4 $10ab$
5

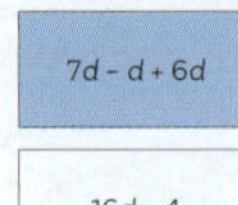

$7d - d + 6d$	$\frac{24d}{2}$	$2d \times 6d$	$\frac{48}{4}d$
$16d - 4$	**$12d$**		$13d^2 - d$
$3 \times 4d$			$d \times 12$
$\frac{24}{2d}$	$12 + d$	$36d \div 3$	$d + 10d - p + p$

6 $5h$ 7 $p + 4q$
8 $\frac{3}{a}$ 9 $-5f + g$
10 $27c^2$ 11 $\frac{1}{6}$
12 4 13 $3m^2$
14 $2ab - a + 5a^2 - b$ 15 $w - 3w^2$
16 $4p^3 + p^2$

Powers (pp. 97–101)

Multiplying powers (p. 97)

1 e^4 2 g^7
3 $5h^4$ 4 $6p^5$
5 z^2 6 n^8
7 a^8 8 b^7
9 $3c^6$ 10 $21g^5$
11 $18cd^7$ 12 $12r^3s^9$

Dividing powers (pp. 98–99)

1 y^3 2 z^2
3 $\frac{1}{a^6}$ 4 $g^3 \div 3$
5 $6a^6$ 6 $\frac{m}{2n}$
7 $\frac{c^6}{d^5}$ 8 $\frac{3b^4}{a^6}$
9

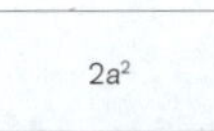
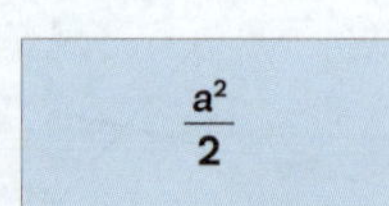
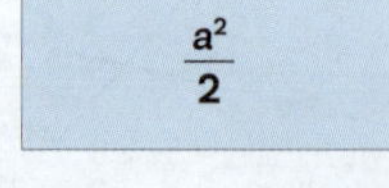

$2a^2$	$2a^6 \div 4a^4$	$14a^3b^5 \div 7ab^5$	$\frac{1}{2}a^2$
$\frac{6a^8}{12a^6}$	**$\frac{a^2}{2}$**		$2a^2 \div 4a^4$
$2a^4bc^2 \div 4a^2bc^2$			$\frac{2a^2}{4}$
$4a^{[illegible]} \div 2a^{[illegible]}$	$\frac{12a^5b}{24a^3b}$	$6a^7b^2 \div 12a^5b^2$	$\frac{24a^{10}b}{12a^8b}$

10 $\frac{1}{z^3}$ 11 $\frac{p^4}{6}$
12 $3e^2$ 13 $\frac{4}{y}$
14 n 15 $\frac{a}{b^2}$

16 s^2t 17 $\frac{x}{y^2}$
18 $\frac{d^4}{4c}$ 19 $2p^4q$
20 $y = \frac{\mathbf{y}}{1} = \frac{\mathbf{6y}}{6} = \frac{3y}{\mathbf{3}} = \frac{\mathbf{y^4}}{y^3} = \frac{5y^2}{\mathbf{5y}}$
21 $\frac{3}{z} = \frac{3z}{\mathbf{z^2}} = \frac{\mathbf{6}}{2z} = \frac{3z^2}{\mathbf{z^3}} = \frac{15z^4}{\mathbf{5z^5}}$
22 $\frac{s}{r^2} = \frac{2s}{\mathbf{2r^2}} = \frac{\mathbf{r^2s}}{r^4} = \frac{3s^2}{\mathbf{3r^2s}} = \frac{5r^2s}{\mathbf{5r^4}}$

Powers of powers (p. 100)

1 x^{12} 2 $16c^6$
3 $125d^{12}$ 4 $49y^{12}z^2$
5 $8g^{12}h^{15}$ 6 $54a^{15}b^{18}$
7 p^{14} 8 s^{18}
9 $36b^{10}$ 10 $64x^{15}$
11 g^2h^8 12 $9b^8c^{10}$
13 $50m^{12}n^{20}$ 14 $1250d^{12}e^3$

Mixing it up (p. 101)

1 $\frac{5a^6}{a^2} = 5a^4$ $(2a^2b)^3 = 8a^6b^2$ $\frac{6a^6b^3}{2a^2} = 3a^3b^4$ $3a \times a^4 = 3a^5$
$\frac{3(2a^2b)^2}{4ab} = 3a^3b$ $8(a^3b)^2 = 8a^6b^3$ $a^2b^3 \times 3ab = 3a^4b^3$ $\frac{15a^4b}{3ab} = 5a^3$

2 $2c^5$ 3 $3m^{11}$
4 p^{12} 5 e^6
6 $\frac{1}{d^4}$ 7 $9y^{10}$
8 $15n^5$ 9 $128p^{15}$
10 $\frac{1}{2z^3}$ 11 $\frac{5}{y^4}$

		Explanation	Correct answer
12	$6f^3 \times 2f^4 = 12f^{12}$	Multiplied the powers instead of adding them.	$12f^7$
13	$18e^{12} \div 6e^3 = 3e^4$	Divided the powers instead of subtracting them.	$3e^9$
14	$(2c^2)^3 = 8c^8$	Cubed the first power (2) instead of multiplying it by 3.	$8c^6$
15	$2(3d^5)^2 = 36d^{10}$	Multiplied 2 by 3 before squaring. Should do 3^2 before multiplying by 2.	$18d^{10}$

Brackets (pp.102–105)

Expanding (pp. 102–103)

1 5 2 14
3 w 4 8
5 20 6 27
7 16 8 15
9 21 10 z
11 5 12 70
13 $4x + 4y$ 14 $5x + 10$
15 $3y - 12$ 16 $14x + 35$
17 $-6x - 24$ 18 $-2y + 16$
19 $4x^2 - 9x$ 20 $-2xy + xz$
21 $10z - 20$ 22 $p^2 - 4p$
23 $-18 + 6g$ 24 $-bc - 4b$

ISBN: 9780170497978

25	$10r + 5s$	**26**	$7x - 14 + 7z$
27	$-2u^2 + 6u$	**28**	$12fg - 6f$
29	$-4a + 8b$	**30**	$-6 + 14p$
31	$-x + 2x^2$	**32**	$2m^3 - 5m^2$
33	$-7y + 4$	**34**	$-10a + 30a^3$

Factorising (pp. 104–105)

1	1, **3**	**2**	1, 2, **4**
3	1, **2**	**4**	1, 2, 3, 4, **6**
5	**1**	**6**	1, **3**
7	1, 2, 4, **8**	**8**	**1**
9	1, g	**10**	1, s
11	1, 1e, 2, 2e, 5, 5e, 10, 10e	**12**	1, 1c, 3, 3c
13	4	**14**	3
15	3	**16**	5
17	x	**18**	2
19	4	**20**	2
21	8	**22**	12
23	5	**24**	10
25	$4x + 3$	**26**	$x - 3$
27	$3 - 2x$	**28**	$x - 5$
29	$5x + 1$	**30**	$5x - 2$
31	$2x + 5$	**32**	$3 - x$
33	$8(x + y)$	**34**	$7(2x - y)$
35	$6(2x - 1)$	**36**	$x(x - 4)$
37	$y(x + 2)$	**38**	$5(4x^2 - 1)$
39	$8(3 - x)$	**40**	$2x(x + 2)$
41	$-7x(x - 2)$ or $7x(2 - x)$	**42**	$6x(3 - x)$
43	$4x(y - 5x)$	**44**	$-5xy(3 + z)$ or $5xy(-3 - z)$

Straight lines (pp. 106–129)

Coordinates (p. 106)

1 **A** (4, 3) **B** (1, -5)
C (-6, 4) **D** (0, 7)
E (-3, -7) **F** (2, 0)

2

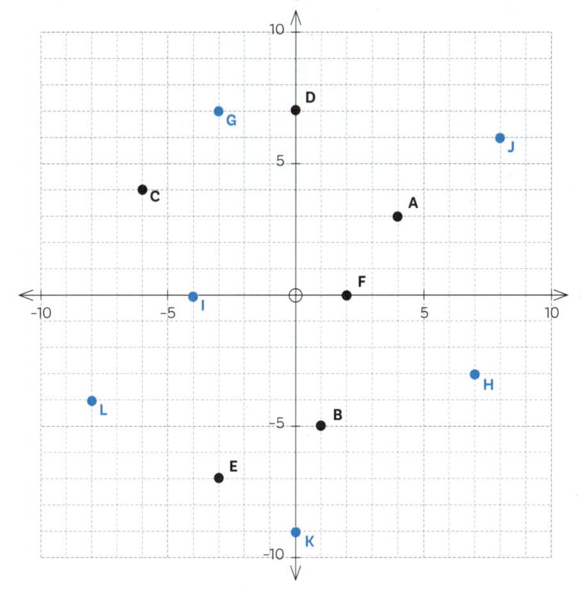

Linear patterns with discrete data (p. 107–111)

1 a

Design number (n)	Number of matchsticks (M)
0	1
1	4
2	7
3	10
4	13
5	16
6	19

Equation: $M = 3n + 1$

b

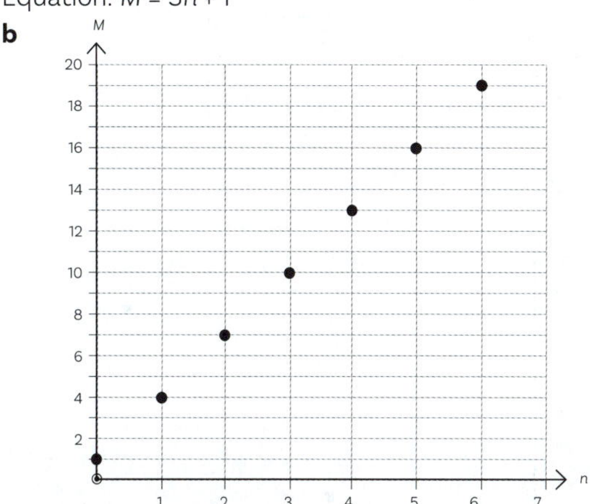

c $M = 3 \times 30 + 1 = 91$
So the 30th design needs 91 matchsticks.

d The 3 represents the number of matchsticks that need to be added for each extra design.
The 1 represents the single matchstick on the left of each design.

2 a

Design number (n)	Number of buttons (B)
0	2
1	6
2	10
3	14
4	18
5	22
6	26

Equation: $B = 4n + 2$

b

c $B = 4 \times 20 + 2 = 82$

ISBN: 9780170497978

So the 20th design needs 82 buttons.

d The 4 represents the number of buttons that need to be added for each extra design.
The 2 represents the two buttons on the left of each design.

3 **a**

Design number (n)	Number of crosses (C)
0	1
1	5
2	9
3	13
4	17
5	21
6	25

Equation: $C = 4n + 1$

b

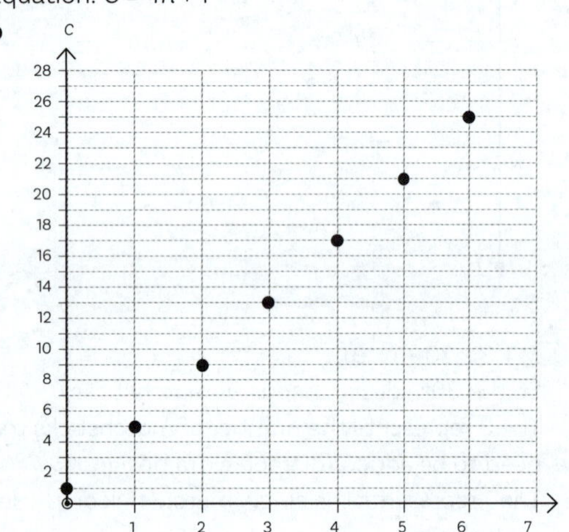

c $C = 4 \times 15 + 1 = 61$
So the 15th design needs 61 crosses.

d The 4 represents the number of crosses that need to be added for each extra design.
The 1 represents the single cross at the centre of each design.

4 **a**

Number of activities (A)	Cost (C)
0	5
1	7
2	9
3	11
4	13
5	15
6	17

Equation: $C = 2A + 5$

b

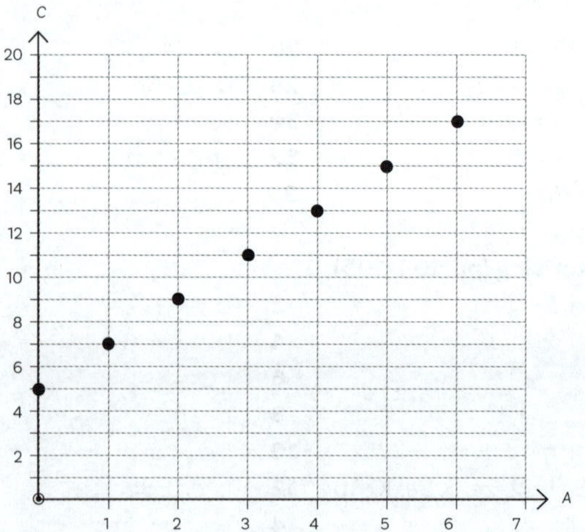

c $C = 2 \times 9 + 5 = 23$
So the total cost if she did nine activities would be $23.

d The 2 represents the cost per activity.
The 5 represents the entry cost to the fair.

The gradient of a line (pp. 112–116)

1 $\frac{3}{4}$

2 $\frac{5}{2}$

3 $-\frac{2}{4}$ or $-\frac{1}{2}$

4 $-\frac{6}{2}$ or $-\frac{3}{1}$ or -3

5 $\frac{6}{5}$

6 $-\frac{1}{4}$

7 $-\frac{8}{2}$ or $-\frac{4}{1}$ or -4

8 $\frac{6}{2}$ or $\frac{4}{4}$ or $\frac{3}{2}$ or $\frac{2}{2}$ or 1

9

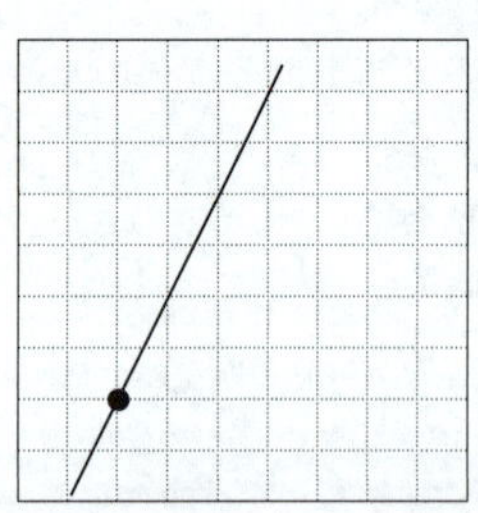

10

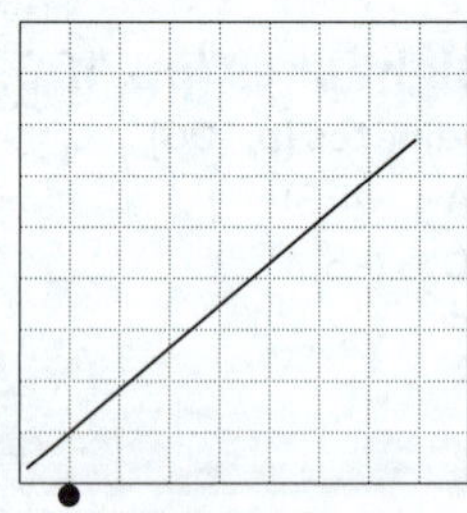

11

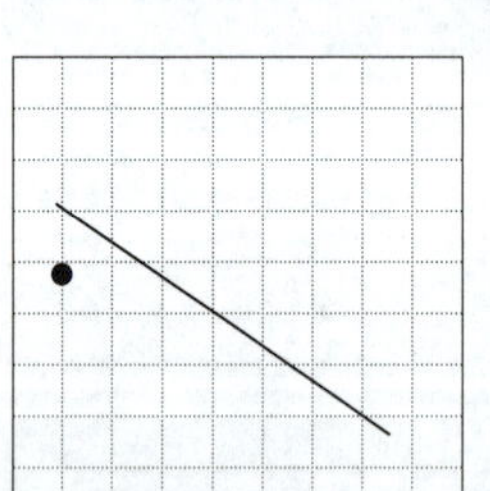

12

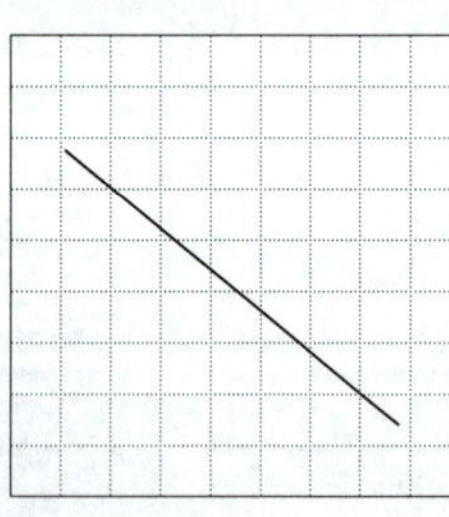

13

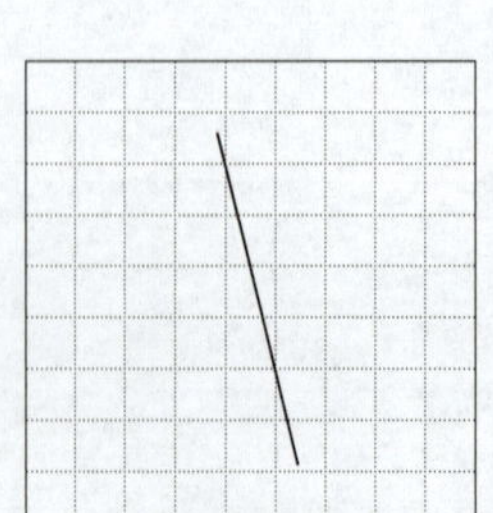

14

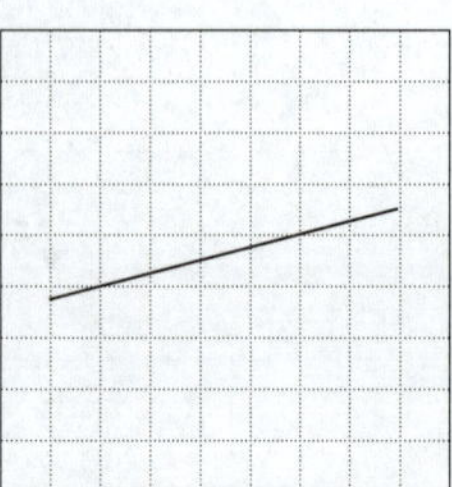

15 $m = \frac{4}{3}$

16 $m = -\frac{1}{3}$

17 $m = \frac{1}{4}$

18 $m = -\frac{3}{5}$

19 $m = -\frac{5}{4}$

20 $m = 2$

ISBN: 9780170497978

Drawing straight lines – continuous data (pp. 117–125)

1

x	$x + 4$	y	Coordinates
0	0 + 4	4	(0, 4)
1	1 + 4	5	(1, 5)
2	2 + 4	6	(2, 6)
3	3 + 4	7	(3, 7)
4	4 + 4	8	(4, 8)

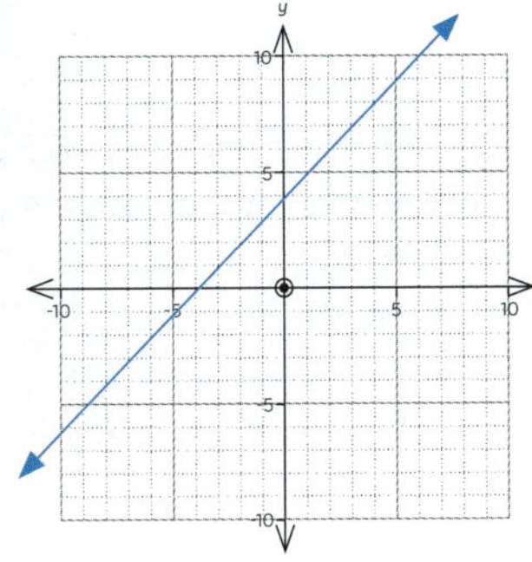

2

x	$3x + 1$	y	Coordinates
0	3(0) + 1	1	(0, 1)
1	3(1) + 1	4	(1, 4)
2	3(2) + 1	7	(2, 7)
3	3(3) + 1	10	(3, 10)
4	3(4) + 1	13	(4, 13)

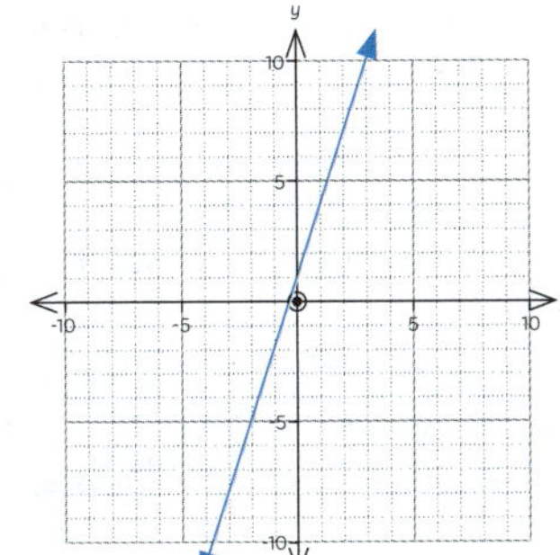

3

x	$\frac{1}{2}x + 3$	y	Coordinates
0	$\frac{1}{2}(0) + 3$	3	(0, 3)
1	$\frac{1}{2}(1) + 3$	$3\frac{1}{2}$	$(1, 3\frac{1}{2})$
2	$\frac{1}{2}(2) + 3$	4	(2, 4)
3	$\frac{1}{2}(3) + 3$	$4\frac{1}{2}$	$(3, 4\frac{1}{2})$
4	$\frac{1}{2}(4) + 3$	5	(4, 5)

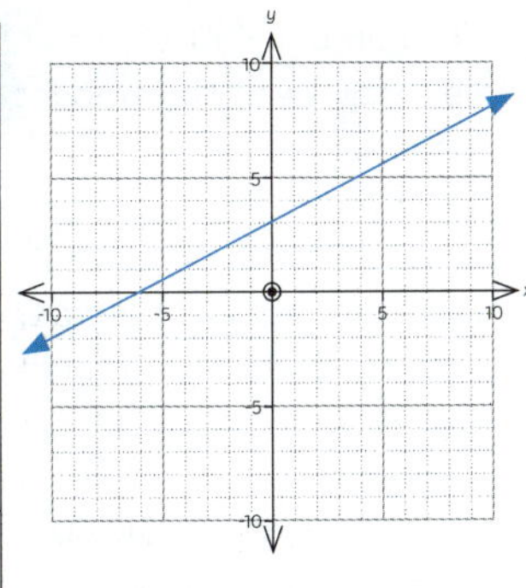

4

x	$-x + 5$	y	Coordinates
0	-0 + 5	5	(0, 5)
1	-1 + 5	4	(1, 4)
2	-2 + 5	3	(2, 3)
3	-3 + 5	2	(3, 2)
4	-4 + 5	1	(4, 1)

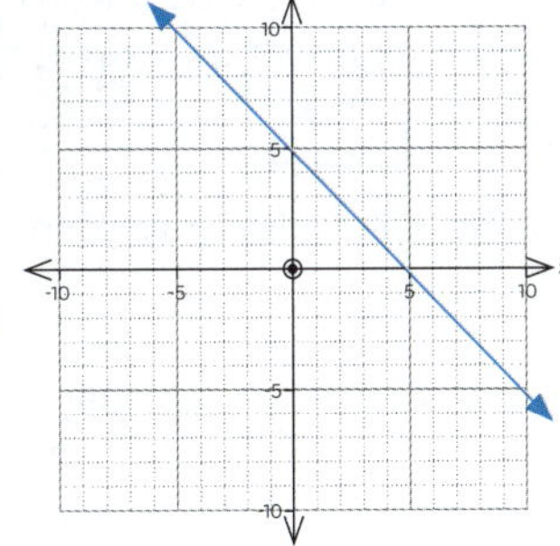

5

x	$2x + 3$	y	Coordinates
0	2(0) + 3	3	(0, 3)
1	2(1) + 3	5	(1, 5)
2	2(2) + 3	7	(2, 7)
3	2(3) + 3	9	(3, 9)
4	2(4) + 3	11	(4, 11)

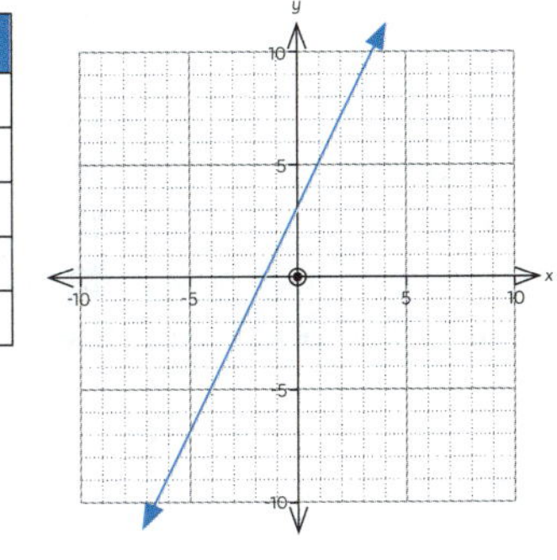

6

x	$-2x - 1$	y	Coordinates
0	-2(0) - 1	-1	(0, -1)
1	-2(1) - 1	-3	(1, -3)
2	-2(2) - 1	-5	(2, -5)
3	-2(3) - 1	-7	(3, -7)
4	-2(4) - 1	-9	(4, -9)

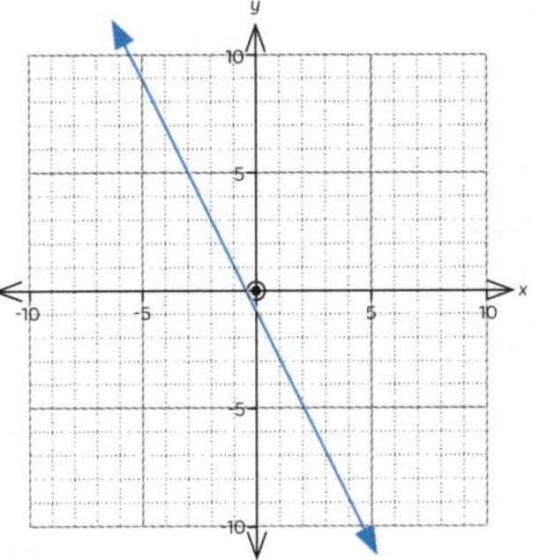

7 $y = -\frac{5}{3}x + 2$

8 $y = \frac{3}{5}x + 2$

9 $y = \frac{5}{3}x - 2$

10 $y = \frac{3}{5}x - 2$

11 $y = -\frac{3}{5}x - 2$

12 $y = -\frac{3}{5}x + 2$

13

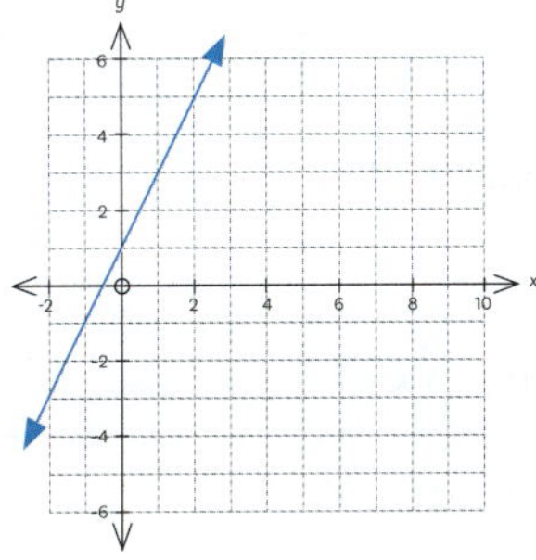

14 $m = -1 \quad c = 3$

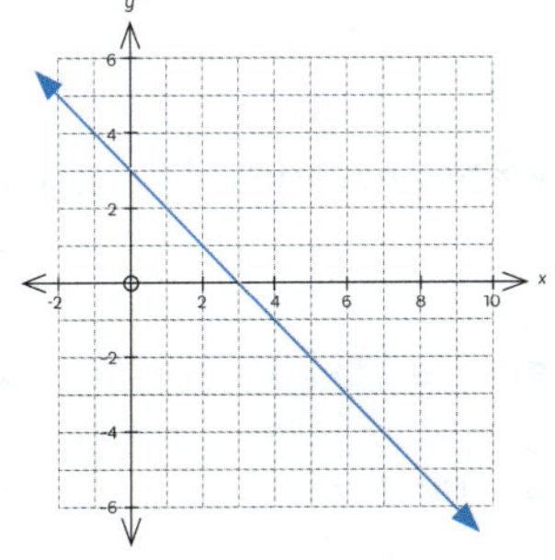

15 $c = -4 \quad m = \frac{1}{2}$

16 $c = 2 \quad m = -\frac{2}{3}$

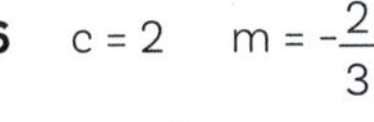

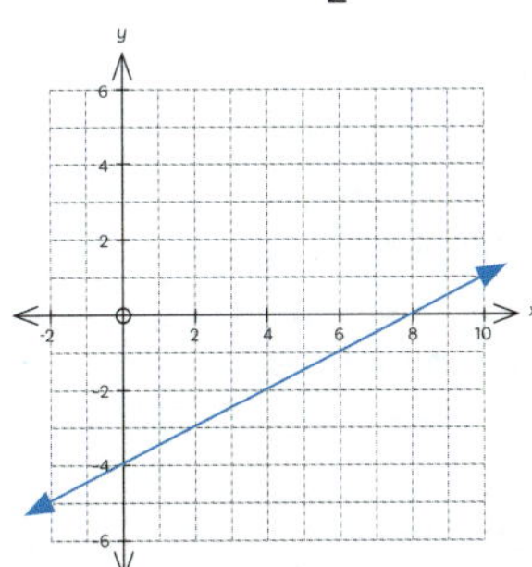

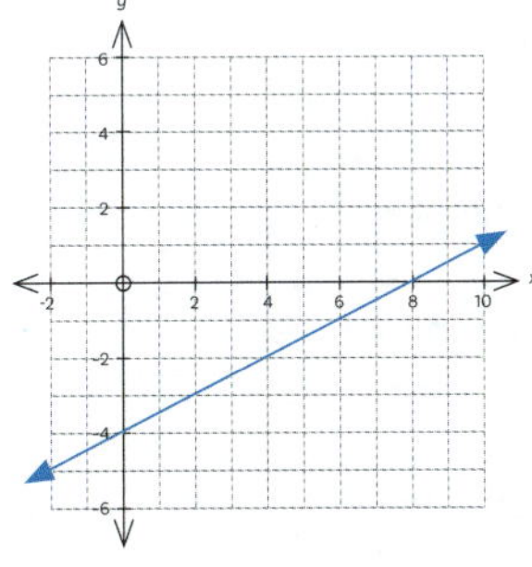

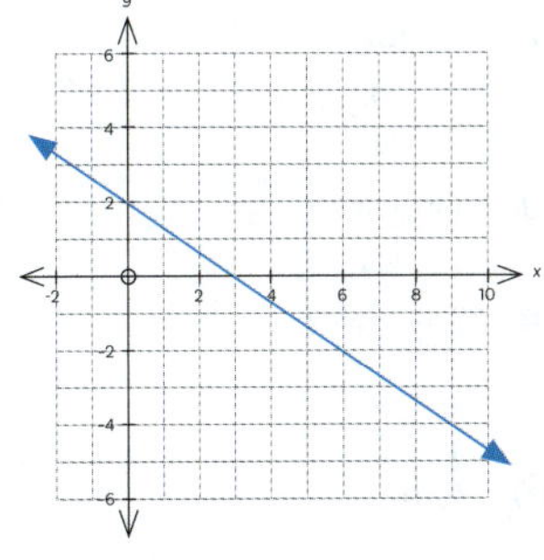

17 $c = -5 \quad m = 3$

18 $c = -\frac{1}{4} \quad m = 0$

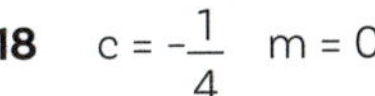

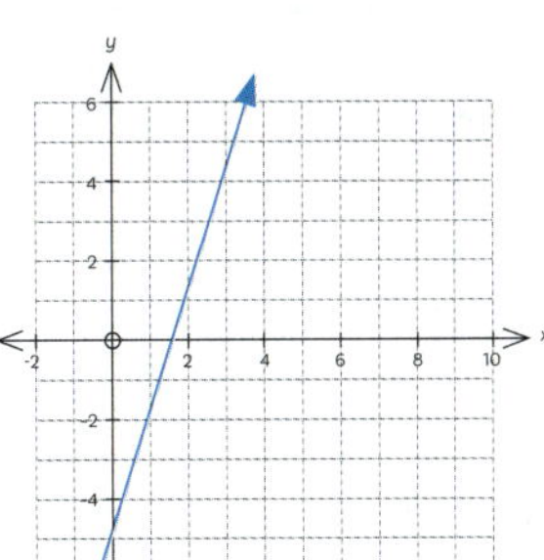

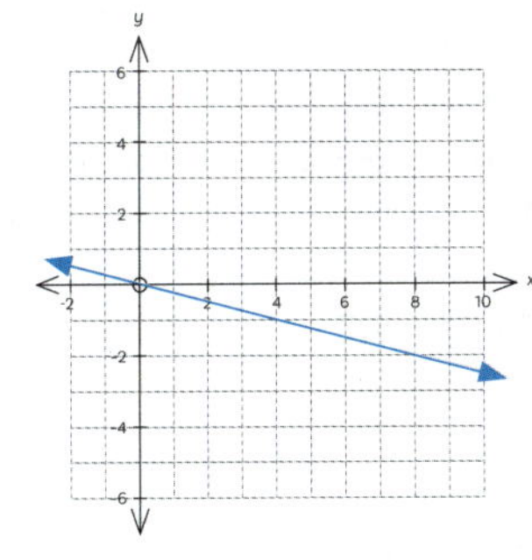

19 $y = 4$

20 $x = 2$

21 $x = -3$

22 $y = 0$

ISBN: 9780170497978

23

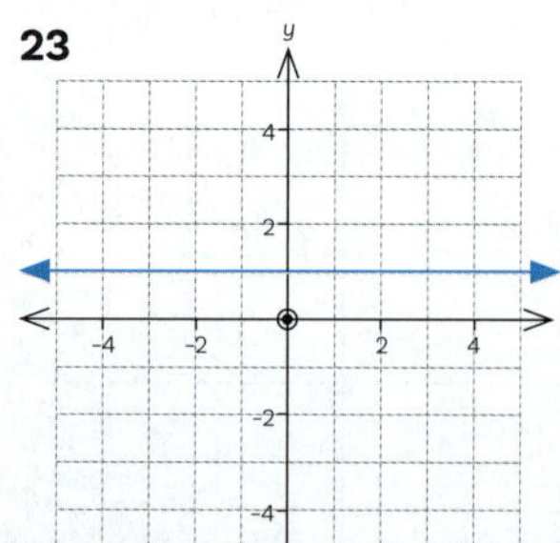

24

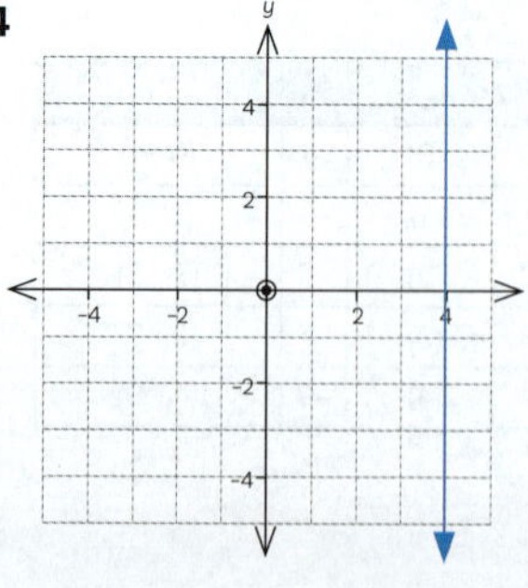

25

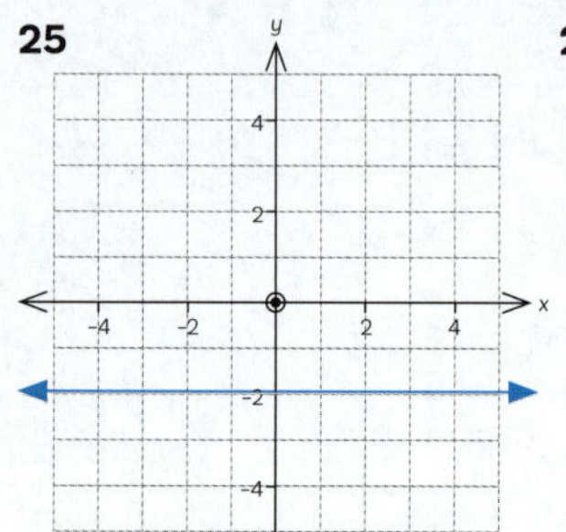

26

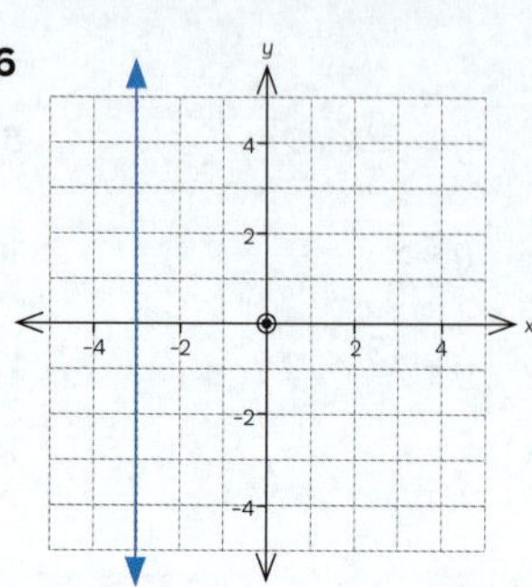

Writing equations from graphs (pp. 126-129)

1 $y = \frac{1}{2}x + 3$ **2** $y = 3x - 5$

3 $y = -\frac{4}{3}x + 2$ **4** $y = -\frac{3}{5}x - 1$

5 Gradient = 1 y intercept = -4
$y = x - 4$

6 Gradient = -2 y intercept = 3
$y = -2x + 3$

7 Gradient = $\frac{3}{4}$ y intercept = -2
$y = \frac{3}{4}x - 2$

8 Gradient = 4 y intercept = 5
$y = 4x - 5$

9 Gradient = $-\frac{3}{2}$ y intercept = 4
$y = -\frac{3}{2}x + 4$

10 Gradient = $\frac{1}{2}$ y intercept = 0
$y = \frac{1}{2}x$

Solving linear equations (pp. 130-144)

One-step equations (pp. 130-132)

1	$y = 1$	**2**	$q = 18$
3	$m = 4$	**4**	$a = 30$
5	$g = 100$	**6**	$h = -5$
7	$s = 52$	**8**	$x = -13.5$
9	$d = 24.5$	**10**	$p = 12.8$
11	$e = 18.2$	**12**	$b = -3$
13	$v = 180$	**14**	$y = 3.75$
15	$p = 2$	**17**	$a = -6.5$
17	$z = 22$	**18**	$b = -14$
19	$d = 0.4$	**20**	$s = 120$
21	$g = -37$	**22**	$m = 23$
23	$e = -19$	**24**	$x = -34$

Forming and solving linear equations (pp. 133-134)

1 Let x represent the length of one side.
$4x = 26$
$x = 6.5$
The length of one side = 6.5 cm.

2 Let x represent the height a year ago.
$x + 1.3 = 7.2$
$x = 5.9$
Height a year ago = 5.9 m.

3 Let x represent the number.
$2x = 19$
$x = 9.5$
The number = 9.5.

4 Let x represent the number.
$x - 10 = 8$
$x = 18$
The number = 18.

5 Let x represent the number.
$x + 2 = 14$
$x = 12$
The number = 12.

6 Let x represent the number.
$\frac{x}{10} = 50$
$x = 500$
The number = 500.

7 Let x represent the amount Ellie earned before her increase.
$x + 1.80 = 19.50$
$x = 17.70$
Ellie earned $17.70 before the increase.

8 Let x represent the amount each student gets.
$8x = 100$
$x = 12.50$
Each student gets $12.50.

9 Let x represent the length of one side of the pentagon.
$5x = 42$
$x = 8.4$
Each side of the pentagon is 8.4 cm long.

10 Let x represent the extra length when the trailer is added.
$5.6 + x = 13.1$
$x = 7.5$ m
The trailer adds 7.5 m to the total length of the two together.

Two-step equations (pp. 135-137)

1	$x = 8$	**2**	$x = 10$
3	$x = 11$	**4**	$x = 6$
5	$x = -6$	**6**	$x = -3.4$
7	$x = 3$	**8**	$x = 16.5$
9	$x = 1$	**10**	$x = 65$
11	$x = 12$	**12**	$x = 6$
13	$x = 84$	**14**	$x = -3$
15	$x = 20$	**16**	$x = -5$
17	$x = -8$	**18**	$x = 24$

19 Let x represent the number.
$5x + 4 = 39$
$x = 7$
The number is 7.

ISBN: 9780170497978

20 Let x represent the number.
$3x - 1 = 11$
$x = 4$
The number is 4.

21 Let x represent the number.
$2x - 11 = 0$
$x = 5.5$
The number is 5.5.

22 Let x represent the number.
$\frac{x}{3} + 4 = 1$
$x = -9.$
The number is −9.

23 Let x represent the number of punnets Jess picked every hour.
$5 + 2x = 19$
$x = 7$
Jess picks 7 punnets an hour.

24 Let x represent the time Freddy spent babysitting.
$8 + 10x = 43$
$x = 3.5$
Freddy babysat for 3.5 hours.

25 Let x represent the length of the unknown sides.
$2x + 2(4.5) = 30$
$x = 10.5$
The unknown sides are 10.5 cm long.

26 Let x represent the length of the unknown sides.
$2x + 18 = 48$
$x = 15$
The unknown sides are 15 cm long.

Equations with variables on both sides (pp. 138–140)

1	$x = 3$	**2**	$x = 2$
3	$x = 4$	**4**	$x = -1$
5	$x = 3$	**6**	$x = -11$
7	$x = 9.5$	**8**	$x = -2$
9	$x = 5$	**10**	$x = -2$
11	$x = 4.2$	**12**	$x = 2$
13	$x = -1$	**14**	$x = -0.375$

15 Let x represent the number.
$2x = 9 - x$
$x = 3$
The number is 3.

16 Let x represent the number.
$3x - 10 = x + 4$
$x = 7$
The number is 7.

17 Let x represent the number.
$\frac{1}{2}x + 5 = x + 1$
$x = 8$
The number is 8.

18 Let x represent the number.
$4x + 7 = 8x + 11$
$x = -1$
The number is −1.

19 Let x represent the length of unknown sides.
$2x + 10 = 6x$
$x = 2.5$
The triangle has sides with lengths 5.5 cm, 2.5 cm and 7 cm.
The sides of the hexagon are 2.5 cm.

Find the errors (p. 141)

	✓ or ×	Correct solution
1	×	$5x - 2 = x - 4$ $4x - 2 = -4$ $4x = -2$ $x = -\frac{1}{2}$
2	×	$7x - 14 = 1 + x$ $6x - 14 = 1$ $6x = 15$ $x = 2.5$
3	✓	
4	✓	
5	×	$2x - 21 = 11x + 33$ $-9x - 21 = 33$ $-9x = 54$ $x = -6$
6	×	$7 - x = 11x - 23$ $7 - 12x = -23$ $12x = -30$ $x = 2.5$

Equations with brackets (pp. 142–143)

1	$x = 2.5$	**2**	$x = 9$
3	$x = 5.5$	**4**	$x = 5$
5	$x = -1$	**6**	$x = -3.5$
7	$x = 0.8$	**8**	$x = 1$
9	$x = -8$	**10**	$x = 19.25$
11	$x = -1$	**12**	$x = 1$
13	$x = 3$	**14**	$x = -2.5$

Mixing it up (p. 144)

Inequations (pp. 145–148)

Inequations with integers (p. 145)

1	$3 < 5$	**2**	$8 > 7$	**3**	$0 < 1$
4	$0 > -1$	**5**	$-5 < -4$	**6**	$3 > -3$

ISBN: 9780170497978

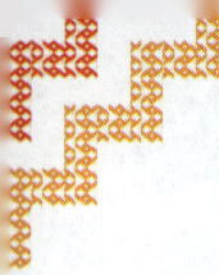

7

Symbols	Possible values of x	Words
x > 2	-6 -5 -4 -3 -2 -1 0 1 2 3 4 5 6	*x is greater than two*
x = 4	-6 -5 -4 -3 -2 -1 0 1 2 3 4 5 6	*x equals four*
x ≤ 3	-6 -5 -4 -3 -2 -1 0 1 2 3 4 5 6	*x is less than or equal to three*
x < 5	-6 -5 -4 -3 -2 -1 0 1 2 3 4 5 6	x is less than 5
x = -1	-6 -5 -4 -3 -2 -1 0 1 2 3 4 5 6	x is equal to -1
x > 5	-6 -5 -4 -3 -2 -1 0 1 2 3 4 5 6	x is greater than 5 or x is greater than or equal to 6
x ≥ 1	-6 -5 -4 -3 -2 -1 0 1 2 3 4 5 6	x is greater than or equal to 1
x < 1 or x ≤ 0	-6 -5 -4 -3 -2 -1 0 1 2 3 4 5 6	x is less than 1 or x is less than or equal to 0
x < -2	-6 -5 -4 -3 -2 -1 0 1 2 3 4 5 6	x is less than -2
x ≥ 3	-6 -5 -4 -3 -2 -1 0 1 2 3 4 5 6	x is greater than or equal to 3
x > -1 or x ≥ 0	-6 -5 -4 -3 -2 -1 0 1 2 3 4 5 6	x is greater than -1 or x is greater than or equal to 0
x ≤ 1	-6 -5 -4 -3 -2 -1 0 1 2 3 4 5 6	x is less than or equal to 1
x ≥ -4	-6 -5 -4 -3 -2 -1 0 1 2 3 4 5 6	x is greater than or equal to -4
x < -3 or x ≤ -4	-6 -5 -4 -3 -2 -1 0 1 2 3 4 5 6	x is less than -3 or x is less than or equal to -4

Inequations on a number line (p. 146)

Symbols	Possible values of x	Words
x < 4	-3 -2 -1 0 1 2 3 4 5	x is less than 4
x > 3.5	-3 -2 -1 0 1 2 3 4 5	x is greater than 3.5
x ≤ 3	-3 -2 -1 0 1 2 3 4 5	x is less than or equal to 3
x ≥ 1	-3 -2 -1 0 1 2 3 4 5	x is greater than or equal to 1
x < -1.5	-3 -2 -1 0 1 2 3 4 5	x is less than -1.5
x > -3	-3 -2 -1 0 1 2 3 4 5	x is greater than -3
x ≤ 0	-3 -2 -1 0 1 2 3 4 5	x is less than or equal to 0

Solving inequations (pp. 147–148)

1 x ≥ 4

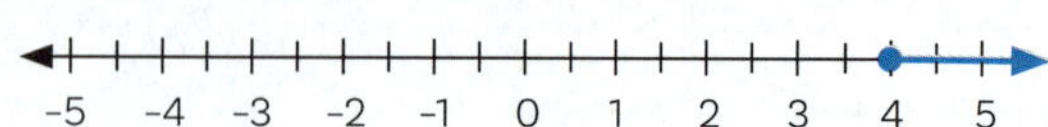

Words: *x* is greater than or equal to 4.

2 x ≤ -2

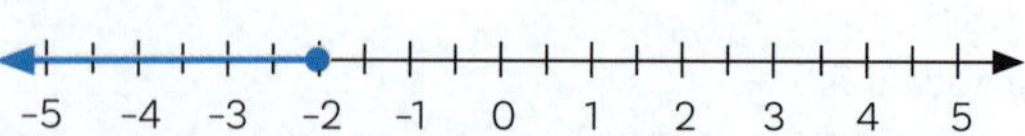

Words: *x* is less than or equal to -2.

3 x > 3

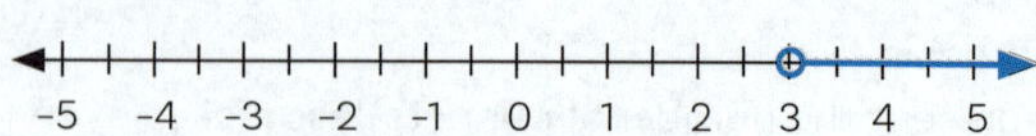

Words: *x* is greater than 3.

4 x < 2

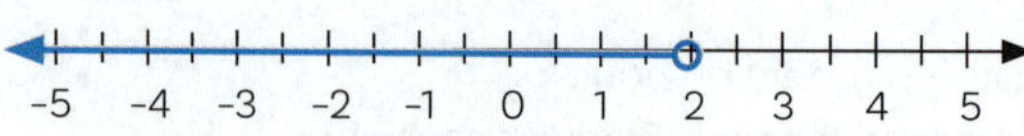

Words: *x* is less than 2.

5 x ≤ -3

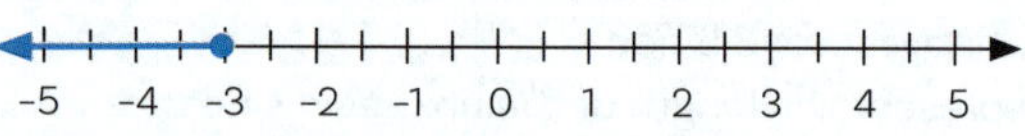

Words: *x* is less than or equal to -3.

6 x ≥ -4

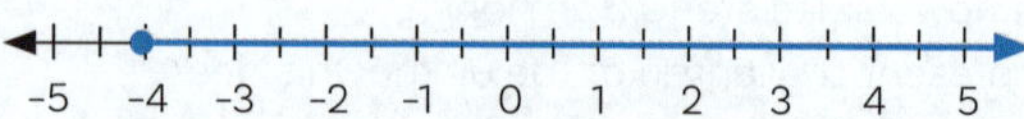

Words: *x* is greater than or equal to -4.

7 x < 3

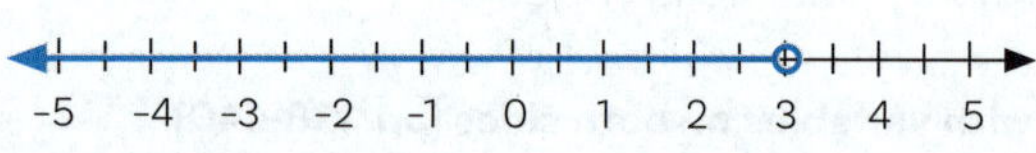

Words: *x* is less than 3.

8 x > -2

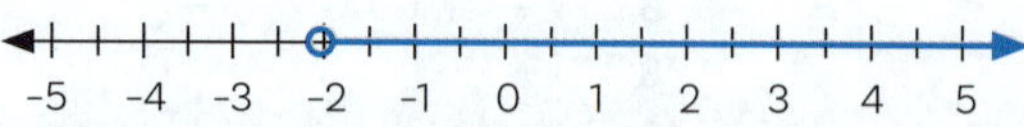

Words: x is greater than -2.

9 x < -3

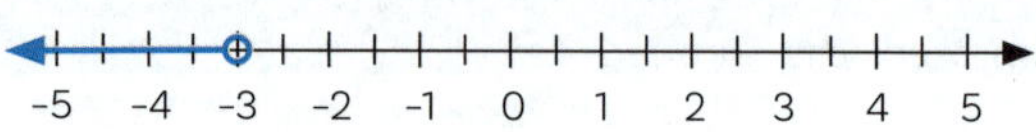

Words: *x* is less than -3.

10 x ≤ -1

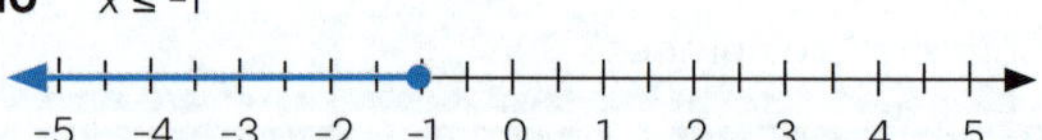

Words: *x* is less than or equal to -1.

11 x ≤ -4

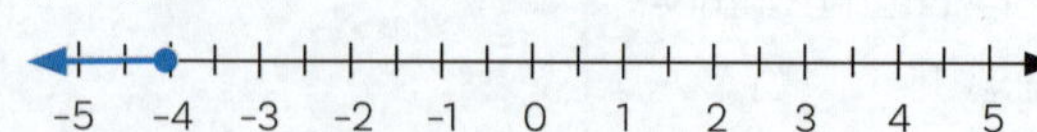

Words: *x* is less than or equal to -4.

12 x ≤ 2

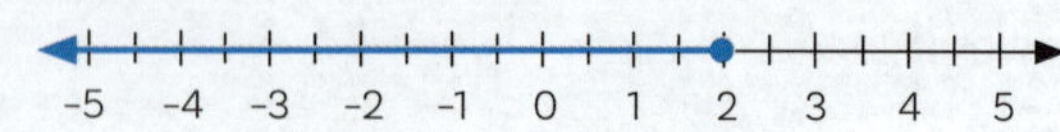

Words: *x* is less than or equal to 2.

 ISBN: 9780170497978

Substitution and formulae (pp. 149–157)

Substitution with one variable (p. 149)

1

Formula	$b = 3$	$b = 5$	$b = 0$	$b = -2$
$A = 4b$	12	20	0	-8
$A = b + 2$	5	7	2	0
$A = 6b - 5$	13	25	-5	-17
$A = 1 + b^2$	10	26	1	5
$A = \frac{1 + b}{2}$	2	3	$\frac{1}{2}$	$-\frac{1}{2}$

2 **a** -15 **b** 7
c -5 **d** -8
e 9 **f** 1

Formulae with one variable (pp. 150–152)

1 **a** $T = \frac{1}{2}c$
b T = 2.5 tablespoons

2 **a** $P = 3s + 4$
b P = 40 cm

3 **a** $A = 15h$
b A = \$82.50
c $A = 17.5h$
d Motel cleaning: 6 x \$15 = \$90.00
Milking shed: 5 x \$17.50 = \$87.50
Motel cleaning earns her slightly more money (\$2.50).
e $A = 10 + 19h$
f A = \$124.00

4 **a** $P = 20 + 16(5 - 1)$
= \$84.00
b $P = 20 + 16(h - 1)$
$= 20 + 16h - 16$
$= 4 + 16h$
c $P = 22 + 15(h - 1)$
$= 7 + 15h$
d Hemi: $P = 20 + 16(4 - 1)$
= \$68
Grace: $P = 22 + 15(4 - 1)$
= \$67
Hemi is paid \$1 more than Grace.
e Georgia gets paid \$24 for the first hour and then \$14 for each extra hour.
f $P = 30 + 14(h - 1) = 16 + 14h$
g Instead of being paid \$24 for the first hour, she is paid \$24 for each of the first two hours, and then \$14 for each extra hour.

Substitution with several variables (p. 153)

1

Formula	$b = 2$, $c = 5$	$b = 9$, $c = 4$	$b = 6$, $c = -2$
$A = 20 - 2bc$	0	-52	44
$A = c(b - 1)$	5	32	-10
$A = (c - b)^2$	9	25	64
$A = \frac{b^2 - 3c}{2}$	$-5\frac{1}{2}$	$34\frac{1}{2}$	21

2 **a** 6 **b** 30
c 181 **d** -6
e 52 **f** 112

Formulae with two or more variables (pp. 154–155)

1 **a** $P = 21.5h + 30e$
b P = \$1070
c Maria is paid \$23 per hour during the week and \$35 per hour at weekends.
d $P = 23h + 8d$

2 **a** $D = 0.75 \times 14$
= 10.5 m
b D = 25.5 m
c 33 m – 25.5 m = 7.5 m

3 **a** $C = 40d + 22h$
b C = \$230.00
c Mike's Machines charges a daily rate of \$70 and \$8 for every hour of use.
d \$250 **e** Harry's Hire, \$20

Rearrangement of formulae (pp. 156–157)

1 $d = \frac{P}{4}$ 2 $I = \frac{V}{R}$

3 $d = \sqrt{A}$ 4 $r = \frac{C}{2\pi}$

5 **a** $d = st$ **b** $t = \frac{d}{s}$

6 $r = \sqrt{\frac{A}{\pi}}$ 7 $P = \frac{100I}{RT}$

8 **a** $m = \frac{2E}{v^2}$ **b** $v = \sqrt{\frac{2E}{m}}$

Understanding instructions in algebra (pp. 158–159)

	Question	Instruction	Answer
1	$2x(x - 3y)$	Expand	$2x^2 - 6xy$
2	$4x - 5y + 2y - x$	Simplify	$3x - 3y$
3	$5x - 9 = 21$	Solve	$x = 6$
4	$\frac{x^3y}{xy^2}$	Simplify	$\frac{x^2}{y}$
5	$6xy^3 + 2x^2y$	Factorise	$2xy(3y^2 + x)$
6	$\frac{x}{2} - 7 = 15$	Solve	$x = 44$
7	$7x + 2x^2$ where $x = 3$	Evaluate	$7x + 2x^2 = 39$
8	$10x^2 - 6x - x - 1 + x^2$	Simplify	$11x^2 - 7x - 1$
9	$20 - 3(2x - 1)$	Expand	$23 - 6x$
10	$A = \pi r^2h$ where $r = 2$ and $h = 3$	Evaluate	$A = 37.7$ (1 dp)

Non-linear relationships (pp. 160–169)

Linear or not? (pp. 160–161)

1 4, 6, 8, 10, 12
Linear

2 1, 4, 9, 16
Non-linear

3 1, 7, 13, 19
Linear

4 20, 12, 7, 4, 2
Non-linear

5 Linear

6 Linear

7 Non-linear

ISBN: 9780170497978

Drawing parabolas (pp. 164-168)

1

x	$x^2 + 3$	y	Point
-3	$(-3)^2 + 3$	12	(-3, 12)
-2	$(-2)^2 + 3$	7	(-2, 7)
-1	$(-1)^2 + 3$	4	(-1, 4)
0	$(0)^2 + 3$	3	(0, 3)
1	$(1)^2 + 3$	4	(1, 4)
2	$(2)^2 + 3$	7	(2, 7)
3	$(3)^2 + 3$	12	(3, 12)

Compared with the graph of $y = x^2$, the parabola $y = x^2 + 3$ has moved up 3.

2

x	$x^2 - 4$	y	Point
-3	$(-3)^2 - 4$	5	(-3, 5)
-2	$(-2)^2 - 4$	0	(-2, 0)
-1	$(-1)^2 - 4$	-3	(-1, -3)
0	$(0)^2 - 4$	-4	(0, -4)
1	$(1)^2 - 4$	-3	(1, -3)
2	$(2)^2 - 4$	0	(2, 0)
3	$(3)^2 - 4$	5	(3, 5)

Compared with the graph of $y = x^2$, the parabola $y = x^2 - 4$ has moved down 4.

3

x	$x^2 + 5$	y	Point
-3	$(-3)^2 + 5$	14	(-3, 14)
-2	$(-2)^2 + 5$	9	(-2, 9)
-1	$(-1)^2 + 5$	6	(-1, 6)
0	$(0)^2 + 5$	5	(0, 5)
1	$(1)^2 + 5$	6	(1, 6)
2	$(2)^2 + 5$	9	(2, 9)
3	$(3)^2 + 5$	14	(3, 14)

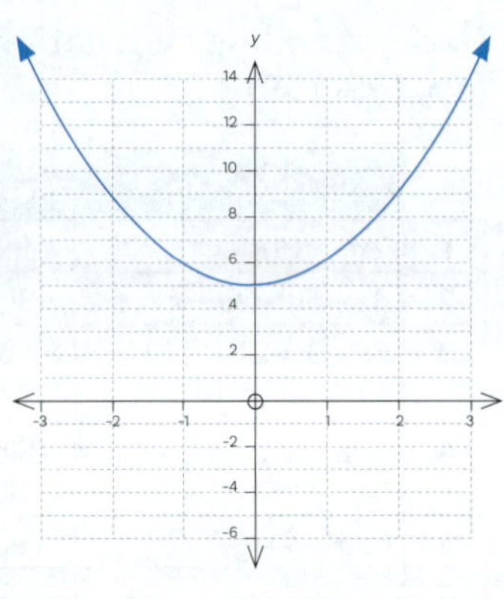

Compared with the graph of $y = x^2$, the parabola $y = x^2 + 5$ has moved up 5.

4

x	$x^2 - 2$	y	Point
-3	$(-3)^2 - 2$	7	(-3, 7)
-2	$(-2)^2 - 2$	2	(-2, 2)
-1	$(-1)^2 - 2$	-1	(-1, -1)
0	$(0)^2 - 2$	-2	(0, -2)
1	$(1)^2 - 2$	-1	(1, -1)
?	$(?)^? - ?$	?	(?, ?)
3	$(3)^2 - 2$	7	(3, 7)

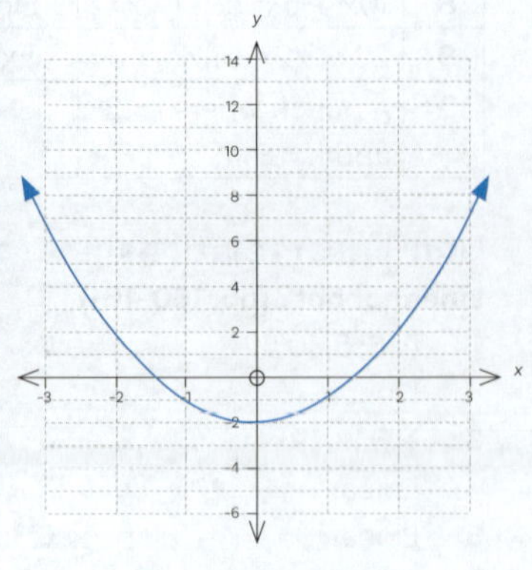

Compared with the graph of $y = x^2$, the parabola $y = x^2 - 2$ has moved down 2.

5

x	$-x^2 + 3$	y	Point
-3	$-(-3)^2 + 3$	-6	(-3, -6)
-2	$-(-2)^2 + 3$	-1	(-2, -1)
-1	$-(-1)^2 + 3$	2	(-1, 2)
0	$-(0)^2 + 3$	3	(0, 3)
1	$-(1)^2 + 3$	2	(1, 2)
2	$-(2)^2 + 3$	-1	(2, -1)
3	$-(3)^2 + 3$	-6	(3, -6)

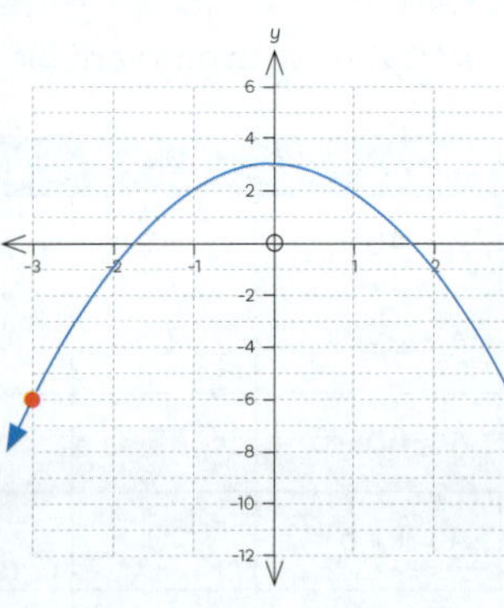

Compared with the graph of $y = -x^2$, the parabola $y = -x^2 + 3$ has moved up 3.

6

x	$-x^2 - 4$	y	Point
-3	$-(-3)^2 - 4$	-13	(-3, -13)
-2	$-(-2)^2 - 4$	-8	(-2, -8)
-1	$-(-1)^2 - 4$	-5	(-1, -5)
0	$-(0)^2 - 4$	-4	(0, -4)
1	$-(1)^2 - 4$	-5	(1, -5)
2	$-(2)^2 - 4$	-8	(2, -8)
3	$-(3)^2 - 4$	-13	(3, -13)

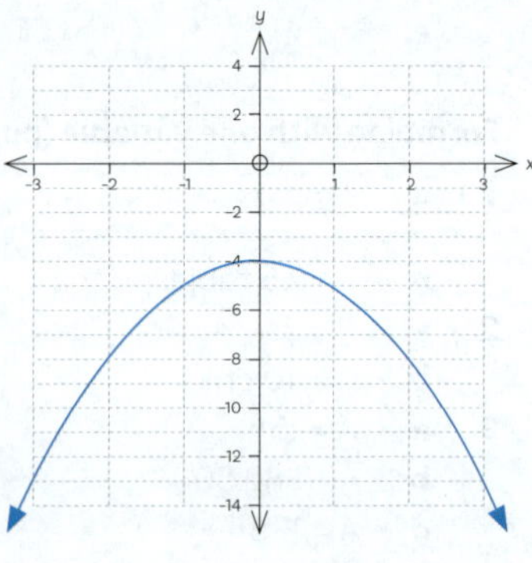

Compared with the graph of $y = -x^2$, the parabola $y = -x^2 - 4$ has moved down 4.

Putting it together (p. 169)

1

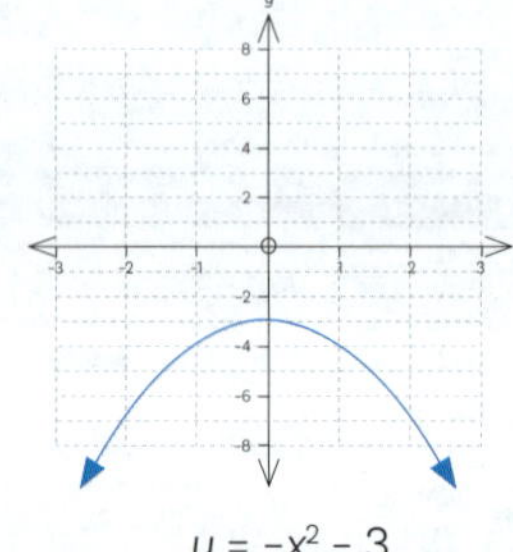

$y = -x^2 - 3$

2

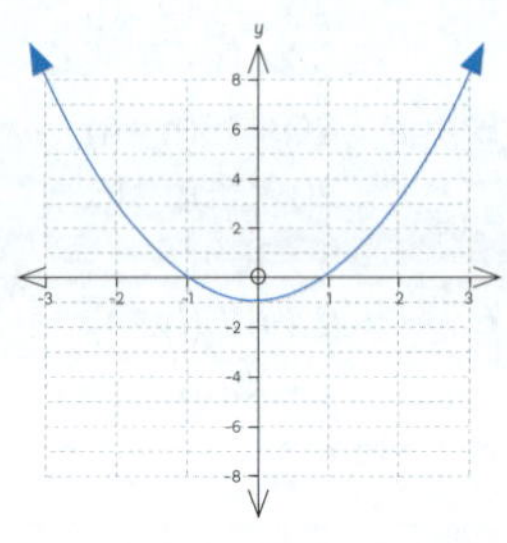

$y = x^2 - 1$

3

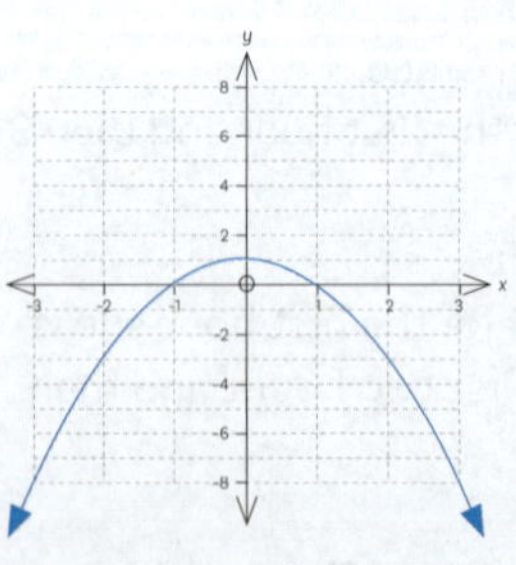

$y = -x^2 + 1$

4

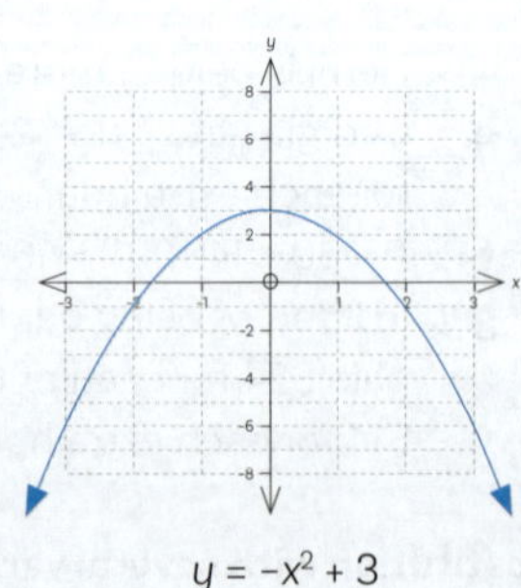

$y = -x^2 + 3$

ISBN: 9780170497978

5

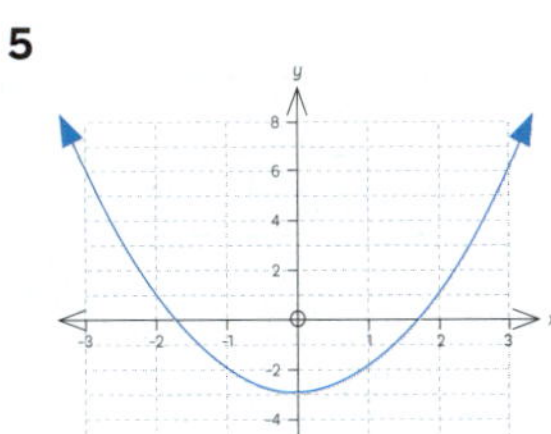

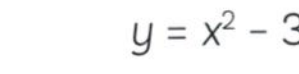

$y = x^2 - 3$

6

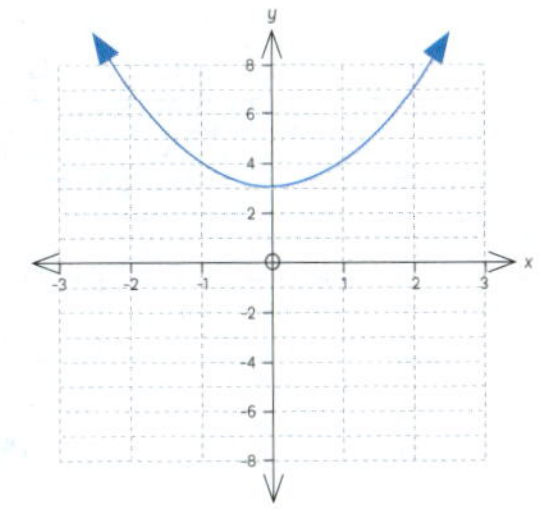

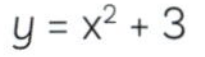

$y = x^2 + 3$

7

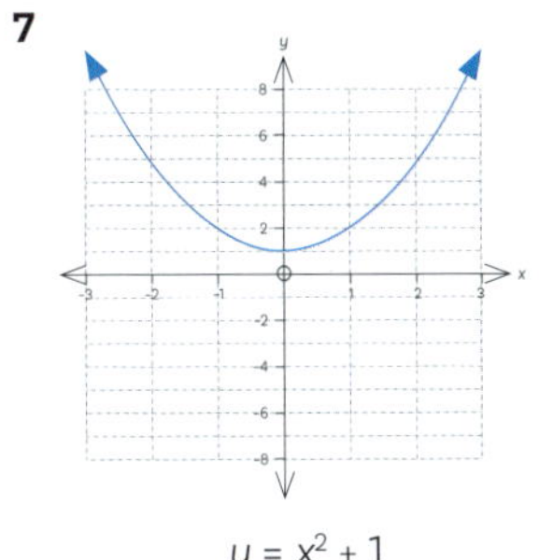

$y = x^2 + 1$

8

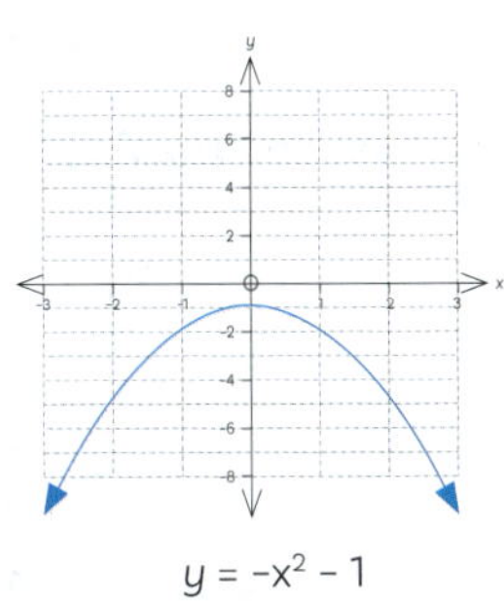

$y = -x^2 - 1$

MEASUREMENT (pp. 170–224)

The language of measurement (p. 170)

Length distance far stretch long wide reach	**Angle** incline slant decline steep gradient pitch slope flat
Temperature warm cold heat hot fever icy	**Time** era long period age
Volume/capacity room bulk space	**Mass** heavy load light

Measuring devices (p. 171)

Length tape measure ruler pedometer odometer	**Capacity** cup syringe teaspoon tablespoon measuring cylinder pipette measuring cup
Mass scales spring balance	**Angle** protractor compass clinometer
Time stopwatch timer clock	**Temperature** thermometer

Units (pp. 172–180)

Abbreviations (shortened versions) for units (p. 172)

Unit of measurement	Shortened version	Used to measure
minute	min	time
metre	*m*	*length*
milligram	mg	mass
kilometre	km	length
tablespoon	Tbsp	capacity
kilogram	kg	mass
cup	c	capacity
hectare	ha	area
gram	g	mass
millimetre	mm	length
litre	L	capacity
calorie	cal	energy
gigabyte	GB	data
tonne	t	mass
centimetre	cm	length
degrees Celsius	°C	temperature
second	s	time
megabyte	MB	data
millilitre	mL	capacity
teaspoon	tsp	capacity
kilojoule	kJ	energy
cubic metre	m^3	volume
square metre	m^2	area
cubic centimetre	cc	volume

Length (pp. 173–174)

1 0.231 m
2 210 mm
3 15 000 cm
4 3010 mm
5 430 000 cm
6 988 800 cm
7 1600 cm
8 9000 μm
9 3000 m
10 0.21 m
11 4 km
12 55 mm
13 2000 mm
14 0.18 cm
15 140 mm
16 2.32 km
17 32 m
18 742 mm

19

0.2 km	105 cm	15 cm	1.2 m	25 mm
200 m	1.05 m	0.15 m	1.2 m	0.025 m

Smallest → Largest

25 mm	15 cm	105 cm	1.2 m	0.2 km

20

0.998 km	980 m	998 001 mm	99 801 cm	989 m
998 m	980 m	998.001 m	998.01	989 m

Smallest Largest

980 m	989 m	0.998 km	998 001 mm	99 801 cm

21 m **22** mm or cm
23 cm **24** km
25 cm **26** mm
27 80 mm **28** 16.5 cm
29 28.65 m **30** 21.1 km
31 1.8 m **32** 12 m
33 4.9 cm

Mass (pp. 175–176)

1 150 000 mg **2** 2.1 kg
3 7.6 g **4** 0.00534 kg
5 3400 kg **6** 8700 g
7 0.52 g **8** 700 kg
9 0.931 t **10** 81 000 mg
11 0.655 kg **12** 23 000 g
13 5.392 kg **14** 2 600 000 mg
15 0.81 kg **16** 92 g
17 53 kg **18** 0.00787 t
19

81 100 g	0.080 t	81 kg	8100 g	810 000 mg
81 100 g	80 000 g	81 000 g	8100 g	810 g

Smallest Largest

810 000 mg	8100 g	0.080 t	81 kg	81 100 g

20

3.39 t	3039 kg	3309 kg	3.93 t	3 039 g
3390 kg	3039 kg	3309 kg	3930 kg	3.039 kg

Smallest Largest

3 039 g	3039 kg	3309 kg	3.39 t	3.93 t

21 kg **22** g
23 g **24** mg
25 t **26** kg
27 145 g **28** 3490 kg
29 23.1 kg **30** 245 g
31 800 g **32** 19 g

Capacity (volume) (pp. 177–178)

1 270 mL **2** 0.54 L
3 1.119 L **4** 9.3 mL
5 2000 mL **6** 5.7 L
7 0.183 L **8** 72 000 mL
9 3100 mL **10** 20.6 L
11 0.005 L **12** 1990 mL
13

0.908 L	809 mL	0.89 L	1.9 L	900 mL
908 mL	809 mL	890 mL	1900 mL	900 mL

Smallest Largest

809 mL	0.89 L	900 mL	0.908 L	1.9 L

14

2.02 L	2002 mL	2220 mL	2.202 L	2.2 L
2.02 L	2.002 L	2.220 L	2.202 L	2.2 L

Smallest Largest

2002 mL	2.02 L	2.2 L	2.202 L	2220 mL

15 350 mL **16** 240 L
17 500 mL **18** 450 L
19 108 000 L **20** 1.6 L
21 5 L **22** 6.5 mL

Appropriate units (p. 179)

1 mL **2** mg
3 m **4** kg
5 kg **6** mL
7 g **8** m
9 mL or g **10** cm
11 L **12** t or kg
13 t **14** m
15 mg **16** kg

Estimating quantities (p. 180)

1. The weight of a hippo is most likely to be 3500 kg.
2. The length of the Auckland Harbour Bridge is most likely to be 1020 m.
3. The capacity of an average human stomach is most likely to be 1.5 L.
4. The mass of a watermelon is most likely to be 5.5 kg.
5. The length of a cricket pitch is most likely to be 20.12 m.
6. The height of the Auckland Sky Tower is most likely to be 328 m.
7. The mass of a kiwi is most likely to be 2.5 kg.
8. The length of a hockey field is most likely to be 91.4 m.
9. The height of a basketball hoop is most likely to be 3.05 m.
10. The amount of air in a balloon is most likely to be 6 L.
11. The mass of a bus is most likely to be 12 000 kg.
12. The length of a standard surfboard is most likely to be 196 cm.
13. The length of a 737 aeroplane is most likely to be 39.47 m.
14. The mass of a loaf of bread is most likely to be 650 g.
15. The capacity of a fish tank most likely to be 150 L.
16. The height of Mt Everest is most likely to be 8849 m.
17. The capacity of a car's fuel tank is most likely to be 50 L.
18. The height of a garden fence is most likely to be 1.8 m.
19. The mass of a laptop charger is most likely to be 400 g.
20. The mass of a tennis ball is most likely to be 57 g.

Time (pp. 181–183)

Converting units (p. 181–182)

1 3 min **2** 1500 min
3 672 hours **4** 4320 hours
5 6 min **6** 96 h
7 4 h **8** 90 min
9 9000 s **10** 5.5 d
11 1.5 h **12** 61
13 250 s **14** 5 h
15 545 min **16** 100 s

 ISBN: 9780170497978

17

299 min	0.2 d	16 800 s	4.9 h
299 min	288 min	280 min	294 min

Smallest — Largest

16 800 s	0.2 d	4.9 h	299 min

18

2.1 d	205 200 s	30 h	3042 min
3024 min	3420 min	3240 min	3042 min

Smallest — Largest

2.1 d	3042 min	30 h	205 200 s

19 minutes
20 months
21 seconds
22 minutes
23 years
24 days
25 19 s
26 2 min
27 45 min
28 1 year
29 20 years
30 2 hours

Stopwatches (p. 183)

1 00:58.42
2 01:09.65
3 12:14.35
4 03:12.05
5

01:25.99	01:52.99	02:09.99	00:26.90	00:25.99

Quickest — Slowest

00:25.99	00:26.90	01:25.99	01:52.99	02:09.99

6 **a** Hazel
b Two minutes, twenty-eight seconds and fourteen hundredths of a second
c 40.27 s
7 1.02 s

Speed (pp. 184–185)

1 4 m/s
2 70 km/h
3 120 km
4 5 s
5 60 km/h
6 5 m/s
7 328 km/h
8 10 m/s
9 120 m
10 270 km
11 14 km
12 15 km
13 5 hours
14 120 s
15 0.5 hours or 30 m
16 60 s
17 7.5 km
18 20 km/h
19 12 km/h
20 100 s

Scales (pp. 186–189)

Reading scales (pp. 186–187)

1 **A** = 0.2 cm
B = 2.8 cm
C = 5.4 cm
2 **D** = 28°
E = 116°
3 550 mL
4 18 V
5 ¾ tank
6 32° or 33°
7 **F** = 250.7 mm
G = 252.3 mm
H = 253.1 mm
8 4.6 x 1000 r/min or 4600 r/min
9 **I** = 255°

Showing values on scales (pp. 188–189)

1 **2**

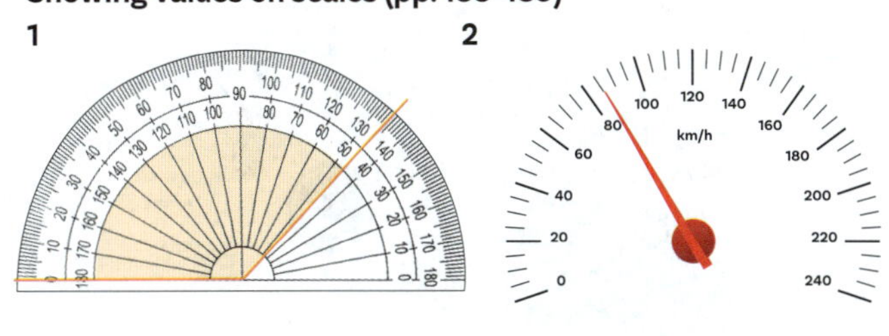

3

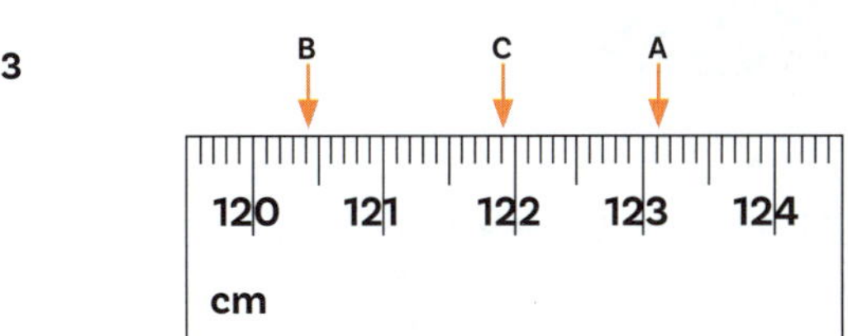

4 **5**

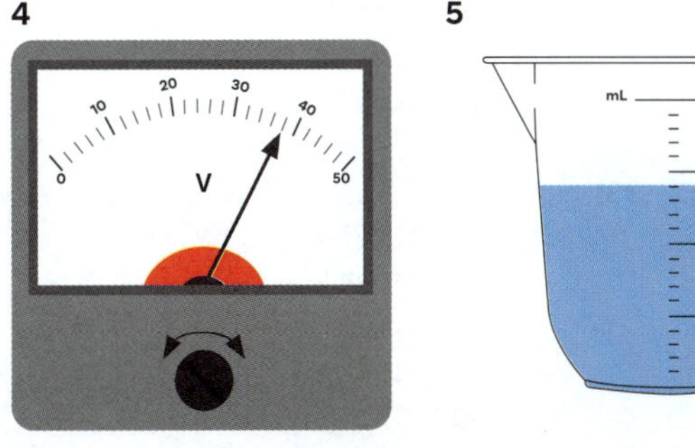

6

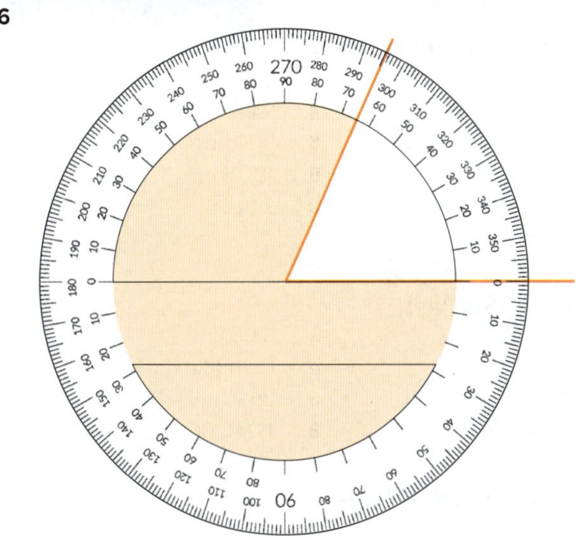

7 **8**

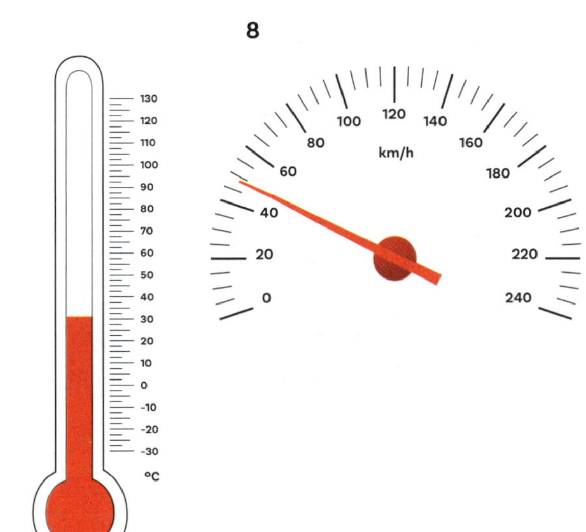

9 10

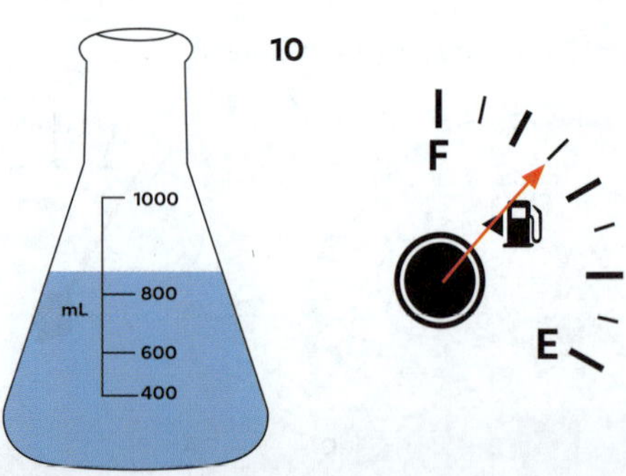

Perimeter (pp. 190–195)

Shapes with linear sides (pp. 190–191)

1	77 mm	2	34 cm
3	7.6 m	4	15 cm
5	30 m	6	10.634 km or 10 634 m
7	15 m	8	12 km
9	50 cm	10	660 m
11	264 m	12	0.4 m

Circles (pp. 192–193)

1	34.56 cm	2	15.71 m
3	487.0 mm	4	11.94 km
5	38.56 cm	6	11.83 m
7	164.3 mm	8	161.1 cm
9	9.740 km	10	119.4 m

Compound shapes (pp. 194–195)

1	28 cm	2	9.96 m
3	694 mm	4	24.47 m
5	6.06 m	6	380 cm
7	288.0 cm	8	180.5 cm
9	23.23 km	10	2.86 m

Area (pp. 196–209)

Units of area (p. 196)

1	0.8 ha	2	0.05 km^2
3	1.5 m^2	4	0.0098 m^2
5	2.5 km^2	6	35.9 ha
7	9.990 m^2	8	1 040 000 m^2

Quadrilaterals (pp. 197–202)

1	48 cm^2	2	81 m^2
3	7 km	4	7 cm

5

7 m 4 m
2 m 14 m
1 m 28 m

6

12 cm 12 cm

7	28 m^2	8	6150 cm^2
9	5850 cm^2 or 0.585 m^2	10	2250 cm^2 or 225 000 mm^2
11	165 cm^2 or 16 500m^2	12	2.3 m^2
13	5 km	14	12 cm

15 16

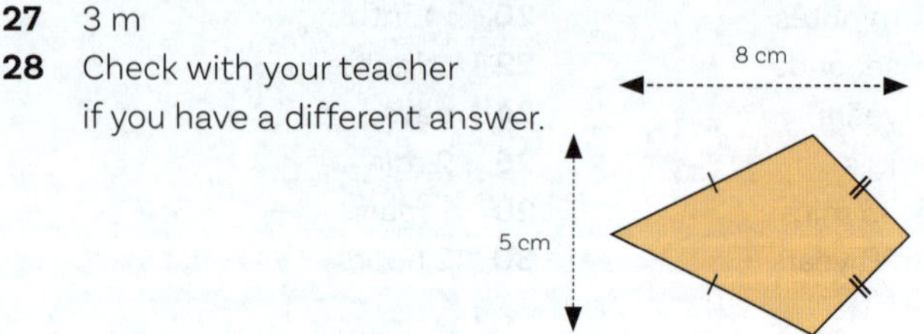

17	10 m^2	18	3000 mm^2
19	112 cm^2	20	210 m^2
21	29.25 m^2	22	80 cm^2
23	8 km	24	4.1 cm
25	1200 mm^2	26	24 cm^2
27	3 m		

28 Check with your teacher if you have a different answer.

8 cm 5 cm

Triangles (pp. 203–204)

1	10 cm^2	2	2000 mm^2
3	2.5 m^2	4	8.82 km^2
5	32.5 cm^2	6	5.25 cm^2
7	5.5 cm	8	3.5 km

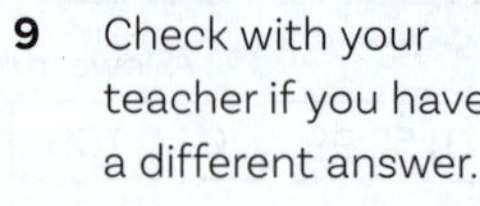

9 Check with your teacher if you have a different answer.

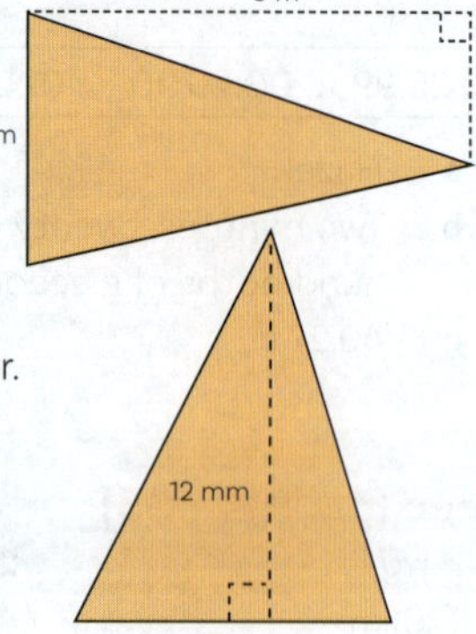

10 Check with your teacher if you have a different answer.

Circles (pp. 205–206)

1	28.27 km^2	2	1963 mm^2
3	380.1 m^2	4	63.62 cm^2
5	39.27 km^2	6	402.1 mm^2
7	12.57 m^2	8	115.5 cm^2
9	6.000 km	10	11.00 cm

Compound shapes (pp. 207–209)

1	66 km^2	2	1400 mm^2
3	138.54 km^2	4	65 m^2
5	217.23 cm^2	6	5950 mm^2
7	65.70 m^2	8	2925 mm^2
9	18.34 km^2	10	4585.55 cm^2
11	815.04 mm^2	12	1299.23 cm^2
13	73.83 m^2	14	48.79 cm^2

Volume (pp. 210–214)

Units of volume (p. 210)

1	0.003 m^3	2	0.0007 m^3
3	4 100 000 cm^3	4	8 L
5	22 000 cm^3	6	9900 cm^3

ISBN: 9780170497978

Cuboids (pp. 211–212)

1 $2856\ cm^3$
2 $10\ m^3$
3 $375\ 000\ mm^3$
4 $180\ 000\ cm^3$
5 $371\ 875\ cm^3$
6 $6.6825\ m^3$
7

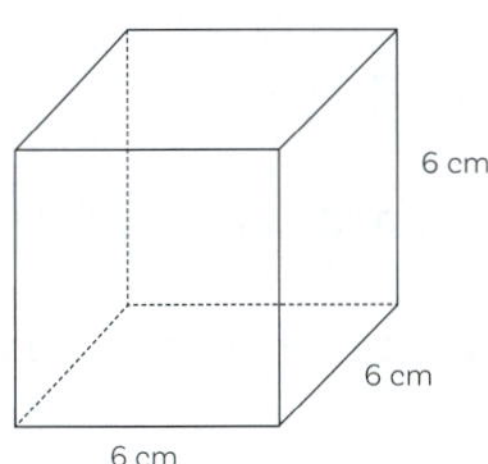

8 11 cm
9 2700 cartons

Compound cuboids (pp. 213–214)

1 $412\ m^3$
2 $31\ 450\ cm^3$
3 $4\ 008\ 000\ mm^3$
4 $60\ cm^2$
5 $29\ 520\ cm^3$
6 $159.216\ m^3$
7 $9900\ cm^3$
8 $528\ 000\ mm^3$
9 $0.45\ m^3$
10 $57\ m^3$

Scaling (pp. 215–217)

Scale factor (p. 215)

1

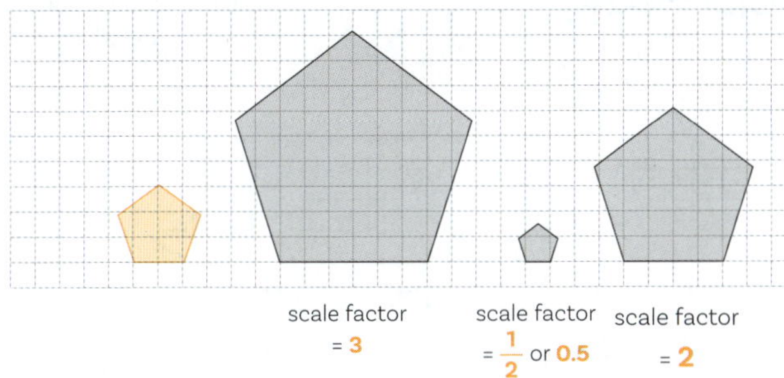

2

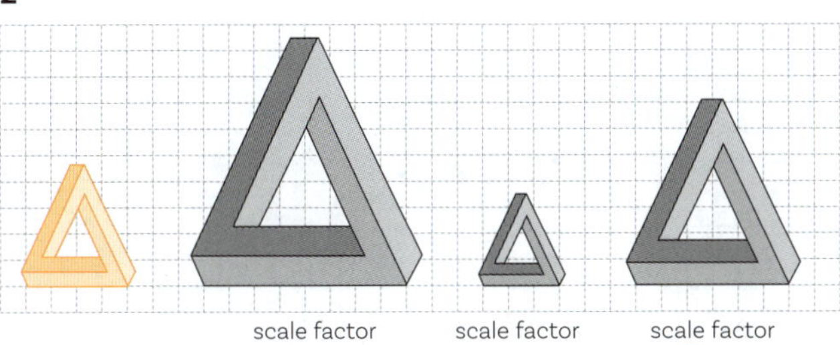

Scale factors for perimeter, area and volume (p. 216–217)

1 **Perimeter original** 16 cm
Perimeter image 48 cm
Area of original $16\ cm^2$
Area of image $144\ cm^2$
2 $27\ m^3$
3 24 cm
4 3
5 72 cm
6 Dimensions: 10 m x 10 m x 10 m
Volume: $1000\ m^3$

The Theorem of Pythagoras (pp. 218–224)

Activity

The area of the **green** square = c^2
The area of the bottom square (containing 1, 2, 3 and 4) = a^2
The area of the smallest square (5) = b^2
So: $c^2 = a^2 + b^2$

Finding the length of the hypotenuse (pp. 219–221)

1 6.40 cm (2 dp)
2 9.90 cm (2 dp)
3 13.04 cm (2 dp)
4 10.82 cm (2 dp)
5 61.22 mm (2 dp)
6 1.70 m (2 dp)
7 53.67 m (2 dp)
8 5.83 cm (2 dp)
9 53.81 m (2 dp)
10 5.06 km (2 dp)
11 65.53 cm (2 dp)
12 60.12 cm (2 dp)

Finding the lengths of short sides (pp. 222–223)

1 59.87 cm (2 dp)
2 3.67 cm (2 dp)
3 6.93 cm (2 dp)
4 91.85 mm (2 dp)
5 2.00 km (2 dp)
6 60.37 m (2 dp)
7 33.35 mm (2 dp)
8 28.32 cm (2 dp)
9 161.25 m (2 dp)
10 91.45 km (2 dp)
11 10.78 cm (2 dp)
12 6.09 m (2 dp)

Mixing it up (p. 224)

1 54.67 cm (2 dp)
2 104.85 m (2 dp)
3 3.59 cm (2 dp)
4 58.59 m (2 dp)
5 78.11 km (2 dp)
6 75.89 m (2 dp)
7 19.80 m (2 dp)
8 6.68 m (2 dp)

GEOMETRY (pp. 225–261)

The language of geometry (p. 225)

1 Supplementary angles
2 Vertex
3 Right angle
4 Obtuse angle
5 Reflex angle
6 Diagonal
7 Adjacent angles
8 Parallel lines
9 Complementary angles
10 Bisector
11 Quadrilateral
12 Acute angle

Angles (pp. 226–236)

Angle revision (pp. 226–227)

1 $x = 113°$
Reason: Vert opp ∠s =
2 $x = 279°$
Reason: ∠s at a point = 360°
3 $x = 57°$
Reason: ∠s on a line = 180°
4 $x = 126°$
Reason: Vert opp ∠s =
5 $x = 157°$
Reason: ∠s at a point = 360°
6 $x = 21°$
Reason: ∠s on a line = 180°
7 $x = 129°$
Reason: Vert opp ∠s =
8 $x = 53°$
Reason: ∠s on a line = 180°

Triangles (pp. 228–230)

1 Right-angled and scalene
2 Isosceles
3 Equilateral
4 Scalene
5 Right-angled and isosceles
6 Isosceles
7 $x = 32°$
Reason(s): ∠s in a Δ = 180°
8 $x = 133°$
Reason(s): Ext ∠ of a Δ = sum of int opp ∠s

ISBN: 9780170497978

9 $x = 102°$
Reason(s): Isosceles Δ and ∠s in a Δ = 180°

10 $x = 57°$
Reason(s): Ext ∠ of a Δ = sum of int opp ∠s

11 $x = 120°$
Reason(s): Equilateral Δ and ext ∠ of a Δ = sum of int opp ∠s

12 $x = 76°$
Reason(s): Isosceles Δ and ∠s in a Δ = 180°

13 $x = 76°$
Reason(s): Ext ∠ of a Δ = sum of int opp ∠s

14 $x = 20°$
Reason(s): Ext ∠ of a Δ = sum of int opp ∠s

15 $x = 42°$
Reason(s): Isosceles Δ and ∠s in a Δ = 180°

16 $x = 114°$
Reason(s): Isosceles Δ and ext ∠ of a Δ = sum of int opp ∠s

Quadrilaterals (p. 231)

1 $x = 117°$
Reason(s): ∠s in a quad = 360°

2 $x = 224°$
Reason(s): ∠s in a quad = 360°

3 $x = 111°$
Reason(s): ∠s in a quad = 360°, ∠s on a line = 180°

4 $x = 75°$
Reason(s): ∠s in a quad = 360°, ∠s at a point = 360°

Angles in special quadrilaterals (p. 232)

Rectangle and square	All the angles in squares and rectangles are **equal** and **right** angles.
Parallelogram and rhombus	In a parallelogram or a rhombus, there are two opposite pairs of **equal** angles.
Trapezium	In an ordinary trapezium, there are **no** equal angles.
Isosceles trapezium	An isosceles trapezium has **two** pairs of **equal** angles.
Right trapezium	A right trapezium has **two** right angles and **two** other angles which are **not** equal.
Kite	In a kite, there is **one** pair of equal angles and the other two angles are **not** equal.

5 $x = 63°$ 6 $x = 60°$
7 $x = 41°$ 8 $x = 65°$
9 $x = 127°$ 10 $x = 127°$
11 $x = 124°$ 12 $x = 114°$

Parallel lines (pp. 234–236)

1 Co-interior 2 Alternate
3 Corresponding 4 Alternate
5 Co-interior 6 Corresponding

7 $x = 137°$
Reason: Alt ∠s =, ∥ lines

8 $x = 129°$
Reason: Corr ∠s =, ∥ lines

9 $x = 133°$
Reason: Co-int ∠s add to 180°, ∥ lines

10 $x = 115°$
Reason: Alt ∠s =, ∥ lines

11 $x = 129°$
Reason: Corr ∠s =, ∥ lines

12 $x = 72°$
Reason: Co-int ∠s add to 180°, ∥ lines

13 $x = 50°$
Reason: Co-int ∠s add to 180°, ∥ lines

14 $x = 51°$
Reason: Alt ∠s =, ∥ lines

15 $x = 60°$ 16 $x = 127°$
17 $x = 64°$ 18 $x = 75°$

2D and 3D shapes (pp. 237–244)

2D and 3D language (p. 237)

1 Vertices 6, Edges 9, Faces 5
2 Vertices 4, Edges 6, Faces 4
3 Vertices 10, Edges 15, Faces 7
4 Vertices 12, Edges 18, Faces 8

Nets (pp. 238–239)

1

ISBN: 9780170497978

2

Isometrics (pp. 240–244)

1

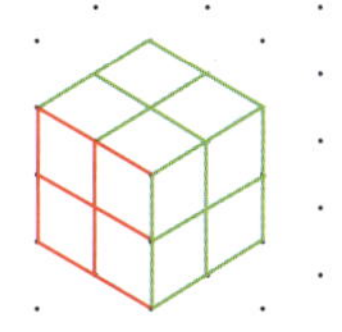

2

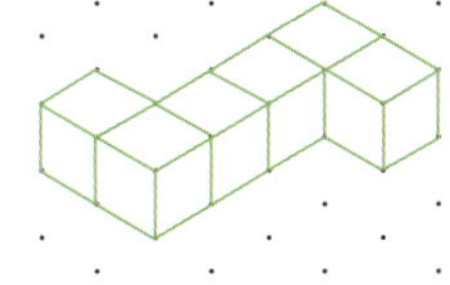

3

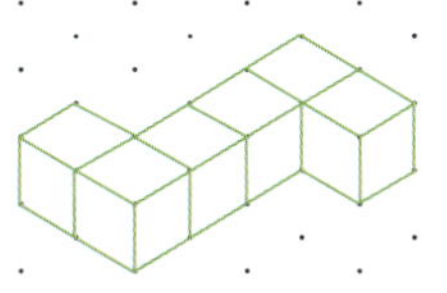

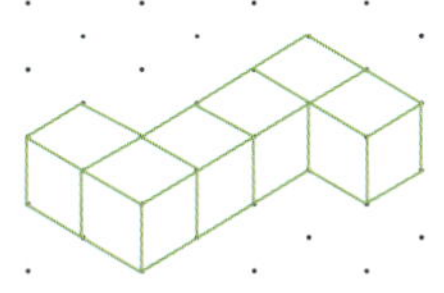

4

5

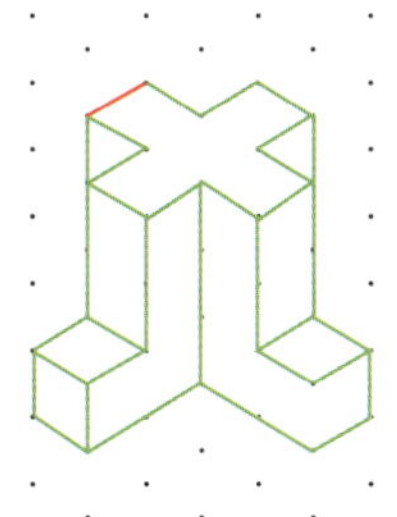

6

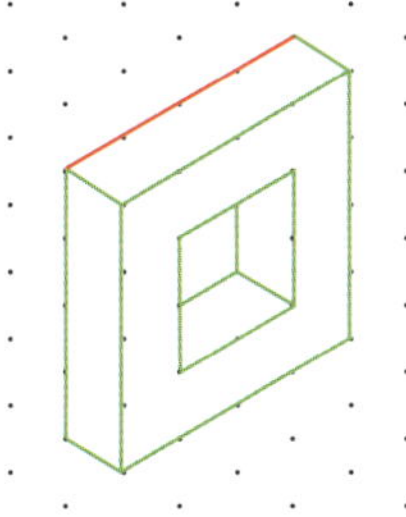

7

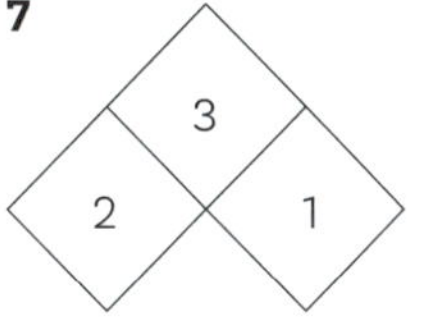

8

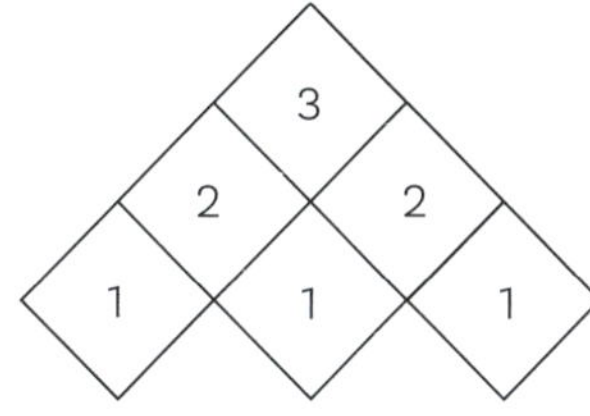

9

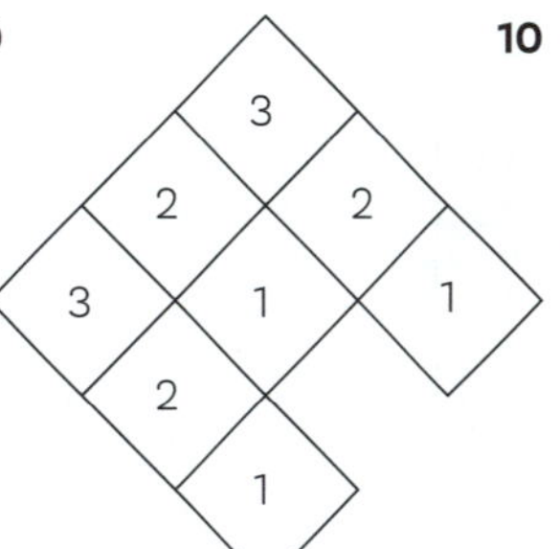

10

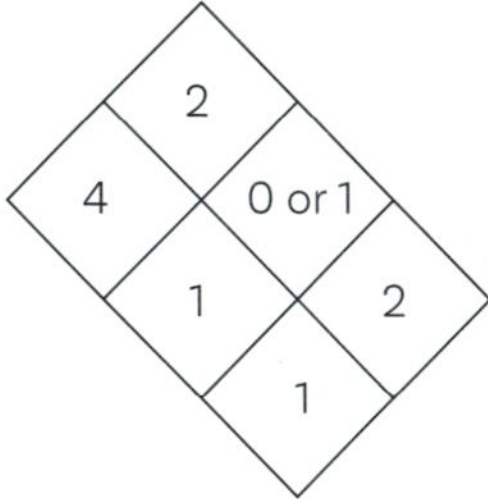

11

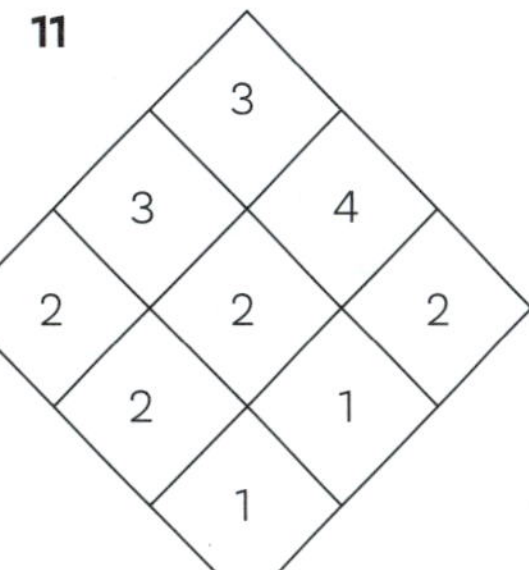

12

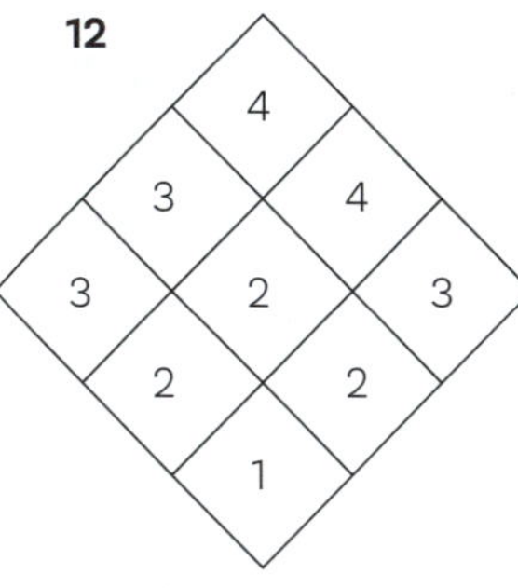

13

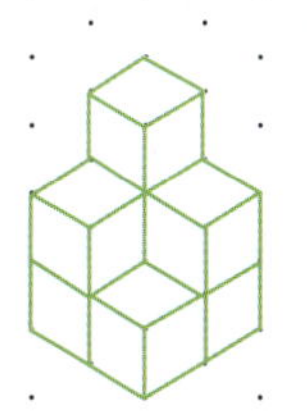

14

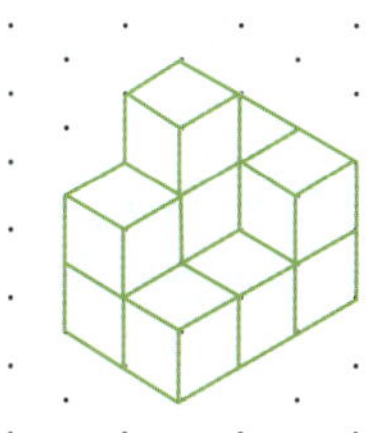

15

16 **B**

17 **D**

18 **A**

19 **C**

Transformation geometry (pp. 245–255)

Translation (pp. 246–248)

1 $\begin{pmatrix}4\\2\end{pmatrix}$

2 $\begin{pmatrix}-2\\4\end{pmatrix}$

3 $\begin{pmatrix}2\\-4\end{pmatrix}$

4 $\begin{pmatrix}-1\\2\end{pmatrix}$

5 $\begin{pmatrix}-4\\-2\end{pmatrix}$

6 $\begin{pmatrix}1\\-2\end{pmatrix}$

7 **Right** one and **up** five
8 **Right** three and **down** six
9 **Left** seven and **up** eight
10 **Left** ten and **down** four
11 Left five and up two
12 Right nine and down eleven
13

$\begin{pmatrix}2\\3\end{pmatrix}$	$\begin{pmatrix}-2\\-1\end{pmatrix}$	$\begin{pmatrix}5\\-2\end{pmatrix}$	$\begin{pmatrix}0\\3\end{pmatrix}$	$\begin{pmatrix}-3\\8\end{pmatrix}$	$\begin{pmatrix}2\\-4\end{pmatrix}$	$\begin{pmatrix}9\\-4\end{pmatrix}$	$\begin{pmatrix}-2\\-3\end{pmatrix}$	$\begin{pmatrix}7\\2\end{pmatrix}$	$\begin{pmatrix}-4\\0\end{pmatrix}$
a	b	c	d	e	f	g	h	i	j

ISBN: 9780170497978

14 $\begin{pmatrix} 5 \\ 2 \end{pmatrix}$

15 $\begin{pmatrix} -6 \\ 3 \end{pmatrix}$

16 $\begin{pmatrix} 3 \\ -3 \end{pmatrix}$

17 $\begin{pmatrix} -3 \\ -4 \end{pmatrix}$

18 $\begin{pmatrix} 5 \\ -2 \end{pmatrix}$

19 $\begin{pmatrix} -5 \\ 0 \end{pmatrix}$

20 $\begin{pmatrix} 7 \\ 1 \end{pmatrix}$

21 $\begin{pmatrix} -8 \\ -1 \end{pmatrix}$

Reflection (pp. 249–251)

1

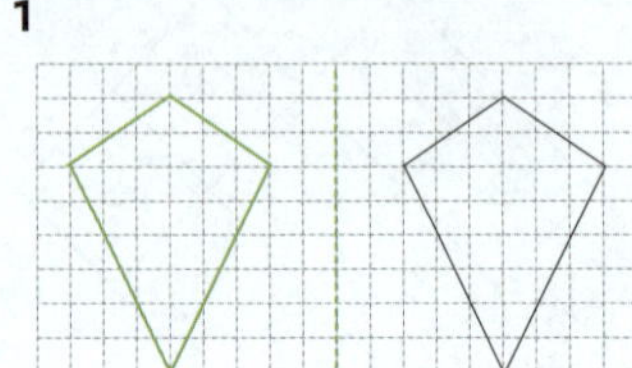

2

3

4

5

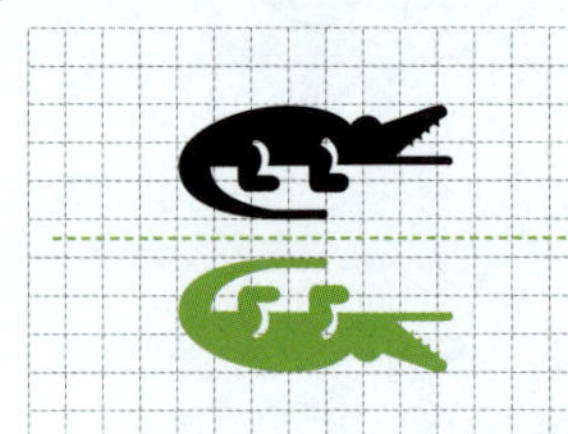

6

7

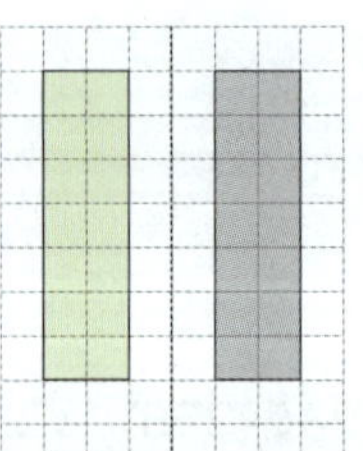

8

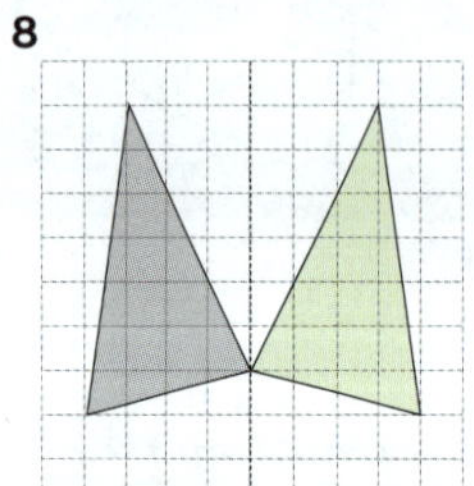

9

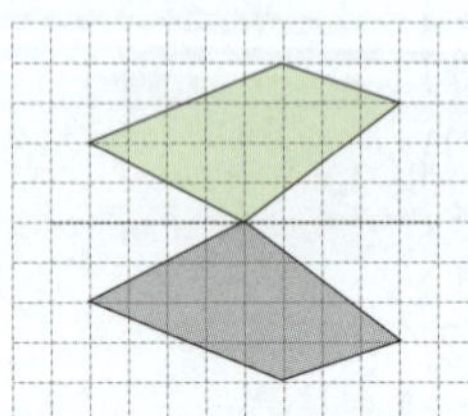

10

11

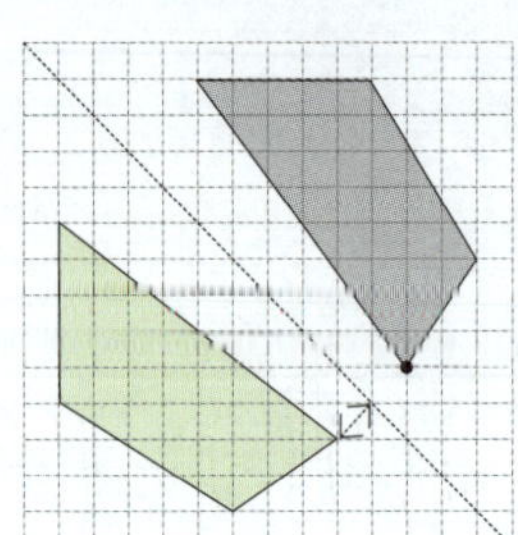

12

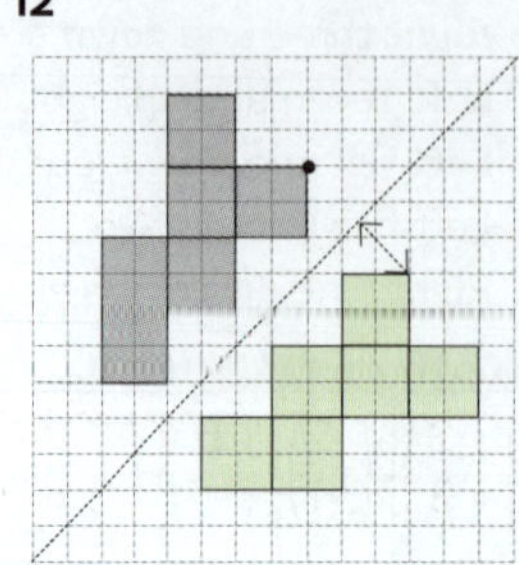

13

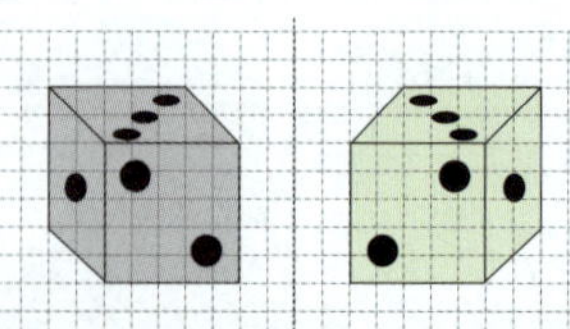

14

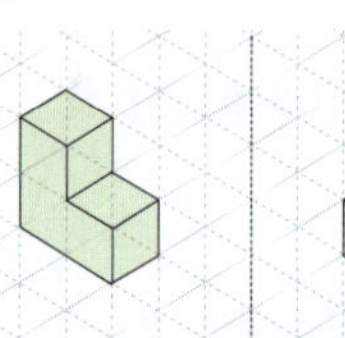

Rotation (pp. 252–255)

1 90°

2 270°

3 180°

4 90°

5

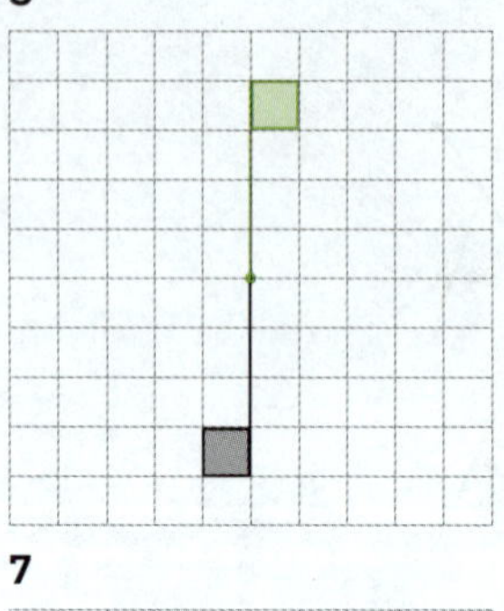

6

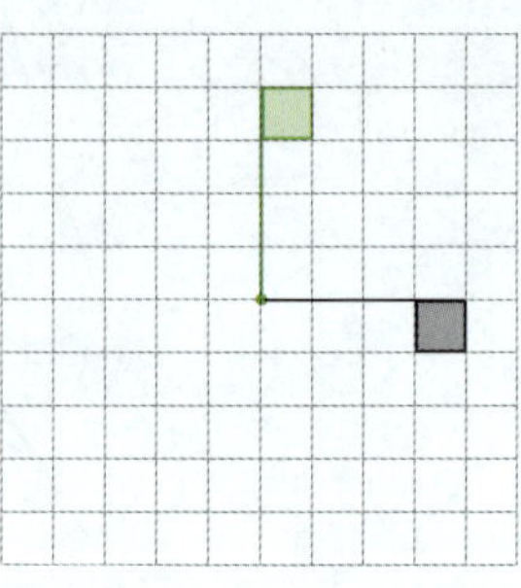

7

8

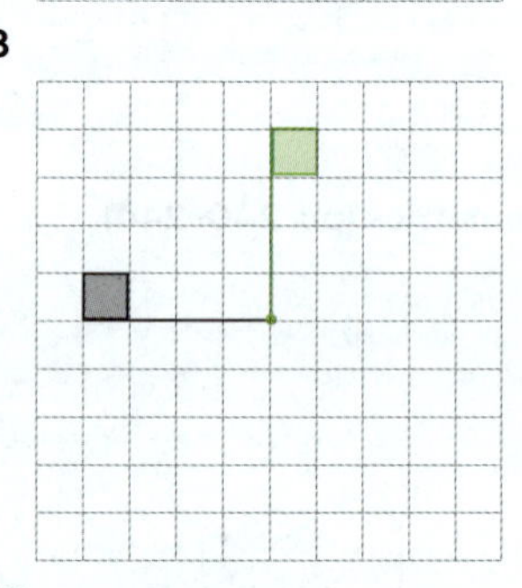

9

10

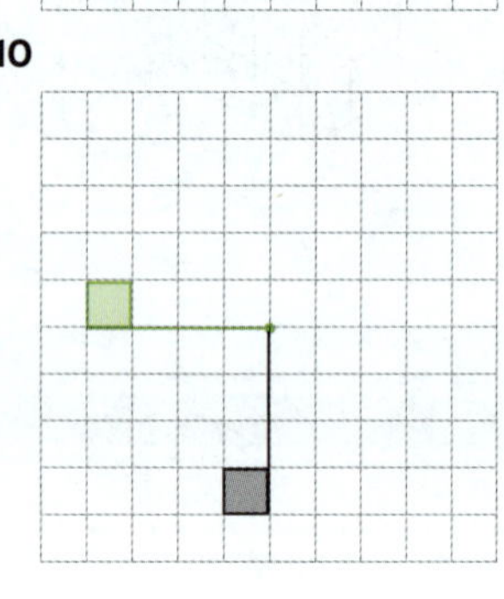

Position and orientation (pp. 256–261)

Directions (pp. 256–257)

1 S **2** NW **3** SW **4** E

5 NE **6** W **7** SE **8** N

9

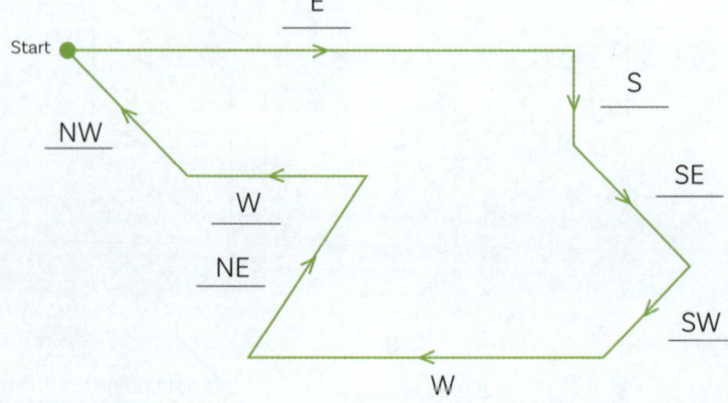

10 **a** South wall **b** Bathroom

c Northeast corner

11 **a** East **b** Southeast

c South **d** Northwest

 ISBN: 9780170497978

Scales (pp. 258–261)

1 a 4.3 or 4.4 m b 5.6 m
c 3.3 or 3.4 m d 1.9 or 2 m
e 1.6 or 1.7 m f 11.9 or 12 m

2 a 1 cm b 5 cm
c 1.5 cm d 0.5 cm
e 3.5 cm

3 2 mm 4 mm 5 mm 8 mm

4
a	Awatuna to Makaka	*North*	3 km
b	Riverlea to Mangawhero	South	5.5 km
c	Makaka to Mahoe	Northeast	11 km
d	Kaponga to Riverlea	West	6 km
e	Auroa to Kapuni	East	8 km
f	Makaka to Kapuni via Auroa	Southeast	16 km

STATISTICS (pp. 262–295)

Throughout this section, you are likely to give answers that differ from those below. If so, ask your teacher.

Problem, plan and data (pp. 263–270)

Thinking about the data (p. 263)

1 Age of the second labrador: 105 years. This is likely to be 10.5 years.
??? for the golden retriever: M. This is probably mistyped and should be a N (they are adjacent on the keyboard).
Cost of food per week for Chihuahua. $49 seems far too much for a very small dog.

2 Does your dog wear a collar most of the time?
Has your dog been desexed?
Does your dog have toys?
Has your dog been micro chipped etc.

Investigative questions (p. 264)

1 Yes
The breed has been recorded for all the dogs.

2 No
We have no information about how well behaved the dogs are.

3 Yes
The sex has been recorded for all the dogs.

4 No
There is information about the cost of food per week, but not the mass of food fed to the dog.

5 Yes
The sex and mass have been recorded for all the dogs.

6 Are the female dogs in Wai-iti older than male dogs?
Are dogs that sleep outside more expensive to feed?
Which breed costs most to feed? etc.

7 Disagree
The five female dogs in the sample of 10 all sleep inside, but it is very unlikely that there isn't one female dog that sleeps outside in the 128 dogs in Wai-iti.

8 Agree
All of the 10 dogs in the sample are less than 35 kg, so it is very unlikely that most of the 128 dogs will be more than 35 kg.

9 Maybe
Two of the 10 dogs in the sample are labradors, so it is possible that it is the most popular breed.

10 Maybe
Both of the labradors in the sample of 10 are male, so it is possible that most labradors in Wai-iti will be male.

Types of questions and identifying variables and groups of interest (p. 265–266)

1 Summary 2 Comparative
3 Summary 4 Comparative
5 Comparative 6 Time series

7	*Number of electric cars*	*Cars in the school car park*
8	Time it takes to get to school	Students in my class
9	Mass of cat	Cats in Wai-iti
10	Position in the classroom	Year 9 and 10 students at Paradise High School
11	Area of paper	Paper planes
12	Number of books borrowed	Members who visit the library
13	Resting heart rate	Members of the football team

Expected findings (pp. 267–268)

1

Reasons (Yes)
They need less energy to keep warm at night. They are more likely to be spoiled and therefore fed more.

Reasons (No)
Their owners are likely to care for them more and make sure they don't get fat. They don't need to build up their fat reserves in order to keep warm at night.

2

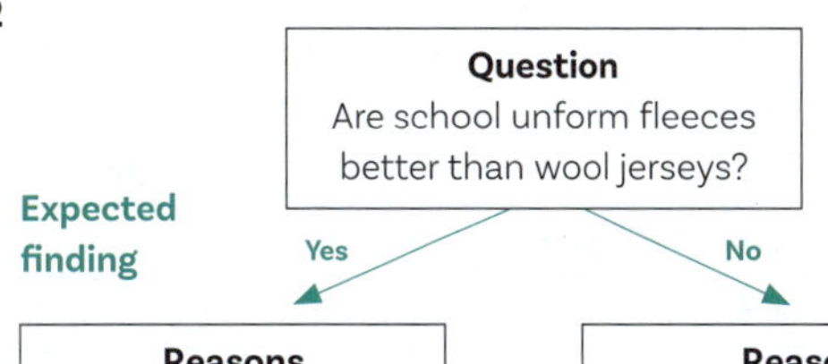

Reasons (Yes)
Fleeces are lighter, cheaper and easier to wash and dry. Wool is itchy.

Reasons (No)
Wool is natural, breathable and warmer.

3 Plane A
Better made, crisper folds, better paper, better design, looks more aerodynamic, etc.
Plane B
Lighter, better design, etc.

4 Yes
With an increased angle, the marble will build up more speed and travel further.

5 a Yes
b Students would spend more time focused on work, less bullying so students would be happier, etc.
a No
b Cellphones are a useful resource for learning in the classroom, etc.

ISBN: 9780170497978

6 **a** Yes
b Taller people are likely to be stronger.
a No
b Tall people are likely to wobble more and further because of their height.

Collection of data (pp. 269–270)

1

✓	Is the student wearing shoes?
×	Is the student wearing a jersey?
✓	Has the student's hair been flattened?
×	Were people's heights measured inside or outside?
✓	Was the data including student names left on the whiteboard after class?
×	Was all the data collected on the same day?
✓	Was the same measuring device used for all students?
✓	When the heights were recorded, were they double-checked?
×	Had the student eaten lunch?
✓	Did the same person do all the measuring?

2 **a** Length of time a student can stand on one foot. Height of student.
b Year 9 and 10 students at Mary's school.
c No
She shouldn't just be getting Year 9 or 10 students who walk past her at interval to do the test. She should test entire classes. There are likely to be sports practices or meetings at interval and these students might be better at standing on one foot.
d

✓	Did you explain what the data was going to be used for?
×	Did you write down the results carefully?
×	Were they wearing correct uniform?
✓	Did you ask people if they would take part?
✓	Were their answers kept private?
×	Did you use the same stopwatch each time?
✓	Was anyone forced or tricked into giving answers?
✓	Could they say no or stop at any time?

Data display (pp. 271–283)

1 *Pie graph*
Descriptive
2 Box plot
Discrete and continuous
3 Scatter plot
Discrete and continuous
4 Tally chart
Discrete and descriptive
5 Bar graph
Descriptive and discrete
6 Line graph
Discrete and continuous
7 Pictograph
Discrete
8 Dot plot
Discrete
9 Histogram
Continuous

Reading axes (pp. 272–273)

1 Major 0.5 Minor 0.1

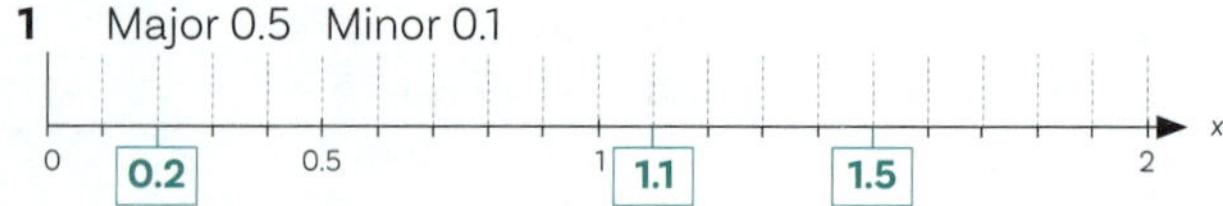

2 Major 0.3 Minor 0.1

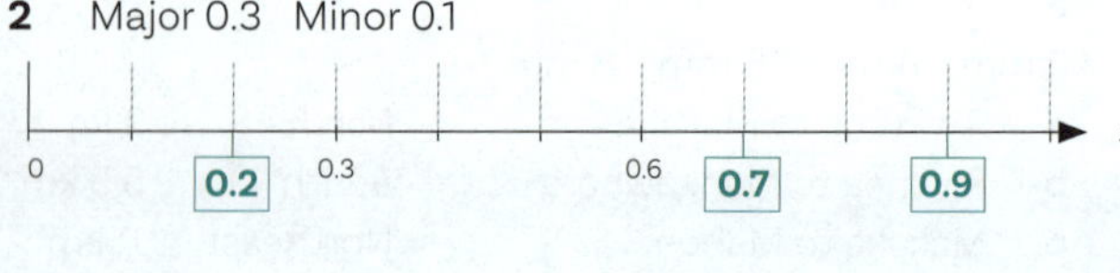

3 **4** **5**

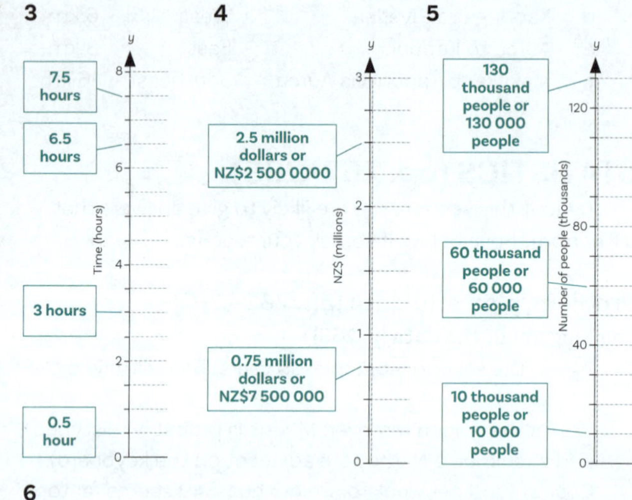

6

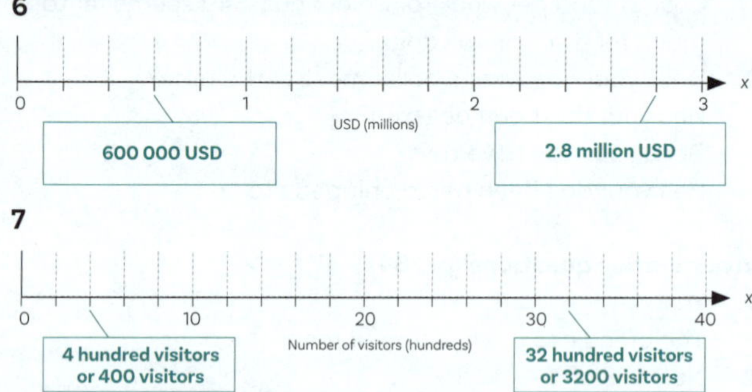

7

Data interpretation (pp. 274–276)

1 **a** Mason **b** 149 or 150
c Theodore **d** 2019, 2020 and 2021
e Elijah
f Agree
Theodore is a more popular name than either Mason or Elijah.

2 **a** 91
b USA and Australia
c 34% (0 dp)
d USA got the most medals. However, if we consider the number of medals per person in the country, Australia is likely to be more successful.

3 **a** Which of these best describe where you come from: Wellington City, the Wellington region, elsewhere in New Zealand, not from New Zealand?
b 26%
c Agree
48% of the visitors come from overseas, so 52% are from New Zealand.

4 **a** 53
b 1.8% (1 dp)

ISBN: 9780170497978

c Can't tell for sure.
We don't know what the conditions for the race will be next year or whether there will be an athlete capable of racing this fast.

5 a 183 cm
b Six All Blacks
c 17% (0 dp)
d Agree
Only one player is shorter than 175 cm.

Scatter plots (pp. 277–283)

1

Day	Coordinates	Description
a	(**21**, **28**)	It was **21**°C and they sold **28** ice creams.
b	(**22**, **42**)	It was **22**°C and they sold **42** ice creams.

c 18
d Temperature: 25°C
Ice creams: 15
e Temperature: 18°C
Ice creams: 40
f

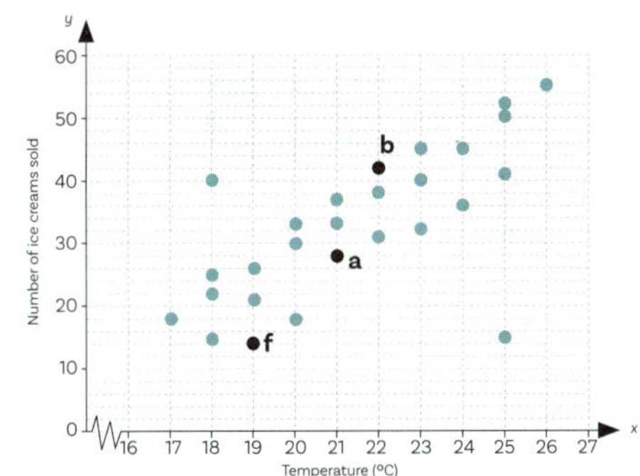

2 a False
b True
c True

3

Teacher	Coordinates	Description
a	(**1**, **7**)	They drank **1** cup of coffee and slept for **7** hours.
b	(**3.5**, **6**)	They drank **3.5** cups of coffee and slept for **6** hours.

c i and **ii**

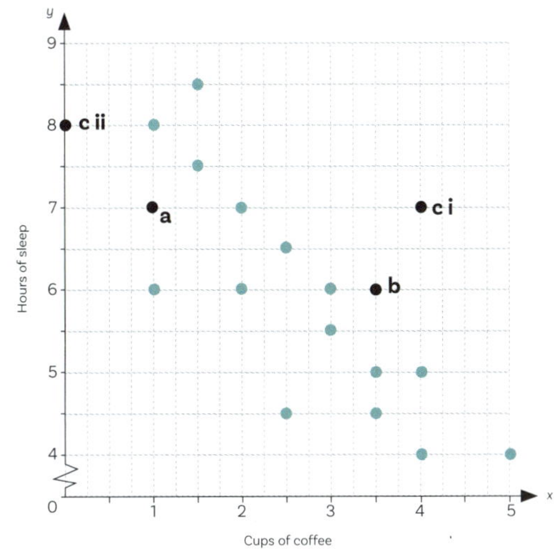

d Seven teachers
e In general, teachers who drank more coffee tended to sleep less.

4 **Direction** Positive
Strength Strong
5 **Direction** Negative
Strength Moderate
6 **Direction** Positive
Strength Weak
7 **Direction** Negative
Strength Strong
8 The graph shows a **positive** relationship between a person's height and the length of their footprint. This means that taller people have **longer** footprints.

9

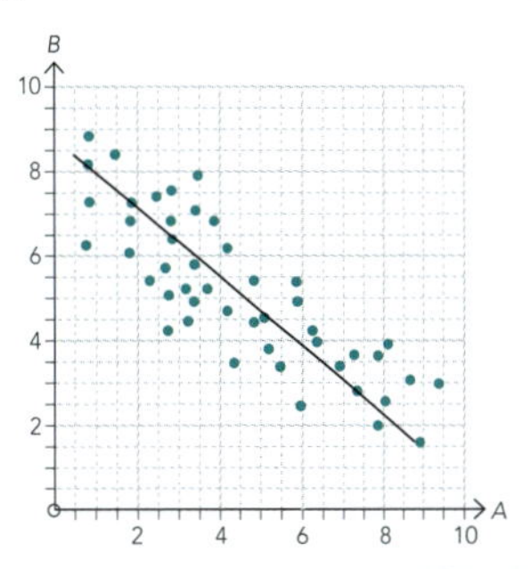

10

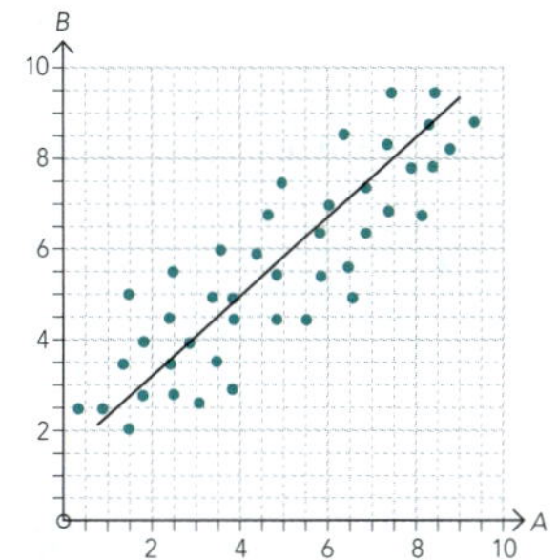

11

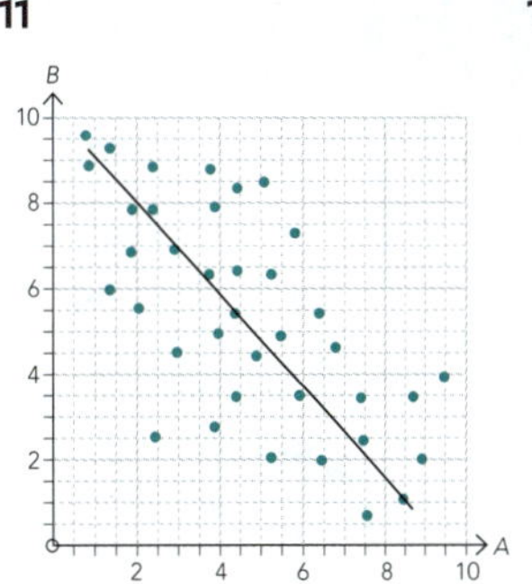

12

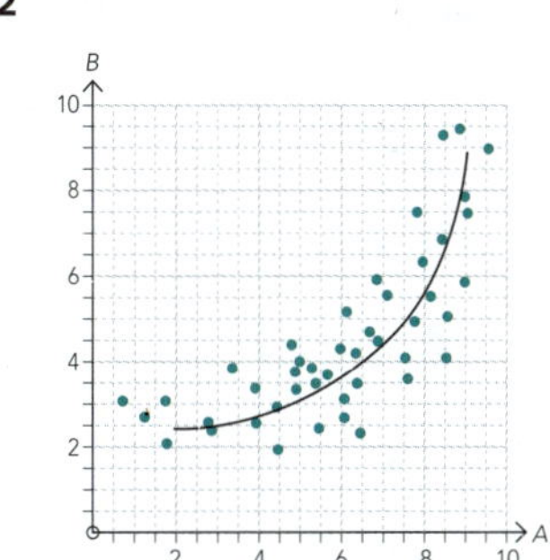

13

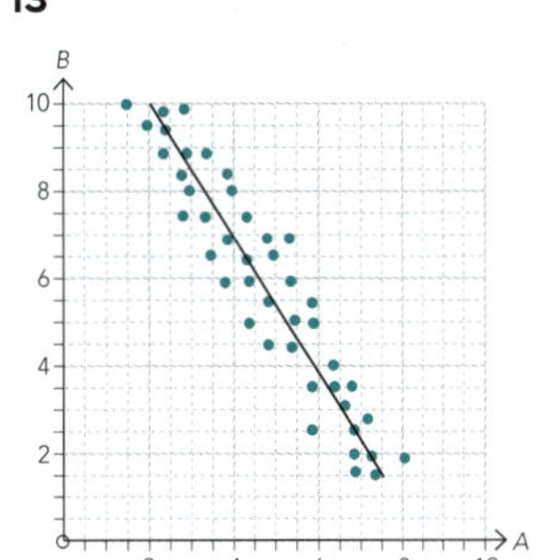

14

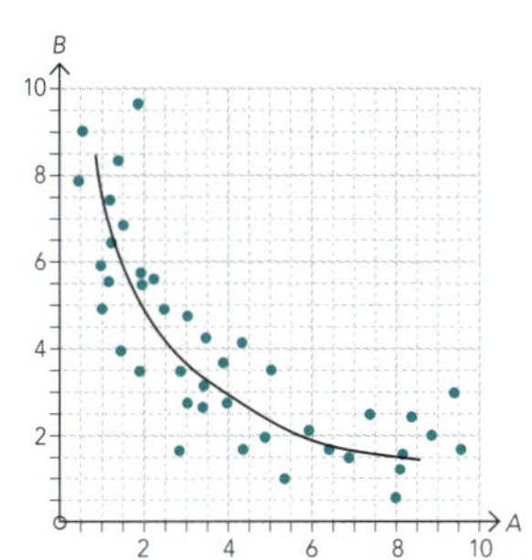

Data analysis (pp. 284–290)

Measures of centre (averages) (pp. 284–286)

1 a $40.\dot{3}$ b 47.4
c The mean for set **b** is **bigger** than that for set **a** because **the 5 reduced the mean for set a**.
2 a 27 b 23.5
3 a 14 b No mode
c 12 and 17

Measures of spread (pp. 287–288)

1. Minimum = 2 | LQ = 6 | Median = 10
   UQ = 16 | Maximum = 20
   Range = 18 | Interquartile range = 10
2. Minimum = 1 | LQ = 5 | Median = 9.5
   UQ = 13 | Maximum = 23
   Range = 22 | Interquartile range = 8
3. Minimum = 2.0 | LQ = 2.3 | Median = 2.95
   UQ = 3.4 | Maximum = 4.0
   Range = 2 | Interquartile range = 1.1
4. Minimum = 9 | LQ = 12 | Median = 13
   UQ = 15 | Maximum = 18
   Range = 9 | Interquartile range = 3
5. Minimum = 3 | LQ = 7 | Median = 10
   UQ = 13 | Maximum = 15
   Range = 12 | Interquartile range = 6

Unusual features (pp. 289–290)

1 Unusual point

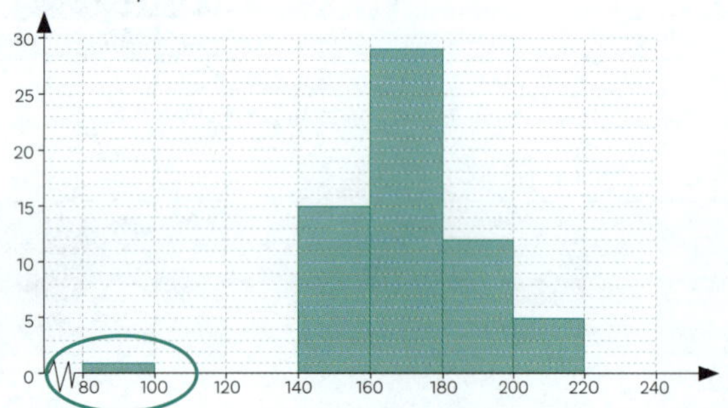

2 Cluster

100 110 120 130 140 150

3

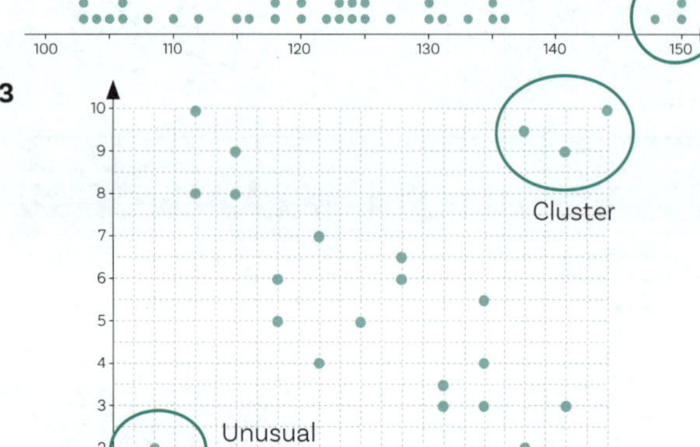

4 45, 59, 35, 47, **11**, 39, 48, 41, 51, 52
Unusual point

5 Unusual point

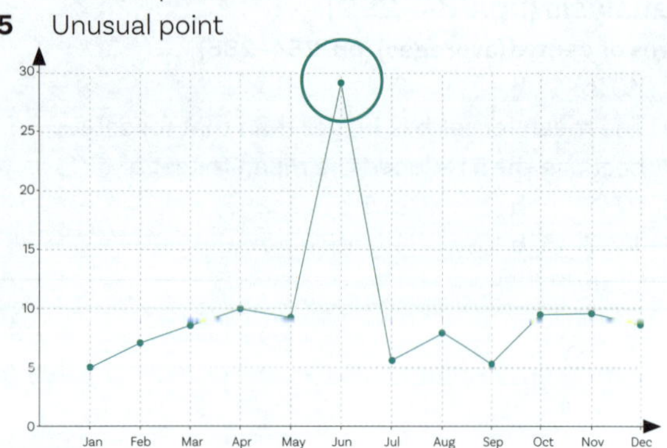

On every other month, the maximum amount is 10 or less, but in June, the value was around 29.

Decision trees (pp. 291–292)

1 a

Frostclaw	Venomshade	Shadowmorph	Gloamwither	Ironhide

b

Horns	Fluffy	Number of eyes	Type
Yes	No	3	Gloamwither
No	Yes	1	Shadowmorph
No	No	3	Ironhide
No	Yes	1	Shadowmorph
Yes	Yes	3	Frostclaw
No	Yes	1	Shadowmorph

c Check your sketch with your teacher. It should have horns, with no fur and multiple eyes.

2 Shadowmorph

3 Venomshade

4 Frostclaw

5 a

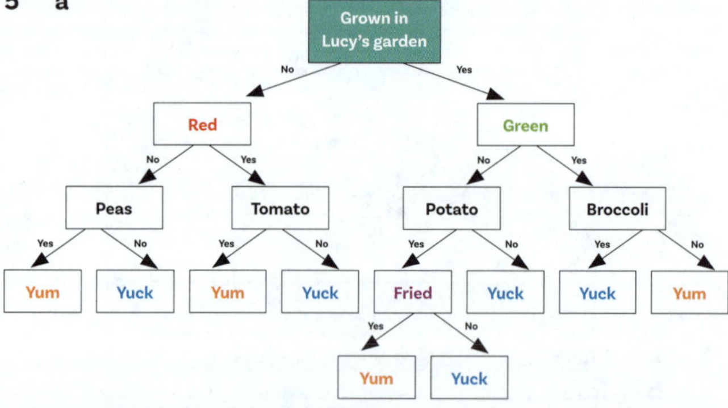

b Fried

c No

d Peas and tomato

e Fried potato and broccoli

f It is grown in the garden, it's not green but it's not a fried potato, so she won't eat it.

Conclusions (pp. 293–295)

1 a The most preferred pet in my year group was a cat, with 44% of students selecting it.
Reasons: It is the only conclusion referring to the group that he surveyed.
The conclusion reflects the data: most students would rather have a cat, not a dog.
The conclusion is supported by a calculation.

b No

c Yes because dogs are very common pets and it was his preference.

d He should have surveyed students from the whole school to reflect his question.
He should have said what question he asked.

ISBN: 9780170497978

2 a The '1.5' books means the x-axis is not regular.
b Most Paradise High School students have read two or three books this year.
Reasons: Doesn't tell us how many books most Paradise High School students read.
Is not accurate – only 20 out of 54 students have read fewer than three books.
Is true and tells us about how many books most have read (30/54).
c Yes
d Yes because it was supported by her data. Students who spend time in the library at lunchtime are likely to be book readers.
e Needs to specify the type of book, e.g. would the Road Code count?
Needs to specify what 'read' means – a little of the book or all of it?
Students leaving the library are likely to have read more books than most, so select a different place.
Lunchtime practices on Thursdays would mean some students couldn't be surveyed, so select a different time.

3 a On most days, his Maths classroom is as warm or warmer than his Science classroom.
b These results do support his expected findings – his Maths classroom is usually warmer than his Science classroom.
c Finley should have considered the time of day when his lessons occurred. Possibly on Wednesday he had Maths early in the morning when it was cold and Science in the afternoon after it had warmed up.
He also should have said when during the lesson he measured the temperature because having a lot of people in a room can make it warmer.

PROBABILITY (pp. 296–309)

The probability scale (p. 296)

1 You may think of different terms. If so, discuss them with your neighbours or your teacher.
1 certain, a sure thing, definite, guaranteed
0.9 *very likely*, almost certain
0.7 likely, good chance, probable
0.5 50-50, maybe, even chance
0.3 unlikely
0.1 very unlikely, slight chance
0 *impossible*, no chance, no way

Sample space (pp. 297–299)

1 a

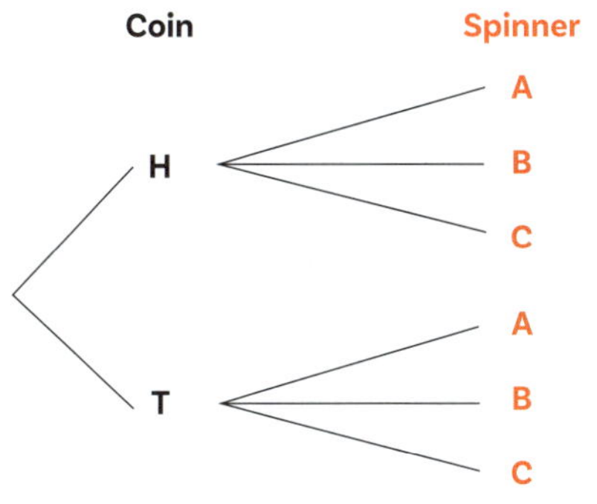

Coin	Spinner
H	A
	B
	C
T	A
	B
	C

Outcomes in sample space: HA, HB, HC, TA, TB, TC
Number of outcomes: 6

b

	A	B	C
H	HA	HB	HC
T	TA	TB	TC

Same result? ✓

c Number of outcomes for the coin = 2
Number of outcomes for the spinner = 3
Multiplying these numbers gives 6
Same result? ✓

2 a

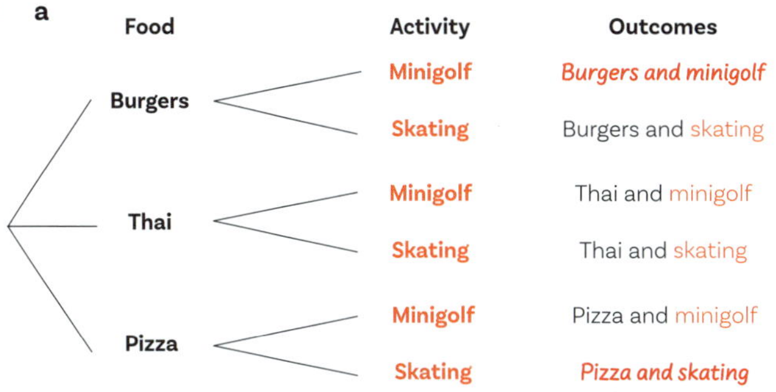

Food	Activity	Outcomes
Burgers	Minigolf	*Burgers and minigolf*
	Skating	Burgers and skating
Thai	Minigolf	Thai and minigolf
	Skating	Thai and skating
Pizza	Minigolf	Pizza and minigolf
	Skating	*Pizza and skating*

b 6

c

	Minigolf	Skating
Burgers	Burgers and minigolf	Burgers and skating
Thai	Thai and minigolf	Thai and skating
Pizza	Pizza and minigolf	Pizza and skating

Same result? ✓

d Number of food x Number of activities = 3 x 2
= 6
Same result? ✓

Ways of calculating probabilities (pp. 300–305)

1 Theoretical
2 Experimental
3 Experimental
4 Theoretical
5 Theoretical

Calculating theoretical probability (pp. 301–303)

1 a \$0, \$5, \$10, \$15, \$20
b 5
c $\frac{1}{5}$ or 0.2
d $\frac{4}{5}$ or 0.8
e $\frac{3}{5}$ or 0.6
f 0

2 a

	1	2	3	4	5	6
R	R1	R2	R3	R4	R5	R6
B	B1	B2	B3	B4	B5	B6
W	W1	W2	W3	W4	W5	W6

b 18
c i $\frac{1}{18}$ or $0.0\dot{5}$
ii $\frac{2}{18}$ or $0.\dot{1}$
iii $\frac{9}{18}$ or 0.5
iv $\frac{3}{18}$ or $0.1\dot{6}$
v 0

ISBN: 9780170497978

3 a

Spinner	Coin	Outcome	Probability
R	H	RH	$P(RH) = \frac{1}{6}$
	T	RT	$P(RT) = \frac{1}{6}$
B	H	BH	$P(BH) = \frac{1}{6}$
	T	BT	$P(BT) = \frac{1}{6}$
W	H	WH	$P(WH) = \frac{1}{6}$
	T	WT	$P(WT) = \frac{1}{6}$

b 6

c **i** $\frac{1}{6}$ or $0.1\dot{6}$ **ii** $\frac{2}{6}$ or $\frac{1}{3}$ or $0.\dot{3}$

iii $\frac{3}{6}$ or $\frac{1}{2}$ or 0.5 **iv** $\frac{2}{6}$ or $\frac{1}{3}$ or $0.\dot{3}$

v 0 **vi** $\frac{2}{6}$ or $\frac{1}{3}$ or $0.\dot{3}$

Calculating probabilities from observations (pp. 304–305)

1 a 8 **b** $\frac{2}{8}$ or 0.25

c $\frac{6}{8}$ or 0.75

2 a 60 **b** $\frac{8}{60}$ or $0.1\dot{3}$

c $\frac{43}{60}$ or $0.71\dot{6}$ **d** $\frac{38}{60}$ or $0.6\dot{3}$

3 a

	Experienced	First time	Totals
Snowboarding	12	44	56
Skiing	18	46	64
Totals	30	90	120

b $\frac{64}{120}$ or $0.5\dot{3}$ **c** $\frac{30}{120}$ or 0.25

d $\frac{44}{120}$ or $0.3\dot{6}$

e Snowboarding had $\frac{12}{56}$ = 0.21 (2 dp) experienced students.

Skiing had $\frac{18}{64}$ = 0.28 (2 dp) experienced students.

So skiing had the greater proportion of experienced students.

Experimental probability investigation (pp. 306–307)

a

Die roll	Total	Probability	
1	2	$\frac{2}{10}$	0.2
2	2	$\frac{2}{10}$	0.2
3	2	$\frac{2}{10}$	0.2
4	0	$\frac{0}{10}$	0
5	1	$\frac{1}{10}$	0.1
6	3	$\frac{3}{10}$	0.3

b No

He did get more sixes than any other number, but he threw the die just 10 times so this might have been by chance.

c Throw the die many more times.

d

	1	2	3	4	5	6
Frequency	卌 卌	卌 |||	卌	卌 卌		卌 ||||	卌 ||
Probability	$\frac{10}{50} = 0.2$	$\frac{8}{50} = 0.16$	$\frac{5}{50} = 0.1$	$\frac{11}{50} = 0.22$	$\frac{9}{50} = 0.18$	$\frac{7}{50} = 0.14$

e No

This was just 50 throws of the die, so these results could still be due to chance.

f

	Total	Probability (2 dp)
6	231	$\frac{231}{1450} = 0.16$
Not 6	1219	$\frac{1219}{1450} = 0.84$

g No

However, the P(6) for the class results was 0.16, which is close to the theoretical probability of $0.1\dot{6}$. So the results suggest that Henry might be wrong.

h

	Henry	Scarlett	Class
Number of tosses	10	50	1450
P(6)	0.3	0.14	0.16
P(not 6)	0.7	0.86	0.84

The probabilities get closer to the theoretical probability of $0.1\dot{6}$.

i 166 667 (not 166 666.7 – you can't throw 0.7 of a 6)

j No

What you have previously rolled does not have any effect on what you roll next.

Simulations (pp. 308–309)

a She has assumed that the numbers of each type of bird card in the boxes are similar.

She has assumed that boxes containing the same bird card have been mixed with other boxes, so a shop doesn't, for instance, have boxes which contain just kea cards.

b Do a lot more trials.

c I would make 1, 2 and 3 represent a kiwi and 4, 5 or 6 represent a fantail.

 ISBN: 9780170497978